macromedia® FLASH™ MX 2004 actionscript

derek franklin / jobe makar

training from the source

Macromedia Flash MX 2004 ActionScript: Training from the Source

Derek Franklin / Jobe Makar

Published by Macromedia Press, in association with Peachpit Press, a division of Pearson Education.

Macromedia Press
1249 Eighth Street
Berkeley, CA 94710
510/524-2178
800/283-9444
510/524-2221 (fax)
Find us on the World Wide Web at:
http://www.peachpit.com
http://www.macromedia.com

To report errors, please send a note to errata@peachpit.com

Printed and bound in the United States of America

ISBN 0-321-21343-2

9 8 7 6 5 4 3 2

CREDITS

Macromedia Press Editor: Angela C. Kozlowski

Editor: Robin Drake

Technical Editors: Steven Heckler, Jeff Tapper

Production Coordinator: Myrna Vladic

Copy Editors: Suzanne Hobbs, Christine McGeever

Compositors: Rick Gordon, Emerald Valley Graphics
Debbie Roberti, Espresso Graphics

Indexer: Julie Bess

Cover Production: George Mattingly, GMD

BIO

Derek Franklin is the Chief Idea Guy at derekfranklin.com. Actually, he's the only guy at derekfranklin.com! He has been involved in the Web since 1995, getting his first taste of Flash in 1997 and never looking back. Derek has won numerous design awards for his work and has authored several best-selling Macromedia Press Flash books, which have been translated into many languages. When he's not writing books, Derek spends his time experimenting with Flash in ways that are completely abnormal, but he likes it! He and his family live in Bloomington, Indiana, which he considers one of the coolest places on the planet.

Jobe Makar is the lead programmer and co-owner of Electrotank, Inc., and winner of several international game awards. The creator of more than 100 Flash games, Jobe has been working with Flash since version 3. He has authored or co-authored several books on Flash, including *Macromedia Flash MX Game Design Demystified*. He has been the lead programmer at Learnimation for four Small Business Innovation Research Awards from the National Science Foundation and the U.S. Department of Education. Jobe currently lives with his wife and entirely too many animals in Raleigh, North Carolina.

ACKNOWLEDGMENTS

Are we done yet?! Those are the words that kept playing through my head the last several months as this wonderful revision was being written and put together. It's not an easy task to do a worthy follow-up to the best-selling MX book of 2002 (according to Amazon.com). It took a lot of time and effort by everybody on the writing, editing, and production team to create this book, and hopefully the passion of everyone involved to do their absolute best shows in the product you hold in your hands. I think it does! Whew! It has taken a lot out of me, personally, but not enough to forget my manners and to thank everyone who was involved. They know who they are, but you might not. Jobe, who could ask for a better co-author, seriously? Angela and Robin, you both did such a great job editing! Thank you for your hard work and patience. To all the rest of the team, please know that I wish I could list all of your names, but you know how those pesky editors are about conserving space. Just be aware that I am very thankful to all of you. And finally, a big "thank you" to you, the reader. Your continued support is always appreciated.

–Derek Franklin

Yes Derek, we are done! It's a great feeling to look back on everything that we have accomplished in this book. You are an author and an artist! As always, we could not have done this alone. There are some amazing people whose efforts and support have contributed as much during the creation of this book as the authors'. Thank you, Angela, for keeping us all on track. Robin, you really have done an amazing job with the editing. Thanks also to the technical editors, Steve Heckler and Jeff Tapper. I thank my colleagues at Electrotank.com for some very helpful conceptual programming conversations.

It would not have been possible to keep my sanity during this process without the support of my family. A big thanks to everyone! Kelly, thank you for your sweet luvin'. Free, you da dog!

–Jobe Makar

DEDICATION

This book is dedicated in loving memory to Chance.

–Jobe Makar

table of contents

introduction

ActionScript is the programming language that enables you to use Macromedia's popular Flash to create highly interactive multimedia-based Web sites, product demos, teaching materials, and more. If you're familiar with the logic of other programming languages, especially JavaScript or Java, ActionScript will seem quite familiar. After you've learned the logic behind how scripting works, as well as the many things it allows you to create and do, chances are you'll wish you had started sooner. Creativity isn't reserved for artists and designers, after all; scripting is another form of creativity, and equally as rewarding. With a thorough knowledge of ActionScript, you can express yourself in many ways you may never have imagined.

This *Training from the Source* course introduces you to the major elements of ActionScript by guiding you through a wealth of step-by-step projects that thoroughly explain not only what's happening, but also why and how. The focus of each project is the teaching of ActionScript; therefore, in nearly all the projects, most graphical elements and other objects not directly related to the lesson are already set up for you. Their purpose in the project, as well as brief descriptions of what they do (if necessary), are always included.

Now that there are two versions of Flash (Standard and Professional), it was a fine balancing act to make this book appealing and useful to users of either version. To that end, users of both versions can benefit from the majority of this book, although there are several lessons that make use of components and functionalities found only within the Professional version.

The curriculum of the course is approximately 26–30 hours in length and includes the following lessons:

- **Lesson 1:** Introducing ActionScript
- **Lesson 2:** Using Event Handlers
- **Lesson 3:** Understanding Target Paths
- **Lesson 4:** Using Object Classes
- **Lesson 5:** Using Functions
- **Lesson 6:** Creating and Manipulating Data
- **Lesson 7:** Creating Custom Classes
- **Lesson 8:** Using Conditional Logic
- **Lesson 9:** Automating Scripts with Loops
- **Lesson 10:** Scripting UI Components
- **Lesson 11:** Getting Data In and Out of Flash
- **Lesson 12:** Using XML with Flash
- **Lesson 13:** Validating Data
- **Lesson 14:** Working with Text Fields
- **Lesson 15:** Controlling Movie Clips Dynamically
- **Lesson 16:** Time- and Frame-Based Dynamism
- **Lesson 17:** Scripting for Sound
- **Lesson 18:** Loading External Assets
- **Lesson 19:** Testing and Debugging
- **Lesson 20:** Maximum-Strength SWFs
- **Lesson 21:** Printing and Context Menus

This book contains more than 40 separate projects, each designed to teach you a specific aspect of ActionScript. These projects are fun, useful, and practical examples of how ActionScript can be used in real-world situations.

Each lesson begins with an overview of the lesson's content and learning objectives. Lessons are divided into individual tasks that help you learn and utilize various aspects of the lesson's topic.

This book is part of the *Training from the Source* series. It contains conceptual information, in-depth material, and step-by-step explanations. In addition, each lesson includes the following special features:

- **Special font for code:** To help you easily identify ActionScript, XML, and HTML code within the book, the code has been styled in a `special font` that's unique from the rest of the text.

- **Bold text:** Bold text is used to identify the names of visual elements in a project, including movie clips, buttons, and text fields.
- **Tips:** Tips contain shortcuts for carrying out common tasks, and ways you can use the skills you're learning to solve common problems.
- **Notes:** Notes provide additional information pertaining to the task at hand.
- **Appendix:** The Appendix contains a list of Flash resources related to many aspects of using Flash, including scripting, design, animation, and usability.

This course is developed to help you build your skills progressively as you work through each lesson. When you've completed the entire course, you'll have a thorough knowledge of ActionScript, including its syntax, capabilities, and the logic behind the way to make it do what you want it to do. As a result, you have the skills necessary to create dynamic, highly interactive Flash content.

The accompanying CD contains all the files necessary to complete each lesson. Files for each lesson appear in a folder titled with the lesson number. It is strongly suggested that you create a folder on your hard drive and transfer all lesson files to that folder prior to beginning the course. The reason is that you'll occasionally be asked to test your work using Flash's Test Movie command. This command creates a test file in the same directory as the Flash file that is being authored. If the authored file was opened from the CD, Flash will attempt to create the test movie on the CD. In almost all cases, this is impossible and will result in an error.

Each lesson folder contains two subfolders: Assets and Complete. The Assets folder contains any media files and initial Flash files needed for the lesson. The files you need are identified at the beginning of each lesson. The Complete folder contains completed files for each step in the project so that you can compare them to your own work or see where you're headed.

The lessons in this book assume that the following statements are true:

- You're familiar with using menus, opening and saving files, and so on for either the Windows or Macintosh operating system.
- Flash MX 2004 (Standard or Professional) is already installed on your machine.
- Your computer meets the system requirements listed in the following section.
- You're generally familiar with Flash's interface, movie and authoring concepts, creating and using movie elements, using the timeline, using basic actions, and working with the Actions panel. If you're not comfortable with any of these tasks, be sure to check out other books from Macromedia Press and Peachpit Press.

A collage of some of the many projects you will script in this course.

MACROMEDIA TRAINING FROM THE SOURCE

The Macromedia *Training from the Source* and *Advanced Training from the Source* series are developed in association with Macromedia, and reviewed by the product support teams. Ideal for active learners, the books in the *Training from the Source* series offer hands-on instruction designed to provide you with a solid grounding in the program's fundamentals. If you learn best by doing, this is the series for you. Each *Training from the Source* title contains hours of instruction on Macromedia software products. They are designed to teach the techniques that you need to create sophisticated professional-level projects. Each book includes a CD-ROM that contains all the files used in the lessons, completed projects for comparison, and more.

MACROMEDIA AUTHORIZED TRAINING AND CERTIFICATION

This book is designed to enable you to study at your own pace with content from the source. Other training options exist through the Macromedia Authorized Training Partner program. Get up to speed in a matter of days with task-oriented courses taught by Macromedia Certified Instructors. Or learn on your own with interactive, online training from Macromedia University. All these sources of training will prepare you to become a Macromedia Certified Developer.

For more information about authorized training and certification, check out *www.macromedia.com/support/training*.

WHAT YOU WILL LEARN IN THIS BOOK

As you work through these lessons, you will develop the skills you need to create and maintain your own Web sites.

By the end of this course, you will be able to do all of the following:

- Plan an interactive project
- Understand ActionScript syntax and how it works
- Use the numerous event handlers to create a variety of interactivity
- Use and understand built-in objects, properties, and methods
- Manipulate text and numbers dynamically to perform specific tasks
- Use functions to centralize your code
- Create custom objects and methods
- Employ conditional logic in your movie to react to varying circumstances
- Use loops to automate scripting tasks
- Use and customize UI components
- Move data in and out of Flash using text files and XML
- Script your applications to communicate with a third-party Web service
- Validate all types of data
- Create text fields dynamically and format text using Cascading Style Sheets
- Dynamically control movies using scripting rather than the timeline
- Employ date, time, and frame-based interactivity
- Script sounds to make your project more engaging
- Load and unload various types of media from your projects
- Test and use Flash's Debugger to maximize your project's code
- Create an application that uses a third-party tool to enhance its functionality beyond Flash's built-in capabilities
- Print Flash content using ActionScript

MINIMUM SYSTEM REQUIREMENTS

Windows

- 600 MHz Intel Pentium III processor or equivalent
- Windows 98 SE, Windows 2000, or Windows XP
- 128 MB RAM (256 MB recommended)
- 275 MB available disk space

Macintosh

- 500 MHz PowerPC G3 processor
- Mac OS 10.2.6
- 256 MB RAM (512 MB recommended)
- 500 MB available disk space

introducing ActionScript

LESSON 1

Introductions form the start of any great relationship. Get ready, then, to be introduced to your new best friend: ActionScript! We believe you'll find ActionScript a satisfying companion—especially as you delve deeper into the relationship. Although you may not necessarily think of scripting as a creative endeavor, a working knowledge of ActionScript can spark all kinds of ideas—ones that will enable you to create dynamic content that can interact with your users on myriad levels. Best of all, you'll get the satisfaction of watching your ideas grow into working models that fulfill your projects' objectives.

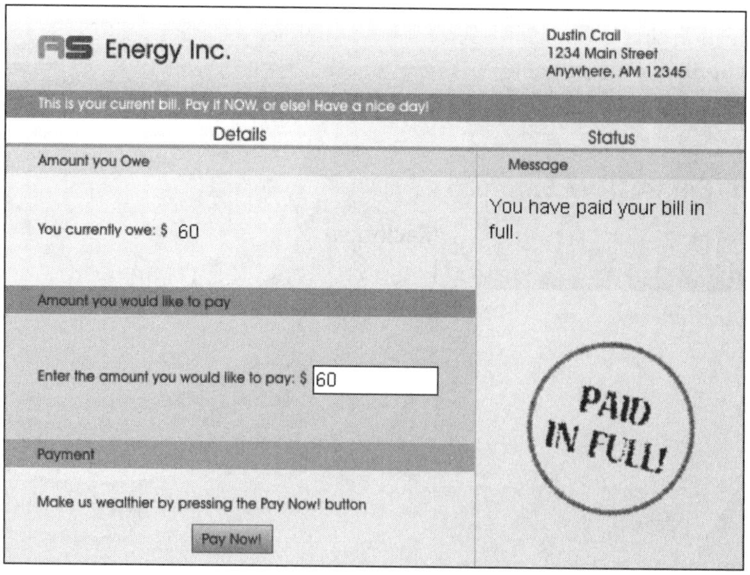

We'll plan, create, and test a highly interactive electric-bill payment system.

In this lesson, we'll introduce previous ActionScripters to version 2.0 of the language. For new users, we'll show you some compelling reasons for learning ActionScript, as well as what makes it tick. And if you're feeling a little shy, sometimes the best thing to do is jump right in—which is exactly what you'll do here as you create and test a complete interactive project before lesson's end.

WHAT YOU WILL LEARN

In this lesson, you will:

- Learn about ActionScript 2.0 and how it differs from ActionScript 1.0
- Discover the benefits of learning ActionScript
- Learn to navigate and use the ActionScript editor
- Learn about script elements
- Plan a project
- Write your first script
- Test your script
- Debug your script

APPROXIMATE TIME

This lesson takes approximately one and one half hours to complete.

LESSON FILES

Starting File:

Lesson01/Assets/electricbill1.fla

Completed Projects:

electricbill2.fla
electricbill3.fla

ACTIONSCRIPT MATURES TO VERSION 2.0

If you've been involved with Flash for any length of time, you've seen it evolve from a simple multimedia tool used for creating animated Web graphics and interactive buttons into a multimedia powerhouse that can play external MP3 files, load graphics, play video, talk to a database, and more.

The passionate and innovative community of Flash developers worldwide drives this evolution, to a large degree. By constantly pushing Flash development to new heights, they make us aware not only of the possibilities, but also of the limitations of what can be done.

Fortunately for us, with each new version of Flash, Macromedia strives hard to address these limitations, providing developers with the tools that enable us to do more cool stuff, in the easiest, most efficient manner.

Since its introduction in Flash 5, ActionScript has enabled Flash-based content to soar to new heights, yet there have been obstacles and limitations discovered along the way.

The execution of ActionScript in the Flash 5 player tended to be slow. Tasks that required milliseconds in other scripting/programming languages took seconds with ActionScript. Ask game programmers and they'll tell you that the speed of processing seemed like a lifetime, and it really limited the kind of interactivity that could be used.

In addition to slow processing speeds, ActionScript in Flash 5, while powerful, wasn't very flexible. There wasn't an easy way of implementing object-oriented programming techniques, which enable the creation of more complex and manageable Flash applications.

ActionScript in Flash MX, though not officially dubbed anything more than ActionScript 1.0 with some enhancements, probably could have rightfully been called ActionScript 1.5. It addressed a number of the processing speed issues that plagued Flash 5 ActionScript. In addition, the capabilities of ActionScript in Flash MX were enhanced in ways that enabled the implementation of common object-oriented programming techniques, including the creation of custom object classes and inheritance. While this was definitely a huge step in the right direction, there was still room for improvement.

With Flash MX 2004, Macromedia has introduced ActionScript 2.0. With it come some new capabilities and, more importantly, some new syntax and a new way of structuring and working with your code.

As we discuss in the next section, the changes are somewhat subtle, but they move ActionScript into the realm of a professional-grade programming language. And with what people are demanding from their Flash applications these days, this is definitely a move in the right direction.

NOTE *If you're just learning ActionScript, feel free to skip this section (which probably won't make sense) and move on to the next.*

DIFFERENCES BETWEEN ACTIONSCRIPT 1.0 AND 2.0

If you're familiar with ActionScript 1.0, you'll find that ActionScript 2.0 is similar, yet it has several subtle but important differences. In this section, we examine some of them so that you can take your hard-earned knowledge of ActionScript 1 and put it to use with ActionScript 2.0.

Before we look at these differences, let us first tell you up front that if you want to stick with what you know (programming in ActionScript 1.0), then by all means, do so. ActionScript 1.0 syntax still works in Flash MX 2004. But while this may be the case, and you do have a choice, we recommend you take the time to learn ActionScript 2.0, for a number of reasons.

First, there may come a time when a version of Flash is released that no longer supports ActionScript 1.0. Time spent learning version 2.0 now will be time you might have to spend down the road anyway. And while we can't guarantee it, don't expect ActionScript to jump to version 3.0 any time soon (if ever), because version 2.0 is now built around professional programming language concepts that have stood the test of time. As a matter of fact, outside of a few syntactical differences, writing ActionScript 2.0 code is not much different from writing Java code.

That's right; if you take the time to learn ActionScript 2.0, you'll be able to quickly transition your knowledge to the Java universe, where industrial-strength, cross-platform applications are standard. Consider learning ActionScript: it's a two-for-one deal!

Second, by its very nature and requirements, ActionScript 2.0 will force you to become a more efficient, organized, and better coder. As you will soon see, ActionScript 2.0 has some very strict requirements about how things are done. It's a lot less forgiving than ActionScript 1.0. This may seem like a bad thing, but it actually prevents you from being too sloppy with your scripts, which can make finding bugs a pain, and which can make updating a project months later an arduous task.

Finally, if speed is important to you, you'll be happy to know that ActionScript 2.0 has been shown to be three to seven times faster than ActionScript 1.0. This speed increase will promote the development of even more robust Flash applications.

Let's next look at some of the main differences you'll find between ActionScript 1.0 and ActionScript 2.0.

Case Sensitivity

In ActionScript 1.0, these variable names referenced the same variable:

```
myVariable
MyVariable
```

In ActionScript 2.0, however, they would be considered two separate variables due to the case difference in their spelling; the first variable begins with a lowercase character, while the second an uppercase character. In fact, all of the following are considered different elements in ActionScript 2.0:

```
myName
MyName
MYNAME
myname
myNAME
```

This case sensitivity rule applies to all elements in ActionScript 2.0, including instance names, keywords, method names, and so on. Thus, while this syntax will stop all sounds from playing:

```
stopAllSounds();
```

this will cause an error:

```
stopallsounds();
```

TIP *One easy way of testing for case errors is to press the Check Syntax button on the Actions panel. Errors resulting from case mismatches will appear in the output window.*

Strict Data Typing

Variables are used to contain data. This data comes in many forms, including strings of text, numbers, true/false values, references to objects such as movie clip instances, and so on. In ActionScript 1.0, when creating a variable, Flash would automatically assign a data type to it. In this example, Flash understood that the value on the right was of the Number data type:

```
myVariable = 36;
```

While Flash will still automatically recognize this variable as holding a Number data type, ActionScript 2.0 introduces what is known as *strict data typing*, which gives you more control over setting a variable's data type. Here's how it works.

When creating a variable with ActionScript 2.0, you use this syntax not only to create the variable, but also to assign its data type at the same time:

```
var myVariable:Number = 36;
```

As you can see, this syntax is not that different from what you're used to using in ActionScript 1.0. The difference is the addition of the `var` keyword, and the explicit declaration that this variable will hold a number, as indicated by the `:Number` syntax.

A variable that will hold a string looks like this:

```
var myOtherVariable:String = "Hello";
```

In addition to assigning data types to regular variables, strict data typing is used in the creation of object instances:

```
var myArray:Array = new Array();
```

and function definitions:

```
function myFunction (name:String, age:Number)
```

NOTE *Both of these types of strict data typing will be explained in greater depth later in the book.*

How can all those extra keystrokes be an enhancement? Well, there are several ways.

If you're familiar with the Actions panel's ability to provide code hints (which we will discuss shortly), you'll be happy to know that strict data typing activates code hinting for named elements. For example, if you create an Array object using the syntax:

```
var myArray:Array = new Array();
```

the Actions panel will recognize from that point forward that any reference to `myArray` is a reference to an Array object, and it will automatically provide Array object code hints whenever you script that object. In some cases, this new ability eliminates the need for a suffix (**_array**, **_xml**, and **_color**, for example), which was one of the ways that Flash MX enabled code hinting for an object. While the new syntax requires a few more keystrokes, you'll save a few because you no longer have to add suffixes to elements' names, so consider it a decent trade-off.

NOTE *You'll notice we said that in some cases the new ability eliminates the need for suffixes. Visual elements (movie clip instances, buttons, text fields, and components, for example) are not created and named in the same manner as data elements. For this reason, suffixes for these elements' names (such as* **_mc**, **_btn**, *and* **_txt***) are still useful. For this book, we will generally use suffixes only for visual elements.*

Code hinting isn't the only benefit to strict data typing. By indicating the type of data a variable will hold, you save the Flash player a whole lot of time trying to figure it out on its own. When the Flash player is running your application, Flash needs to keep track of the type of data each variable contains. If you use strict data typing, you make this process a lot easier and less processor-intensive for the Flash player. As a result, your scripts will execute much faster. If you want to increase the speed of your applications, use strict data typing.

Finally, strict data typing can be a very simple way of helping you uncover bugs in your code. Here's an example:

```
var favoriteBand:String;
```

This line of script creates a variable named `favoriteBand`, which has been strictly typed to hold a String.

Later in your script you assign this variable a value or give it a new one using the syntax:

```
favoriteBand = "The Beatles";
```

However, if somewhere in your script you use something like this syntax:

```
favoriteBand = 46;
```

the Output panel will open and display a "Type mismatch" error when you attempt to export (compile) your movie. This is an error indicating that you've attempted to assign an incorrect value type to a variable. In our example, we've attempted to assign a numeric value (Number data type) to a variable that has been set up to hold a string value.

This functionality can help prevent a number of bugs that can result from simple mistakes you might make when assigning values to variables.

Class Structure

Perhaps the biggest change in ActionScript 2.0 is the way that object-oriented programming is implemented. For example, with ActionScript 1.0, a custom class of objects was defined this way:

```
_global.Person = function (name, age){
  this.name = name;
  this.age = age;
}
```

In ActionScript 2.0, the same class is created using this syntax:

```
class Person {
  var name:String;
  var age:Number;
  function Person (name:String, age:Number){
    this.name = name;
    this.age = age;
  }
}
```

Notice the use of the new `class` keyword. This syntax is very similar to the syntax for creating classes of objects in Java. As you learn more about this syntax (which we won't discuss in detail at this point), you'll quickly see its benefits over ActionScript 1.0.

Another subtle difference in creating custom classes of objects between ActionScript 1.0 and 2.0 is that the script that contains the class definition must exist in its own external **.as** file. This means that the script for defining the `Person` class would need to be saved as an external **.as** file (which is nothing more than a text file with a **.as** file extension) named **Person.as**. This is different from ActionScript 1.0, which allows you to place the code for a class definition on Frame 1 of a movie clip's timeline. This is no longer possible when creating content for the Flash 7 player. Class definitions must exist in an external **.as** file. We'll discuss this functionality in Lesson 7, "Creating Custom Classes." For now, be aware of the difference.

NOTE *You can still place scripts on frames, buttons, etc., but class definitions must exist in their own* **.as** *files.*

To make the creation of **.as** files as easy as possible, Flash MX 2004 now provides a stand-alone ActionScript editor, which is separate from the Actions panel, and which is used for nothing more than the creation and saving of **.as** files. Later in this lesson, we'll look at both the Actions panel and the stand-alone ActionScript editor.

There are other differences between ActionScript 1.0 and ActionScript 2.0, but this brief overview should provide you with enough insight to get started if you've worked with ActionScript 1.0.

SIMILARITIES BETWEEN ACTIONSCRIPT 1.0 AND 2.0

Okay, up to this point we've only talked about everything that's different between the two versions of ActionScript. But what about them is the same? What hard-earned knowledge of ActionScript 1.0 that you currently have is still applicable to ActionScript 2.0? Fortunately, plenty!

You still control movie clips with this syntax:

```
myMovieClip_mc.gotoAndPlay(15);
```

You still create conditional statements the same way:

```
if (myNumber1 + myNumber2 == 20 && enabled != true){
  //actions;
}
```

or looping statements this way:

```
for (i = 0; i <= myVariable; ++i){
  //actions;
}
```

Expressions are still created the same way:

```
myVariable = (myNumber1 / 2) + (myNumber2 + 15);
```

And scripts can still be assigned to button and movie clip instances using the `on()` and `onClipEvent()` event handlers.

WHY LEARN ACTIONSCRIPT?

Today, if you're a Flash developer, one thing is certain: animation skills, no matter how phenomenal, are no longer enough. A firm grasp of ActionScript is essential because without it, only the most elementary interactivity is possible. By acquiring an in-depth knowledge of ActionScript, you can:

- Provide a personalized user experience
- Achieve greater control over movie clips and their properties
- Animate elements in your movie programmatically—that is, without using the timeline
- Get data in and out of Flash to create forms, chat programs, and more
- Create dynamic projects that respond to the passage of time or the current date
- Dynamically control sound volume and panning
- Do much more

Add to these benefits the fact that viewing and interacting with Flash content can be more than just a Web experience. Flash can create self-running applications or mini-programs that operate independently of the browser—a capability more people are putting to use to create games, learning applications, and more. If you want to do this, too, you need at least an intermediate knowledge of ActionScript.

ACTIONSCRIPT ELEMENTS

ActionScript is a language that bridges the gap between what you understand and what Flash understands. As such, it allows you to provide both action-oriented instructions (do this) and logic-oriented instructions (analyze this before doing that) in your Flash project. Like all languages, ActionScript contains many different elements, such as words, punctuation, and structure—all of which you must employ properly to get your Flash project to behave the way you want it to. If you don't employ ActionScript correctly, you'll find that interactivity either won't occur or won't work the way you intended. Many of these elements, as well as several other elements such as logical statements and expressions, will be covered in more detail throughout the book.

To begin to understand how ActionScript works, look at this sample script, which contains many of the essential elements that make up a typical script. After the script is a discussion of these elements and their role in the script's execution.

We can assume that this script is attached to a button:

```
on (release) {
  //set the cost of the mug
  var mugCost:Number = 5.00;
  //set the local sales tax percentage
  var taxPercent:Number = .06;
  //determine the dollar amount of tax
  var totalTax:Number = mugCost * taxPercent;
  //determine the total amount of the transaction
  var totalCost:Number = mugCost + totalTax;
  //display a custom message
  myTextBox_txt.text = "The total cost of your transaction is " + totalCost;
  //send the cashRegister_mc movie clip instance to frame 50
  cashRegister_mc.gotoAndPlay (50);
}
```

Although at first glance this may look like Latin, once you become acquainted with some of its elements, you'll understand.

NOTE *Other script elements (for example, objects, functions, loops, properties, and methods) are discussed in detail throughout the book.*

Events

Events occur during the playback of a movie and trigger the execution of a particular script. In our sample script, the event that triggers the script is `on (release)`. This event signifies that when the button to which this script is attached is released, the script will execute. Every script is triggered by an event, and your movie can react to numerous events—everything from a button being pressed to text changing in a text field to a sound completing its playback, and more. We will discuss events in depth in Lesson 2, "Using Event Handlers."

Actions

These form the heart of your script. An action is usually considered to be any line that instructs Flash to do, set, create, change, load, or delete something.

Here are some examples of actions from the sample script:

```
var mugCost:Number = 5.00;
cashRegister_mc.gotoAndPlay (50);
```

The first line creates a variable named `mugCost`, sets its data type as Number (indicating the variable will hold a numeric value), and sets the value of the variable to `5.00`. The second line tells the **cashRegister_mc** movie clip instance to begin playing at Frame 50 of its timeline.

Generally speaking, most of the lines in a script that are within curly braces ({}) are actions. These lines are usually separated by semicolons (we'll discuss punctuation shortly).

Operators

These include a number of symbols (=, <, >, +, –, *, &&, etc.) and are used to connect two elements in a script in various ways. Take a look at these examples:

- `var taxPercent:Number = .06;` assigns a numeric value of .06 to the variable named `taxPercent`
- `amountA < amountB` asks if `amountA` is less than `amountB`
- `value1 * 500` multiplies `value1` times 500

Keywords

These are words reserved for specific purposes within ActionScript syntax. As such, they cannot be used as variable, function, or label names. For example, the word `on` is a keyword and can only be used in a script to denote an event that triggers a script, such as `on (press)`, `on (rollOver)`, `on (rollOut)`, and so on. Attempting to use keywords in your scripts for anything other than their intended purpose will result in errors. Other keywords include `break`, `case`, `class`, `continue`, `default`, `delete`, `do`, `dynamic`, else, extends, finally, for, function, get, if, implements, import, interface, in, instanceof, new, null, private, public, return, set, static, switch, this, throw, try, typeof, undefined, var, void, while, and with.

Data

A dynamic script almost always creates, uses, or updates various pieces of data during its execution. Variables are the most common pieces of dynamic data found in scripts and represent pieces of data that have been given unique names. Once a variable has been created and assigned a value, that value can be accessed anywhere in the script simply by inserting the variable's name.

NOTE *Variable names are case sensitive:* `myVariable` *and* `MyVariable` *are not the same.*

In our sample script, we created a variable named `mugCost` and assigned it a value of 5.00. Later in the script, the name of that variable is used to refer to the value it contains.

Curly Braces

Generally, anything between opening and closing curly braces signifies an action or set of actions the script needs to perform when triggered. Think of curly braces as saying, "As a result of this–{do this}." For example:

```
on (release) {
  //set the cost of the mug
  var mugCost:Number = 5.00;
  //set the local sales tax percentage
  var taxPercent:Number = .06;
}
```

Semicolons

Appearing at the end of most lines of scripts, semicolons are used to separate multiple actions that may need to be executed as the result of a single event (similar to the way semicolons are used to separate thoughts in a single sentence). This example denotes six actions, separated by semicolons:

```
var mugCost:Number = 5.00;
var taxPercent:Number = .06;
var totalTax:Number = mugCost * taxPercent;
var totalCost:Number = mugCost + totalTax;
myTextBox_txt.text = "The total cost of your transaction is " + totalCost;
cashRegister_mc.gotoAndPlay (50);
```

Dot Syntax

Dots (.) are used within scripts in a couple of ways: One is to denote the target path to a specific timeline. For example, `_root.usa.indiana.bloomington` points to a movie clip on the main (`_root`) timeline named **usa**, which contains a movie clip named **indiana**, which contains a movie clip named **bloomington**.

Because ActionScript is an object-oriented language, most interactive tasks are accomplished by changing a characteristic (*property*) of an object or by telling an object to do something (*invoking a method*). When changing a property or when invoking a method, dots are used to separate the object's name from the property or method being worked with. For example, movie clips are objects; to set the rotation property of a movie clip instance named **wheel_mc**, you would use the syntax:

```
wheel_mc._rotation = 90;
```

Notice how a dot separates the name of the object from the property being set.

To tell the same movie clip instance to play, invoking the `play()` method, you would use the syntax:

```
wheel_mc.play()
```

Once again, a dot separates the name of the object from the method invoked.

Parentheses

These are used in various ways in ActionScript. For the most part, scripts employ parentheses to set a specific value that an action will use during its execution. Look at the last line of our sample script that tells the **cashRegister_mc** movie clip instance to go to and play Frame 50:

```
cashRegister_mc.gotoAndPlay (50);
```

If the value within parentheses is changed from 50 to 20, the action still performs the same basic task (moving the **cashRegister_mc** movie clip instance to a specified frame number); it just does so according to the new value. Parentheses are a way of telling an action to work based on what's specified between the parentheses.

Quotation Marks

These are used to denote textual data in the script. Because text is used in the actual creation of the script, quotation marks provide the only means for a script to distinguish between instructions (pieces of data) and actual words. For example, `Derek` (without quotes) signifies the name of a piece of data. On the other hand, `"Derek"` signifies the actual word "Derek."

COMMENTS

These are lines in the script preceded by two forward slashes (//). When executing a script, Flash ignores lines containing comments. They indicate descriptive notes about what the script is doing at this point in its execution. Comments enable you to review a script months after it was written and still get a clear idea of its underlying logic.

You can also create multi-line comments using the syntax:

```
/* everything between
here is considered
a comment */
```

INDENTING/SPACING

Although not absolutely necessary, it's a good idea to indent and space the syntax in your code. For example:

```
on (release) {
var mugCost:Number = 5.00;
}
```

will execute the same as:

```
on (release) {
  var mugCost:Number = 5.00;
}
```

However, by indenting code, you make it easier to read. A good rule is to indent anything within curly braces to indicate that the code within those braces represents a *code block*, or chunk of code, that is to be executed at the same time. (The AutoFormat feature of the Actions panel takes care of most of this for you.) You can *nest* code blocks within other code blocks—a concept that will become clearer as you work through the exercises.

For the most part, white space is ignored within a script. For example:

```
var totalCost:Number = mugCost + totalTax ;
```

will execute in the same way as:

```
var totalCost:Number =mugCost+totalTax;
```

While some programmers feel that extra white space makes their code easier to read, others believe it slows them down to insert spaces. For the most part, the choice is yours. There are a couple of exceptions: variable names cannot contain spaces; nor can you put a space between an object name and an associated property or method. While this syntax is acceptable:

```
myObject.propertyName
```

this is not:

```
myObject. propertyName
```

In addition, there must be a space between the var keyword used when creating a variable, and the actual name of the variable. This is correct:

```
var variableName
```

but this is not:

```
varvariableName
```

USING THE ACTIONS PANEL/ACTIONSCRIPT EDITOR

Obviously, the premise of this book requires you to concentrate on writing scripts. It's a good idea to get familiar with the tools you'll use in Flash to do so. In this, your first exercise, you'll learn some of the basics of creating scripts with the ActionScript editor.

NOTE *The purpose of this book is to teach ActionScript, not so much how to use the Flash interface. This discussion will be concise, providing enough information to help you progress through the book. For a more extensive look at the many features of the Actions panel, pick up the Macromedia Flash* Visual QuickStart Guide.

1) With Flash open, choose File > New and choose Flash Document from the list of choices. Press OK.

This step creates a new Flash document. It's usually a good idea to give your document a name and save it, so we'll do that next.

2) From the File menu, choose Save As. In the dialog box that appears, navigate to any folder on your hard drive where you would like to save this file (it's not important where, really), name it *myFirstFile.fla*, and press the Save button.

After you press Save, the tab at the top of the document window will reflect the name of your new file.

3) Open the Actions panel by choosing Window > Development Panels > Actions.

Let's look at the various sections of the Actions panel.

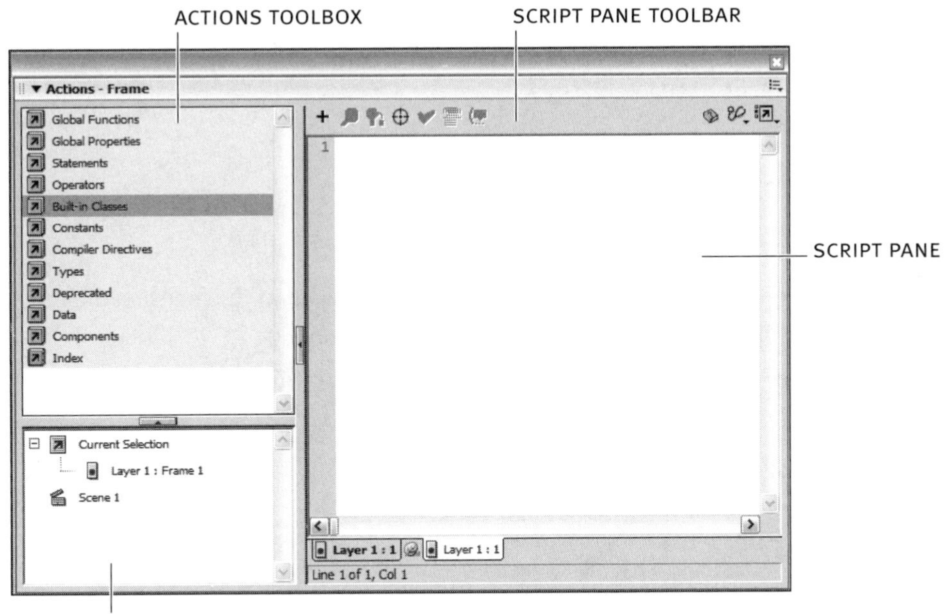

The *Script pane* is where you add ActionScript. You type into this window just as you would a word processor. The script that appears in this window changes, depending on the currently selected element in the Flash authoring environment. For example, selecting a keyframe on Frame 10 allows you to place a script on that frame if one doesn't already exist; if that frame already contains a script, it will be displayed for editing.

The *Actions toolbox* contains a categorical list of ActionScript elements. Double-clicking an icon (a book with an arrow) opens or closes a category in the list. The toolbox is designed to provide a quick way of adding script elements to your scripts for further configuration. You can add script elements to the Script pane by double-clicking the element's name in the toolbox window, or by clicking and dragging it to the Script pane.

The *Script Navigator* displays a hierarchical list of elements (frames, buttons, movie clip instances) in your projects that contain scripts. Clicking an element will display the script attached to it in the Script pane, allowing you to navigate quickly through the scripts in your project for editing purposes. Only elements with scripts attached to them appear in the Script Navigator.

The *Script pane toolbar* appears above the Script pane and provides a series of buttons and commands, enabling you to add to or edit the current script in the Script pane in various ways.

In the next steps, we'll explore the capabilities and functionalities of the ActionScript editor. Let's look first at code hinting.

4) In the Script pane, type:

```
myMovieClip_mc.
```

NOTE *Let's assume this is the name of a movie clip instance we've placed in our movie.*

Immediately after you type the dot (.), a drop-down menu provides a list of actions applicable to movie clip instances.

Why did the editor provide a list of commands for movie clip instances? It's because of the name we chose for our movie clip instance. Notice that we added **_mc** to the movie clip instance's name. This suffix enables the editor to automatically identify **myMovieClip_mc** as a movie clip instance and provide a drop-down list of appropriate commands when you type that name in the Script pane.

Common suffixes for visual movie elements include **_btn** for buttons and **_txt** for text fields. We will be using these suffixes for visual elements throughout this book.

Other, nonvisual elements, such as Sound and Date objects, have suffixes as well, but instead of using suffixes for nonvisual elements, we'll instead be utilizing a new functionality in Flash MX 2004, which we'll demonstrate next.

For a complete list of suffixes, consult the ActionScript Dictionary.

5) Select the current script and delete it. In its place, type:

```
var mySound:Sound = new Sound();
```

This line of script creates a new Sound object named mySound. Creating a Sound object using this syntax identifies mySound as a Sound object to the ActionScript editor. As a result, referencing this object by its name later in the script will cause a drop-down menu of appropriate Sound object–related commands to appear automatically. Let's test it.

6) Press Enter/Return to go to the next line in the Script pane, and type:

```
mySound.
```

Once again, immediately after typing the dot, you see a drop-down menu with a list of actions applicable to Sound objects.

You can create a new Sound object using this syntax:

```
mySound = new Sound();
```

but this syntax will not activate the functionality of code hinting when you script that object, as the syntax in Step 5 does.

To help you grasp this concept, let's look at a couple more examples.

This code activates Color object–related code hinting for the myColor Color object:

```
var myColor:Color = new Color();
```

This code does not:

```
myColor = new Color();
```

This code activates Date object–related code hinting for the myDate Date object:

```
var myDate:Date = new Date();
```

This code does not:

```
myDate = new Date();
```

NOTE *To clarify, in this book we will be using suffixes only when naming visual elements such as movie clip instances, text fields, and buttons. This is because visual elements are not created in the same manner as the description in this step. Using suffixes in their names is the only way to activate code hinting when referencing them in the ActionScript editor.*

Let's look next at another type of code hint available in the ActionScript editor.

7) Select the current script and delete it. Type in its place:

```
getURL(
```

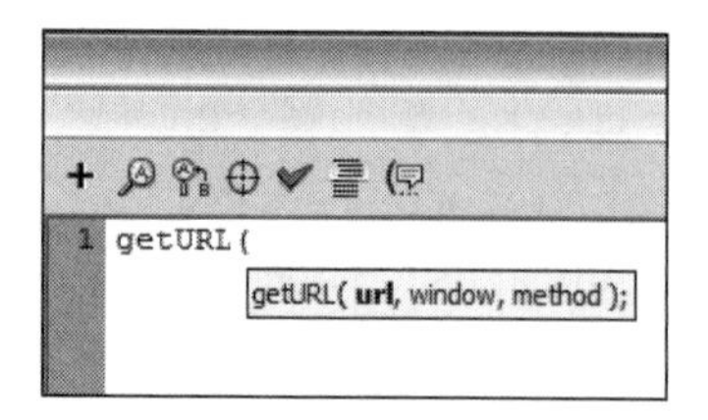

Once you type the opening parenthesis, a code hint ToolTip will appear. This functionality becomes active when you type the code for an action that has definable parameters, such as the `getURL()` action. The currently definable parameter will appear in bold text within the ToolTip. As you enter various parameter data (separated by commas), the ToolTip will be updated to display the currently definable parameter in bold text. The ToolTip will disappear once you type the closing parenthesis for the action.

You can manually display code hints at any time by placing the insertion point (cursor) at a location where code hints normally appear automatically (such as just after the opening parenthesis of an action), then pressing the Code Hint button on the Script pane toolbar.

Other buttons on the toolbar allow you to find words in your scripts, replace words in your scripts (a great feature if you change the name of something), insert target paths, check scripts (without having to spend extra time to actually export the entire movie), and autoformat your scripts (allowing the editor to handle the job of formatting your scripts in an easy-to-read manner).

The last aspect of the ActionScript editor that we'll discuss here is its ability to create **.as** files.

8) From the File menu, choose New and select ActionScript File from the list of choices. Press OK.

This step creates a new ActionScript file, ready for editing in the ActionScript editor.

The ActionScript editor looks very similar to how it looked in the previous steps. The most noticeable difference is the fact that while the interface elements of the editor are active, the rest of Flash's interface is dimmed out. Flash enters this "limited" mode when you edit **.as** files. The reason is that in this mode its sole purpose is to enable you to create and edit **.as** files. Drawing tools and other panel functionalities have no meaning in this context.

TIP *You can rid the interface completely of dimmed-out interface elements by pressing F4. Pressing F4 again brings them back.*

Another noticeable change is the disappearance of the Script Navigator. Once again, because this mode is meant for editing **.as** files, the concept of navigating various scripts in a project has no meaning, and the Script Navigator is nonexistent in this mode. Other than these differences, the ActionScript editor works in the same manner as previously discussed in this exercise.

When you create **.as** files (as you'll be doing later in the book), you save them by choosing File > Save and providing a name.

NOTE *In most cases in this book, unless otherwise stated,* ***.as*** *files (once we begin creating them) should be saved in the same directory as your main* ***.fla*** *files.*

One last thing to note about the Flash authoring environment is that two tabs now appear at the top of the document window. One tab represents the Flash document we created in Step 1, and the other represents the open ActionScript file we just created. Clicking on these tabs allows you to switch easily between authoring the Flash document and the ActionScript file. Flash automatically switches editing modes when you do.

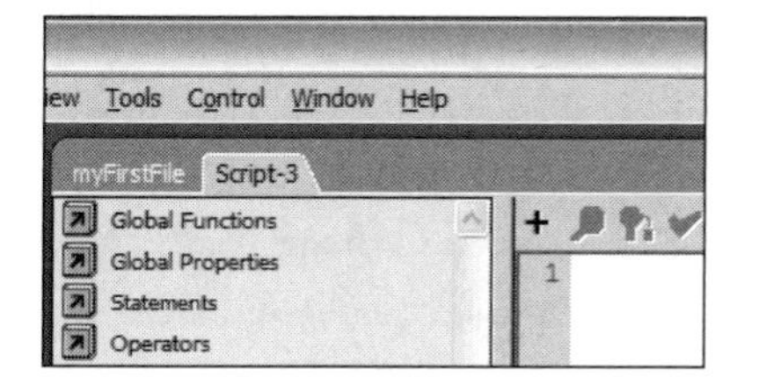

This completes the exercise. Next, you start creating your first application.

PLANNING A PROJECT

When creating a project that contains a generous amount of ActionScript, it's wise to do some planning up front. Dealing with problems in the idea stage makes a lot more sense than dealing with them in the development stage, where they often require more time and cause frustration before they are fixed. We guarantee you'll save time in the long run.

Many issues must be addressed before you even open Flash and start scripting. A good way to go about this is to ask yourself a series of questions.

WHAT DO YOU WANT TO OCCUR?

This is the most important question in the script planning process. Be as clear, informative, and visual as possible in your answer, but avoid going into too much detail.

For the project we discuss in this lesson, we want to create a scene that acts as a front end for paying an electric bill. We want the amount of the bill to be loaded into the movie from an external source, a text file. We want to allow the user to enter an amount to pay into a text box. When a button is pressed, the amount the user paid will be compared to the amount he or she owed, and a visual and textual representation (a custom message) of the result—overpaid, underpaid, or paid in full—will be presented. When the user releases that button, we want the visual and textual elements in the scene to return to their original state. The script that accomplishes this will be the main script in the project.

WHAT PIECES OF DATA DO YOU NEED TO TRACK?

In other words, what numbers or values in the application are integral to its function? In our case, that data is the amount of the electric bill. We will also need to keep track of the difference between what the user owes and what he or she has paid, so that we can display that value in custom messages.

WHAT NEEDS TO HAPPEN IN THE MOVIE PRIOR TO A SCRIPT BEING TRIGGERED?

In our project, the amount of the electric bill must be established in the movie before anything else can happen. Because the primary goal of our project is to compare the amount of the electric bill with the amount the user chooses to pay, if the amount of the electric bill isn't established when the movie first plays, there will be nothing to compare when the script is executed. Creating and setting data prior to a script's being executed, or when a movie first plays, is known as *initializing* the data—a common practice in scripting and something that's usually transparent to the user.

At this point, you need to start thinking about how the data—the amount of the electric bill—will get into the movie. You can place it within the movie when you author it, or you can have it loaded from an external source (for example, a server or text file) when the movie plays. For our project, we opt for the latter: We use a simple script to load a text file containing the amount of the electric bill into the movie. The text file loaded into the movie to provide data is known as a *data source*.

WHAT EVENT WILL TRIGGER THE MAIN SCRIPT?

In our case, the answer is obvious: a button press. However, all kinds of events can trigger a script in Flash, so it's important to give some thought to this question. Does something need to happen when a user moves, presses, or releases the mouse, or when he or she presses a key on the keyboard? How about when a movie clip first appears in the scene? Or does the event need to happen continually (the whole time the movie is playing)? We'll discuss such events in detail in the next lesson.

ARE THERE DECISIONS TO BE MADE WHEN THE MAIN SCRIPT IS TRIGGERED?

When the main script in our movie is triggered, the amount the user enters to pay needs to be compared with the amount he or she owes to determine whether the payment amount is too much, too little, or right on target. The answers to these questions will determine the custom message to display as well as what other visual elements are visible on the screen.

WHAT ELEMENTS MAKE UP THE SCENE? HOW DO THEY FUNCTION?

Our scene will be made up of a number of elements, some of which we need to name so that ActionScript can use, control, and/or interact with them. To trigger the script, our scene will need a button, which will look like a pay button found on many sites.

We also need a dynamic text field to display the amount of the bill; we'll name this text field **owed_txt**. In addition, we need an input text field where the user can enter the amount he or she wishes to pay; we'll name this text field **paid_txt**. We also need a dynamic text field to display the custom message generated by the script; we'll name this text field **message_txt**. Finally, we'll add a graphic of a rubber stamp in the form of a movie clip instance with four visual states. Initially, the stamp will not be visible. If the user has not paid enough, a stamp will appear, indicating underpayment. A stamp showing payment in full will appear if the user pays the exact amount, and another showing overpayment if the user overpays. This rubber-stamp movie clip instance will be named **stamp_mc**.

WHAT WILL YOUR SCENE LOOK LIKE?

Use whatever means you want—an illustration program or a pencil and napkin—to create a rough graphical representation of your scene (both its appearance and the action that will take place), as shown in the diagram below. Include all the information you've gathered at this point. This important part of the planning process is often called *storyboarding*.

As you grow more proficient at ActionScript and develop additional projects, you'll soon be able to ask (and answer) the previous planning questions intuitively. However, no matter what your skill level, storyboarding remains an essential part of the planning process.

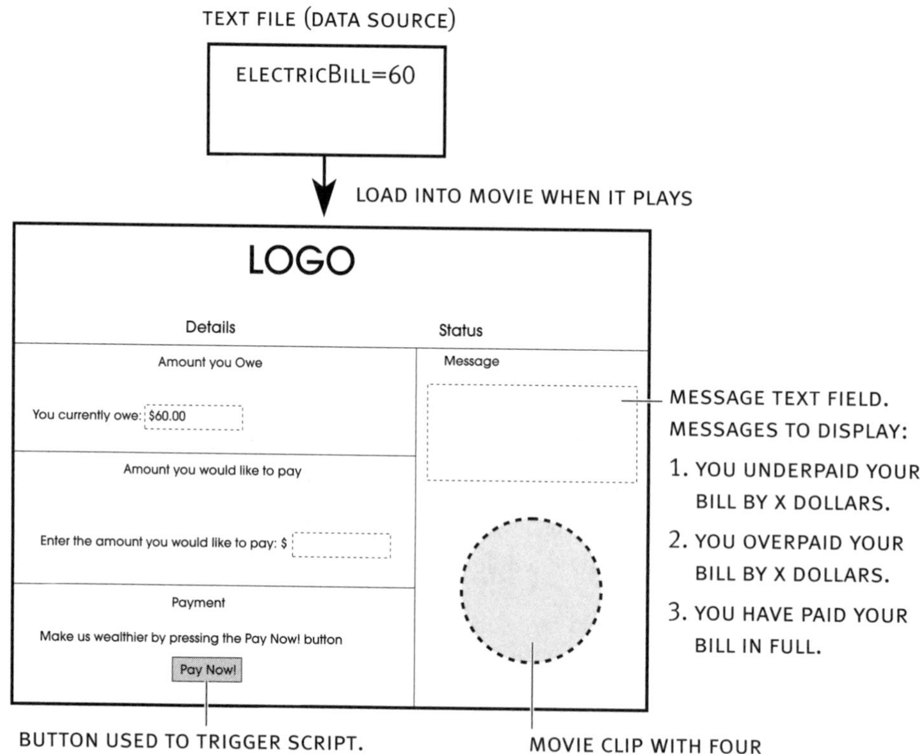
TEXT FILE (DATA SOURCE)
ELECTRICBILL=60
LOAD INTO MOVIE WHEN IT PLAYS
LOGO
Details
Status
Amount you Owe
Message
You currently owe: $60.00
Amount you would like to pay
Enter the amount you would like to pay: $
Payment
Make us wealthier by pressing the Pay Now! button
Pay Now!
MESSAGE TEXT FIELD.
MESSAGES TO DISPLAY:
1. YOU UNDERPAID YOUR BILL BY X DOLLARS.
2. YOU OVERPAID YOUR BILL BY X DOLLARS.
3. YOU HAVE PAID YOUR BILL IN FULL.
BUTTON USED TO TRIGGER SCRIPT. WHEN PRESSED, THE AMOUNT PAID IS COMPARED TO THE AMOUNT OWED AND SCENE ACTS ACCORDINGLY. WHEN BUTTON IS RELEASED, ELEMENTS IN SCENE ARE RESET.
MOVIE CLIP WITH FOUR GRAPHICAL STATES:
1. NONE
2. UNDERPAID
3. OVERPAID
4. PAID IN FULL

WRITING YOUR FIRST SCRIPT

Now that we have all the information we need, as well as a rough storyboard for our project, let's assemble it.

1) Open Windows Notepad or Apple Simple Text to create a new text file and type `&electricBill=60`.

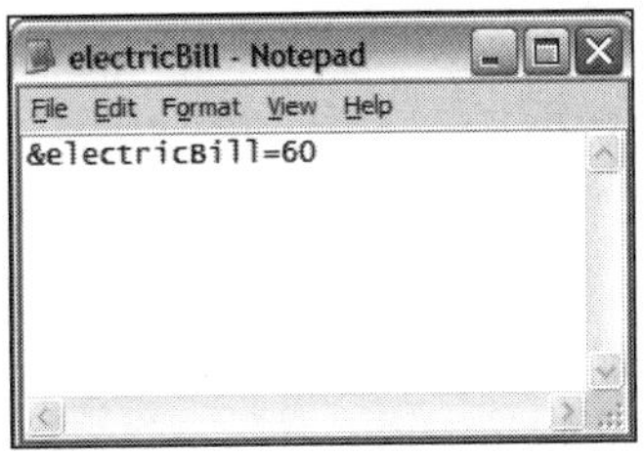

In the first part of this exercise we create the source for the data to be loaded into our movie when it plays. For our project, this data source contains a value representing the amount of the electric bill. When Flash loads this text file, it interprets this line of text and creates within the movie a piece of data (called a *variable)* named `electricBill` and assigns it a value of 60. The value of this variable will be used in several ways in our project.

NOTE *Loading data into Flash from external sources is discussed in detail in Lesson 11, "Getting Data In and Out of Flash." Variables are discussed in detail in Lesson 6, "Creating and Manipulating Data."*

2) Name the text file *Electric_Bill.txt* and save it in the folder that contains the files for this lesson. Open *electricbill1.fla* in the Lesson01/Assets folder.

With the exception of setting up scripts, our project elements are largely in place. (Remember, the focus of this book is ActionScript, *not* how to use Flash.)

Our project's main timeline contains five layers. The layers will be named in such a way that their content is evident. Currently, the Actions layer is empty.

3) Open the Property Inspector and select the text field to the right of the text that reads `"You currently owe:"`. In the Property Inspector, give this text field an instance name of *owed_txt*.

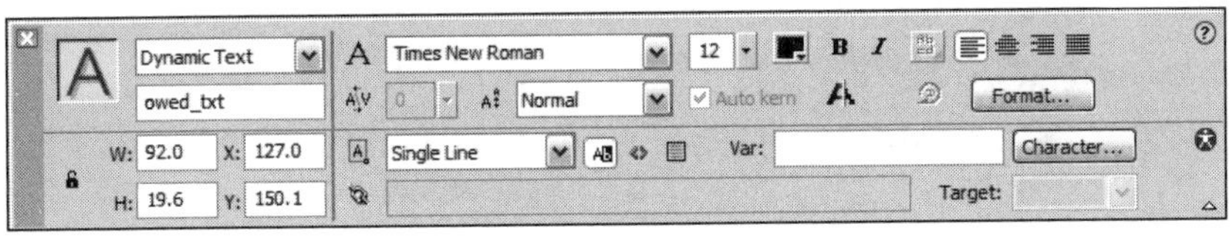

Because this text field will be used to display the amount of the electric bill, we've named it **owed_txt**. We add the **_txt** suffix to this text field's name so that when we create the script that references it, code hints will appear.

4) With the Property Inspector open, select the text field to the right of the text that reads `"Enter the amount you would like to pay:"`**. In the Property Inspector, give this text field an instance name of *paid_txt*.**

The text field you selected is an input text field. It will be used to accept input from the user—specifically, the amount he or she wants to pay toward the electric bill. We've entered zero (0) in this text field, so that's the amount that will appear initially when our movie plays.

5) With the Property Inspector open, select the text field on the right of the stage, under the label `"Status"`**. In the Property Inspector, give this text field an instance name of *message_txt*.**

This text field will be used to display a custom message to our user, depending on how much he or she chooses to pay.

6) Select the stamp movie clip instance (it appears as a tiny white circle below the *message_txt* text field) and name it *stamp_mc*.

Because our script will affect this movie clip instance, we must give the movie clip instance a name so that we can tell the script what to do with it. This movie clip instance has four frame labels (*none*, *underpaid*, *paid_in_full*, and *overpaid*) on its timeline that represent how it will look under various conditions. Initially, it will appear as *none*.

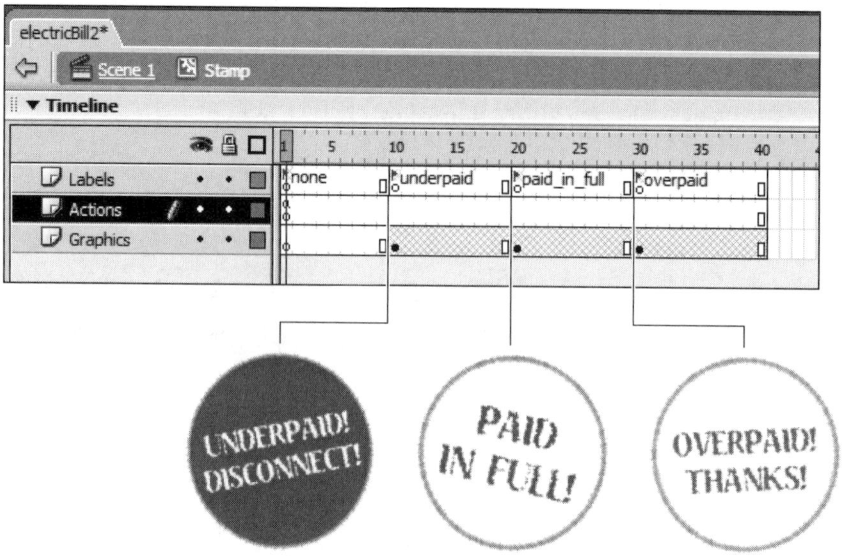

In the script we're about to set up, we want the movie clip to move to the *underpaid* label if the user pays less than what he or she owes, which causes the Underpaid stamp graphic to appear. If the user pays the exact amount, we want to send the clip's timeline to the frame label *paid_in_full*, which causes the Paid in Full stamp graphic to appear. If the user pays too much, we want the clip's timeline to go to the frame labeled *overpaid*, causing the Overpaid stamp graphic to appear.

Now that our scene elements are named, we're ready to script. Begin by instructing our movie to load the data from the external text file.

7) With the Actions panel open, select Frame 1 of the Actions layer, and enter the script:

```
var externalData:LoadVars = new LoadVars();
```

ActionScript uses LoadVars objects to load and store data that comes from an external source. The LoadVars object in our example is the external text file named **Electric_Bill.txt** that we created earlier.

In the next steps we add a script that loads the data in our external text file into this object, for use by Flash.

8) Add this script below the current script on Frame 1:

```
externalData.onLoad = function(){
  owed_txt.text = externalData.electricBill;
}
```

With these three lines of script, we tell Flash what to do once data from our text file has finished loading into the `externalData` LoadVars object. We've used the `onLoad` event to trigger the execution of the rest of the script. Essentially, this script is saying, "When data has finished loading (`onLoad`) into the `externalData` LoadVars object, execute the following function." (You'll learn more about functions in Lesson 5, "Using Functions.")

The function does one thing: it sets the value of the `text` property of the **owed_txt** text field instance to equal the value of `externalData.electricBill`. This requires a bit of explanation.

Our LoadVars object is named `externalData`. As mentioned earlier, this object is used to load and store data loaded from an external source. Our text file contains a single piece of data named `electricBill`, which has a value of 60. When this data is loaded into the `externalData` LoadVars object, it becomes part of that object. Thus, `externalData.electricBill` holds a value of 60 once the data from the external text file has been loaded. If our external text file contained other pieces of data, they could be referenced using the syntax:

```
externalData.name
externalData.address
externalData.phone
```

You'll remember that **owed_txt** is the instance name we assigned to the text field used to display what the customer owes. Thus, the function will cause the number 60 to appear in the **owed_txt** text field.

Text fields are objects that have numerous properties. One of the properties of a text field instance is its `text` property. This property is used to designate the text displayed in an instance. The script demonstrates how this property is used to set the text displayed in the text field instance named **owed_txt**. Notice that a dot (.) separates the object name from the name of its property. In ActionScript, this is how you indicate that you want to work with something specific concerning the object—in this case, one of its properties.

Here you'll also notice the use of an operator between two elements—an object property and a variable (and its value). Here, the equals sign (=) is used to tell the script to assign the value of the `externalData.electricBill` variable to the `text` property of the **owed_txt** text field instance.

9) Add this script below the current script on Frame 1:

```
externalData.load("Electric_Bill.txt");
```

Actions - Frame

```
1 var externalData:LoadVars = new LoadVars();
2 externalData.onLoad = function(){
3     owed_txt.text = externalData.electricBill;
4 }
5 externalData.load("Electric_Bill.txt");
```

Actions : 1

Line 5 of 5, Col 40

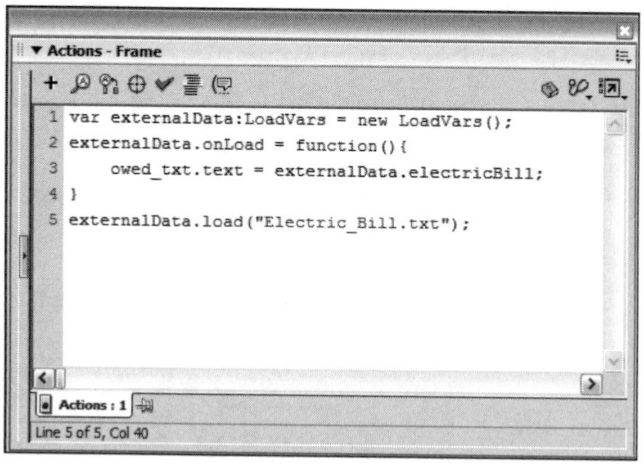

This line of script tells Flash to begin loading of the external data. It does so using the `load` command, which is a special command used by LoadVars objects. The command requires that you specify the URL of the external data to be loaded. In our case, it's the text file named **Electric_Bill.txt**. This is an example of setting a parameter value.

Recall that earlier we discussed how some actions had configurable parameters, and the parameter value you provided would determine how the action worked. In this case, the `load` action allows us to enter the URL to a text-based data source anywhere on our hard drive or on the Web. The command always works in the same manner (it loads data from an external source), but the location of the data source (the parameter value) can vary. You'll find that many actions in ActionScript work in this manner.

The script required for loading data from our external text file into Flash is complete. Let's do a quick review.

First, we created a LoadVars object named `externalData` for loading and holding our external data. Next, we told the `externalData` object to execute an action after data had finished loading into it. Finally, we initiated the process of loading the external data.

Are you wondering why we told the script what to do with the loaded data before we loaded the data? While it may not be obvious, it's the logical thing to do. Look at nature. For example, our stomachs are preprogrammed to process food. Imagine the mess that would ensue if we had to eat a complete meal before our stomachs knew what to do with the food. The same principle applies here. Scripting generally requires that you script how to handle various consequences, before they actually occur.

NOTE *We've placed this script on Frame 1 of our movie so that it will be executed as soon as the movie begins playing—important because our movie needs the* `electricBill` *value in order for the script that we'll be adding to the Pay Now! button to work.*

Now it's time to set up the script for the Pay Now! button.

10) With the Actions panel open, select the Pay Now! button and enter this script:

```
on (press) {
  var amountPaid:Number = Number(paid_txt.text);
  var amountOwed:Number = Number(owed_txt.text);
}
```

This script executes when the button it is attached to is pressed. In the script, this event is followed by an opening curly brace ({), a couple lines of script, and a closing curly brace (}). These curly braces indicate, "Do these two things when the button is pressed."

In the first line of the script, a variable named amountPaid is created and its value is set to equal that displayed in the **paid_txt** text field instance—with a twist. Normally, anything entered in a text field is considered text. Thus, even if a value of 100 appears in the text field as numerals, it's considered text (consisting of the characters 1, 0, and 0, or "100" with quotes) rather than the number 100 (without quotes).

NOTE *The fact that Flash considers everything entered in a text field to be text is a default behavior. Even though the user might not add quotes while typing into a text field, Flash adds them so that the movie knows that the value is a text value.*

You can think of the Number() function as a specialized tool that allows you to convert a text value to a numerical value in such a way that ActionScript recognizes it as a number instead. You need to place the text you want to convert between the parentheses of the function. For example:

```
var myNumber:Number = Number("945");
```

will convert the text **"945"** to the number 945 (no quotes) and assign that number value to the variable named myNumber. In our script, we used the Number() function and placed a reference to the text value to be converted between the parentheses of the function. If the user types **"54"** (text initially) into the **paid_txt** field, the Number() function causes amountPaid to be given a numeric value of 54 as well.

TIP *The Number() function has its limitations: you can use it only to convert something that is potentially a number in the first place. For example, Number("dog") results in NaN (not a number) because a numeric conversion is not possible.*

The next line in the script in Step 10 does essentially the same thing, except that the value of amountOwed is set to equal the converted-to-a-number value displayed in the **owed_txt** text field instance. You'll remember that this text field instance displays the amount of the electric bill. Thus, after the conversion takes place, amountOwed is given a value of 60.

The reason for converting the values in the text fields in this manner is that most of the rest of the script will be using them to make mathematical evaluations or calculations—it needs to see them as numbers, not text, in order for them to work.

In summary, when the button is pressed, the text values displayed in the **paid_txt** and **owed_txt** text fields are converted to numbers. These number values are assigned to the variables named amountPaid and amountOwed, respectively. These variable values will be used in the remainder of the script.

11) With the Actions panel still open, add these lines to the script created in the previous step. Add them within the curly braces ({}), just below where it says `var amountOwed:Number = Number(owed_txt.text);`**:**

```
if (amountPaid < amountOwed) {
  var difference:Number = amountOwed - amountPaid;
  stamp_mc.gotoAndStop ("underpaid");
  message_txt.text = "You underpaid your bill by " + difference + " dollars.";
} else if (amountPaid > amountOwed) {
  var difference:Number = amountOwed - amountPaid;
  stamp_mc.gotoAndStop ("overpaid");
  message_txt.text = "You overpaid your bill by " + difference + " dollars.";
} else {
  stamp_mc.gotoAndStop ("paid_in_full");
  message_txt.text = "You have paid your bill in full.";
}
```

Because we added these lines of script *within* the curly braces of the `on (press)` event, they are also executed when the button is pressed.

This part of the script is broken into three parts, identified by the lines:

```
if (amountPaid < amountOwed)
else if (amountPaid > amountOwed)
else
```

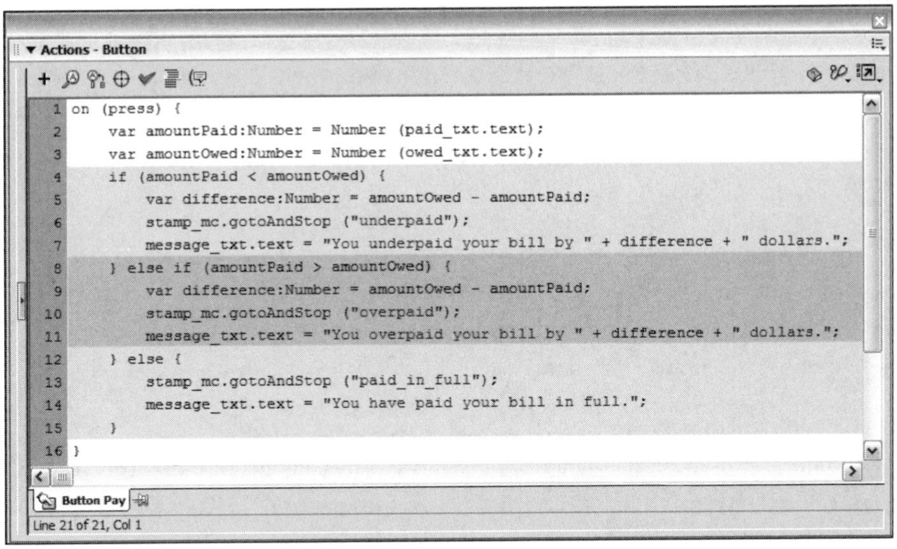

These three lines represent a series of conditions the script will analyze when executed. The condition to be analyzed in each case is specified between the parentheses. Underneath each of these lines in the script are several lines of indented script (between additional curly braces), which represent the actions that will be executed if that particular condition proves true. Here's how it works:

When our Pay Now! button is pressed, we want our script to determine whether the amount the user enters to pay is more than, less than, or equal to the amount owed. That's what the three conditions our script analyzes are all about. Let's review the first condition, which looks like this:

```
if (amountPaid < amountOwed) {
  var difference:Number = amountOwed - amountPaid;
  stamp_mc.gotoAndStop ("underpaid");
  message_txt.text = "You underpaid your bill by " + difference + " dollars.";
}
```

The first line uses a less-than operator (<) to compare the value of one variable to another. It basically states, "If the amount the user enters to pay (`amountPaid`) is *less* than the amount he or she owes (`amountOwed`), take these actions." These actions are only executed if this condition is `true`. And if they are executed, it's as a group, which is why they're placed within their own set of curly braces. The first action creates a variable named `difference` and assigns it a value of `amountOwed` minus `amountPaid`. If the user has entered 40 as the amount to pay, `difference` would have a value of 20 (`amountOwed` – `amountPaid`, or 60 – 40). It's important to note that any equation to the right of the equals sign is calculated prior to assigning the calculated value to the item to the left. The next line tells the **stamp_mc** movie clip instance to go to and stop at the frame labeled *underpaid*, causing the Underpaid stamp to appear. The last line will generate a custom message to be displayed in the **message_txt** text field.

We call this a *custom* message because of the way the message is constructed within the script. Note the use of the `difference` variable in this line: the value of `difference` is inserted in the middle of this message between the two sections of quoted text and the plus signs. If `difference` has a value of 20, this message would read: "You underpaid your bill by 20 dollars."

Remember that anything within quotes is considered plain text. Because `difference` is not enclosed in quotes, ActionScript knows that it references a variable's name and thus will insert that variable's value there. The plus sign (+) is used to concatenate (join) everything to create a single message. The equals (=) sign is used to assign the final, concatenated value to the `text` property of the **message_txt** text field.

If the amount the user enters to pay is the same as what's owed, or more, this part of the script is ignored and the next part of the script is analyzed. It reads:

```
else if (amountPaid > amountOwed) {
  var difference:Number = amountOwed - amountPaid;
  stamp_mc.gotoAndStop ("overpaid");
  message_txt.text = "You overpaid your bill by " + difference + " dollars.";
}
```

The first line here states, "If the amount the user enters to pay is more than the amount he or she owes, take these actions." The actions executed here are variations on the ones discussed previously, with minor differences. The first difference is that the **stamp_mc** movie clip instance is sent to the frame labeled *overpaid*, which displays the Overpaid stamp. The second difference comes in the wording of the custom message. Instead of saying **underpaid**, here it says **overpaid**. The actions in this section are executed only if the user pays more than what's owed. If that's not the case, these actions are ignored and the last part of the script is analyzed. It reads:

```
else {
  stamp_.gotoAndStop ("paid_in_full");
  message_txt.text = "You have paid your bill in full.";
}
```

Here, the script doesn't begin by asking if `amountPaid` is more or less than `amountOwed` (as it did in the first two sections). This is because the script continues to this point only if the user has entered the exact amount owed—this part of the script will execute only if neither of the first two sections does.

In the end, when the button is pressed, only one of these three sets of actions will execute. As a result, the **stamp_mc** movie clip instance will appear a certain way and a custom message will appear in the **message_txt** text field.

When the Pay Now! button is released, we want the elements in our scene to reset so that they appear as they did when the movie first played. Let's add that functionality.

12) With the Actions panel open and the Pay Now! button selected, enter these lines at the end of the current script:

```
on (release) {
  stamp_mc.gotoAndStop ("none");
  message_txt.text = "";
}
```

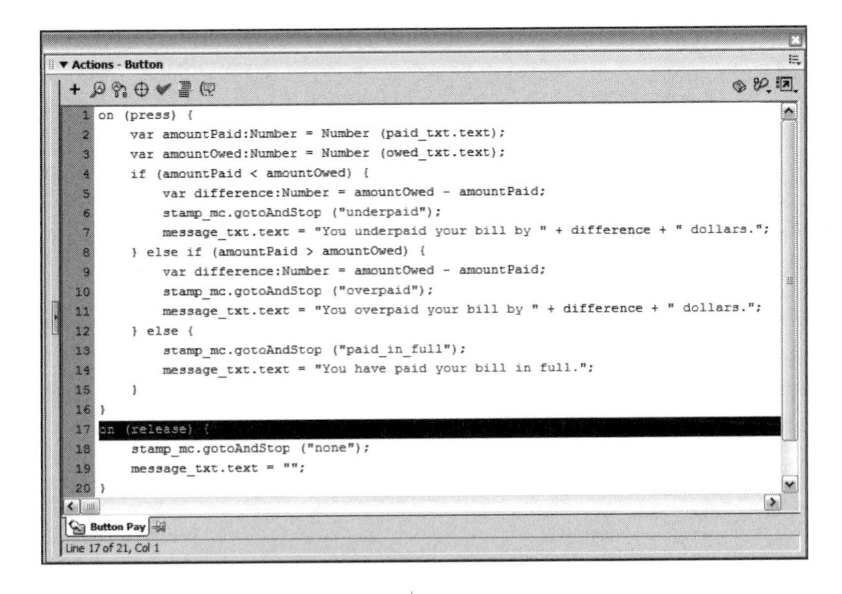

This script is triggered when the button is released. It will send the **stamp_mc** movie clip instance to the frame labeled *none* and empty the **message_txt** text field, returning these scene elements to their original state.

13) Save this file as *electricBill2.fla* in the same directory where you saved the *Electric_Bill.txt* file created earlier.

We'll use this file in the next exercise in this lesson.

TESTING YOUR FIRST SCRIPT

It would be pure fantasy to believe ActionScripts always work exactly as planned. Just as it's easy to forget a comma or to misspell a word when writing a letter, it's easy to make mistakes when writing scripts—regardless of how familiar you are with ActionScript. However, unlike your letter recipients, Flash is unforgiving when it comes to script errors. In scripting, errors mean bugs, and bugs mean your script either won't work at all or won't work as planned. Luckily, Flash provides some handy ways to test scripts and stamp out bugs.

1) If *electricBill2.fla* isn't already open, open it now.

This is the file we set up in the last exercise. In this exercise, we'll test the project's functionality from within Flash's testing environment.

2) From Flash's menu bar, choose Control > Test Movie.

This command creates a fully functional version of your exported movie and displays it in Flash's testing environment. Although there are all kinds of ways you can test your movie in this environment (determining overall file size, streaming capability, and appearance), we're interested in testing its interactive features—which means doing everything we can to mess it up.

TIP *Enlist as many friends and colleagues as possible to help you test your project. This way you have a greater chance of testing every possible scenario and thus finding all the potential bugs.*

3) Enter various amounts in the `"Enter the amount you would like to pay:"` **text field, then press the Pay Now! button.**

- *Enter an amount less than 60.* If you enter 35 in this text field, the message, "You underpaid your bill by 25 dollars" should appear and the **stamp_mc** movie clip instance should show the Underpaid stamp.

- *Enter an amount more than 60.* If you enter 98 in this text field, the message, "You have overpaid your bill by 38 dollars" should appear and the **stamp_mc** movie clip instance should show the Overpaid stamp. This is what should happen. What really happens is that the message shows an overpayment of –38 dollars, not 38 dollars. We log this bug as an error and continue testing.
- *Enter the exact amount of 60.* If you enter 60 into this text field, the message, "You have paid your bill in full" should appear and the **stamp_mc** movie clip instance should show the Paid in Full stamp.
- *Erase everything in this field.* If you do this and press the Pay Now! button, you get a message stating, "You have paid your bill in full" and the **stamp_mc** movie clip instance will show that you paid your bill in full. Obviously, this is wrong; we log this as an error and continue testing.
- *Enter some text.* If you enter anything beginning with a letter and press the Pay Now! button, you get the message, "You have paid your bill in full" and the **stamp_mc** movie clip instance will show the Paid in Full stamp—another obvious mistake, which we log as an error.

TIP *When you find bugs while testing a complex project, sometimes it's best to stop testing and begin the bug-stomping process immediately (as opposed to logging several bugs first, then attempting to fix them all at once). The reason is that when attempting to eliminate a bug, you may unwittingly introduce a new one. Fixing several bugs at once could result in several new bugs—obviously not what you want. By fixing bugs one at a time, you can better concentrate your bug-squashing efforts and avoid a lot of needless backtracking.*

As you know, our project contains three bugs:

- If a user overpays his or her bill, the overage is shown as a negative number in the custom message that is displayed.
- If a user chooses not to pay anything, our project functions incorrectly.
- If a user enters text rather than a numeric value, our project functions incorrectly.

Let's consider why these bugs occur. In the case of the first bug, we know that the numeric value that appears in this dynamic message is based on the value of the `difference` variable that's created when the script is executed. In addition, we know that the problem occurs only if the user pays *more* than the amount of the bill. Thus, the problem lies in the way `difference` is calculated when the user overpays his or her bill. We'll review that part of our script.

As for the other two bugs, our script is set up to act in various ways when executed, depending on what amount the user enters to pay. However, we forgot to account for the possibility that the user might not enter anything, or that he or she might enter text, both of which cause our project to act funny. We'll make a slight addition to the script to account for this possibility.

4) Close the testing environment and return to the authoring environment. Select the Pay Now! button and modify Line 9 of the script, which currently reads: `var difference:Number = amountOwed - amountPaid;` **to read** `var difference:Number = amountPaid - amountOwed;`**.**

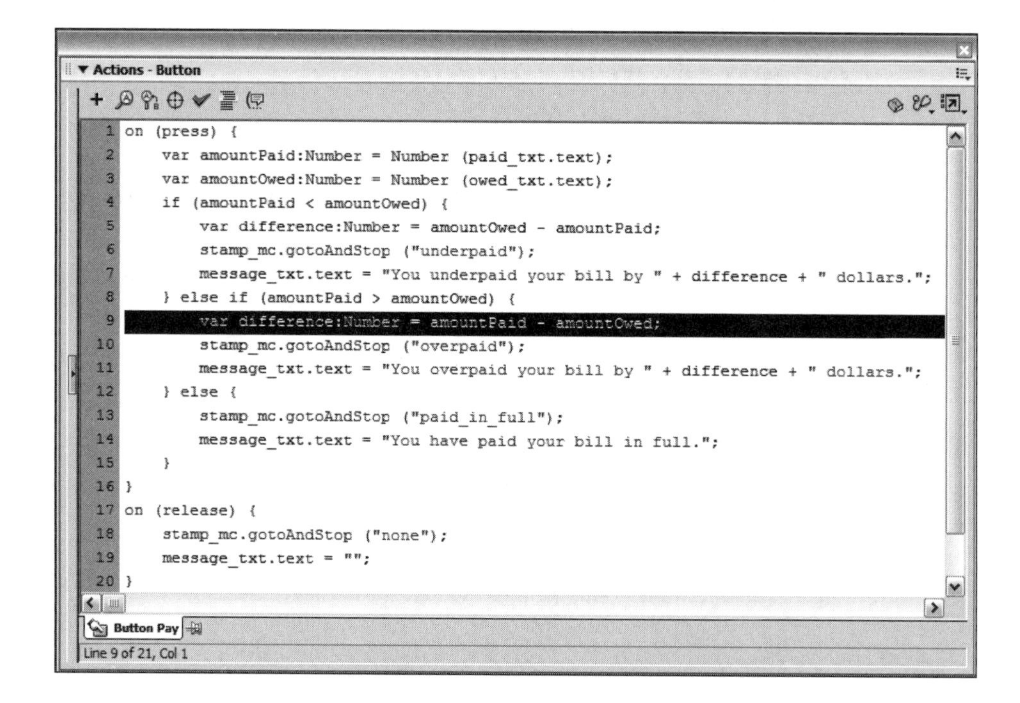

In reviewing the section of the script that determines what happens when `amountPaid` exceeds `amountOwed`, we discover that `difference` is calculated by subtracting `amountOwed` by `amountPaid`. How is this a problem? If the user pays 84 dollars, the difference being calculated is 60 – 84 (or `amountOwed` minus `amountPaid`). Subtracting a larger number from a smaller number results in a negative number. To fix the problem, we simply switch the position of `amountOwed` and `amountPaid` in the line of script that sets the value of `difference`. Now, the smaller number is subtracted from the larger one, resulting in a positive number.

NOTE *You don't need to modify the other area in the script where the value of* `difference` *is set, because that area is only executed when the user pays less than he or she owes, in which case the value will be calculated properly.*

5) With the Pay Now! button selected and the Actions panels still open, make this addition and modification to the `if` statement:

Addition:

```
if (isNaN (amountPaid)) {
  message_txt.text = "What you entered is not a proper dollar amount. Please try
   again.";
}
```

Modification to what used to be the initial `if` statement:

```
} else if (amountPaid < amountOwed) {
  var difference:Number = amountOwed - amountPaid;
  stamp_mc.gotoAndStop ("underpaid");
  message_txt.text = "You underpaid your bill by " + difference + " dollars.";
}
```

Notice that with this addition and modification, what used to be the first condition that was analyzed has now been relegated to the second condition. Modifying the script in this way will cause this new condition to be analyzed first.

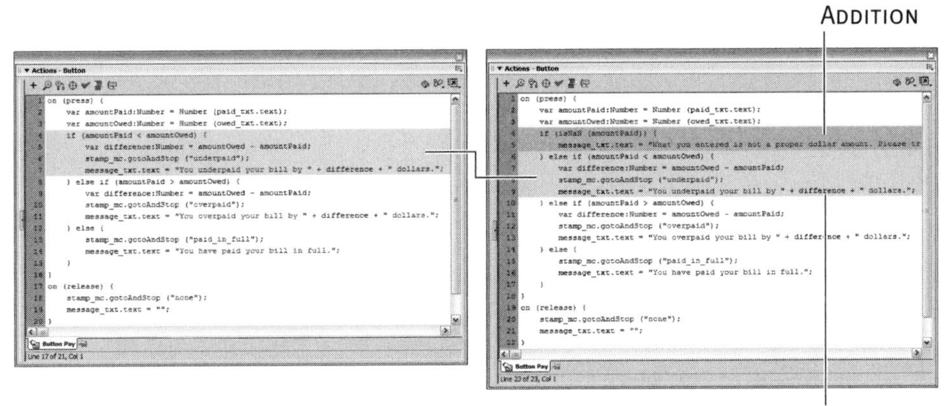

This addition allows the script to deal with the contingency that the user enters nothing or enters text as the amount to pay. It says that when the Pay Now! button is pressed, if the value of `amountPaid` is not a number (or `isNaN`), do nothing in the scene but display a message that asks the user to enter a proper dollar amount.

If the amount entered cannot be converted to a numerical value (for example, "frog") or if the field is left blank, this part of the script executes. The `isNan()` function is another special tool that ActionScript provides to take care of simple yet critical tasks. Notice that instead of inserting a literal value between the parentheses of this function (such as "cat" or 57), we've placed a reference to a variable's name (in this case, `amountPaid`). This causes the value that the variable holds to be analyzed.

NOTE *The `isNaN()` function and its uses are covered in greater detail throughout the book.*

We made this the first condition to look for because it's the most logical thing to check when the script is first executed. If the user enters a numeric value, this part of the script is ignored and the rest of the script works as expected.

6) From Flash's menu bar, choose Control > Test Movie. In the exported test file, enter various amounts in the `"Enter the amount you would like to pay:"` **text field and press the Pay Now! button.**

At this point the movie should work properly under all circumstances.

7) Close the testing environment and return to the authoring environment. Save this file as *electricBill3.fla*.

Congratulations! You've completed your first lesson.

WHAT YOU HAVE LEARNED

In this lesson, you have:

- Been introduced to ActionScript 2.0, and learned the differences and similarities between ActionScript 2.0 and ActionScript 1.0 (pages 6–15)
- Familiarized yourself with the various elements that make up a script (pages 15–20)
- Learned to use the ActionScript editor (pages 20–25)
- Planned and developed an ActionScript project (pages 26–28)
- Written the project script (pages 29–38)
- Tested the script, searching for bugs (pages 38–39)
- Fixed bugs to complete the project (pages 39–42)

using event handlers

LESSON 2

We push buttons, we push people, we even push people's buttons, all with a single purpose: to elicit a response. The Macromedia Flash way of saying this is that for every *event* there is an action.

In a Flash environment, the responses that come from pushing, holding, moving, entering, and leaving are triggered by *event handlers*. Event handlers represent the first step in getting your movie to do anything interactive—which is why a thorough understanding of them is vital.

We'll create several projects in this lesson, including this self-running presentation that uses frame events to provide the user with a hands-free experience.

WHAT YOU WILL LEARN

In this lesson, you will:

- Learn how event handlers are used in scripts
- Determine the best event handler for the job
- Use mouse/button/keyboard events to control interactivity
- Create a self-running presentation using frame events
- Use clip events to create an interactive project
- Orchestrate multiple events to accomplish a task
- Define and use event handler methods
- Learn about Listeners and how to use them

APPROXIMATE TIME

This lesson takes approximately two hours to complete.

LESSON FILES

Starting Files:

Lesson02/Assets/MouseEvents1.fla
Lesson02/Assets/FrameEvents1.fla
Lesson02/Assets/ClipEvents1.fla
Lesson02/Assets/OrchestratingEvents1.fla
Lesson02/Assets/CarParts1.fla
Lesson02/Assets/Listeners1.fla

Completed Projects:

MouseEvents2.fla
FrameEvents2.fla
ClipEvents2.fla
OrchestratingEvents2.fla
CarParts2.fla
Listeners2.fla

WHAT EVENT HANDLERS DO

Many computer programs allow users to accomplish tasks by dragging and dropping items on the screen, resizing windows, making adjustments with sliders, and creating artistic masterpieces using "virtual" art tools—all modes of interaction determined by the way in which the software has been programmed to deal with various events (mouse presses, mouse movements, keyboard input, and so on).

Event handlers orchestrate your movies' interactivity by controlling when scripts are triggered. They provide a "when" to a script so that it executes only when something specific occurs. Every script in your movie is triggered by an *event*—a user rolling over a button or pressing a key, your movie's timeline reaching a certain frame, and so on.

In ActionScript, event handlers (with the exception of frame events) usually represent the first lines in a script. For example:

```
When this happens (event) {
  do this;
  do this;
}
```

Frame events occur when the timeline reaches a frame that contains a script. When you place a script on a frame, you don't need to identify a frame event to trigger that script because the timeline reaching the frame is enough to cause it to execute. If the script were placed in a frame, it would look like this:

```
do this;
do this;
```

The better you understand event handlers, the more control you'll have over the user's experience. By using event handlers properly, you can create immersive environments the user will enjoy.

CHOOSING THE RIGHT EVENT HANDLER

Using event handlers properly presents one of the biggest challenges for ActionScript users—perhaps because most of us haven't given much thought to how things happen around us, and how to apply what we know when we create interactive environments. However, being mindful of how things and people interact in the real world can go a long way toward helping you re-create such interactions in your Flash movies.

As we introduce you to Flash's many event handlers, we'll examine some of the ways in which their use can be translated into real-world events. As you review these events, remember what you learned at the beginning of this lesson: in Flash, for every event, there is an action (or reaction).

NOTE *Later in the lesson we'll discuss event handler methods, which are an extension of the standard event handlers.*

USING MOUSE EVENTS

Mouse events control the execution of scripts when the mouse interacts with a button or movie clip instance. You use them to emulate things you might do with your hands.

MAKING CONTACT: `on (press)`

In the physical world, when you touch or press something—a person or an ice cube—you expect a reaction: the person responds, the ice cube melts. The `on (press)` event handler works great for emulating touching, grabbing, or just plain pushing, as well as the results of any of these actions. You can use this event handler to trigger a script when the cursor is above a button or movie clip instance and the mouse button is pressed.

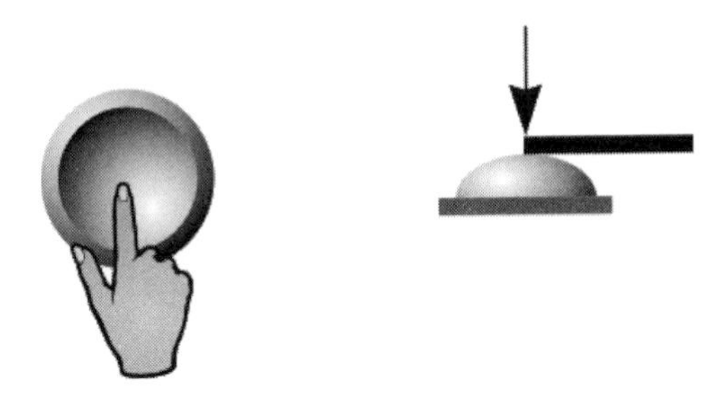

LETTING GO: `on (release)`

When you release something or cease to make contact with it, you're usually finished interacting with it and ready to move on. This event handler—which emulates letting go of something (or dropping it)—is the most direct way of allowing the user to make your movie take action. It's often used on buttons or movie clip instances to trigger actions. You use it to trigger a script when the mouse button is released (it was first pressed while it was over a button or movie clip instance).

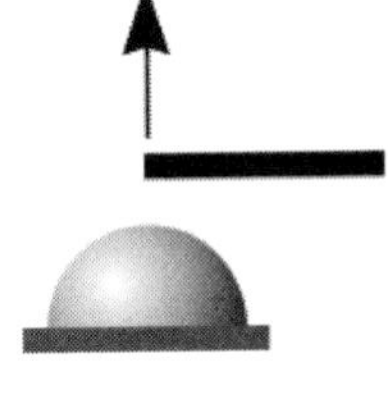

PULLING, SNAPPING: `on (releaseOutside)`

Imagine a deck of cards sitting on a table: you push down on the top card with your finger, drag it away from the deck, and then let your finger up. In Flash, this deck of cards could represent a button that the user presses, drags away from, then releases. You can use this event handler to trigger a script when your user has pressed a movie button or movie clip instance but released the mouse away from it, making this event handler useful for emulating pulling or snapping.

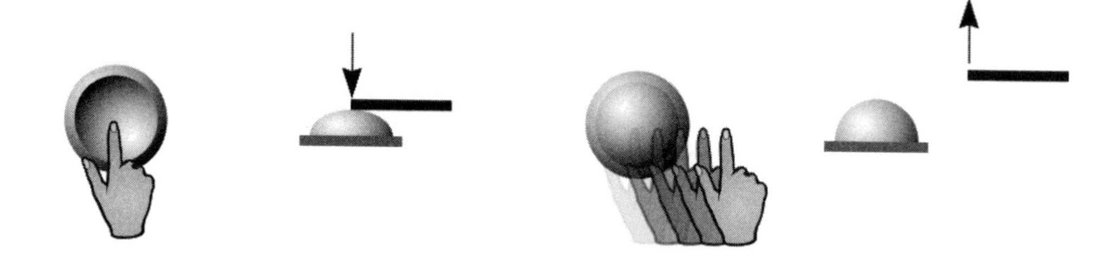

KEYBOARD CONTROL: `on (keyPress)`

You use this event to program your movie to trigger a script when a user presses a letter, number, punctuation mark, symbol, or arrow key; or the Backspace, Insert, Home, End, Page Up, or Page Down key.

OVER BUT NOT TOUCHING: `on (rollOver)`

You can place your hand over a hot stove and feel the heat without actually touching the stove. Consider using this event handler to emulate the way objects are affected by other objects that radiate heat, cold, light, air, and so on—with the button or movie clip instance as the radiation source. You can also use this event handler to display information about what a button or movie clip instance does before it's pressed (similar to a ToolTip or an HTML hotspot graphic). You employ this event handler to trigger a script when the user places his or her mouse over a button or movie clip instance.

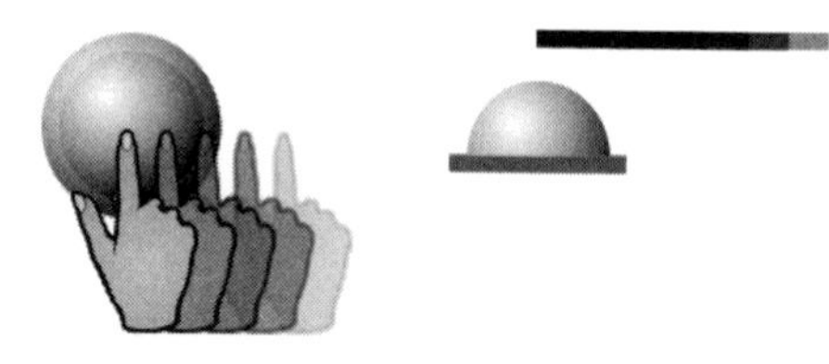

NO LONGER ON TOP OF: `on (rollOut)`

Obviously, when you move your hand away from that stove, you cease to feel the heat it's radiating and your hand cools down. That's what this event handler emulates. You can use this event handler to trigger a script when the user moves the mouse away from a button or movie clip instance it was formerly over.

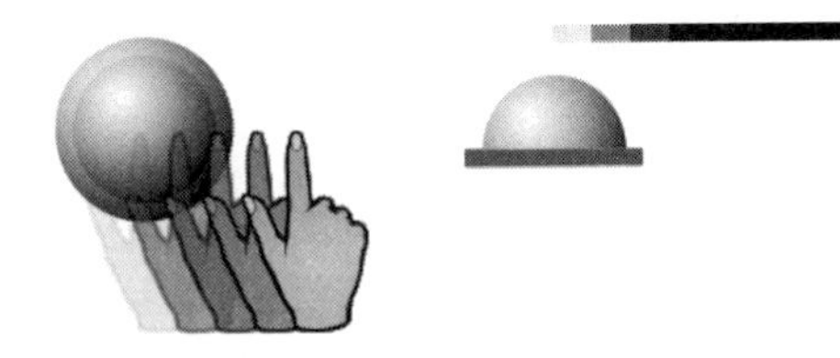

GROOVES, BUMPS, RUBBING: `on (dragOver)`

The act of rubbing entails a back-and-forth motion across an area. When a shoe is being shined (cloth dragged over it), for example, it gets slicker with each pass (action). This event handler lets you emulate this type of activity in your movie by triggering a script each time the mouse passes over the same movie button or movie clip instance while the mouse button remains pressed.

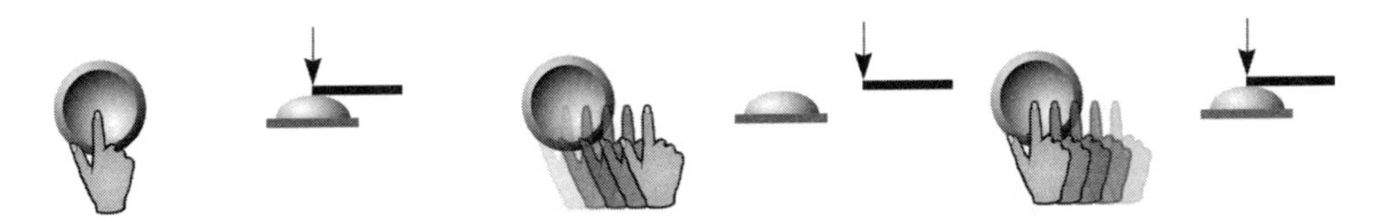

OOPS: `on (dragOut)`

This event handler allows you to emulate what can happen when you press or touch something but then pull away—as if you were to touch someone by accident and quickly pull your hand away once you realize your mistake. You can use this event handler to trigger a script when the user places the pointer over a movie button or movie clip instance, presses the mouse button, and drags it away from the movie button or movie clip instance (while still pressing the mouse button).

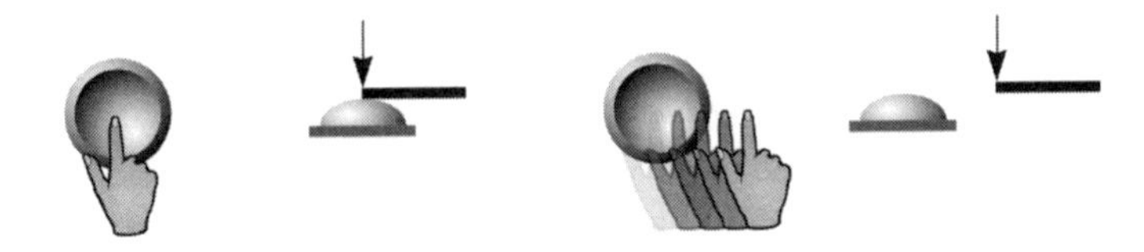

In this exercise, we'll create a fingerprint scanner that interacts with the user in various ways. In the process, you'll learn several creative uses for these event handlers, enabling you to emulate rubbing, snapping, and more.

1) Open *MouseEvents1.fla* in the Lesson02/Assets folder. Open the Scene panel and Property Inspector.

We're focusing on the ActionScript that makes this project work, so most of the elements are already in place. Let's get acquainted with what's on the stage.

The Scene panel shows that our project contains two scenes, Scan and Playroom. We'll begin our work in the Scan scene, which contains five layers that are named according to their content.

If you select the box in the bottom center of the screen, you'll see in the Property Inspector that this is a dynamic text field with an instance name of **message_mc**.

If you select the hand graphic, you'll notice in the Property Inspector that this is a movie clip instance named **hand_mc**. The black box in the middle of the screen is also a movie clip instance; this one is named **scanner_mc**. On top of this movie clip instance is a button that appears to be a square piece of glass. Soon we'll attach several scripts to this button.

2) Lock the Scanner button layer and double-click the scanner movie clip instance in the middle of the stage to edit it in place.

You are now looking at this movie clip's timeline. The overall functionality of this movie clip is not important (move the playhead to see how it appears visually at various points). It is, however, important to be aware of the six frame labels on its timeline. One of the functions of the several scripts we'll attach to our Glass button (on the main timeline) will be to move this movie clip's timeline to these various labels whenever a particular mouse event occurs.

3) Return to the main timeline. With the Actions panel open, select Frame 1 of the Actions layer and add the script:

```
stop ();
Mouse.hide();
startDrag ("hand_mc", true);
message_txt.text = "Please place your finger on the scanner and press down.
Release after 2 seconds.";
```

The first action prevents the movie from moving past this scene until we instruct it to do so. The second action hides the mouse cursor because we will be using the **hand_mc** movie clip instance as a custom cursor. The third action instructs Flash to drag this instance and move it around the screen as if the instance were the normal mouse cursor. The `true` parameter in this action automatically centers the dragged clip's center on the tip of the mouse cursor. The last action places the initial text in the text field named **message_txt**.

Because these actions are on Frame 1 of the first scene, they occur as soon as the movie begins to play.

4) With the Actions panel still open, unlock the Scanner button layer, select the button on that layer (which appears as a square sheet of glass), and add the script:

```
on (rollOver) {
  scanner_mc.gotoAndPlay ("Active");
  message_txt.text = "Please press on the screen to continue.";
}
```

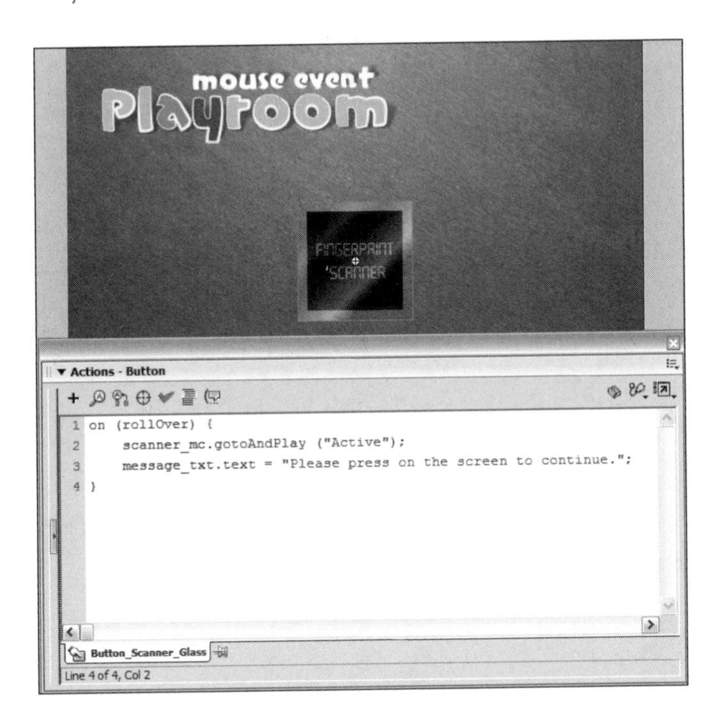

When the hand moves over the Glass button, we want to give the impression that it's being "sensed" by the scanner. The rollOver event lets us do that by triggering an action when the hand first hovers over the button. This event handler triggers two actions: it sends the **scanner_mc** movie clip instance to the Active frame, where a short animation provides a visual cue that the scanner is active and ready to be pressed. It then changes the text being displayed in the **message_txt** text field.

5) Add this script just below the current script:

```
on (rollOut) {
  scanner_mc.gotoAndPlay ("Inactive");
  message_txt.text = "Please place your finger on the scanner and press down.
  ⇒Release after 2 seconds.";
}
```

As you can see from this addition, a single button can respond to multiple events.

This script (and the rollOut event that triggers it) addresses what happens when the mouse moves away from the button without pressing it. In this case, the **scanner_mc** movie clip instance is sent to the Inactive frame, where a short animation provides a visual cue that the scanner is resetting.

The next action in this script changes the text displayed in the **message_txt** text field. This is the same text that appears when the movie is first played, once again giving the impression that the scanner has been reset.

6) Add this script just below the current script:

```
on (press) {
  scanner_mc.gotoAndPlay ("Scan");
  message_txt.text = "Now scanning...";
}
```

When the user presses the button and holds it down, this script is triggered. The first action sends the **scanner_mc** movie clip instance to the frame labeled Scan, where a short, repeating animation of scan lines moving up and down on a scanner provides a visual cue that a scan is taking place.

The next action in this script changes the text displayed in the **message_txt** text field.

7) Add this script below the current script:

```
on (dragOut) {
  scanner_mc.gotoAndPlay ("Error");
  message_txt.text = "An error has occurred. You have removed your finger prior to
  ⇒processing. Please try again.";
}
```

This script, and the dragOut event that triggers it, addresses what happens when the mouse button is pressed while over the button but then is dragged away from it while remaining pressed. The thinking here is that the user pressed the button to start the scanning process but then pulled away, abruptly ending the scan. As a result, the **scanner_mc** movie clip instance is sent to the frame labeled Error, where a short animation provides a visual cue that there was an error in the scan.

The next action in this script changes the text displayed in the **message_txt** text field.

8) Add this script below the current script:

```
on (release) {
  scanner_mc.gotoAndPlay ("Process");
  message_txt.text = "Processing your scan...";
}
```

When the user presses the button and releases it, this script is triggered. The first action sends the **scanner_mc** movie clip instance to the frame labeled Process, where a short animation indicates that something is being processed and then cleared. At the end of this animation, a frame action instructs the main timeline to go to the Room frame and stop. This frame label is actually on Frame 1 of the Playroom scene, the next scene in our project. This functionality allows an action on the movie clip's timeline to move the main timeline between scenes.

The next action in this script changes the text displayed in the **message_txt** text field.

You've now finished setting up this scene. During playback, with proper user interaction, our project should progress to the Playroom scene. Let's continue our work there.

9) With the Scene panel open, click the scene named Playroom.

This scene contains seven layers, named according to their contents.

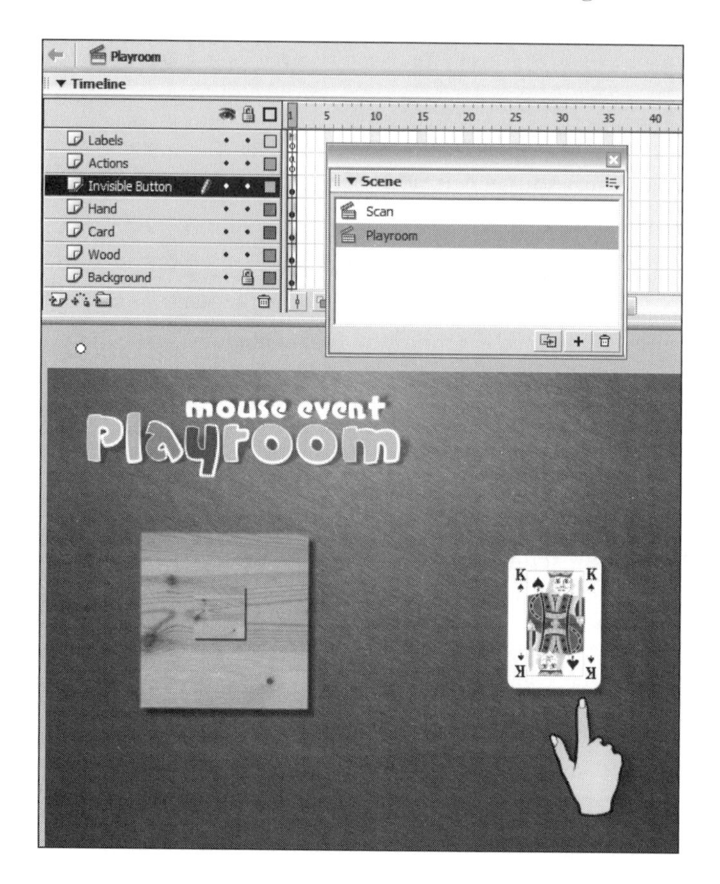

In this scene, we attach mouse events to movie clip instances to facilitate interactivity—and in doing so demonstrate how you can employ mouse events in almost the same fashion on buttons as on movie clip instances. In the upper-left portion of the work area, just above the stage, a small circle represents an empty movie clip instance (no graphical content). We'll attach a couple of mouse events to this instance. In the middle of the square piece of wood is a smaller piece of wood, which is a movie clip instance named **bump_mc**. We'll place a mouse event on this instance that allows us to emulate sanding this bump away. The card on the right side of the stage is a movie clip instance. We'll script this instance to "snap" into place when it's clicked and dragged.

10) With the Actions panel open, select Frame 1 of the Actions layer and add this script:

```
startDrag ("hand_mc", true);
```

This action is the same as the one in the previous scene that enabled the **hand_mc** movie clip instance to be dragged around the stage. Although the mouse remains hidden when the timeline moves from one scene to another (as our project is set up to do), dragging of objects needs to be reinitiated whenever a scene changes, which is what this step does.

11) With the Actions panel still open, select the small piece of wood (with an instance name of *bump_mc*) and add this script:

```
on (dragOver) {
  this._alpha = this._alpha - 10;
}
```

If the user presses and holds down the mouse button while moving the cursor back and forth over this instance, its opacity will decrease by 10 percent with each pass (`dragOver`). After 10 passes, the bump will be invisible, producing the effect of rubbing away the bump.

The way this script works is simple: with each `dragOver` event, we set the movie clip instance's `alpha` property (transparency) to equal its current value minus 10. The term `this` is a contextual reference to the object to which the script is attached.

NOTE *For more information about the term* `this`*, as well as other target paths, see Lesson 3, "Understanding Target Paths."*

12) With the Actions panel still open, select the *card_mc* movie clip instance and add the following script:

```
on (releaseOutside) {
  this._x = _root._xmouse;
  this._y = _root._ymouse;
}
```

If the mouse is placed on top of the instance, pressed, moved away from the instance (while remaining pressed down), and then released, this script will be executed. The script will move the **card_mc** movie clip instance's x and y positions to match the x and y positions at the time the event occurs. In other words, suppose the **card_mc** movie clip instance is on the left side of the stage. If the user places the mouse over the instance, presses and holds down the mouse button, drags the cursor away from the instance (to the right side of the stage, for example), and releases the mouse button, the **card_mc** instance's position will snap to the right side of the stage—the cursor's location on release of the mouse button.

13) With the Actions panel open, select the empty movie clip instance (above the stage) and add this script:

```
on (keyPress "<Space>") {
  _root.bump_mc._alpha = 100;
}
on (keyPress "<Left>") {
  _root.gotoAndStop (1);
}
```

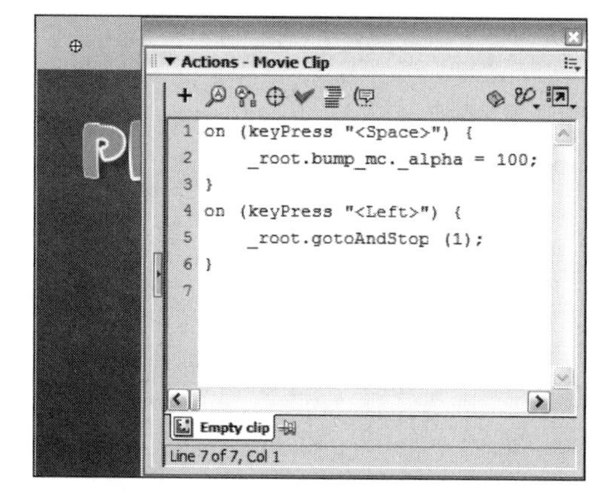

Here we've added two keyPress events to this movie clip instance. Note that you don't need to place the instance on a visible portion of the stage because the actions attached to it are triggered by keyboard presses rather than cursor interaction.

The first keyPress event is triggered when the user presses the Spacebar. When this occurs, the transparency of the **bump_mc** movie clip instance is reset to 100, making it fully visible again (in case it had been rubbed away).

The second keyPress event is triggered when the user presses the Left Arrow key. When this occurs, the main timeline (_root) is sent back to Frame 1, which contains the Scan scene where the user must scan his or her fingerprint again to return to the Playroom.

This completes the scripting for our project.

14) From the menu, choose Control > Test Movie to see the movie in action.
Interact with the scanner and elements in the Playroom to solidify your understanding of how these events work.

15) Close the test movie to return to the authoring environment. Save your project as *MouseEvents2.fla*.
This completes the exercise. You should now have a thorough understanding of mouse events and the ways you can use them to enhance your projects.

MAKING THE MOST OF ATTACHING MOUSE EVENTS TO MOVIE CLIPS

Movie clip instances can also have attached mouse events (as shown in the preceding exercise). To make the most of this powerful capability, you need to be aware of a few things:

- To cause a movie clip to be treated as a button, simply attach a mouse event to it. Under most circumstances, you cannot attach both mouse events and clip events to a single instance. However, you can use event handler methods (discussed later in this lesson) to set a movie clip instance to react to both mouse and clip events.
- When a movie clip instance is assigned mouse events so that Flash recognizes it as a button, it retains all of its movie clip functionality.
- When a movie clip instance is assigned mouse events so that Flash recognizes it as a button, a hand cursor will appear when the user places his or her mouse over it. If you want a movie clip instance to act like a button but don't want the hand cursor to appear, set the `useHandCursor` property of the instance to `false` with a `rollOver` event:

  ```
  on (rollOver) {
    this.useHandCursor = false;
  }
  ```

  The `useHandCursor` property can be set for button instances as well (covered later).
- Although you can place mouse events on movie clip instances, you cannot place clip events on button instances (as we'll discuss later in this lesson).
- Button instances can be assigned instance names, and they have properties similar to movie clip instances (for example, `_alpha`, `_rotation`, `_y`, and so on). Thus, if you give a button an instance name of **myButton_btn**, you can change its transparency using `myButton._alpha = 50`.
- Although you can assign instance names to buttons (and they're treated similarly to movie clip instances, employing properties and methods), buttons aren't independent timelines, while movie clips are—an important thing to remember when using the term `this` as a target path. For example, if you were to place the following script on a movie clip instance, the instance itself would rotate:

  ```
  on (press) {
    this._rotation = 30;
  }
  ```

  However, if you were to place the same script on a button, the button's parent will rotate. Think of it this way: movie clip instances *are* timelines, even when attaching mouse events so that Flash recognizes them as buttons. In addition to having properties and methods, buttons can be given instance names. They are still *part* of a timeline, not timelines themselves.

You might ask, because movie clips can be treated as buttons while they maintain all of their powerful movie clip instance capabilities, why use standard buttons at all? Primarily because a button's up, over, and down states are still much easier to re-create and implement using an actual button. For quick and easy button functionality, use button instances. For highly sophisticated button functionality, use movie clip instances with mouse events attached to them.

- If you use a movie clip instance as a button, you can place three special frame labels (`_up`, `_over`, `_down`) on a movie clip's timeline to easily facilitate the movie clip button's appearance when the mouse interacts with it (though you aren't *required* to do this in order to use a movie clip instance as a button).

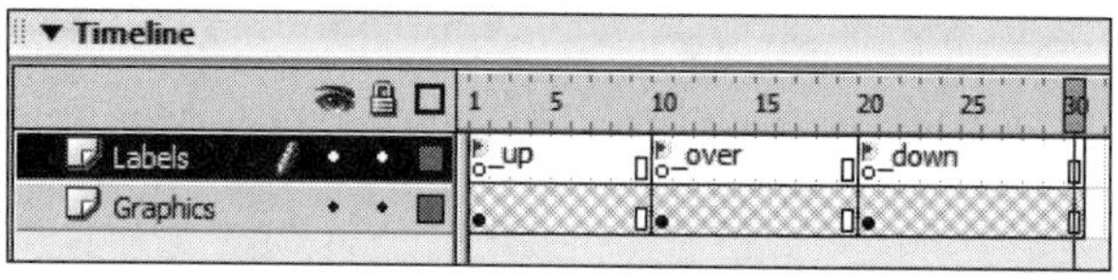

- By default, the *hit area* of a movie clip button will be the shape and area of any graphical content it contains. You can change the hit area at any time by defining its `hitArea` property. For example, this script will set a movie clip instance as the `hitArea` of a movie clip button:

```
myClipButton_mc.hitArea = _root.myHitClip_mc;
```

  This property is available only to movie clip buttons, not standard buttons.

USING FRAME EVENTS

Frame events are probably the easiest events to understand. When you attach a series of actions to a keyframe on the timeline, Flash executes those actions when the movie reaches that frame during playback. Frame events are great for triggering actions based on the passage of time or actions that need to be synchronized with elements currently visible on the stage.

NOTE *Many projects need to have a number of things set in place as soon as they begin to play. Known as* initializing, *this process usually involves creating data or establishing certain aspects of the movie's functionality. For this reason, many developers place a number of actions on Frame 1 of the main timeline to implement this initialization process. These actions are used to create variables and arrays as well as to define functions—all of which may be needed soon after the movie begins to play.*

In the next exercise, we'll create a simple self-running presentation that displays pictures and related text sequentially, using frame events.

1) Open *FrameEvents1.fla* in the Lesson02/Assets folder. Open the Property Inspector.

First, let's get acquainted with what's on the stage.

This 200-frame scene contains six layers (named according to their content), five text fields, three buttons, and two movie clip instances. The movie will begin playing at Frame 1, displaying a picture and associated text on the screen. We will place actions on Frame 200 to advance the picture, and send this timeline back to Frame 1 to repeat the process. Because our movie is set to play at 20 frames per second, each picture (and the information it contains) will be visible for 10 seconds (200 frames divided by 20 frames a second) before moving on. If you select the center picture in the left portion of the stage, the Property Inspector indicates that this is a movie clip instance named **pictures_mc** that itself contains several pictures: these pictures form the basis of our slide show. Soon, we'll add frame events to this clip's timeline. The other movie clip instance, **indicator_mc**, appears as a small white circle in the lower-right corner of the stage. This instance contains a short animation that alerts the user that the picture is about to change in case he or she wants to pause the presentation.

The three text fields to the right of the **pictures_mc** movie clip instances have instance names of (in clockwise order) **date_txt, country_txt**, and **caption_txt**. Using frame events, these fields will be filled with information related to the currently displayed picture. Two other text fields appear above and to the left of our control buttons (Play, Stop, and Rewind). The text field above these buttons is named **warning_txt** because this is where text will be displayed indicating that the picture is about to change. To the left of the control buttons is a text field named **balloon_txt**. When the user rolls over one of the control buttons, the function of that button will be shown here.

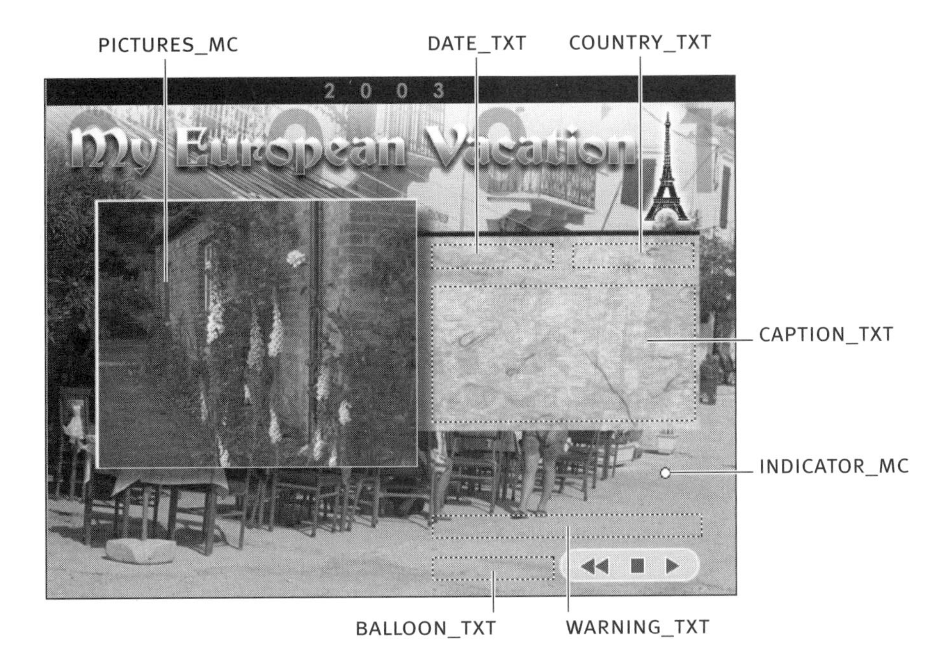

2) Double-click the *pictures_mc* movie clip instance in the middle of the stage to edit it in place.

You're now looking at this movie clip's timeline. It contains two layers labeled Pix and Actions. The Pix layer contains five keyframes, each of which contains a different picture (move the playhead to view these pictures). The Actions layer contains six blank (empty) keyframes. We'll explain shortly why this layer has one more keyframe than the Pix layer.

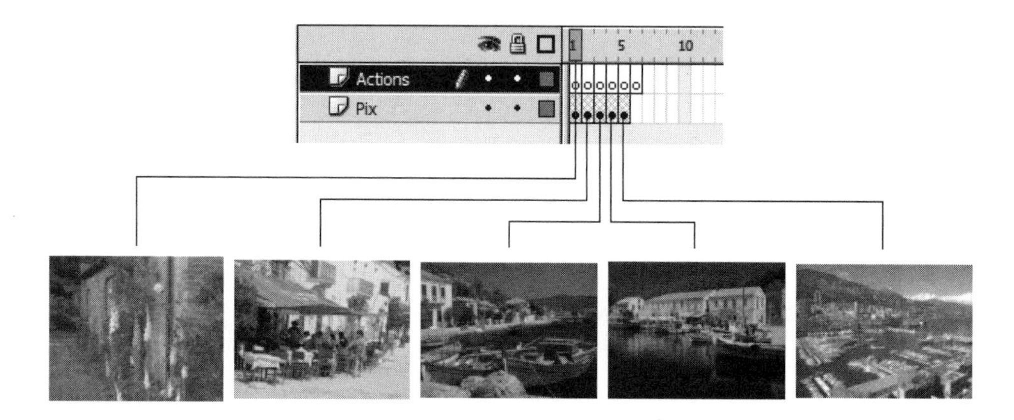

Now let's fill these empty keyframes with scripts.

3) With the Actions panel open, select Frame 1 on the Actions layer and add the script:

```
stop ();
_root.date_txt.text = "June 15th";
_root.country_txt.text = "Scotland";
_root.caption_txt.text = "Isn't this a beautiful place?";
```

The first action will prevent this movie clip from playing beyond Frame 1 until we instruct it to do so.

The next three actions place text into the appropriate text fields on the main timeline. This textual information relates to the graphic that appears on Frame 1 of the Pix layer on this timeline. In other words, whenever this timeline is on this frame, the visible picture and the text displayed in the text fields will coincide with one another.

4) With the Actions panel open, select Frame 2 on the Actions layer and add the script:

```
_root.date_txt.text = "June 16th";
_root.country_txt.text = "Italy";
_root.caption_txt.text = "The food was excellent!";
```

When this movie's timeline is moved to Frame 2, these three actions will update the respective text in the appropriate text fields on the main timeline. This textual information relates to the graphic that appears on Frame 2 of the Pix layer on this timeline.

5) With the Actions panel open, select Frames 3, 4, and 5 on the Actions layer and add these scripts:

Place on Frame 3:

```
_root.date_txt.text = "June 17th";
_root.country_txt.text = "Greece";
_root.caption_txt.text = "We went for a boat ride.";
```

Place on Frame 4:

```
_root.date_txt.text = "June 18th";
_root.country_txt.text = "France";
_root.caption_txt.text = "We took another boat ride.";
```

Place on Frame 5:

```
_root.date_txt.text = "June 19th";
_root.country_txt.text = "Monaco";
_root.caption_txt.text = "The mountains were amazing!";
```

Each of these sets of actions has the same effect as the previous two sets; the only difference is that these are triggered when this movie's timeline is moved to Frames 3, 4, and 5, respectively.

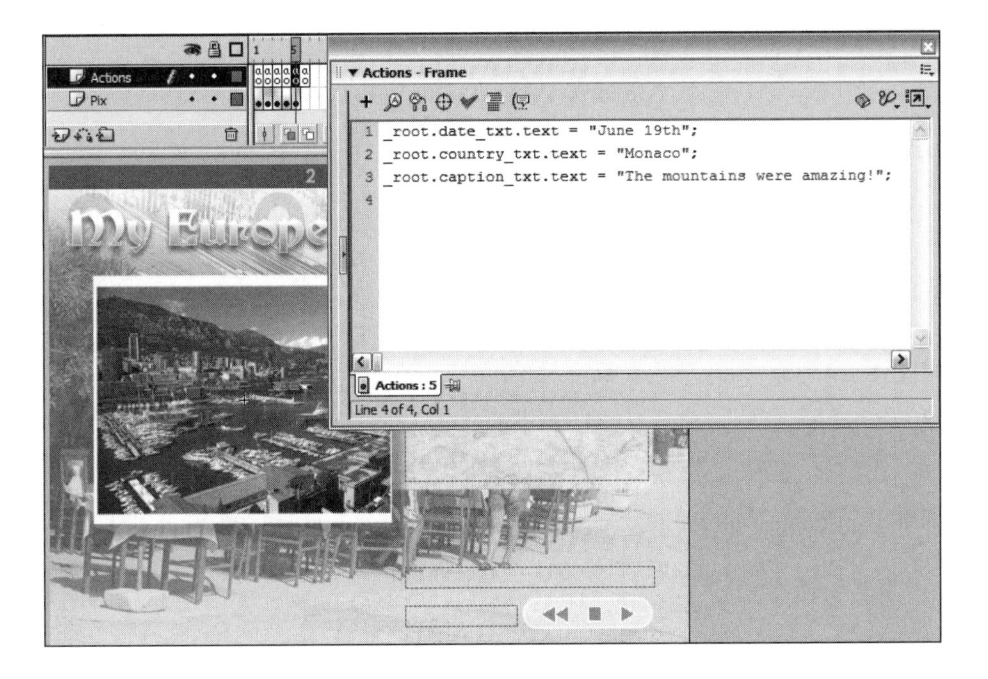

6) With the Actions panel open, select Frame 6 on the Actions layer and add the script:

```
gotoAndStop (1);
```

We advance through the frames in this movie clip dynamically by telling Flash to go to the next frame in the timeline—we won't use frame numbers or labels. We run out of pictures after Frame 5, and this script is triggered when the movie clip is advanced to the next frame (Frame 6), immediately sending the timeline back to Frame 1 and the first picture. Our demonstration loops through these five graphics until the presentation is stopped or the user exits it.

It should be easy to add more pictures and text to the presentation. Let's set up the functionality that advances our presentation through these graphics.

7) Return to the main timeline. With the Actions panel open, select the keyframe on Frame 140 and add this script:

```
warning_txt.text = "The picture will change in 3 seconds.";
indicator_mc.gotoAndPlay ("On");
```

Eventually, Frame 200 will contain a script to advance the picture being displayed. Our movie is set to play at 20 frames per second, so placing this script on Frame 140 will cause it to be executed three seconds (200 frames minus 140 frames equals 60 frames, or 3 seconds) prior to the picture change.

The first action displays a warning message in the **warning_txt** text field instance indicating that the picture will change in three seconds. The next action sends the **indicator_mc** movie clip instance to the frame labeled On, where a short animation acts as a visual cue that the picture is about to change.

8) With the Actions panel open, select the keyframe on Frame 160 and add this script:

```
warning_txt.text = "The picture will change in 2 seconds.";
```

This action updates the message in the **warning_txt** text field to indicate that the picture will be changing in two seconds.

9) With the Actions panel open, select the keyframe on Frame 180 and add the following script:

```
warning_txt.text = "The picture will change in 1 second.";
```

This action updates the message in the **warning_txt** text field to indicate that the picture will be changing in one second.

10) With the Actions panel open, select the keyframe on Frame 200 and add this script:

```
pictures_mc.nextFrame();
warning_txt.text = "";
gotoAndPlay (1);
```

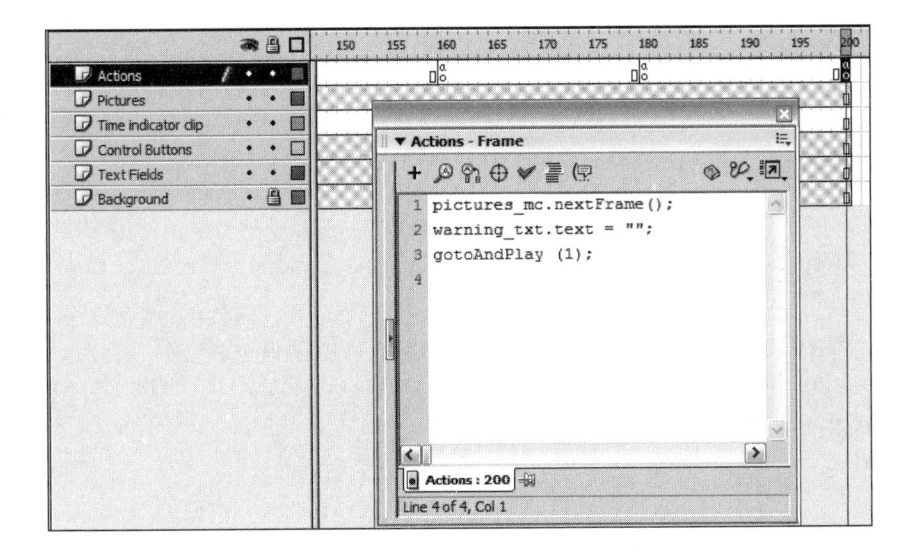

This set of actions represents the foundation that makes our presentation work. If the act of displaying a picture and its associated text for 10 seconds is a *cycle*, these actions would be executed at the end of each cycle.

The first action advances the **pictures_mc** movie clip instance to the next frame of its timeline. Doing so will cause the next picture to be displayed and the frame actions on that frame to be triggered. This will cause the text info for that picture to be displayed as well.

The next action clears all text from the **warning_txt** text field because the warning phase is complete—at least for several seconds.

The last action sends the main timeline back to Frame 1, which continues to play, and the entire process is repeated.

We want to let the user control the presentation's playback, so that will be our focus in the next few steps.

11) With the Actions panel open, select the triangular button on the control panel and add this script:

```
on (release) {
  play ();
}
on (rollOver) {
  balloon_txt.text = "Play";
}
on (rollOut) {
  balloon_txt.text = "";
}
```

This button responds to three events. When the user presses and releases the button, the main timeline plays (though obviously only if the presentation was stopped in the first place). When the user rolls the mouse pointer over the button, the word "Play" will appear in the **balloon_txt** text field (providing the user with a visual cue about what the button does). When the user rolls the mouse away from the button, the **balloon_txt** text field is cleared.

12) With the Actions panel open, select the square button on the control panel and add this script:

```
on (release) {
  stop ();
}
on (rollOver) {
  balloon_txt.text = "Stop";
}
on (rollOut) {
  balloon_txt.text = "";
}
```

This button is also set up to respond to three mouse events. When the user presses and releases the button, the main timeline will stop (though only if it was playing in the first place). When the user rolls the mouse pointer over the button, "Stop" is displayed in the **balloon_txt** text field (to cue the user about what the button does); and when the user moves the mouse away from the button, the **balloon_txt** text field is cleared.

13) With the Actions panel open, select the double-triangle button on the control panel and add this script:

```
on (release) {
  gotoAndPlay (1);
  pictures_mc.gotoAndStop (1);
  warning_txt.text = "";
}
on (rollOver) {
  balloon_txt.text = "Rewind";
}
on (rollOut) {
  balloon_txt.text = "";
}
```

When this button is pressed and released, the main timeline and the **pictures_mc** movie clip instance are sent back to Frame 1. This action resets the presentation to its original state, regardless of how it has progressed. The next action will display the word "Rewind" in the **balloon_txt** text field when the user rolls the mouse pointer over the button (to cue the user about what the button does). The `rollOut` event empties the **balloon_txt** text field when the user moves the mouse away from the button.

14) From the menu, choose Control > Test Movie to see the movie in action.

View the presentation from start to finish to get a feel for how it works. Use the control buttons to control playback.

15) Close the test movie to return to the authoring environment. Save your work as *FrameEvents2.fla*.

You have completed the exercise. Used properly, frame events can aid in creating highly interactive presentations you can add to easily.

USING CLIP EVENTS

When a movie clip instance with attached scripts enters a scene, that scene can take on a new look, feel, and function through the use of *clip events*. These events allow actions to be triggered when an instance enters or leaves a scene, when the user moves the mouse around in the scene, and in other ways.

This section describes the various clip events and provides real-world analogies for their uses. Note that you can use clip events only with scripts attached to movie clip instances.

PRESENCE: `onClipEvent (load)`

When someone or something enters a room or an area, there can be all kinds of ripple effects: the demeanor of people already in the room changes; the environment can be affected in some way; even the person (or thing) entering the room can change as a result of what's going on inside. This event handler provokes a similar response by triggering a script when a movie clip instance enters a scene—useful for initializing the movie clip, for having it be affected by the environment it's entering, or for having it affect the environment.

ABSENCE: `onClipEvent (unLoad)`

If a movie clip instance can affect a scene when it enters, it can also affect the scene when it leaves (sometimes in the opposite way). You can use this event handler to trigger a script when a movie clip instance exits a scene.

POWER, ENERGY: `onClipEvent (enterFrame)`

When an object is given energy or power, it usually signifies that it is taking action on a continuous basis. Consider a clock: without power it sits motionless and useless. If you provide power to it, it ticks, the hands on the face move, and you're able to use it to tell time. This event handler is used to trigger a script continuously, at the same rate as that of your movie as it plays. If your movie's frame rate is set to 20 frames per second, the scripts this event handler triggers are executed 20 times a second. This event handler has many powerful applications, as you'll learn from lessons throughout this book.

MOVEMENT: `onClipEvent (mouseMove)`

Think of this event as a motion detector within your movie. If a movie clip instance is present in the scene to which this clip event is attached, a set of actions can be executed each time the user moves the mouse—even if it's just a pixel. This event allows you to create motion-related interactivity—for example, the ability to detect movement direction (right, left, up, and down), current mouse position, and more.

COMPUTER-BASED INTERACTION: `onClipEvent (mouseDown)`, `onClipEvent (mouseUp)`, `onClipEvent (keyDown)`, `onClipEvent (keyUp)`

Because the mouse and keyboard are designed to interact with computers, these clip events don't have real-world equivalents. However, they do provide a means of executing scripts when the user presses (or releases) the mouse button or specific keys. While these events may seem similar to the `press`, `release`, and `keyPress` events described earlier in this lesson, they're a bit more powerful. Using the `keyUp` and `keyDown` clip events, you can create key-combinations, or keyboard shortcuts, in your application so that action is taken when a sequence of keys is pressed. In contrast, the `keyPress` mouse event allows a single key to initiate action. The `mouseUp` and mouseDown clip events are different from the press and release mouse events because while the latter only trigger scripts when the user interacts directly with a button, the mouseDown and mouseUp events trigger scripts when the mouse is pressed or released *anywhere* on the stage.

Receiving Instructions: onClipEvent (data)

In real life, incomplete instructions can lead to all sorts of problems. The same holds true in Flash. Because Flash lets you load various types of data (variables, external SWFs, JPGs) from external sources into movie clip instances, this event handler plays a vital role because it triggers a script, attached to an instance, only after this data has been *completely* loaded into it from the source. In doing so, it prevents you from receiving the types of errors that result from incomplete instructions. You can use this event to re-execute actions (refresh) if data is loaded into the clip more than once.

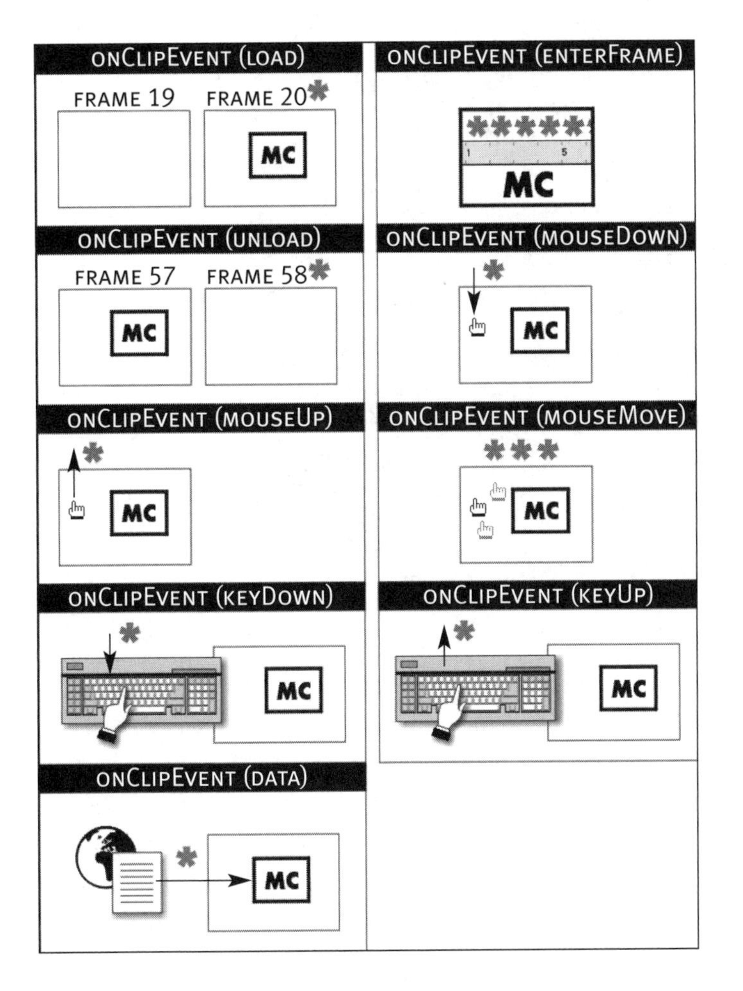

This is a visual representation of how clip events are triggered. The down arrow represents pressing the mouse button or a key. The up arrow represents releasing the button or key. The asterisk represents an occurrence of the event.

In the next exercise, we'll create a project that simulates a burglar's getting caught in the act. The burglar's presence (or absence) will determine how the scene plays, and the burglar himself will be programmed to respond to the environment in various ways using clip events.

1) Open *ClipEvents1.fla* in the Lesson02/Assets folder. Open the Property Inspector.

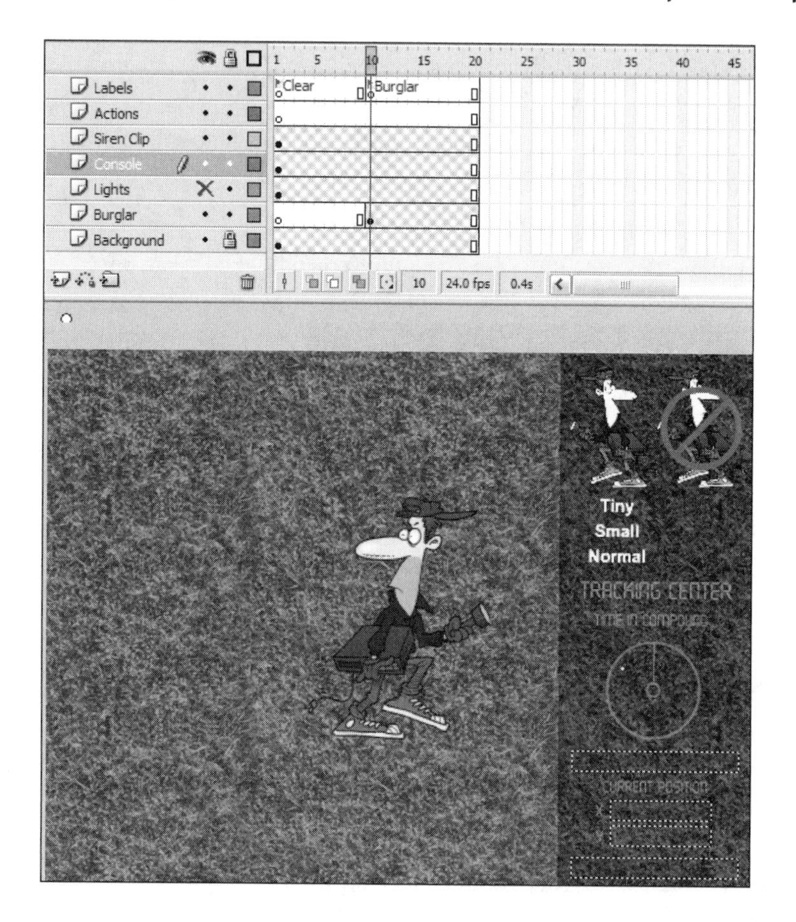

This project contains a single scene that includes seven layers named according to their content. Take special note of the two frames with labels. The one labeled Clear represents the scene without the burglar, and the one labeled Burglar introduces the burglar into the scene. (Move the playhead between these frames to get a handle on this concept because it will be critical to the success of our project.) The burglar graphic is actually a movie clip instance named **burglar_mc**, which will contain most of the scripts that control our movie's interactivity (more on that in a bit). The **burglar_mc** movie clip instance is the only movie element that appears and disappears when the user navigates between these two frame labels; all other elements are constantly present. Let's look at these constantly present elements.

At the top-right of the stage are four buttons. The one that depicts the burglar with the international sign for "No" (red circle with a line through it) on top will eventually be set up to move the scene to the Clear frame, thus "removing" the burglar from the scene. The other three buttons—Tiny, Small, and Normal—will be used to dictate our burglar's size.

Below these buttons is a light-green circle graphic: a movie clip instance named **timer_mc**. We will program **timer_mc** to spin when the burglar is in the scene, giving the sense that it's tracking time.

Below the **timer_mc** movie clip instance is a text field named **timeAmount_txt**. Here, we will be incrementing a number as long as the burglar is present—once again to give the sense that we're tracking time.

Below this text field are two more text fields, one with an *X* beside it, the other with a *Y*. We'll program our burglar to follow the mouse as it moves around. These text fields—**mouseXPosition_txt** and **mouseYPosition_txt**, respectively—display the current x and y coordinates of the **burglar_mc** movie clip instance as it moves.

Below these text fields is the last text field. Named **message_txt**, this text field will provide the current status of our environment ("All Clear," "ALERT!" and so on).

Our scene contains only two other elements—both movie clip instances that need to be examined in depth to be understood.

2) Double-click the small circle in the top-left of the work area, just above the stage, to edit this movie clip in place.

This movie clip has an instance name of **siren_mc**. With its timeline visible, you can see that it's made up of three layers and two frame labels. At the frame labeled On, there's a siren sound on the timeline. When this movie's timeline is sent to that frame label, the sound will play. This will be used to simulate an alarm being turned on. The other frame label on this timeline, Off, contains no sound; when the timeline is sent to that frame, the alarm will cease playing.

3) Return to the main timeline. On the Lights layer, click the Show Layer button (red *X*) to reveal a big black box that covers the entire stage. Double-click it to edit this movie clip in place.

This movie clip has an instance name of **lights_mc**. With its timeline visible, you can see that it's made up of four layers and five frame labels. This movie clip is used to simulate various light angles in the movie. We'll be scripting our project so that when the burglar moves to a particular area of the screen, the appropriate light will come on.

For example, if he moves left, the left "light" will come on (frame labeled Left). On the Sound layer, we've placed a sound at each one of the frame labels that gives the audio effect of a big switch being toggled (the light is turning on).

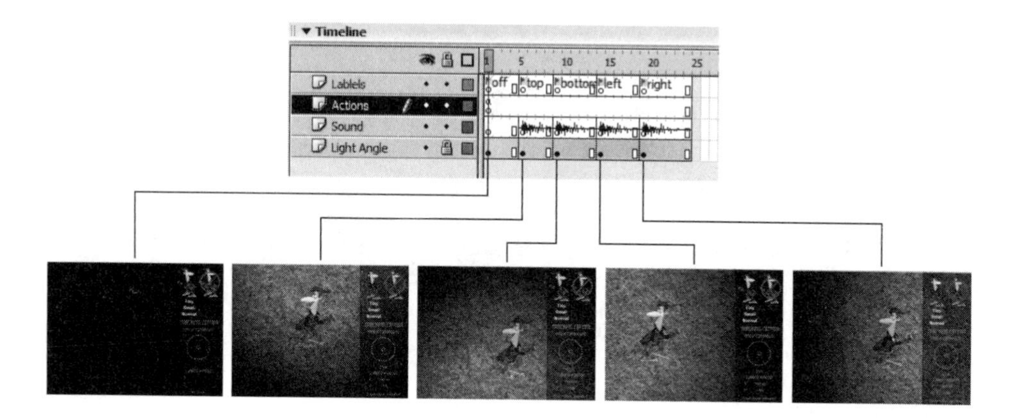

Now that the introductions are complete, it's time to start scripting!

4) Return to the main timeline. On the Lights layer, press the Hide Layer button to hide the big black area that is the *lights_mc* movie clip instance. With the Actions panel open, select Frame 1 on the Actions layer and attach this script:

```
message_txt.text = "All Clear";
var time:Number = 0;
var size:Number;
stop ();
```

The first line places the text "All Clear" in the **message_txt** text field as soon as the movie plays. Whenever the timeline is sent back to this frame label, this action will execute again. Knowing this, we can deduce that whenever "All Clear" appears in the **message_txt** text field, the main timeline is at Frame 1 and the burglar is not present. An understanding of this functionality will prove important in a moment.

The next two lines of script create the `time` and `size` variables, which both hold numeric values. We haven't assigned values to the `size` variable yet, but some of the scripts we add later will do so.

The last line stops the timeline from moving past this frame until we instruct it to do so.

5) With the Actions panel open, select the Tiny button and attach this script:

```
on (release) {
  if (message_txt.text == "All Clear") {
    size = 50;
    gotoAndStop ("Burglar");
  } else {
    burglar_mc._xscale = 50;
    burglar_mc._yscale = 50;
  }
}
```

When this button is pressed and released, it will take one of two sets of actions, depending on whether the main timeline is on the frame labeled Clear (no burglar) or the one labeled Burglar (burglar is present). In essence, this script says that if the **message_txt** text field contains the text "All Clear" (which it will whenever the main timeline is on Frame 1 and the burglar is not present), set the value of the `size` variable to `50` and move the main timeline to the frame labeled Burglar. At this frame the burglar will be present. The `size` variable will eventually be used to set the size of the burglar when he first appears in the scene. If **message_txt** does not contain "All Clear," these actions are ignored and the ones below them are executed instead. This also means that the main timeline is currently at the frame labeled Burglar and the **burglar_mc** movie clip instance is present in the scene. If this is the case, these actions will scale the vertical and horizontal size of the **burglar_mc** movie clip instance to 50 percent of its original size.

6) With the Actions panel open, select the Small button and attach this script:

```
on (release) {
  if (message_txt.text == "All Clear") {
    size = 75;
    gotoAndStop ("Burglar");
  } else {
    burglar_mc._xscale = 75;
    burglar_mc._yscale = 75;
  }
}
```

This is just a variation of the script attached to the button in the preceding step. The only difference is that `size` is given a value of `75` and the two actions that scale the **burglar_mc** movie clip instance (if present in the scene) scale it to 75 percent.

7) With the Actions panel open, select the Normal button and attach this script:

```
on (release) {
  if (message_txt.text == "All Clear") {
    size = 100;
    gotoAndStop ("Burglar");
  } else {
    burglar_mc._xscale = 100;
    burglar_mc._yscale = 100;
  }
}
```

Once again, this is just a variation of the script attached to the button in the preceding step. The only difference is that `size` is given a value of 100, and the **burglar_mc** movie clip instance (if present) is scaled to 100 percent, or its original size.

8) With the Actions panel open, select the No Burglar button and attach this script:

```
on (release) {
  gotoAndStop ("Clear");
}
```

This button does one thing: it moves the main timeline to the frame labeled Clear, where the **burglar_mc** movie clip instance does not exist. When the timeline is moved back to Frame 1, the actions we set up in Step 4 execute again.

In summary, the Tiny, Small, and Normal buttons are used to make the burglar appear or to resize him. The button we just configured makes the burglar disappear.

The rest of the scripting for our project will be placed on the **burglar_mc** movie clip instance.

9) With the Actions panel open and the main timeline at the frame labeled Burglar, select the *burglar_mc* movie clip instance and attach this script:

```
onClipEvent (load) {
  startDrag (this, true);
  this._xscale = _root.size;
  this._yscale = _root.size;
  _root.lights_mc.gotoAndStop("bottom");
  _root.mouseXPosition_txt.text = _root._xmouse;
  _root.mouseYPosition_txt.text = _root._ymouse;
  _root.message_txt.text = "ALERT!";
}
```

This set of actions is triggered when this movie clip first appears (`load`), or when it reappears in the scene as a result of the timeline's being moved to this frame. The first action causes the **burglar_mc** movie clip (`this`) to become draggable. The next two actions scale the movie clip's horizontal and vertical size based on the current value of the `size` variable, which exists on the root (main) timeline. Remember that we set this variable with one of our three buttons (Tiny, Small, or Normal). When one of the buttons is pressed, the `size` variable is set to a value of 50, 75, or 100 (depending on which button was pressed); the main timeline is sent to the frame containing this movie clip instance; and, on loading, the value of the `size` variable is used to set the size of the burglar.

The next action tells the **lights_mc** movie clip instance to move to the frame labeled *bottom*. At this label it appears that light is shining from the bottom of the screen. This is just a default setting. We'll make the **light_mc** movie clip instance a bit more dynamic in a moment.

The next two actions display the mouse's current x and y positions in the text fields on the root timeline (**mouseXPosition_txt** and **mouseYPosition_txt**, respectively).

The last action displays the text "ALERT!" in the **message_txt** text field on the root timeline to indicate that the burglar is now present.

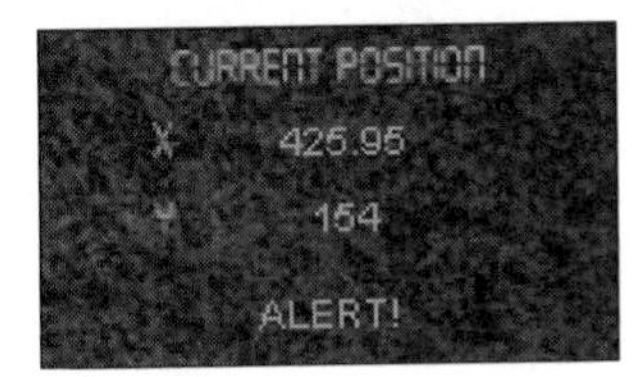

10) Add this script just below the end of the current one:

```
onClipEvent (enterFrame) {
  _root.time++;
  _root.timeAmount_txt.text = _root.time;
  _root.timer_mc._rotation = _root.timer_mc._rotation + 1;
}
```

Here, the `enterFrame` event controls three actions that are executed 24 times a second (because this type of event executes actions at the same rate at which the movie plays).

The first action uses the `time` variable on the main timeline (which we created in Step 4), to hold the value of an incrementing number. Using the ++ operator, each time the `enterFrame` event occurs (24 times a second), the value of this variable is incremented by 1. This syntax is the same as writing the following script:

```
_root.time = _root.time + 1;
```

The next action is used to display the incrementing value of the `time` variable in the **timeAmount_txt** text field.

The last action rotates the **timer_mc** movie clip instance by 1 degree, 24 times a second. This will produce the effect of the timer being turned on while the burglar is present.

NOTE *Because this script exists on the* **burglar_mc** *movie clip instance, it will execute only while that instance is present in the scene.*

11) Add this script just below the end of the current one:

```
onClipEvent (mouseMove) {
  if (_root._xmouse > Number(_root.mouseXPosition_txt.text) + 10) {
    _root.lights_mc.gotoAndStop("right");
    _root.message_txt.text = "Intruder is moving East";
  } else if (_root._xmouse < Number(_root.mouseXPosition_txt.text) - 10) {
    _root.lights_mc.gotoAndStop("left");
    _root.message_txt.text = "Intruder is moving West";
  } else if (_root._ymouse > Number(_root.mouseYPosition_txt.text) + 10) {
    _root.lights_mc.gotoAndStop("bottom");
    _root.message_txt.text = "Intruder is moving South";
  } else if (_root._ymouse < Number(_root.mouseYPosition_txt.text) - 10) {
    _root.lights_mc.gotoAndStop("top");
    _root.message_txt.text = "Intruder is moving North";
  }
  _root.mouseXPosition_txt.text = _root._xmouse;
  _root.mouseYPosition_txt.text = _root._ymouse;
}
```

The actions in this script are triggered every time the mouse is moved. An `if/else if` statement compares the mouse's current position with its last known position, and then acts accordingly. We'll examine the first comparison in the statement; having done that, the rest should be self-explanatory.

Before we continue, it's important to note that the `load` event we set up in Step 9 contained two actions that set the text displayed in the **mouseXPosition_txt** and **mouseYPosition_txt** text fields based on the x and y positions of the mouse when the **burglar_mc** movie clip is loaded. We will now use those text values in the comparisons made in this script. Since the information displayed in the fields will be used in mathematical comparisons in our `if/else if` statement, their values have to be converted to numbers using the `Number()` function. Thus, the script sees them as numeric values rather than text values.

The first part of this script states that if the *current* horizontal position of the mouse (`_root._xmouse`) is greater than the value of **mouseXPosition_txt** plus 10, two actions will be executed. By checking the mouse's current position against its last recorded position, we can determine in which direction it's moving. For example, if the current horizontal position of the mouse (`_root._xmouse`) is 300 and the previously recorded position (as displayed in the **_root.mouseXPosition_txt** text field) was 200, we know the mouse has moved to the right. In this case, our script would trigger two actions: one to move the **lights_mc** movie clip instance to the frame labeled *right* (where the light appears to come from the right part of the stage) and one to display the message "The intruder is moving East" in the **message_txt** text field. The `if` statement uses four comparisons to determine whether the mouse has moved right, left, up, or down.

NOTE *Keep in mind that although the mouse can move in two directions simultaneously (for example, up and right in a diagonal direction), our script gives single-direction movement precedence. This means that right-left movements are of higher priority than up-down movements. If the mouse moves both left and down, the script will detect only the left movement. The reason is that the `if` statement first looks to see if the mouse has moved right. If it has, the two actions for dealing with this movement are executed, but no other part of the `if` statement is executed. If the mouse hasn't moved right, that part of the `if` statement is ignored, and our script checks whether the mouse has moved left. If it has, the two actions for dealing with this movement are executed, but no other part of the `if` statement is executed. This same process continues when checking for down and up movements. In essence, once a movement in any single direction has been detected, the rest of the script is ignored. Because the `if` statement looks for right, left, down, and up movement in that order, if it detects right and left movements first, down and up movements won't matter.*

On a side note, you'll notice that in each comparison we add or subtract 10 from the value of **mouseXPosition_txt** or **mouseYPosition_txt** so that the mouse must move at least 10 pixels from its last recorded position before *any* action will occur. If we didn't do this, the mouse's movement on screen would look like firecrackers going off—that is, visually too intense.

The last two actions of this script (placed just before the last curly brace in the script) record the current x and y positions of the mouse so that the next time this script is executed (when the mouse is moved), these values can be used in the comparison process of the `if` statement again. Because these values are placed in the **mouseXPosition_txt** and **mouseYPosition_txt** text fields, each time the mouse is moved and these values are updated, the changes are displayed in those fields as well.

In essence, this script compares the current position of the mouse against its previously recorded position; takes appropriate action based on whether the mouse has moved left, right, up, or down; and records the mouse's current position for the next time the mouse is moved.

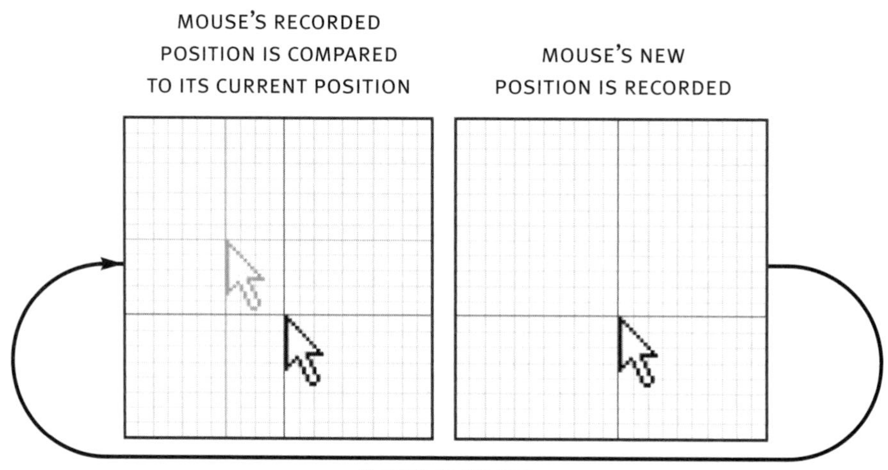
MOUSE'S RECORDED POSITION IS COMPARED TO ITS CURRENT POSITION
MOUSE'S NEW POSITION IS RECORDED
MOUSE IS MOVED

12) Add this script after the current one:

```
onClipEvent (unload) {
  _root.time = 0;
  _root.timeAmount_txt.text = _root.time;
  _root.timer_mc._rotation = 0;
  _root.message_txt.text = "All Clear";
  _root.mouseXPosition_txt.text = "";
  _root.mouseYPosition_txt.text = "" ;
  _root.lights_mc.gotoAndStop ("Off");
}
```

This script dictates what happens when this movie clip instance (**burglar_mc**) is unloaded, or is no longer in the scene (as a result of the main timeline's moving to a frame where the burglar doesn't exist). This occurs when the No Burglar button is clicked and the main timeline is moved to the Clear frame (which is actually Frame 1).

The actions restore the elements to their original state (that is, before the burglar appeared in the scene). The first one resets the `time` variable to `0`. The next action sets what is displayed in the **timeAmount_txt** text field to the value of `time` (making it `0` as well). The next action resets the `rotation` property of the **timer_mc** movie clip instance to `0`; the action after that displays "All Clear" in the **message_txt** text field. The subsequent two actions clear the **mouseXPosition_txt** and **mouseYPosition_txt** text fields, and the last action moves the **lights_mc** movie clip instance to the frame labeled Off. This last action turns the scene black again.

13) Add this script after the current one:

```
onClipEvent (mouseDown) {
  this.gotoAndStop("right");
  _root.message_txt.text = "Intruder is confused";
}
```

When the mouse button is pressed anywhere on screen, these two actions are executed. The first sends the **burglar_mc** movie clip instance (`this`) to the frame labeled *right*. At this label, the intruder appears to be looking to his right. In addition, a short audio clip plays of him saying, "Oh, no!" The second action causes the **message_txt** text field to display "Intruder is confused."

14) Add this script after the current one:

```
onClipEvent (mouseUp) {
  this.gotoAndStop("left");
  _root.message_txt.text = "Intruder is running";
}
```

When the mouse button is released anywhere on screen, these two actions are executed. The first sends the **burglar_mc** movie clip instance (`this`) to the frame labeled *left*. At this label, the intruder appears to be looking to his left. The second action causes the **message_txt** text field to display "Intruder is running."

15) Add this script after the current one:

```
onClipEvent (keyDown) {
  _root.siren_mc.gotoAndStop("on");
  _root.message_txt.text = "Backup has been called";
}
```

When any key is pressed, two actions are executed. The first sends the **siren_mc** movie clip instance to the frame labeled *on*, causing a siren to be heard. The second action causes the **message_txt** text field to display "Backup has been called."

16) Add this script after the current one:

```
onClipEvent (keyUp) {
  stopAllSounds();
  _root.siren_mc.gotoAndStop("off");
  _root.message_txt.text = "Silent alarm activated";
}
```

When any key is released, these three actions are executed. The first stops all sounds, including the currently playing siren. The second action sends the **siren_mc** movie clip instance to the frame labeled *off* (causing the siren to be turned off). The last action causes the **message_txt** text field to display "Silent alarm activated."

NOTE *Because the* `mouseDown/mouseUp` *and* `keyDown/keyUp` *clip events are attached to the* **burglar_mc** *movie clip instance, none has an effect until that instance appears in the scene.*

The scripting of our project is complete.

17) Choose Control > Test Movie to test the functionality of our project.

Press one of the buttons on the top-right corner of the stage to make the burglar appear. When he appears, notice how the environment changes. Move him around to see what changes his movement provokes. Press the button to remove him and notice what happens. When the burglar is in the scene, click the mouse or press the Spacebar on the keyboard. Most of our movie's interactivity depends on the **burglar_mc** instance being present in the scene, showing how introducing a single instance into the scene can change its dynamics completely.

18) Close the test movie and save your work as *ClipEvents2.fla*.

This completes the exercise.

ORCHESTRATING MULTIPLE EVENTS

As you've probably figured out by now, different events can occur simultaneously in your movie. For example, the user can have the mouse button pressed down (triggering a `press` mouse event) while moving the mouse around the screen (triggering a `mouseMove` clip event). By writing scripts that work in harmony while multiple events are occurring, you can add powerful interactivity to your projects.

In this exercise, you'll orchestrate several events to simulate a cue ball's being hit with a pool stick. Although there are some quite sophisticated ways of doing this, we take an intermediate approach.

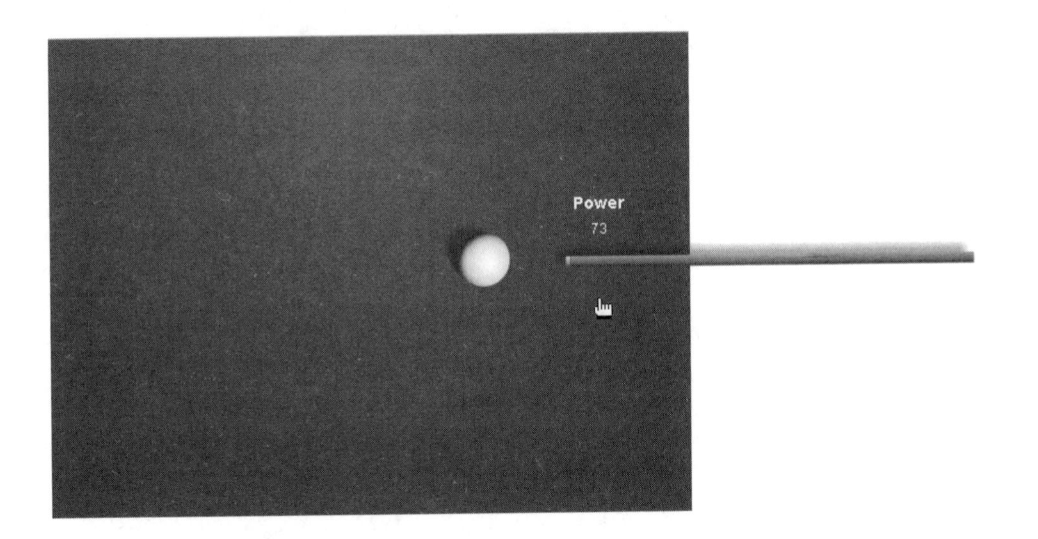

1) Open *OrchestratingEvents1.fla* in the Lesson02/Assets folder.

This project contains a single scene with six layers that are named according to their contents.

The white cue ball is a movie clip instance named **ball_mc**. We'll soon be attaching some scripts to this clip. To the right of this instance is a transparent-blue rectangle—an invisible button that will contain some scripts, which when used in tandem with those on the **ball_mc** movie clip instance will facilitate the interactivity we seek. To the right of this button is a graphic of a pool stick. This is a movie clip instance named **stick_mc**. The timeline of this movie clip contains two frame labels, Starting and PullBack. At the Starting label, the stick is up against the ball. At the PullBack label, the stick is animated so that it looks like it's being pulled to the right, in anticipation of hitting the ball. Just above the pool stick is a text field instance named **powerAmount_txt** that displays the power at which the ball is hit, based on how far the stick has been "pulled" to the right.

We're going to set up our project so that when the user presses, pulls away from, and releases the invisible button, the distance between the point where it was first pressed and where it was released will be calculated. That amount will be used to move the ball to the left. The greater the distance, the farther the ball will move to the left.

Let's begin the scripting process by first creating and declaring some variables our project will eventually use.

2) With the Actions panel open, select Frame 1 and add this script:

```
var power:Number;
var hitAmount:Number;
var trackMouse:Boolean;
var mouseStart:Number;
var mouseEnd:Number;
```

These lines of script are used to declare the five variables our project will use. All but one will hold numeric values. `trackMouse` will be used to hold a Boolean value of `true` or `false`.

3) With the Actions panel open, select the invisible button and add this script:

```
on (press) {
  ball_mc._x = 360;
  ball_mc._y = 180;
  power = 0;
  powerAmount_txt.text = power;
  hitAmount = 0;
  trackMouse = true;
  mouseStart = _root._xmouse;
}
```

Notice the location of this button. It's placed at the tip of the pool stick, just between the stick and the ball—a logical spot because, as the point of impact, it's also the best place from which to "pull back."

Most of the actions in this script have an initializing effect in our project and are triggered when the mouse button is first pressed. Since we know that the user may want to hit the ball more than once, the first two actions are necessary in order to move the ball back to its initial horizontal (x) and vertical (y) positions, essentially resetting it for the next hit. The next action sets the value of `power` to `0`. This variable's value—which will be used to determine how hard the ball is hit—will change as the pool stick is pulled back. The value must be reset to `0` at the beginning of each hit. The next action simply displays the current value of the `power` variable in the **powerAmount_txt** text field.

A script placed on the **ball_mc** movie clip instance will use the value of `hitAmount` to determine the distance the ball should move. We'll set up that script in a moment.

The next action in the script sets the value of `hitAmount` to `0`. Because this variable's value will change after the ball is hit, this action is used to reset the value when the button is pressed.

The next action sets the value of trackMouse to true. All you need to understand at this point is that this variable's value acts like a switch for turning on a script that will be attached to the **ball_mc** movie clip instance.

The last action records the current horizontal position of the mouse when the button is pressed and places that value in the variable named mouseStart. Shortly, this value will be used to determine the force (hitAmount) at which the ball is hit.

4) With the Actions panel open, add this script at the end of the current script:

```
on (dragOut) {
  stick_mc.gotoAndPlay ("PullBack");
}
```

When the user moves away from the invisible button (with the mouse button still pressed), this action is executed (the dragOut event occurs), moving the **stick_mc** movie clip instance to the PullBack frame. Here the stick appears to pull back—a nice visual hint to emulate the action occurring onscreen.

5) With the Actions panel open, add this script at the end of the current script:

```
on (releaseOutside) {
  stick_mc.gotoAndStop ("Starting");
  mouseEnd = _root._xmouse;
  hitAmount = mouseEnd - mouseStart;
  trackMouse = false;
}
```

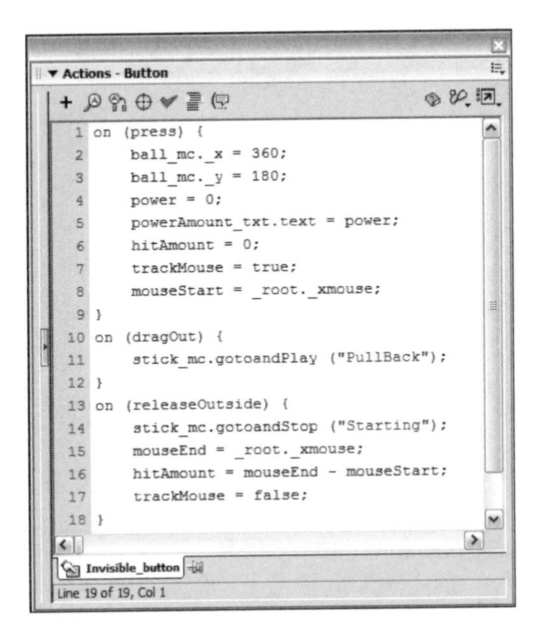

When the invisible button is pressed, moved away from (with the mouse button still pressed), and released (the releaseOutside event occurs), these actions are executed. Because the act of pressing, dragging, then letting go is similar to what you would employ when using a slingshot, we'll use it here to emulate the pool stick's hitting the ball.

The first action moves the **stick_mc** movie clip instance to the frame labeled Starting. The stick appears in its starting position, against the ball. This, along with the ball's being set in motion (which we'll discuss in a moment), gives the appearance of the ball's being hit and then moved.

The next action records the mouse's horizontal position at the time it's released. We now have the mouse's horizontal position when the invisible button was first pressed (mouseStart) as well as when it was released (mouseEnd). Now let's take a look at how the next action uses these two values.

The value of hitAmount is determined by subtracting mouseStart from mouseEnd. If mouseStart equals 200 and mouseEnd equals 300, hitAmount is assigned a value of 100. This represents the distance the mouse moved from the time the button was first pressed to the time it was released—in other words, the "force" with which our ball was hit, and how far it will move to the left.

The last action sets the value of trackMouse to false. All you need to understand here is that this value acts like a switch for turning off a script that will be attached to the **ball_mc** movie clip instance. Remember that when the button is pressed, this value is set to true, turning the script on. Thus, this script is turned on when the button is pressed, and turned off when it's released outside. (We'll explain the script we're turning on and off shortly.)

The only thing left to do is attach a couple of scripts to the **ball_mc** movie clip instance. One will move the ball; the other will use the trackMouse variable we've been discussing.

6) With the Actions panel open, select the *ball_mc* movie clip instance and add this script:

```
onClipEvent (enterFrame) {
  if (_root.hitAmount > 5) {
    this._x = this._x - 10;
    _root.hitAmount = _root.hitAmount - 2;
  }
}
```

This script uses an enterFrame event handler to execute. It contains an if statement that looks at the value of hitAmount on the root timeline before taking action. (Remember that the value of hitAmount is set by the functionality of our invisible button and is used to determine how hard the ball will be hit.)

The script states that if the value of hitAmount is more than 5, move the **ball_mc** movie clip instance (this) to its current x position minus 10 (this moves it left) and deduct 2 from the value of hitAmount. As long as hitAmount is more than 5, these actions will be executed 24 times per second because we've used the enterFrame event. As a result, the **ball_mc** movie clip instance will move 10 pixels to the left 24 times a second. Because the second action subtracts 2 from the value of hitAmount each time it's executed, the value of this variable will eventually drop below 5, which will cause this script to stop executing. It will begin executing again only when hitAmount is assigned a value greater than 5, which, once again, is the functionality the button provides. This is a perfect example of orchestrating several events to accomplish a single interactive goal.

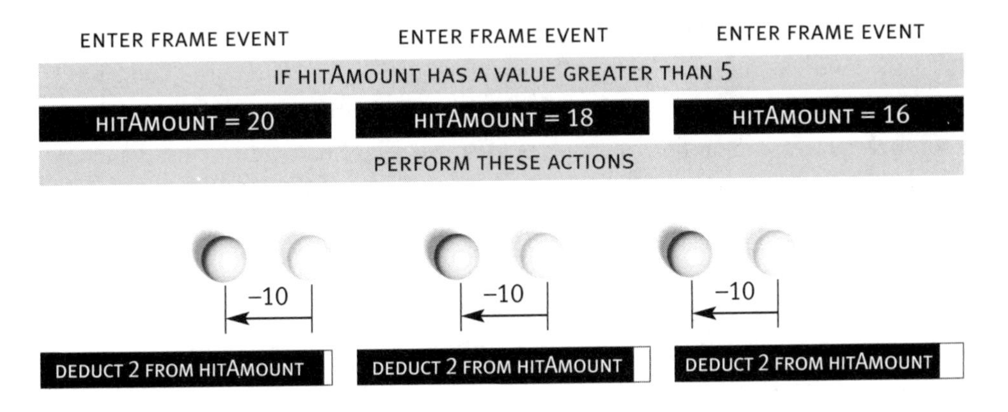

7) Add this script at the end of the current one:

```
onClipEvent (mouseMove) {
  if (_root.trackMouse == true) {
    _root.power = _root._xmouse -_root.mouseStart;
    _root.powerAmount_txt.text = _root.power;
  }
}
```

This script uses a mouseMove event handler to execute. It also contains an if statement that looks at the value of trackMouse on the root timeline before taking action. Remember that the value of this variable is set to true when the invisible button is pressed but false when it's released. Because this script takes action only if its value is true, alternating the value of this variable—as we do with various mouse events—has the effect of turning the script on and off.

The script states that if the value of `trackMouse` is `true`, set the value of the variable named `power` to equal the difference between the mouse's current horizontal position minus the value of `mouseStart`. Remember that `mouseStart` is the recorded horizontal position of the mouse at the moment the invisible button is pressed. The next action is used to display the value of `power` in the **powerAmount_txt** text field. Because these actions are executed whenever the mouse is moved (and `trackMouse` has a value of `true`), they provide a real-time display of the power used to hit the ball.

NOTE *In the end, the value displayed in the* ***powerAmount_txt*** *text field is the same as that assigned to the variable* `hitAmount`*, which determines how far the ball moves when hit.*

The concept you need to grasp here is the idea of turning clip event–based scripts on and off using scripts triggered by mouse events—a capability that gives you a great deal of control in an interactive environment. You'll see many more examples of this technique throughout this book.

8) Choose Control > Test Movie.

Press the mouse on the tip of the pool stick and move your mouse to the right. You'll notice the interaction. Release the mouse after pulling a distance and notice how the pool stick hits the ball and the ball moves to the left, based on the amount of power applied. After completing the process, try it again. Each time the ball is hit with a different amount of power, it moves accordingly.

9) Close the test movie to return to the authoring environment and save your work as *OrchestratingEvents2.fla*.

This step completes the exercise.

UNDERSTANDING EVENT HANDLER METHODS

Although we've discussed a number of events thus far, we've really just scratched the surface of Flash reactions. You already know that scripts react to all kinds of triggers: interaction with the mouse, the timeline's reaching a specific frame, movie clip instances entering a scene. But did you know that by using event handler methods, you can make your scripts execute when sounds finish playing, when the stage is resized, or when the text in a text field changes? You can even use event handler methods to extend the functionality of the events we've already used in this lesson.

Although event handler methods and standard event handlers are used for the same basic purpose (that is, executing a script when something happens in your movie), you must implement them a bit differently.

By now, you know how to set up a script to be executed as the result of an event. For example, this script is attached to a movie clip instance named **myMovieClip_mc** and is executed whenever the mouse button is pressed while the instance is present in the scene:

```
onClipEvent(mouseDown) {
  this._rotation = 45;
}
```

This script will rotate the movie clip instance by 45 degrees when the mouse button is pressed.

Using an event handler method, the following script would be placed on a frame of the timeline to accomplish the same purpose, rotating **myMovieClip_mc** whenever the mouse button is pressed:

```
myMovieClip_mc.onMouseDown = function() {
  this._rotation = 45;
}
```

Instead of using `onClipEvent` to define the event handler (as shown in the first script), here we use a dot (.) to separate the name of the object (in this case **myMovieClip_mc**) from the event to which it needs to react. And to reiterate, we've placed this script on a frame rather than attached it to the instance.

Don't worry about the use of `function()` in the script. We'll provide an in-depth discussion of functions in Lesson 5, "Using Functions." All you need to know about this use of `function()` is that it's a necessary part of the syntax for implementing the event handler method.

NOTE *To execute a particular function when an event handler method is defined, change the syntax to* `myMovieClip.onMouseDown = nameOfFunction;`.

The actions in the second line of the script (between the curly braces) define what needs to happen when the event occurs.

Because this script describes how the **myMovieClip_mc** instance reacts to the `onMouseDown` event, that instance must exist in the scene at the time the event handler method is defined. This will attach the defined functionality to the instance. By the same token, event handler methods assigned to objects are removed when the object leaves the scene (or is otherwise removed). If the object appears in the scene again, any event handler methods will need to be defined again.

At first glance, you may be wondering how event handler methods are much different from regular events, and if there are any advantages of using one over the other. That's what we'll discuss next.

NOTE *Event handler methods play a large role in the way custom objects are set up to react to events. For more information, see Lesson 7, "Creating Custom Classes."*

USING EVENT HANDLER METHODS

All standard event handlers have equivalent *event handler methods* (also called *callback functions* or *function callbacks*). For example:

`on (press)` is `buttonName_btn.onPress` or `movieClipName_mc.onPress`

`on (release)` is `buttonName_btn.onRelease` or `movieClipName_mc.onRelease`

`on (enterFrame)` is `movieClipName_mc.onEnterFrame`

In addition, these event handler methods exist but have no standard event equivalents:

Buttons/Movie Clips

```
nameOfClipOrButton.onKillFocus
nameOfClipOrButton.onSetFocus
```

Sound Objects

```
nameOfSoundObject.onLoad
nameOfSoundObject.onSoundComplete
nameOfSoundObject.onID3
```

Text Fields

```
nameOfTextField.onChanged
nameOfTextField.onKillFocus
nameOfTextField.onScroller
nameOfTextField.onSetFocus
```

Stage Objects

```
Stage.onLoad
```

StyleSheet Objects

```
nameOfStyleSheet.onResize
```

ContextMenu Objects

```
nameOfContextMenu.onSelect
```

ContextMenuItem Objects

```
nameOfContextMenuItem.onSelect
```

LoadVars Objects

```
nameOfLoadVarsObject.onLoad
```

SharedObject Objects

```
nameOfSharedObject.onStatus
```

LocalConnection Objects

```
nameOfLocalConnection.allowDomain
nameOfLocalConnection.onStatus
```

NetConnection Objects

```
nameOfNetConnection.onStatus
```

NetStream Objects

```
nameOfNetStream.onStatus
```

XML Objects

```
nameOfXMLObject.onData
nameOfXMLObject.onLoad
```

XMLSocket Objects

```
nameOfXMLSocketObject.onClose
nameOfXMLSocketObject.onConnect
nameOfXMLSocketObject.onData
nameOfXMLSocketObject.onXML
```

You can use numerous events to trigger a script. Because some of these objects are intangible (for example, Sound, LoadVars, and XML), defining event handler methods on a keyframe of the timeline is the only way to execute a script when an event occurs in relation to that object (in contrast to buttons and movie clip instances, which you can select on the stage and to which you can directly attach scripts).

NOTE *We will discuss and use many of these event handler methods throughout this book. For more information, see the ActionScript dictionary.*

By attaching a script to a button or movie clip instance using a regular event handler, you pretty much lock down not only what happens when an event occurs but also the events that actually trigger execution of a script. For example:

```
on (press) {
  gotoAndPlay(5);
}
```

If you were to attach this script to a button, the button would react *only* to the `press` event, performing a single action when that event occurred. To give you an idea of the power and flexibility of event handler methods, assume there's a button instance on the stage named **myButton_btn**. By placing the following script on Frame 1 of the main timeline (assuming the button exists at that frame), you define how that button will react to certain events:

```
myButton_btn.onPress = function() {
  stopAllSounds();
}
myButton_btn.onRelease = function() {
  myMovieClip_mc._xscale = 50;
}
```

When pressed, the button will halt all sounds; when released, it will horizontally scale **myMovieClip_mc** to 50 percent of its original size.

However, by moving that timeline to Frame 2—which contains the following script (assuming the button exists at Frame 2)—you would change the button's function completely:

```
myButton_btn.onPress = null
myButton_btn.onRelease = null
myButton_btn.onRollOver = function() {
  stopAllSounds();
}
myButton_btn.onRollOut = function() {
  myMovieClip_mc._xscale = 50;
}
```

By using `null`, you prevent the button from continuing to react to an `onPress` or `onRelease` event—and instead instruct it to react to the two newly defined events.

TIP *You can also delete an event handler method using this syntax:* `delete myButton_btn.onPress`.

By using event handler methods, we can change the button's functionality and the events it reacts to—a powerful capability.

Event handler methods also come in handy for dynamically created objects. Because the act of dynamically creating an object involves putting an object in your movie that wasn't there when the movie was authored, you can't set up the object to react to an event by selecting it (it hasn't been created yet). This is where event handler methods become really useful. Take a look at this sample script:

```
_root.createEmptyMovieClip("newClip_mc", 1);
_root.newClip_mc.onEnterFrame = function(){
  myVariable++;
}
_root.newClip_mc.onMouseMove = function(){
  myCursorClip_mc._x = _root._xmouse;
  myCursorClip_mc._y = _root._ymouse;
}
```

After creating a movie clip instance named **newClip_mc**, we immediately use event handler methods to define what that instance will do when certain events occur.

In the next exercise, we place event handler methods on Frame 1 of our movie to define how scene elements react to various events. The idea behind this project is that when the user selects a particular text field (or types text into a field), elements in the scene will react and other elements will be dynamically configured to react to various mouse and clip events.

NOTE *Although we have used event handlers attached directly to button and movie clip instances thus far in the book, we will be using event handler methods a lot more extensively from this point on. The reason is twofold. First, they're a lot more flexible and dynamic. And second, they allow us to script various elements from a central location—the timeline—which is a recommended practice by Macromedia due to the fact that scattering scripts throughout your project (placed on various instances) makes the project more difficult to debug and manage.*

1) Open *CarParts1.fla* in the Lesson02/Assets folder.

This project contains a single scene with eight layers that are named according to their contents.

The Background layer contains the main background graphic. The CarClip layer contains the red car at the top-left of the stage—a movie clip instance named **car_mc**. That movie clip's timeline contains a couple of movie clip instances, **wheel1_mc** and **wheel2_mc**, which represent the wheels of the car. The next layer, Text Fields, contains three text fields: **text1_txt, text2_txt**, and **text3_txt**. As you will see, the way in which the user interacts with these text fields will dictate how the project functions.

The next layer, Arrows, contains three small arrow movie clip instances: **arrow1_mc, arrow2_mc**, and **arrow3_mc**. These arrows appear below each text field and will be set up to move horizontally along the bottom of the text field as text is entered and removed in a field. The next layer, Wheel, contains the movie clip **wheelClip_mc**, which will be dynamically scripted to react to the `onEnterFrame` event only when the **text1_txt** text field has been selected. The layer above that, Speedometer, contains a movie clip instance named **speedClip_mc** whose timeline contains a short animation of a needle rotating in a gauge, as well as a revving sound. When the clip is played, these animations make the clip appear to operate like the real thing. This instance will be dynamically scripted to play when the `onPress` event occurs—but only after the **text2_txt** text field has been selected. The next layer, Fan, contains a movie clip instance named **fanClip_mc**, which will be set up to react to the `onEnterFrame` event only when **text3_txt** has been selected. Finally, Frame 1 of the Actions layer will contain most of the script for our project.

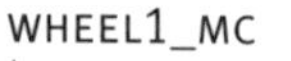

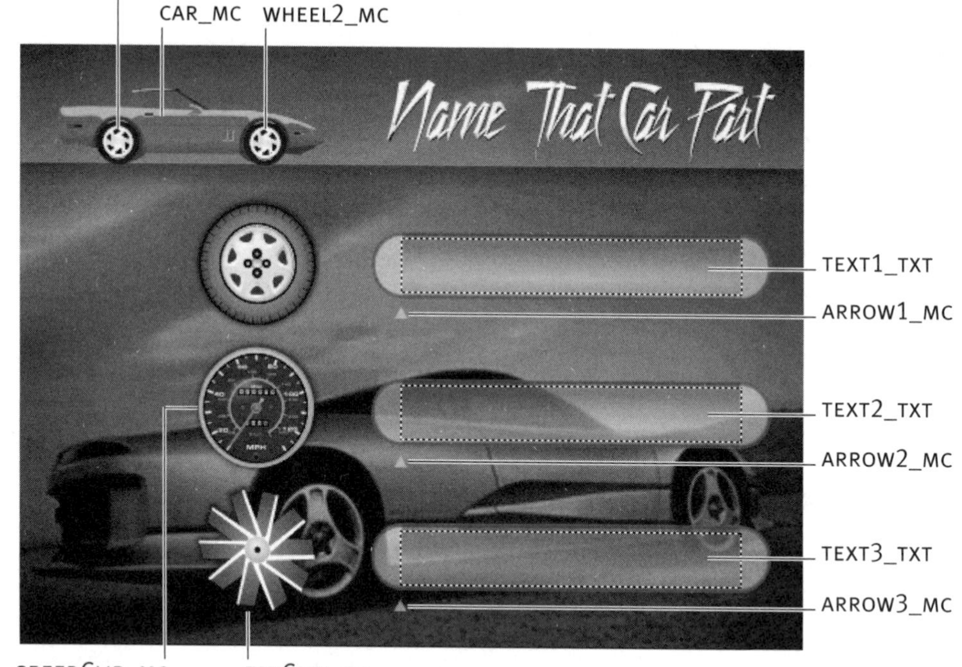

2) With the Actions panel open, select Frame 1 and add this script:

```
text1_txt.onChanged = function(){
  car_mc._x += 2;
  car_mc.wheel1_mc._rotation += 10;
  car_mc.wheel2_mc._rotation += 10;
  arrow1_mc._x = text1_txt._x + text1_txt.textWidth;
}
```

This script defines what happens when the text in the **text1_txt** text field is changed (added to or deleted).

The first action is used to move the **car_mc** instance two pixels to the right by adding 2 to its current x property. The next two actions rotate the **wheel1_mc** and **wheel2_mc** movie clip instances (which are in the **car_mc** instance) by adding 10 degrees to their current rotation values. This will cause them to appear to spin as the car moves right.

NOTE *As shown in an earlier script, using* + *and* = *in the script is the same as saying, "Add the value on the right of the equals sign to the current value of what is identified on the left"—which in this case is the rotation value of the* **wheel1_mc** *and* **wheel2_mc** *movie clip instances.*

The last action moves **arrow1_mc** horizontally so that it appears just below the last letter in the **text1_txt** text field. It does this by adding the horizontal location of **text1_txt** (its _x property) to the width of the text in the field. The sum of this amount will position **arrow1_mc** appropriately. Every time text is changed (`onChanged`) in **text1_txt**, these actions will be triggered.

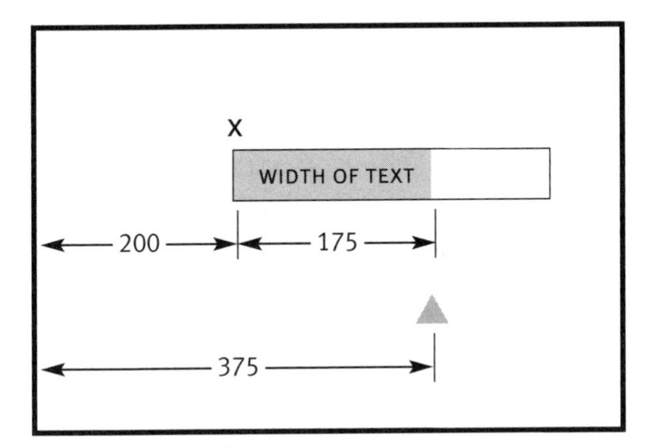

3) With the Actions panel open, add this script below the script you just added:

```
text1_txt.onSetFocus = function(){
  wheelClip_mc.onEnterFrame = function(){
    this._rotation += 30;
  }
  speedClip_mc.onPress = null;
  fanClip_mc.onEnterFrame = null;
}
```

This script defines what happens when the **text1_txt** text field has been given focus or clicked. (To "focus" on a field means to make it the active field, into which the user can immediately enter information.)

When this event handler method is triggered, it does an interesting thing: it configures three other event handler methods. Yes, they are that flexible. First, **wheelClip_mc** is set to react to the `onEnterFrame` event so that it will spin by an additional 30 degrees each time the event is triggered (24 times a second). This will cause it to spin as soon as **text1_txt** is selected. Because we will be adding script in the next couple of steps that will enable **speedClip_mc** and **fanClip_mc** to react to `onPress` and `onEnterFrame` events, respectively, the next two actions are used to remove that functionality when **text1_txt** is selected.

The next additions to the script are just a variation on what has been added so far.

4) With the Actions panel open, add this script below the script you just added:

```
text2_txt.onChanged = function(){
  car_mc._x += 2;
  car_mc.wheel1_mc._rotation += 10;
  car_mc.wheel2_mc._rotation += 10;
  arrow2_mc._x = text2_txt._x + text2_txt.textWidth;
}
```

Syntactically and functionally, this script is the same as the script shown in Step 2—with two exceptions. First, it's executed when the text in the **text2_txt** text field changes. Also, the last action is used to move **arrow2_mc** horizontally so that it appears just below the last letter in the **text2_txt** text field.

5) With the Actions panel open, add this script just below the script you just added:

```
text2_txt.onSetFocus = function(){
  wheelClip_mc.onEnterFrame = null;
  speedClip_mc.onPress = function(){
    this.play();
  }
  fanClip_mc.onEnterFrame = null;
}
```

This script is a variation of the script in Step 3. It dictates what occurs when **text2_txt** is given focus (selected). You'll notice that the **speedClip_mc** instance is set up to react to an `onPress` event. Pressing the **speedClip_mc** instance after **text2_txt** has been given focus will cause that instance to play. The other actions prevent the **wheelClip_mc** and **fanClip_mc** instances from reacting to the `onEnterFrame` event that other parts of the script define. As you may have realized, the idea behind this functionality is to enable the instance to the left of a text field to react to an event when the field is given focus, but prevent it from reacting to that event when another field is given focus.

6) With the Actions panel open, add this script below the script you just added:

```
text3_txt.onChanged = function(){
  car_mc._x += 2;
  car_mc.wheel1_mc._rotation += 10;
  car_mc.wheel2_mc._rotation += 10;
  arrow3_mc._x = text3_txt._x + text3_txt.textWidth;
}
text3_txt.onSetFocus = function(){
  wheelClip_mc.onEnterFrame = null;
  speedClip_mc.onPress = null;
  fanClip_mc.onEnterFrame = function(){
    this._rotation += 20;
  }
}
```

Once again, this script is a variation of those presented in previous steps. It dictates what occurs when **text3_txt** is given focus or when text within that field changes.

7) Choose Control > Test Movie.

Click the top text field (**text1_txt**); that text field will be given focus and the **wheelClip_mc** instance will begin spinning. As you type text into the field, two things will occur: the **car_mc** movie clip instance will move to the right, with its wheels spinning, and the arrow underneath the field will continue to appear just below the last character in the field. Try clicking the **speedClip_mc** movie clip: notice that nothing happens. Click **text2_txt**, and that fact changes: the **wheelClip_mc** instance will quit spinning, and clicking the **speedClip_mc** instance will make that instance play. Clicking **text3_txt** will cause the **speedClip_mc** instance to become inactive again, but the **fanClip_mc** instance will begin spinning.

8) Close the test movie to return to the authoring environment and save your work as *CarParts2.fla*.

This step completes the exercise.

USING LISTENERS

Just as a single transmitter broadcasts radio waves to thousands of radio receivers, some events can be "broadcast" to any number of objects so that they respond accordingly. You do this by employing what are known as *Listeners*—events that can be broadcast to objects that have been "registered" to listen for them (*listening objects).*

Suppose you wanted an object (sound, movie clip, text field, array, or custom) to react to a certain event's being triggered in your movie. You would first create an event handler method for that object:

```
myTextField_txt.onMouseDown = function(){
  myTextField_txt.text="";
}
```

Here we've set up a text field named **myTextField_txt** to react when the mouse button is pressed. The `onMouseDown` event is not a standard event that a text field can react to, and at this point it still won't. For the text field to react to this event, you must *register* the text field as a Listener for the event. You can do so by adding this code:

```
Mouse.addListener(myTextField);
```

Here the text field is registered with the Mouse object because the `onMouseDown` event is a Listener of that object. Now, whenever the mouse button is pressed, the event handler method we created earlier will execute. You can set up any number of objects for a single Listener event as long as the object has been given an event handler method to deal with the event, and the object has been registered to listen for that event. If you no longer want an object to listen for an event, you can *unregister* it using this syntax:

```
Mouse.removeListener(myTextField);
```

Listeners give you a bit more flexibility for scripting how your projects react to various events.

NOTE *Not all events can be treated as Listeners. With this in mind, be aware of which events are listed as Listeners in the Actions toolbox. If an event is not listed as a Listener, other objects cannot be set up to listen to it.*

In the next exercise, in honor of the new History panel found in Flash MX 2004, we'll create our own History panel, named Bygones, using Listeners. Our panel will be used to indicate the following information:

- When the mouse button has been pressed, and where it was pressed
- If a key has been pressed, and which one
- If the stage has been resized, and to what new size

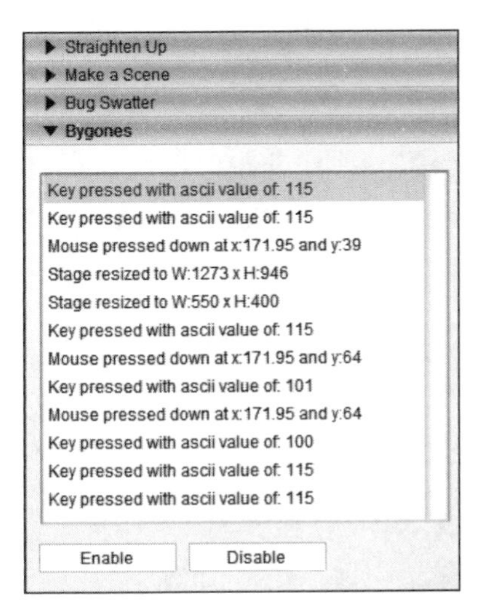

1) Open *Listeners1.fla* in the Lesson02/Assets folder.

This project contains a single scene with four layers that are named according to their contents.

The Background layer contains all of the nonfunctional interface graphics. The Components layer contains a List component instance named **historyList_lb** (in which **_lb** stands for ListBox).

NOTE *For more information on components, see Lesson 10, "Scripting UI Components."*

The Buttons layer contains two buttons: one named **enable_btn**, and the other named **disable_btn**. Obviously, the **enable_btn** button will be used to activate the Bygones panel's functionality, while the **disable_btn** will be used to deactivate it.

The Actions layer is currently empty but will eventually contain all the scripts for this project.

2) With the Actions panel open, select Frame 1 of the Actions layer and add this script:

```
var historyArray:Array = new Array ();
```

This line of script creates an Array object named `historyArray`. An Array object is simply an object that can hold multiple pieces of data in indexed positions. You can think of it as a mini-database. Look at this example:

```
var directions:Array = new Array();
```

The script creates a new Array object named `directions`. We fill this object with data in this manner:

```
directions[0] = "North";
directions[1] = "East";
directions[2] = "South";
directions[3] = "West";
```

Our `directions` array now contains four pieces of data. To access data in the array, you use this syntax:

```
myTextField_txt.text = directions[2];
```

The script will cause "South" (the text in index position 2 of the array) to appear in the text field.

In the case of this project, we will be using the historyArray Array object to store information about recorded interactions. For example, a new piece of data will be added to historyArray each time the mouse button is pressed, a key is pressed, or the stage is resized. If the mouse button has been pressed twice and three keys have been pressed, historyArray will contain five items. These five items will each be text descriptions of the particular interaction.

NOTE *For more information about arrays and how to use them, see Lesson 6, "Creating and Manipulating Data."*

3) Add this script below the script added in the preceding step:

```
historyList_lb.setDataProvider(historyArray);
```

The List component we placed in our project is used to provide a mechanism to display the data that will be added to the historyArray Array object. This line of script tells the **historyList_lb** List component to use the historyArray Array object as its data source. As a result, when we add a new item to the historyArray Array object, it will appear in the **historyList_lb** List component.

4) Add this script below the script added in the preceding step:

```
historyArray.onMouseDown = function () {
  this.unshift ("Mouse pressed down at x:" + _root._xmouse + " and y:" +
  ⇒_root._ymouse);
  historyList_lb.setSelectedIndex (0);
};
```

This script tells the historyArray Array object what to do when the mouse button is pressed. The onMouseDown event is not one that an Array object can normally respond to, but because this event is also a Listener event of the Mouse object, any object—including our Array object—can be programmed to listen for it when it is triggered. This is only part of the equation that makes this work, however. Eventually, we'll tell the Mouse object to register the historyArray to listen for its events using this syntax:

```
Mouse.addListener(historyArray);
```

We won't do this yet. We explained it here to help you understand that using Listeners is a two-step process. Let's discuss what this script does.

The script is triggered when the mouse button is pressed. It adds a new item to our historyArray using this syntax:

```
this.unshift(item to add);
```

Because this line of our script exists *within* the overall script that tells historyArray how to react to onMouseDown events, this, in this context, is a relative reference to the historyArray Array object. It could have also been written this way:

```
historyArray.unshift(item to add);
```

unshift() is a method that an Array object can use to place a new item in the first position of its index, while moving (shifting) all existing items up one position. The data you want to add is placed within the parentheses. According to the directions Array object we discussed earlier, this syntax:

```
directions.unshift("North");
```

would place the value "North" in index 0 of the directions Array object:

```
directions[0]; //has a value of "North"
```

Using the unshift() method again:

```
directions.unshift("East");
```

places the value "East" in index position 0, while moving the value "North" up to index position 1:

```
directions[0]; //has a value of "East"
directions[1]; //has a value of "North"
```

In our script, then, every time the mouse button is pressed, the unshift() method is executed and adds the information in the parentheses (which we'll discuss in a moment) to index 0 of historyArray, while moving existing items in the array up one index position. As a result, what appears in the **historyList_lb** List component will be updated as well.

Let's look at the information that gets added to the array each time the mouse button is pressed and the unshift() method is executed. Our script shows that what is added looks like this:

```
"Mouse pressed down at x:" + _root._xmouse + " and y:" + _root._ymouse
```

This represents the structure of the information that will be added to our panel each time the mouse button is pressed. In this case, the x and y positions of the mouse (_root._xmouse and _root._ymouse, respectively) are captured and inserted into the message. When the mouse is pressed down, if it has an x position of 350 and a y position of 100, the message that gets inserted into the historyArray Array object reads as follows:

```
"Mouse pressed down at x:350 and y:100"
```

Once this gets added to historyArray, this information will also appear in our List component, as a result of earlier scripting of our historyArray (Step 3) to feed data to the List component. Pretty simple, don't you think?

In the script we added in this step, the last line before the final curly brace reads:

```
historyList_lb.setSelectedIndex (0);
```

This will cause the top item in the **historyList_lb** List component to be highlighted. This is simply for cosmetic purposes, so that the last piece of data added to the list will always stand out.

Next, we script historyArray to listen for when the user presses a key on the keyboard. Fortunately, this script is similar to the one we just discussed.

5) Add this line of script below the one added in the preceding step:

```
historyArray.onKeyDown = function () {
  this.unshift ("Key pressed with ascii value of: " + Key.getAscii ());
  historyList_lb.setSelectedIndex (0);
};
```

This part of our script tells historyArray what to do when a key on the keyboard is pressed. The onKeyDown event specified here is not one that Array objects can normally respond to. But because it is an available Listener event of the Key object, we can use it to program our Array object to do something when a key is pressed.

This script also uses the unshift() method described in the preceding step. As you can see, this again refers to the historyArray Array object. Thus, whether the mouse button or a key on the keyboard is pressed, the message generated by our script is placed into index 0 of our single Array object (while moving all existing index items up one index number). As a result, our List component will display *all* messages generated from mouse clicks and key presses.

The message created when a key is pressed is built around this syntax:

```
"Key pressed with ascii value of: " + Key.getAscii ()
```

This part of the script uses the `Key.getAscii()` method to determine the ASCII code for the currently pressed key on the keyboard.

As a result, if the Spacebar is pressed, it generates a message that looks like this:

```
Key pressed with ascii value of: 32
```

NOTE *For a complete list of ASCII values, consult the ActionScript dictionary that comes with Flash.*

As described in Step 4, `historyList_lb.setSelectedIndex (0);` will highlight the first item in the **historyList_lb** List component. This action causes all the recently added items to always appear highlighted.

Finally, let's script `historyArray` to listen for when the stage is resized.

6) Add this line of script below the one added in the preceding step:

```
historyArray.onResize = function () {
  this.unshift ("Stage resized to W:" + Stage.width + " x H:" + Stage.height);
  historyList_lb.setSelectedIndex (0);
};
```

This script is similar to the last two. It scripts `historyArray` to react to the resizing of the stage (using the `onResize` event, which is a Listener event of the Stage object). The message generated by this script will also be added to `historyArray`. If the stage is resized to a width of 550 and a height of 400, this message will read:

```
Stage resized to W:550 x H:400
```

It's time to register `historyArray` with the Mouse, Key, and Stage objects so that it can begin reacting to the events those objects generate. Before we do, however, let's do a test, just so you understand the importance of this registration process.

7) Choose Control > Test Movie.

When the movie appears, you can press the mouse button, type keys, and resize the stage to your heart's content, but nothing happens. Simply scripting the `historyArray` Array object to react to these events doesn't mean it will react. Not yet, at least. Let's go back to the authoring environment and finish the job.

8) Close the test window to return to the authoring environment. Open the Actions panel and add this script at the end of the current script:

```
enable_btn.onRelease = function () {
  Mouse.addListener (historyArray);
  Key.addListener (historyArray);
  Stage.addListener (historyArray);
};
```

This script will execute when the Enable button (named **enable_btn**) is pressed and released. It registers the `historyArray` Array object as a Listener of the Mouse, Key, and Stage objects. As a result, the functionality we scripted in the previous steps will come to life when the project is tested again and the Enable button is pressed.

9) Add this script at the end of the current script:

```
disable_btn.onRelease = function () {
  Mouse.removeListener (historyArray);
  Key.removeListener (historyArray);
  Stage.removeListener (historyArray);
};
```

```
Actions - Frame
1  var historyArray:Array = new Array ();
2  historyList_lb.setDataProvider (historyArray);
3  historyArray.onMouseDown = function () {
4      this.unshift ("Mouse pressed down at x:" + _root._xmouse + " and y:" + _root._ymouse);
5      historyList_lb.setSelectedIndex (0);
6  };
7  historyArray.onKeyDown = function () {
8      this.unshift ("Key pressed with ascii value of: " + Key.getAscii ());
9      historyList_lb.setSelectedIndex (0);
10 };
11 historyArray.onResize = function () {
12     this.unshift ("Stage resized to W:" + Stage.width + " x H:" + Stage.height);
13     historyList_lb.setSelectedIndex (0);
14 };
15
16 enable_btn.onRelease = function() {
17     Mouse.addListener (historyArray);
18     Key.addListener (historyArray);
19     Stage.addListener (historyArray);
20 }
21 disable_btn.onRelease = function() {
22     Mouse.removeListener (historyArray);
23     Key.removeListener (historyArray);
24     Stage.removeListener (historyArray);
25 }
Actions : 1
Line 9 of 25, Col 26
```

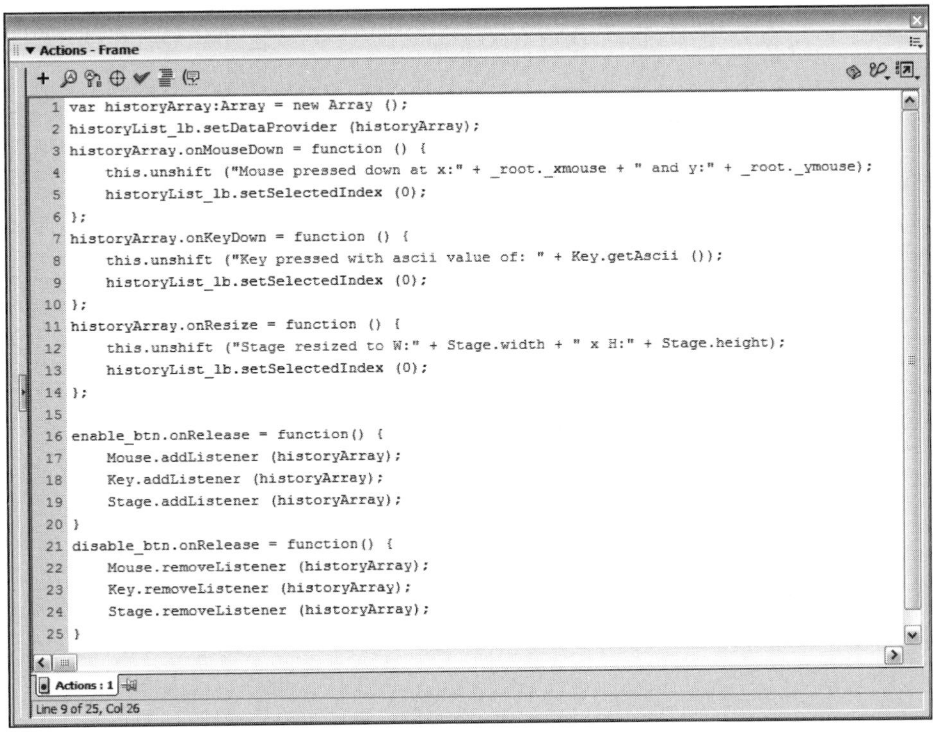

This script will execute when the Disable button (named **disable_btn**) is pressed and released. It does just the opposite of the script added in the preceding step. Using `removeListener()`, it *unregisters* the `historyArray` Array object as a Listener of the Mouse, Key, and Stage objects. As a result, `historyArray` will no longer react to Mouse, Key, and Stage events (until the Enable button is pressed again).

Let's test the project now.

10) Choose Control > Test Movie.

When the movie appears, press the Enable button to activate the Bygones panel. Press the mouse button, type on your keyboard, and resize the window the movie is playing in. Each time you perform one of these actions, `historyArray` will trigger a script as it was set up to do. As a result, you'll see updated information displayed in the List component, representative of the way you are interacting with the movie. Press the Disable button to turn off the functionality of the Bygones panel.

That's all there is to using Listeners.

As a side note, be aware that the Mouse, Key, and Stage objects can generate a total of seven Listener events. While the registering process (shown in Step 8) registers `historyArray` to listen for all of these objects, it is scripted to react to only three of them. For example, the following line in our script:

```
Mouse.addListener(historyArray);
```

registers `historyArray` to listen to *all four* Mouse Listener events, but it is only scripted to react to the `onMouseDown` event. For `historyArray` to react to the other three Listener events, you would need additional scripts (as described in Steps 4 through 6).

11) Close the test movie to return to the authoring environment and save your work as *Listeners2.fla*.

This completes the exercise and the lesson.

WHAT YOU HAVE LEARNED

In this lesson, you have:

- Learned how event handlers are used in scripts (pages 44–46)
- Determined the best event handlers for specific types of jobs (pages 46–49)
- Used mouse/button/keyboard events to control interactivity (pages 50–58)
- Created a self-running presentation using frame events (pages 58–65)
- Used clip events to create an interactive project (pages 65–78)
- Orchestrated various events to create a highly interactive environment (pages 78–84)
- Used event handler methods to dynamically set how an object reacts to an event (pages 84–94)
- Learned what Listeners do and how to use them (pages 94–102)

understanding target paths

LESSON 3

Communication is an important part of our everyday lives. We communicate by telephone, email, postal mail, and so on. Because nearly everyone communicates in a similar fashion, without a system of individual identification it would be impossible to route those communications from one person to another. We have unique phone numbers, email addresses, and street addresses—all of which to help ensure that communication intended for us actually reaches us.

Just as phone numbers, email addresses, and street addresses lead communication to its intended recipient, Macromedia Flash *target paths* lead one timeline to another, allowing them to communicate. In this lesson, we'll take a look at the target paths used in typical Flash projects and show you how to use Flash's powerful ability to have timelines talk to each other—a capability you'll use to give your projects more depth and sophistication.

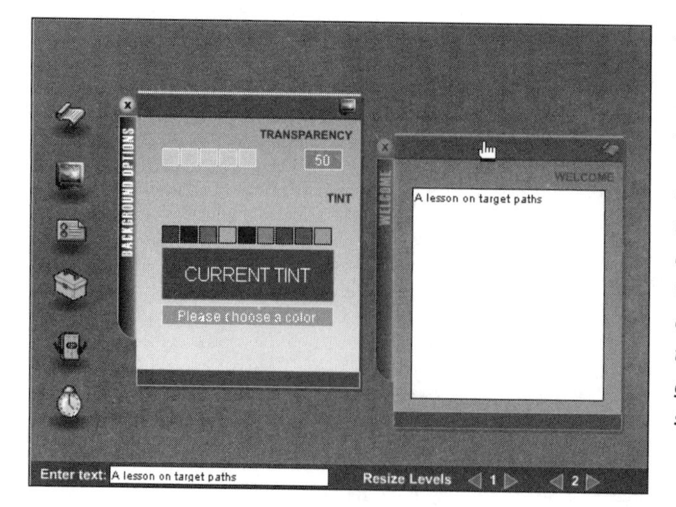

A thorough understanding of target paths and how to use them will enable you to create sophisticated applications where independent timelines can work together to perform tasks. The "windowed" Flash application shown here (which we'll create in this lesson) is an excellent example of the way target paths can be used to give a project more depth and sophistication.

WHAT YOU WILL LEARN

In this lesson, you will:

- Gain an understanding of the hierarchy of timelines in Flash movies
- Learn about absolute and relative target paths
- Learn how movies communicate with each other
- Use the parent-child relationship in movies to create an "effect" clip
- Control specific timelines within a single project
- Control movies loaded into levels
- Learn how to make global references to various ActionScript elements

APPROXIMATE TIME

This lesson takes approximately one and one half hours to complete.

LESSON FILES

Starting Files:

Lesson03/Assets/currentTarget1.fla
Lesson03/Assets/rootTarget1.fla
Lesson03/Assets/parentTarget1.fla
Lesson03/Assets/movieclipTarget1.fla
Lesson03/Assets/backgroundControl1.fla
Lesson03/Assets/textBox1.fla
Lesson03/Assets/levelTarget1.fla
Lesson03/Assets/levelTarget3.fla
Lesson03/Assets/backgroundControl2.fla

Completed Projects:

currentTarget2.fla
rootTarget2.fla
parentTarget2.fla
movieclipTarget2.fla
textBox2.fla
levelTarget2.fla
levelTarget4.fla
backgroundControl3.fla

UNDERSTANDING MULTIPLE TIMELINES

Every project includes a main timeline. But projects also include movie clip instances that have timelines of their own. You can use the `loadMovie()` action to add external SWFs to a project, thereby adding even more timelines. Therefore, a single project can have many separate timelines, all of which can act independently, with their own variables, properties, objects, and functions.

However, these timelines can also work together: one timeline can control another. In fact, any timeline present in a scene can tell another present timeline to do something. (Timelines are considered *present* as long as they exist in the Player movie window. If a movie clip instance appears in your movie for 40 frames, it's considered present—and targetable—only during those 40 frames.)

The communication lines for these movie elements are provided by target paths—addresses to objects (movie clip instances, for example) that describe the overall area in which the object exists and narrow that area with each subsequent level. To better understand this concept, take a look at the following example. The target path to one of your authors would look something like this:

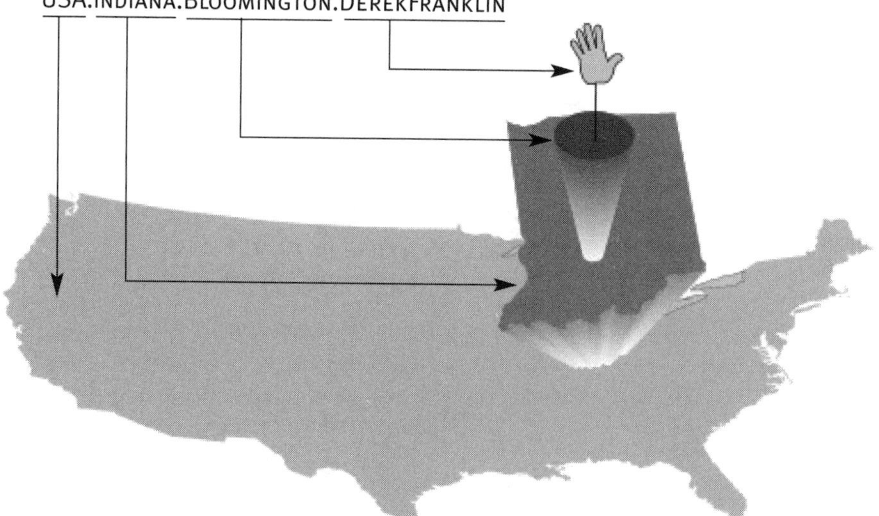

This target path contains four levels, separated by dots, with each subsequent level smaller in size and scope until you reach the target: Derek Franklin. This is what's known as an *absolute path*—the complete and absolute location of Derek Franklin here on Earth. If someone in Australia wanted to communicate with Derek (using a hypothetical communication system), he or she would use this absolute address.

In addition to absolute target paths, there are also *relative target paths*—a slightly trickier concept to understand, so let's consider an example. If someone in Bloomington wanted to communicate with Derek (who is also in Bloomington), a lot of the information included in the absolute path would be unnecessary (country, state, city) because both people exist in a position relative to one another: Bloomington. The following *relative path* would suffice:

```
DerekFranklin
```

Relative paths are powerful because they enable you to script a "chunk" of timelines to work together, in a unique way, based on their relationship. As long as these timelines' relative relationship remains the same, they'll continue to work together—even if you move them to another location in your project, or to another project altogether.

Think of a Flash project as a hierarchy of movies, where timelines exist within other timelines and where the main, or *root*, movie serves as the starting point (see the section titled "Targeting the Main Movie" on page 114). When timelines exist in a hierarchical structure, as they do in Flash projects, it is critical that you understand how to address, or *target*, a timeline using target paths.

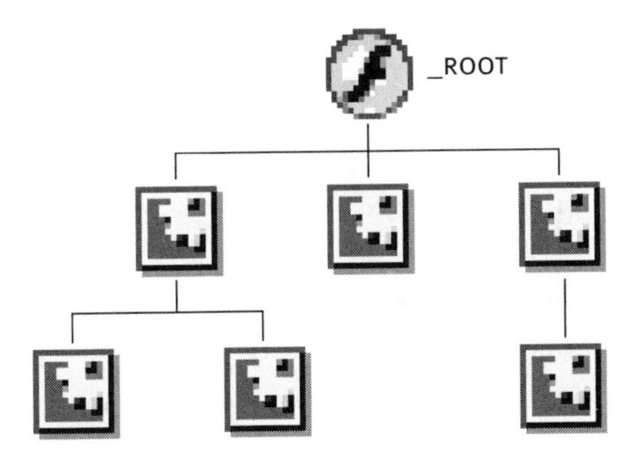

You will use target paths not only to alter timelines but to access their data, functions, objects, and so on.

TARGETING THE CURRENT MOVIE

Whenever a script is placed in a timeline, such as on a frame or on a button, and the target for those actions is that same timeline, the target for the actions in that script is the current movie. This is sort of like telling yourself to do something. For example, if you were to tell yourself to stand up, that action could be said to be targeting the "current" person—you—because you gave *and* responded to the command (you're both the commander *and* the person taking orders). If you were to script this action, it would look like this:

```
standUp();
```

Note that the action doesn't include a target path. This is because the action targets the current movie: if you were to tell yourself to stand up, you wouldn't normally address yourself prior to giving the command. In much the same way, Flash understands that when an action doesn't include a target path, it's meant to affect the timeline where the script resides.

Another way to address the current movie in a script is by preceding an action with the term `this`, like so:

```
this.standUp();
```

In essence, you're saying, "With this timeline, take the following action." We'll provide greater detail about this later in the book. For now, remember that in all cases, the following syntax is interchangeable when addressing the current movie:

```
action ();
this.action ();
```

Keep in mind that your project may contain many scripts on various timelines that don't contain target paths. When this is the case, each script affects its own timeline or the current movie.

In the next exercise, we'll target the current movie for several timelines, using no target path and the term `this` interchangeably. We use both because we want you to grow accustomed to the use of `this` as well as how it relates to the current referenced object. You will have opportunities to use it in more advanced ways later.

1) Open *currentTarget1.fla* in the Lesson03/Assets folder.

This project consists of a single scene with four layers, each named according to its content. The Background layer contains four keyframes. At each of these keyframes the background is a different color. (Move the playhead back and forth to see this in action.) In the middle of the stage is a movie clip instance of a very rounded fellow.

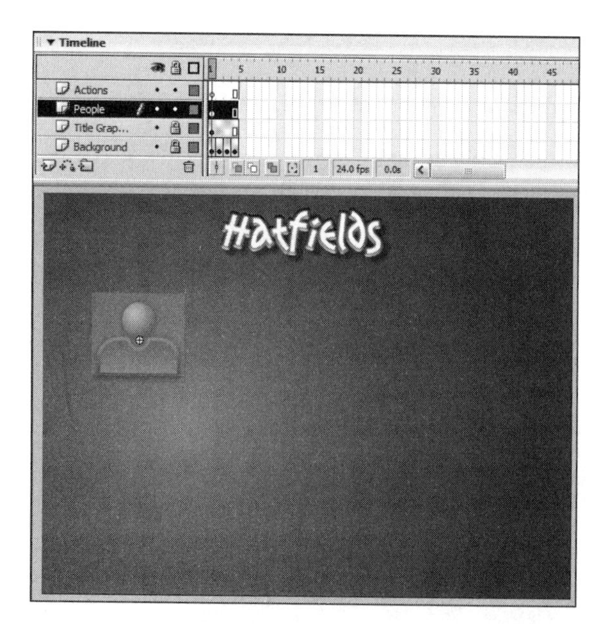

In our first scripting task, we'll instruct the main timeline to move to a random frame when it begins playing, causing a random background color to appear. After that, we'll work with the movie clip instance in the middle of the stage, script it to do something, add a few family members, and then script them to do something as well.

2) Select Frame 1 of the main timeline and add the following script:

```
var colorNumber:Number;
colorNumber = random (4) + 1;
this.gotoAndStop (this.colorNumber);
```

The keyframe on Frame 1 of the main timeline is currently selected, meaning that the main timeline is the current movie in the context of this script. As a result, any action you enter in the Actions panel without a target path (or that uses `this`) will affect this timeline.

After declaring that `colorNumber` will contain a number, the second line in the script generates a random number between 1 and 4 and assigns it to `colorNumber`. By using `random (4)` we ask Flash to generate a random number with four possible values, always beginning with zero—0, 1, 2, or 3. By adding 1 (+1), the possible values generated become 1, 2, 3, or 4—a necessity because the last line in the script tells the current movie to go to and stop at a frame number based on the random value assigned to `colorNumber`. Timelines don't have a Frame 0, so `colorNumber` can't contain a value of less than 1. As a result of this script, one of the background colors displays at random when the movie begins.

Notice that no target path is used on line 2 when assigning the value of `colorNumber` (for example, `this.colorNumber = random(4) + 1;`) ; however, the term `this` is placed before the variable's name in the last line. The two syntax types are interchangeable and reference the current timeline. In this case, the current timeline is the main timeline because Frame 1 of the main timeline is where this script exists.

The timeline that is considered the "current" timeline in a script is determined completely by where the script exists. In other words, the main timeline is considered the current timeline, relative to the script in this step, because this script is placed on Frame 1 of the main timeline. If you were to move this script to Frame 1 of a movie clip's timeline, the target for these actions would cease being the main timeline and would instead become the movie clip where the script was placed.

The next few steps should help you more fully understand this concept.

3) Double-click the movie clip instance in the middle of the stage to edit it in place.
You'll need a solid understanding of this movie clip's timeline to complete several of the exercises in this lesson, so let's take a minute now to get acquainted with it.

This timeline has two frame labels: Quiet and Speak. At the Speak label, a text balloon appears that includes a text field named **balloon_txt**. We will soon create a script that displays text within this text field whenever the timeline is moved to the Speak label.

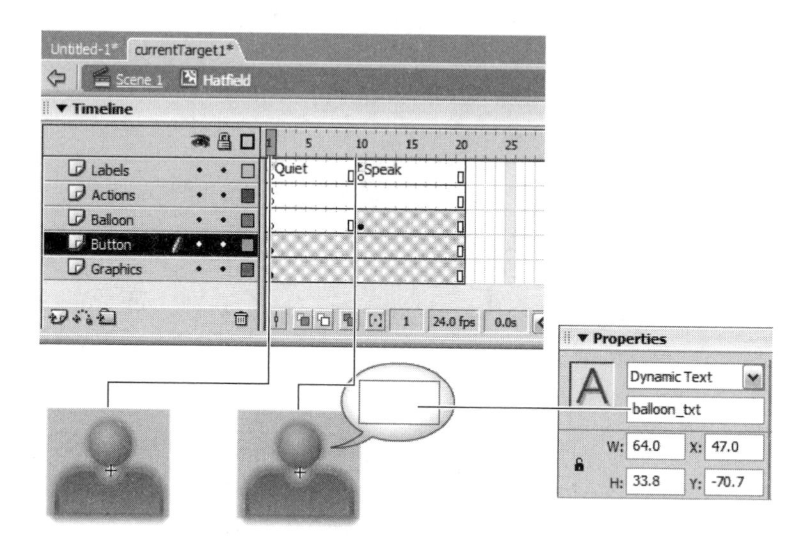

The Button layer of this timeline contains an invisible button that's placed on top of all graphics on this timeline. We will script this button in the next step.

Finally, Frame 1 of this timeline's Actions layer contains a `stop()` action to prevent the timeline from moving past this frame until we instruct it to do so.

4) With the Actions panel open, select the invisible button and add this script:

```
on (press) {
  startDrag (this);
  gotoAndStop ("Speak");
  balloon_txt.text = words;
}

on (release) {
  stopDrag ();
  this.gotoAndStop ("Quiet");
}
```

The first set of actions is executed when this button is pressed, causing the movie clip instance to become draggable. Next, the same timeline is sent to the frame labeled Speak. In addition, we set the text to be displayed in the **balloon_txt** text field to the value of `words`—the name of a variable that will contain a string of text. We will define the value of this variable shortly.

As the script shows, when the invisible button is released (the mouse button is released), dragging stops and the timeline is sent to the frame labeled Quiet.

Once again, the important thing to remember in this script is that either a target path has not been defined in front of the actions, or `this` has been used. In either case, the target is understood to be the current timeline, which is the timeline that this button is a part of.

5) Return to the main timeline. With the Library panel open, drag two more instances of the Hatfield movie clip onto the stage. Choose Control > Test Movie to test what you've done so far.

The first thing you'll notice is that the main timeline goes to a random frame to display one of the background colors on Frames 1 through 4. This is a result of the script on Frame 1 of the main timeline, which we added in Step 2 of this exercise.

Press any of the instances, and you'll notice that they become individually draggable and that their text balloons appear. The concept to grasp here is that the invisible button that enables this functionality is part of the *master* movie clip itself (see Step 4). Thus, each instance of that clip contains this button as well as the script that makes it work (*instances* are nothing more than exact copies of the master clip).

Recall that the script on the button is set up to make the timeline it is part of (the current timeline) draggable when the button is pressed. Because each instance is considered a separate timeline, only the instance that contains the currently pressed button will be dragged when the button is pressed. When actions are placed on the master clip's timeline or a button *inside* the master clip (as demonstrated here), and those actions target its own timeline, each instance of the movie clip inherits that scripted functionality. Think of this as "genetically" programming instances based on the same master movie clip so that they all have a fundamental function.

Using clip event handlers, we can give each instance its own personality, on top of what it is "genetically" programmed to do. Let's look at that technique next.

6) Close the test window to return to the authoring environment. With the Actions panel open, select one of the three instances on the stage and add the script:

```
onClipEvent (load) {
  var words:String;
  words = "I'm Derek";
  this._xscale = 75;
  _yscale = 75;
}
```

You learned in Lesson 2, "Using Event Handlers," that clip events (`load`, `enterFrame`, `mouseMove`, and so on) are event handlers attached to movie clip instances. As such, clip events allow you to script actions that affect single movie clip instances rather than every instance of a movie clip, as demonstrated in the previous steps. As a result, you would use clip events—*outside* the movie clip's timeline—to script characteristics unique to specific movie clip instances, but you would script shared traits *inside* the movie clip's timeline (on a frame or button inside the clip) so that all instances of that movie clip would inherit those characteristics. Both sets of actions target the current timeline, but they do so with a different scope.

If you were to extend this metaphor to people, you would think of shared traits (the things you script inside your movie clip's timeline) as our common capacity to think, feel, and move—things we all inherit. Unique characteristics (the things you script outside your movie clip's timeline) could include name, size, and location—things that are individual to each of us.

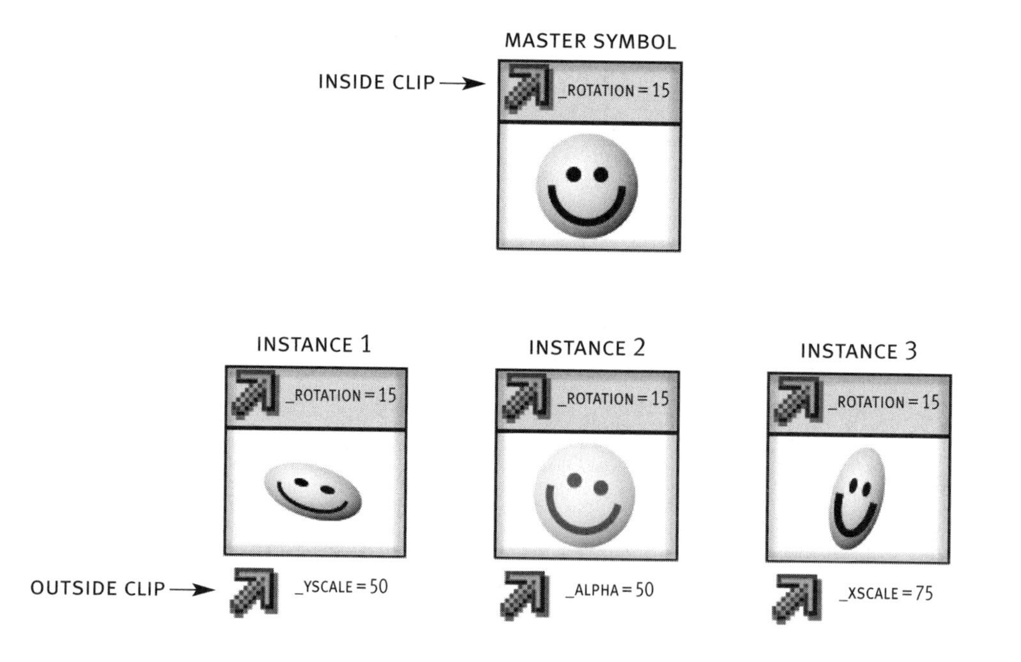

The script in this step is executed when the instance loads or first appears in the movie. The first action assigns a text value to `words`. When this action is executed, the name and value of this variable are stored in this instance. Remember that the value of this variable is used to set the text that is displayed in the **balloon_txt** text field mentioned in Step 4.

The next two actions in this step scale the instance by 75 percent.

7) With the Actions panel open, select one of the other two instances on the stage and add this script:

```
onClipEvent (load) {
  var words:String;
  words = "I'm Ashlie";
  _x = 400;
  _y = 300;
}
```

This script is similar to the one in Step 6 except that it sets the value of `words` to `"I'm Ashlie"` and, on loading, moves this instance to a location 400 pixels horizontally from the left of the stage and 300 pixels vertically from the top of the stage.

8) With the Actions panel open, select the last instance on the stage and add the script:

```
onClipEvent (load) {
  var words:String;
  words = "I'm Kathy";
}
onClipEvent (mouseMove) {
  this._rotation = this._rotation + .5;
}
```

When this instance is loaded, the first action will change the value of `words`. A second clip event rotates the instance half a degree each time the mouse is moved.

9) Choose Control > Test Movie to see what we've done so far.

On loading, you'll see that our scripts have caused several things to occur: the instance we scripted in Step 6 is now 75 percent smaller than the other two. The second instance we scripted can be seen at the x and y coordinates we told it to go to on loading. The third instance rotates as the mouse is moved. Press any of these movie clip instances to see that you can still drag as before, but the text balloon now includes text that's customized for each instance. Again, remember that while scripts placed *inside* the movie clip they target will affect all instances of that clip, clip events attached to individual instances let you customize each instance.

10) Close the testing environment to return to the authoring environment. Save this file as *currentTarget2.fla*.

We will build on this file (with a few modifications) in the next exercise.

TARGETING THE MAIN MOVIE

The main (*root*) movie represents the main timeline of an SWF. All of your project's other timelines exist, in some way, inside this one.

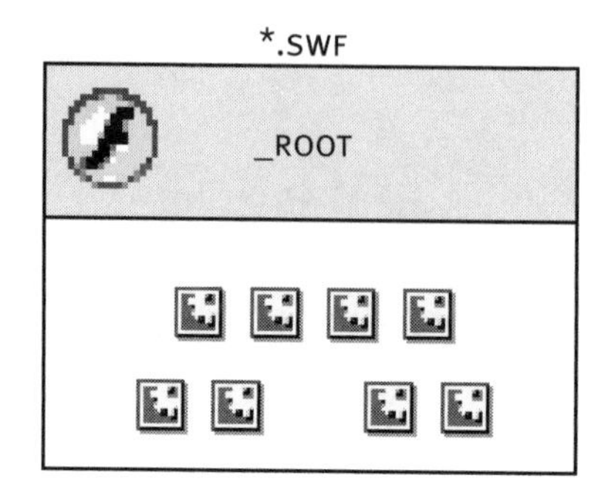

Targeting the main timeline is simple. The syntax is:

```
_root.play();
```

You can place this script on any timeline, exactly as shown, and it will always cause the main timeline to play.

NOTE *An external movie (SWF) loaded into a level is also considered a root timeline. In the section "Targeting Movies on Levels," we'll explain how this affects your scripting.*

1) Open *rootTarget1.fla* in the Lesson03/Assets folder.

This file is identical to the one we just finished working on except that two buttons appear on the lower-right portion of the stage. We will script these buttons to resize the main timeline when they are clicked. We will then copy these buttons, place them inside our movie clip instances, and—without modifying the target paths used in the script—demonstrate how you can use `_root` to target the main timeline apart from any other timeline in the SWF.

2) With the Actions panel open, select the button with the minus sign over it and add the script:

```
on (release) {
  _root._xscale = _root._xscale - 10;
  _root._yscale = _root._yscale - 10;
}
```

When this button is pressed and released, the main timeline's size will be reduced by 10 percent. Because the button to which we're attaching this action resides on the main timeline—which is also the timeline affected by the button—this script doesn't require a target path. We use an absolute target path here to demonstrate its universal effectiveness.

3) With the Actions panel open, select the button with the plus sign over it and add the script:

```
on (release) {
  _root._xscale = _root._xscale + 10;
  _root._yscale = _root._yscale + 10;
}
```

This script is similar to the one in Step 2 except that when this button is pressed and released, the main timeline's size will *increase* by 10 percent.

4) Drag-select both buttons and the text on top of the buttons and copy them. Double-click one of the movie clip instances on the stage to edit it in place. Paste the buttons on the *Change root Buttons* layer on the movie clip's timeline, and center them just below the current graphics.

Although these copies of the buttons on the main timeline exist within this movie clip timeline, the actions attached to them still target the main timeline because a `_root` target path always refers to the main timeline of the movie (the SWF).

5) Choose Control > Test movie to test the project.

The first thing you'll notice is that every instance of our movie clip includes the buttons. In addition, the buttons appear in their original placement—on the lower-right portion of the stage. Click any of these buttons (on the main timeline, or within a movie clip instance) and you get the same result: the main timeline is resized. As it resizes, however, something interesting occurs: the other timelines are resized as well. This resizing is due to the parent-child relationship between the main timeline and the movie clip instances on it—we'll discuss this topic in more detail in the next exercise.

6) Close the testing environment to return to the authoring environment. Save the project as *rootTarget2.fla*.

We build on this file (with a few modifications) in the next exercise.

TARGETING A PARENT MOVIE

Flash allows you to place one timeline inside another—this is what you're doing whenever you add a movie clip instance to the main timeline. However, even movie clip instances can contain other movie clip instances many levels deep. Placing one timeline inside another creates a *parent-child relationship* between the timelines. The parent is the timeline that *contains* the other movie; the child is the movie *contained* within the other timeline.

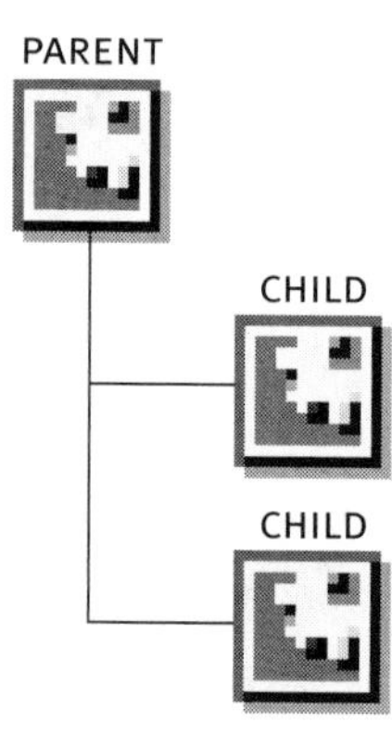

A child movie can easily tell its parent what to do (not so easy in real life!) using the following syntax:

```
_parent.play();
```

To understand how it works, imagine placing a movie clip instance named **myMovieClip_mc** on the main timeline and then placing another movie clip instance named **myOtherMovieClip_mc** inside **myMovieClip_mc**. The absolute target path of the movie structure would look like this:

```
_root.myMovieClip_mc.myOtherMovieClip_mc
```

If you wanted an action on **myOtherMovieClip_mc**'s timeline to cause **myMovieClip_mc**'s timeline to go to Frame 50, you would use this syntax:

```
_parent.gotoAndPlay(50);
```

You could place this same syntax on **myMovieClip_mc**'s timeline, and it would cause the main timeline to go to Frame 50 because the main timeline is that movie clip's parent.

In the next exercise, we'll place movie clips inside movie clips, creating parent-child relationships. Such relationships can have all sorts of ramifications within a project, helping you make your movies more interactive. You will also create a simple "effect" clip that you can drag and drop into any timeline, causing that timeline to do something.

1) Open *parentTarget1.fla* in the Lesson03/Assets folder.

The only difference between this file and the file we worked on in the last exercise is that the buttons set up to scale the main timeline have been removed to avoid confusion.

2) Double-click one of the movie clip instances on the stage to edit it in place. With the Library panel open and the Child Clip layer selected, drag an instance of the Hatfield Child movie clip onto the stage, just to the right of the graphics in the current movie clip.

You've just placed one movie clip within another, creating a parent-child relationship: the movie clip instance you just dragged onto the stage is the child, and the timeline you dragged it to is the parent. The child's timeline is set up in the same manner as the parent's timeline. It contains an invisible button that, when pressed, will drag the instance and display a text balloon. The text field in this balloon is named **balloon_txt**, just as it is in the parent movie.

NOTE *For visual clarity, you might want to resize the* **Hatfield Child** *movie clip to 50 percent of its original size, but you aren't required to do so.*

3) With the Actions panel open, select the child movie clip instance and add the script:

```
onClipEvent (load) {
  var words:String;
  this.words = _parent.words + "'s kid";
}
```

When this movie clip instance is loaded—loading occurs simultaneously with the parent's loading because the child resides on Frame 1 of its parent timeline—data is transferred from the parent to the child. The action can be translated like this: "Make the value of `words` in *this* timeline equal to the value of `words` in the *parent* timeline, plus the text `'s kid`." Thus, if `words` has a value of `"I'm Derek"` in the parent, then `words` will have a value of `"I'm Derek's kid"` in the child. Let's test it.

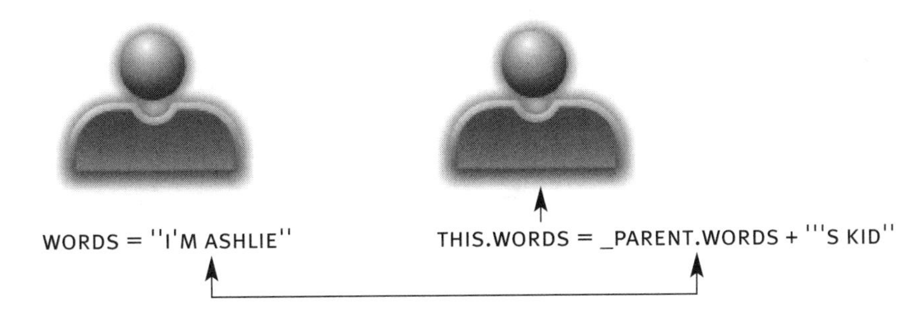
WORDS = "I'M ASHLIE"
THIS.WORDS = _PARENT.WORDS + "'S KID"

4) Choose Control > Test Movie to view the project up to this point.

The first thing you'll notice when the movie plays is that each of our instances now includes a child movie clip instance. If you click one of the child movie clip instances, not only does it become draggable, but its text balloon appears with text indicating who its parent is. This is the functionality we set up in the previous step.

Click and drag one of the parent movies and you'll notice that its child is dragged as well. The same thing occurs with the parent movie that rotates as the mouse moves: its child movie rotates along with it.

Data-wise, a child movie clip is independent of its parent: Data in one timeline does not affect data in the other unless you program it to do so. Graphically, however, it's another story. Size, position, transparency, and other graphical changes made dynamically to a parent movie clip will automatically affect its children in the same way. However, changes to a child have no inherent effect on a parent. If you want child clips to affect parent clips, you must specifically program them to do so. This means you can program groups of timelines to work together but remain separate from other groups in the project.

Let's look at another use of this parent-child relationship between timelines.

5) Close the testing environment to return to the authoring environment. With the Library panel open, double-click the Swirl Clip movie clip instance.

This step puts Flash in Symbol Editing mode with the Swirl Clip's timeline visible. This clip contains no graphical data, just four empty keyframes to which we will add scripts.

6) With the Actions panel open, select Frames 1, 2, 3, and 4 and add these scripts:

Place on Frame 1:

```
_parent._x = _parent._x - 1;
_parent._xscale = _parent._xscale - 1;
```

Place on Frame 2:

```
_parent._y = _parent._y - 1;
_parent._yscale = _parent._yscale - 1;
```

Place on Frame 3:

```
_parent._x = _parent._x + 2;
_parent._xscale = _parent._xscale - 1;
```

Place on Frame 4:

```
_parent._y = _parent._y + 2;
_parent._yscale = _parent._yscale - 1;
```

The makeup of these scripts isn't terribly important—what's important is that the actions all target the parent movie clip, and when an instance of the Swirl Clip is placed inside a timeline, its parent will appear to spiral away into nothingness. Let's demonstrate.

7) Return to the main timeline. With the Library panel open and the Swirl Clip layer selected, drag a Swirl Clip instance onto the stage. Choose Control > Test Movie to test the project.

As soon as the movie begins to play, the main timeline begins to swirl away into nothingness—an effect achieved by the movie clip instance we dropped into it. You can apply this effect to any timeline by placing that same movie clip instance inside it, which we'll do next.

8) Close the test window to return to the authoring environment. Select the Swirl Clip instance on the main timeline and choose Edit > Cut. Double-click one of the Hatfield movie clip instances to go to its timeline. With the Swirl Clip layer selected, choose Edit > Paste in Center to paste the Swirl Clip into this timeline. Choose Control > Test Movie to test the project.

When the movie plays, the main timeline no longer swirls away—every instance of the Hatfield movie clip does instead. This is because once the Swirl Clip instance was moved, the main timeline ceased being its parent and the Hatfield movie clip became its parent instead. Getting a movie clip to swirl away is just the tip of the iceberg when it comes to exploiting the ability to create drag-and-drop behaviors.

To create more sophisticated behaviors, you can use the parent target path to target many levels up:

```
_parent._parent._alpha = 50;
```

9) Close the test window to return to the authoring environment. Save your work as *parentTarget2.fla*.

This step completes the exercise.

TARGETING MOVIE CLIP INSTANCES

When you drag a movie clip instance into a timeline and assign it an instance name, that name (as well as the clip's relationship to other timelines) determines its target path. For example, if you place a movie clip instance on the main timeline and give it an instance name of **alien_mc**, the movie clip instance's absolute target path is as follows:

```
_root.alien_mc
```

You can use this syntax in a script in any timeline of your project to communicate with this particular instance.

You could also use the relative path:

```
alien_mc
```

to target the instance from the main timeline because it's a child movie of the main timeline.

If you were to place this same movie clip instance inside another movie clip instance named **spaceship_mc**, which resided on the root timeline, the absolute target path would become the following:

```
_root.spaceship_mc.alien_mc
```

Because the relationship between the root timeline and the **alien_mc** movie clip instance has changed, the root timeline must now use this relative path to target it:

```
spaceship_mc.alien_mc
```

In addition, because the **spaceship_mc** movie clip instance is now in the same position relative to the **alien_mc** movie clip instance as the root timeline was before, the **spaceship_mc** instance can now target the **alien_mc** movie clip instance like this:

```
alien_mc
```

In the next exercise, you will target specific movie clips based on their names and positions relative to the timeline that contains the script.

1) Open *movieclipTarget1.fla* in the Lesson03/Assets folder.

This file picks up where we left off in the last exercise. We will name the various instances on the stage so that we can target them in a script.

2) With the Property Inspector open, select each instance on the stage and name it according to the value that the instance assigns to `words` (plus *_mc*) when it loads.

For example, if the selected instance were to set the value of `words` to `"I'm Derek"` on loading, you would name this instance **Derek_mc**. Do the same for the other instances on the stage.

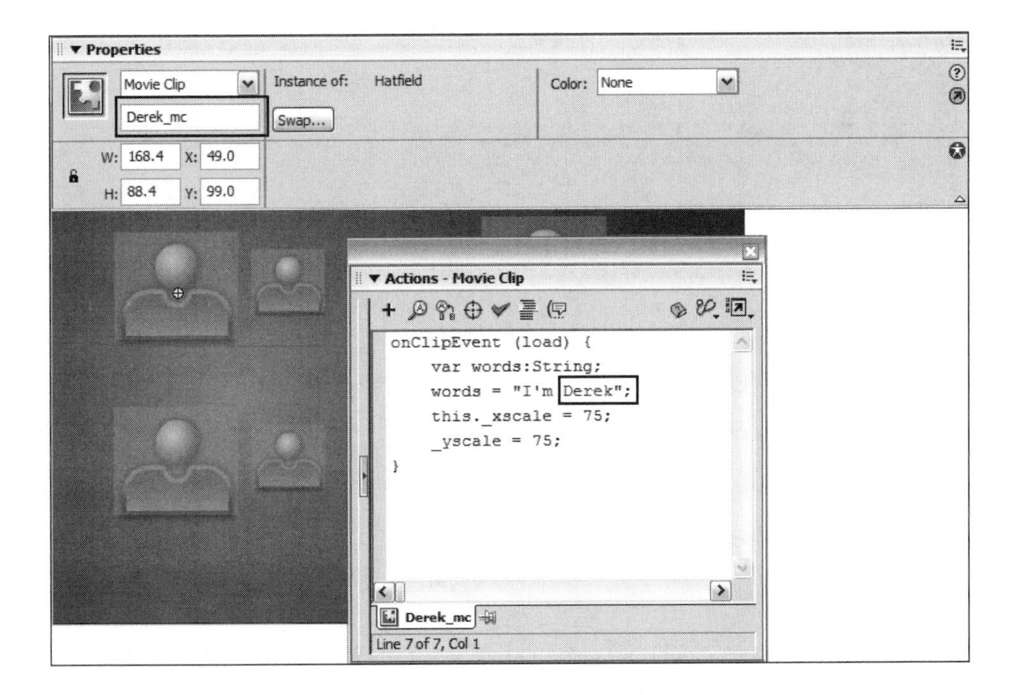

3) Double-click one of the instances to edit it in place. Inside this timeline is an instance of the Hatfield Child movie clip. With the Property Inspector open, select the instance and name it *myKid_mc*. Return to the main timeline.

You can now target six movie clip instances from any other timeline. Their absolute target paths are as follows:

```
_root.Derek_mc
_root.Derek_mc.myKid_mc
_root.Kathy_mc
_root.Kathy_mc.myKid_mc
_root.Ashlie_mc
_root.Ashlie_mc.myKid_mc
```

4) With the Actions panel open, select the instance named *Kathy_mc*. At the end of the current script (where it reads `this._rotation = this._rotation + .5;`), add the script:

```
myKid_mc._rotation = myKid_mc._rotation + 20;
_root.Derek_mc.myKid_mc._xscale = _root.Derek_mc.myKid_mc._xscale + .5;
_root.Derek_mc.myKid_mc._yscale = _root.Derek_mc.myKid_mc._yscale + .5;
_root.Ashlie_mc.myKid_mc._y = _root.Ashlie_mc.myKid_mc._y - .5;
```

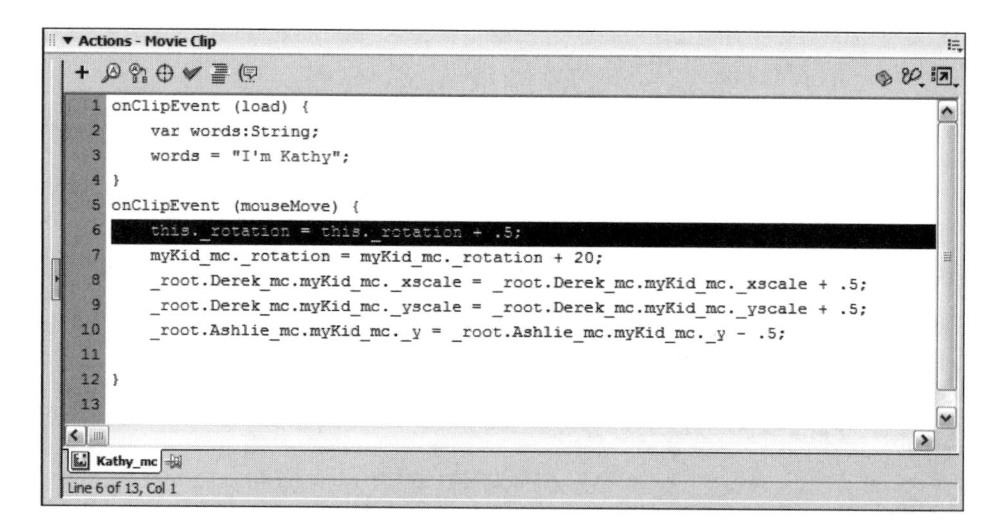

The placement of these lines of script dictates that they are to be triggered with each mouse movement. Because this script is attached to the instance named **Kathy_mc**, the first action uses a relative target path to target the **myKid_mc** instance within **Kathy_mc**. This action sets the `rotation` property of this instance to its current value plus 20 every time the mouse is moved. The next two actions use absolute target paths to target the **myKid_mc** instance inside the **Derek_mc** instance. These actions cause that instance to grow by 0.5 percent each time the mouse is moved. The last action uses an absolute target path to target the **myKid_mc** instance inside the **Ashlie_mc** instance. Each time the mouse is moved, the instance will move 0.5 pixels up from its current position.

5) Choose Control > Test Movie to test the project.

As you move the mouse, the **myKid_mc** movie clip instances we targeted should perform the actions we scripted for them.

6) Close the test movie to return to the authoring environment. Save your file as *movieclipTarget2.fla*.

This step completes the exercise, as well as our use of this file in this lesson.

TARGETING MOVIES ON LEVELS

With the `loadMovie()` action, Flash enables you to load more than one **.swf** file into the Flash player window simultaneously (something you'll learn how to do in the exercise that follows, and that we discuss more in Lesson 18, "Loading External Assets"). SWFs exist in the Flash player window in what are known as *levels*. Functionally, levels (for holding SWFs) are similar to layers (for holding content) on a timeline: they are a plane of existence, a depth that puts a loaded SWF and all its content on top of or below other movies that have been loaded in the player window. You can load hundreds of external **.swf** files into various levels in the player window.

When you use the `loadMovie()` action to load a movie into a level, you must assign a level number to which the movie will be loaded. However, you don't need to load movies into sequential levels. You can assign arbitrary numbers, such as 46 or 731, if you prefer. Once a movie has been loaded into a level, its target path is its level number. For example, if you were to load a movie into Level 37, movies on other levels would target that movie using this target path:

```
_level37
```

To tell the main timeline on this level to stop, you would use the following syntax:

```
_level37.stop ();
```

NOTE *The first movie to appear in the player window automatically loads into Level 0.*

A level's target path is the key to controlling the SWF loaded there, including its main timeline and any movie clip instances it may contain.

Because you're loading multiple SWFs into the player window using the `loadMovie()` action, it's important to note that each SWF's main timeline is considered the `_root` timeline in relation to other movies within that SWF. Thus, although an SWF loaded into a level might be addressed as `_level37` by movies on other levels, the main timeline of that SWF can be addressed as `_root` by movie clip instances within that same SWF. This means that if movies have been loaded into 15 levels, there are a total of 16 root movies, including the one on Level 0. Whenever a timeline targets another timeline on that same level, it can use a relative target path.

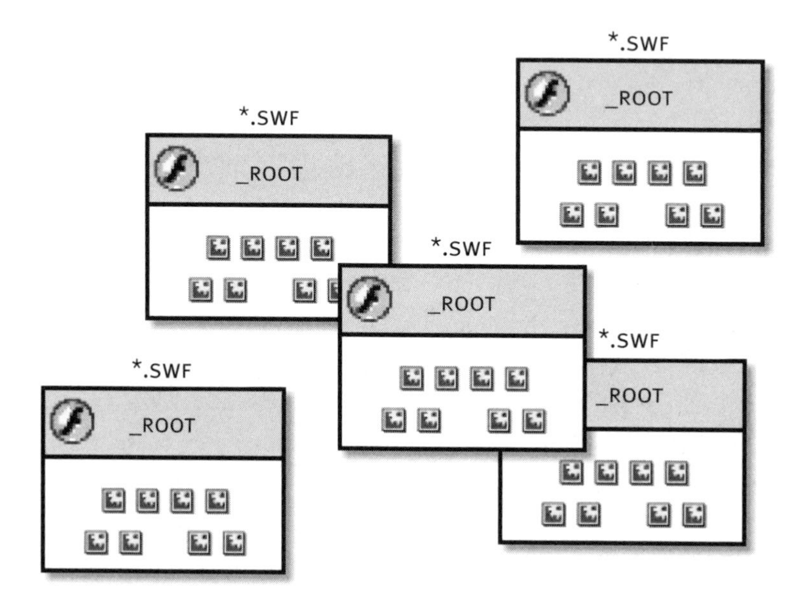

In the next exercise, we'll load movies into Levels 1 and 2 and control them from Level 0.

1) Open *backgroundControl1.fla* in the Lesson03/Assets folder.

This is the movie that will be loaded into Level 1. It looks like an operating system dialog box, and it contains a single scene made up of six layers, each of which is named according to its content.

In the next exercise, we'll script the functionality of many of the buttons you see. For now, we'll make the window draggable, as well as allow it to be closed.

2) With the Actions panel open, select Frame 1 on the main timeline and add the script:

```
_visible = false;
```

This action, because it exists on Frame 1, will cause this movie (which will eventually be loaded into Level 1) to become invisible upon loading, giving the effect of a closed window when it is initially loaded. A script on Level 0 will be used to "open" the window (make it visible).

3) With the Actions panel open, select the round Exit button (with an *X* on it) and add the script:

```
on (release) {
  _visible = false;
}
```

The script in Step 2 is used to make the movie invisible when it is *initially* loaded, but the script on this button will be used to "close" the window (make it invisible) if it has been "opened" (made visible). Shortly, we'll be creating the script that "opens" this window (makes it visible).

4) With the Actions panel open, select the rectangular invisible button at the top of the dialog box and add the script:

```
on (press) {
  _alpha = 50;
  startDrag (this);
}

on (release) {
  _alpha = 100;
  stopDrag ();
}
```

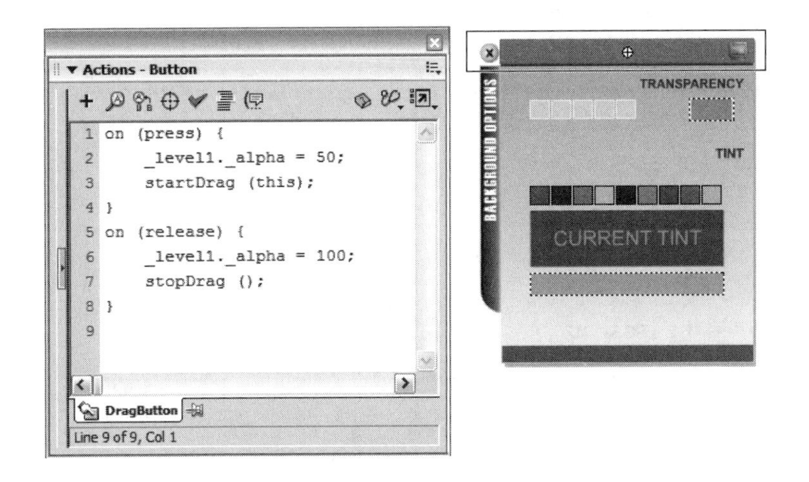

When this button is pressed, this movie will become 50 percent transparent as well as draggable. When the button is released, the movie will once again become 100 percent opaque and dragging will stop—thus emulating the effect of a draggable dialog box.

It's important to note that because we know this movie will be loaded into Level 1, this syntax would work, too:

```
on (press) {
  _level1._alpha = 50;
  startDrag (this);
}

on (release) {
  _level1._alpha = 100;
  stopDrag ();
}
```

Notice in this script that the actions that change the movie's transparency now contain absolute target paths to Level 1 (`_level1.alpha = 50;`). Although this syntax will work, there's a major disadvantage to using it. For the purpose of this project, we *know* this movie will be loaded into Level 1, so we could comfortably use an absolute target path to Level 1 in our script. If our project were a bit more dynamic, it might allow this movie to be loaded arbitrarily into any level—Level 82, for example. In that case, the line of script that changes the `alpha` property would not work because it would target the movie on Level 1, not the movie loaded into Level 82. Using a relative path in these scripts (by not using a target path at all, as shown in the first script in this step), ensures that the movie can be loaded into any level and that all of its scripts will continue to work properly.

5) Export this movie as *backgroundControl.swf* in the Lesson03/Assets folder.

This step creates an **SWF** from our project, which will be loaded into Level 1.

6) Save your work as *backgroundControl2.fla*.

We'll work with this file again in the next exercise.

7) Open *textBox1.fla* in the Lesson03/Assets folder.

This movie will be loaded into Level 2. As with the last movie we worked on, this movie resembles an operating system dialog box. It contains a single scene made up of four layers, each of which is named according to its content.

All of the scripts we're adding to this file are the same, and they work in the same manner as those we added to the previous file. The only difference is that they affect *this* movie, which is loaded into Level 2.

8) With the Actions panel open, select Frame 1 on the main timeline and add the script:

```
_visible = false;
```

This action targets the movie that will be loaded into Level 2. This script makes the movie on Level 2 invisible, just as the script in Step 2 made the movie on Level 1 invisible.

9) With the Actions panel open, select the round Exit button (with an *X* on it) and add the script:

```
on (release) {
  _visible = false;
}
```

This button will be used to "close" the window if it has been made visible.

10) With the Actions panel open, select the rectangular invisible button at the top of the dialog box and add the script:

```
on (press) {
  _alpha = 50;
  startDrag (this);
}

on (release) {
  _alpha = 100;
  stopDrag ();
}
```

When this button is pressed, the movie in Level 2 will become 50 percent transparent as well as draggable. When the button is released, that movie will once again become 100 percent opaque and dragging will cease—the same effect as that described in Step 4.

You're finished scripting this movie for now.

11) Export this movie as *textBox.swf* in the Lesson03/Assets folder.

This creates an SWF from our project, which will be loaded into Level 2.

12) Save your work as *textBox2.fla*.

We'll work with this file again in the next exercise.

13) Open *levelTarget1.fla* in the Lesson03/Assets folder.

This is the movie that will be loaded into the player initially (into Level 0, but we don't need to define this). We will add actions to this movie to load **backgroundControl.swf** into Level 1 and **textBox.swf** into Level 2. We will then add actions that enable us to control these movies.

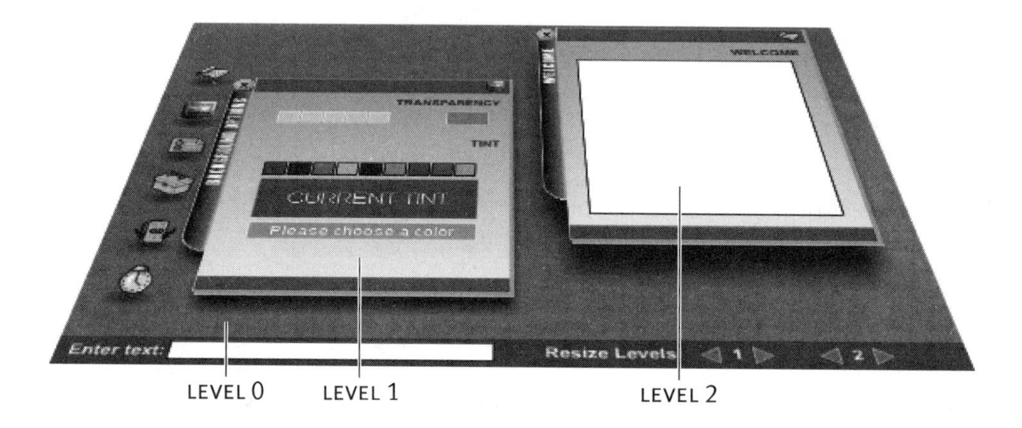

This file takes the appearance of an operating system desktop. It contains a single scene composed of four layers, each named according to its content.

14) With the Actions panel open, select Frame 1 and add the script:

```
loadMovieNum ("backgroundControl.swf", 1);
loadMovieNum ("textBox.swf", 2);
```

The first action loads **backgroundControl.swf** into Level 1, and the second action loads **textBox.swf** into Level 2.

Remember that both of these movies are set up to become invisible on loading. To make them visible, we must script two of the buttons on our desktop—we'll do this next.

15) With the Actions panel open, select the button that resembles a computer icon (on the left of the stage) and add the script:

```
on (release) {
  _level1._visible = true;
}
```

This action makes the movie loaded into Level 1 visible, emulating the effect of a dialog box opening. As you can see, targeting a movie loaded into a level is straightforward.

16) With the Actions panel open, select the button that resembles a paper scroll (on the left of the stage) and add the script:

```
on (release) {
  _level2._visible = true;
}
```

This script has the same effect as the script on the computer icon button, but this script will make the movie loaded into Level 2 visible when the button is pressed.

Next, let's set up the buttons that will be used to scale the movies on Levels 1 and 2.

17) With the Actions panel open, select the left-arrow button (to the left of the "1" at the bottom of the screen) and add the script:

```
on (release) {
  _level1._xscale = _level1._xscale - 5;
  _level1._yscale = _level1._yscale - 5;
}
```

When this button is pressed and released, the horizontal and vertical proportions of the movie on Level 1 will be scaled down to their current values minus 5.

18) With the Actions panel open, select the right-arrow button (to the left of the "1" at the bottom of the screen) and add the script:

```
on (release) {
  _level1._xscale = _level1._xscale + 5;
  _level1._yscale = _level1._yscale + 5;
}
```

These actions have the same effect as those discussed in Step 17 except that they *increase* the horizontal and vertical proportions of the movie on Level 1.

19) With the Actions panel open, place these actions on the buttons on either side of the "2" at the bottom of the screen:

Place on left-pointing button:

```
on (release) {
  _level2._xscale = _level2._xscale - 5;
  _level2._yscale = _level2._yscale - 5;
}
```

Place on right-pointing button:

```
on (release) {
  _level2._xscale = _level2._xscale + 5;
  _level2._yscale = _level2._yscale + 5;
}
```

These actions have the same effect as those discussed in Steps 17 and 18 except that they control the movie loaded into Level 2.

20) Choose Control > Test Movie to test the project's functionality.

When this project begins playing, **backgroundControl.swf** is loaded into Level 1 and **textBox.swf** is loaded into Level 2. However, you may remember that we set up these movies to be invisible on loading. Clicking either of the icon buttons on the desktop we scripted will show the appropriate movie on that level. With the movies visible, press the scale buttons at the bottom of the screen to see how movies loaded into levels can be targeted. You can also drag these movies using the drag buttons we set up, or you can close one of these "dialog box" windows by pressing the Exit button on either.

21) Close the testing environment to return to the authoring environment and save your work as *levelTarget2.fla*.

We will use a slightly modified version of this file in the next exercise.

TARGETING MOVIE CLIP INSTANCES ON LEVELS

Targeting a movie clip instance that exists within an SWF loaded into a level is a straightforward process: input the level number of the SWF that holds the movie clip, followed by the instance name itself. An instance called **cuteDog_mc** within an SWF loaded on Level 42, for example, would have this target path (relative to movies on other levels):

```
_level42.cuteDog_mc
```

If **cuteDog_mc** itself contained a movie clip instance named **tail_mc**, that instance's target path would be:

```
_level42.cuteDog_mc.tail_mc
```

Although we've used absolute paths in these examples (because we're targeting timelines on different levels), remember that you can use relative target paths to target timelines on the same level.

In this exercise, we'll build on our operating system project by targeting movie clip instances in SWFs loaded into levels, and we'll show you how to use simple data from one level in another.

1) Open *levelTarget3.fla* in the Lesson03/Assets folder.

This is like the file to which we added scripts in the last exercise, with one addition: the timeline now includes a layer called Colors Clip.

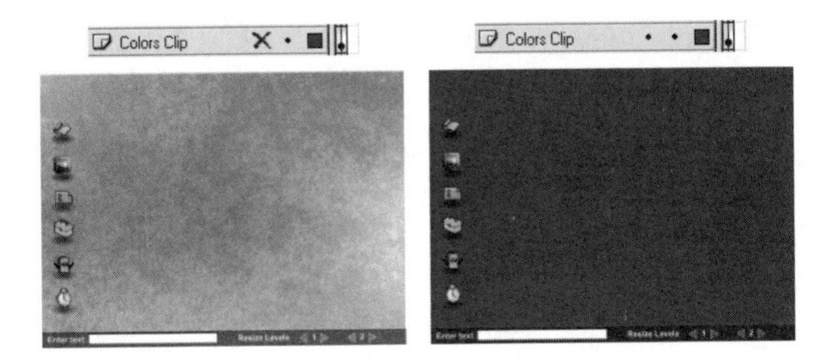

2) Press the Show Layer button (with the big red *X*) on the Colors Clip layer to reveal the content of this layer.

You should now see a purple box that covers the entire stage. This box is a movie clip instance named **colors_mc**. This movie clip instance will act as a color layer above the multicolored textured background you see when this instance is not visible. Changing the color and transparency of this instance will make it seem as if the textured background on the desktop is changing. Soon we'll script the movie that's loaded into Level 1 (**backgroundControl.swf**) to change colors and control transparency of this instance.

3) Double-click the *colors_mc* movie clip instance to edit it in place.

The timeline of the **colors_mc** movie clip instance is composed of a single layer that contains several frame labels. At each of these frame labels, the colored box on stage is filled with the color associated with that frame label's name. We will control this clip's color by sending it to different labels on its timeline. Initially the clip will be purple because this is the color at Frame 1, and that frame includes a `stop()` action to prevent the timeline from moving until we instruct it to do so.

4) Return to the main timeline. With the Property Inspector open, select the text field in the lower-left portion of the stage, next to where "Enter Text:" is displayed.

Looking at the Property Inspector, you'll notice that this is an input text field named **inputText_txt**. Here the user can enter any text he or she wants, and that text will be displayed in a text field in the movie loaded into Level 2 (**textBox.swf**). Next, we'll set up the script that creates this functionality.

5) With the Actions panel open, select the button on the desktop that resembles a scroll of paper, and add this script just below `_level2._visible = true;`:

```
_level2.inputText_txt.text = _level0.inputText_txt.text;
```

A text field named **inputText_txt** in the movie that gets loaded into Level 2 has the same name as the text field in this movie, as we discussed in the preceding step. When this button is pressed, this action will set the value of the text field on Level 2 to the same value as the text field in this movie. This is a simple example of how data can be transferred between timelines.

6) With the Actions panel open, select Frame 1 of the main timeline and add this script just below `loadMovieNum ("textBox.swf", 2);`:

```
_level0.colors_mc._alpha = 50;
```

This action will make the **colors_mc** movie clip instance (which resides on the Colors Clip layer) 50 percent transparent when the movie begins to play. We used a target path of `_level0` for this action—even though it's not required—to reinforce your understanding that the first movie to load (this movie) is automatically loaded into Level 0.

7) Export this file as *levelTarget.swf* in the Lesson03/Assets folder.
We'll play this file at the end of this exercise.

8) Save this file as *levelTarget4.fla*.
We're finished scripting this file.

9) Open *backgroundControl2.fla* in the Lesson03/Assets folder.
This is the same file we used in the last exercise—the one that gets loaded into Level 1 of our project. In the previous exercise, we scripted it to become invisible on loading, to close when the Exit button is pressed, and to become draggable when the invisible button at the top of the box is pressed. Here, we'll enhance its functionality by enabling it to control the **colors_mc** movie clip instance that resides on Level 0. We'll attach scripts to the many square buttons that you see.

Before we begin scripting, you need to familiarize yourself with several of the elements on the stage. On the left, just below the word "Transparency," you'll see a dynamic text field named **alphaAmount_txt**. You will use it in two ways: to display the current transparency of the **colors_mc** movie clip instance on Level 0, and to display the amount of transparency that will be applied to that instance when any of the five Transparency buttons are rolled over. To the left of this text field are five square buttons that will be scripted to change the transparency of the **colors_mc** movie clip instance.

Below these buttons are nine additional buttons that resemble color swatches. These buttons will be set up to send the **colors_mc** movie clip (Level 0) to the various frame labels on its own timeline. Below these buttons is a movie clip instance named **currentColor_mc**, which is essentially a smaller version of the **colors_mc** movie clip instance. Its timeline has similar color boxes and frame labels to those of the **colors_mc** movie clip instance. This movie clip instance will display the current color applied over the textured background on the desktop (Level 0). Below this movie clip instance is another text field, **colorName_txt**, which displays the name of the color as the mouse rolls over the color swatches above it.

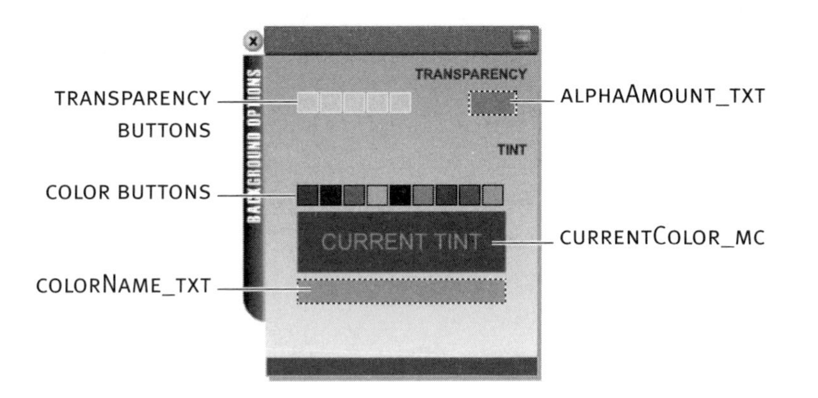

10) With the Actions panel open, select the square transparency button on the far left of the *alphaAmount_txt* text field and add the script:

```
on (rollOver) {
  alphaAmount_txt.text = 0;
}

on (release) {
  _level0.colors_mc._alpha = 0;
}

on (release, rollOut) {
  alphaAmount_txt.text = _level0.colors_mc._alpha;
}
```

This button will be used to set to 0 the transparency of the **colors_mc** movie clip instance on Level 0.

The first action will display 0 in the **alphaAmount_txt** text field when the button is rolled over. This is simply to provide the user with feedback about the amount of transparency this button will apply. With the next action, when the button is released, the alpha property of the **colors_mc** movie clip instance is set to 0, which makes it transparent. (Note the simplicity of this target path: level number followed by instance name.) The next action will set the value displayed in the **alphaAmount_txt** text field to the current transparency of the **colors_mc** movie clip instance when the button is released or the mouse is rolled away from it.

You can attach the same script to the buttons to the right of this one and replace the 0 values with 25, 50, 75, and 100, respectively.

11) With the Actions panel open, select the purple Color Swatch button (the first one on the left) and add the script:

```
on (rollOver) {
  colorName_txt.text = "Purple";
}

on (release) {
  currentColor_mc.gotoAndStop ("Purple");
  _level0.colors_mc.gotoAndStop ("Purple");
}

on (release, rollOut) {
  colorName_txt.text = "Please choose a color";
}
```

This button will set the color of the **colors_mc** movie clip instance on Level 0 by moving that timeline to the appropriate frame label.

The first action will display Purple in the **colorName_txt** text field when the button is rolled over to tell the user what color tint this button will apply. When the button is released, two actions are executed: the first sends the **currentColor_mc** movie clip instance to the frame labeled Purple. This will change the box below the Color Swatch buttons to purple, indicating that this is the current tint. The next action sends the **colors_mc** movie clip instance on Level 0 to the frame labeled Purple, causing the textured background on Level 0 to take on a purple tint (depending on its current transparency). The last action will reset the text in the **colorName_txt** text field to read Please choose a color.

You can attach this same script to the buttons on the left of this one, simply replacing the three areas that have `Purple` values with `Maroon`, `Lavender`, `SkyBlue`, `DeepBlue`, `Orange`, `GrassGreen`, `SeaGreen`, and `Pink`, respectively.

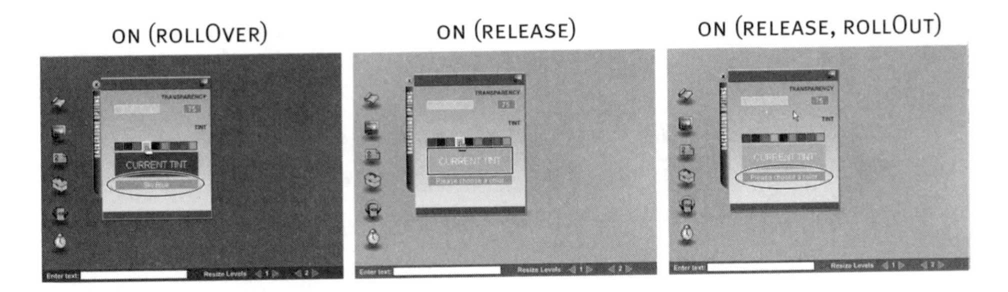

12) Export this movie as *backgroundControl.swf* in the Lesson03/Assets folder.

This creates an **SWF** from our project, which will be loaded into Level 1, overwriting a previously saved version from the last exercise.

13) Save your work as *backgroundControl3.fla*.

We're finished with this file.

14) Locate the *levelTarget.swf* file you created and double-click it to open and play it.

As soon as this file begins to play, **backgroundControl.swf** is loaded into Level 1 and **textBox.swf** is loaded into Level 2—both of which are made invisible on loading. The **colors_mc** movie clip instance that overlays the textured background is currently tinted purple and has a transparency of 50 percent.

Enter some text in the text field at the bottom of the screen and press the button on the screen that resembles a scroll of text. This button was set up to make Level 2 visible, as well as to feed this text to a text field on that level.

Press the button resembling a computer monitor to make the movie on Level 1 visible. This movie controls the color and transparency of the **colors_mc** movie clip instance on Level 0. Press the Transparency and Color buttons in this movie to see how they affect that movie clip instance.

TIP *As discussed at the beginning of this lesson, timelines can contain their own data, functions, and objects. While we haven't addressed these topics yet, it's prudent to briefly discuss a few points about how target paths relate to these dynamic elements, because most projects are set up so that a dynamic element on one timeline can be used by another.*

For example, a variable may be named **myVariable**. *Suppose that variable exists in a movie clip instance named* **myMovieClip_mc**, *which itself is inside a movie loaded into Level 74. To use this variable in any of your scripts on any timeline, you would place the appropriate target path in front of the variable name, like this:*

```
_level27.displayText_txt.text =_level74.myMovieClip_mc.myVariable;
```

The same principle applies to function calls:

```
_root.anotherMovieClip_mc.myFunction();
```

or any type of object:

```
_parent.myObject
```

The importance of this mechanism will become more evident as you progress through the lessons in this book.

UNDERSTANDING MULTIPLE IDENTITIES

As you've learned in this lesson, you can target a single timeline in many ways, depending on its relationship to the timeline targeting it, and your own needs and personal preferences. The graphic shows the interchangeable target paths that can be used when one movie targets another.

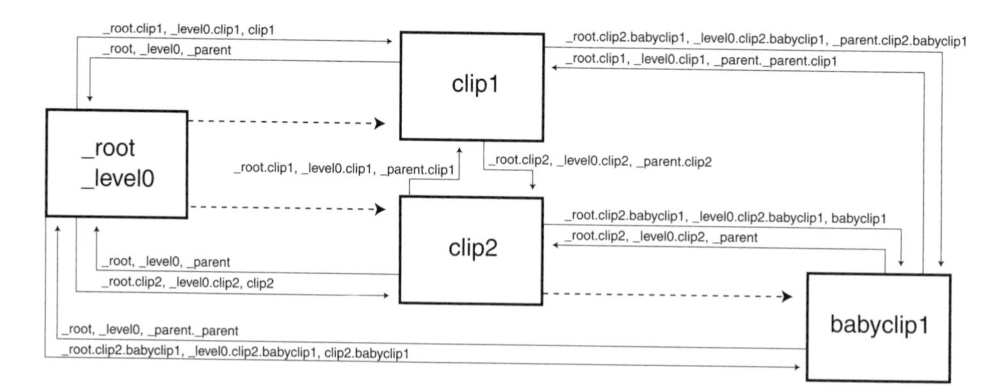

Solid lines and arrows represent one movie targeting another. Dotted lines and arrows represent child movies.

CREATING AND REFERENCING GLOBAL ELEMENTS

There's no denying that even with a thorough understanding of target paths, it's sometimes hard to keep track of them—especially when you have timelines within timelines within timelines. As you might imagine, target paths can become quite long. To help simplify things, ActionScript provides access to a *global object*. As a global element, this special Flash object exists apart from any specific timeline and is omnipotent in relation to your Flash project: you can reference it from any timeline *without* a target path and take advantage of its power to reference other timelines and the variables, functions, and other dynamic elements they contain.

Let's take a look at how you create a global element and how you convert an element with a target path into a global element.

Creating a global element, such as a variable, is as simple as this:

```
_global.myVariable = "hello";
```

Because this variable is now a global element, you can reference it from any timeline by its name:

```
_root.myMovieClip_mc.favoriteGreeting = myVariable;
```

or

```
_root.favoriteGreeting = myVariable;
```

You can also use the global identifier to create global functions (see Lesson 5, "Using Functions"):

```
_global.myFunction = function(){
  //actions...
}
```

To call the function from any timeline, use its name:

```
myFunction();
```

The same syntax is used to create instances of objects (see Lesson 4, "Using Object Classes"):

```
_global.myDateObject_date = new Date();
```

You can easily convert an element with a target path (such as a movie clip instance) so that it can be referenced globally—that is, without a path. For example, suppose a movie clip instance in your project has a target path of `_root.car_mc.engine_mc.piston_mc`. If you want to make it easier to reference this instance, you give it a global address:

```
_global.myPiston_mc = _root.car_mc.engine_mc.piston_mc;
```

To control that instance, you simply reference its global address from any timeline:

```
myPiston_mc.play();
```

Is there a benefit to using a global element? It's a matter of preference as well as what a given project dictates. In general, though, any element you use frequently or that's used by a number of timelines is a good candidate for becoming a global element.

One thing to keep in mind, though, is that naming collisions can occur when you use global elements—that is, an element in a timeline (for example, a variable) may end up with the same name as a global element. For example, suppose you have a global variable named `myVariable`. Suppose you also have a movie clip instance named **myMovieClip_mc**, which contains a variable named `myVariable`. You have a global variable *and* a variable in a movie clip instance, both with the same name.

You would have a problem if **myMovieClip_mc** attempted to reference the global variable named `myVariable` using this:

```
myVariable
```

This is because this timeline has its own local variable named `myVariable`. If you use this syntax, Flash won't be able to tell whether the script is referencing the local variable (within the movie clip instance) or the global one—a conflict it resolves by automatically referencing the closest variable to the timeline itself, which is the local one.

An easy way to avoid these naming collisions is to preface global element names with a small *g:*

```
gMyVariable
gFavoriteColor
```

TIP *Another thing to remember is that a global element uses memory that can be freed only by deleting the global element. Therefore, using lots of global elements may not be an efficient use of memory.*

WHAT YOU HAVE LEARNED

In this lesson, you have:

- Learned about Flash timelines and absolute and relative target paths (pages 104–107)
- Learned how to control multiple clip instances (pages 107–113)
- Controlled the main timeline of a project (pages 114–115)
- Used the parent-child relationship in movies to create an "effect" clip (pages 116–120)
- Controlled specific timelines within a single project (pages 120–123)
- Controlled movies loaded into levels (pages 123–136)
- Learned how to create global references to various ActionScript elements (pages 137–138)

using object classes

LESSON 4

Every day you use objects to perform any number of activities. You may have used Tupperware to store fresh cookies to prevent them from becoming stale, or the trash can to store a fruitcake from your Aunt Sally. *Objects* are items designed to meet specific needs. You can use them to perform tasks of their own (for example, a VCR playing or recording a movie), or you can employ them as simple storage devices.

Using Macromedia Flash, you can create objects that perform tasks or store something (such as data), in much the same way as real-world objects. As a matter of fact, you'll probably be pleasantly surprised at how familiar Flash objects seem, once you understand basic concepts of how they work. While Flash allows you to create your own

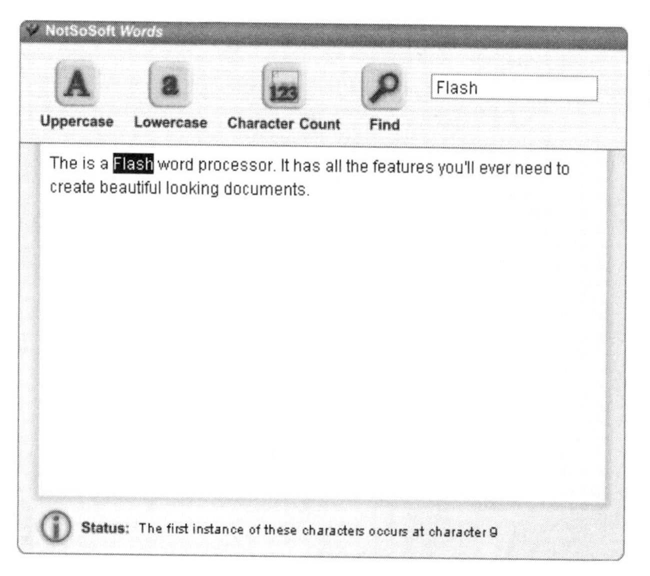

This Flash word processor is one of the projects you'll create in this lesson.

kinds of custom objects (a topic we'll cover in Lesson 7, "Creating Custom Classes"), it provides a number of built-in objects (organized in what are known as *classes*), ready for immediate use in your projects. In this lesson, we'll introduce you to many of these built-in classes of objects, explain their functionality, and help you gain experience using them.

WHAT YOU WILL LEARN

In this lesson, you will:

- Learn what objects/object classes are and why they are useful
- Get acquainted with the various classes of objects available in ActionScript
- Use the Color class
- Create an interactive scene using the Key object class
- Create a word processor using properties and methods of the String and Selection object classes

APPROXIMATE TIME

This lesson takes approximately 45 minutes to complete.

LESSON FILES

Starting Files:

Lesson04/Assets/Clown1.fla
Lesson04/Assets/balloon1.fla
Lesson04/Assets/wordProcessor1.fla

Completed Projects:

Clown2.fla
balloon2.fla
wordProcessor2.fla

WHAT OBJECTS ARE AND WHY THEY'RE USEFUL

ActionScript objects allow you to perform all sorts of interactive tasks with Flash. They provide a means for you to work with text, sound, color, dates, and more, in very dynamic ways.

As you'll soon learn, ActionScript objects, while intangible, are very much like their physical counterparts. They have characteristics known as *properties*, which can be changed with a script, and they have abilities, known as *methods*, which allow them to perform various tasks. We'll discuss both of the aspects of objects in depth in a moment.

The primary benefit of using objects in ActionScript is that they allow you to program and manipulate data, colors, sound, dates, et cetera, in a context that makes sense to humans—we're all familiar with the idea of objects having characteristics and abilities.

UNDERSTANDING THE CONCEPT OF OBJECT CLASSES

At the introduction of this lesson, when we introduced the phrase, "classes of objects," you probably scratched your head wondering what in the world the phrase meant. It's actually a simple yet important concept to understand in the world of object-oriented programming. We'll touch on it briefly here to acquaint you with its meaning. A more in-depth discussion can be found in Lesson 7, "Creating Custom Classes," where you'll create your own custom classes of objects.

"Classes of objects" (or *object classes*, or simply *classes*), is an organizational phrase used to denote sets of objects with similar characteristics and abilities. You've probably heard the terms upper class, middle class, or working class to describe groups of people that fit a certain mold due to their finances or capabilities. The same general idea applies to the concept of classes of objects in ActionScript. Each object you use in ActionScript belongs to a specific class that defines the general characteristics and abilities of the objects in it. To help you grasp this concept in the realm of ActionScript, let's look at an example.

Perhaps you've noticed that all movie clip instances you place in your project have a `_width` or `_alpha` property (among a lot of other common properties), or that you can control every movie clip instance's timeline using the `gotoAndPlay()` action (also known as a *method*). This is because Flash contains a MovieClip class (it's hidden from you, but it exists). This class defines the general capabilities of every movie clip instance you use in your project. While each movie clip instance might look different, they all have the same basic properties and abilities. This is similar to how humans walk, talk, and sneeze (common abilities), but each human's way of doing it is unique. We are all part of the Human class, so to speak.

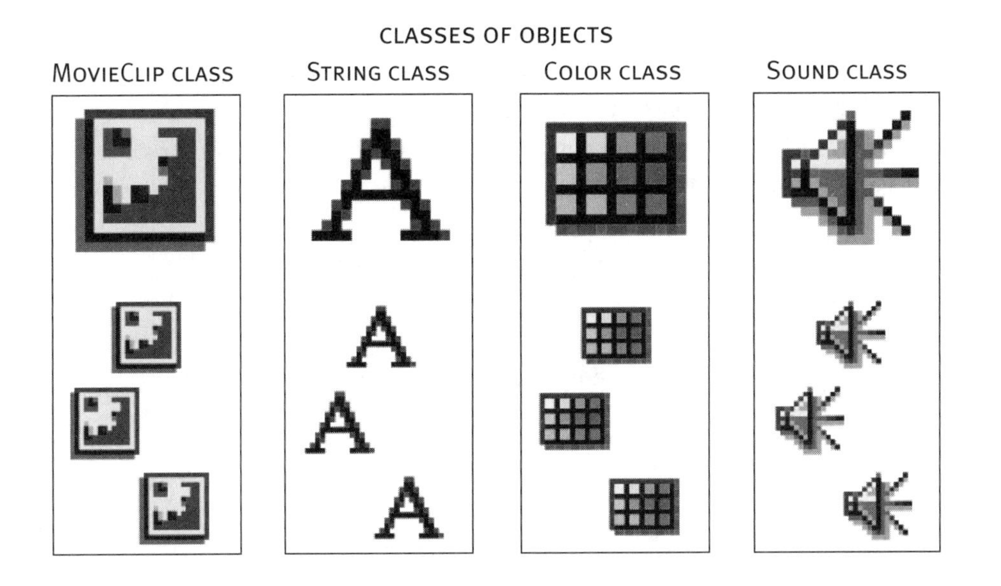

It's important to realize that when building your Flash projects, you create and use *instances* of various classes of objects, rather than placing the actual class in your project. It's a subtle but important distinction.

For example, when you drag a movie clip onto the stage, you're actually creating an *instance* of the MovieClip class. When you create a dynamic text field, you're creating an *instance* of the TextField class. You will usually work with instances (also known simply as objects) in Flash, as opposed to the actual class (although this can be done, and you will learn how in Lesson 7, "Creating Custom Classes"). A class is often referred to as a blueprint, while an instance of that class is thought of as the resulting usable object that you work with, based on that blueprint.

As we mentioned, classes of objects are defined by two primary characteristics: their *properties* and *methods*. Let's take an in-depth look at both.

NOTE *In the discussion that follows, the term* object *refers to an instance of a class. For example, if we mention an object named* `mySound`, *we are referring to an instance of the Sound class named* `mySound`.

Properties

Many but not all classes of objects have properties—values that represent characteristics belonging to instances of that class. In the real world, a car has properties like color, make, model, and horsepower. If your project had a Car class and you had created an instance of it named `myCar`, you might access the value of its properties in this manner:

```
var carColor:String = myCar.color;
var carTopSpeed:Number = myCar.topSpeed;
```

Several classes of objects in Flash have properties. For example, instances of the MovieClip class have property values that represent their transparency, visibility, horizontal position, vertical position, and rotation. Changes to any of these properties affect the movie clip instance's appearance or functionality, just as giving a car a paint job or changing its engine would alter the car. You can use property values of various objects in your scripts to set values elsewhere. Assume that a script in your project moves your car at a speed based on its horsepower. That line of script might look like this:

```
var speedFactor:Number = myCar.horsepower;
```

Here, the value of `speedFactor` is dependent on the value of the `horsepower` property of `myCar`.

Let's look at one more example of a property and how it's used in ActionScript.

The length of a string is a property of a String object. For example, the length of the term "Flash" is 5 because it contains five characters. In ActionScript, this would be written like this:

```
var name:String = "Flash";
var lengthOfName:Number = name.length;
```

The first line of code creates a variable called `name` whose value is the string `"Flash"`. The second line creates a variable called `lengthOfName` whose value is that of the `length` property of the `name` object (5). Although property names associated with movie clips are *usually* preceded by an underscore (`_alpha` and `_rotation`, for example), the property names of most objects are *not* preceded by an underscore. MovieClip properties break from what is considered the norm because their properties were first introduced in Flash 4, when ActionScript had a much different form than it has today.

Methods

A method represents a task that instances of a class of objects can perform. If you think of VCRs as a class of objects, methods of that class would include the abilities to play, record, stop, rewind, fast forward, and pause. The syntax representing the methods of our VCR class would look like this:

```
play();
rewind();
record();
```

In order for an instance of the VCR class to invoke (use) a method of its class, the syntax requires that you first indicate the name of the VCR class instance, followed by a dot and the name of the method:

```
myVCR.record();
```

This tells the VCR instance named `myVCR` to start recording.

The parentheses included with the method sometimes allow you to invoke the method in a unique way using a parameter or set of parameter values. Using the VCR example again, let's say you wanted to record a TV show on Channel 8 from 10:00 p.m. to 11:00 p.m. on September 9. The script required to perform this task might look like this:

```
myVCR.record("8", "10:00 pm", "11:00 pm", "September 9");
```

Commas separate the method parameters. Keep in mind that parameter values can be hard coded as shown, or they can be dynamic values such as variables. You can even use other methods as parameters. (You'll learn more about parameter values in the next lesson.)

Although many ActionScript object classes have methods that accept parameters, not all do. Some methods simply perform tasks that don't require special settings. For example, the `stop()` method of the MovieClip class allows you to stop the playback of a movie clip instance—nothing more, nothing less, thus additional parameters are unnecessary.

Each class of objects has a unique set of methods—it makes sense because each has a specific function.

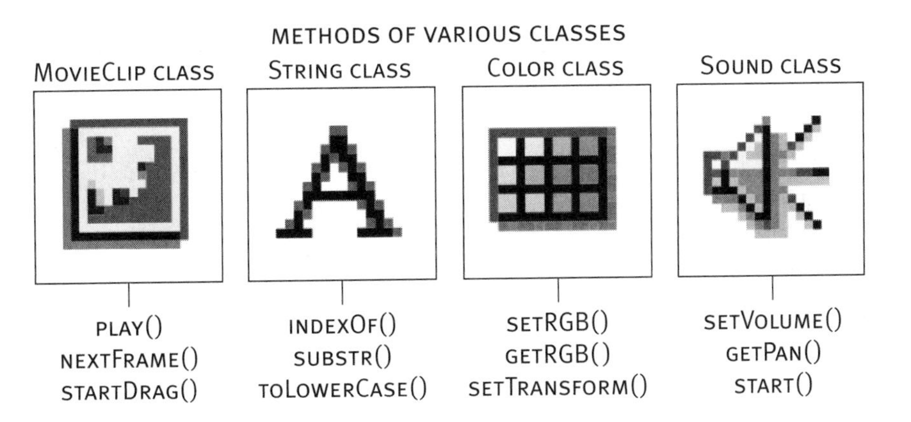

The various methods used by object classes in ActionScript perform all sorts of tasks, including:

- Getting and setting values
- Doing conversions (for example, converting a negative number to a positive)
- Indicating whether something is true or false
- Activating or deactivating something
- Manipulating something (such as text or numbers)

We'll demonstrate some of these tasks in this lesson and many others throughout the book.

BUILT-IN OBJECT CLASSES

In the next section, we'll briefly review many of the built-in object classes that ActionScript provides, as well as some ways they are used. Before we do, however, it's important to discuss how to actually get instances of classes into your project in the first place, so you can begin to utilize their power and functionality.

You can create object instances in one of two ways. To create a new instance of the MovieClip, Button, or TextField class, you create it on the stage or drag it onto the stage from the library. However, only MovieClip, Button, and TextField instances can be created in this way. To create an instance of any other class, you must use a *constructor*—a simple line of code that tells Flash to create an object instance of a particular class. A constructor looks like this:

```
nameOfInstance:nameOfClass = new nameOfClass();
```

If you wanted to create an instance of the Sound class, the constructor would look like this:

```
mySound:Sound = new Sound();
```

Whenever you create an object instance, you must give it a unique name. This allows you to change a property or invoke a method as it relates to that particular instance (remember, an instance inherits all the properties and methods of the class to which it belongs). We'll demonstrate the concept in examples. As you gain programming experience, you'll begin to understand when you should use constructors.

While instances of the MovieClip, TextField, and Button classes can be created on the stage manually by dragging them from the library, they can also be created dynamically using ActionScript.

NOTE *Object names follow the same naming conventions as variables, which means they can't contain spaces, symbols, or a number as the first character.*

Some object classes are known as *top-level classes*, which means you can't create instances of them using the methods we've shown. What differentiates these classes from those of which you create instances? Top-level classes represent and control global functionalities within your project. Take, for example, the Mouse class, which controls cursor visibility (among other things). You have just one cursor, so it wouldn't make sense to be able to create instances of this class; instead, you use the methods available to it, to do various things with the mouse. Look at the example:

```
Mouse.hide()
```

This line of script hides the cursor. Notice that the name of an instance is not referenced in relation to the `hide()` method. Instead, the *name of the top-level class* is referenced (in this case, Mouse), followed by the name of the method you wish to use. Similar syntax is used with any top-level class. As we go through the rest of this lesson, we'll introduce you to other top-level classes and the syntax required to use them.

In the Actions panel under the Built-in Classes book, you can access all of Flash's built-in classes, each of which is contained in one of these five subbooks:

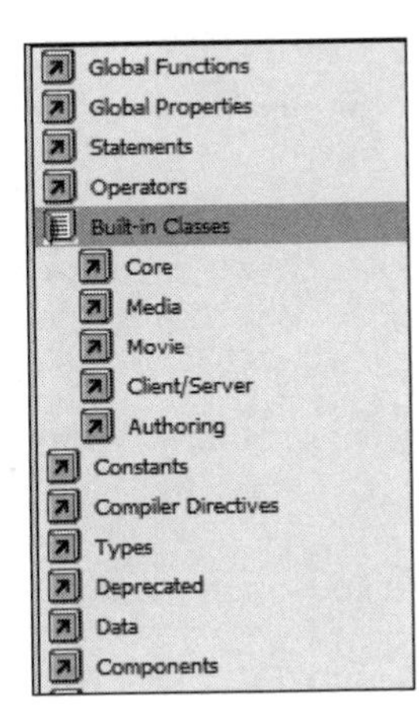

- Core. These classes deal with information storage and manipulation, not including information that's being moved into or out of Flash itself.
- Media. These classes assist with manipulating sound and video in your Flash movie, such as playing sounds, gaining access to the system camera, and streaming video.
- Movie. These classes deal with visual content and system-related information such as movie clips, text fields, the stage, and accessibility.
- Client/Server. These classes control the movement of information in and out of Flash.
- Authoring. These classes assist you in creating custom actions and custom components.

The following describes many of the built-in classes available in ActionScript as well as where and how you might use them. We'll indicate whether a class is a top-level class (creating instances is not required), or not, in which case you must create individual instances.

Accessibility Class (Top-Level)

This class contains read-only information about the computer's ability to use a screen reader:

```
Accessibility.isActive();
```

This script returns a result of either true or false. If the result is true, the user's computer can employ a screen reader.

Array Class (Instances)

An array is a storage device for multiple pieces of information. Arrays store information that can be set and referenced using a numbering system. For example:

```
var cakeType:Array = new Array();
cakeType[0] = "Chocolate";
cakeType[1] = "Angel Food";
cakeType[2] = "Baked Alaska";
```

The first line creates a new instance of the Array class called cakeType using the Array constructor. The next lines place data inside that array.

The Array class contains many useful methods that will help you add, remove, and sort array items from instances of that class.

NOTE *For more on arrays, see Lesson 6, "Creating and Manipulating Data."*

Boolean Class (Instances)

Instances of the Boolean class store one of two values, true or false. You can create a Boolean object by using the Boolean constructor or by using the = assign operator. For example:

```
var toggle:Boolean = new Boolean(false);
```

and

```
var toggle:Boolean = false;
```

create identical objects.

Button Class (Instances)

When you place a button on the stage, you create an instance of the Button class. Only MovieClip and TextField objects are created in a similar fashion—that is, by placing actual instances on the stage. The Button class contains properties and methods that allow you to control the appearance, tab order, functionality, and more of button instances.

Capabilities Class (Top-Level)

This class contains information about the user's computer, such as screen resolution and whether it can play sounds. The following script places the horizontal resolution of the user's computer into myVariable:

```
var myVariable:Number = System.capabilities.screenResolutionX;
```

TIP *Being able to access computer information allows you to create movies that tailor themselves to the capabilities of your user's computer. For example, you can determine whether a handheld computer is accessing the movie and, if so, redirect the user to a page designed expressly for handheld devices.*

Color Class (Instances)

You use an instance of this class to change a movie clip's color dynamically. When you create a Color object, you point it at a particular movie clip. Using the Color class's methods, you can alter your movie clip's color. You create a Color object using the Color class constructor method:

```
var myColor:Color = new Color(pathToTimeline);
```

Later in this lesson you'll complete an exercise using an instance of the Color class.

ContextMenu Class (Instances)

The context menu is the menu seen in the Flash player when you right-click (Control-click on the Macintosh). This class is used in conjunction with instances of the ContextMenuItems class (described shortly) to create customized context menus (with custom commands), which appear when the user right-clicks (or Control-clicks) a visual element in the Flash player window. This class also allows you to enable or disable any and all of the built-in context menu commands (such as Play, Stop, and Print) even as your movie plays.

This script creates a new ContextMenu object named myCustomMenu:

```
var myCustomMenu:ContextMenu = new ContextMenu();
myCustomMenu.hideBuiltInItems();
myCustomMenu.builtInItems.print = true;
myMovieClip_mc.menu = myCustomMenu;
myButton_btn.menu = myCustomMenu;
myTextField_txt.menu = myCustomMenu;
```

The second line of the script uses the hideBuiltInItems() method to hide all the built-in menu commands, and the third line enables the Print command so that it will appear when the menu is opened. The last three lines assign the custom menu to a movie clip, button, and text field instance. Right-clicking (or Control-clicking) any of these instances will cause the custom menu to appear.

Settings...
Print...
About Macromedia Flash Player 7...

ContextMenuItems Class (Instances)

This class is used in conjunction with the ContextMenu class (described just above) to create items that appear in a custom context menu. Your Flash project can be scripted to capture when a user clicks a custom menu item so that you can have a specific action or actions occur. For example, you can create a custom context menu that will allow a user to right-click in your project and choose to mute the volume.

NOTE *You will see more on the ContextMenu and ContextMenuItems classes in Lesson 20, "Maximum-Strength SWFs".*

Date Class (Instances)

With this class you can access the current time as local time or Greenwich Mean Time, as well as easily determine the current day, week, month, or year. To create a new instance of the Date class, you use the Date class constructor method. This example demonstrates one use of the Date class:

```
var now:Date = new Date();
var largeNumber:Number = now.getTime();
```

The example creates a variable called `largeNumber`, whose value is the number of milliseconds since midnight January 1, 1970.

NOTE *We will use the Date object in Lesson 16, "Time- and Frame-Based Dynamism."*

Error Class (Instances)

The Error class was introduced in Flash MX 2004 to help with managing errors in your projects. An error is whatever you define an error to be (a number was too large or too small, for example). When an error occurs, a new instance of the Error class is instantiated—this is known as "throwing" an error. With the Error class you can capture errors and write code to handle them so that your application behaves well, rather than acting in an unpredictable way.

You will see more on the Error class in Lesson 19, "Testing and Debugging."

Key Class (Top-Level)

You use the Key class to determine the state of the keys on the keyboard—for example, whether the Caps Lock key is toggled on, which key was pressed last, and which key or keys are currently pressed.

You will complete an exercise using this object later in this lesson.

LoadVars Class (Instances)

Flash allows you to load data into a movie from an external source. Using the LoadVars class, Flash can load in variables from a specified URL (which can be a standard text file). For example:

```
var myObj:LoadVars = new LoadVars();
myObj.load("http://www.mysite.com/myFiles/file.txt");
```

In the example, all of the loaded variables become properties of the `myObj` LoadVars instance.

Math Class (Top-Level)

With the Math class, you can perform many useful calculations and have the result returned. Here's one:

```
var positiveNumber:Number = Math.abs(-6);
```

The script uses the absolute value method of the Math object to convert the –6 to a positive number.

Mouse Class (Top-Level)

The Mouse class controls cursor visibility and allows you to set up Listeners to track mouse activity. Here is an example:

```
Mouse.hide();
```

The script hides the mouse from view. The mouse is still active, but it is not visible.

MovieClip Class (Instances)

You create instances of this most familiar class either in the authoring environment (by placing them on the stage), or with ActionScript actions such as `createEmptyMovieClip()` and `duplicateMovieClip()`—*not* by using the constructor function. Movie clip instances have many properties and methods that are used frequently in an interactive project. Here's an example:

```
myClip_mc.gotoAndStop("Menu");
```

With this script, a movie clip with an instance name of **myClip_mc** will be sent to the frame labeled Menu.

MovieClipLoader Class (Instances)

This class provides a way for you to easily load and gain access to information during the load of an SWF or JPG into a target movie clip or level. With an instance of the MovieClipLoader class, you know the file size of the external asset you are loading as well as how much of it has been loaded. By continually checking to see how much of the asset has been loaded, you can build a progress bar that indicates how far along an asset is in the loading process.

The MovieClipLoader class also provides a way for you to be informed of when the asset has finished loading.

NOTE *This class will be used in Lesson 18, "Loading External Assets."*

NetConnection Class (Instances)

The NetConnection class is used together with the NetStream class to play external Flash Video (FLV) files from an HTTP address or a hard drive.

NetStream Class (Instances)

The NetStream class provides methods and properties for controlling the playback of external Flash Video (FLV) files.

NOTE *You will see more on the NetConnection and NetStream classes in Lesson 18, "Loading External Assets."*

Number Class (Top-Level)

You can create a Number class instance by using its constructor method or by assigning a number as the value of a variable. For instance:

```
var age:Number = new Number(26);
```

is equivalent to:

```
var age:Number = 26;
```

The `new Number()` constructor method is rarely used, however, because creating a new number without the constructor takes less effort and achieves the same result.

Object Class (Instances)

No, it's not a typo: there is an Object class! You can use this generic class—which is also known as ActionScript's root class (meaning it's the highest in the class hierarchy) in various ways. By employing the properties and methods available to it, you can affect and modify other object classes (such as those listed in this section). It also comes in handy for creating object instances that hold information about the current user, or instances that track chunks of related data (to name just a couple of uses).

The following is the syntax for creating a generic object:

```
var names:Object = new Object();
names.cat = "Hayes";
```

The first line of script creates a new object called names. The second line adds a variable (property) to the object called cat. The variable is considered a property of this object.

In Lesson 7, "Creating Custom Classes," we'll show you how to create your own custom classes of objects (better than generic objects!) as well as how to create properties and methods for your custom class. Once you know how to do this, you can create objects and classes that do precisely what you want.

PrintJob Class (Instances)

Previous versions of Flash left much to be desired in the area of printing. For example, various frames on the timeline had to be specified as printable *before* the movie was exported to an SWF file. In addition, printing content from multiple timelines opened multiple Print dialog boxes. Flash MX 2004 provides a much-improved way to handle printing. With the PrintJob class you are able to dynamically specify frames from various timelines to print from a single Print dialog box.

NOTE *This class is used in Lesson 21, "Printing and Context Menus."*

Selection Class (Top-Level)

You use the Selection class to retrieve information or set characteristics relating to selected items in your movies, especially text in text fields. When the cursor is in an area of a text field, that field is said to be "in focus." You can employ the Selection class to set the focus to a specific text field, to find out which text field is currently in focus, or even to programmatically select specific chunks of text in a field so that it can be manipulated in some way. Here's an example of one use of the Selection class:

```
Selection.setFocus("firstName");
```

The script sets into focus the input text field with the instance name of firstName.

You'll complete an exercise using this class later in this lesson.

Sound Class (Instances)

You use instances of the Sound class to control sounds—for example, setting volume and adjusting left and right speaker pan settings. To learn more about this class, see Lesson 17, "Scripting for Sound."

Stage Class (Top-Level)

With the Stage class, you can control and get information about characteristics of the stage, such as alignment. For example:

```
Stage.height
```

The script returns the height of the stage in pixels.

String Class (Instances)

You use the String class to manipulate and get information about strings of text. You can create a new string by using the String class constructor method or by putting quotes around a value when setting a variable. For example:

```
var bird:String = new String("Robin");
```

is the same as:

```
var bird:String = "Robin";
```

You'll use this class to complete an exercise later in this lesson.

StyleSheet Class (Instances)

The StyleSheet class is used to define a set of style rules for text. It can then be applied to a text field which makes the text in that text field adhere to the style rules (such as font size and color). The StyleSheet class is useful because you can have several text fields use the same style. If you decide to change something about the style, such as the text color, then all the text fields that use the style will be affected. In addition, external Cascading Style Sheet (CSS) files can be used, providing a way to achieve a uniform look to text content both on your CSS-enhanced Web pages and the Flash content embedded in them (since both can make use of a single style sheet definition). This script creates a new StyleSheet object, then loads an external CSS file into that object.

```
var myStyleSheet = new TextField.StyleSheet();
myStlyeSheet.load("externalStyleSheet.css");
```

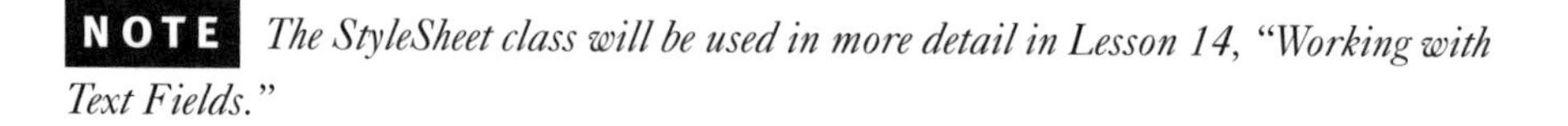

NOTE *The StyleSheet class will be used in more detail in Lesson 14, "Working with Text Fields."*

System Class (Top-Level)

This class contains information about your user's computer system, such as the operating system, the language being used, and all the properties of the Capabilities object.

One of the System class's properties is a string called `serverString` that contains a list of the system capabilities (concatenated into one string). You can send this list to the server so that you can store or use the information it contains. To access the string, use:

```
System.capabilities.serverString
```

TextField Class (Instances)

Using this class, you can dynamically create a new text field and control most of its characteristics—for example, setting the format of the text field or the scrolling of text. Instances of this class are created when a text field is placed on the stage while you're authoring your movie, or created dynamically using the `createTextField()` method. We'll use this object later in this lesson.

TextFormat Class (Instances)

Instances of the TextFormat class are used to change the format/style of text displayed in text fields. Once it's created, you apply the instance of the TextFormat class to a text field using the `setTextFormat()`or `setNewTextFormat()` methods:

```
nameOfTextField_txt.setTextFormat(nameOfFormatObject);
```

XML Class (Instances)

XML is one of the most popular standards for formatting data—it's no surprise when you consider that XML-formatted data lets all kinds of applications transfer information seamlessly. Using Flash, you can create an XML object (which is an instance of the XML class) to store an XML-formatted document that can then be sent from or loaded into XML objects. Here's one use of the XML object:

```
var myXML:XML = new XML();
myXML.load("myFile.xml");
```

The script creates a new XML object and loads an XML-formatted file into that object.

NOTE *In Lesson 12, "Using XML with Flash," you will learn more about using the XML class.*

XMLSocket Class (Instances)

Flash also allows you to set up a persistent connection with a *socket server*—an application that runs on a Web server. The socket server waits for users to connect to it. Once connected, the socket server can transfer information between all connected users at very fast speeds, which is how most chat systems and multiplayer games are created. An XML socket is so named because it uses the XML format as the standard for transferred information.

You can create an XMLSocket object instance by using the XMLSocket class constructor method. The following is an example of one use of this type of object:

```
var mySocket:XMLSocket = new XMLSocket();
mySocket.connect("http://www.electrotank.com", 8080);
```

This script creates a new instance of the XMLSocket class and opens up a connection with a socket server. See Lesson 12, "Using XML with Flash," for a detailed description of socket servers and the XMLSocket class, as well as an exercise in creating your own chat application.

Covering every built-in class in detail is beyond the scope of this book. However, throughout the lessons we'll use many of these classes in various ways, and provide detailed instructions about how and why we're using them. The following exercises will concentrate on just a few of these classes to give you a general idea of how you can use them.

USING THE COLOR CLASS

To use a Color object, you must first create it using the Color class constructor. Here's the syntax for creating a new Color object:

```
var myColor:Color = new Color(shirt_mc);
```

The script creates a new instance of the Color class named `myColor` and associates it with a movie clip instance named **shirt_mc**.

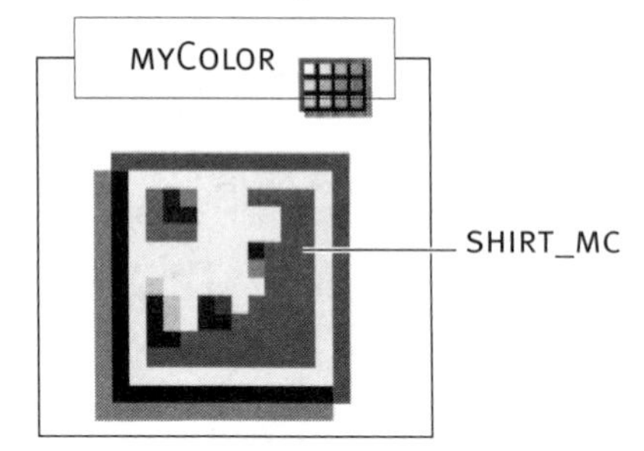

You can create the object anywhere. The constructor accepts one parameter: the path to the movie clip it should modify. If you want to create a Color object with ActionScript from within a movie clip that will reference itself, you would use `this` as the path. For example, this script:

```
var myColor:Color = new Color(this);
```

creates a new instance of the Color object on the movie clip instance that contains this script.

NOTE *As with any class instance, you can create many instances of the Color class in a single project and associate them with various timelines, providing you with dynamic control over the color of many instances simultaneously.*

The most common Color object method is `setRGB()`, which changes the color of the movie clip instance specified as the parameter when the object was created. Here's an example of one use of `setRGB()`:

```
var myColor:Color = new Color(shirt_mc);
myColor.setRGB(0xFF3300);
```

The script creates a new Color object named `myColor` and then uses the `setRGB()` method to change the color of the `shirt_mc` movie clip instance to red. This method accepts a parameter (`0x`) followed by the hex value for a color. The `0x` parameter is a reserved character combination that tells Flash that a hexadecimal number follows.

The number system we're accustomed to using is called *base 10*, which means 10 numbers are used for all values (0 through 9). In other words, all other numbers (28; 6,403; 496; 300, 439; and so on) can be described using a combination of these 10. Hexadecimal numbers, in contrast, are *base 16*, which means their values are expressed using numbers *and* letters: 0 through 9, and A through F. Using this method, you can create hexadecimal values of 00 to FF, with 00 being a base 10 value of 0, and FF a base 10 value of 255.

However, you don't absolutely have to know hex values to describe certain colors when using the `setRGB()` method. Instead, if you know the RGB value of a color, you can convert it to a hexadecimal value dynamically using the Number class and the `parseInt()` function—we'll cover this topic in the next exercise (though we won't cover it in detail).

In this exercise you'll create a simple interactive scene in which you'll be able to change the color of a clown's hair using several buttons.

1) Open *Clown1.fla* in the Lesson04/Assets folder.

The content has already been created and placed on the stage, so we can focus on the ActionScript involved in changing the color of a movie clip. The main timeline has four layers: Actions, Background, Clown Hair, and Buttons.

The Clown Hair layer contains a movie clip instance named **hair_mc**. You will be changing the color of this instance with ActionScript.

The Buttons layer contains five circular, colored buttons. These buttons have instance names based on their respective colors: **red_btn**, **green_btn**, **blue_btn**, **yellow_btn**, and **rainbow_btn**. You'll be adding ActionScript to the first frame of the main timeline, which will change the color of the **hair_mc** movie clip when any of the five buttons is clicked.

2) With the Actions panel open, select Frame 1 of the main timeline and add the script:

```
red_btn.onRelease = function() {
  var hairColor:Color = new Color(hair_mc);
  hairColor.setRGB(0xCC0000);
};
```

This script assigns a callback function to the `onRelease` event of the **red_btn** instance.

The callback function (lines 2 and 3) tell Flash to create a new Color object named `hairColor` when this button is released and to associate that object with the **hair_mc** movie clip instance. This function also uses the `setRGB()` method to change the color of this Color object (hence the **hair_mc** movie clip instance) to `CC0000`, which is the hex value for the red in the middle of the button.

3) On the same frame, below the script added in the preceding step, add this script:

```
yellow_btn.onRelease = function() {
  var hairColor:Color = new Color(hair_mc);
  hairColor.setRGB(0xFFCC00);
};
```

This script is identical to the script used to assign the onRelease callback to the red button, except for the color value used in the setRGB() method, the value of which is the hex value for the yellow in the middle of the button. When a user clicks the yellow button, it will execute this callback and the clown's hair will turn yellow.

4) With Frame 1 still selected, add this script to the bottom of the current script:

```
green_btn.onRelease = function() {
  var hairColor:Color = new Color(hair_mc);
  hairColor.setRGB(0x009900);
};
```

The hex value for green is 009900 and is used in the setRGB() method in the same manner as in the two preceding scripts.

5) Add a similar script for the *blue_btn* instance:

```
blue_btn.onRelease = function() {
  var hairColor:Color = new Color(hair_mc);
  hairColor.setRGB(0x336699);
};
```

As with the three other buttons, this script creates a Color object that it uses to change the color of the **hair_mc** movie clip instance.

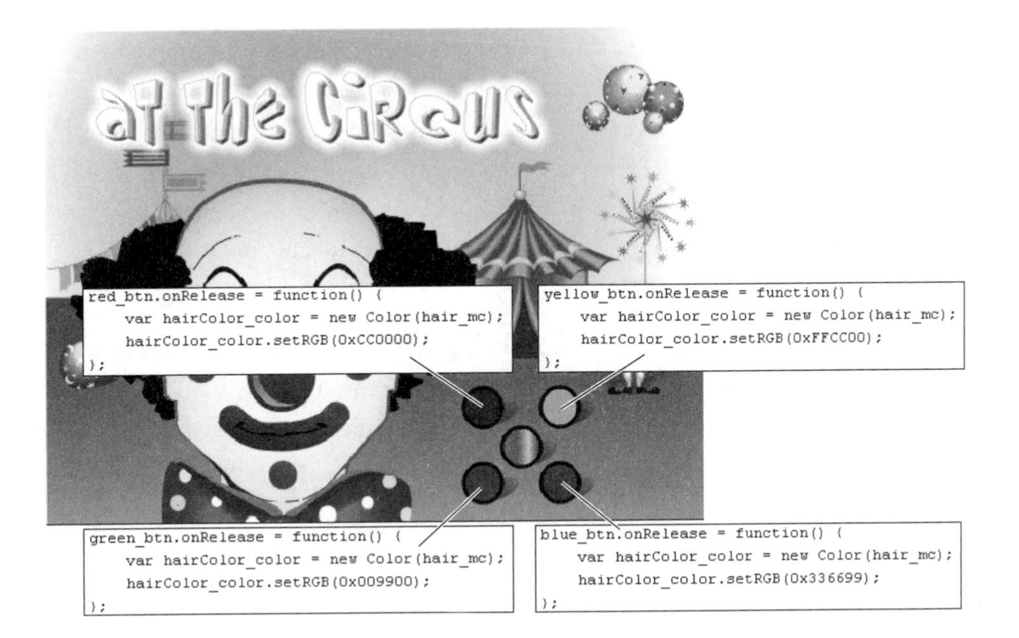

Now it's time to test your work.

6) Choose Control > Test Movie. Click the four buttons to view the color changes.

Every time you click one of these buttons, Flash creates a new Color object and associates it with the **hair_mc** movie clip instance. The setRGB() method available to Color objects is then used to change the color of that instance.

NOTE *Although in this exercise a Color object is created on each button, an object needs to be created only once—after which it exists as part of the timeline. Any changes to that object can be made by using methods available to that object.*

Now let's use ActionScript to change the clown's hair color to a random color.

7) Close the test movie to return to the authoring environment. With the Actions panel open, select Frame 1 and add this script to the end of the current script:

```
rainbow_btn.onRelease = function() {
  var R:Number = random(256);
  var G:Number = random(256);
  var B:Number = random(256);
  var colorHexString:String = R.toString(16)+G.toString(16)+B.toString(16);
  var colorHex:Number = parseInt(colorHexString, 16);
  var hairColor:Color = new Color(hair_mc);
  hairColor.setRGB(colorHex);
};
```

There are two ways to describe a color programmatically: with its RGB (red, green, blue) value or with its hex value. There are three separate RGB values, each of which can have a numeric value between 0 and 255. The RGB value of red, for instance, is R=255, G=0, B=0. The corresponding hex value (for the same color of red) is FF0000. The idea behind the first five lines of this script is to generate a random RGB value, convert it to a hex value, then use that value in the setRGB() method at the bottom of the script.

Lines 2, 3, and 4 of the script create variables R, G, and B, whose values are random numbers between 0 and 255. The next line of ActionScript uses the toString() method of the Number object to convert a base 10 number to a base 16 string value. Let's assume, for example, that when this script is executed, the following R, G, and B values will be generated:

```
R = 45
G = 202
B = 129
```

The next line of the script says to convert the value of R to a base 16 value, then convert it to a string, and then do the same thing with G and B. Using the plus (+) operator to put the converted values together, the variable colorHexString will have a string value of "2DCA81". This needs to be converted to a hex number (same value as the string value, without the quotes) to use the `setRGB()` method. To do this, you use the `parseInt()` function.

The last two lines of the script create a new Color object pointing to the **hair_mc** movie clip instance and then change its color to the random value just created.

NOTE *This script can randomly generate more than 16 million possible colors.*

8) Choose Control > Test Movie, and click the rainbow-colored button several times.

The **hair_mc** movie clip instance changes randomly. You can even modify this technique to randomly generate colors within a certain range.

9) Close the test movie and save your work as *Clown2.fla*.

You should now be able to easily change the color of any movie clip instance at any time.

USING THE KEY CLASS TO ADD INTERACTIVITY

The Key class is a useful tool for capturing key events from the user (that is, user interaction with the keyboard). You can employ the Key class for tasks such as these:

- Determining whether a specific key is currently pressed
- Determining the last key pressed
- Obtaining the key code value of the last key pressed
- Adding a Listener that watches for a key event
- Determining whether a certain key (such as Caps Lock) is toggled on or off

The Key class is a top-level class, which means you cannot create a new instance of it. The most common use of the Key class is to determine whether a specific key is pressed. You would use this syntax to determine whether a key is being pressed:

```
Key.isDown(Key.TAB);
```

The script uses the `isDown()` method of the Key class to determine whether the Tab key is currently pressed down. It returns a result of either `true` or `false`. The parameter of the `isDown()` method can reference either a specific key in the Key class or the key code of a specific key. Every key on your keyboard has a special number associated with it, called a *key code*. For example, the Tab key can be referenced using `Key.TAB`, or by the number 9, which is its ASCII equivalent. This script is the essentially the same as the preceding one:

```
Key.isDown(9);
```

In the next simple exercise, you'll move a hot air balloon around the screen using your keyboard and the Key class.

1) Open *balloon1.fla* in the Lesson04/Assets directory.

This movie contains three layers: Background, Balloon, and Actions. On the Balloon layer, you'll see a movie clip instance of a hot air balloon with an instance name of **balloon_mc**. The Background layer simply displays an image. In this exercise, you'll place actions on the first frame of the Actions layer.

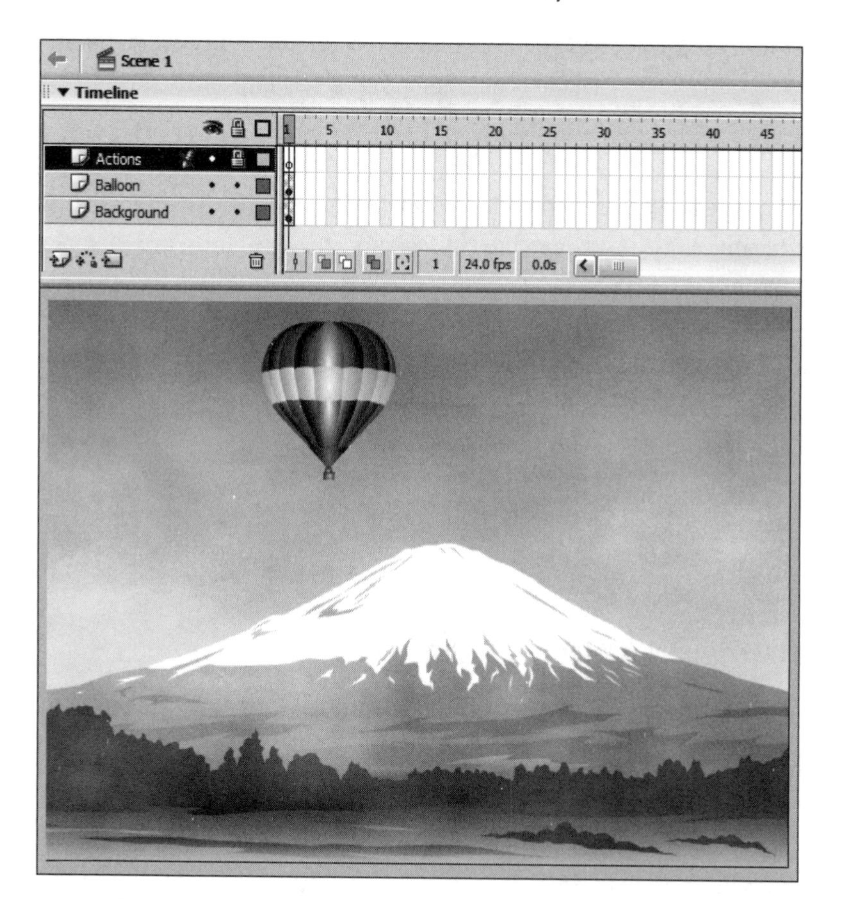

2) With the Actions panel open, select Frame 1 in the Actions layer and add this script:

```
var speed:Number = 3;
```

At the end of this exercise, you should be able to move the balloon with your arrow keys. Every time you press the key, the balloon should move a certain amount. When the movie first starts, this script creates a variable called speed, which determines how much the balloon moves every time you press a key. When used in the following scripts, this value represents a distance of 3 pixels.

3) With Frame 1 still selected, add this script at the end of the current script:

```
_root.onEnterFrame = function() {
  if (Key.isDown(Key.RIGHT)) {
    balloon_mc._x += speed;
  } else if (Key.isDown(Key.LEFT)) {
    balloon_mc._x -= speed;
  }
};
```

This script uses an onEnterFrame event handler method to evaluate a conditional statement. Key.RIGHT references the Right Arrow key, and Key.LEFT references the Left Arrow key. Each time this statement is evaluated, the **balloon_mc** movie clip instance is moved to its current x position *plus* the value of speed if the Right Arrow key is pressed (moving the instance to the right). However, if the Right Arrow key is not pressed, that part of the script is ignored and the next part is evaluated—if the Left Arrow key is pressed, the movie clip instance is moved to its current x position *minus* the value of speed (moving the instance to the left).

4) Add this ActionScript to the enterFrame **clip event:**

```
if (Key.isDown(Key.UP)) {
  balloon_mc._y -= speed;
} else if (Key.isDown(Key.DOWN)) {
  balloon_mc._y += speed;
}
```

This script is similar to the ActionScript we added in the preceding step. However, here the `if` statement reacts to the Up and Down Arrow keys rather than the Right and Left Arrow keys. The first part of this statement says that if the Up Arrow key is pressed, the movie clip instance is moved to its current y position *minus* the value of `speed` (moving the instance up). If the Down Arrow key is pressed, the instance is moved to its current y position *plus* `speed` (moving the instance down).

5) Choose Control > Test Movie. Use the Left, Right, Up, and Down Arrow keys to control the movement of the hot air balloon.

The conditional statements you wrote are performed in each frame of the `onEnterFrame` clip event. If one of the keys is detected to be in the down state, the balloon will be moved accordingly.

6) Close the test movie and save your work as *balloon2.fla*.

Now you know how to capture a keypress and make something happen as a result. This script has many applications, including paging through a slide show or making a game.

WORKING WITH STRING AND SELECTION CLASSES

As one of the most commonly used classes, the String class uses methods that can be helpful for modifying and building *strings*—quote-enclosed values that contain information (like the name `"Jobe"`) that can be easily understood by humans.

```
var message:String = "No shoes, no service!";
```

The script creates a variable named `message` whose value is a string. In such cases, you can think of the variable itself as a String object (an instance of the String class)—which means you can use String class methods to manipulate its value.

Let's look at a few examples.

The `toUpperCase()` method of the String class forces a string to become all uppercase letters:

```
message = message.toUpperCase();
```

The script modifies the variable `message` to contain `"NO SHOES, NO SERVICE!"` For the opposite effect—that is, to force the entire string to become all lowercase letters—you would apply `toLowerCase()` in the same fashion.

Note that the text value of a text field instance (the text within the field) is considered an instance of the String object. If `message` were the name of a text field instance, the previous script could be rewritten like this:

```
message.text = message.text.toUpperCase();
```

Although it is most common to create a String object the easy way (`var message:String = "Hello"`), it is also possible to create a String object by using the constructor of the String class.

```
var message:String = new String("Hello");
```

Is there any advantage to using one over the other? Not really: every project is different, and you may find cases where one seems to be more appropriate than the other. To review, you can create an instance of the String object by:

- Using a constructor (for example, `var myNewStringObject:String = new String("Hello");`). The String object is identified as `myNewStringObject`.
- Assigning a string value to a variable. The String object is identified as the name of the variable.
- Creating a text field. The String object is identified as the text property of the field, as in `nameOfTextField.text`.

Another useful method of the String class—`indexOf()`—lets you find the first occurrence of a character or group of characters in a string. The result returned is a number corresponding to the *letter index* where the string starts. A letter index is the number of a character in relation to the whole string. The first character in a string has an index of 0, the second has an index of 1, and so on. If the `indexOf()` method finds no occurrences of the character or group of characters, it returns a value of `-1`. Here's an example of one use of the `indexOf()` method:

```
message_txt.text = "No shoes, no service!";
var firstS:Number = message_txt.text.indexOf("s");
```

The variable `firstS` will be assigned a value of `3` because that's the character number of the first *s* encountered (the first *s* in *shoes*).

STRING INDEX VALUES

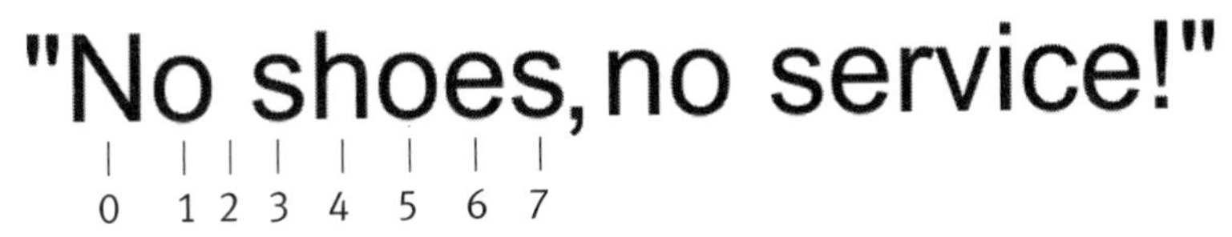

It can sometimes be useful to determine the number of characters in a string. This is easy to do because all instances of the string class have a `length` property. You can often use string length to validate user-input information in a text field. Perhaps you want a user to enter a valid zip code: you know that it must be five characters in length. By checking the length property of the zip code, you could create a simple validation script:

```
zipCode_txt.text = "27609";
var zipLength:Number = zipCode_txt.text.length
if (zipLength == 5) {
  // Correct length of zip code
} else {
  // Invalid zip code
}
```

The first line sets the text value shown in the **zipCode_txt** text field. (We assume this is what the user has entered.) The next line creates a variable named `zipLength` and assigns it a value based on the length property of **zipCode_txt.text**—in this case `5`, because that's the number of characters the **zipCode_txt** field contains. The last part of the script uses an `if` statement to take one set of actions if `zipLength` equals 5 and another if it doesn't.

The Selection class allows you to control various aspects of the currently focused text field, including highlighting text, getting and setting the caret's (current insertion point) position and more. A text field is considered focused if the user's cursor is placed there. Because only one text field can be focused at a time, there's no need to create an instance of the Selection class; you can use it directly (the Selection class is a top-level class). By clicking on a text field, the user dictates which one has focus. However, you can use the `setFocus()` method to override the user's current choice—important since you can only use other Selection class methods on the text field currently in focus. (As you'll see in the next exercise, you can't always rely on the user to select—and thus bring into focus—the proper text field.)

One last method of the Selection class allows you to highlight portions of text dynamically—without the user's help. The method `Selection.setSelection(param1, param2)` includes two parameters: the character index of where the selection starts and the character index of where the selection should end. For example, you have a text field that contains the text `"Derek is the craziest person I know"`. To highlight the word *craziest* (assuming its text field is in focus), you would use:

```
Selection.setSelection(13, 20);
```

In this exercise, you'll create a simple word processor using many of the String and Selection class methods we've discussed.

1) Open *wordProcessor1.fla* in the Lesson04/Assets folder.

This file has three layers: Background, Buttons, and Actions. The Background layer contains the image of the word processor window as well as text fields. The Buttons layer contains the four buttons that appear at the top of the word processor window. Starting from the left, the buttons have these instance names: **upper_btn, lower_btn, count_btn**, and **find_btn**.

There are three text field instances on the stage. The largest one, in the center, represents the text document. It has an instance name of **inputField_txt**. The next text field, to the right of the Find button, is appropriately called **findField_txt**. When the movie is played, the user will be able to enter a character or string of characters into this text field, which will be searched against the contents in the **inputField_txt** text field. The search results will be displayed in the third text field, at the bottom of the window, which is called **status_txt**. This text field is also used to display the results when counting the number of characters in the document.

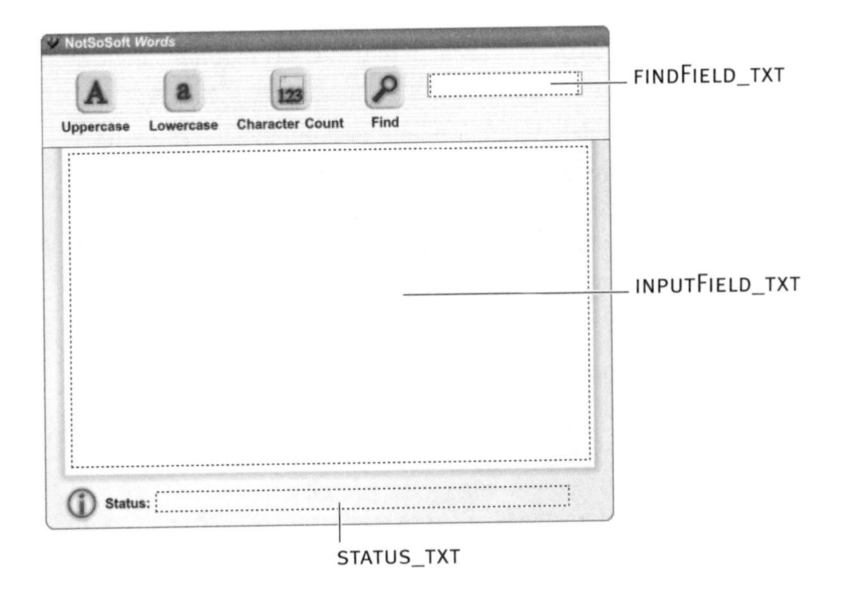

2) With the Actions panel open, select Frame 1 in the Actions layer and add the script:

```
upper_btn.onRelease = function() {
  inputField_txt.text = inputField_txt.text.toUpperCase();
};
```

Flash interprets this script as saying, "On release of the button called **upper_btn**, make all of letters in the **inputField_txt** text field uppercase." When the button is clicked, the contents of the **inputField_txt** text field are reassigned with uppercase letters.

3) Add this script to the same frame:

```
lower_btn.onRelease = function() {
  inputField_txt.text = inputField_txt.text.toLowerCase();
};
```

This script is similar to the one added in the preceding step. On release of the **lower_btn** button, the **inputField_txt** text field is reassigned with all lowercase characters.

4) Add this script, which counts the number of characters in the *inputField_txt* text field:

```
count_btn.onRelease = function() {
  status_txt.text = "There are "+inputField_txt.text.length+" characters in the
current document";
};
```

This script counts the number of characters in the **inputField_txt** text field and displays a message about the character count results in the **message_txt** text field. The Length property of the **inputField_txt** text field is determined and inserted in the middle of the message. The message is built dynamically by adding, `"There are"` plus the value of the `length` property, plus the ending part of the message, `"characters in the current document"`. If the document has 50 characters, the message will read, `"There are 50 characters in the current document"`.

5) Add this script to search and highlight text:

```
find_btn.onRelease = function() {
  var result:Number = inputField_txt.text.indexOf(findField_txt.text);
  if (findField_txt.text != "" && result>=0) {
    status_txt.text = "The first instance of these characters occurs at character
"+result;
    Selection.setFocus("_root.inputField_txt");
    Selection.setSelection(result, result+findField_txt.text.length);
  } else {
    status_txt.text = "That string could not be found";
  }
};
```

This script is the most complex one in this exercise. The first line sets the value of the `result` variable using the `indexOf()` method of the String object. Here, we're asking the script to look in the **inputField_txt** text field and find the index number of the first occurrence of the character or group of characters entered into the **findField_txt** text field. In the end, `result` will have a value of –1 (no occurrence was found) or 0 to the string length (depending on how many characters are in the document). For example, if the first occurrence is found at index 13 (the fourteenth character), `result` will have a value of 13. This value plays an important part in the rest of the script.

RESULT = INPUTFIELD_TXT.TEXT.INDEXOF(FINDFIELD_TXT)

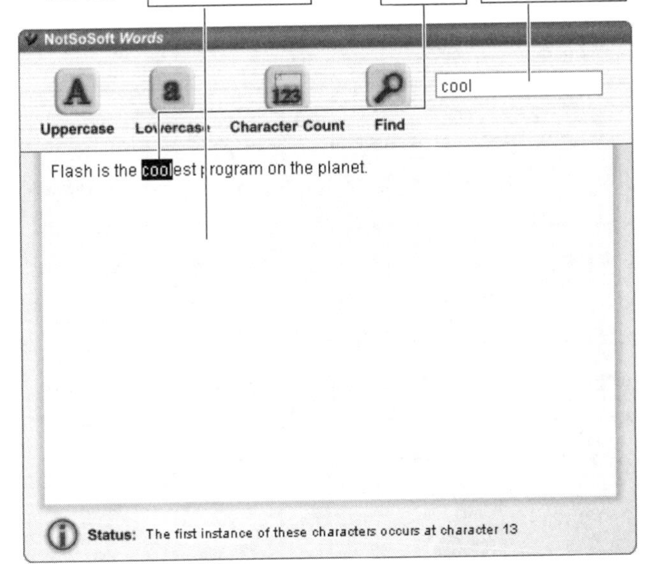

The next part of the script uses an `if` statement to carry out one of two sets of actions, depending on whether a couple of conditions prove true. The first part of the statement looks at the text values of **findField_txt** and the numeric value of `result`. It says that if **findField_txt** is not empty (this makes sure that the **findField_txt** text field has not been left blank) *and* the value of `result` is equal to or greater than 0 (which it will be if an occurrence of the characters entered is found), do the actions below. The `else` part of the statement deals with what happens if neither of these conditions is met. In this case, nothing will happen except that the **status_txt** text field will display the text, `"That string could not be found"`.

Assuming that both conditions are true, let's look at what the three actions under the first part of the `if` statement do. The first action will display a dynamic text message in the **status_txt** text field. The message is built dynamically by adding `"The first instance of these characters occurs at character"` plus the value of `result`. If `result` has a value of 7, the message will read, `"The first instance of these characters occurs at character 7"`. The next two actions use methods of the Selection class to highlight the character or characters in the **inputField_txt** text field that were searched for and found. You'll remember that a text field must have focus before any of the Selection object methods can be used on the field. Because we want to highlight text in the **inputField_txt** text field, we use this line to ensure that this field has focus before the next Selection method is used on it:

```
Selection.setFocus("_root.inputField_txt");
```

The next line of script uses another Selection method to highlight text in the currently focused text field. This line reads:

```
Selection.setSelection(result, result + findField_txt.text.length);
```

We've used a couple of dynamic values with this method to determine where the selection begins and ends. Because we want the selection to start at the point where the first occurrence was found, we use the value of `result` as the starting point of the selection. The ending point of the selection is determined by adding the value of `result` to the value of the `length` property of the **findField_txt** text field. How does this work? Assume you typed `I like my dog very much` in the **inputField_txt** text field. Next, in the **findField_txt** text field, you search for `dog`. When the script is executed, `result` will have a value of `10` (the first occurrence of `dog` is at the eleventh character), and **findField_txt.text.length** will be `3` (because the word `dog` is currently in this field, and it is three characters long). Using these values, the script could be written like this:

```
Selection.setSelection(11, 11 + 3);
```

or

```
Selection.setSelection(11, 14);
```

This will highlight characters 11 through 14, which is where `dog` appears in the **inputField_txt** text field.

6) Choose Control > Test Movie.

Type something into the **inputField_txt** text field and press the Uppercase and Lowercase buttons. Press the Count Characters button to determine how many characters the document contains. Finally, try out the search function by entering one or more characters into the **findField_txt** text field and pressing the button.

7) Close the test movie and save your work as *wordProcessor2.fla*.

You can see how easy it is to use the methods associated with the String and Selection classes—a good thing since you'll find yourself using the String class frequently to both validate and reformat data.

WHAT YOU HAVE LEARNED

In this lesson, you have:

- Learned what objects are and why they are useful (pages 140–145)
- Become acquainted with the various built-in object classes available in ActionScript (pages 146–156)
- Used the Color class (pages 156–161)
- Created an interactive scene using the Key class (pages 161–164)
- Created a word processor using properties and methods of the String and Selection classes (pages 164–170)

using functions

LESSON 5

When programming, you may find yourself using the same chunks of code repeatedly—either by copying and pasting them or by rewriting the same lines of ActionScript. There is a way to write ActionScript just once and reuse it anytime with a single action. You do this with *functions* and the action by which you execute a function is a *call* or a *function call*. Functions are real time-savers—during both development and code maintenance—because they reduce the amount of code you need to write or modify.

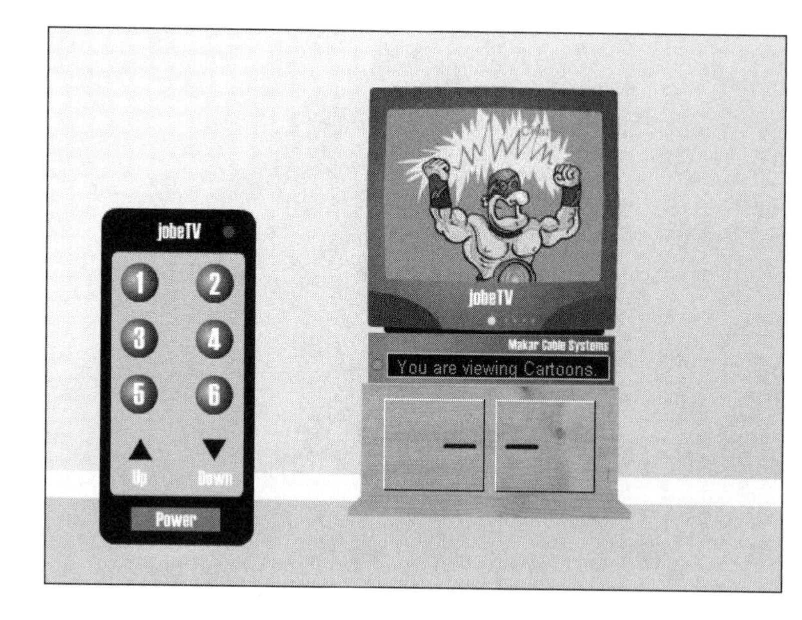

You will create several functions that allow you to turn a Flash-TV on and off and change its channels. A Flash-TV is a simple Flash app that acts like a TV and remote control.

Think of a function as a mini-program that serves a specific purpose within another application. You can use it to perform a set of specific actions, or you can feed it information and output a result—or you can do both. Functions provide a powerful and versatile way to script your project.

In this lesson, you'll learn how to create and use functions while developing a remote control for a Flash-made television set.

WHAT YOU WILL LEARN

In this lesson, you will:

- Create a function
- Call a function
- Add parameters to a function
- Create a function that returns a result
- Use local variables

APPROXIMATE TIME

This lesson takes approximately one and one half hours to complete.

LESSON FILES

Starting File:

Lesson05/Assets/television1.fla

Completed Project:

television4.fla

CREATING FUNCTIONS

Before you use a function, you must create or define it. You can do this by using one of two possible syntaxes.

SYNTAX 1

This code describes the first syntax:

```
function myFunction (parameter1:DataType,parameter2:DataType,etc.) {
  //actions go here;
}
```

The code represents the most common way of creating a function, as well as the syntax we'll use most frequently in this lesson. You'll see that the function declaration begins with the word `function`, followed by the name of the function (which can be anything you choose, as long as it follows typical naming conventions). Following the function name is an area enclosed by parentheses. You can leave this area blank, or you can fill it with information (parameter data) that the function can use. By leaving the area within the parentheses blank, you create a "generic" function—that is, one that performs the same way whenever it's called (used). If your function contains parameters, it will perform in a unique way each time it's called based on the parameter information it receives. Giving the function information in this way is called *passing in arguments* or *passing in parameters*. You can use as many parameters as you want. We'll tell you how to use parameter data a bit later in this lesson.

Following the optional parameter area is an open curly brace, followed by a carriage return and then some actions before the curly brace that concludes the function. In the space between the curly braces, you write the actions that you want your function to perform. These actions can also make use of any parameter information passed to the function (as you will see soon).

TIP *You can create a function skeleton (that is, a function that does not yet contain any actions) in the Actions panel by clicking Statements > User-Defined Functions, then double-clicking the function command.*

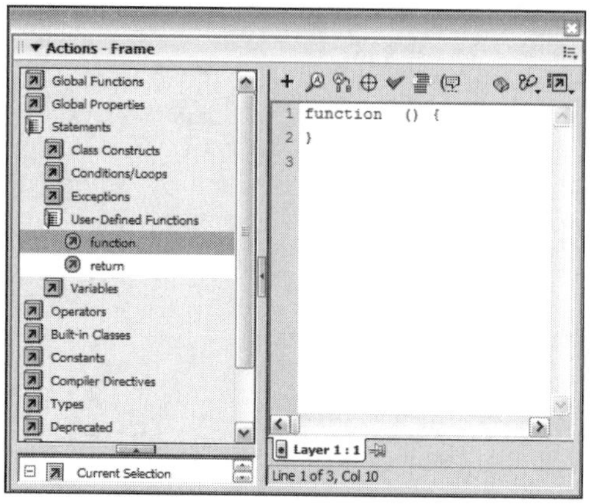

SYNTAX 2

This code represents the second syntax for creating functions:

```
myFunction = function (parameter1:DataType,parameter2:DataType,etc.)
  {/* actions go here */
};
```

You would use this syntax to create a function dynamically or to define your own custom *method* of an object (which we'll discuss in Lesson 7, "Creating Custom Classes"). The only difference between this syntax and Syntax 1 is in the way the function name is assigned: the function name appears first, and the syntax for defining how the function will work follows the = assignment operator.

Now that you understand the basic syntax for creating/defining a function, let's look at how a function is used, or called.

If a function contains no parameters, it can be called using the following syntax:

```
myFunction();
```

When you call a function, you're telling Flash to execute all the actions within that function. If `myFunction()` contained 20 actions, all of them could be executed by using this single line of script.

If a function has been defined to accept parameter data, you can use the following syntax to call it:

```
myFunction(parameter1, parameter2);
```

If `parameter1` had a value of `cat` and `parameter2` had a value of `36`, then those two values would be sent to the function, for use by the actions within the function definition. At a later time, the same function could be called, but different parameter values sent. This would result in the same function's working in a slightly different way from the first example, because the actions within the function would be making use of different parameter values.

The foregoing examples assume that the function and function call reside on the same timeline. Just as each timeline contains its own variables and objects, each timeline also contains any functions you've defined there. To call a function on a specific timeline, you need to place the target path to that timeline in front of the function call, like this:

```
_root.clip1.clip2.myFunction();
```

In this exercise, you'll create a Power button on a television remote control. With this button, the Flash-TV can be toggled on and off using a function.

TIP *A function can be called dynamically based on a value—for instance,* `_root[aVariableName]();`*. Thus, if* `aVariableName` *had a value of* `"sayHello"`*, the function call would actually look like* `_root.sayHello();`*.*

1) Open *television1.fla* in the Lesson05/Assets folder.

The movie's structure has already been created. The Actions layer is where you will include all of the ActionScript for this exercise. On the TV layer, a movie clip instance named **tv_mc** has three layers on its timeline: the bottom layer (Television) is a graphic, and the layer above that (Screen) contains a movie clip instance called **screen_mc** (which is then masked by the layer above that). The **screen_mc** movie clip instance itself includes two layers and two frames, and contains graphical content that represents the various "programs" seen when changing channels on the TV.

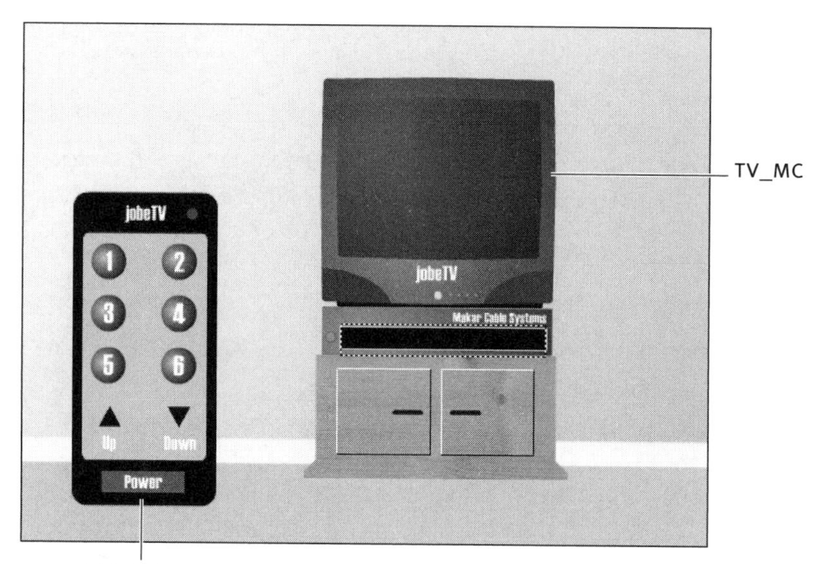

On the main timeline, a layer named Remote contains a movie clip instance named **remote_mc**. Inside **remote_mc**, you'll find a layer that contains most of the remote-control graphics, including a movie clip with an instance name of **light_mc**, as well as another layer that contains the buttons for the remote. The numbered buttons have instance names of **channel1_btn** through **channel6_btn**. Under the numbered buttons are the Up and Down channel buttons whose instance names are **up_btn** and **down_btn**, respectively. The bottom button, Power, has an instance name of **power_btn**.

2) Select Frame 1 of the Actions layer on the main timeline. With the Actions panel open, add the script:

```
var tvPower:Boolean = false;
function togglePower() {
  var newChannel:Number;
  if (tvPower) {
    newChannel = 0;
    tvPower = false;
  } else {
    newChannel = 1;
    tvPower = true;
  }
  tv_mc.screen_mc.gotoAndStop(newChannel+1);
  remote_mc.light_mc.play();
}
```

The first line of this script creates a variable named `tvPower`, which is used to track the current state of the TV. A value of `true` means the television is on; `false` means the television is off. The television will appear off initially, so `tvPower` is set to `false`.

The next 11 lines represent a function definition for `togglePower()`. When called, this function will toggle the television power on and off. No parameters are passed into this function. Because this script exists on Frame 1, our `togglePower()` function is defined and a variable called `tvPower` is set to `false` as soon as the frame is loaded (that is, when the movie begins to play).

TIP *Because functions must be defined before they can be called, it's common practice to define all functions on an early frame in your movie so that they can be called at any time after that.*

The first part of the function uses an `if` statement to analyze the current value of `tvPower`. If `tvPower` is `true` (TV is on) when the function is called, the actions in the function change it to `false` (off) and set the value of the `newChannel` variable to 0; otherwise (`else`), `tvPower` is set to `true` and `newChannel` to 1. Using the `if` statement in this manner causes the value of `tvPower` to be set to its opposite each time the function is called, thus toggling the value of `newChannel`. By the time this statement is finished, `newChannel` has a value of `0` or `1`.

The function then sends the **screen_mc** movie clip instance (which is inside the **tv_mc** movie clip instance) to a frame based on the current value of `newChannel + 1`. You must add 1 to the value of `newChannel` to prevent the timeline from being sent to Frame 0 (`newChannel` will sometimes contain a value of 0, and there's no such thing as Frame 0 in a Flash movie timeline). In the end, this part of the function will send the **screen_mc** movie clip instance to Frame 1 (showing a blank TV screen) or Frame 2 (showing Channel 1).

The function finishes by telling the light on the remote control to play, which causes it to blink, providing a visual indication that a button has been pressed.

There is now a function on Frame 1 of the main, or root, timeline. Although this function contains several actions, none of them is executed until the function is called.

3) With the Actions panel still open, add this script to the end of the current actions (after the function definition):

```
remote_mc.power_btn.onRelease = togglePower;
```

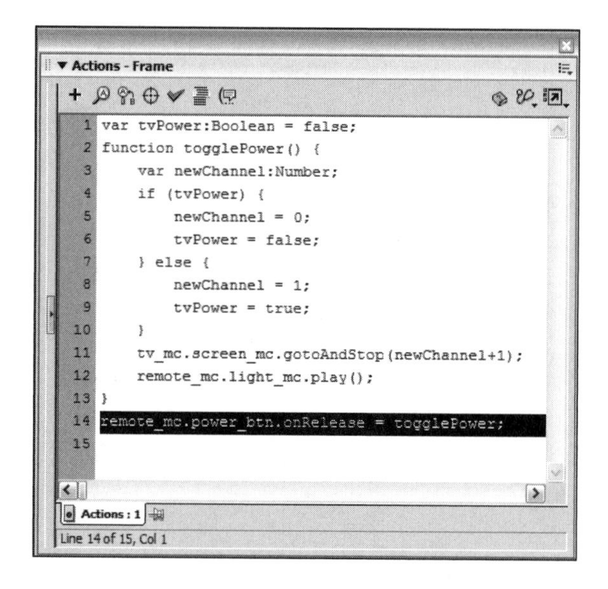

The Power button for the remote control has an instance name of **power_btn** (and it exists inside the **remote_mc** movie clip instance). This line of ActionScript assigns an `onRelease` event handler to the Power button: our `togglePower` function. Every time the Power button is clicked, the `togglePower()` function is called, causing the actions within the function to be executed.

4) Choose Control > Test Movie. Then click the Power button several times to view the TV on/off functionality you've created.

Every time you press the Power button, the `togglePower()` function is called so that all the actions within that function are performed. As mentioned, the actions within the function toggle the state of the TV.

5) Close the test movie and save your work as *television2.fla*.

You have now created and used a function! In the next section, we'll build on this idea to create a more powerful and versatile function.

ADDING PARAMETERS TO FUNCTIONS

In the preceding exercise, you learned how to create a function and call it. In this exercise, you'll add parameters to a function and learn how to use them. Here's the syntax for creating a function that accepts parameters:

```
function convertToMoonWeight (myWeight:Number){
  var weightOnMoon:Number = myWeight/6.04;
}
```

The sole parameter for this function is named `myWeight`. The value of that parameter is also used *within* the function definition (near the end of the second line), just as if it were a preexisting variable. Notice that you should associate a data type with the parameter in the function definition. In this case, the parameter `myWeight` represents a numeric value.

Here's an example of the syntax used to call this function:

```
convertToMoonWeight(165);
```

Here you can see that we added a numeric value of `165` to the function call. This value is sent to the function being called so that it can perform its specified functionality, based on that value. In this example, the value of `165` in the *function call* is assigned to the `myWeight` parameter in the *function definition*. The result looks something like this:

```
function convertToMoonWeight (165){
  var weightOnMoon:Number = 165/6.04;
}
```

Thus, in our example, sending a value of `165` to our `convertToMoonWeight()` function would set the value of `weightOnMoon` to 165/6.04, or `27.32`.

The `myWeight` parameter is replaced with the value sent to the function when it is called. The great thing about this is that whenever we call our function again, we can send it a different value, which will result in the `weightOnMoon` variable's being set to a different value as well. Take a look at these function calls to the `convertToMoonWeight()` function:

```
convertToMoonWeight(190);
convertToMoonWeight(32);
convertToMoonWeight(230);
```

Each of these function calls is to our single function, but because different values are sent to the function in each call, the function performs the same action (converting that value to moon weight) using the different values.

NOTE *Parameters you define for a function have meaning only within that function. In our example,* `myWeight` *has no meaning or use outside of the function itself.*

When sending values to a function, you can also use variables in your function call, as in the following:

```
convertToMoonWeight(myVariable);
```

When you do this, the current value of the variable is passed to the function.

Functions can also be made up of multiple parameters, like this:

```
function openWindow(url:String, window:String){
getURL(url, window);
}
```

This function definition contains two parameters, `url` and `window`, separated by a comma. The function contains a single action, `getURL()`, which makes use of these two parameters. Making a call to this function looks like this:

```
openWindow("http://www.yahoo.com", "_blank");
```

The function call also *sends* two values, separated by a comma, to the function: a URL and the HTML target for opening the specified URL. These parameter values are used by the function in order to perform its specified functionality. In this case, the function call would result in *yahoo.com* opening in a new browser window.

When defining multiple parameters in a function definition, remember their order within the parentheses. Respective values that are defined in the function definition should be listed in that same order in the function call.

Here's a function call to the `openWindow()` function that won't work because the parameters of the function definition dictate that the URL should be listed first in the function call:

```
openWindow("_blank", "http://www.yahoo.com");
```

NOTE *When a function is called, a temporary array called* `arguments` *is created. This array contains all parameters passed to the function—even if you specified none when defining your function. Here is an example of how to access the* `arguments` *array:*

```
function traceNames() {
  trace("This function was passed " + arguments.length + "arguments");
  trace("The value of the first argument is: " + arguments[0]);
  trace("The value of the second argument is: " + arguments[1]);
}
traceNames("Kelly","Chance");
```

In this example, these strings appear in the output window:

```
This function was passed two arguments
The value of the first argument is: Kelly
The value of the second argument is: Chance
```

Accessing the *arguments* array enables you to create functions that can adapt their functionality based on how many parameters are passed to them. For more information about arrays, see Lesson 6, "Creating and Manipulating Data."

In this exercise, you'll add functionality to the numeric keypad on the remote control and to the TV channel Up and Down buttons, allowing them to change the channel displayed on the TV screen. The numeric buttons work by calling a function and passing in the number of the channel to jump to. You will also modify the `togglePower()` function slightly.

1) Open *television2.fla*.

We continue to work with the file you completed in the preceding exercise. Before we do, however, it's important to note the structure of the **screen_mc** movie clip instance, which is inside the **tv_mc** movie clip instance. The **screen_mc** movie clip instance's timeline has graphical content on Frames 1 through 7. This content represents the "off" state of the TV (on Frame 1), as well as six channels of programming that our TV will be set up to receive.

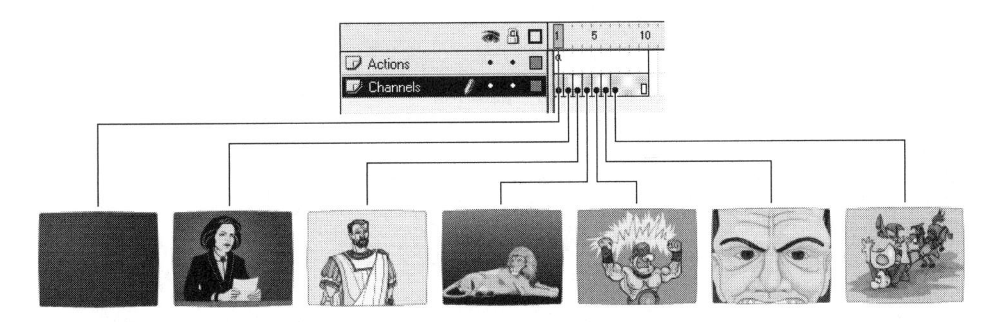

2) Select Frame 1 of the Actions layer on the main timeline and open the Actions panel. Add this ActionScript just below the line that reads `var tvPower:Boolean = false;`**:**

```
var currentChannel:Number;
```

In this exercise we create functions that change the channel of the TV, including incrementing and decrementing the TV channel. To increment or decrement a channel, you need to have the current channel stored. The script declares a new variable called `currentChannel`, which will be used to store the numeric value of the current TV channel.

3) With Frame 1 still selected, add this script just below the end of the last function definition:

```
function changeTheChannel(newChannel:Number) {
  if (tvPower) {
    currentChannel = newChannel;
    tv_mc.screen_mc.gotoAndStop(newChannel+1);
    remote_mc.light_mc.play();
  }
}
```

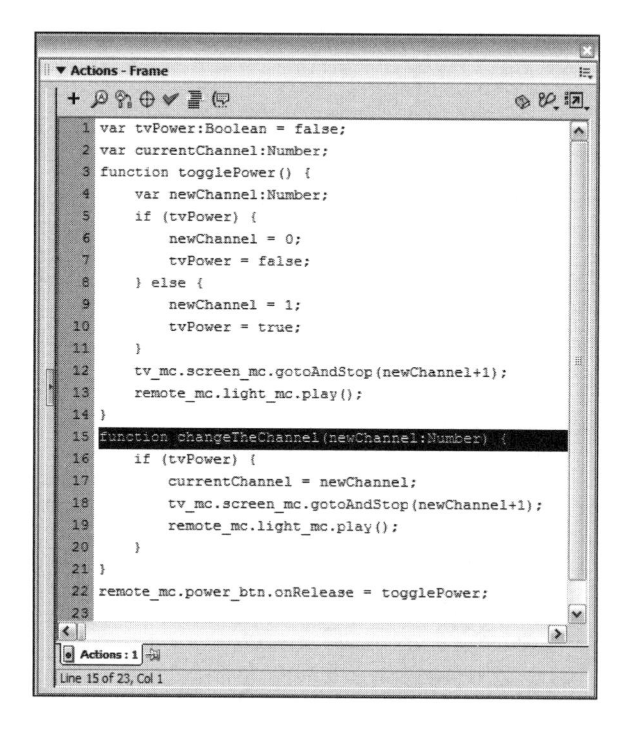

You have just created a function that accepts a parameter. This function changes the TV channel based on the parameter value received (`newChannel`). All of the actions the function performs are enclosed in an `if` statement, which is used to allow channels to be changed *only* if `tvPower` is `true`. The function then sets a variable used to store the current channel of the television to the value of the parameter value sent to the function.

The next two lines should be familiar from the `togglePower()` function we discussed in the preceding exercise: they set the frame in the **screen_mc** movie clip instance (causing the television to change channels) and instruct the light on the remote control to blink. To understand how this function works, consider a simple example. Assume this function call is made:

```
changeTheChannel(4);
```

The function would ask whether tvPower is true (TV is on) before doing anything else. If it is, currentChannel is given a value of 4 (the same as the parameter passed to the function). Next, the **screen_mc** movie clip instance is moved to a frame based on the parameter value passed to the function, plus 1 (or 4 + 1). The **screen_mc** instance is moved to Frame 5.

Your newly created function is ready for use. Next, we'll add onRelease event handlers to each of the numeric buttons to call changeTheChannel().

4) Add this script to the end of the current script on Frame 1:

```
remote_mc.channel1_btn.onRelease = function() {
  changeTheChannel(1);
};
remote_mc.channel2_btn.onRelease = function() {
  changeTheChannel(2);
};
remote_mc.channel3_btn.onRelease = function() {
  changeTheChannel(3);
};
remote_mc.channel4_btn.onRelease = function() {
  changeTheChannel(4);
};
remote_mc.channel5_btn.onRelease = function() {
  changeTheChannel(5);
};
remote_mc.channel6_btn.onRelease = function() {
  changeTheChannel(6);
};
```

You just added an event handler function to each of the numeric buttons on the remote control (you'll remember that **remote_mc** contains six buttons named **channel1_btn** through **channel6_btn**—thus the basis for the syntax used). When one of those buttons is clicked, it will call the changeTheChannel() function and pass it a channel number. In this way we are able to use the same function with several different buttons and have the result depend on a parameter that was passed in.

NOTE *Functions that are created as the result of the assign operator (=) are considered to be actions. All actions should be terminated with a semicolon. Therefore, each function definition above ends with a semicolon, whereas the normal function syntax does not.*

5) Choose Control > Test Movie. Press the Power button on the remote control to turn on the TV, and then use the numeric keypad on the remote control to change the channels.

If you press the channel buttons before turning on the television, the changeTheChannel() function will not perform the change request. If the television is on and you press one of the channel buttons, that button number is passed into the changeTheChannel() function and the **screen_mc** movie clip instance will move to the correct frame (channel).

6) Close the testing movie to return to the authoring environment. With the Actions panel open, select Frame 1 of the Actions layer.

This frame now contains two function definitions, one for turning the TV on and off, and another for changing channels using the numeric buttons on the remote control keypad. However, you'll notice some redundancy between these functions: Both are set up so that when either is called, it tells the remote control light to blink as well as sends the **screen_mc** movie clip instance to the correct frame. It's best to fix this type of redundancy whenever possible, so we'll correct this problem now.

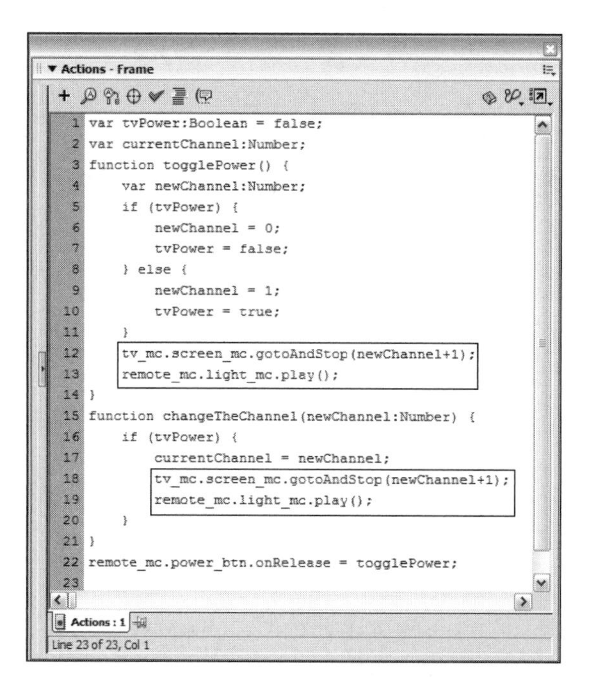

7) With the Actions panel still open, modify the `togglePower()` **function to read:**

```
function togglePower() {
  if (tvPower) {
    changeTheChannel(0);
    tvPower = false;
  } else {
    tvPower = true;
    changeTheChannel(1);
  }
}
```

This function now makes use of the `changeTheChannel()` function to change the channel when the power is turned on or off. When the TV is turned on, the `togglePower()` function makes a call to the `changeTheChannel()` function and passes in the number 1. This means that every time the TV is turned on, it will start on Channel 1. When it is turned off, it goes to Channel 0 (the off state of the TV screen). This demonstrates how one function can contain a call to another.

NOTE *Notice that in the first part of the* `if` *statement in Step 7, the call to the* `changeTheChannel()` *function happens before* `tvPower` *is set to* `false`. *This is because we defined the* `changeTheChannel()` *function so that it works only if* `tvPower` *is* `true` *(which it is if this part of the statement is executed). If* `tvPower` *were set to* `false` *first, the function call of* `changeTheChannel(0)` *would do nothing. The* `else` *part of the statement works just the opposite: The value of* `tvPower` *is set to* `true` *first, before the function call. Once again, this is because* `tvPower` *must have a value of* `true` *before the function call will have an effect.*

Let's create some functions that will allow us to increment and decrement channels using the Up and Down arrows on the remote.

8) Select the first frame of the Actions layer on the main timeline and open the Actions panel. Insert this script in the frame, just below `tvPower:Boolean = false;`**:**

```
var numberOfChannels:Number = 6;
```

This line of code creates a variable called `numberOfChannels` and assigns it a value of 6. This variable will be used in a function (which we'll create in a moment) that will be used to increment channels each time it's called. Remember that the **screen_mc** movie clip instance contains graphics representing only six channels; this value of 6 represents the total number of channels our TV can display and will be used to prevent the incrementing of channels beyond Channel 6. Let's see how this works.

9) Add this script at the end of the currently selected frame:

```
function channelUp () {
  if (currentChannel + 1 <= numberOfChannels) {
    changeTheChannel(currentChannel + 1);
  }
}
```

This function—which does not accept parameters—bumps up the channel by 1 each time the function is called. However, it uses a "safety mechanism" to prevent going beyond Channel 6. Recall that a variable named `currentChannel` is set every time the `changeTheChannel()` function is called (see Step 3). The value of this variable represents the channel currently displayed minus 1. Thus, if Channel 4 is currently displayed, this variable's value will be 3. Before the channelUp() function will execute, it uses an if statement to determine whether the current channel incremented (the value of currentChannel + 1) will still be less than or equal to the upper channel limit (the value of numberOfChannels, or 6). If the condition is satisfied, the changeTheChannel() function is called with a parameter that has a value of the current channel plus 1. This will cause the next channel to be displayed. This if statement contains no accompanying else statement: if the condition is not satisfied, this means that Channel 6 is currently displayed and no further actions are performed.

10) Add this script at the end of the currently selected frame:

```
function channelDown () {
  if (currentChannel - 1 >= 1) {
    changeTheChannel(currentChannel - 1);
  }
}
```

Like the channelUp() function, this function does not accept parameters. When called, it determines whether the value of the currentChannel variable *decremented* by 1 is greater than or equal to the lower bound of 1, thus preventing the user from "channeling down" beyond Channel 1. If this condition is satisfied, the changeTheChannel() function is called and passed the value of the currentChannel minus 1. This will cause the previous channel to be displayed. As with the if statement in the channelUp() function definition, this if statement contains no accompanying else statement. If the condition is not satisfied, it means that Channel 1 is currently displayed and no further actions will be performed.

It's time to add function calls to the Up and Down buttons on our remote control that will use the channelUp() and channelDown() functions we created.

11) Add this script at the end of the current script on Frame 1:

```
remote_mc.up_btn.onRelease = channelUp;
```

This line of ActionScript assigns an event handler to the onRelease event of the **up_btn** instance inside the **remote_mc** movie clip instance. Every time the button is clicked, the channelUp() function will be called. When the current channel reaches its upper limit (as defined by the numberOfChannels variable), the channels will no longer increment.

12) Add this script:

```
remote_mc.down_btn.onRelease = channelDown;
```

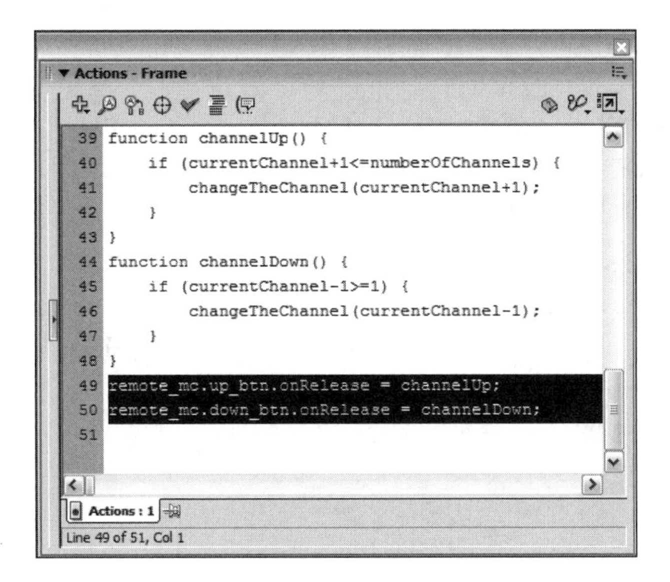

As with the Up button in Step 11, this script assigns an event handler to the **down_btn** button instance in the **remote_mc** movie clip instance. Every time this button is pressed, `channelDown()` is called and the `currentChannel` variable is decremented (as long as it's greater than the lower limit). The television is then set to the correct channel.

13) Choose Control > Test Movie. Turn on the television using the Power button, and use the Up and Down buttons to change channels.

Notice that you can select any channel, and from there use the Up and Down buttons to change the channels. Using a variable that stores the current channel and functions, as you have done here, makes this type of functionality simple.

14) Close the test movie and save your work as *television3.fla*.

You have created a functional remote control for a television. In the next exercise, you'll use functions in a new way while adding functionality for the cable box in our project to display a text description of the current channel's content.

USING LOCAL VARIABLES AND CREATING FUNCTIONS THAT RETURN RESULTS

The variables you've created and used so far can be accessed at any time by any script in the Flash movie. In contrast, *local* variables are special variables you can create and use only within the scope of a function definition. In other words, a local variable is created within the function definition, used by the function when it's called, then deleted automatically when that function has finished executing. Local variables exist only within the function where they are created.

Although local variables are not absolutely required in ActionScript, it's good programming practice to use them. Applications that require many and frequent calculations create a lot of variables and will slow applications over time. By using local variables, however, you minimize memory usage and help prevent *naming collisions*, which occur when your project gets so big you unknowingly create and use variable names that are already in use. However, local variables in one function definition can have the same names as local variables within another function definition—even if both definitions exist on the same timeline. This is because Flash understands that a local variable has meaning only within the function definition where the variable was created.

There is only one way to create a local variable manually, and you have been using this syntax for four lessons. Here's the syntax:

```
var myName:String = "Jobe";
```

This variable becomes a local variable by simply being declared *within* a function definition, using the keyword `var`.

To better grasp this concept, consider this example.

In the previous exercise, we declared (created) the variable `currentChannel` on Frame 1 of the main timeline using the following syntax:

```
var currentChannel:Number;
```

Because the line of script that created the variable was on Frame 1 of the main timeline, and it *didn't* exist within a function definition, `currentChannel` became a variable of the main timeline. If we place this exact syntax within a function definition, `currentChannel` is considered a local variable (belonging to the function only); it exists only when the function is called and is deleted immediately upon the completion of the function's execution. Think of local variables as temporary variables, for use within functions.

If you need to create a timeline variable from within a function, do not use the var syntax when declaring it. Declare the variable like this:

```
name = "Jobe";
```

TIP *It is best to create timeline variables outside of function definitions. Declaring a timeline variable outside of a function is considered good practice because you group all your timeline variables together. When coming back to your code months later or having another programmer look at your code, this variable organization will be appreciated.*

Multiple local variables can be declared within a function definition on a single line using this syntax:

```
var firstName:String = "Jobe", lastName:String = "Makar", email:String =
"jobe@electrotank.com";
```

Returning Results from a Function Call

Not only do functions simply execute sets of actions; you can also use them like mini-programs within your movie, processing information sent to them and returning values. Take a look at this function definition:

```
function buyCD(availableFunds:Number, currentDay:String):Boolean{
  var myVariable:Boolean;
  if(currentDay != "Sunday" && availableFunds >= 20){
    myVariable = true;
  }else{
    myVariable = false;
  }
  return myVariable;
}
```

The values of two parameters—availableFunds and currentDay—are sent to the function when it is called. The function processes those values using an if/else statement. At the end of this function, myVariable will contain a value of true or false. Using the return statement (as shown at the bottom of the function definition), the value of myVariable is returned to where the function was called. To understand this, take a look at how this function is called in the following script:

```
var idealCircumstances:Boolean = buyCD(19, "Friday");
if(idealCircumstances == true){
  gotoAndPlay("Happiness");
}else{
  gotoAndPlay("StayHome");
}
```

Pay particular attention to the line that reads:

```
var idealCircumstances:Boolean = buyCD(19, "Friday");
```

To the right of the = sign is our actual function call, which sends the values of 19 and "Friday" to the buyCD() function for processing. If you recall how our function was defined, these values are used to determine a true or false value for myVariable. Sending these particular values (19, "Friday") to the function causes myVariable to evaluate to a value of false. Because the last line of code in our function says return myVariable;, the value of myVariable is returned to the script where the function was called. So,

```
idealCircumstances = false;
```

In essence, we used a function call to assign a value to the variable idealCircumstances. This happens in a split second. After a value has been assigned, the value of idealCircumstances can be used in the rest of the script, as our example demonstrates.

idealCircumstances:Boolean = **buyCD(19.00, "Friday")**

buyCD(availableFunds:Number, currentDay:String)

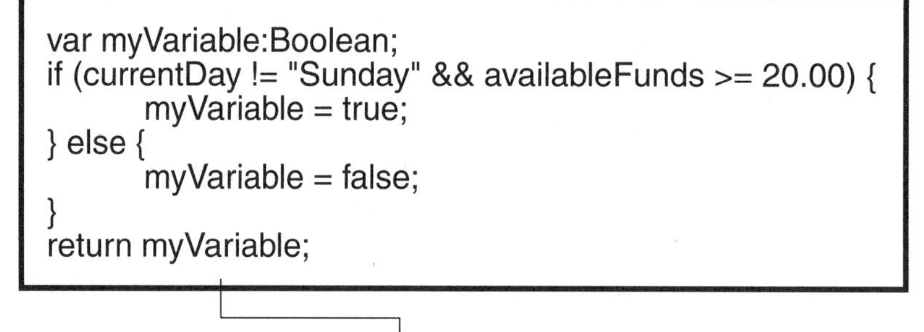
var myVariable:Boolean;
if (currentDay != "Sunday" && availableFunds >= 20.00) {
myVariable = true;
} else {
myVariable = false;
}
return myVariable;

idealCircumstances = **false**

TIP *You can use the* return *action to return any data types, including variable values, arrays, or any other objects.*

Now that you understand that functions can return values, it's a good time to point out a minor addition to our function definition syntax. The first line of our buyCD() function definition looks like this:

```
function buyCD(availableFunds:Number, currentDay:String):Boolean{
```

Between the closing parenthesis and the curly bracket on the end, we've placed the syntax `:Boolean`. This addition is to indicate that the function returns a value whenever it is called. In this case, the function returns a `true` or `false` value, hence the reason for using `:Boolean`. A function set up to return a numeric value would be written this way:

```
function myNumberFunction(param1:Number, param2:Boolean):Number{
  //actions
}
```

A function set up to return a string value, this way:

```
function myNumberFunction(param1:Number, param2:Boolean):String{
  //actions
}
```

A function set up to return an Array object, this way:

```
function myNumberFunction(param1:Number, param2:Boolean):Array{
//actions
}
```

and so forth.

If a function doesn't return a value at all (like the functions used in this lesson's projects so far), the function should be written this way:

```
function myNumberFunction(param1:Number, param2:Boolean):Void{
  //actions
}
```

Notice the use of `:Void` to indicate that this function does not return a value.

Although the functions we used in this lesson have not made use of this syntax (they still work properly), using this syntax is considered good practice and should improve the speed of ActionScript execution. The speed increase may be noticeable only if your project contains many functions.

In this exercise, using both local variables and a function that returns a value, you'll script the cable box display in our project, which displays the name of the current channel. You will create a function that builds the text to be displayed on the cable box.

1) Open *television3.fla*.

This file continues where the last exercise left off. We'll focus on the movie clip that has an instance name of **cableBox_mc** (and which looks like a cable box). This movie clip instance contains a simple graphic and a text field with an instance name of

cableDisplay_txt. This text field will be filled with different channel names, depending on the channel selected.

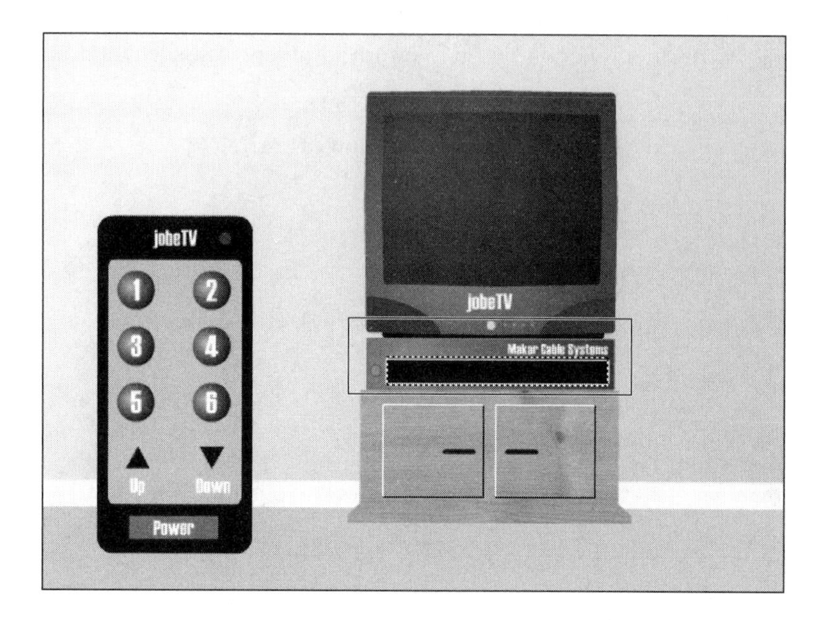

2) With the Actions panel open, select Frame 1 on the main timeline and enter this script just below where it says `numberOfChannels = 6;`**:**

```
var channelNames:Array =
["","News","Classics","Family","Cartoons","Horror","Westerns"];
```

You just created an array named `channelNames`. This array contains names that will be dynamically inserted into a string of text that will be displayed inside the cable box. The seven string elements in this array are separated by commas (the first may not be easily discernible because it's an empty string of `""`). Each one of these elements has an associated *index* value, beginning with 0. For example, `channelNames[0] = ""` (empty), `channelNames[1] = "News"`, `channelNames[2] = "Classics"`, and so on. This is important to understand as we progress.

NOTE *For more information on arrays, see Lesson 6, "Creating and Manipulating Data."*

Let's create a function that uses the text elements in this array to display a message in the cable box.

3) With the frame still selected, enter this script at the end of all scripts on Frame 1:

```
function displayCableText():String {
  var displayText:String;
  if (currentChannel != 0) {
    displayText = "You are viewing "+channelNames[currentChannel]+".";
  } else {
    displayText = "";
  }
  return displayText;
}
```

NOTE *This is defined after the other functions but before the event handler assignments, but it really doesn't matter where it's defined. It's just a matter of preference to have it one place over another.*

This script defines the `displayCableText()` function, which accepts no parameters. It is used to dynamically build a string of text that will eventually appear in the **cableDisplay_txt** text field within the **cableBox_mc** movie clip instance. The function then takes this string and returns it using the `return` action. The function contains a conditional statement that checks to make sure the television channel is not the channel associated with the TV being in the off state (0). If the condition is satisfied, a local variable named `displayText` is created, and a line of text is dynamically built from the `channelNames` array as well as the current value of `currentChannel`. For example, if the value of `currentChannel` is `4` at the time this function is called and executed, this would essentially be the same as the following:

```
displayText = "You are viewing " + channelNames[4] + ".";
```

Because `Cartoons` exists at index position 4 of the `channelNames` array, it can be broken down further:

```
displayText = "You are viewing Cartoons";
```

If the first part of the conditional statement is not satisfied (`else`), the local variable `displayText` is set with no value (or simply `""`). The function ends by returning the value of `displayText`. But where does this value actually get returned to? We'll explain that in the next step. Because `displayText` has been specified as a local variable (using `var`), it's removed from memory as soon as its value is returned.

4) With the Actions panel still open, modify the `changeTheChannel()` function by inserting this code after the fifth line of the function definition:

```
cableBox_mc.cableDisplay_txt.text = displayCableText();
```

You have modified `changeTheChannel()` so that each time a channel is changed and the `changeChannel()` function is called, the **cableDisplay_txt** text field (inside the **cableBox_mc** movie clip instance) will be updated with the correct text. This line of ActionScript sets the value of the text field instance **cableDisplay_txt** (which is actually the dynamic text field in our cable box) using the returned value of the `displayCableText()` function. Thus, the `displayCableText()` function is called, goes to work, and comes up with a value. That value is inserted after the = sign. This is what's meant by a function *returning* a value. The value the function comes up with is returned to the line of script that called the function. This is also a great example of how using functions can be a real time-saver. We've enhanced `changeTheChannel()` in a single location, but any script that calls the function will automatically execute this enhancement as well—very efficient!

5) Choose Control > Test Movie. Select the Power button to turn the television on. Change the channel a few times.

Every time you select a button that changes the channel, the cable box is updated with the name of the channel you're watching. You have created a simple application that uses six functions to perform several tasks.

6) Close the test movie and save your work as *television4.fla*.

You're finished with this file. You'll apply what you've learned here in lessons to come.

WHAT YOU HAVE LEARNED

In this lesson, you have:

- Learned how functions can make scripting a project much more efficient (pages 172–174)
- Created functions using various syntaxes (pages 174–178)
- Passed arguments into functions while calling them (pages 179–187)
- Used local variables (pages 188–189)
- Returned and used the results of calling a function (pages 189–191)
- Called functions from within other functions (pages 191–195)

creating and manipulating data

LESSON 6

When you use Flash to create an application, you use the Text tool to enter information directly onto the stage. Text that you enter in this manner is said to be *hard coded* because it's permanent once the SWF file is published. If you want to alter data that's hard coded into your Flash application, you must edit the Flash source file—a cumbersome and unnecessary process because Flash lets you define areas where text can be displayed dynamically. Instead of being set when the SWF is published, dynamic data is processed and stored at run time (while the SWF file is running), which means you can change it as often as you want. *Dynamic data* can be user-supplied information, data loaded from another file, or even information you can't control, such as the current time. You can use this type of data to display information, make decisions, manipulate the position of movie clips, and much more.

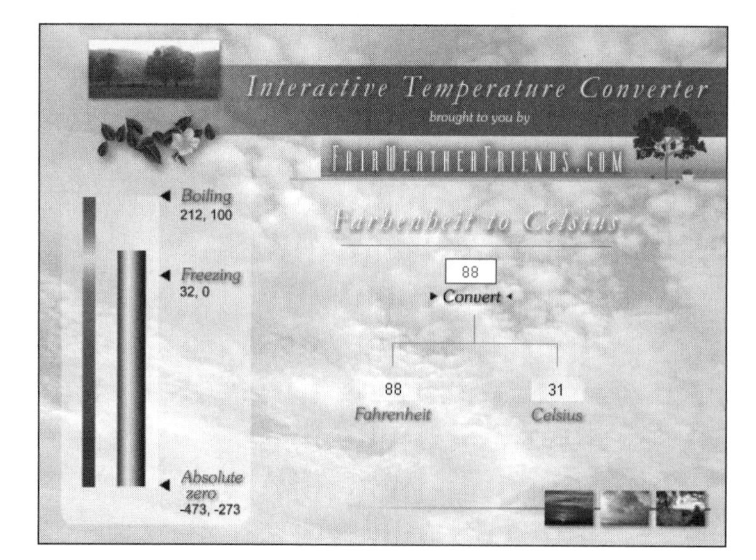

This temperature converter manipulates data by converting values from one scale to another—Fahrenheit to Celsius.

In this lesson, you'll learn how to create objects, variables, and arrays (all elements of a data-driven project), as well as how to manipulate data already within your project (such as numbers and strings of text) in order to display your data in new and useful ways.

WHAT YOU WILL LEARN

In this lesson, you will:

- Learn the power of dynamic data
- Create text fields
- Create variables
- Create arrays
- Store information in objects
- Retrieve information from storage dynamically
- Build expressions
- Learn about precedence
- Manipulate numbers with the Math class
- Gain experience with the methods of the String class

APPROXIMATE TIME

This lesson takes approximately one and one half hours to complete.

LESSON FILES

Starting Files:

Lesson06/Assets/newsFlash1.fla
Lesson06/Assets/tempConverter1.fla
Lesson06/Assets/madlibs1.fla

Completed Projects:

newsFlash5.fla
tempConverter2.fla
madlibs2.fla

CREATING VARIABLES

You have created many variables in Lessons 1–5. Here in Lesson 6, we formally introduce variables and how they are created.

Each timeline in your project can contain its own set of variables—containers, so to speak, for storing information (data). When you create variables, you must give them names—monikers you cannot change, though you can alter their contents. Here's the syntax for creating a variable:

```
var myFullName:String = "Jobe Makar";
```

The script declares a new variable, associates a data type with that variable, and gives the variable data to store.

By using `var` followed by a space, you indicate that the next string of letters is the declaration of a variable. After the variable name (the string of letters after `var`) you add a colon. The Actions panel gives you a drop-down list of data types you can add after the colon, or you can type the data type yourself. The assignment operator (=) sets what is found to its right as the value of the variable. Above, `"Jobe Makar"` is the value of `myFullName`.

NOTE *As you learned in Lesson 1, "Introducing ActionScript," by associating a data type with a variable you allow the Flash player to assist you in debugging scripts. If you declare a variable as a string but later attempt to assign a number as a value, the Flash player will catch this error and report it to you when you export your movie (at "compile time").*

You can also declare a variable without giving it a value. For example:

```
var myFullName:String;
```

The script tells the Flash Player that when the variable `myFullName` is used at some point in the future, it should have a String value.

It is also possible to create a variable this way:

```
myFullName = "Jobe Makar";
```

This script is a valid way to create a variable. However, creating a variable in this manner is no longer recommended. It is now recommended to use the `var` syntax so that you can make full use of data typing and for good memory management.

NOTE *You can name a variable anything, as long as you follow some simple rules. The name must begin with a character or underscore, and it cannot contain spaces, special characters (@, #, $, %, and so on), or punctuation marks. Even though you might not receive an error from Flash if you use a special character for a variable name, it can still cause unplanned behavior.*

TIP *Name your variables according to the data they contain—for example,* `numberOfDays`*,* `favoriteDogsName`*,* `totalTax`*, and so on—so you can remember and use them easily throughout your project.*

Once you create a variable and assign it a value, you can use that value in any script simply by referencing its name. For example:

```
var myFavoriteNumber:Number = 66;
```

This code creates a variable named `myFavoriteNumber` and assigns it a value of `66`. To use that value in a script, you use syntax like this:

```
myButton_btn.onRelease = function() {
  gotoAndStop (myFavoriteNumber); // Moves the timeline to frame 66
  cat_mc._xscale = myFavoriteNumber; // Scale cat movie clip instance 66%
  ⇒vertically
};
```

Variables derive their power from universally available data—that is, information that can be used in any script. If the value of your variable changes, the scripts that use it will execute differently because some of the actions are based on the current value of that variable.

<table>
<tr><th>Data Storage</th><th>Scripts</th></tr>
<tr><td rowspan="3">var myFavoriteNumber:Number = 66</td><td>gotoAndStop (myFavoriteNumber);</td></tr>
<tr><td>cat_mc._xscale = myFavoriteNumber;</td></tr>
<tr><td>if (userInput > myFavoriteNumber);
  message_txt.text = "Lower it, buddy!';
} else {
  message_txt.text = "That's fine!";
}</td></tr>
</table>

The three main types of variable values are String, Boolean, and Number. A String is a text value. For example, `var myFullName:String = "Jobe Makar"` has the String value `"Jobe Makar"`. Strings are most often used to store text, such as in the example `var latestNews:String = "We just got a new dog!"` String values are defined using quotation marks (`""`). The syntax `var myFavoriteNumber:String = "27"` assigns a text value of `"27"` to `myFavoriteNumber`, *not* a number value of `27`.

A Boolean value is a `true` or `false` value such as the following:

```
var playMusic:Boolean = true;
```

In programming, Boolean values are often used to indicate whether something is on or off: A script can look at the Boolean's current state (on or off, true or false) and act accordingly. For example, if you were to create a music toggle button for a Flash movie, you might want to set a Boolean variable to store the music's state—on or off (`var musicPlaying:Boolean = true` or `var musicPlaying:Boolean = false`). You could attach a script to the button so that when clicked, it would check to see if the music was on or off (`true` or `false`). If the music were currently on (`true`), the idea would be to turn the music off and then switch the value of the variable to `false`. If the music were off (`false`), the music would need to be turned on and the value of the variable set to `true`. Because the value of `musicPlaying` is switched between `true` and `false` with each successive button click, the script on the button would evaluate its current value and turn the music on or off.

NOTE *In Lesson 8, "Using Conditional Logic," we'll cover Boolean values and their uses in more depth.*

A Number value is just that, a number. Numbers are used to store numeric values—often for mathematical use. You can use numeric values for people's ages, for scores in a game, and to track the number of times someone has clicked a button—to name just a few uses. Here's how you would create a variable and assign a number value to it:

```
var radius:Number = 32;
```

Instead of assigning direct values (or literals)—for example, 32, "dog," or something else—to variables, you can use an expression to set the value. An expression is a phrase—or a collection of variables, numbers, text, and operators—that evaluates to a string, number, or Boolean value. For example:

```
var bottlesOfBeerOnTheWall:Number = 99;
var oneFellDown:Number = 1;
var bottlesLeft:Number = bottlesOfBeerOnTheWall - oneFellDown;
```

The third line in this script uses an expression to set the value of `bottlesLeft`. The expression substitutes the values of the variables (99 and 1) and performs a subtraction. The end result is that the variable `bottlesLeft` is assigned a value of 98. It's important to note that the structure of the expression determines whether it will result in a string, Boolean, or number value.

When using expressions to set variable values, the expression doesn't have to be lengthy. Take a look at this example:

```
var someone:String = "Jobe Makar";
var coffeeBoy:String = someone;
```

A variable called someone is created in the first line of the script. In the second line, the value of the coffeeBoy variable is set to the string "Jobe Makar" by referencing the value of someone. If the value of someone changes later, coffeeBoy will not reflect the change.

NOTE *A variable can also gain its value as the result of a function. For more on this topic, see Lesson 5, "Using Functions."*

A Flash project can contain many timelines, each with its own set of dynamic data (variables, arrays, and so on). The timeline where dynamic data resides depends on the timeline on which it was placed when it was created. This script creates a variable named myVariable in the current movie:

```
var myVariable:Number = 100;
```

The next script creates a variable named myVariable and places it on the root (main) timeline:

```
_root.myVariable = 100;
```

Notice the use of a target path in this variable's creation. Using target paths in this manner, you create or access data on a specific timeline.

Note that using a target path to create a variable restricts you from using the recommended var syntax to declare a variable. Take a look at this:

```
var _root.myVariable:Number = 100;
```

The script is not valid. Try typing it into the Actions panel and selecting the Check Syntax button. You receive an error. You can properly declare a variable on a timeline only from the timeline itself (a script attached to a frame or button in the timeline). This does not mean that you can't change the value of a variable properly from another timeline, but it's recommended that you first declare the variable in that timeline. For example, let's say you have **myClip1_mc** and **myClip2_mc** movie clip instances. In **myClip1_mc** you have the following code:

```
var myVariable:Number = 100;
```

In **myClip2_mc**, you can then change the value of the variable that is living in **myClip1_mc** with the following code:

```
_parent.myClip1_mc.myVariable = 200;
```

By coding in this manner, you can still make use of the strict typing of variables in Flash while allowing variables to be modified from another timeline.

You can also create variables directly on objects. However, you cannot use the `var` syntax when doing so. For example:

```
var person:Object = new Object();
person.name = "Jobe";
```

It's perfectly acceptable code—but there is no way to use the `var` syntax for creating the `name` variable on the object without defining your own class of objects. (In Lesson 7, "Creating Custom Classes," you learn to create variables on an object while using the `var` syntax, but the concept covers new topics, so we won't discuss it here.)

Because dynamic text fields can be used to display the value contained in a particular piece of data, in this exercise you set and use variables that ultimately control what's displayed on the screen for a news site project.

1) Open *newsFlash1.fla* in the Lesson06/Assets folder.

This file currently contains no actions, but the frame and movie clip structure have already been created.

The main timeline has two frame labels, Initialize and Sit. The first, Initialize, is where you create the data for this project. The other label, Sit, will contain actions used to pull out the data to be displayed in various places on screen.

Move to the Sit frame label and you'll see that graphics have already been created and inserted. The screen doesn't yet contain any text fields to display data.

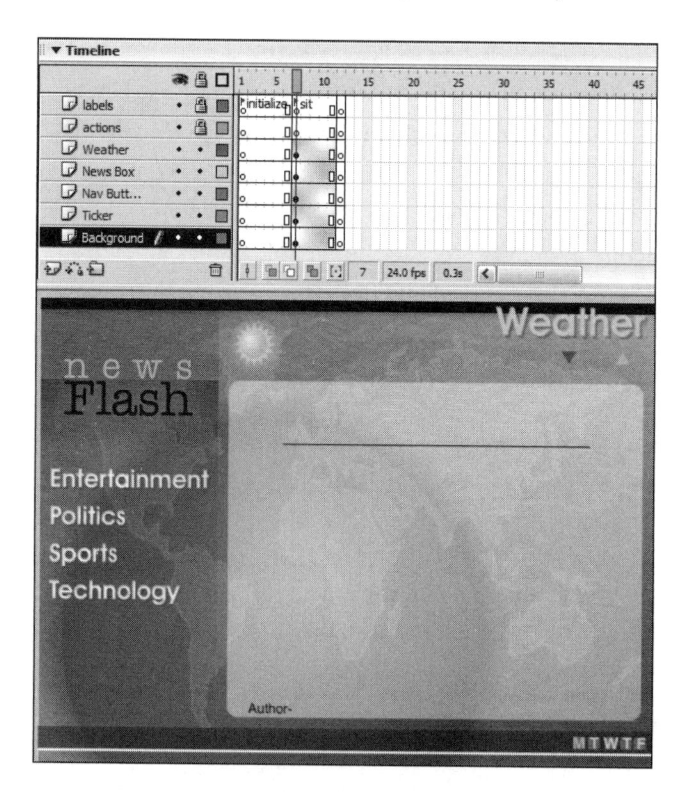

2) Select Frame 1 of the Actions layer on the main timeline. Open the Actions panel and enter the script:

```
// ----Monday------ --
var monday:Object = new Object();
monday.date = "Monday, August 25 2003";
// ----Tuesday------ --
var tuesday:Object = new Object();
tuesday.date = "Tuesday, August 26 2003";
```

To structure the data for this application, you'll use objects—each of which will be named for a different day of the week and will store all the news for that day accordingly. Note that we only discuss the ActionScript for Monday and Tuesday because the ActionScript for the rest of the week works in the same way.

Entering the preceding script on Frame 1 of the timeline creates the objects `monday` and `tuesday`. You add a date variable (object property) on each object to store each day's date.

3) Save your work as *newsFlash2.fla*.

You've created the objects, properties, and variables needed so far. You'll create more variables in a later exercise.

CREATING ARRAYS

Suppose you have a guest list for a party: You can store the information in ActionScript with variables like these:

```
var name1:String = "John Smith";
var name2:String = "Kelly McAvoy";
var name3:String = "Joyce Rendir";
var name4:String = "Tripp Carter";
```

If Kelly tells you she can't make it to your party, aside from being upset that only three people will be attending, you'll have to rename the variables beneath her name and shift them up your list. You can simplify this tedious task—as well as many other similar data storage and manipulation chores—by using arrays.

Think of arrays as supervariables: While a regular variable can only contain a single value, an array can contain multiple values—which means you could store that entire guest list in a single array.

However, you must create an array in order to use it. Because arrays are objects (instances of the Array class), you use the Array class constructor method to create them. Here's the syntax to create an array:

```
var myArray:Array = new Array();
```

You can populate an array with values separated by commas when you create it, like this:

```
var guestList:Array = new Array("John Smith","Kelly McAvoy","Joyce
⇒Rendir","Tripp Carter");
```

Or you can use this syntax:

```
var guestList:Array = ["John Smith","Kelly McAvoy","Joyce Rendir","Tripp Carter"];
```

Each value in an array is identified by an index number—0, 1, 2, and so on—that denotes its position in the array. In the array we just created, `"John Smith"` has an index number of 0, `"Kelly McAvoy"` has an index number of 1, and so on. To access a value in an array, you would use this syntax:

```
var myFavoriteGuest:String= guestList[1];
```

Here, the variable `myFavoriteGuest` is assigned a value of `"Kelly McAvoy"` because this is the value that exists at index position 1 in our `guestList` array.

The `guestList` array was created with four elements. You can add or modify elements at any time by referencing the specific element in the array. For example, this script will update the value at index 2 from `"Joyce Rendir"` to `"John Rendir"`:

```
guestList[2]="John Rendir";
```

An array element can contain any data type, including strings, numbers, and Boolean values, as well as entire objects. An array element can even contain another array. You'll learn more about arrays and methods of the Array class in later lessons. The next exercise—in which you'll use arrays to store groups of related information for each day of the week—represents just the beginning.

NOTE *You cannot use the* `var` *syntax when you're creating an array on an object unless you're building your own custom class of objects. This concept is discussed in Lesson 7, "Creating Custom Classes."*

1) With *newsFlash2.fla* still open, select Frame 1 of the Actions layer. Add this script after the `monday.date = "Monday, August 25 2003"` **variable set:**

```
monday.weather = new Array();
monday.weather[0] = "Rainy";
monday.weather[1] = "Very wet";
monday.weather[2] = 85;
monday.weather[3] = 62;
```

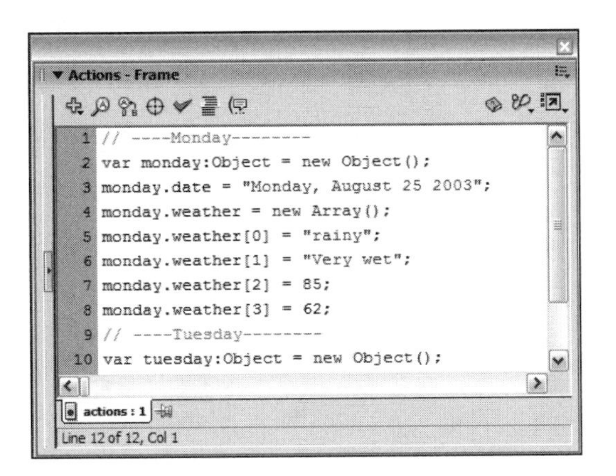

You created an array called `weather` that's used to store weather data. The array is on the object `monday`. Remember: you store all information pertaining to Monday on the `monday` object.

On the frames that contain graphics, you'll see a small weather icon (which currently displays the sun, as shown in the following figure). This icon is a movie clip instance whose timeline contains three frame labels that hold weather icons that correspond to three different weather conditions. The frame labels are Sunny, Rainy, and Stormy. The value of the first element (the 0th index) of the `weather` array will be used later to send this movie clip instance to the correct frame. Here it's set to "Rainy" because Monday is supposed to be rainy. The second element of the `weather` array contains a blurb about Monday's weather, which will be displayed later on the screen.

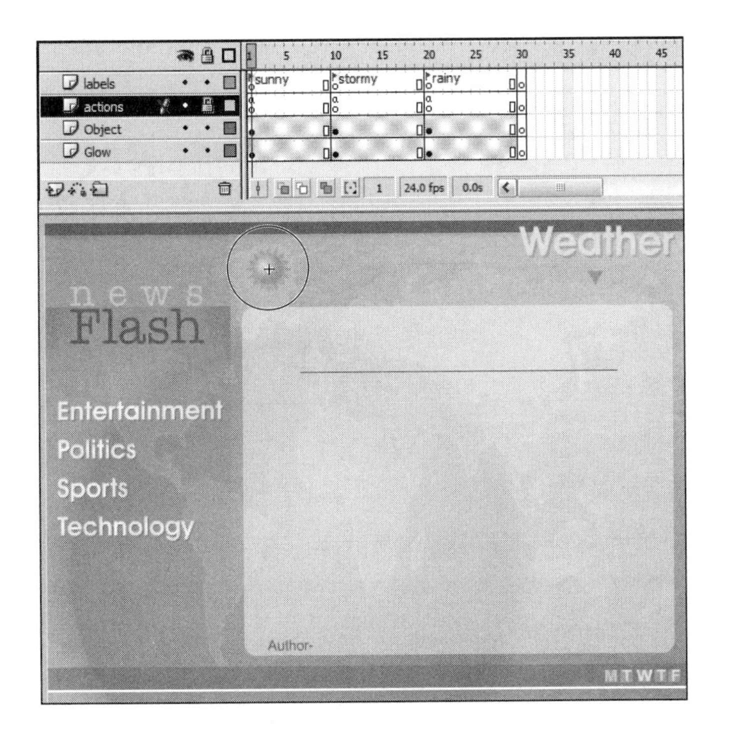

The high and low temperatures for Monday are stored in the third and fourth elements of the `weather` array, respectively. These values will be accessed later so that they can be displayed on the news page.

You have just created an array that stores four pieces of related information in a way that is easily accessible.

2) With Frame 1 still selected, insert this script after `tuesday.date = "Tuesday, August 26 2003";`**:**

```
tuesday.weather = new Array();
tuesday.weather[0] = "Sunny";
tuesday.weather[1] = "Beautiful Day!";
tuesday.weather[2] = 90;
tuesday.weather[3] = 73;
```

You have created another array named `weather`, but this array is on the `tuesday` object. It contains weather information pertaining to Tuesday. The first element of this array contains the value `"sunny"` so that the weather icon movie clip instance will display a sun. The value of each array element here is different from that of the `weather` array for Monday, but the index numbers of corresponding values are the same: although the high temperatures for Monday and Tuesday are different, they're both stored at the Number 2 index position in each array.

Now that you've created and structured your weather data, it's time to create and structure some news stories.

3) Create arrays to contain news articles for individual categories by entering this script after `monday.weather[3] = 62`**:**

```
monday.entertainment = new Array();
monday.entertainment[0] = "MTV is 22!";
monday.entertainment[1] = "The popular TV network MTV has now been on the air for
⇒22 years...";
monday.entertainment[2] = "Jobe Makar";
monday.politics = new Array();
monday.politics[0] = "Presidential Election 2004";
monday.politics[1] = "Candidates are preparing for a year-long campaign...";
monday.politics[2] = "Happy Camper";
monday.sports = new Array();
monday.sports[0] = "Head Tennis";
monday.sports[1] = "The Head Atlantis tennis racquet is one of the most popular
⇒racquets in history...";
monday.sports[2] = "Jane Doe";
monday.technology = new Array();
monday.technology[0] = "BajillaHertz Processors!";
monday.technology[1] = "The BajillaHertz processor has just hit the shelves and
⇒is faster than light...";
monday.technology[2] = "John Doe";
```

This news site can display four sections of stories: entertainment, politics, sports, and technology, as indicated by the navigation buttons on the left of the screen. For each of these sections, we created an array and stored information about one article for that Monday. In the first section of this step, we created an array called `entertainment`. The first element of the `entertainment` array stores the news story's headline; the second element contains the actual news article; and the third element stores the name of the author. The `politics`, `sports`, and `technology` arrays contain the same type of information (headline, story, and author) at the same index positions.

Although this information will be accessed on a later frame, by building a logical object-oriented storage structure for it now you ensure that it will be easy to access when needed.

4) Add this news article script after `tuesday.weather[3] = 73`:

```
tuesday.entertainment = new Array();
tuesday.entertainment[0] = "Amazing Sci-Fi";
tuesday.entertainment[1] = "Sentrillion Blazers is the must see sci-fi movie of
⇒the year!...";
tuesday.entertainment[2] = "Jobe Makar";
tuesday.politics = new Array();
tuesday.politics[0] = "No Child Left Behind";
tuesday.politics[1] = "School systems protest the yearly testing criteria...";
tuesday.politics[2] = "John Doe";
tuesday.sports = new Array();
tuesday.sports[0] = "Ryder Cup Begins";
tuesday.sports[1] = "The European golf tournament you have been waiting for has
⇒just begun...";
tuesday.sports[2] = "Jane Doe";
tuesday.technology = new Array();
tuesday.technology[0] = "KatrillaHertz Processor";
tuesday.technology[1] = "The KatrillaHertz processor is just out and is twice as
⇒fast as the BajillaHertz chip...";
tuesday.technology[2] = "John Doe";
```

This script stores the headlines, stories, and authors for the four news sections on Tuesday. The array names are the same as they were for Monday; the only difference is the information stored. Tuesday's information structure is exactly the same as that for Monday.

5) Save your work as *newsFlash3.fla*.

You have created the information storage structure for your news site. Because all of the script we created so far is placed on Frame 1, this data will be created as soon as the movie begins to play. Next you will add the capability to retrieve the information and display it on screen.

CREATING DYNAMIC TEXT FIELDS AND RETRIEVING INFORMATION

In Flash, there are three types of text objects: static, input, and dynamic.

You compose static text on the stage using the Text tool. However, because you can't change the font, font size, or content of any static text area once an SWF file is created, you use static text for text that you'll only need to change occasionally. Web site navigation buttons, for example, are good candidates for static text.

Input text defines a text area that can be edited by users at run time. In other words, it's where users enter text. Input text fields are generally employed to gather from the user textual information that your movie uses or sends to a server for processing. This type of text field is commonly found in Flash forms.

A dynamic text field is a text area on the stage that can be populated, or filled with text as a movie plays—which means the text can change as the movie plays. A dynamic text field can also be set to display simple HTML-formatted text. A news section of a Flash Web site is a good example of where dynamic text would be useful. When you use a dynamic text field to display HTML-formatted text, you set attributes such as color, font, and hyperlinks dynamically.

NOTE *All input and dynamic text fields placed in a project are instances of the Text Field object. As such, you can control and change them using properties and methods of that class.*

You configure text fields using the Property Inspector. If you select the text tool from the Tools panel and open the Property Inspector from Window > Properties, you'll see that it includes a drop-down menu (at the top) where you can select one of the three text types (static, dynamic, or input). Depending on which text type you select, different text options are available.

If you select Static Text from the drop-down list in the Property Inspector, you can choose from these options:

- **Use Device Fonts.** If you select this option, Flash will use fonts installed on the user's computer rather than any special fonts you've included.
- **Selectable.** If you select this option, the mouse cursor will change to an I-bar so that on mouse-over the text can be highlighted and copied.
- **Bold.** Selected text is bolded.
- **Italic.** Selected text is italicized.
- **Alignment.** You can change the alignment of the text to be left-aligned, right-aligned, centered, or justified using the appropriate paragraph icon.

- **Text Orientation.** Choose whether text in a static text field appears horizontally or vertically.
- **Format.** Clicking this button brings up the Format Options dialog box, where you can adjust indenting, line spacing, and margins.
- **Character Display Attributes.** You can choose the font, point size, and kerning for the text using this option.
- **Position Attributes.** At the bottom-left of the Property Inspector is information about the screen position and the height and width of the text field.
- **URL Link.** Enter a URL here to make the text field respond as regular hyperlinked text.
- **Alias Text.** By default, this option is turned on. While on, the text in the selected text field is smoothed. When off, the text is not smoothed.

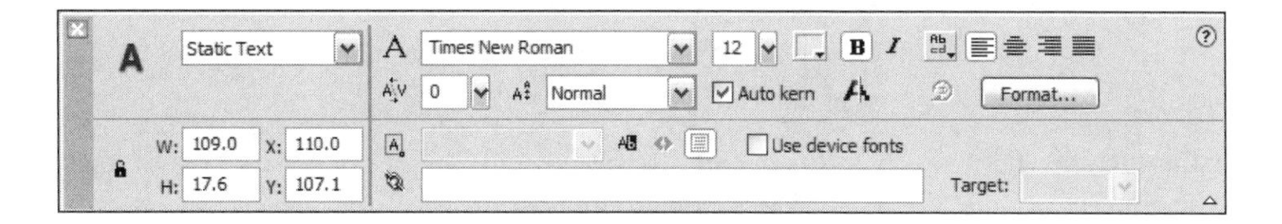

If you choose Input Text from the drop-down list, you have these options:

- **Single Line, Multiline, Multiline No Wrap, Password.** If you select Single Line, only one line of text can be entered in this text field. Additional options impose restrictions on the length of that line. If you select Multiline, multiple lines of text can be entered, and lines that exceed the width of the text field will automatically wrap to the next line. The Multiline No Wrap selection prevents text from wrapping. Text that extends beyond the boundaries of the text field is simply not shown. With Password selected, stars serve as visual replacements for anything you type (and the computer remembers the correct content).
- **Instance Name.** Assigning instance names to input text and dynamic text fields lets you use ActionScript to control or access information from a text field. If you gave a text field an instance name of **box_txt**, for example, you could access its text using the reference **box_txt.text**.
- **Var.** You can also give text fields variable names. When you assign a variable name directly to a text field, its contents always reflect the value of that variable. Likewise, if the text field is modified, the value of the variable changes to match the modified field.

NOTE *The ability to assign variables to text fields is a holdover feature from Flash 5. This functionality may be useful on rare occasions, but in most cases you should assign instance names to your text fields. This makes available a lot of scripting functionality not available to text fields when they have been assigned variable names.*

- **HTML.** Although input text fields are usually employed to accept user input, you can also use them to display dynamically generated text. If you select this option, the text field will be able to interpret any HTML 1.0 code (tags for bold, underline, and so on) that's included in the dynamic text that populates the field.
- **Border/Bg.** If selected, this option will add a white background and black border to the text box—a useful way to automatically show where the text field is located on the screen. If you leave this option unselected, the user might not be able to see where the input field is located on the stage.
- **Maximum Characters.** This option allows you to limit the number of characters that can be entered into the text field. (If this option is set to 0, users can enter an unlimited number of characters.)
- **Character.** When you click this button, you're presented with the Character Options dialog box, which enables you to configure several display options pertaining to the currently selected text field. One of these options is to embed this text field's fonts into the SWF at the time it's published, allowing Flash to display very smooth edges on your text.

TIP *Embedding fonts in a text field increases the file size of the SWF from about 1KB to 40KB, depending on the font and the characters that you choose to embed.*

All of the options for Input Text are also available for Dynamic Text, which also has this additional option:

- **Selectable.** This is the same as the Selectable option for Static Text.

In the next exercise you'll create all the needed text fields for the News Flash Web site. All of the text fields used here are dynamic text fields.

1) With *newsFlash3.fla* still open, move the playhead to the frame labeled Sit.

On this frame you see the News Flash site graphics. On the left side of the stage four buttons correspond to news sections. In the upper-middle portion of the stage there's a movie clip instance that contains several weather icons. The name of this movie clip instance is **icon_mc**. The top-right of the screen shows an arrow pointing up and an arrow pointing down. The high and low weather temperatures will be displayed here. On the bottom-right, you'll see a movie clip that shows the letters *M T W T F* referring to the five business days in a week; this clip has an instance name of **days_mc**.

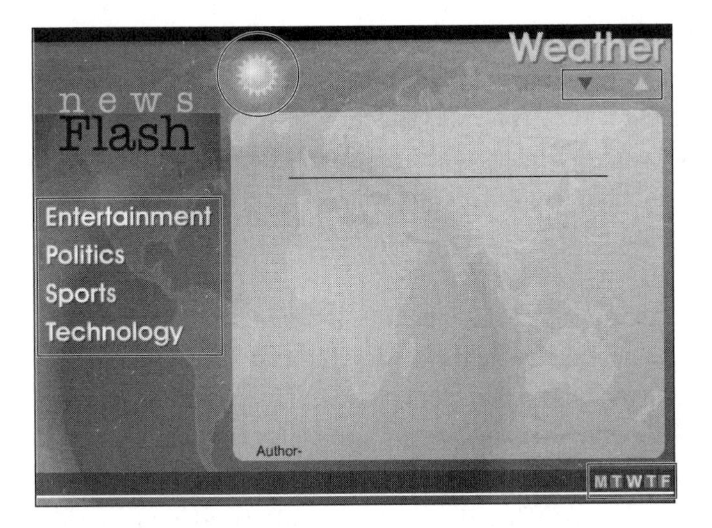

2) Select the Weather layer. Select the Text tool from the toolbar and open the Property Inspector. Select Dynamic Text from the drop-down list.

In the next several steps you'll create dynamic text fields in various areas of the stage. Once you create a text field, you edit the instance name in the Property Inspector.

3) Create a text field to the right of the weather icon by clicking on the stage. Adjust the width of this text field to approximately 150 pixels. Change the font of the text to _sans and the font size to 14.

This text field will display info about the day's weather. The text that will be dynamically placed in this field should be white. To make sure this is the case, choose White from the Property Inspector while the text field is selected. All of the text fields created for this project will be either white or black. Make sure that Single Line (rather than Multiline) is displayed in the Property Inspector.

4) With the text field still selected, edit its instance name in the Property Inspector to read *weatherBlurb_txt*.

This text field is now complete. Whenever the value for `weatherBlurb_txt.text` is set in the main timeline, the information displayed in this text field is updated.

5) Click and drag to create two text fields on this layer, one to the left of the blue arrow and another to the right of the blue arrow in the Weather section of the site. Change the font size to 13. Assign the instance name *low_txt* to the left text field and *high_txt* to the one on the right.

These two text fields will display the low and high temperatures for the selected day.

6) Select the News Box layer. With the Text tool still selected, click and drag to create another text field the width of the light-blue area just above the black line on the stage. Change the current font to _typewriter and the font size to 20, and select the Bold option. Using the Properties Inspector, choose the Center option for the text. Give the text field the instance name *headline_txt*.

This text field displays the headline of an article with the Courier font.

7) Click and drag to create another text field under the *headline_txt* text field approximately the size of the unoccupied light-blue area. Change the current font to _sans, the font size to 12, and the current color to Black. Select Multiline from the drop-down list. Assign the instance name *article_txt* to this text field.

This text field is where the actual article will be displayed. When the value for `article_txt.text` is set in the main timeline, the information displayed in this text field is updated.

8) Click and drag to create another text field about 130 pixels wide just to the right of the word *Author* on the bottom of the light-blue area. Change the Properties Inspector so that Single Line is selected. Assign this text field the instance name *author_txt*.

Like the other text fields, the information displayed in this text field will be updated whenever the value for `author_txt.text` is changed.

9) Select the Ticker layer. Click and drag to create another text field in the bottom-left of the screen, positioned on the dark gray bar. Change the current font to _sans, White, Bold, with a font size of 14. Assign this text field the instance name *date_txt*.

This text field will display the date of the day you select to view the news.

10) Save your work as *newsFlash4.fla*.

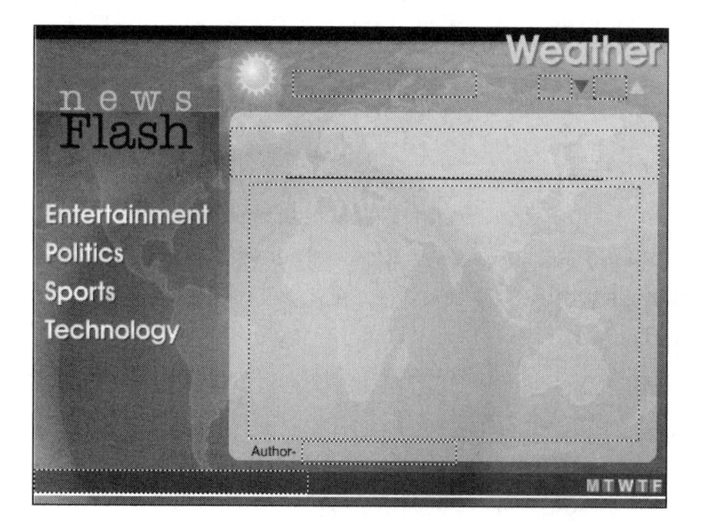

You have created all of the visual areas on the stage that will contain dynamic data. However, you still need to retrieve the stored information and use it to populate the text fields.

RETRIEVING THE DATA

Now that you've created a data-storage architecture, you need to develop a way to retrieve the information from storage—and that involves some new syntax that provides a means of writing a dot syntax path dynamically. Square brackets are used to evaluate an expression. Here's how it works. Assume we have three variables that contain animal sounds:

```
var dog:String = "bark";
var cat:String = "meow";
var duck:String = "quack";
```

We'll create a variable and assign it a text value of "dog", "cat", or "duck" (note that these text values have the same names as the variables we just mentioned). We'll start with "dog":

```
var currentAnimal:String = "dog";
```

Using this syntax, we can access the value of the variable named dog:

```
var animalSound = this[currentAnimal];
```

Here, animalSound is assigned a value of "bark". The expression to the right of the equals sign looks at currentAnimal and sees that it currently contains a string value of "dog". The brackets surrounding currentAnimal tell ActionScript to treat this value as a variable name. Flash sees this line of script like this:

```
var animalSound:String = this.dog;
```

Because dog has a value of "bark", that's the value assigned to animalSound. If we were to change the value of currentAnimal to "cat," animalSound would be assigned a value of "meow".

Note that you must use this in the expression to include the target path of the variable used to set the dynamic variable name (in this case currentAnimal), because it relates to the variable to the left of the equals sign (in our case animalSound). Using this denotes that these two variables are on the same timeline. If animalSound existed in a movie clip instance's timeline while currentAnimal was on the root (main) timeline, the syntax would look like this:

```
var animalSound:String = _root[currentAnimal];
```

Here are a couple of other examples:

```
var animalSound:String = _parent[currentAnimal];
var animalSound:String = myMovieClip[currentAnimal];
```

This syntax is critical to the way you retrieve information from the objects in this exercise. Remember that all the objects are built with the same array names and structure; they have different parent object names (`monday` and `tuesday`). We can use the aforementioned syntax to dynamically access the data in these objects based on the current value of a variable.

1) With *newsFlash4.fla* open, select Frame 1 of the Actions layer. Open the Actions panel and enter these variables at the end of the current script:

```
var day:String = "monday";
var section:String = "entertainment";
```

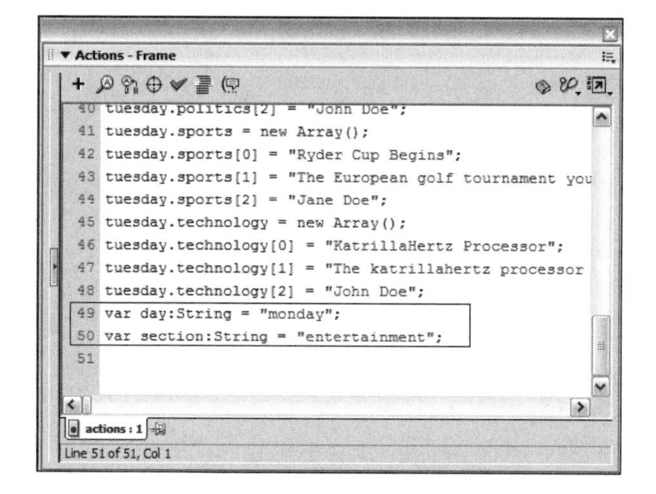

When the application plays for the first time, we want Monday to appear initially, and entertainment news to be displayed. The two variables set in Step 1 allow us to accomplish this—you'll see how in the next few steps.

NOTE *These variables are known as initializing variables. Because the information our application displays depends on the buttons the user clicks, these variables provide some starting settings prior to user input.*

2) Select the frame labeled Sit in the Actions layer. Enter this script in that frame:

```
function refresh(category) {
  section = category;
}
```

This function is called when any of the section buttons is clicked. The button events that call this function will be added later in this exercise.

The purpose of this function (by the end of this exercise) is to refresh what is shown on the screen based on the current values of the `day` and `section` variables (which were initially set to `"monday"` and `"entertainment"`, respectively, in Step 1 of this exercise).

Currently there is only one line of ActionScript inside this function definition. It updates the value of the `section` variable to that of the parameter value passed to the function. If the Entertainment button is clicked, it will call this function and pass it a value of `"entertainment"`. The function will then assign the `section` variable a value of `"entertainment"`. We'll explain the purpose over the next several steps as we add more actions to this `refresh()` function.

3) Add this script at the end of the `refresh()` function:

```
date_txt.text = this[day].date;
```

This script uses the syntax we introduced at the beginning of this exercise. The text displayed in the **date_txt** field is set by dynamically referencing another variable. Because `day` initially has a value of `"monday"` (as set in Step 1), ActionScript sees the code as this:

```
date_txt.text = monday.date;
```

You'll remember that `monday.date` contains the text value of `"Monday, August 25 2003"` and **date_txt** is the name of the text field in the bottom-left portion of the screen. As a result of this action, `"Monday, August 25 2003"` will be displayed in the **date_txt** text field.

You can begin to see how dynamically named variables can be useful. If the variable `day` had a value of `"tuesday"`, this line of code would reference the `date` variable in the object called `tuesday`.

4) With the current frame still selected, add this script to the end of the `refresh()` function:

```
days_mc.gotoAndStop(day);
icon_mc.gotoAndStop(this[day].weather[0]);
weatherBlurb_txt.text = this[day].weather[1];
```

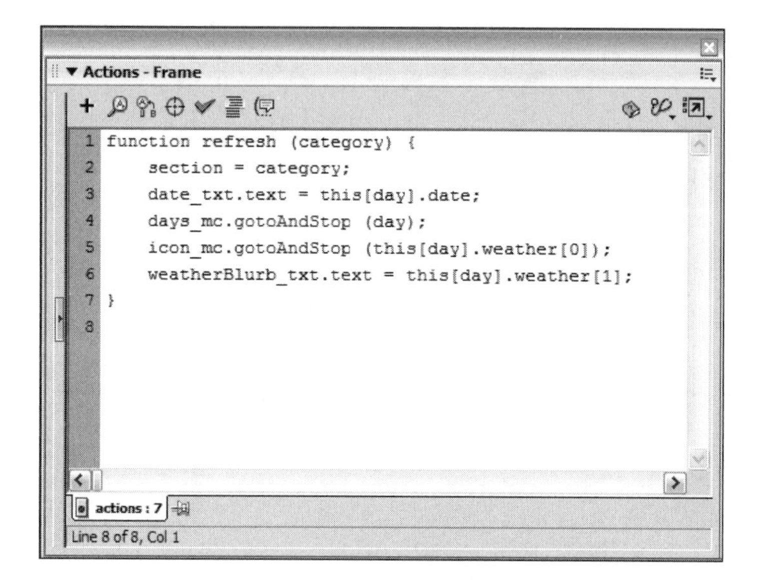

These three actions depend on the current value of `day` (which we set to an initial value of `"monday"` in Step 1) when they are executed. Here's how.

The movie clip instance named **days_mc** in the bottom-right portion of the stage contains five buttons (M, T, W, T, and F, with instance names of **monday_btn** through **friday_btn**) that will enable the user to select the day's news that he or she wishes to see. This movie clip also contains five frame labels (Monday, Tuesday, and so on), one for each day of the business week. Each of the frame labels displays a different day in yellow. The first line of the script tells the **days_mc** movie clip instance to go to the appropriate frame, based on the current value of `day`. This cues the user to which day's news he or she is viewing. Because `day` has an initial value of `"monday"`, that day will initially appear in yellow.

The weather icon (instance name **icon_mc**) contains three frame labels, one for each weather type (Sunny, Stormy, and Rainy). Remember that the zero element of the `weather` array in the `monday` and `tuesday` objects contains one of these three values. The second line of the script dynamically pulls that value from the `weather` array using the correct object and sends the **icon_mc** movie clip instance to the correct frame. Flash sees :

```
icon_mc.gotoAndStop(this[day].weather[0]);
```

as

```
icon_mc.gotoAndStop(this.monday.weather[0]);
```

Let's take it a step further. Consider that `monday.weather[0]` has a value of `"Rainy"`:

```
icon_mc.gotoAndStop("rainy");
```

In the same way, the last action will populate the **weatherBlurb_txt** text field with the value of `monday.weather[1]`, which is `"Very wet"`.

Keep in mind that if `day` had a value of `"tuesday"`, these actions would be executed based on the respective values in the `tuesday` object.

5) Add this script to end of the `refresh()` function:

```
high_txt.text = this[day].weather[2];
low_txt.text = this[day].weather[3];
```

Using the same syntax as in the preceding step, the **high_txt** and **low_txt** text fields are populated by referencing the second and third elements of the `weather` array dynamically.

6) Add these actions to the `refresh()` function:

```
headline_txt.text = this[day][section][0];
article_txt.text = this[day][section][1];
author_txt.text = this[day][section][2];
```

The dynamic referencing performed in this step is one level deeper into the storage objects than the dynamic referencing was in Step 5. We're trying to dynamically pull information about a news article from an object and an array because the day can be either Monday or Tuesday and the section can be Entertainment, Politics, Sports, or Technology. The initialization variables you set in Step 1 of this exercise set `section = "entertainment"`. Using the values of our initialization variables, Flash will read the three lines of ActionScript like this when the `refresh()` function is executed:

```
headline_txt.text = this.monday.entertainment[0];
article_txt.text = this.monday.entertainment[1];
author_txt.text = this.monday.entertainment[2];
```

The only text field instances affected by the current `section` variable are **headline_txt**, **article_txt**, and **author_txt**.

7) Add this function call to the end of the frame:

```
refresh(section);
```

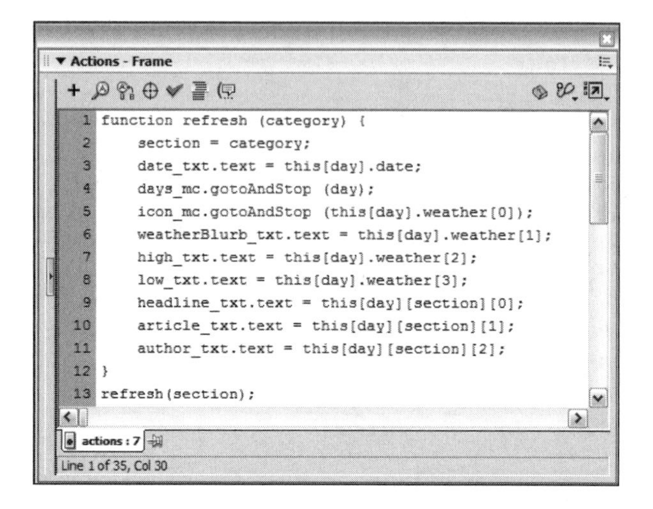

This script calls the function we created and passes it the current value of the `section` variable, to which we gave an initial value of `"entertainment"`. As a result, the function will cause our project to initially display Monday's entertainment news. Although the news displayed in our project will be highly dependent on choices the user makes by pressing buttons (which we will script momentarily), this function call has an initializing effect: it determines what is displayed before the user makes the first choice.

8) Enter a `stop()` action after the `refresh()` function.

When you test the movie, you don't want the entire movie to loop repeatedly. Instead, the movie will initialize the storage variables on Frame 1 and move to the Sit label and populate the text fields on the screen. The `stop()` action keeps the movie from playing past the Sit frame.

9) Choose Control > Test Movie.

Your on-screen text fields should be populated with information pertaining to Monday entertainment. The weather icon movie clip should display the correct icon, and the **days_mc** movie clip instance (on the bottom-right) should have the *M* (for Monday) highlighted.

10) Close the test movie to return to the authoring environment. Add this script to the bottom of the frame you have been working with:

```
entertainment_btn.onRelease = function() {
  refresh("entertainment");
};
```

This scripts the Entertainment button so that when it is released, the `refresh()` function is called and the string `"entertainment"` is passed as the section name. This changes the display to an entertainment-related article if one isn't already showing.

11) Add these button event handlers for the remaining three news section buttons:

```
sports_btn.onRelease = function() {
  refresh("sports");
};
politics_btn.onRelease = function() {
  refresh("politics");
};
technology_btn.onRelease = function() {
  refresh("technology");
};
```

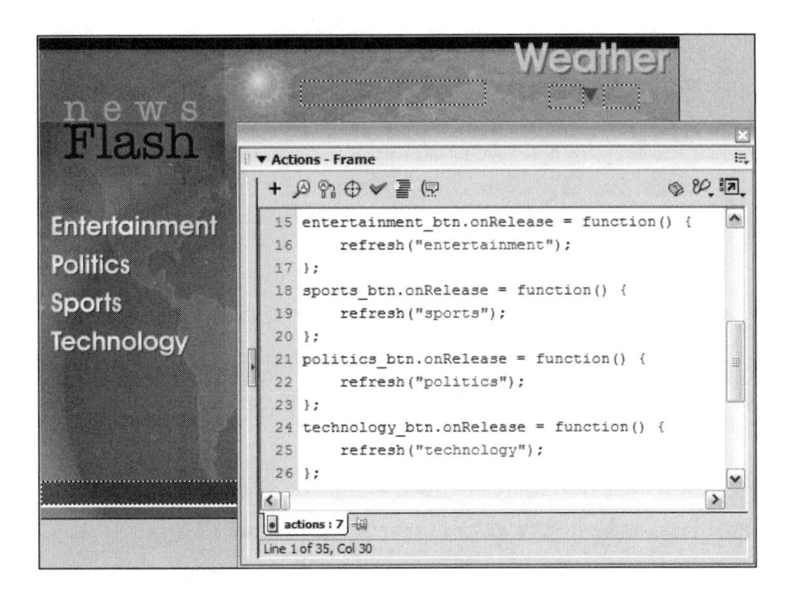

This script does the same thing the ActionScript attached to the Entertainment button does—the only difference is in the string value passed into the `refresh()` function. The Politics button passes in `"politics"`, the Sports button passes in `"sports"`, and the Technology button passes in `"technology"`.

12) Choose Control > Test Movie. Click the four category buttons to see the headlines, articles, and authors change.

The information should change very easily now. It would be easy to add more sections of news stories using this object-oriented technique.

13) Close the test movie to return to the authoring environment. Select the frame we've been adding script to and add these button event handlers for the buttons found in the *days_mc* movie clip instance:

```
days_mc.monday_btn.onRelease = function() {
  day = "monday";
  refresh("entertainment");
};
days_mc.tuesday_btn.onRelease = function() {
  day = "tuesday";
  refresh("entertainment");
};
```

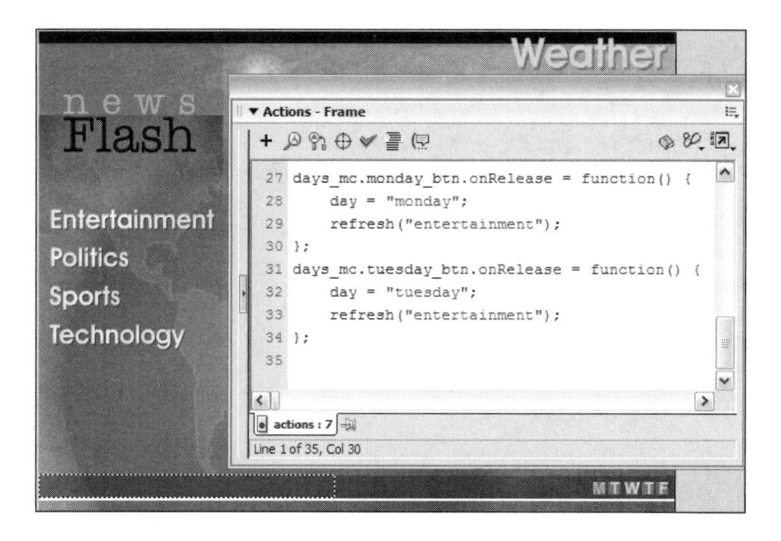

Earlier in this exercise, we mentioned that the **days_mc** movie clip contains five buttons for the five business days of the week. They are named **monday_btn** through **friday_btn**. In this step we add event handlers for the `onRelease` event of the **monday_btn** and **tuesday_btn** buttons.

When the **monday_btn** button is released, it changes the `day` variable to `"monday"` and calls the `refresh()` function, passing `"entertainment"`. This action changes the current day to `"monday"` and the current news section to `"entertainment"`. Likewise, when the **tuesday_btn** is released, the `day` variable to changed to `"tuesday"` and the news section is changed to `"entertainment"`.

14) Choose Control > Test Movie. Click the M and T on the bottom-right of the screen to change the display. Notice that the weather and date change.

The way we've coded this makes it easy to add day objects without changing the information retrieval code.

15) Close the test movie and save your work as *newsFlash5.fla*.

You have completed a project in which displayed information is retrieved dynamically from a logical storage structure. The next logical step in a project like this would be to put all of our project's data into a database or text file. The information would then be grabbed and routed into the storage structure you created. We'll cover loading information in and out of Flash in Lesson 11, "Getting Data In and Out of Flash," and Lesson 12, "Using XML with Flash."

BUILDING EXPRESSIONS

As we mentioned earlier in this lesson, an expression is a phrase—or a collection of variables, numbers, text, and operators—that evaluates to a value. To understand this concept, take a look at this example:

```
var oneDozen:Number = 6 * 2;
```

To the right of the equals sign, you see `6 * 2`—this is an expression. When this script is executed, the expression `6 * 2` is replaced by the result of 6 multiplied by 2, or 12. Thus, `oneDozen` equals 12.

An expression can contain variables, arrays, even function calls—anything that, when evaluated, returns a value. For example:

```
var total:Number = subTotal + tax;
```

The value of `total` is based on the result of adding the variable `subTotal` to the variable `tax`. The expression is `subTotal + tax`.

```
var discount:Number = totalPrice * employeeDiscount[2];
```

The value of `discount` is based on the result of multiplying the variable `totalPrice` by the value of the third element in the `employeeDiscount` array; `totalPrice * employeeDiscount[2]` is the expression.

Here:

```
var usDollars:Number = 10;
var japaneseYen:Number = convertToYen(usDollars);
```

the value of `japaneseYen` is based on the value returned by a call to the `convertToYen()` function—making the function call itself the expression.

NOTE *For more information about functions, see Lesson 5, "Using Functions."*

Expressions are used to do the following:

- Set variable values
- Set array element values
- Determine whether conditions are being met (using the comparison operators)
- Dynamically name movie clips, variables, and objects
- Call functions dynamically
- And more

Expressions enable you to avoid hard-coding values that will remain the same no matter what. By assigning and manipulating values via expressions, you can make the data used by your scripts dynamic—resulting in more interactive projects. Many of the scripts in this book rely on expressions—that's because without them, your project plays back in exactly the same way each time it's viewed.

OPERATORS

Operators are the marks within an expression that control the way in which the expression's values are evaluated. The operators you use will depend on the ways in which you need to manipulate values.

NOTE *In this section we review both arithmetic and string operators. For information about logical and comparison operators, see Lesson 8, "Using Conditional Logic."*

ARITHMETIC OPERATORS

Even if you're not very familiar with ActionScript, you'll recognize most of the arithmetic operators. These operators are used in expressions to manipulate numeric values.

- **Addition operator (+).** Adds two numeric values together. For example, `var totalCost:Number = productPrice + tax` adds the two variables to arrive at a final result.
- **Increment operator (++).** A shorthand method for adding 1 to a value. For example, `++myAge` increases the value of the `myAge` variable by 1—the equivalent of `myAge = myAge + 1;`
- **Subtraction operator (–).** This operator subtracts two values and can be used in the same way as the addition operator. For example, `var moneyInWallet = paycheck - moneySpent` subtracts one value from another to return a new number.

- **Decrement operator (--).** This operator reduces the value of a variable by 1. For example, `--bottlesOfBeerOnTheWall` takes a bottle of beer from the wall.
- **Multiplication operator (*).** This operator multiplies one numeric value by another. For example, in `var hoursPerWeek:Number = 24 * 7` the number of hours per week is the product of these two numbers being multiplied together.
- **Division operator (/).** Divides one numeric value by another. For example: `var hourlyRate:Number = payCheck / hoursBilled` divides the value of `hoursBilled` into the value of `payCheck`.
- **Modulo operator (%).** Divides the value on the left by the value on the right and returns the value of the remainder. For example, in `4 % 2` the result would be 0 because 4 can be evenly divided by 2; hence there is no remainder. In `7 % 3`, the result is 1 because 3 divides into 7 twice with a remainder of 1. Here's an illustration of how it works:

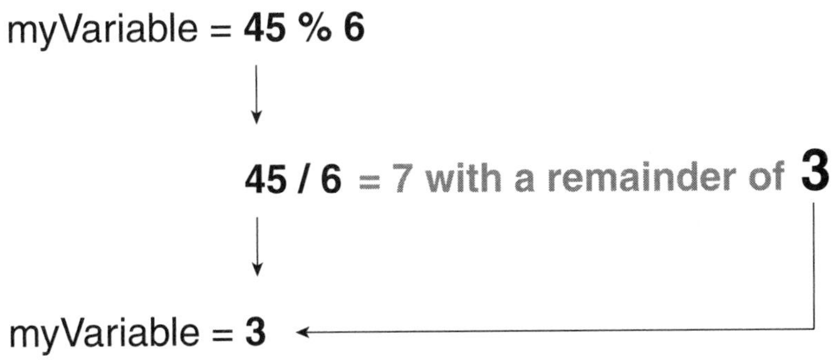

myVariable = **45 % 6**

↓

45 / 6 = 7 with a remainder of **3**

↓

myVariable = **3** ←

STRING OPERATORS

Unlike numbers, which can be manipulated using several different operators, strings can be manipulated by only one operator—the concatenation operator (they can also be manipulated using various methods of the String class, however). Although other operators work with strings (namely assignment operators and comparison operators), they cannot be used to *directly* manipulate a string. (For more on comparison operators, see Lesson 8, "Using Conditional Logic.")

- **Concatenation operator (+).** Concatenation means to link or join two or more things—exactly what this operator does with strings of text in ActionScript. The concatenation operator—which uses the same symbol as the addition operator—joins two text strings to create a single string. For example:

  ```
  var birthDayMessage:String = "You are " + age + " years old.";
  ```

  If `age` has a value of `26`, then the plus symbol joins the three parts of the message together to form "You are 26 years old."

PRECEDENCE

Expressions can often include several operators. When this is the case, it's important to understand the order in which parts of the expression are evaluated, or the *order of precedence*. A value can't be involved in two mathematical operations simultaneously—that is, you can't subtract from a value at the same time you're using that value to multiply another number (like the `5` in the expression `var myNumber:Number = 20 * 5 - 3;` in which one of these evaluations must be completed before the other can begin). Based on the rules of precedence, expressions are evaluated in this order:

1. Data in parentheses is evaluated before data outside parentheses. For precise control over how an expression is evaluated, you can nest part of an expression in parentheses.
2. Multiplication and division are evaluated before addition or subtraction. Because multiplication and division have equal precedence, evaluation occurs from left to right when both are used (in the absence of parentheses).
3. Addition and subtraction are evaluated last. Because these operations have equal precedence, evaluation occurs from left to right when both are used (in the absence of parentheses).

Let's take a look at a few examples:

```
var myVariable:Number = 5 + 7 - 3;
```

Because addition and subtraction have the same precedence, this expression is simply evaluated from left to right, with `myVariable` being assigned a value of 9.

```
var myVariable:Number = 5 + 7 * 3;
```

Because multiplication takes precedence over addition, 7 is multiplied by 3, then 5 is added to that result. In the end, `myVariable` is assigned a value of 26.

```
var myVariable:Number = (5 + 7) * 3;
```

Because data in parentheses takes precedence, 5 is added to 7, then that result is multiplied by 3. In the end, `myVariable` is assigned a value of 36.

```
var myVariable:Number = ((2 + 8) * (4 - 2)) / 5;
```

Even though multiplication and division usually take precedence over addition and subtraction, nested parentheses are used to add 2 to 8, then to subtract 2 from 4. These two results are multiplied, then divided by 5. The result is that `myVariable` is assigned a value of 4. Here is an illustration of this operation:

```
var myVariable:Number = ((2 + 8) * (4 - 2)) / 5
                ↓
myVariable = (10 * 2) / 5
                ↓
myVariable = 20 / 5
                ↓
myVariable = 4
```

MANIPULATING NUMERICAL DATA USING MATH

Earlier in this lesson, we introduced you to the numeric operators, which perform simple arithmetic in your expressions. Flash's Math class allows you to access a variety of useful methods for further manipulating numbers. We'll introduce a few of the most commonly used methods of the Math class here. You'll use many of the other methods in other lessons in this book.

Common methods of the Math class include:

- `Math.abs()` The absolute-value method is used to return the scalar (positive) value of a number. For example: `var distance:Number = Math.abs(here - there);` If subtracting the value of `there` from `here` results in a negative value (for example, –375), the `Math.abs` method will convert it to a positive value (for example, 375), ensuring a positive result.
- `Math.round()` The round method accepts a number as a parameter and returns an integer. If the digit in the tenth placeholder of the number is 5 or greater, the number is rounded to the next highest integer; if it's less than 5, it's rounded to the next lowest integer. For example: `var cupsOfCoffee:Number = Math.round(3.7);` Because 7 is greater than or equal to 5, this number is rounded up to the next highest integer, 4.
- `Math.floor()` This method works like `Math.round()` except that it always rounds down to the next lowest integer.
- `Math.ceil()` This method works like `Math.round()` except that it always rounds up to the next highest integer.
- `Math.sqrt()` The square-root method accepts a positive number as an argument and returns the square root of that number. For example: `var answer:Number = Math.sqrt(9); answer;` is assigned a value of 3.

In this exercise, using operators, expressions, and Math class methods, you will write a simple algorithm that will convert Fahrenheit temperatures to Celsius. You will also program a thermometer to display the correct mercury level.

1) Open *tempConverter1.fla* in the Lesson06/Assets folder.

All of the symbols and text fields have been created and are on the stage so that we can focus on ActionScript. The main timeline contains four layers: Actions, Thermometer, Temperature Input, and Background.

The Background layer contains the main graphics. The Temperature Input layer contains an input text field with an instance name of **temperature_txt**. This is where the temperature to be converted will be input. This layer also contains two additional text fields, **fahrenheit_txt** and **celsius_txt**, which will be used to display those values. Also on this layer is a button containing the text "Convert." The Thermometer layer contains a movie clip instance named **mercury_mc** that will be scaled vertically to indicate the proper temperature.

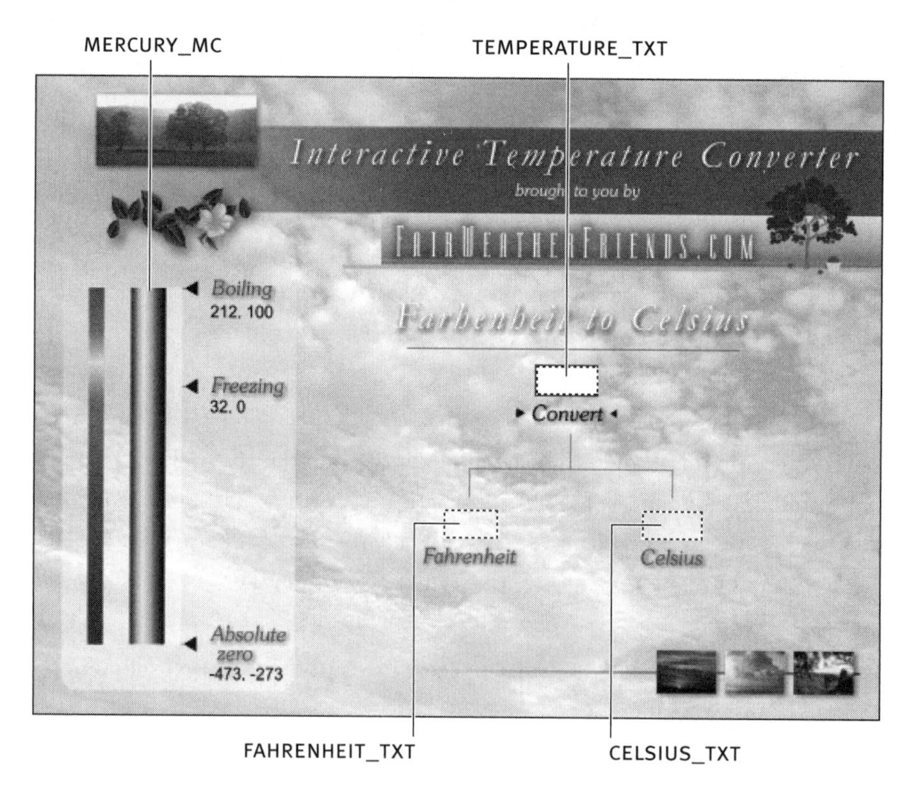

2) With the Actions panel open, select Frame 1 of the Actions layer and add the script:

```
function changeTemp () {
}
```

The script represents the beginning of a function definition. Ultimately, this function will be executed when the Convert button is pressed, and it will do the following:

1. Convert a Fahrenheit value to Celsius.
2. Make sure that the Fahrenheit value entered to convert is within the range on the thermometer.
3. Scale the mercury on the thermometer to the correct height.

3) At the beginning of the function definition you started in the preceding step, create these variables:

```
var boilingPoint:Number = 212;
var absoluteZero:Number = -460;
```

Our thermometer covers a large temperature range—from absolute zero (approximately –460 degrees Fahrenheit) to the boiling point of water (212 degrees Fahrenheit), temperatures that will be treated as the highest and lowest acceptable input temperatures.

4) To ensure that the input temperature is within acceptable limits, add this script after `var absoluteZero:Number = -460`**:**

```
if (temperature_txt.text > boilingPoint) {
  temperature_txt.text = boilingPoint;
} else if (temperature_txt.text < absoluteZero) {
  temperature_txt.text = absoluteZero;
}
fahrenheit_txt.text = temperature_txt.text;
```

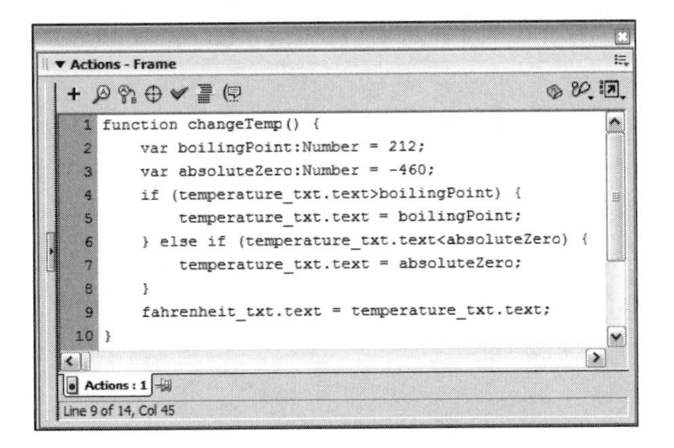

This part of the function is an `if/else if` statement that acts as a data filter. It says that if the value the user inputs (`temperature_txt.text`) is greater than the value of `boilingPoint` (which is 212), the user-input value will be automatically set *to* the value of `boilingPoint`. Otherwise, if the user inputs a value less than `absoluteZero`

(–460), that value will be automatically set to the value of absoluteZero. After the filter, the value of temperature_txt.text is set to display in the **fahrenheit_txt** text field instance.

Filter statements such as this are used frequently in programming because functions rarely accept all possible input extremes.

5) After the statement we added in the preceding step, add this expression, which is used to convert Fahrenheit to Celsius:

```
celsius_txt.text = Math.round((5 / 9) * fahrenheit_txt.text - 17.777);
```

The expression to the right of the equal sign converts a Fahrenheit value to Celsius. This expression sets the value of celsius_txt.text, which is the name of the corresponding text field on the stage. This line is used to display the converted value in that text field.

Notice the use of parentheses in the expression. As Flash executes this line of code, it will evaluate the first part of the expression that it can find that is fully enclosed in parentheses (in this case, 5 / 9). Flash performs the multiplication, then the subtraction. The Math.round() method is not invoked until its entire argument is evaluated and replaced with a numeric result. This method will then round the final, resulting value to the next integer up or down, depending on the value in the tenth place of the argument.

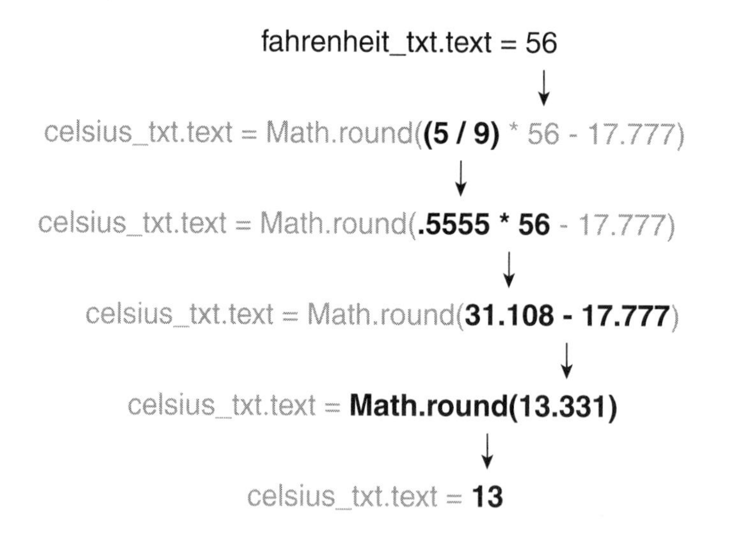

6) Add these lines at the end of the current script:

```
var scalePercent:Number = (Math.abs(absoluteZero - fahrenheit_txt.text) /
Math.abs(absoluteZero - boilingPoint)) * 100;
mercury_mc._yScale = scalePercent;
```

These two lines first create a variable to store the percent used to scale the **mercury_mc** movie clip instance; then they use that value to scale it.

The expression used to set the value of `scalePercent` is based on the ratio of the difference between absolute zero and the temperature submitted when compared against the full temperature range. To help you understand, let's assume that the user has entered a value of 56 in the **fahrenheit_txt** text field. We know that `absoluteZero` equals –460 and that `boilingPoint` equals 212. The expression is evaluated like this:

```
(Math.abs(-460 - 56) / (Math.abs(-460 - 212)) * 100;
```

or

```
(Math.abs(-516) / (Math.abs(-672)) * 100;
```

or

```
((516) / (672)) * 100;
```

or

```
(.767) * 100
```

or

```
76.7
```

The absolute-value method of the Math class is used here to ensure that the expression evaluates to a positive percentage value. (A negative percentage value wouldn't make sense in the context of this script.)

The second line of the script scales the **mercury_mc** movie clip instance vertically using the value of `scalePercent`. Thus, the instance is scaled to 76.7 percent of its original value, which works well because the **mercury_mc** movie clip was built in Flash to be the maximum height when at normal size (100 percent).

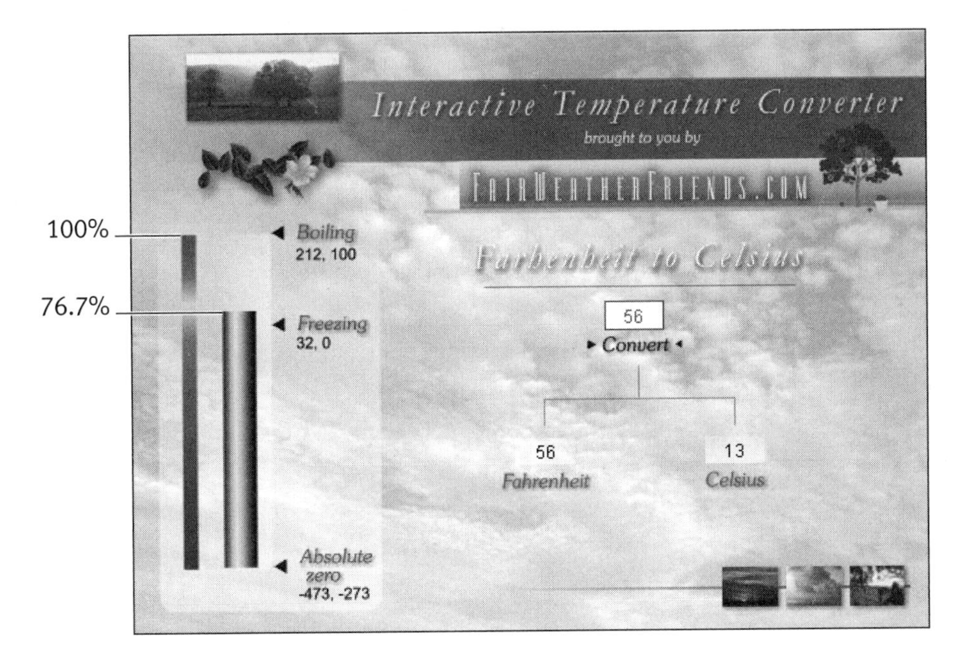

7) Add this button event handler to the selected frame (outside and below the `changeTemp()` function definition):

```
convert_btn.onRelease = function() {
  changeTemp();
};
```

When the **convert_btn** button is released, the `changeTemp()` function you just built will be called.

8) Choose Control > Test Movie. Enter a temperature value and press the button.

When the button is pressed, you'll see the **mercury_mc** movie clip scale appropriately. The **celsius_txt** and **fahrenheit_txt** fields on the screen will also get populated with data. Try entering a temperature that falls outside the acceptable range, and you'll see that the filter `if/else if` statement catches and replaces it with either the upper or lower boundary.

9) Close the test movie and save your work as *tempConverter2.fla*.

You have now used the Math class in an expression. With it, you converted Fahrenheit to Celsius and scaled a movie clip based on a percent calculated.

MANIPULATING STRINGS

So far, we've dealt mostly with numbers. Now it's time to learn about the powerful methods of the String class, to which you were introduced in Lesson 4, "Using Object Classes." Using String class methods, you can find specific characters in a string, change the case of the string, reverse the characters in the string, and more.

Here are some of the most commonly used String class methods:

- `length` This String class property returns the number of characters in a string. For example: `var numCharacters:Number = userName.length;` Here the value of `numCharacters` is based on the number of characters in the `userName` variable. If `userName` is `"Jobe"`, the result is `4`.
- `substr(start, length)` The `substring()` method, which returns part of a string, accepts two parameters: starting index and the length (or number) of characters to count (including starting character). If the length parameter is omitted, this method will by default count until the end of the string. For example: `name.substr(1, 2);` If the value of `name` is `"Kelly"`, the result would be `"el"`. The letter `e` has an index of 1, and the number `2` tells the substring to include two letters.

- `toLowerCase()` This method forces all of the letters in a string to be lowercase. For example: `message.toLowerCase();` If the value of `message` is `"Hello"`, the result is `"hello"`.
- `toUpperCase()` This method forces all of the letters in a string to be uppercase. For example: `message.toUpperCase();` If the value of `message` is `"Hello"`, the result is `"HELLO"`.

NOTE *As explained in Lesson 4, "Using Object Classes," the* `text` *property of a text field instance can also be considered an instance of the String class—and can be manipulated as such. For example,* `myTextField_txt.text.toUpperCase();` *causes all the text in the* ***myTextField_txt*** *text field to appear in uppercase letters.*

In this exercise, you create a simple, silly word-game application. You enter words in a basic form, and a paragraph will be generated.

1) Open *madlibs1.fla* in the Lesson06/Assets folder.

This file includes three layers: Background, Text Fields, and Actions. The Background layer contains the main site graphics. The Text Fields layer contains five input text fields, a dynamic display text field, and a Submit button (we'll use the Actions layer in a moment).

The five input text fields are, from the top down, **verb1_txt**, **propernoun_txt**, **verb2_txt**, **adjective_txt**, and **noun_txt**. These will allow the user to enter words that will be used to generate the paragraph. The bigger text field at the bottom-right of the stage is named **paragraph_txt** and will be used to display the paragraph.

2) With the Actions panel open, select Frame 1 of the Actions layer and add the following script:

```
function generate () {
}
```

This is the beginning of a function definition. This function will be called when the Submit button is pressed. The final version of this function will take all the user-input words and modify them when needed. A sentence of text will be generated that includes these input words.

3) With Frame 1 still selected, add these four lines to the `generate()` function definition:

```
verb1_txt.text = verb1_txt.text.toLowerCase();
verb2_txt.text = verb2_txt.text.toLowerCase();
adjective_txt.text = adjective_txt.text.toLowerCase();
noun_txt.text = noun_txt.text.toLowerCase();
```

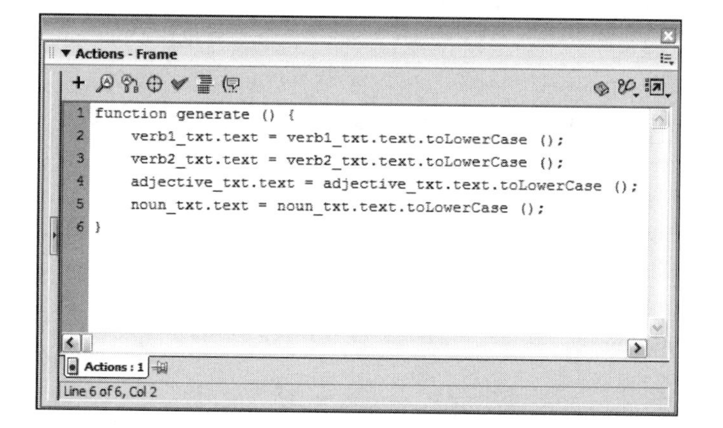

These four actions force the text entered into the corresponding text fields to be lowercase—primarily for grammatical reasons (none of these fields will include proper nouns or represent the first word in the sentence).

4) Add the following script to the end of the current `generate()` function, after `noun_txt.text = noun_txt.text.toLowerCase():`

```
propernoun_txt.text = propernoun_txt.text.substr(0, 1).toUpperCase() +
⇒propernoun_txt.text.substr(1).toLowerCase();
```

In the script, propernoun_txt.text makes reference to the **propernoun_txt** text field on the stage, which is used to enter a person's name. For grammatical reasons, the leading character in a person's name (that is, the character at index 0) should be capitalized and the rest of the letters lowercased. To ensure that this is the case, we use the substr() method in our expression. You can use two methods concurrently and in a contiguous fashion.

First, propernoun_txt.text.substr(0, 1) returns the first letter of the value of propernoun_txt.text, which it is then forced to uppercase by the toUpperCase() method. The string concatenation operator (+) is then used to concatenate the first half of the expression with the second. The second half also uses the substr() method. The difference here is that it begins counting with the character at index 1 (the second letter). Because the length value (the second parameter of the substr() method) is not specified, it finds the rest of the characters in the string and uses the toLowerCase() method to make those letters lowercase.

As a result, "kelly" would be changed to "Kelly", and "kElLy" to "Kelly".

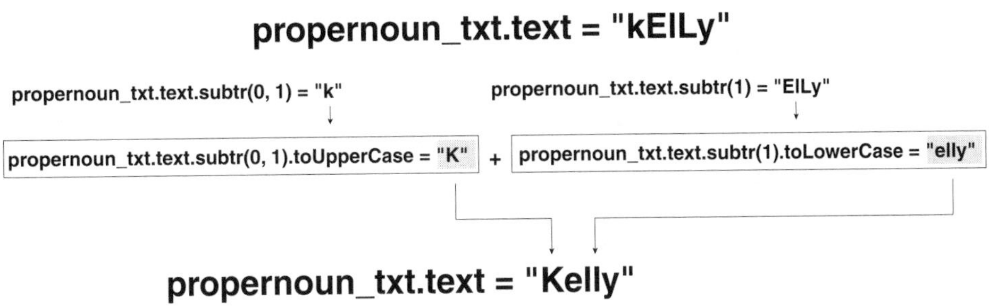

propernoun_txt.text = "kElLy"

propernoun_txt.text.subtr(0, 1) = "k"

propernoun_txt.text.subtr(1) = "ElLy"

propernoun_txt.text.subtr(0, 1).toUpperCase = "K" + propernoun_txt.text.subtr(1).toLowerCase = "elly"

propernoun_txt.text = "Kelly"

5) Add this line of script to the generate() function:

```
paragraph_txt.text = "You " + verb1_txt.text + " into love with " +
⇒propernoun_txt.text + " when you " + verb2_txt.text + " " + propernoun_txt.text
⇒+ " eating a " + adjective_txt.text + " "+noun_txt.text + ".";
```

This script uses the concatenation operator several times to insert various variable values in hard-coded text strings to build a complete sentence.

NOTE *When concatenating several strings, be careful that each string section has opening and closing quotes; if any are missing, an error will result.*

6) Add this button event handler to the bottom of the frame:

```
generate_btn.onRelease = function() {
  generate();
};
```

When the button is released, the `generate()` function you just created will be called.

7) Choose Control > Test Movie.

Enter text into each of the input text boxes, press the Submit button, and read the sentence you created. Try it again, this time entering text with varying case. You'll see how easy it is to manipulate strings with ActionScript.

8) Close the test movie and save your work as *madlibs2.fla*.

Now you know something about using methods of the String class—an important aspect of learning ActionScript, since text plays an important role in many projects and you need to know how to manipulate it. The exercises in this section introduced you to the basics. As you continue through the book, you'll find additional examples of ways to control text to suit your project's needs.

WHAT YOU HAVE LEARNED

In this lesson, you have:

- Learned about and created variables (pages 196–203)
- Created arrays and accessed them dynamically (pages 203–207)
- Created text fields and learned the common uses of each type (pages 208–213)
- Stored information in objects and retrieved it dynamically (pages 213–221)
- Explored expressions (pages 221–223)
- Learned about precedence in ActionScript (pages 224–225)
- Used the Math class to modify data (pages 225–230)
- Used the String class to modify strings and build a sentence (pages 230–234)

creating custom classes

LESSON 7

As an ActionScript programmer, you can create an unlimited variety of applications. The more experience you gain, the more you'll realize how often you end up writing code that performs certain custom tasks over and over again. For example, let's say that last month you created an address book application for a client. This month you learn that you need to create an employee directory for the same client. Immediately you'll notice that there are many similar features between an address book and an employee directory. In fact, an employee directory may have all the features of the address book, plus some extras. If you created an address book class for the address book application, you would be able to reuse it for the employee directory application.

In this lesson, you will create several custom classes whose functionality will be plugged into several movie clips, allowing instances of those clips to perform customized tasks.

Creating custom classes helps promote code reusability and is essential for well-written object-oriented programming. In this lesson, you will be introduced to the syntax and concepts needed to create custom classes and you will gain experience writing your own classes.

WHAT YOU WILL LEARN

In this lesson, you will:

- Learn class syntax and terminology
- Learn about classpaths and how they're used
- Learn about private, public, and static members, and how to use them
- Use inheritance to extend a class
- Use overriding
- Create custom object classes
- Associate a custom class with a movie clip in the library

APPROXIMATE TIME

This lesson takes approximately two hours to complete.

LESSON FILES

Starting Files:

Lesson07/Assets/CurrencyConverter1.fla
Lesson07/Assets/PetParade1.fla

Completed Projects:

CurrencyConverter2.fla
PetParade2.fla
Animal.as
Dog.as
Cat.as

CLASSES, TOP-LEVEL CLASSES, AND INSTANCES

Basically, a *class* is a definition or blueprint of how an object is made up and how it should act. For example, an instance of the Array class (an Array object) can store multiple pieces of information in numerically indexed locations (`myArray[0]`, `myArray[1]`, `myArray[2]`, and so on). How can the array do this? It knows how to do this because it was defined that way by the Array class. The Array class has hidden logic and definitions (code) that work behind the scenes to define the way an Array object works and how it's used. Think of a class as a template from which objects are created. This is a vague description of a class, but as you progress through this lesson and are introduced to more concepts, terminology, and examples, you'll gain a better understanding of what a class really is.

A class generally exists to produce an instance of itself on demand. You create an instance of a class by invoking the *constructor method* of that class. For example:

```
var myArray:Array = new Array():
```

The action to the right of the equals sign, `new Array()` in this example, executes the constructor method of the Array class. You cannot use the Array class directly. You must create an instance of the class to use any of its properties and methods. When creating the array instance, the Array class creates an object and then populates it with properties and methods. In a sense, the Array class is similar to a factory for array objects. When asked, it creates and returns an Array object.

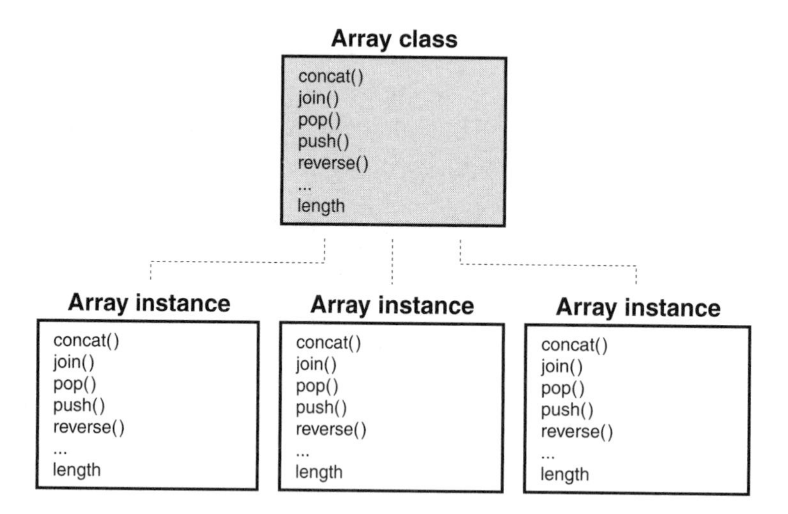

There also are classes that you can use without the need to create an instance. This type of a class is called a *top-level* class. Examples of this type of class include the Math, Mouse, and Key classes. When you think about it, top-level classes make sense. Is there ever really a need to have more than one instance of the Mouse class or the Math class? With the Math class, you simply pass a number into a method and a result is returned. The Math class doesn't store any of the information that you feed it, so only one copy is needed. On the other hand, arrays store unique data, so it wouldn't make sense to access the Array class directly because you would only be able to have one array.

TIP *Some programmers call a top-level class a* singleton.

CREATING A CLASS

The code for defining an ActionScript class exists in its own **.as** file (remember that the **.as** file extension stands for *A*ction*S*cript). Only one class can be defined per file. If you create 13 classes, you have to create 13 **.as** files. A class file is nothing more than a text file containing ActionScript code. The name of each class file is the name of the class followed by the **.as** file extension. For example, if you create a TestClass class, it has to exist in a file with this exact name: **TestClass.as**.

NOTE *It's considered good coding practice to give classes a name beginning with an uppercase letter.*

A class file can be created from within the Macromedia Flash authoring environment by opening the ActionScript editor (File > New > ActionScript File) or by using the text editor of your choice, such as Notepad. Using the built-in editor offers the advantage of built-in features such as code hinting that make the job of creating a custom ActionScript class much easier.

Simply creating a text file with an **.as** extension doesn't automatically make it a functional class file. The contents of the file must be ActionScript whose syntax defines the class (including its methods and properties). For example, the following code, inside the **TestClass.as** file, is the beginning of a valid class file:

```
class TestClass {
}
```

The statement `class` tells the compiler (the part of Flash that handles the creation of SWF files) that everything that follows in this file is considered part of a class definition (for defining the TestClass class). After the `class` statement is the name of the class being created: TestClass. The name of the class must be the same as the name of the **.as** file that contains the code defining the class; therefore, the TestClass class definition must be in a file named **TestClass.as**.

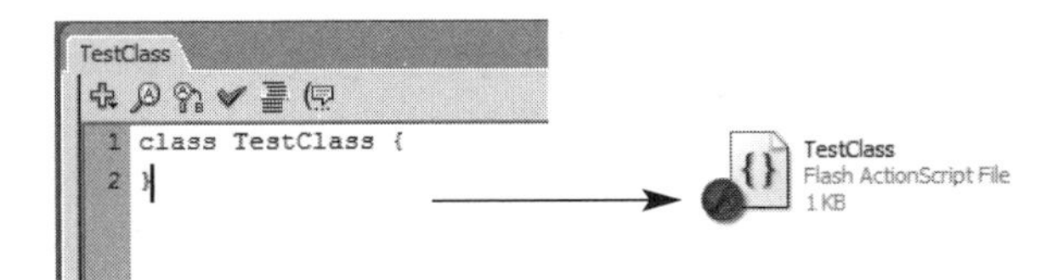

A class file defines characteristics about the class by creating properties and methods. The properties and methods of a class are referred to as *members*, and they are all defined within the outermost curly braces of the class. Consider the following example:

```
class Cube {
  var length:Number = 3;
  var height:Number = 2;
  var width:Number = 7;
  function getVolume():Number {
    return length * height * width;
  }
}
```

In this example, the properties `length`, `height`, and `width` and the method `getVolume()` are all members of the Cube class.

To create a new instance of a class to use its functionality in your project, the class must have a constructor method defined. The constructor must have the same name as the class. Let's modify the Cube class we just created to contain a constructor method and accept parameters so that we can create a custom cube instance:

```
class Cube {
  var length:Number;
  var height:Number;
  var width:Number;
  function Cube(tempLength:Number, tempHeight:Number,tempWidth:Number) {
    length = tempLength;
    height = tempHeight;
    width = tempWidth;
  }
  function getVolume():Number {
    return length * height * width;
  }
}
```

After coding the Cube class, you save it as an **.as** file named **Cube.as** in the same directory as your Flash authoring file. (Alternatively, you can place your **.as** class files elsewhere, which we'll discuss in a moment.) You would create a new instance of the Cube class on a frame in your Flash authoring file in the following way:

```
var myCube:Cube = new Cube(3, 2, 7);
```

You can then get the volume of the `myCube` object this way:

```
var volume:Number = myCube.getVolume();
```

By default, the properties and methods available to an instance of a class are fixed by the properties and methods defined in its class file. For example, the Cube class file defines three properties (`length`, `height`, and `width`) and one method (`getVolume()`). As a result, the myCube instance of the Cube class can access those particular properties and that method:

```
myCube.length //has a value of 3
myCube.height //has a value of 2
myCube.width //has a value of 7
myCube.getVolume() // returns a value of 42
```

The myCube properties can be set using the following syntax:

```
myCube.length = 6;
myCube.height = 4;
```

and so on. But if you attempt to add a property or method to the myCube instance that was not defined in its class file, such as:

```
myCube.color = "red";
```

an error will result when you export your movie. This principle helps you eliminate bugs in your code. Here's how. In your application, perhaps Cube instances shouldn't have color properties, and instead you meant to assign a color property to the myCup instance of the Cup class, which would have been acceptable. When you export your movie, Flash's compiler sees that you've set the color property for an instance of the Cube class. It then looks at the Cube class definition to see whether the color property has been defined there. If not, Flash assumes that the code is wrong, and an error results. This setup helps you to script object instances in a nearly foolproof manner; no object instance is allowed to perform an action unless that action is explicitly permitted by the class definition.

While this can be a great way to help you debug your applications—because Flash displays an error when you attempt to use an object in the wrong way—there may be times when you *do* want instances of a custom object class to be able to add or access properties and methods that were not defined in its class file. This is possible, too. You would simply need to add the dynamic class modifier to the class definition (notice the first line):

```
dynamic class Cube {
  var length:Number;
  var height:Number;
  var width:Number;
  function Cube(tempLength:Number, tempHeight:Number, tempWidth:Number) {
    length = tempLength;
    height = tempHeight;
    width = tempWidth;
  }
  function getVolume():Number {
    return length * height * width;
  }
}
```

With the addition of the `dynamic` modifier, all instances of the Cube class, including the `myCube` instance we created earlier, can add any property or method, regardless of whether that property or method was originally defined in the Cube class file.

NOTE *Some of Flash's built-in classes—for example, MovieClip, LoadVars, and SharedObject—are dynamic classes, which is why you can dynamically add properties and methods to instances of these classes. Other built-in classes—such as TextField and Sound—are not dynamic; if you attempt to add properties to instances of these classes, Flash displays errors when you export your movie.*

There are a couple important points to note about classes and class members.

Although you're not required to use strong typing syntax (`:Number`, `:Array`, `:String`, and so forth) when creating a class, this strategy is highly recommended. Strong typing is useful because it helps prevent bugs.

You can create instances of a custom class from any timeline within your project, in the same manner as you do with any of Flash's built-in classes; therefore, an instance of our custom Cube class can be created on the main timeline, or any movie clip's timeline.

THE CLASSPATH

So far you have been introduced to the basics of the class syntax and creating a class file. What you haven't yet learned is how class files relate to Flash authoring files—how they're used in tandem.

If you want to use a custom class in a Flash project to create instances of that class, Flash must know where to find its class file. This section explores how to instruct a Flash file to load and use a custom class. As with many things in Flash, there are several techniques.

When compiling an SWF file from an FLA file, Flash checks to see whether you created an instance of a custom class. If a custom class is being used, Flash attempts to load that custom class to include it inside the SWF file. The directories in which Flash searches for the class are called the *classpath*. If the class file is found within the classpath, the compiler includes the class in the SWF. If the class file is not found, the compiler reports an error.

Two classpaths are recognized when authoring an FLA file: one classpath is global, and the other is at document level. The global classpath is the same no matter which FLA file you're authoring. The document-level classpath can be changed for a specific FLA file without affecting the classpaths seen by other FLA files.

The Global Classpath

By default, the global classpath points to two separate directories. The first is the directory in which your current Flash document resides. For example, if you're editing an FLA that's saved on your hard drive in a directory called MyTest, the MyTest directory is recognized as a global classpath for that FLA. You can place class files used by your project in that directory and Flash will find them. The global classpath also points to the directory that contains the class files and interfaces for Flash's built-in classes.

NOTE *The global class directory can be found in the Flash MX 2004 program folder. On Windows XP, it's in the following location:*

Program Files\Macromedia\Flash MX 2004\en\First Run\Classes

Class files placed in this directory are immediately available for use by any **FLA** *you author.*

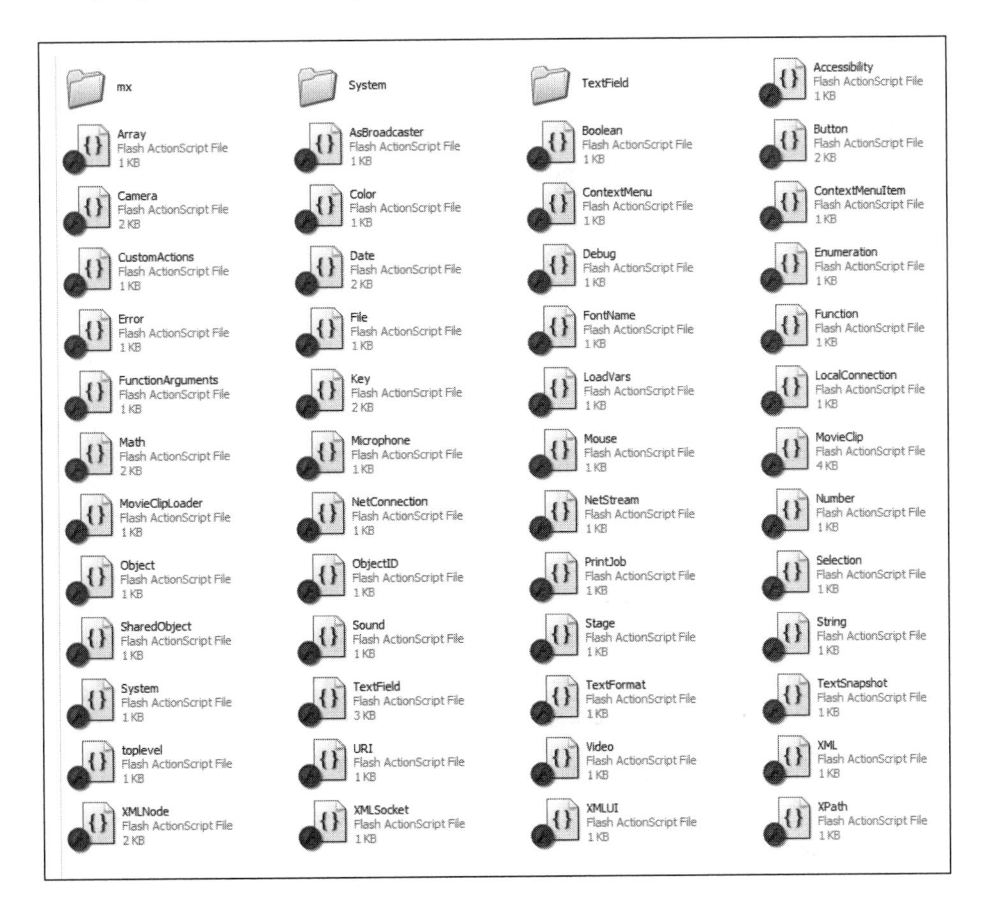

To understand how the classpath works, let's consider an example. If you create an instance of a custom class in an FLA, such as the following:

```
var addresses:AddressBook = new AddressBook();
```

during the compiling process (or when you select the Check Syntax option in the Actions panel), the global classpath will be searched for a file called **AddressBook.as**. If found, that file is loaded and included in the SWF. If no such file is found, you get a compile error.

You can edit the global classpath by adding or removing directories with the following process:

1) Select Edit > Preferences.

2) Click the ActionScript tab.

3) Click ActionScript 2.0 Settings.

4) Use the options in this dialog box to add to or edit the list of directories in the classpath.

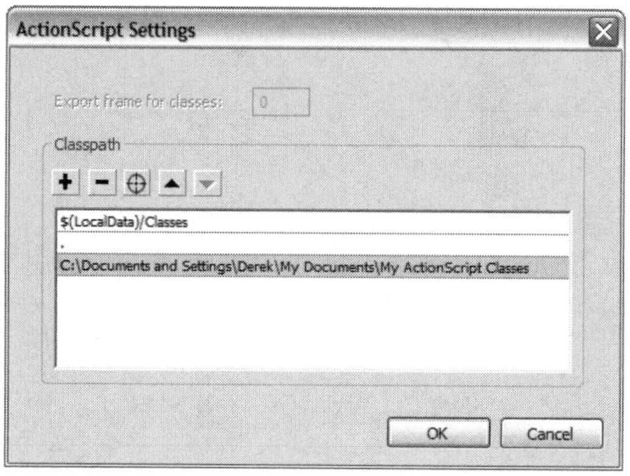

THE DOCUMENT-LEVEL CLASSPATH

The document-level classpath is empty by default. You can add any number of directories to this classpath to make Flash search for necessary classes while compiling an authoring file to an SWF. This classpath exists only for the current FLA file.

Editing the document-level classpath is a useful option when you want to specify a directory or list of directories that contain class files specific to the current application. If you added these directories to the global classpath, every FLA file or ActionScript file that you edited would include them in the search for the class files to add to an SWF during compile.

To edit the document-level classpath, follow these steps:

1) Select File > Publish Settings.

2) Select the Flash tab.

3) Click the Settings button next to ActionScript 2.0.

4) Use the options in this dialog box to add to or edit the list of directories in the classpath.

Notice that a field called Export Frame for Classes in this dialog box was dimmed in the global classpath version. By default, all class files included in the compiled SWF are initialized on Frame 1 of the movie. Including class files that beef up the SWF file size might cause a lag when loading the SWF file over the Internet, because the data from the class files must be downloaded to the end user's computer before Frame 1 can be rendered.

In many cases, including the class files adds only a tiny amount to the total SWF file size because these files are relatively small. But if you run into a problem when loading this data before Frame 1, you can change the frame number in the Export Frame for Classes field. For example, this would allow you to include a two- or three-frame loading animation in the first few frames of the SWF that loops while the data from the class files and the rest of the SWF are loaded.

PACKAGES AND IMPORTING CLASSES

You have learned that a classpath points to one or more directories. Each of these directories can contain class (**.as**) files. In addition to containing class files, a classpath directory can contain subdirectories. A subdirectory in a classpath directory is known as a *package*, and can contain class files and more directories, called *subpackages*.

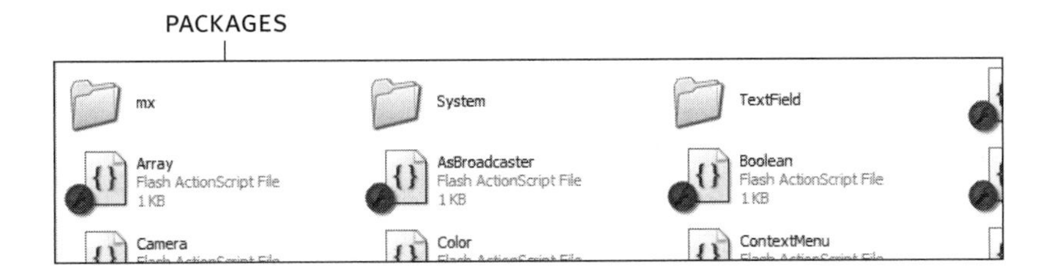

Keeping classes in packages is a good way to keep them organized. You might have hundreds of class files after just a few months of programming with Flash. Saving these classes in a logical directory structure makes them easier to locate, and can help you avoid class-name conflicts with multiple projects.

When you use packages, the class file syntax changes slightly, and can complicate instantiating an instance of that class.

As shown earlier, this is the basic syntax used to create a class called TestClass:

```
class TestClass {
  function TestClass() {
    //Constructor
  }
}
```

The rule that we didn't mention earlier is that the name declaration of the class must contain the path to the class file from the root classpath directory in which the class resides. The TestClass class above assumes that the class file is not in any package, but is sitting directly in a classpath directory. However, if we decided to create the TestClass class in a package called TestPackage, the class definition would look like this:

```
class TestPackage.TestClass {
  function TestClass() {
    //Constructor
  }
}
```

The text after the `class` keyword contains not only the name of the class (TestClass) but the overall path where it exists. In this case, TestClass exists inside the TestPackage directory, which itself exists in a classpath directory.

Suppose you created an address book class for Macromedia. Because you're a very organized person, you created a logical package (directory) structure for your class file. The class definition might look like this:

```
class Clients.Macromedia.AddressBook {
  function AddressBook() {
    //Constructor
  }
}
```

This class is contained in the Macromedia directory, which is in the Clients directory, which is in a classpath directory.

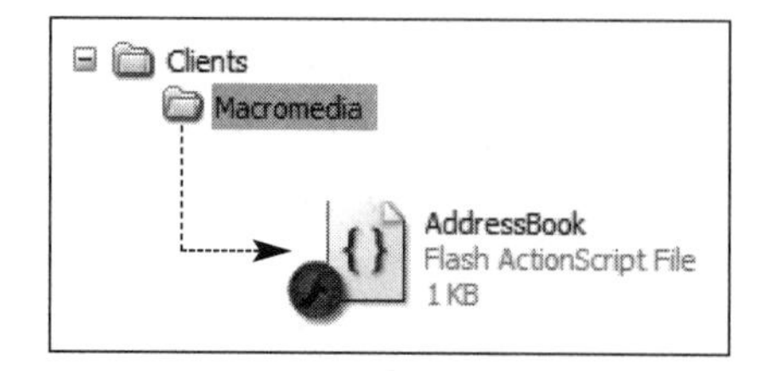

To create an instance of a class that's in a package, you must use the full package path. For example:

```
var myInstance:TestPackage.TestClass = new TestPackage.TestClass();
```

Notice that the data type and the constructor are referenced using the full path. As you can imagine, working with long class names such as this can make for a lot of typing if you're creating many instances. But there's a way to use the abbreviated name of your class (the class name without package path)—by *importing* the class. You can import a class by using the `import` statement followed by the path to the class. For example:

```
import TestPackage.TestClass;
```

After the `import` statement, you can work with the class by using the abbreviated name. For example:

```
import TestPackage.TestClass;
var myInstance:TestClass = new TestClass();
```

You can import all class files in a package by using an asterisk (*) in place of a class name. For example:

```
import TestPackage.*
```

This line of ActionScript imports all classes found in the TestPackage package. It doesn't import any classes from subpackages.

The `import` statement allows you to use the abbreviated class name only within the frame on which the statement appeared. If you import TestPackage on Frame 1, you cannot use the abbreviated name on Frame 2 unless Frame 2 also imports TestPackage.

You've been introduced to a lot of new concepts up to this point, and now it's time to get your hands dirty. In this exercise, you will create a simple custom class and use it in a Flash document.

1) Open Flash. Select File > New. Select ActionScript File from the list. Save the file as *CurrencyConverter.as*.

You have just created an empty ActionScript file that will contain a class called CurrencyConverter. This class will allow you to convert an amount of currency from U.S. dollars (USD) to Great Britain pounds (GBP) or vice versa.

Later in the exercise, you will add just a few lines of script to an **FLA** file to use the functionality of the CurrencyConverter class.

NOTE *When creating an ActionScript file, which in this case is a class file, Flash gives you a full-screen ActionScript window in which to type. You don't have access to the normal Flash user interface elements, such as the drawing tools or components.*

2) With the ActionScript file open, add the following line of ActionScript to start the class definition:

```
class CurrencyConverter {
```

The first word, `class`, tells Flash that what follows is a class definition. Not all ActionScript files contain a class, so this definition is necessary.

The text just after the `class` keyword is the name of the class. Remember that the name of the class must also contain the path to the class from a root classpath directory. The FLA file that will use this class (which we'll create in a moment) will be saved in the same directory as the class file (which is considered a global classpath); therefore, using just the name of the class is acceptable. If we decided to save this class file into a subdirectory called Currency, we would name the class Currency.CurrencyConverter.

The last character in the previous ActionScript is an opening curly brace (`{`). The last character that we will add in the class is the closing curly brace (`}`). Everything between these two braces defines the properties and methods of the class.

3) Add the following variable declaration on the next line:

```
var exchangeRate:Number;
```

The purpose of this class is to convert USD to GBP or GBP to USD. The `exchangeRate` variable stores the exchange rate ratio between GBP and USD. If the value of `exchangeRate` were 0.634731, for example, there would be .634731 GBP for one USD. This exchange rate will be used by a method of this class to convert the currency.

The value of the `exchangeRate` variable is set via the constructor method of the CurrencyConverter class, which we'll define next.

4) Add the following constructor method:

```
function CurrencyConverter(rate:Number) {
  exchangeRate = rate;
}
```

To use this class, you must be able to create an instance of it. A *constructor method* is a function that defines actions to take when creating a new instance of the class. It must have the same name as the class—but without the path to the class (if applicable).

This constructor method takes one parameter, rate, which is used to set the value of exchangeRate when an instance is created.

The way the constructor method is set up allows us to create a new instance of the CurrencyConverter class in the following manner:

```
var myConverter:CurrencyConverter = new CurrencyConverter(.54321);
```

5) Add the following method, which will be used to convert the currency:

```
function convert(convertTo:String, amount:Number):Number {
  var result:Number;
  if (convertTo == "USD") {
    return amount / exchangeRate;
  } else if (convertTo == "GBP") {
    return amount * exchangeRate;
  }
  return result;
}
```

This method definition is nothing more than a function, as you learned in Lesson 5, "Using Functions." We call it a *method* simply to indicate that it's a function specifically designed to work with a particular class—in this case, our custom CurrencyConverter class. This function accepts two parameters—convertTo and amount—and returns a numeric value that represents the converted value. The convertTo variable is a string that specifies to which currency type the amount parameter should be converted. If the amount should be converted to USD, the amount is divided by the value of exchangeRate to arrive at a result; otherwise, the amount is multiplied by the value of exchangeRate. The last line in this method returns the result variable.

6) Add a closing curly brace (}) on the last line of the class to close the definition. Save the file.

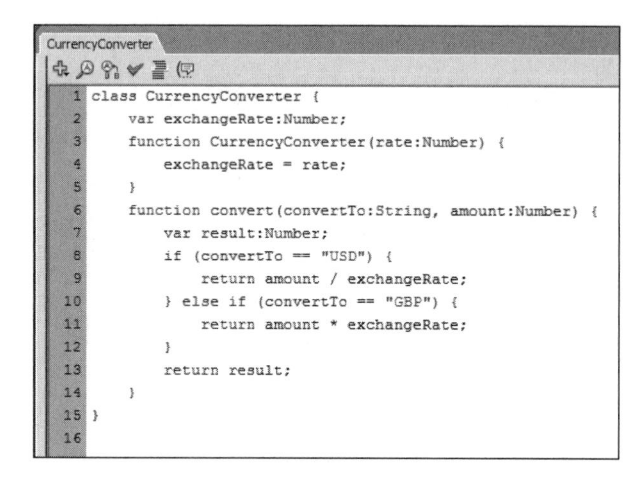
CurrencyConverter
class CurrencyConverter {
var exchangeRate:Number;
function CurrencyConverter(rate:Number) {
exchangeRate = rate;
}
function convert(convertTo:String, amount:Number) {
var result:Number;
if (convertTo == "USD") {
return amount / exchangeRate;
} else if (convertTo == "GBP") {
return amount * exchangeRate;
}
return result;
}
}

You have created a class file! The next thing that we need to do is create and use an instance of this class in a Flash movie.

7) Open *CurrencyConverter1.fla* in the Lesson07/Assets directory.

Notice that this FLA contains only one layer called Actions, and one frame. The objective of this exercise is simply to create a custom class and then learn how to use it in an FLA file. Over the next three steps you'll add the four lines of ActionScript needed to accomplish this goal.

8) Select Frame 1, open the Actions panel, and create the following variable:

```
var rate:Number = 0.634731;
```

This is the exchange rate that we'll pass into the constructor method of the CurrencyConverter class when creating a new instance of it. When we invoke the `convert()` method, it will use this value to perform the conversions.

9) Create a new instance of the CurrencyConverter class by adding this code:

```
var converter:CurrencyConverter = new CurrencyConverter(rate);
```

The name of the instance that we're creating is `converter`. It has a data type of CurrencyConverter. By using the statement `new CurrencyConverter(rate)`, we create a new instance of the CurrencyConverter class. The value of `rate` was passed in to set the exchange rate that this instance will use.

When the FLA is compiled into an SWF, the compiler sees that CurrencyConverter is used as if it were a class; therefore, the compiler searches the classpath directories for a class named CurrencyConverter. If the compiler finds the class, it adds the class to the SWF. If the compiler doesn't find the class, a compile error is reported.

10) Add the following final two lines of ActionScript to convert some currency and to show the result:

```
var result:Number = converter.convert("USD", 130.5);
trace(result);
```

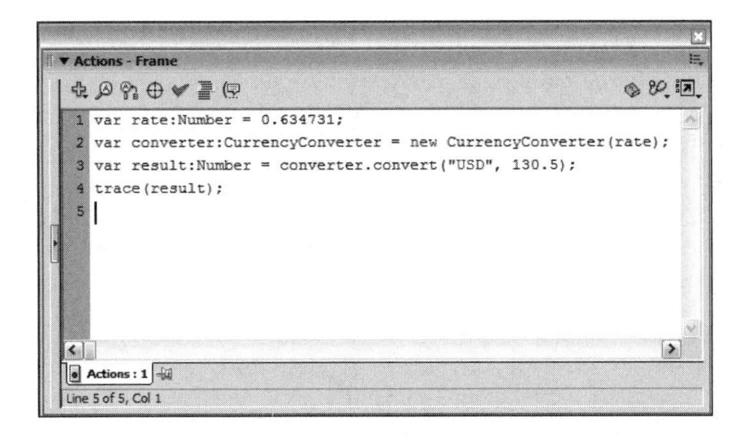

The name of the CurrencyConverter instance created in Step 9 is `converter`. Here we call the `convert` method on the `converter` instance. In the first parameter, we pass in the currency to which we want the number converted. The second parameter is the amount that we want converted. A result is returned and stored in a variable called `result`. In the final line, a `trace` action shows the value of `result` in the Output window.

11) Select Control > Test Movie to test your work.

The Output window should pop up and display a number. When the SWF was compiled, the compiler detected the use of a class called CurrencyConverter, searched the classpath directories for that class, and included the class in the SWF. The ActionScript in the SWF then created a new instance of the class and used it to perform a task.

12) Close the test movie and save your work as *CurrencyConverter2.fla*.

In this exercise, you created a class and then used it in a Flash movie. As this lesson progresses, you'll learn much more about classes and gain more experience working with them.

GETTERS AND SETTERS

As you're well aware by now, when you create an instance of a class you're actually creating an object. Often these objects have properties, as defined by their class files. For example, look at this class definition:

```
class State {
  var population:Number;
  function State() {
    //Constructor
  }
}
```

This defines the State class. This class has a single property named `population`, which is obviously used to hold the number of people in the state.

Creating an instance of this class would look like this:

```
var northCarolina:State = new State();
```

You can now set the value of the `population` property of the `northCarolina` instance in the following manner:

```
northCarolina.population = 8000000;
```

While this may seem fine, problems can arise if you need to change the way in which the value of `population` is determined. Right now, `population` represents a number, so setting a new numeric value involves nothing more than entering the new number. But what if the instances of the State class need to be updated so that when setting the value of `population`, a growth percentage of 5 percent is factored in automatically? You could edit every script in every project that references this property to read similar to this:

```
northCarolina.population = 8000000 + (8000000 * .05);
```

But all that editing would take a lot of work. It's better to make your classes versatile enough to handle this kind of change simply by updating the class file. This is where *getters* and *setters* become useful. Look at the updated State class definition:

```
class State {
  var population:Number;
  function State() {
    //Constructor
  }
  function setPopulation(num:Number){
    population = num + (num * .05);
  }
  function getPopulation():Number{
    return population;
  }
}
```

As defined by the class now, setting and getting the population property are handled by methods, which can be used in the following way:

```
northCarolina.setPopulation(8000000); //automatically adds a 5% growth
⇒rate when set
northCarolina.getPopulation(); // returns a value of 8400000
```

Either of these getter or setter methods could be changed or enhanced as needed from within the class definition. As a result, all scripts in all projects that use the State class would automatically reflect the new functionality.

Because of the versatility of getters and setters, getting and setting property values directly is considered bad coding practice. Set up and use getter and setter methods instead.

IMPLICIT get AND set METHODS

Now that you understand the power and efficiency of using getter and setter methods, it's time to introduce alternate syntax that might seem a 180-degree turn from what you just learned. Look at the following updated State class definition:

```
class State {
  var statePopulation:Number;
  function State() {
    //Constructor
  }
  function set population(num:Number){
    statePopulation = num + (num * .05);
  }
  function get population():Number{
    return statePopulation;
  }
}
```

While it might not be obvious, the names of the setPopulation() and getPopulation() methods have been changed to set population and get population, respectively. This change converts the methods to what are known as *implicit* get and set methods. What does this mean? You get the best of both worlds—property values can be set or retrieved within the class file by using functions, but referencing them in a script is as easy as this:

```
northCarolina.population = 8000000;
```

or this:

```
var myVariable:Number = northCarolina.population;
```

With this syntax, it seems as if we're once again referencing the `population` property directly, but we're actually calling either the `set population` or `get population` method (depending on the task) to take care of the state's population. Notice that we changed the name of the `population` property to `statePopulation`. If we hadn't done this, using the following syntax:

```
northCarolina.population = 8000000;
```

would result in an error. Flash wouldn't know if we were attempting to set the property named `population` or invoking the `set population` set method, because doing either requires the same syntax. Changing the `population` property name to `statePopulation` solves this problem.

NOTE *Using implicit get and set methods offers no technical advantages over using the getter and setter methods described in the previous section, other than saving a few keystrokes.*

DEFINING MEMBERS

Not all class members are created equal. Using special keywords, members can be configured in various ways, allowing you to specify how the member is accessed and the scope of its influence. Next, we'll discuss what this means and how you can use this functionality when creating class members.

PUBLIC AND PRIVATE MEMBERS

By default, all members of a class (its properties and methods) are public. This means that the property or methods of that class can be accessed by instances of that class. Look again at our State class definition:

```
class State {
  var statePopulation:Number;
  function State() {
    //Constructor
  }
  function setPopulation(num:Number) {
    statePopulation = num + (num * .05);
  }
  function getPopulation():Number {
    return statePopulation;
  }
}
```

The members in this class, statePopulation, setPopulation(), and getPopulation(), are all publicly accessible by instances of the class. For example, the following script:

```
northCarolina.statePopulation = 8000000;
```

shows us setting the value of statePopulation directly. As mentioned in the preceding section, while this property is used to hold a numeric value representing the state's population, it's better to use getter and setter methods to get and set the value, which our class definition has been set up to do. In other words, statePopulation should be a variable that cannot be directly accessed from outside the class definition. To make this change, you use the private and public keywords to indicate each member's access in a class:

```
class State {
  private var statePopulation:Number;
  function State() {
    //Constructor
  }
  public function setPopulation(num:Number) {
    statePopulation = num + (num * .05);
  }
  public function getPopulation():Number {
    return statePopulation;
  }
}
```

statePopulation has been declared as a private member of the class. As a result, only code within the class definition itself, such as the setPopulation() and getPopulation() methods, can access it directly. Attempting to access it from an instance in the following way:

```
northCarolina.statePopulation = 8000000;
```

results in an error.

Any property or method can be declared private or public, as you see fit.

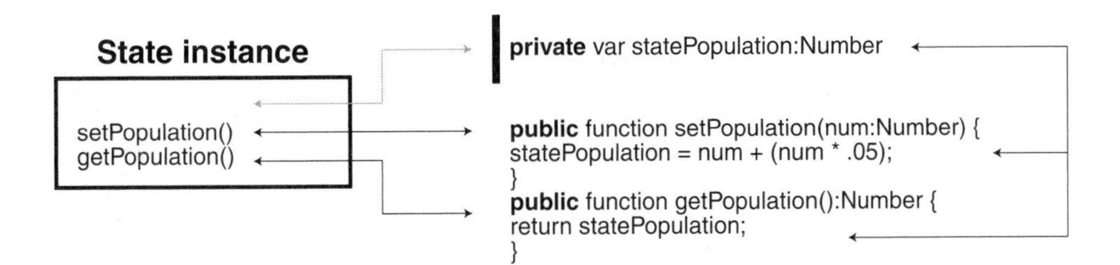

Why would you want to hide some members in this way? Because a robust class definition often has many properties and methods that are used to take care of tasks internally; they have functionality built into them that should not be exposed for use outside the class. Let's look at a real-world example.

When most people use a computer, all they want to know is how to turn it on and off, and how to interact with it via the keyboard and mouse. Most people aren't interested in knowing how it works internally (information about how the hardware is sending data through the circuits or the way the hard drive is reading and writing data—the internal workings of the computer that are important, but that don't affect how it's used). In the same sense, it's not necessary to open all the functionalities of a class to direct access from an instance of that class. A class may have 10 properties and 15 methods internally that affect how instances of that class work, but maybe only 3 or 4 methods that should be directly referenced from an instance.

In the long run, setting member access helps prevent bugs because, as mentioned earlier, it prevents you from scripting an object in a way that you shouldn't. If you attempt to use an object in the wrong way (attempting to use or access a private class member that should only be used internally, within the class), Flash displays an error and lets you know that you need to reexamine your code.

Static Members

By default, every member of a class is duplicated within an instance whenever that instance is created. Consider the State class example that we've used a few times in this lesson. For every new instance of that class, a copy of the `statePopulation` property is created within the instance. This makes sense because every state has its own population. In other words, while every instance of the State class has a `statePopulation` property, the value of that property may differ for each instance.

There may be circumstances, however, when you need a property that is not only accessible by every instance of a class, but has a universal value across all instances. This is the functionality that *static* properties provide.

If a property is static, it's created in memory only once. All instances of the class see the same copy of this member. If any instance of the class edits the value of the property, all instances of the class see the new value.

Take the following class as an example:

```
class Star {
  static var starsInTheSky:Number = 1000000000;
  function Star() {
    //Constructor
  }
  function setTotalStars(num:Number) {
    starsInTheSky = num;
  }
  function getTotalStars():Number {
    return starsInTheSky;
  }
}
```

The property `starsInTheSky` has been specified as `static`, and is used to store the total number of stars that can be seen in the sky. If we were to create several instances of this class, as follows:

```
var star1:Star = new Star();
var star2:Star = new Star();
var star3:Star = new Star();
```

referencing the `starsInTheSky` property from any one of these instances would result in the same value:

```
star1.starsInTheSky //has a value of 1000000000
star2.starsInTheSky //has a value of 1000000000
star3.starsInTheSky //has a value of 1000000000
```

If a star goes supernova or another star is born, the `setTotalStars()` method can be executed to change the value of `starsInTheSky`. When the value is changed, say to `1000000037`, all Star class instances see the following new value:

```
star1.starsInTheSky //has a value of 1000000037
star2.starsInTheSky //has a value of 1000000037
star3.starsInTheSky //has a value of 1000000037
```

NOTE *Yes, we're using code that directly accesses a property (something we told you earlier not to do). This is done strictly to demonstrate the universality of static members.*

When would this kind of functionality be useful? Imagine having a class in which each instance has to load data from the same URL. If the URL was created as a `static` property of the class, it could be changed at a later time and all of the instances would automatically load from the new URL.

Methods can be static, too. Take a look at the following example:

```
class Sky {
  static var starsInTheSky:Number = 1000000000;
  static function setTotalStars(num:Number) {
    starsInTheSky = num;
  }
  static function getTotalStars():Number {
    return starsInTheSky;
  }
}
```

This class has the `starsInTheSky` static property and two static methods—`setTotalStars()` and `getTotalStars()`.

Similar to static properties, static methods have a universal functionality. These methods can be called from any instance to update and return the value of `starsInTheSky`.

An interesting aspect about static methods (and properties) is that they can be accessed simply by referencing the class name, followed by the name of the method, such as:

```
Sky.setTotalStars(999999999); //One star died
var numStars:Number = Sky.getTotalStars();
```

In this example, we've used the class name (Sky) instead of an instance name to invoke both the `setTotalStars()` and `getTotalStars()` methods. This makes sense due to the class-wide functionality of static methods and properties. You've used similar syntax when invoking methods of the Math class, which has several static methods:

```
Math.round();
Math.random();
Math.floor();
Math.ceil();
```

and so on.

NOTE *A class method (static or not) can change the value of a static property, but a static method cannot change the value of an instance-based property.*

UNDERSTANDING INHERITANCE

A class can gain (inherit) all members from another class. This is called *inheritance*. The class that's gaining the members is called a *subclass* and the class from which it inherits is called the *superclass*. If B is a subclass of A, B is said to *extend* A.

Inheritance promotes code reusability. It allows you to give functionality to other classes without having to rewrite code that would be redundant. This concept will be much clearer by the end of this lesson.

Imagine for a moment that you're writing the ActionScript for a game. This game has a hero, controlled by the user, and lots of simple enemy characters. The enemies are not the same as the hero, but they share a number of similarities, such as the ability to walk, get hurt, heal, and die. If you program separate Hero and Enemy classes, you end up rewriting much of the same code to handle these common capabilities. So it makes sense to create a general class that programs these common capabilities—let's call it the Character class—and then create additional classes (Hero and Enemy) that inherit all the functionality of the Character class as well as extend that functionality, each in unique ways. The Hero class might extend the Character class with the capability to be controlled via a user interface, and the capability to wield many types of weapons. The Enemy class might extend the Character class with the capability to use an artificial intelligence algorithm to govern its movement.

In this example, the base superclass (Character) is written once, and two subclasses (Hero and Enemy) extend the functionality of the base class to make new and unique classes. Let's look at how this is done.

Let's assume that a Character class has already been created, given properties and methods, and saved as **Character.as**. A subclass of the Character class (we'll use the Hero class) is created by using the keyword `extends` in the class definition. For example:

```
class Hero extends Character {
  function Hero() {
    //Constructor
  }
}
```

The first word, `class`, says that what follows is a class definition. The next word, `Hero`, gives a name to the class. Next you see `extends Character`. This statement instructs Flash at compile time to give the Hero class all the methods and properties found in the Character class (the Hero class *inherits* from the Character class). In addition to inheriting from the Character class, the Hero class can also be given functionality (properties and methods) unique to itself.

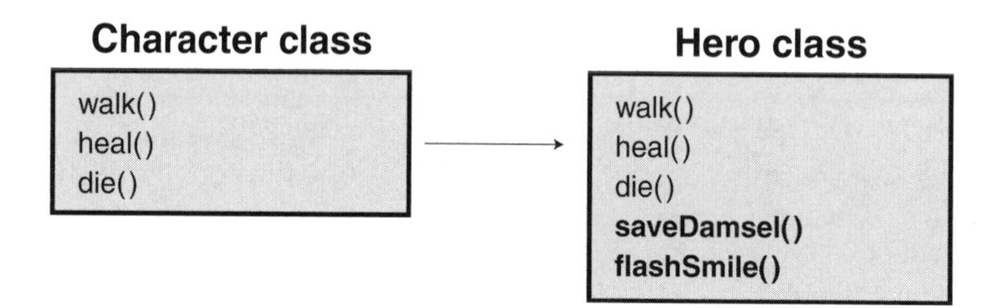

A class can only extend (inherit from) one other class. For example, if Hero extends Character, it cannot extend any other class; however, Hero can extend Character and then MyHero can extend Hero, and so on.

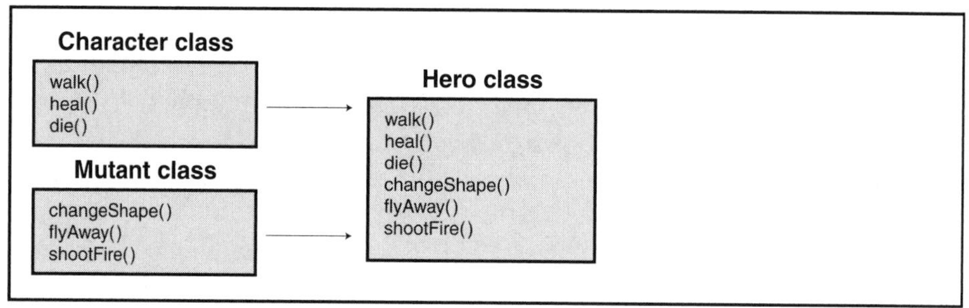

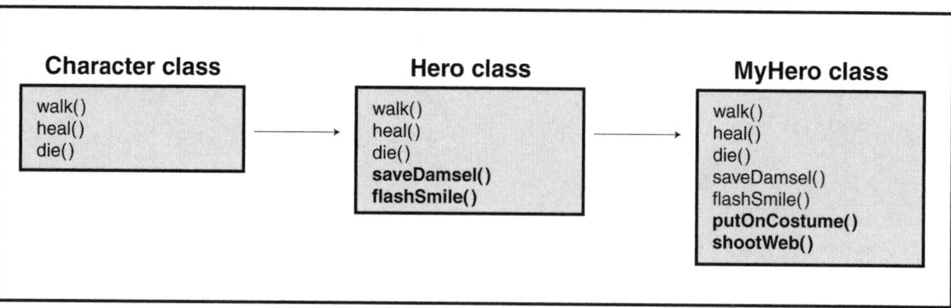

When a class extends another class, the resulting subclass gains all the properties and methods of the superclass; however, those properties and methods can still be changed or enhanced. Replacing a property value or method of the superclass with a new one in the subclass is called *overriding*. Let's look again at the Character class example to help you get a better understanding of this concept.

Let's say that both the Hero and Enemy classes extend the Character class, and the Character class has a `die()` method. As a result of inheritance, both the Hero and Enemy classes inherit the functionality of the `die()` method, as well as all the other members of the Character class. But let's say you want heroes and enemies to die in a different manner than the inherited `die()` method allows. In this case, you would simply define a new `die()` method in the Hero and Enemy classes. Creating a method in a subclass with the same name as an inherited method from its superclass causes the functionality of the subclasses' method to take precedence over the inherited method.

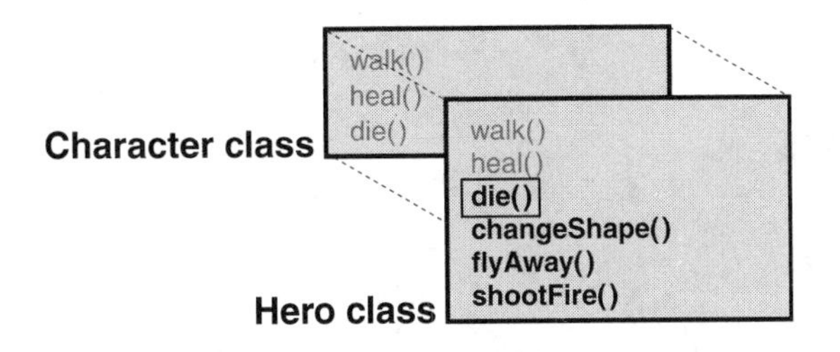

Being able to override properties and methods in this way is useful in creating object-oriented code.

In the following exercise, you'll put into practice most of the concepts you've learned in this lesson so far. You'll create a class called Animal and program the Animal class with several capabilities, including running and stopping, as most animals can do. You'll also create a Cat class that extends Animal by giving Cat animals the capability to meow. (Because the Cat class extends the Animal class, the Cat class inherits the functionality of the Animal class; Cat animals automatically can run and stop.) In addition, you'll create a Dog class that extends the Animal class in a manner similar to that of the Cat class, except that Dog animals will be able to bark. When you've finished scripting these classes, you'll associate the Cat and Dog classes with different movie clips in the library. As a result of this association, each instance of one of those clips that you drag into your project will take on the characteristics of the class with which it's associated.

In this exercise, you'll gain experience creating classes, extending a class, overriding methods and properties, and working with instances of custom-made classes. Let's get started!

1) Open *PetParade1.fla*.

The first order of business is to become familiar with the contents of this FLA. There are three layers in this project file. The Background layer holds the background graphics; the Assets layer currently contains six buttons named **dogRun_btn**, **dogStop_btn**, **dogSound_btn**, **catRun_btn**, **catStop_btn**, and **catSound_btn**. The Actions layer is currently empty, but will eventually contain script.

For this exercise, it's also important to understand the assets in the library because they will play an integral role in how the final application works.

2) Choose Window > Library to open the Library panel.

The library contains a folder, two sound clips, and three movie clips. The folder contains miscellaneous elements that you're free to examine, but you won't work with them directly in this exercise.

The three movie clips are named Dog Clip, Cat Clip, and Balloon. Dog Clip and Cat Clip are the graphical and interactive representations of the Dog class and Cat class. This is important to understand; things that we program the Dog and Cat classes to do will be graphically and interactively carried out by instances of the Dog Clip and Cat Clip movie clips. The Balloon movie clip will be used and explained later in the exercise.

The two sound clips named **Meow.mp3** and **Bark.mp3** represent the sounds that our Cat and Dog animals will make. If you right-click (Control-click on a Macintosh) either of these sounds and then choose Linkage from the menu that appears, you see that the **Meow.mp3** sound has been given an identifier of Meow, and the **Bark.mp3** sound has been given an identifier of Bark. Steps 10 and 12 in this exercise will explain how these sounds are used.

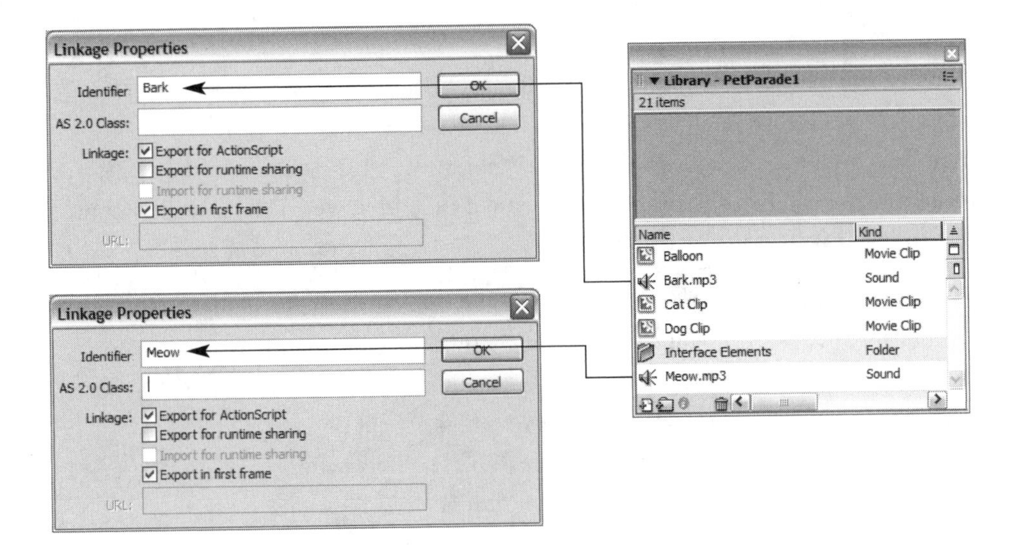

Now that you're familiar with the project's assets, it's time to begin creating the class files that it will use.

NOTE *You will be creating and working with several files in this exercise. As we progress through the steps, keep all the files open. You will be instructed when to tab between the files.*

3) Create a new ActionScript file called *Animal.as* in the Lesson07/Assets folder. Add the following script to the *Animal.as* file:

```
class Animal extends MovieClip {
  private var speed:Number;
  function Animal() {
    this.speed = 5
  }
```

The first line gives the class a name, Animal, and then specifies that this class extends the MovieClip class. This means that instances of the Animal class inherit all the functionalities (properties and methods) of movie clips—properties such as `_x` and `_name`, as well as methods such as `gotoAndPlay()` and `loadMovie()`. This is your first experience creating a new class that inherits from another class. You can think of this technique as taking the basic functionality of movie clips and extending it in a way that's appropriate for programming how Animals work. This will become clearer as we progress through the steps.

TIP *Any of Flash's built-in classes can be extended in this way. With this capability, for example, you can create an enhanced Sound, TextField, or Array class to fit your needs exactly.*

The line following the class declaration defines a private variable named speed that will used by the class. Remember that private variables can only be accessed and used by scripts within the class definition—not directly by instances of the class. The speed variable will be used by a method named run() that we'll create in a moment. This method will be used to move a movie clip based on the value of speed.

The final three lines of the ActionScript in this step define the constructor method for the Animal class. Remember that scripts within the constructor are executed at the moment that an instance of the class is created. Because the Dog and Cat classes inherit from the Animal class, any scripts placed here will be executed when an instance of the Dog class or Cat class is created. The only action here is to set the value of speed in relation to this. this is a reference to an instance created from the class. In other words, whenever an instance of the Animal class is created, that instance is given an initial speed value of 5. We'll add more scripts to the Animal class constructor later in the exercise.

4) After the class constructor, add the following script to handle making an animal run:

```
function run() {
  this.onEnterFrame = function() {
    this._x += this.speed;
  };
}
```

The run() method is used to put instances of the Animal class into motion. When an instance of the Animal class invokes this method, an onEnterFrame event is attached to that instance (this). The action within the event moves the instance along its x axis by the value of the speed variable. Remember that in Step 3 we set the initial value of speed in the constructor method to 5. When an instance of the Animal class invokes this method, it will begin moving five pixels at a time, 24 times per second (the frame rate of our movie). The instance will continue to move until stopped with the stop() method.

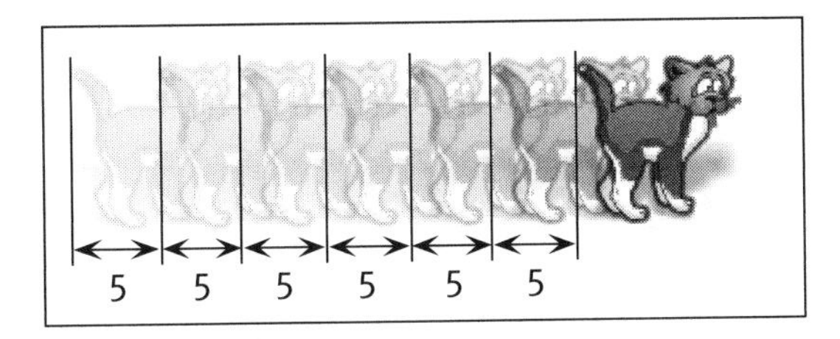

5) Next, add the following `stop()` method:

```
function stop() {
  delete this.onEnterFrame;
}
```

This method stops the instance from moving, simply by deleting the `onEnterFrame` event from the instance.

6) End the definition of the Animal class with a closing curly brace (}); then choose File > Save to save the class file.

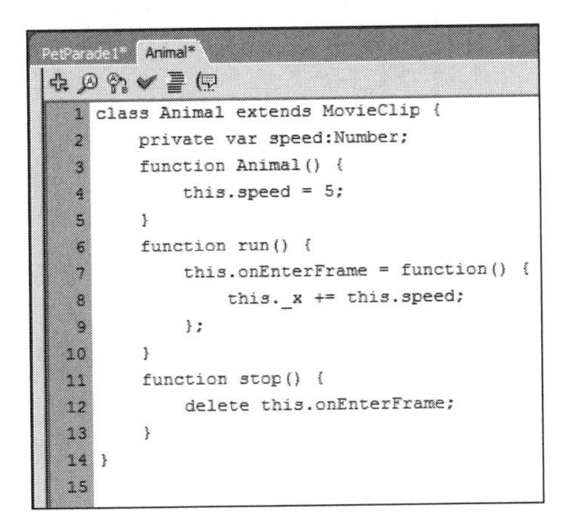

PetParade1*
Animal*
class Animal extends MovieClip {
private var speed:Number;
function Animal() {
this.speed = 5;
}
function run() {
this.onEnterFrame = function() {
this._x += this.speed;
};
}
function stop() {
delete this.onEnterFrame;
}
}

You've created the Animal class. Next you'll create the two subclasses (Dog and Cat) that extend Animal.

7) In the same directory as *Animal.as*, create a new ActionScript file named *Cat.as*. Start the class definition with the following script:

```
class Cat extends Animal {
```

The first two words tell Flash that you're creating a new class called Cat. The next two words, `extends Animal`, tell Flash that this class inherits every method and property of the Animal class, including `run()` and `stop()`. We used similar syntax when defining the Animal class; it extended the MovieClip class. As a result, not only does the Cat class get all the capabilities of the Animal class, but those of the MovieClip class as well. Inheritance trickles down like this as long as you continue extending classes.

In the following steps, we'll program the Cat class to deal with functionalities unique to cats. Running and stopping is something that most animals can do; that's why those functionalities were defined in the more general Animal class, from which the Cat class inherits. The great thing about object-oriented inheritance is that we could create 50 more classes (based on different animals) that all extend the Animal class, but to change the way in which each class handles running we would simply edit the `run()` method in the Animal class file. We'll demonstrate this principle later in the exercise.

Let's set up the unique features of the Cat class.

8) Below the line of script that defines the Cat class, create a property to store the sound object for a Cat instance:

```
private var catSound:Sound;
```

We won't need to access the `catSound` property from outside the class, so it's declared as a private variable. The `meow()` method (created in Step 10) will use the `catSound` property.

9) Create the following constructor method for the Cat class:

```
function Cat() {
  this.speed = 1;
}
```

When a new instance of the Cat class is created, its `speed` property is given a value of 1. In Step 3, we created a variable named `speed` in the Animal class constructor method and gave it an initial value of `5`. Because the Cat class inherits from the Animal class, it automatically inherited that property and its value. You may be wondering why we're setting it again here. Instances of the Animal class will still have a `speed` value of `5`, but instances of the Cat class will have a `speed` value of `1`. We're *overriding* the inherited value with a value specific to cats.

Overriding an inherited property value involves nothing more than using the name of the property you want to override—the `speed` property in this case—and assigning it a new value. As a result, when an instance of the Cat class is created, its `speed` property is set to `1`.

Properties and methods defined in a class always have precedence over properties and methods inherited from another class with the same name; therefore, instances of the Cat class will see and use the `speed` value of 1 as opposed to a value of 5.

The `run()` and `stop()` methods of the Animal class are still inherited, and still work with instances of the Cat class as they were defined in the Animal class file, because we haven't overridden them with methods of the same name in the Cat class (we won't override those methods in this exercise).

10) Create a method called `meow()` that plays a meowing sound when called:

```
function meow() {
  catSound = new Sound(this);
  catSound.attachSound("Meow");
  catSound.start();
}
```

When called, this method creates a new sound object and stores it in the private variable `catSound`. This object has the sound in the Library with a linkage identifier of Meow attached to it. The sound is played by calling the `start()` method of the sound object. Because this method is defined in the Cat class, only instances of the Cat class can call it.

11) End the definition of the Cat class by adding the closing curly brace (}); then choose File > Save to save the class file.

You have completed the first subclass of Animal. Next you'll create another subclass of Animal, the Dog class.

12) In the same directory as *Animal.as*, create a new ActionScript file called *Dog.as*. Define this class as follows:

```
class Dog extends Animal {
  private var dogSound:Sound;
  function Dog() {
    this.speed = 2;
  }
  function bark() {
    dogSound = new Sound(this);
    dogSound.attachSound("Bark");
    dogSound.start();
  }
}
```

This class is similar to the Cat class. The first line of ActionScript names the class Dog and extends the Animal class.

Next, a property called `dogSound` is created. This property will be used to store the sound object used to play the dog's barking sound.

The constructor method sets the value of `speed` to `2`, overriding the value of the property with the same name in the Animal class; instances of the Dog class will all have a `speed` property with a value of `2`.

Similar to the `meow()` method discussed in Step 10, the `bark()` method creates a new sound object and stores it as `dogSound`. The method attaches the sound with the linkage identifier of Bark and then plays the sound.

In the end, Dogs and Cats both `run()` and `stop()`, as most Animals do, but Dogs run at a `speed` of `2` and Bark, while Cats run at a `speed` of `1` and Meow.

13) Choose File > Save to save the Dog class file.

For the moment, our class files are complete. We'll return to the Animal class file shortly, but it's time to open the actual project file to plug in these class files and their functionality.

14) *PetParade1.fla* should already be open in the authoring environment. Click its tab to make *PetParade1.fla* the active window.

The first order of business is to associate our Dog and Cat classes with the Dog Clip and Cat Clip movie clips in the Library.

15) With the Library panel open, right-click (Control-click on a Macintosh) the Cat Clip movie clip and choose Linkage from the menu that appears. In the Linkage Properties dialog box, select the Export for ActionScript option; then enter `cat` in the Identifier field and `Cat` (the first letter must be uppercase) in the AS 2.0 Class field. Click OK.

Although you configured several settings in this step, the one you need to focus on is the AS 2.0 Class field. By entering a value of `Cat` in this field, you're associating the Cat Clip movie clip in the library to the Cat class you created. This means that all instances of the Cat Clip movie clip you place in your project will take on the functionality defined in the Cat class file. As a result, these instances can `run()`, `stop()`, and `meow()`, as you will soon see.

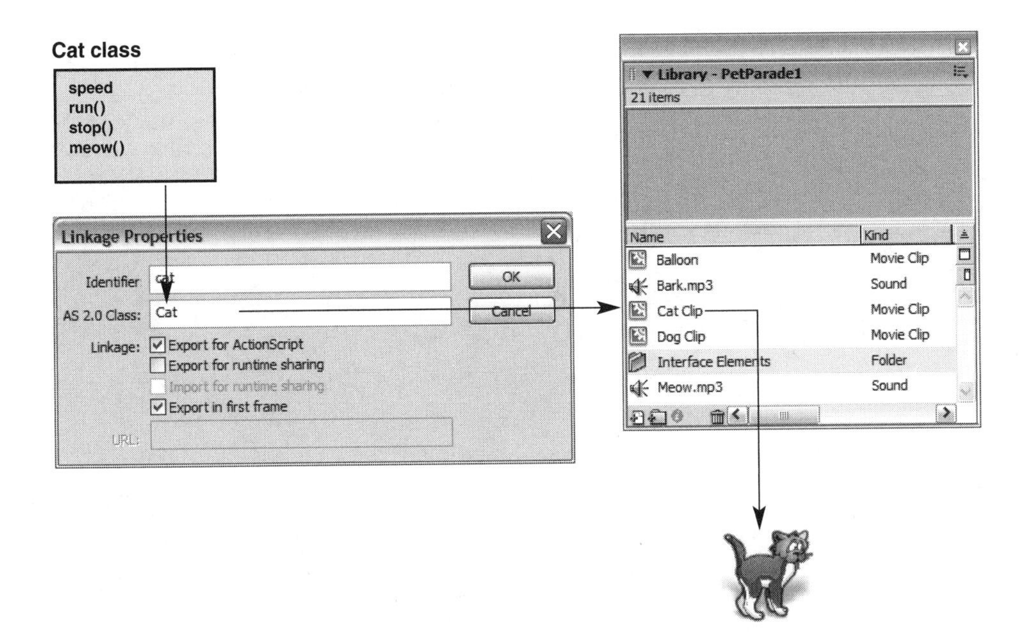

16) Right-click (Control-click on a Macintosh) the Dog Clip movie clip and choose Linkage from the menu that appears. In the Linkage Properties dialog box, select the Export for ActionScript option; then enter `dog` **in the Identifier field and** `Dog` **(the first letter must be uppercase) in the AS 2.0 Class field. Click OK.**

This step associates the Dog Clip movie clip with the Dog class. As a result, all instances of the Dog Clip movie clip you place in your project can `run()`, `stop()`, and `bark()`. This is a great feature of Flash that allows you to create highly interactive class-based movie clips. You simply create a custom class and then associate that class with a movie clip; you instantly have a custom movie clip.

NOTE *To use this feature, the associating class (which in this case is Dog) must inherit from the MovieClip class somewhere up the line.*

17) Click and drag instances of the Dog Clip and Cat Clip movie clips onto the stage. Give the Dog Clip instance the name *dog_mc* and give the Cat Clip instance the name *cat_mc*.

Next, we'll add scripts to cause these instances to perform the actions that cats and dogs do, based on what we programmed into our custom class files.

18) With the Actions panel open, select Frame 1 of the Actions layer and add the following button events to control the *dog_mc* movie clip instance:

```
dogRun_btn.onRelease = function() {
  dog_mc.run();
};
dogStop_btn.onRelease = function() {
  dog_mc.stop();
};
dogSound_btn.onRelease = function() {
  dog_mc.bark();
};
```

When the **dogRun_btn** is clicked, the `run()` method of the Dog class is called and the **dog_mc** instance starts moving. Remember that the Dog class inherits the `run()` method from the Animal class. The method is set up to move the calling instance horizontally, using an `onEnterFrame` event (added in Step 4). The amount by which the instance is moved is based on its internal `speed` value. We programmed the Dog class to set this value to `2` for all instances created from the Dog class; therefore, when the `run()` method is called in relation to the **dog_mc** movie clip instance, that instance will move two pixels at 24 times a second.

dogStop_btn calls the `stop()` method to stop the dog from moving, and the **dogSound_btn** instance makes the dog bark. When clicked, it calls the `bark()` method.

19) Add the following button events to control the *cat_mc* movie clip instance:

```
catRun_btn.onRelease = function() {
  cat_mc.run();
};
catStop_btn.onRelease = function() {
  cat_mc.stop();
};
catSound_btn.onRelease = function() {
  cat_mc.meow();
};
```

As with the buttons that control the **dog_mc** instance, these will make the **cat_mc** instance run, stop running, and make a sound. The cat's sound is a meow, so the `meow()` method is called when the **catSound_btn** instance is clicked.

Whew! It's finally time to test your work.

20) Select Control > Test Movie. When the movie appears, click the buttons at the bottom of the stage to see the results. Then close the test movie to return to the authoring environment, but leave the Library panel open for the next exercise.

As the movie is being exported, Flash pulls in code from the external Animal, Dog, and Cat class files as it detects the references to these classes in our project. The dog and cat can both run, stop, and make sounds, all based on the code in our class files.

We're not finished quite yet. To help solidify your understanding of inheritance, we're going to make a few enhancements to the Animal class so you can see how easy it is to update an object-oriented/inheritance-based project.

1) The Library panel should still be open from the preceding exercise. Double-click the *Balloon* movie clip to edit its timeline.

This movie clip's timeline is simple. It contains a transparent white box and a text field instance called **name_txt**. The name of this field is important to remember.

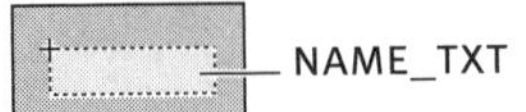

2) Return to the main timeline. In the library, right-click (Control-click on a Macintosh) the Balloon movie and select Linkage from the menu that appears. In the Linkage Properties dialog box, give this movie clip an identifier of *balloon*; then click OK.

This identifier will be used in a moment to dynamically attach this movie clip to our animal movie clip instances when the mouse rolls over them.

3) *Animal.as* should still be open. Click its tab to make *Animal.as* the active window.

Over the next several steps we'll add functionality to this class; by extension, that new functionality will filter down into the Dog and Cat classes because they inherit from this class.

4) Insert the following line of script just below `private var speed:Number;`:

```
private var name:String;
```

This step creates a new private property called `name` in the Animal class. This variable will eventually be used to hold the name we give to instances of the Animal class, or, by extension, the Dog and Cat classes.

5) Insert the following method just below the end of the `stop()` method definition:

```
function setName(tempName:String){
  this.name = tempName;
}
```

This step creates a setter method called `setName()` that accepts a single parameter, `tempName`. The parameter value that's passed in is used to set the `name` property of an instance. For example:

```
dog_mc.setName("Fido");
```

will set **dog_mc**'s `name` property to have a value of `"Fido"`.

In a moment, we'll add script that will invoke the `setName()` method to set the `name` properties of both the **dog_mc** and **cat_mc** instances. First we'll add several lines of script to the Animal constructor function.

6) Insert the following line of script into the Animal constructor method, just below `this.speed = 5`:

```
this.name = "Animal";
```

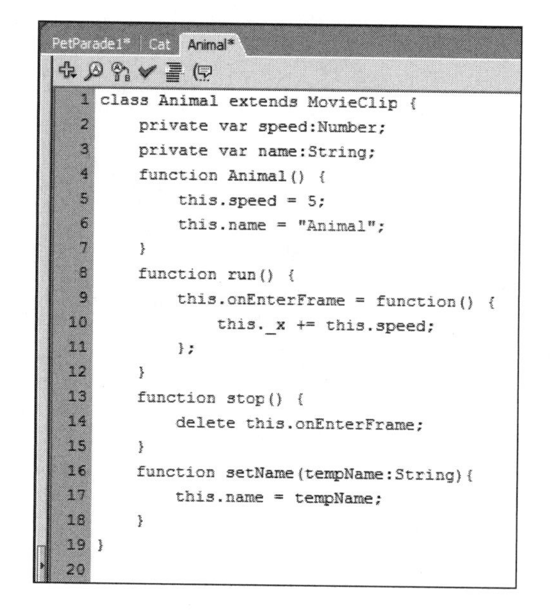


```
1  class Animal extends MovieClip {
2      private var speed:Number;
3      private var name:String;
4      function Animal() {
5          this.speed = 5;
6          this.name = "Animal";
7      }
8      function run() {
9          this.onEnterFrame = function() {
10             this._x += this.speed;
11         };
12     }
13     function stop() {
14         delete this.onEnterFrame;
15     }
16     function setName(tempName:String){
17         this.name = tempName;
18     }
19 }
20
```

Remember that the script inside the constructor function is executed as soon as an instance of the class is created. In our project, because the Dog and Cat classes inherit from Animal, and the Dog Clip and Cat Clip movie clips in the library are associated with the Dog and Cat classes, when an instance of either clip appears in the movie this constructor function is executed in relation to the instance.

With the line of script in this step, we give a default `name` value to instances of the Animal class as well as the Dog and Cat classes. So when **dog_mc** and **cat_mc** first appear in the movie, each will have a default `name` value of `Animal`. This value can be changed as a result of the `setName()` method we added in Step 5, which we'll use shortly.

7) Insert the following script below the script you just added in Step 6:

```
this.onRollOver = function() {
  this.useHandCursor = false;
  this.attachMovie("balloon", "balloon_mc", 0);
  this.balloon_mc._x = this._xmouse;
  this.balloon_mc._y = this._ymouse - 50;
  this.balloon_mc.name_txt.text = this.name;
};
```

This script assigns an `onRollOver` event to instances of the Animal class. This script executes when the **dog_mc** or **cat_mc** instance appears on the stage and the user rolls the mouse over the instance. The purpose of this script is to display the value of the instance's `name` property in a little window based on the Balloon clip in the library (we discussed the Balloon clip in Step 1).

NOTE *Flash MX allowed events of a class to be defined outside the constructor method of the class. This is no longer possible in ActionScript 2.0.*

The first line of the function sets the instance's `useHandCursor` property to `false`; therefore, the hand cursor won't appear when the instance is rolled over. The next line attaches the movie clip with the *balloon* identifier in the library. The attached instance is given a name of **balloon_mc** and a depth of `0`. The next two lines position the newly attached instance so that it appears at the same x position as the mouse, but 50 pixels less than the y position of the mouse; therefore, the balloon will appear slightly offset from the mouse cursor.

Remember that the Balloon movie clip has a text field instance called **name_txt** on its timeline. When you attach that clip and give it an instance name of **balloon_mc**, you can set the text displayed in that field by referencing it as follows:

```
this.balloon_mc.name_txt.text
```

The last line of the script uses this reference to display the `name` property of the instance in the text field.

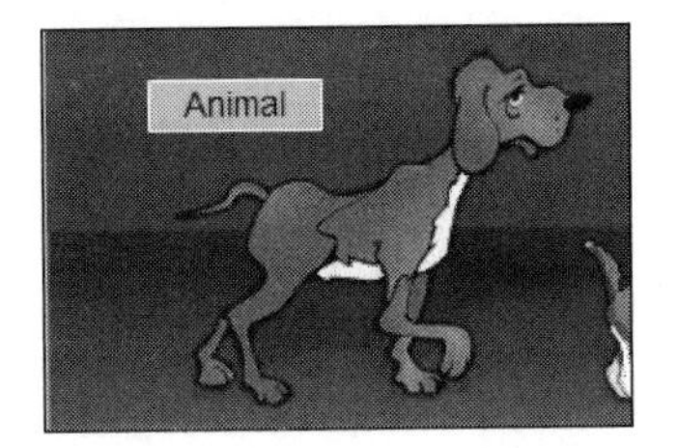

Let's create the functionality that will remove the balloon when the user rolls away from the instance.

8) Insert the following script below the script you just added in Step 7:

```
this.onRollOut = function() {
  this.balloon_mc.removeMovieClip();
};
```

This script removes the **balloon_mc** movie clip instance when the user rolls away.

Let's add one last bit of functionality, allowing instances to be dragged and dropped.

9) Insert the following script below the script you just added in Step 8:

```
this.onPress = function() {
  this.startDrag(false);
}
this.onRelease = function(){
  this.stopDrag();
}
```

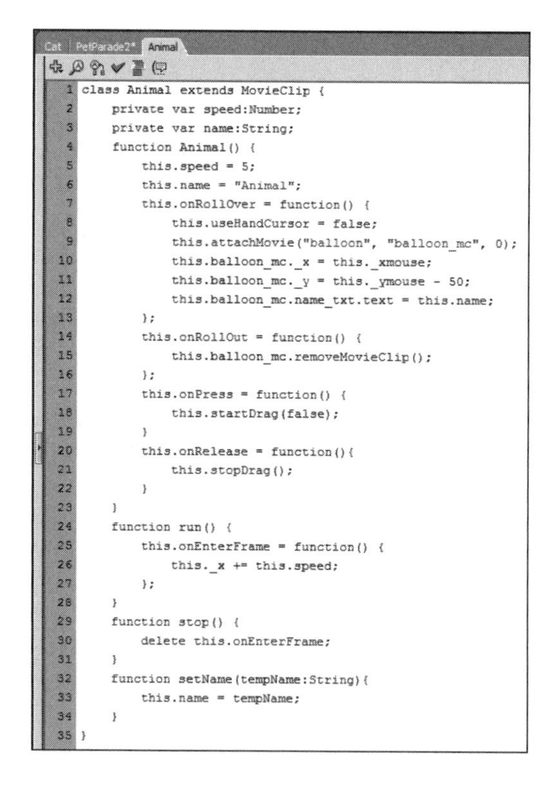

As a result of this script, when an instance is pressed it will become draggable, and dragging will stop when the instance is released.

10) Choose File > Save to save the Animal class file with its new functionality.

The Animal class is now complete. All that's left to do is to return to the **FLA** for this project and add a couple of lines of script.

11) *PetParade1.fla* should already be open in the authoring environment. Click its tab to make *PetParade1.fla* the active window. With the Actions panel open, select Frame 1 of the Actions layer and add the following script at the end of the current script:

```
dog_mc.setName("Fido");
cat_mc.setName("Fluffy");
```

These two lines of script utilize the new `setName()` method created in the Animal class file in Step 5. The `name` property of the **dog_mc** instance is set to `"Fido"` and the `name` property of the **cat_mc** instance is set to `"Fluffy"`. These new values override the default `name` value for Animal instances, discussed in Step 6.

This property value will appear in a balloon when the instance is rolled over. Let's do one final test.

12) Choose Control > Test Movie.

When the movie appears, you can move the mouse over either the dog or cat and the animal's name will appear in a balloon. You can also click and drag either instance.

The important thing to realize about this new functionality is that it was set up in a single file—the Animal class file. All instances that inherited from this class automatically inherited this new behavior when the class file was updated. We hope that you can now appreciate the power of inheritance, and how it allows you to create more manageable projects.

13) Close the test movie and save your work as *PetParade2.fla*.

Due to page constraints, most of the projects in the remainder of the book will not use a class-based object-oriented structure. However, the concepts you learned here can be applied in class-based projects you create on your own.

WHAT YOU HAVE LEARNED

In this lesson, you have:

- Explored the terminology and syntax of classes (pages 236–242)
- Learned how to use classpaths (pages 242–254)
- Learned about private, public, and static members, and how to use them (pages 254–258)
- Used inheritance to extend a class (pages 259–260)
- Become familiar with overriding (pages 260–261)
- Created custom object classes (pages 262–271)
- Associated a custom class with a movie clip in the library (pages 271–275)

using conditional logic

LESSON 8

Every day we're confronted with all kinds of situations, large and small, that require us to make decisions about what actions we'll take. Although we may not be doing it consciously, we're constantly saying to ourselves, "If this is the case, I need to do that." If it's hot, wear shorts; if it's rainy, wear pants; and so on. This process of taking different actions based on current *conditions* (circumstances) is known as *conditional logic*, and it's something we all apply naturally.

A successful rocket launch demands perfect conditions. This lesson's project will emulate a launch to demonstrate some of the principles and techniques used in conditional logic.

Conditional logic is a critical component of interactivity. It allows you to program your project to react intelligently—to the movement or position of the mouse, to the current day of the week, to many other dynamic conditions that exist as your movie plays. By employing conditional logic, you transform simple linear presentations and animations into dynamic projects that offer a unique experience each time they're viewed.

In this lesson, we'll introduce you to some of the ways in which you can use conditional logic to bring about graphical changes in your movies based on varying conditions.

WHAT YOU WILL LEARN

In this lesson, you will:

- Learn how to use `if`, `if/else`, and `if/else if` statements to control the flow of a script
- Explore the various operators used in conditional logic
- Script a project to react to various conditions
- Create a scripted boundary to restrict an object's movement
- Turn a script on and off using conditional logic
- Program a project to react to user interaction
- Learn how to detect and react to object collisions

APPROXIMATE TIME

This lesson takes approximately one hour to complete.

LESSON FILES

Starting File:

Lesson08/Assets/rocketLaunch1.fla

Completed Project:

rocketLaunch6.fla

CONTROLLING A SCRIPT'S FLOW

Typically, actions in your scripts execute consecutively, from beginning to end—a sequence that represents your script's flow. Using *conditional logic*, you can control this flow by scripting specific actions to execute *only* when specific conditions are met or exist in your movie. By implementing conditional logic in your scripts, you give your movie the ability to make decisions and take action based on various conditions you've set, and your movie takes on more dimension as a result. You'll use the *conditional statements* or phrases described in this lesson to implement conditional logic in your scripts.

IF/THEN STATEMENTS

At the heart of conditional logic is the simple `if/then` statement. Here's an example:

```
if (moneySaved > 500) {
buyStuff();
}
// next line of actions…
```

The `buyStuff()` function is called only if the variable `moneySaved` has a value greater than 500. If `moneySaved` is equal to or less than 500, the `buyStuff()` function call is ignored and actions immediately below the `if` statement are executed.

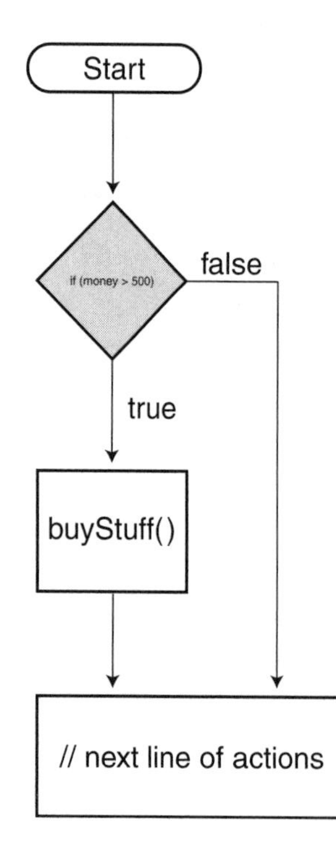

At its core, a conditional statement looks at a *circumstance* (placed within parentheses) and determines whether that circumstance is true or false. If the circumstance is true, actions within the statement are executed; if the circumstance is false, the actions are ignored. When you create an `if` statement, you state, essentially:

```
if (...what is shown here is true) {
  Do this;
}
```

The data you place within parentheses represents the condition to be analyzed. The data within the curly braces ({}) represents the actions to be taken if the condition exists.

As in real life, sometimes an `if` statement needs to analyze multiple conditions before taking a single action or set of actions. For example:

```
if (moneySaved > 500 && billsPaid == true) {
  buyStuff();
}
```

The AND operator (`&&`) has been added to the statement so that now the `buyStuff()` function is called only if `moneySaved` is more than 500 *and* `billsPaid` has a value of `true`. If either condition is false, `buyStuff()` will not be called.

Using the OR operator (`||`) allows you to take a slightly different approach:

```
if (moneySaved > 500 || wonLottery == true) {
  buyStuff();
}
```

The `buyStuff()` function is called if *either* `moneySaved` has a value greater than 500 *or* `wonLottery` has a value of `true`. Both conditions need not be true for the `buyStuff()` function to be called, as was the case when using the AND operator (`&&`) in the earlier example.

You can mix the AND and OR operators to create sophisticated conditional statements like this one:

```
if (moneySaved > 500 && billsPaid == true || wonLottery == true) {
  buyStuff();
}
```

In this script, the `buyStuff()` function is called only if `moneySaved` is more than 500 *and* `billsPaid` has a value of `true`, *or* if `wonLottery` has a value of `true`.

The following table shows a list of the common operators (known as *comparison operators* because they're used to compare values) used in conditional logic, with brief descriptions and examples of how they're used.

Operator	**Description**	**Example**	**Execute the function if...**
==	Checks for equality	`if (name == "Derek")`	`name` has an exact value of `Derek`
!=	Checks for inequality	`if (name != "Derek")`	`name` has a value other than `Derek`
<	Less than	`if (age < 30)`	`age` has a value less than `30`
>	Greater than	`if (age > 30)`	`age` has a value greater than `30`
<=	Less than or equal to	`if (age <= 30)`	`age` has a value less than or equal to `30`
>=	Greater than or equal to	`if (age >= 30)`	`age` has a value greater than or equal to `30`
&&	Logical AND	`if (day == "Friday" && pmTime > 5)`	`day` has a value of `Friday` and `pmTime` has a value greater than `5`
||	Logical OR	`if (day == "Saturday" || day == "Sunday")`	`day` has a value of `Saturday` or `Sunday`

A common mistake when checking equality is to insert a single equals sign (`=`) where a double equals sign (`==`) belongs. Use a single equals sign to assign a value (for example, `money = 300`). Use a double equals sign to check for equality: `money == 300` does not assign a value of `300` to `money`. Rather, it asks whether `money` has a value of `300`.

NOTE *Although number comparisons are straightforward—after all, most of us understand that 50 is less than 100—text-value comparisons are less obvious.* `Derek` *doesn't equal* `derek` *even though the same letters are used. With string values,* `A` *has a lower value than* `Z`*, and lowercase letters have greater values than uppercase letters. Thus, if* `A` *has a value of 1,* `z` *has a value of 52 (*`ABCDEFGHIJKLMNOPQRSTUVWXYZabcdefghijklmnopqrstuvwxyz`*).*

If/Else If Statements

An `if/else if` statement is similar to the basic `if` statement except that it enables your script to react to multiple conditions. Here's an example:

```
if (money > 500) {
  buyTV("35 inch");
} else if (money > 300) {
  buyTV("27 inch");
}
```

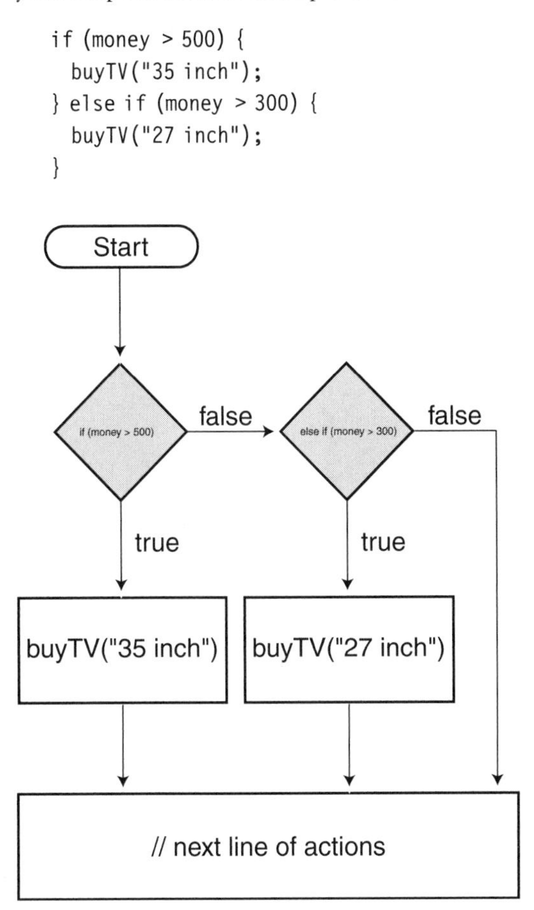

This script executes various actions depending on the value of `money`: "If `money` has a value greater than 500, buy the 35-inch TV." If `money` has a value less than 500, this part of the script is ignored and the next condition is examined. The next condition says that if `money` has a value greater than 300, buy the 27-inch TV. Thus, if `money` has a value of `450` when this script is executed, the first part of the statement is ignored (because 450 is not greater than 500), but the second part of the statement is executed (because a value of 450 *is* greater than 300). If `money` has a value less than 300, both parts of this statement are ignored.

You can create several lines of `if/else if` statements that react to dozens of conditions.

If/Else Statements

An `if/else` statement allows your script to take action if no conditions in the statement prove true. Consider this the fail-safe part of the statement.

```
if (money > 500) {
  buyTV("35 inch");
} else if (money > 300) {
  buyTV("27 inch");
} else {
  workOvertime ();
}
```

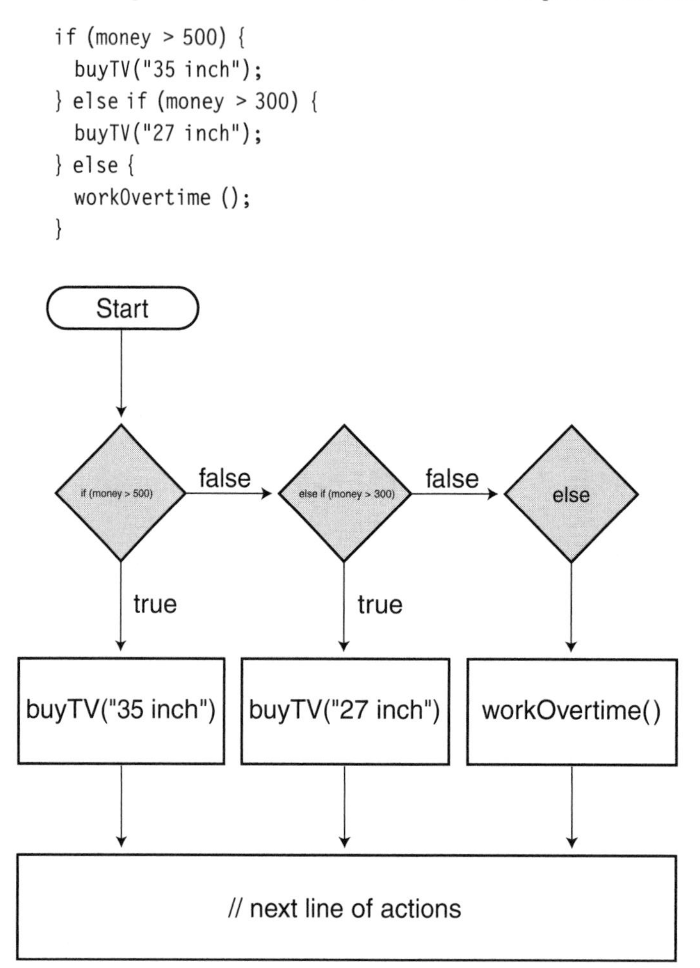

In this script, if `money` doesn't have a value of at least 300, neither of the conditions analyzed is true; as a result, neither of the actions that follow the conditions will be executed. Instead, the actions following the `else` part of the statement are executed—it's a bit like saying this:

```
if (...this is true) {
  // Do this
} otherwise, if (...this is true) {
  // Do this
} otherwise, if none of the conditions above is true {
  // Do this
}
```

CONDITIONAL STATEMENT VARIATIONS

The statements we've discussed so far (and the syntax used) form the basis of most of the conditional logic you'll use in your projects. However, as with most things in ActionScript, there's more than one way to script a conditional statement. Let's look at a couple of these variations and how you might use them to shorten your code and make it easier to read. The following variations have no programmatic advantage over the versions we've already discussed. How you take advantage of them is determined by personal preference.

A `switch` statement, which is a variation on the `if/else` statement, can be useful if you want a script to take a specific set of actions when an exact value exists. For example:

```
switch (favoriteBand) {
case "Beatles":
  gotoAndPlay("Beatles");
  break;
case "U2":
  gotoAndPlay("U2");
  break;
default:
  gotoAndPlay("Slim Whitman");
}
```

A single expression in parentheses (usually a variable) is evaluated once. The value of the expression is compared with the values for each `case` in the structure. If a match exists, the block of code associated with that `case` is executed. If no match is found, the `default` statement at the end is executed. `break` is used in each `case` to prevent the code from automatically running into the next `case` if a match has already been found. Each `case` can check string values (as shown in the example), numeric values, and Boolean values of `true` and `false`. (For Boolean values, however, the variation we describe next represents an easier and more appropriate technique.)

The *ternary operator* (`?:`) lets you write a simple `if/else` statement in one line. Here's an example:

```
var myMood:String = ((money > 1000000) ? "Happy" : "Sad");
```

If the condition within the parentheses evaluates to `true`, the first expression (`"Happy"`) is set as the value of `myMood`. If the condition evaluates to `false`, the second expression (`"Sad"`) is used. This single line of ActionScript accomplishes the same thing as the following code:

```
if (money > 1000000) {
  myMood = "Happy";
} else {
  myMood = "Sad";
}
```

Here's an example of an extended way to use the ternary operator:

```
var myMood:String = "I'm " + ((money > 1000000) ? "happy" : "sad");
```

In this example, myMood will have a value of either "I'm happy" or "I'm sad" depending on whether the value of money is greater than or less than 1000000.

The ternary operator is commonly used to toggle variable states. Here's an example:

```
var playSound:Boolean = (playSound) ? false : true;
```

Every time this script is executed, the variable playSound is changed from true to false or from false to true.

DETERMINING CONDITIONS

Your project may contain numerous conditions you can use to control the way your script works or interacts with the user. Although a condition can take many forms, at its core it represents a circumstance that is either true or false. Conditional statements look for common conditions like these:

- One object comes into contact with another object
- Something is on or off
- A movie clip's position, size, or other property is greater than, less than, or equal to another value
- The user has a specific interaction with the mouse or keyboard
- Text or numeric values are greater than, less than, or equal to another value
- Any combination of the conditions above

REACTING TO MULTIPLE CONDITIONS

For a successful rocket launch to occur, a number of conditions must be met. One of the most important variables affecting a rocket launch is weather, which helps determine not only how the rocket is propelled but how it's controlled. In the following exercise, we'll begin scripting a project so that the rocket will react differently based on randomly generated weather conditions.

1) Open *rocketLaunch1.fla* in the Lesson08/Assets folder.

This file contains a single scene made up of eight layers, named according to their contents. Let's look at the various elements in the scene.

The Weather layer contains a movie clip instance the size of the movie itself. This movie clip, named **weather_mc**, represents the background sky in the scene. Its timeline contains three frame labels: Sunny, Rainy, and Night. At each of these frame labels, the sky graphic changes to match the name of the label. At Sunny, the sky appears sunny; at Rainy, it appears overcast; at Night, it looks dark.

The Ground/Central Graphics layer contains the mountains, ground, and main Central Command graphics. There is also a small movie clip instance of a red dot, which blinks to indicate the launch location on the globe.

The Rocket layer obviously contains our rocket—that is, a movie clip instance named **rocket_mc**. Its timeline contains two frame labels: `off` and `on`. At the `off` label, the rocket doesn't show a flame; at the `on` label, it does, providing a visual indicator of the rocket in motion.

The Control Panel layer contains several elements, the most conspicuous of which is the red Launch button named **launch_btn**. This button will be used not only to launch the rocket but also to reset the scene after a launch has been attempted. Below this button is a movie clip instance named **thrustBoost_mc** that includes the text "Thrusters." This clip also contains two frame labels: `on` and `off`. At the `on` label, the text appears big and red to provide a visual indication that thrust is being applied to the rocket. This layer's last element is a text field in the lower-right portion of the stage with an instance name of **weatherText_txt**. This text field provides a textual indication of current weather conditions.

The Status layer contains a movie clip instance named **status_mc** that appears as a small circle in the middle of the sky. It looks this way because the first frame of its timeline contains no graphical content. This clip provides a text message about the launch's success or failure. There are three frame labels on this movie clip's timeline: *off*, *abort*, and *success*. At the *off* frame label, the status displays no text. At the *abort* label, a text message appears: "Launch Aborted." At the *success* label, a different text message appears: "Launch Successful."

The Launch Window layer contains a movie clip instance named **launchWindow_mc**, showing two red bars. The space between the red bars represents the launch window—the area the rocket must pass through to have a successful launch.

The Sound Clips layer contains a movie clip instance named **sounds_mc** that also appears as a small circle just above the stage, on the left side. Its timeline contains frame labels named *intro*, *launch*, *abort*, and *success*. At each of these labels is an appropriate sound clip (the *launch* label has a launch sound, the *abort* label has an abort sound, and so on). Various scripts will send this clip to these frame labels to provide audio effects for the project.

The Actions layer will contain all the scripts for this project. Let's begin.

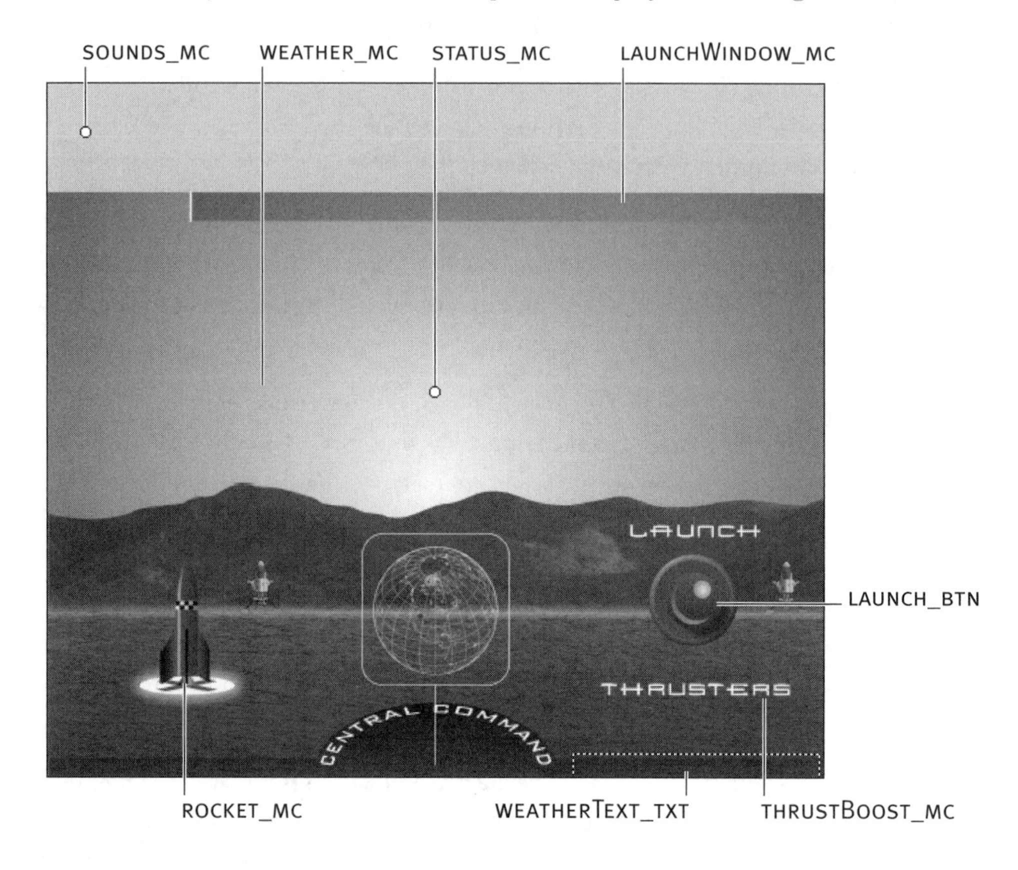

2) With the Actions panel open, select Frame 1 of the Actions layer and add the following script:

```
var noThrust:Number;
var thrust:Number;
function setWeatherConditions(){
var randomWeather:Number = random (3);
var conditions:String;
if (randomWeather == 0) {
    conditions = "Sunny";
    noThrust = 3;
    thrust = 6;
} else if (randomWeather == 1) {
    conditions = "Rainy";
    noThrust = 2;
    thrust = 4;
} else {
    conditions = "Night";
    noThrust = 1;
    thrust = 2;
}
}
```

The first two lines of this script declare two variables: `noThrust` and `thrust`. (We'll elaborate on the purposes of these two variables in a moment.) This function is used to make the project react to random weather conditions. The function's first action sets the value of the `randomWeather` variable, based on a randomly generated number (from three possibilities: 0, 1, or 2). The next line declares the `conditions` variable, which will be used later in the function.

NOTE *You may wonder why the first two variables (`noThrust` and `thrust`) are declared outside the function definition, yet `randomWeather` and `conditions` are declared within the function definition. The `randomWeather` and `condition` variables will be used only within this function definition, so they need to exist only as local variables of the function. The `noThrust` and `thrust` variables will be used later, by other parts of the script. Because `noThrust` and `thrust` must exist as timeline variables, they're created outside the function definition, and the function is used to set their values. For more information on functions, see Lesson 5, "Using Functions."*

Next, an `if` statement within the function definition analyzes the value of `randomWeather` so that the values of three other variables can be set. If `randomWeather` has a value of `0`, the variable named `conditions` is created on this timeline and assigned a string value of `"Sunny"`. In addition, the values of `noThrust` and `thrust` are set to `3` and `6`, respectively. If the value of `randomWeather` isn't 0, that part of the statement is ignored, at which point an `else if` statement checks whether `randomWeather` has a value of `1`. If so, the variables are instead assigned values of `"Rainy"`, `2`, and `4`, respectively. If the value of `randomWeather` isn't 1, that part of the statement is ignored, at which point the actions following the `else` statement are executed.

Remember that an `else` statement enables you to define what happens if none of the previous conditions in the statement has proven true but you still want *something* to happen. In this case, if the previous conditions proved false, the actions under the `else` statement are executed, setting the value of the variables we've been discussing to `"Night"`, `1`, and `2`, respectively.

The value of the `conditions` variable will be used in a moment to set how the weather will appear graphically in the scene. The other two variables will soon be used to establish how fast the **rocket_mc** instance will move based on the weather condition generated.

3) Add this script after the end of the `if` statement (but within the function definition):

```
weather_mc.gotoAndStop (conditions);
weatherText_txt.text = "Weather: " + conditions;
```

These two actions occur as soon as the `if` statement is analyzed, and both use the value of `conditions` to react in unique ways. The first action moves the **weather_mc** movie clip instance to a frame label based on the value of `conditions`. If `conditions` has a value of `"Rainy"`, the **weather_mc** movie clip instance moves to that frame label, where the weather appears rainy. The next action determines what will be displayed in the **weatherText_txt** text field in the lower-right portion of the stage. If `conditions` has a value of `"Rainy"`, this text field displays `Weather: Rainy`.

IF (RANDOMWEATHER == 0) IF (RANDOMWEATHER == 1) ELSE

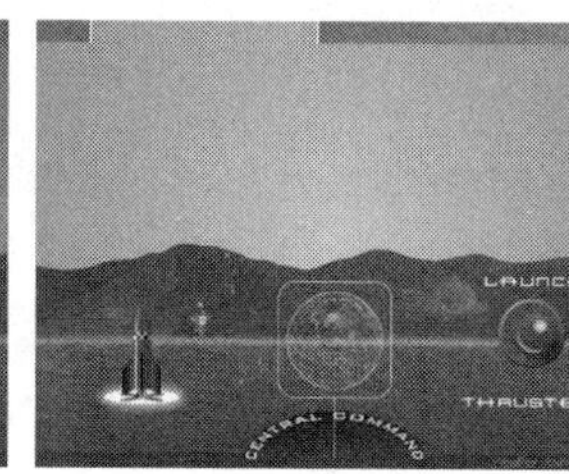

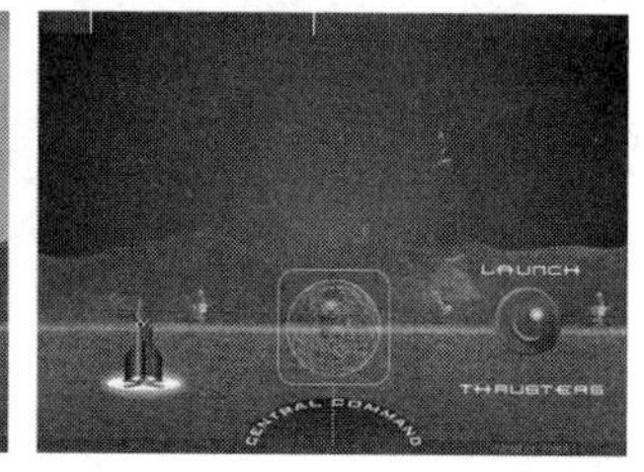

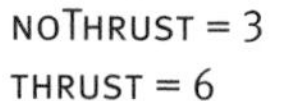
NOTHRUST = 3
THRUST = 6

NOTHRUST = 2
THRUST = 4

NOTHRUST = 1
THRUST = 2

4) Add this script at the end of the function definition:

```
setWeatherConditions();
```

This script calls the `setWeatherConditions()` function as soon as the movie begins to play.

5) Choose Control > Test Movie to test the functionality of the project at this point.
As soon as the movie plays, the script we just added in the preceding steps is executed. The graphical representation of the weather, as well as the text displayed in the lower-right portion of the screen, are affected by the random number generated in the script.

NOTE *Repeated testing may give you different results each time.*

6) While still in the testing environment, choose Debug > List Variables.
This step opens the Output window, allowing you to see the values of variables on different timelines. A quick glance reveals the values of the `thrust` and `noThrust` variables in the main timeline. We'll use these values shortly.

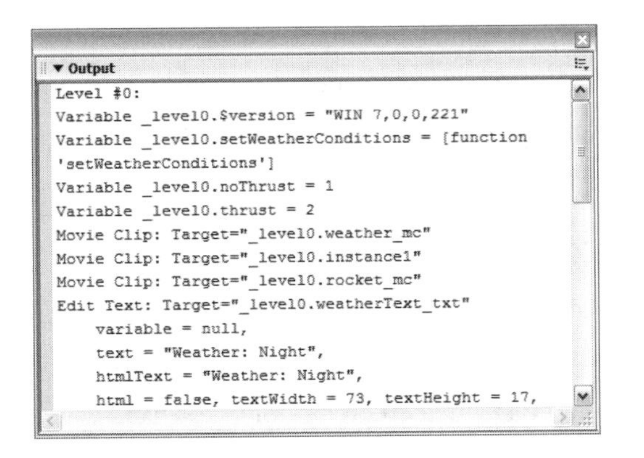
Output
Level #0:
Variable _level0.$version = "WIN 7,0,0,221"
Variable _level0.setWeatherConditions = [function
'setWeatherConditions']
Variable _level0.noThrust = 1
Variable _level0.thrust = 2
Movie Clip: Target="_level0.weather_mc"
Movie Clip: Target="_level0.instance1"
Movie Clip: Target="_level0.rocket_mc"
Edit Text: Target="_level0.weatherText_txt"
variable = null,
text = "Weather: Night",
htmlText = "Weather: Night",
html = false, textWidth = 73, textHeight = 17,

7) Close the test environment to return to the authoring environment, and save your work as *rocketLaunch2.fla*.

We'll build on this file in the next exercise.

DEFINING A BOUNDARY

We contend with boundaries every day. Although boundaries can take many forms—physical, financial, mental—in the end they're nothing more than an indication of a limit. To make a boundary work, you define its limits and take appropriate action when (or just before) those limits are exceeded. Think of driving a car: lines on the road define the boundaries within which the car is supposed to remain. If you're approaching the line on the left (the left boundary), you move the steering wheel to adjust; if you're approaching the line on the right, you adjust in the opposite direction—conditional logic in action! Written in ActionScript, those actions might look like this:

```
if (car_mc._x < leftOfRoad) {
  turnWheel ("right");
} else if (car_mc._x > rightOfRoad) {
  turnWheel ("left");
}
```

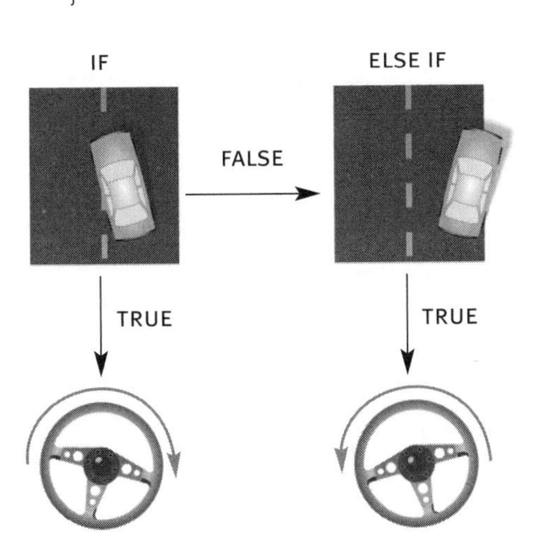
IF
ELSE IF
FALSE
TRUE
TRUE

To make a boundary work in Flash, you must define its limits and use an `if` statement to check the affected element each time an event occurs that might cause the element to exceed its defined boundaries. This concept will become clearer as we progress through the following exercise.

For example, boundaries in Flash might be used to do the following:

- Prevent the properties of movie clip instances (including `x`, `y`, `alpha`, `xscale`, `yscale`, and so on) from being changed beyond specified amounts
- Invoke an action (property change or method) when an element is within or exceeds a specified boundary
- Prevent data values from exceeding defined limits (useful when validating data)

In the following exercise, we'll dynamically animate the red bars at the top of the project to represent a moving "launch window" through which the rocket must pass to complete a successful launch.

1) Open *rocketLaunch2.fla*.

We'll continue building on the file you worked with in the preceding exercise.

2) With the Actions panel open, select Frame 1 of the Actions layer and add this script at the end of the current script:

```
var direction:String;
function launchWinMove(){
  if (launchWindow_mc._x < 0) {
    direction = "right";
} else if (launchWindow_mc._x > 550) {
    direction = "left";
}
if (direction == "right") {
    launchWindow_mc._x = launchWindow_mc._x + 3;
} else {
    launchWindow_mc._x = launchWindow_mc._x - 3;
}
}
_root.onEnterFrame = launchWinMove;
```

Three changes occur with this added script: you create the `direction` variable, define the `launchWinMove()` function (which uses the `direction` variable), and set the `launchWinMove()` function to be triggered with an `onEnterFrame` event. Let's look at how the function works.

The two red bars at the top of the stage are part of the composite movie clip instance named **launchWindow_mc**. The function in this step uses two `if` statements to move this movie clip instance back and forth from left to right. Triggering this function using the `onEnterFrame` event causes these statements to be evaluated 24 times per second (the frame rate of the movie).

The first statement analyzes the position of the **launchWindow_mc** instance as it moves within a specified boundary. The statement says that if the horizontal (x) position of this instance is less than 0—that is, its center point exceeds the left boundary of the stage—set the value of `direction` to `"right"`. If the horizontal position is greater than 550—its center point exceeds the right boundary of the stage—set the value of `direction` to `"left"`. The value of `direction` changes *only* if one of the limits of the boundary is exceeded. This will occur as a result of the movie clip instance being put into motion in the next `if` statement. This statement says that if `direction` has a value of `"right"`, move the instance to its current horizontal position *plus* 3. This action moves the instance to the right. Otherwise (`else`), if `direction` has a value of `"left"`, move the instance to its current horizontal position *minus* 3. This action moves the instance to the left. When these two `if` statements are analyzed and their actions executed 24 times a second, the red bars are set into motion, but the movement of the bars is restricted to a specified area.

NOTE *When creating boundaries in your scripts, note which event handler might cause an element to exceed a boundary, and use that event to analyze the boundary conditional statement. For example, if you want to take a specific action whenever a movie clip instance's vertical position exceeds an established boundary while being dragged around the stage, the* `mouseMove` *event handler would be an ideal choice because it can easily cause a dragged movie clip instance to exceed its boundary.*

These two `if` statements in our script work in harmony. The direction of the movement in **launchWindow_mc** is determined by the boundary it last exceeded (which sets the value of `direction` to either `"left"` or `"right"`)—that is, movement is in the opposite direction of the boundary exceeded. Eventually a boundary will be exceeded again, and the process will be repeated in the opposite direction. In other words, if `direction` has a value of `"right"`, the instance will move right, eventually exceeding the right part of the boundary—at which point the value of `direction` is set to `"left"` and the process is reversed.

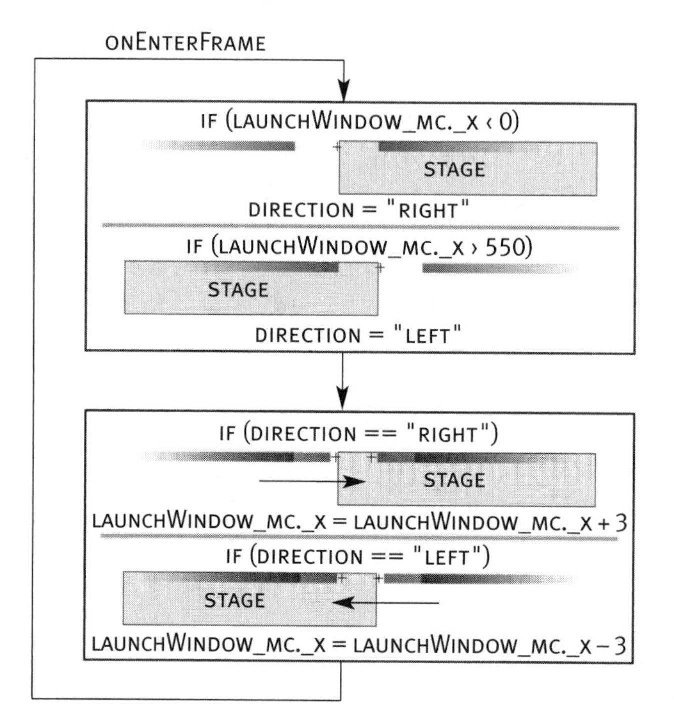

The instance's initial position on the stage is one pixel past the left boundary. When this script is first executed, `direction` is set to `"right"` and the instance moves to the right.

3) Choose Control > Test Movie to test the project's functionality so far.

When the movie plays, the red bars are set into motion. When either boundary defined in Step 2 is exceeded, the bar moves in the opposite direction.

4) Close the test environment to return to the authoring environment, and save your work as *rocketLaunch3.fla*.

We'll build on this file in the next exercise.

TURNING POWER ON/OFF

Sometimes certain actions execute *only* if something is turned on. A car is a real-world example: try driving the car without starting it and you won't get far. A car is designed so that it will run only after you've given it power by turning on the ignition. In similar fashion, something can happen in your movie to trigger your script's functionality (to turn it on).

Think of it this way: events power scripts by triggering actions. The scripts themselves represent the mechanism, or "machine," for accomplishing various tasks. Conditional logic can be used as an on/off switch in your scripts, allowing actions to execute—as the result of an event—only under certain circumstances.

For example, consider this script:

```
function clockEnabled(power:Boolean){
  if(power == true){
    clock_mc.onEnterFrame = function () {
      this._rotation += 1;
    }
  }else{
    delete clock_mc.onEnterFrame;
  }
}
```

When this function is called, it's passed a value of `true` or `false`, such as:

```
clockEnabled(true);
```

The conditional statement within the function checks this value and reacts accordingly. If the value `true` is passed to the function, an `onEnterFrame` event is attached to the **clock_mc** movie clip instance, causing it to rotate 1 degree with each `onEnterFrame` event. As a result, the clock appears to have its power turned on. If you wanted to "unplug" the clock's power, you'd simply call the function again, passing it a value of `false`:

```
clockEnabled(false);
```

The function checks this value and reacts accordingly. In this case, the conditional statement is set up so that sending the function a value of `false` causes the `onEnterFrame` event to be deleted, causing the clock to stop its rotation. The function call essentially becomes the on/off switch for the clock.

Many desktop software applications make use of this scripting functionality to allow users to turn program capabilities on and off through preference settings in dialog boxes. Because Flash projects are usually steeped in multimedia and animation—which are often triggered by an executing script—you can use this on/off capability to restrict a script's power until you need it, essentially turning off timelines, animations, and more.

The next exercise uses these scripting concepts to put the rocket into motion only after the Launch button has been clicked and released.

1) Open *rocketLaunch3.fla*.

We'll continue building on the file you worked with in the preceding exercise.

2) With the Actions panel open, select Frame 1 of the Actions layer and add this script at the end of the current script:

```
var rocketLaunched:Boolean = false;
var speed:Number = noThrust;
```

The first line creates the `rocketLaunched` variable and assigns it an initial value of `false`. This variable will be used to track whether the rocket is in motion (the importance of the `rocketLaunched` variable is discussed in the next exercise). The initial value is `false` because the rocket is initially stationary.

The purpose of the second line of script is to set the value of a variable named `speed` to the value of `noThrust`. The `setWeatherConditions()` function created in the first exercise of this lesson sets the values of `thrust` and `noThrust` based on the value of `randomWeather`. When this line of script is executed, `noThrust` will have a value of 1, 2, or 3—that is, the value that `speed` is set to. (The value of the `speed` variable will be used to set the intital speed of the rocket.)

3) Add this function definition after the script you just added in Step 2:

```
function rocketLaunch(){
  rocketLaunched = true;
  sounds_mc.gotoAndPlay("launch");
  rocket_mc.gotoAndStop("on");
  rocket_mc.onEnterFrame = function(){
    this._y -= speed;
    if(this._y < _y){
      launchSuccess();
    }
  }
}
```

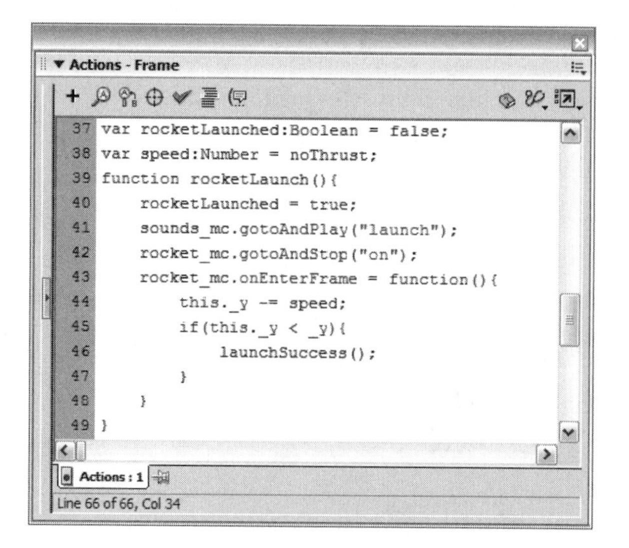

The rocketLaunch() function sets the rocket into motion. In a moment, we'll set up a Launch button to call this function. First, let's take a look at what happens when this function is called. The function begins by setting the value of rocketLaunched to true, indicating that the rocket has been put into motion. The next line sends the **sounds_mc** movie clip instance to the frame labeled *launch*, where an audio clip of a rocket blasting off will play. The next line sends the **rocket_mc** instance to the frame labeled *on*, causing flame to appear at the bottom of the rocket.

Next, an onEnterFrame event handler is dynamically attached to the **rocket_mc** instance; the script within the event handler is executed at the frame rate of our movie, 24 frames per second.

The first line within the event handler moves the rocket to its current vertical position, minus the value of speed. We've used a scripting shortcut of

```
this._y -= speed
```

to denote the longhand version of

```
this._y = this._y - speed
```

Remember that the value of speed is set to the value of noThrust, as described in Step 2. If speed is set to 2, with each onEnterFrame event the _y property value of **rocket_mc** will be decreased by 2, causing it to move upward.

NOTE *Remember that the use of* this *in an event handler method is a direct reference to the object to which the event handler method is attached. As such,* this._y *in this step is a reference to the _y property of the* **rocket_mc** *movie clip instance.*

With the **rocket_mc** movie clip instance moving upward, its y position will eventually exceed the y position of the stage (the top of the stage). The if statement within the event handler method checks for this occurrence. Because this if statement is within the onEnterFrame event handler, the condition is checked 24 times a second. When it becomes true, the launchSuccess() function is called, turning off power to the rocket.

4) Add the following function definition after the current script:

```
function launchSuccess(){
  rocketLaunched = false;
  status_mc.gotoAndStop("success");
  sounds_mc.gotoAndPlay("success");
  rocket_mc.gotoAndStop("off");
  delete rocket_mc.onEnterFrame;
}
```

This function is called when the rocket's y position exceeds that of the stage. It begins by setting the value of the `rocketLaunched` variable to `false`, indicating that the rocket has completed its ascent and is no longer moving. The next line sends the **status_mc** movie clip instance to the frame labeled *success*, causing the message "Launch Successful" to appear in the middle of the screen. The next line sends the **sounds_mc** movie clip instance to the frame labeled *success* on the clip's timeline. At this label, a short audio clip plays, indicating that the launch was successful. The last line deletes the `onEnterFrame` event handler method from the **rocket_mc** movie clip instance. Because the rocket has moved beyond the boundary of the stage, this event handler method, which moves the rocket upward, is no longer necessary. Power to the rocket is turned off.

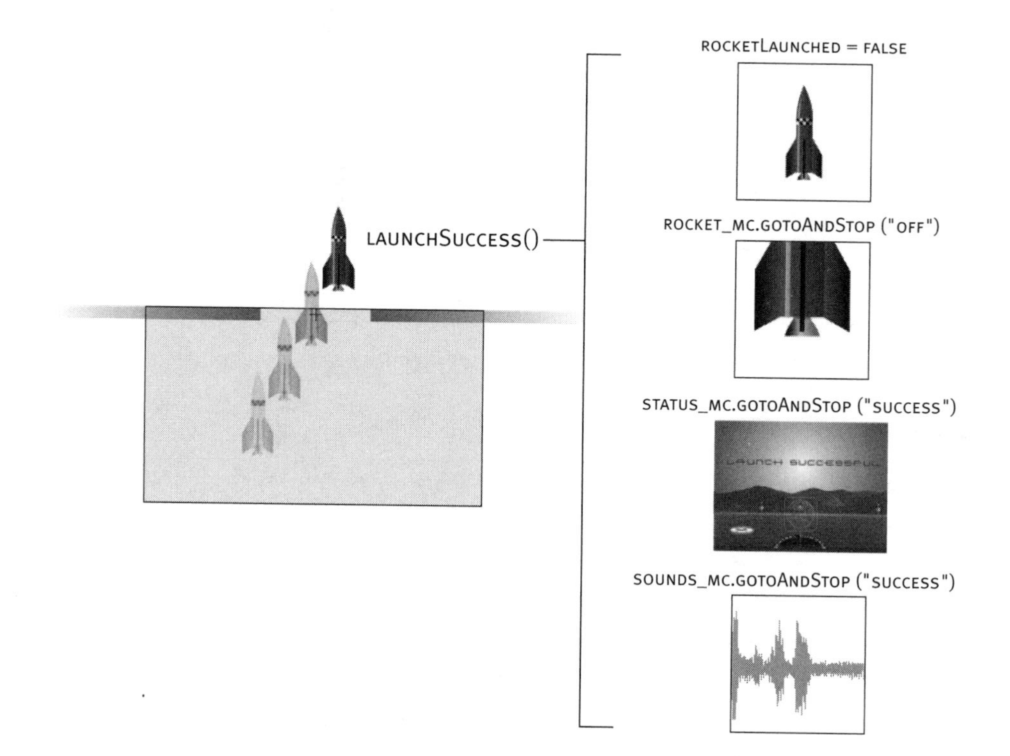

5) Add this line of script at the end of the current script:

```
launch_btn.onRelease = rocketLaunch;
```

Here we've set our Launch button, named **launch_btn**, to call the `rocketLaunch()` function when the button is clicked and released. This action causes the functionality we discussed in Steps 3 and 4 to execute. Let's try it.

6) Choose Control > Test Movie.

Click the Launch button and the rocket begins moving upward. As soon as it moves past the top of the stage, any further movement stops and the application provides visual and auditory indicators showing that the launch was successful.

We want the user to be able to launch the rocket more than once, so let's add a script to enable this functionality.

7) Close the test movie to return to the authoring environment. With the Actions panel open, select Frame 1 of the Actions layer and add the following script at the end of the current script:

```
function rocketReset(){
  rocketLaunched = false;
  status_mc.gotoAndStop("off");
  sounds_mc.gotoAndPlay("intro");
  rocket_mc.gotoAndStop("off");
  rocket_mc._x = 98;
  rocket_mc._y = 352;
  delete rocket_mc.onEnterFrame;
}
launch_btn.onPress = rocketReset;
```

The first part of this script defines a function named `rocketReset()`. The purpose of this function is to reset the elements in the scene to their original states. The function first resets the value of `rocketLaunched` to `false`. The three lines that follow reset the **status_mc**, **sounds_mc**, and **rocket_mc** movie clip instances to their initial frame labels. The next two lines place the **rocket_mc** movie clip instance back on the launch pad. The last line in the function definition removes the `onEnterFrame` event handler from the **rocket_mc** movie clip instance, essentially turning it off for the purpose of resetting the scene. The last line sets the Launch button to call this function whenever the button is clicked.

8) Choose Control > Test Movie to test the functionality of the project up to this point.

Click and release the Launch button to set the rocket into motion. Holding down the Launch button at this point will reset the scene. Releasing it again restarts the launch process.

9) Close the test environment to return to the authoring environment, and save your work as *rocketLaunch4.fla*.

We'll build on this file in the next exercise.

REACTING TO USER INTERACTION

Users interact with a movie via the mouse or the keyboard, either of which can be used in a number of ways—moving the mouse pointer around the screen, clicking and releasing buttons or keys, and so forth. Using conditional logic, you can script a movie to react in various ways based on the user's interaction with the movie.

In the following exercise, you'll add functionality that allows the user to press the Spacebar on the keyboard to apply "thrusters" that move the rocket upward at a quicker-than-usual pace.

1) Open *rocketLaunch4.fla*.

We'll continue building on the file you worked with in the preceding exercise.

When the movie first begins to play, the `setWeatherConditions()` function is called and takes several actions based on the value of a variable named `randomWeather`: it displays a random weather graphic and sets the values of the variables `thrust` and `noThrust`. The variable `thrust` is given a value double that of `noThrust` at the time the variables are set. If `noThrust` has a value of `2`, for example, `thrust` has a value of `4`. Farther down in the script we've been building, the `speed` variable is set to the value of `noThrust`. If `noThrust` has a value of `2`, for example, `speed` has the same value. (Remember that the value of `speed` is used to determine how fast the rocket moves upward.) In this exercise, we'll set the value of `speed` to either `thrust` or `noThrust`, depending on whether the Spacebar is pressed.

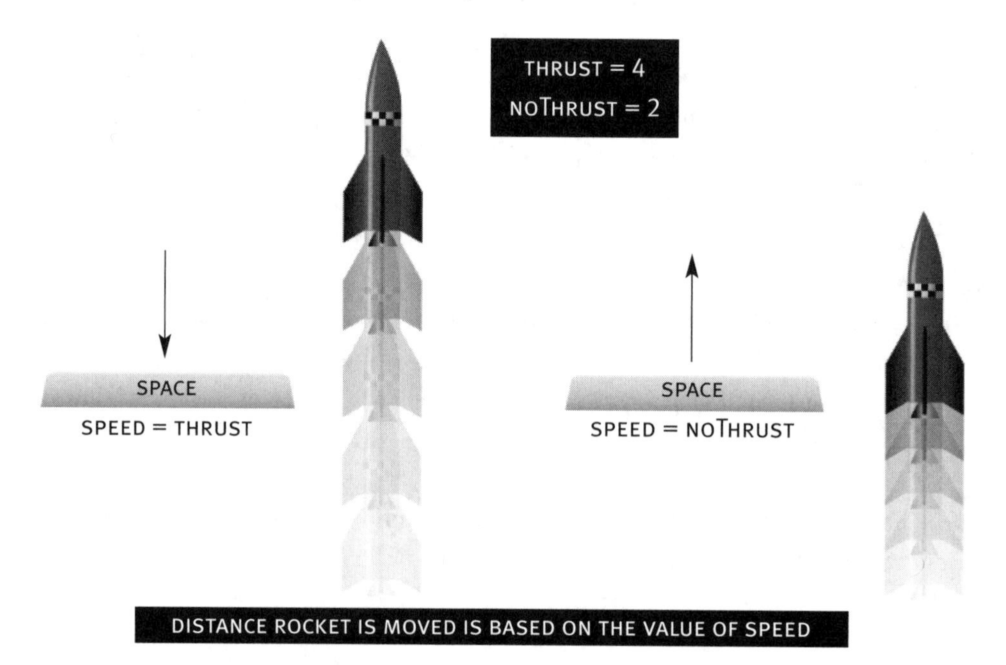

2) With the Actions panel open, select Frame 1 of the Actions layer and add this script at the end of the current script:

```
function rocketThrustIncrease(){
  if(rocketLaunched && Key.isDown(Key.SPACE)){
    speed = thrust;
    thrustBoost_mc.gotoAndStop("on");
  }
}
_root.onKeyDown = rocketThrustIncrease;
```

The first part of this script defines a function named `rocketThrustIncrease()`. The `if` statement in this function looks for two conditions: whether `rocketLaunched` has a value of `true` *and* whether the Spacebar is pressed. If both conditions are true when this function is called, two actions within the `if` statement are executed. The first action sets the value of `speed` to the value of `thrust` to move the rocket upward at twice its current rate. The next action tells the **thrustBoost_mc** movie clip instance (just below the Launch button in the scene) to go to the frame labeled *on*, where big red text displays the word "Thrusters."

NOTE *We check the value of* `rocketLaunched` *in the* `if` *statement because the two actions within the statement should not be executed if the rocket is stationary.*

The last line in this script sets the `rocketThrustIncrease()` function to be called whenever a key is pressed on the keyboard. When a key is pressed, the function is called; before it executes any actions, the function evaluates whether the rocket is in motion and whether the key being pressed is the Spacebar.

We also need a mechanism that allows the rocket to return to its initial speed. That's what the next script does.

3) Add this script after the script you just added in Step 2:

```
function rocketThrustReset(){
  if(!Key.isDown(Key.SPACE)){
    speed = noThrust;
    thrustBoost_mc.gotoAndStop("off");
  }
}
_root.onKeyUp = rocketThrustReset;
Key.addListener(_root);
```

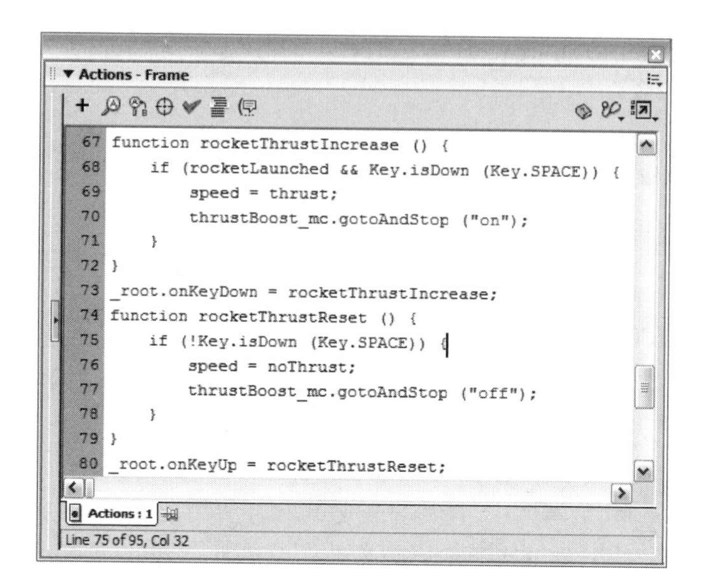

Actions - Frame
67 function rocketThrustIncrease () {
68 if (rocketLaunched && Key.isDown (Key.SPACE)) {
69 speed = thrust;
70 thrustBoost_mc.gotoAndStop ("on");
71 }
72 }
73 _root.onKeyDown = rocketThrustIncrease;
74 function rocketThrustReset () {
75 if (!Key.isDown (Key.SPACE)) {
76 speed = noThrust;
77 thrustBoost_mc.gotoAndStop ("off");
78 }
79 }
80 _root.onKeyUp = rocketThrustReset;
Actions : 1
Line 75 of 95, Col 32

This script's syntax is similar to that of the script in Step 2, but this script works in the opposite manner. For starters, the `rocketThrustReset()` function is called whenever a key is *released* on the keyboard. A conditional statement within the function definition checks whether the Spacebar *is not* pressed. If the Spacebar is not pressed, two actions are executed. The first action resets the value of `speed` to the value of `noThrust` (the initial value of `speed`). The next action tells the **thrustBoost_mc** movie clip instance to go to the frame labeled *off*, where the text "Thrusters" appears as it did initially.

The last line registers the `_root` timeline to listen for `Key` events. (Typically, timelines don't need to be registered to listen for events such as `onEnterFrame`, `onLoad`, and so on in order to access the event's functionality.)

4) Choose Control > Test Movie to test the functionality of your project so far.

Click and release the Launch button. As soon as you release the button, the rocket is set into motion. Pressing the Spacebar should cause the rocket to move upward at twice its current speed. Releasing the Spacebar should return the rocket's speed to its initial value.

5) Close the test environment to return to the authoring environment, and save your work as *rocketLaunch5.fla*.

We'll build on this file in the next exercise.

DETECTING COLLISIONS

Many Flash applications, especially games, are able to detect object collisions—one of the most easily understood applications of conditional logic.

To detect collisions between two objects (movie clip instances), ActionScript provides the `hitTest()` method of the MovieClip class. Using this method in conjunction with a conditional statement allows you to take action when two movie clips collide. You define in the script the various actions you want to take, depending on which object is hit. Take a look at the following script:

```
myBody_mc.onEnterFrame = function() {
  if (hitTest ("wallOfCotton_mc")) {
    pain = 0;
  } else if (hitTest ("wallOfCardboard_mc")) {
    pain = 5;
  } else if (hitTest ("wallOfBricks_mc")) {
    pain = 10;
  }
}
```

If the movie clip instance to which this event handler is attached (**myBody_mc**) collides with the movie clip instance named **wallOfCotton_mc**, `pain` is set to `0`. If **myBody_mc** collides with **wallOfCardboard_mc**, `pain` is set to `5`. Finally, if **myBody_mc** collides with **wallOfBricks_mc**, `pain` is set to `10`. The `hitTest()` method is very straightforward.

In the following exercise, we use the `hitTest()` method in conjunction with a conditional statement to take specific action if the **rocket_mc** movie clip instance collides with either of the two red bars (the launch window) that are in motion. If the rocket hits either bar, the launch aborts; if the rocket passes through the space between the bars, the launch is successful.

1) Open *rocketLaunch5.fla*.

This step builds on the file you worked with in the preceding exercise.

2) Double-click *launchWindow_mc* at the top of the stage to edit this clip in place.

This movie clip instance contains other two movie clip instances: the red bars, with one flipped horizontally in the opposite direction of the other. The red bar on the left is named **leftGuide_mc** and the one on the right is named **rightGuide_mc**. Because both of these bars are movie clip instances, you can use them to react to a collision with the **rocket_mc** movie clip instance.

3) Return to the main timeline. With the Actions panel open, select Frame 1 of the Actions layer and add the following script:

```
launchWindow_mc.onEnterFrame = function () {
  if (this.leftGuide_mc.hitTest ("_root.rocket_mc")
  ⇒|| this.rightGuide_mc.hitTest ("_root.rocket_mc")) {
    launchAbort ();
  }
};
```

The script attaches an `onEnterFrame` event handler to the **launchWindow_mc** movie clip instance. The script executes at our project's frame rate of 24 frames a second.

The conditional statement within this script does one thing: using the `hitTest()` method and the OR logical operator (`||`), it checks whether the **rocket_mc** movie clip instance has collided with the **leftGuide_mc** *or* **rightGuide_mc** movie clip instance, which are both inside the **launchWindow_mc** movie clip instance. If at any time either condition proves `true`, the `launchAbort()` function is called. Let's create that function, and wrap up our work on this project.

4) Place this function definition at the end of the current script:

```
function launchAbort () {
  rocketLaunched = false;
  status_mc.gotoAndStop ("abort");
  sounds_mc.gotoAndPlay ("abort");
  rocket_mc.gotoAndStop ("off");
  rocket_mc._x = 98;
  rocket_mc._y = 352;
  delete rocket_mc.onEnterFrame;
}
```

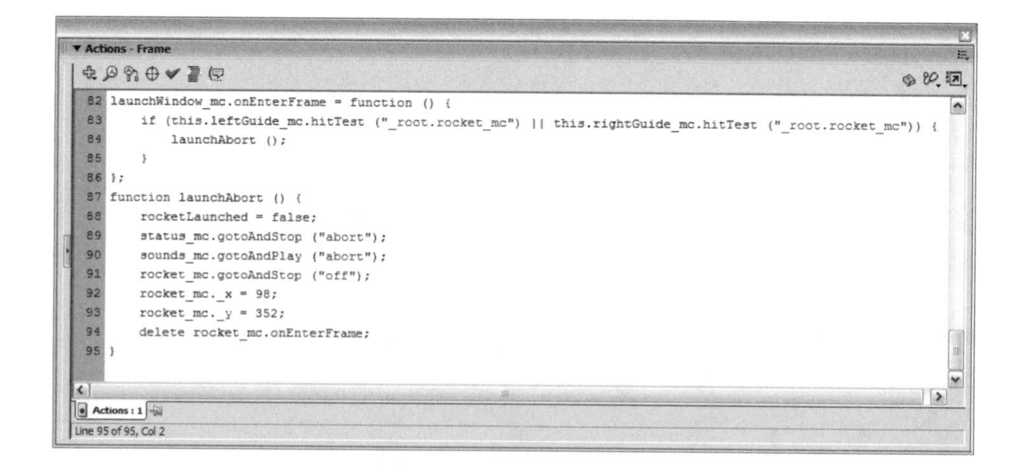

This function works in almost the same manner as that of the `rocketReset()` function we created earlier in this lesson. The difference is that both the **status_mc** and **sounds_mc** movie clip instances are moved to the frame labeled *abort* in the `launchAbort()` function.

Scripting for our project is complete. Let's do a final test.

5) Choose Control > Test Movie to test your project.

Click and hold down the Launch button to experience what happens at prelaunch. Release the button to launch the rocket. Apply thrusters with the idea of getting the rocket through the space between the red bars. If you get through, the launch will be successful; if you don't, it will abort.

6) Close the test environment to return to the authoring environment, and save your work as *rocketLaunch6.fla*.

This step completes the exercise and this lesson.

By using conditional logic in your scripts, you can greatly increase your project's dynamism and provide a unique experience to every person who interacts with it.

WHAT YOU HAVE LEARNED

In this lesson, you have:

- Learned how to use `if`, `if/else`, and `if/else if` statements to control the flow of a script (pages 276–278)
- Learned about the operators used in conditional logic (pages 279–280)
- Scripted a project to react to various conditions (pages 281–289)
- Created a scripted boundary to restrict an object's movement (pages 289–292)
- Turned a script on and off using conditional logic (pages 292–297)
- Programmed a project to react to user interaction (pages 298–300)
- Learned how to detect and react to object collisions (pages 301–303)

automating scripts with loops

LESSON 9

We all have to perform repetitive tasks. Whether complicated or simple, a repetitive task requires performing at least one step in a process repeatedly. For example, if you were sending out 100 wedding invitations, repetitive tasks in that process could include folding papers, stuffing envelopes, sealing envelopes, and affixing stamps—you'd do each task 100 times. In ActionScript, performing a set of repeated steps (*actions*) multiple times is called *looping*. ActionScript lets you loop through a set of actions as many times as needed, which means that instead of writing an action (or set of actions) several times, you can write it once and loop through it any number of times. In this lesson, you'll learn how to use the three loop types that ActionScript offers.

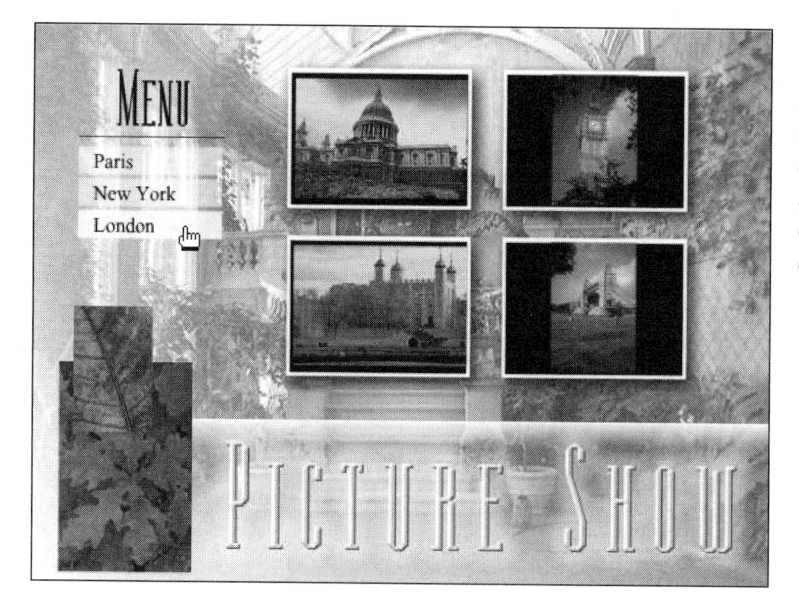

The drop-down list as well as the two-by-two grid of pictures in this application will be created dynamically by using loops.

WHAT YOU WILL LEARN

In this lesson, you will:

- Discover the usefulness of loops
- Learn about the types of loops
- Set loop conditions
- Create a nested loop
- Use loop exceptions

APPROXIMATE TIME

This lesson takes approximately 45 minutes to complete.

LESSON FILES

Starting Files:

Lesson09/Assets/pictureShow1.fla
Lesson09/Assets/phoneNumberSearch1.fla

Completed Projects:

pictureShow3.fla
phoneNumberSearch2.fla

WHY LOOPS ARE USEFUL

Loops enable Flash to perform an action (or set of actions) repeatedly, which means that with just a few lines of ActionScript, you can force an action to be executed several thousand times. In ActionScript, you use loops for tasks that would be difficult or impossible without loops. For example:

- Creating dynamically generated drop-down lists
- Validating data
- Searching text
- Dynamically duplicating movie clips
- Copying the contents of one array to a new array
- Detecting collisions in games between projectiles and objects

You can use loops to automate any number of tasks, such as dynamically creating movie clip instances. Suppose your project called for 100 evenly spaced instances of the same movie clip. You could drag one instance from the library and then create a four- or five-line looping statement to duplicate the instance 100 times and position each duplicate on the stage automatically—a great improvement over dragging 100 instances from the library and aligning each one manually.

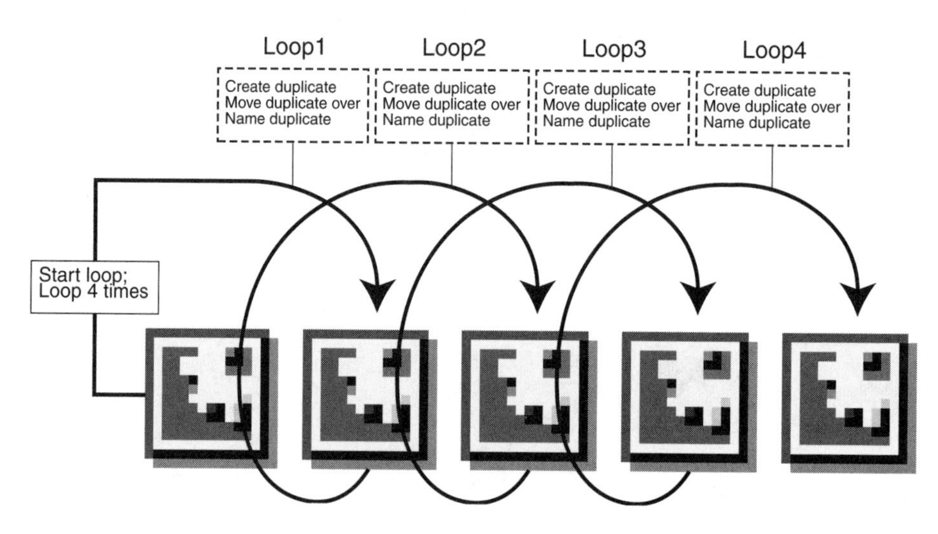

Loops are also dynamic. Suppose you scripted a loop to create a menu of 15 choices (buttons) dynamically. By altering the loop slightly, you could add and remove choices dynamically. In contrast, adding or removing a button from a *manually* created menu involves adding or removing the choice and then moving all of the other choices up or down one position, and perhaps even rescripting here and there.

As you progress through this lesson (and the rest of the book), you'll see the value of using loops in your scripts.

TYPES OF LOOPS

ActionScript can take advantage of three loop types, all of which perform an action (or set of actions) while a specific condition is true.

while Loop

The syntax for creating this common type of loop is as follows:

```
while (someNumber < 10) {
  // perform these actions
}
```

The expression someNumber < 10 is the condition that determines the number of *iterations* (passes through the statement) that the loop will perform. With each iteration, the actions inside the loop are executed. The logic that determines how the condition is evaluated (and how the loop is exited) is discussed shortly, in the section "Writing and Understanding Loop Conditions."

Here's an example of the while loop:

```
while (myClip_mc._y < 0) {
  myClip_mc._y += 3;
}
```

This script moves the **myClip_mc** movie clip instance along the y axis until its position is greater than 0.

for Loop

The for loop is a compact, all-in-one looping solution for loops that rely on incrementing or decrementing a variable. The for loop lets you initialize a loop variable, set the loop condition, and increment or decrement that variable—all in one line of ActionScript. The for loop is typically used to perform an action or set of actions based on the value of an incremental variable—walking an array, for example, or applying actions to a list of movie clips. Here's the syntax of the for loop:

```
for (var someNumber:Number= 0; someNumber < 10; ++someNumber) {
  // perform these actions
}
```

The three elements separated by semicolons within the parentheses are used to specify the number of iterations the loop will perform. In this example, the variable someNumber is created and assigned an initial value of 0. The script states next that as long as someNumber is less than 10, the loop executes the actions contained in the loop. The last element in the parentheses specifies that someNumber will be incremented by 1 with each loop iteration, eventually causing someNumber to have a value of 10, which means that the loop will cease after nine iterations.

The for loop is structured to be used primarily to loop through a set of actions a specified number of times. Here's the same example given for the earlier while loop, but now using the for loop syntax:

```
for (var i:Number=0; i<=10 ; ++i) {
  myClip_mc.duplicateMovieClip("myClip_mc" + i, i);
}
```

This for loop duplicates **myClip_mc** 10 times.

for...in Loop

This loop is used to loop through all of an object's properties. Here's the syntax:

```
for (var i:String in someObject) {
  trace(i);
}
```

The i in the loop is a variable that, with each loop iteration, temporarily stores the name of the property referenced by the variable. The value of i can be used in the actions within the loop. For a practical application, consider the following script:

```
var car:Object = new Object();
car.color = "red";
car.make = "BMW";
car.doors = 2;
var result:String;
for (var i:String in car) {
  result +=  i + ": " + car[i] + newline;
}
```

First, a generic object is created and named car. The next three lines assign properties (think of them as variables within the car object) and corresponding values to the car object. Next, a for...in loop is set up to loop through all of the car object's properties, using i as the variable that temporarily stores the name of each property. The value of i is used in the action within the loop. When the loop is finished, result holds a string of text that contains the name of each property as well as its value.

On the first iteration of the loop, i has a String value of doors (because that was the name of the last property defined). During the first loop, the expression that sets the value of result looks like this:

```
result = result + "doors" + ": " + 2 + newline;
```

After the first loop, result will have this String value:

```
"doors: 2"
```

In the expression that sets the value of `result`, the variable `i` (without brackets) refers to the property *name* (such as `doors`, `make`, or `color`). Using `car[i]` (that is, placing `i` between brackets) is the same as writing `car.doors`, and is a reference to that property's *value*.

PROPERTIES

LOOP3	COLOR = "RED"	i="COLOR" CAR[i] = "RED"
LOOP2	MAKE = "BMW"	i="MAKE" CAR[i] = "BMW"
LOOP1	DOORS = 2	i="DOORS" CAR[i] = 2

When the loop is complete, `result` will have the following String value:

```
"doors: 2
make: BMW
color: red"
```

Because the `car` object has three properties, the `for...in` loop in this script will perform only three iterations automatically.

NOTE *When you create a property on an object, it's stored in an* associative array. *In a regular array, elements are referenced by number, starting with 0. In contrast, elements in an associative array are referenced by name. The* `for...in` *loop in this section loops through the associative array that contains all of these references in a specific timeline or object.*

This type of loop has a variety of uses. You might use a `for...in` loop to find information, for example, such as the following details:

- Name and value of every variable in a timeline or object
- Name of every object in a timeline or object
- Name and value of every attribute in an XML document

WRITING AND UNDERSTANDING LOOP CONDITIONS

For the rest of this lesson, we'll focus on the `while` loop. The actions within this type of loop are performed continuously—as long as the condition evaluates to `true`. For example:

```
var i:Number = 0;
while (i < 10) {
  // perform these actions
}
```

The condition in the loop is `i < 10`. This means that as long as the value of `i` is less than 10, the statement is true and the actions within the loop are repeated. However, the looping statement is missing a key ingredient; it doesn't have a means by which the condition eventually becomes false. Without this functionality, the loop could continue forever, and in the real world endless loops cause applications to freeze. Flash can't do anything else until the looping statement completes its job. To prevent an endless loop in the example, the value of `i` must be incremented so that its value eventually equals 10, at which point the condition proves false and the loop stops.

You can use the increment operator (++) to handle incrementing a loop. Here's an example:

```
var i:Number = 0;
while (i < 10) {
  //perform these actions
  ++i
}
```

Incrementing the value of `i` causes the loop to perform 10 iterations. The value of `i` is initially set to `0`. However, with each loop that value increases by 1. On the tenth loop, `i = 10`, which means that `i < 10` is no longer true and the loop halts. Here's a shortcut that accomplishes the same goal:

```
var i:Number = 0;
while (++i < 10) {
  // perform these actions
}
```

This loop performs 9 iterations. The value of `i` is initially set to `0`. However, with each iteration (including the first), that value is incremented by 1 within the conditional statement of the loop itself. On the tenth loop, `i = 10`, which means that `i < 10` is no longer true, and the loop halts.

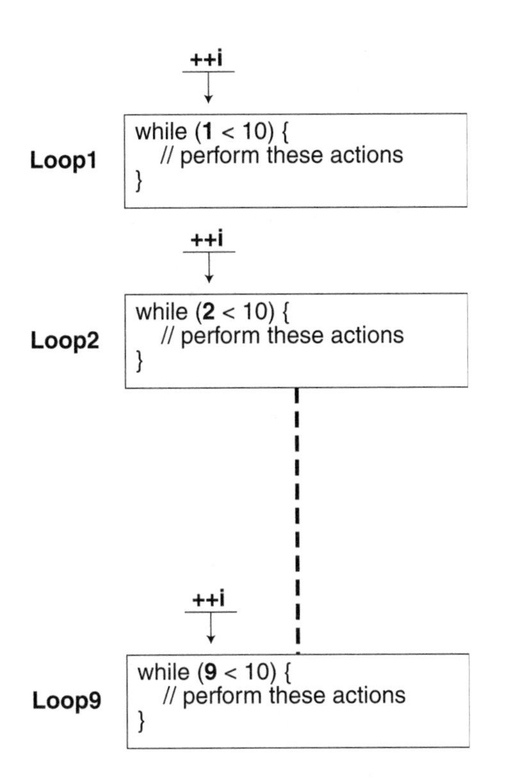

You can also use the decrement operator with a loop, which might look something like this:

```
var i:Number = 10;
while (--i > 0) {
  // perform these actions}
}
```

Alternatively, you can write this script using a `for` loop as follows:

```
for (var i:Number = 10; i>0; --i) {
  // perform these actions
}
```

The condition in a loop doesn't have to depend on an incremented value; it can be any sort of condition. It can also be the result of a function call that returns a value of `true` or `false`, like this:

```
while (someFunction()) {
  // perform these actions
}
```

In the following exercise, you create a drop-down list using a `while` loop.

1) Open *pictureShow1.fla* in the Lesson09/Assets folder.

The main timeline includes three layers: Background, Dynamic Elements, and Actions. The Actions layer contains all the ActionScript for this project. Not surprisingly, the Background layer contains the project's background graphic. The Dynamic Elements layer includes four movie clip instances: three above the stage that contain pictures, and an instance on the stage named **dropDownList_mc** that contains a button named **menu_btn** and another movie clip instance named **item_mc**. The **item_mc** instance is made up of two elements: a dynamic text field with an instance name of **itemName_txt**, and a button that appears as a semitransparent white box and has an instance name of **list_btn**. The **itemName_txt** instance plays an important part in this exercise because it will be duplicated in a process to generate clickable menu choices dynamically.

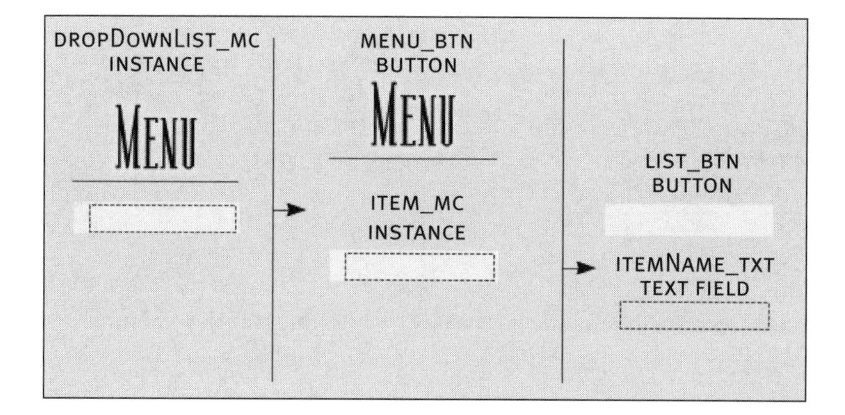

2) With the Actions panel open, select the frame in the Actions layer and add these two lines:

```
var buttonNames:Array = ["Paris", "New York", "London"];
dropDownList_mc.item_mc._visible = false;
```

The first action in this script creates an array named `buttonNames`, which contains names that will appear in the drop-down list. The second action makes the **item_mc** movie clip instance invisible. (Because you'll be using the **item_mc** movie clip instance only as a template for creating duplicates, the instance itself doesn't need to be visible.)

3) Add this function after the script you just added in Step 2:

```
function populateList() {
  var spacing:Number = dropDownList_mc.item_mc._height + 2;
  var numberOfButtons:Number = buttonNames.length;
}
```

When complete, this function duplicates the **item_mc** movie clip instance, aligns the duplicates under the Menu button, and changes the text displayed in the duplicated instances.

Because this function dynamically generates the list of choices, we need to consider vertical spacing between the list-choice buttons in the script. In its first action, this function creates a variable named `spacing`. This variable's value is determined by retrieving the height of the **item_mc** movie clip instance and adding 2 to that value. The loop uses the resulting value to set the spacing between the top of one duplicated movie clip instance and the top of the next movie clip instance underneath.

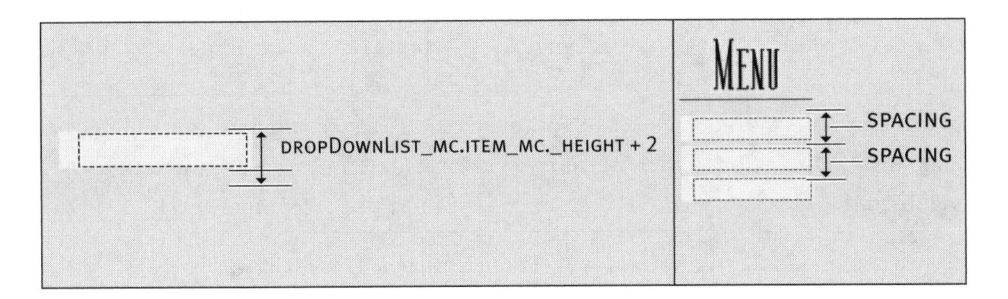

The `numberOfButtons` variable gets its value from the length of the `buttonNames` array (that is, the number of elements that the array contains). The `while` loop (added in the next step) used to build the drop-down list will use value of `numberOfButtons` to determine the number of iterations to perform. Because the length of `buttonNames` is currently `3` (the array contains three city names), the loop we set up will loop three times, creating a list button with each loop. If we placed another city's name in the array, the value of the `length` property of `buttonNames` would be `4`, which means that the loop would adjust accordingly and create four list buttons.

4) Add this script to the `populateList()` function after the last line of code in the function:

```
var i:Number = -1;
  while (++i < numberOfButtons) {
  var name:String = "item" + i;
  dropDownList_mc.item_mc.duplicateMovieClip(name, i);
  dropDownList_mc[name].itemName_txt.text = buttonNames[i];
  dropDownList_mc[name]._x = 0;
  dropDownList_mc[name]._y = i * spacing;
  dropDownList_mc[name].pictureID = i + 1;
  dropDownList_mc[name].list_btn.onRelease = function() {
    itemClicked(this._parent.pictureID);
  };
}
```

You've just scripted a while loop that duplicates the **item_mc** movie clip instance as needed for the drop-down list, positions the duplicates, and gives each duplicate a name to display.

Before the loop is defined, the script creates a local variable named i and assigns it the value -1.

NOTE *The letter* i *is commonly used as the name of an incremental variable in loops.*

The next line of the script starts the while loop and defines the condition that makes the loop continue working. It states, "As long as the incremented value of i is less than the value of numberOfButtons, keep looping." When the loop begins, i has a value of 0; although i is initially assigned a value of -1, the increment operator (++) increments its value by 1 prior to each loop, including the first. Because numberOfButtons has a value of 3 (as discussed in Step 3), and i is incremented by 1 with each iteration, the condition that this loop analyzes will prove false after three iterations.

The first action in the script creates a variable called name, which is assigned a dynamic value based on the current value of i. Because that value is incremented with each iteration of the loop, name is assigned a value of item0 in the first iteration of the loop; item1 in the second iteration, and so on. The next line uses the duplicateMovieClip() method to create a new instance of the **item_mc** movie clip. The two parameters in this method are separated by a comma: the first assigns an instance name to the duplicate that's created, and the other parameter assigns the duplicate a depth (think of this as the *stacking order*). As defined in the method's parenthetical syntax, we use the current value of the name variable (dynamically set with the previous action) as the instance name of the duplicate, and we use the current value of i to set the depth.

For the next four actions in the loop, dropDownList_mc[name] references the name of the duplicate just created. As discussed in Lesson 6, "Creating and Manipulating Data," this special syntax provides a dynamic way of referencing a variable name in ActionScript. In the loop's first iteration, name is assigned a value of item0. With the first iteration of the loop, these lines of script could be rewritten this way:

```
dropDownList_mc.item0.itemName_txt.text = buttonNames[i];
dropDownList_mc.item0._x= 0;
dropDownList_mc.item0._y = i * spacing;
dropDownList_mc.item0.pictureID = i + 1;
```

With each loop iteration, the value of name is updated and used to name the duplicate created. These actions reference the duplicated instance.

Each duplicate contains the two elements included in the original **item_mc** movie clip instance: the white button named **list_btn** and the dynamic text field named **itemName_txt**. The third line in the looping statement,

```
dropDownList_mc[name].itemName_txt.text = buttonNames[i];
```

sets the value of **itemName_txt.text** (and the text that will be displayed over the button) in the duplicated instance. That value is set by using the current value of `i` to reference a string in the `buttonNames` array created in Step 2. In the loop's first iteration, the value of `i` is `0`, which means that the value of **itemName_txt.text** would be `buttonNames[0]`, or the first element in that array, the text string `"Paris"`.

The next two lines of script position the duplicated instance on the stage. As shown in the script, each of the duplicates will have the same x position, `0`. The y position of the duplicate is dynamic, and is determined by multiplying the variable `i` by `spacing`. This action has the effect of spacing the duplicates an equal distance apart vertically.

After executing the two lines of script that position the movie clip, the loop creates a variable named `pictureID` inside the duplicated instance. The value assigned to the variable is based on the current value of `i + 1`. This variable will not be used until the next exercise, where it will be employed to determine the set of pictures to display.

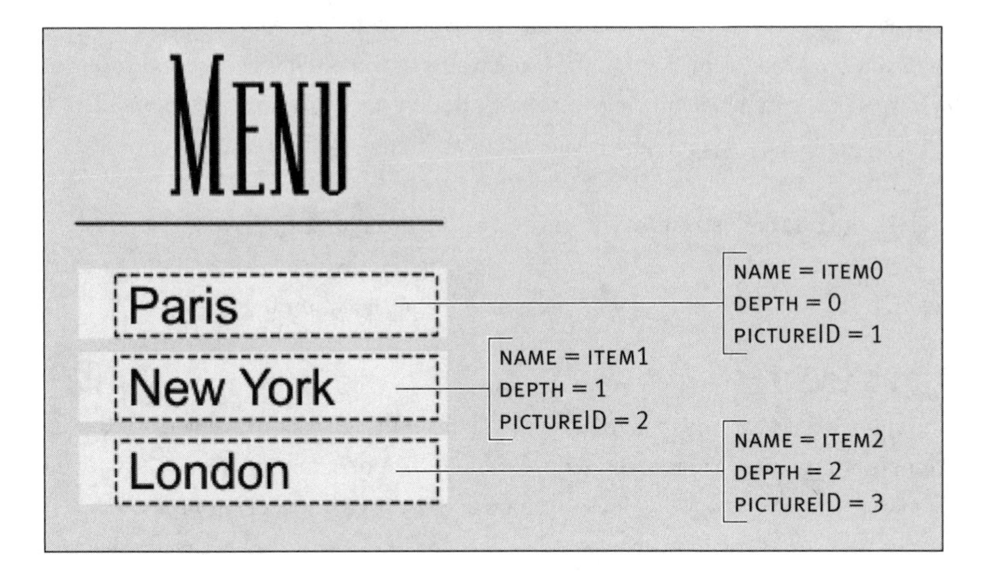

Finally, this loop adds an `onRelease` event handler to the **list_btn** button in each newly duplicated movie clip. When released, the button calls a function named `itemClicked()` on the main timeline and passes in the `pictureID` variable. You'll add the `itemClicked()` function in the next exercise.

The call to the itemClicked() function within the onRelease event handler references the pictureID variable with the following script:

```
this._parent.pictureID;
```

To grasp this syntax concept, it's important to understand the *path* between the pictureID variable and the **list_btn** button. The pictureID variable exists within the duplicated movie clip instance that also contains **list_btn**. The pictureID data exists not within the button (button instances can't hold data), but within the button's *parent*, which is the duplicated movie clip instance. For the button to reference a variable that exists in its parent, the button must step back one level (_parent) to get to the pictureID variable: hence this._parent.pictureID.

5) Add this script after the populateList() function:

```
dropDownList_mc.menu_btn.onRelease = function() {
  populateList();
};
```

When the Menu button is released, the populateList() function is called and a set of list buttons appears. (The list buttons were created dynamically by the function.)

6) Choose Control > Test Movie. Click the Menu button to test your script.

When you click the Menu button, the populateList() function is called, and several duplicates of the **item_mc** movie clip instance are created, positioned, and populated with text—all nearly instantaneously.

7) Close the test movie and save your work as *pictureShow2.fla*.

You created a drop-down list using a while loop. In the next exercise, you put this list to work by making something happen when you click a list item.

NESTED LOOPS

Loops provide a great way of automating a set of scripting tasks. However, loops can accomplish more than the repetitive execution of a set of actions. A *nested loop*—that is, a loop placed inside another loop—can be useful for creating a looping sequence that executes a set of actions, changes a bit, executes those same actions again, changes a bit, and so on. Here's an example of a nested loop:

```
var i:Number = 0;
while (++i <= 10) {
  var j:Number = 0;
  while (++j <= 10) {
    // perform these actions
  }
}
```

The actions in the loops will be executed 100 times. Here's the underlying logic: the outer loop (which uses i) is set to loop 10 times. With each iteration of this outer loop, two things occur: the variable j is reset to 0, which then enables the inner loop (which uses j) to loop 10 times itself. In other words, on the first iteration of the outer loop, the inner loop will loop 10 times; on the second iteration, the inner loop will again loop 10 times; and so on.

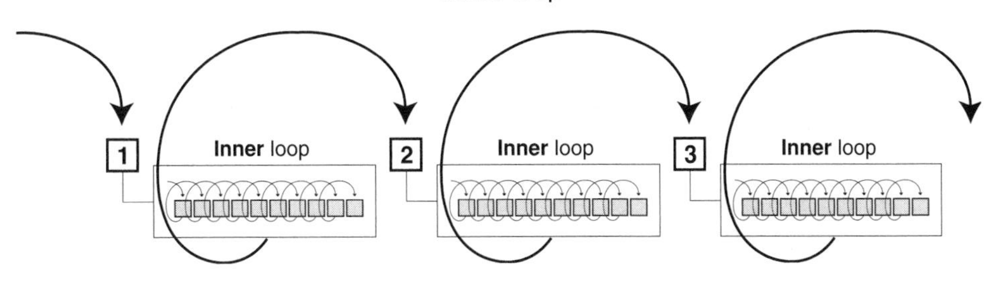

Nested loops are great for breaking repetitive tasks into a hierarchical process. To help you understand this concept, think about writing a letter. A letter represents a nested-loop process in which you start on line 1 and write perhaps 100 characters, drop to line to 2 and write 100 characters, and so on. If your letter is 25 lines long, a script to do the work might look something like this:

```
var i:Number = 0;
while (++i <= 25) {
  var j:Number = 0;
  while (++j <= 100) {
    // type a character
  }
  // drop down to the next line
}
```

Keep in mind that you aren't restricted to nesting just one loop inside another; you can use as many loops within loops as your project requires.

In the following exercise, you use nested loops to create a grid of images that appear when an item in the drop-down list is selected.

1) Open *pictureShow2.fla*.

On the top of the stage are three movie clip instances: **pictures1_mc**, **pictures2_mc**, and **pictures3_mc**. In this exercise, you duplicate one of these three movie clips (depending on which item in the drop-down list is selected) to form a grid of images onscreen.

2) With the Actions panel open, select Frame 1 in the Actions layer and add this function after the current script on that frame:

```
function itemClicked(pictureID:Number) {
  var picToDuplicate:String = "pictures" + pictureID + "_mc";
  var xSpacing:Number = 160;
  var ySpacing:Number = 120;
  var xStart:Number = 190;
  var yStart:Number = 30;
}
```

The preceding exercise set up the duplicated **list_btn** button instances to call this function and pass it a parameter value (`pictureID`) when clicked. When it's finished, this function will copy one of the three `pictureID` movie clip instances at the top of the stage four times, forming a two-by-two grid, and then send each duplicated instance to a unique frame to display an image.

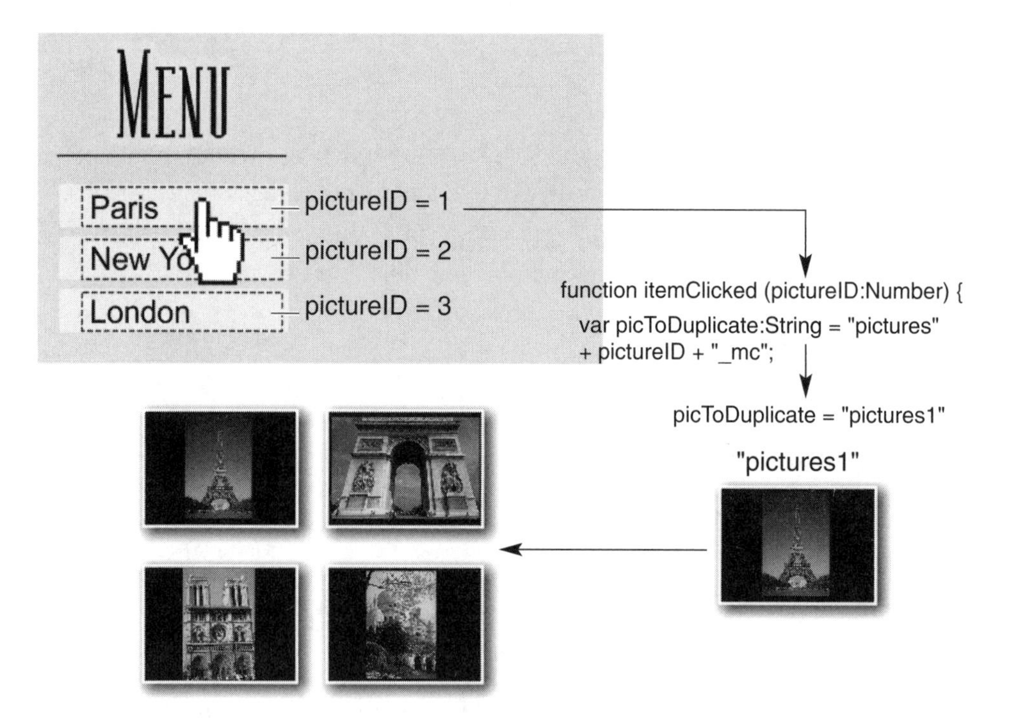

The first line in this function creates a variable called `picToDuplicate`. This variable's value—which is based on the `pictureID` value of 1, 2, or 3 that was passed to the function when it was called—is then set to **picture1_mc**, **picture2_mc**, or **picture3_mc**, which happen to be the names of the instances containing pictures on the stage. We'll use this value later in this function definition to identify which instance to duplicate.

The xSpacing variable represents the amount of space to allot between the left sides of the two movie clip instances found on the same horizontal row. The ySpacing variable indicates the space between two movie clips in the same column. The values of these spacing variables are arbitrary and will depend largely on the amount of space you like between movie clips.

The next two variables, xStart and yStart, represent the starting position of the first duplicated movie clip in relation to the stage. Any subsequent movie clip duplicates are positioned relative to this point.

3) Add this script at the bottom of the itemClicked() **function definition:**

```
var v:Number = 0;
var i:Number = -1;
while (++i < 2) {
  var j:Number = -1;
  while (++j < 2) {
    ++v;
    var name:String = "pictures" + v;
    _root[picToDuplicate].duplicateMovieClip(name, v);
    _root[name]._x = xStart + i * xSpacing;
    _root[name]._y = yStart + j * ySpacing;
    _root[name].gotoAndStop(v);
  }
}
```

This loop contains a nested loop—the portion of the function that actually creates the two-by-two grid of movie clip instances. A single loop would create a single column of movie clip instances. In contrast, a nested loop creates two instances in a column, alters the script slightly to "move" the column coordinates, and creates another two instances in a column (which we'll explain in a moment). Let's look at the logic that allows it to work.

The outer loop, beginning at line 3 of the script, increments i by 1 (++i), setting an initial value of 0. The condition of this outer loop says, "As long as i is less than 2, execute the actions below." Because 0 < 2, the actions within the loop are executed. The first action sets the value of j to -1. Then a nested (inner) loop appears that uses the value of j. First, j is incremented by 1 (++j) and a condition is set that says, "As long as j is less than 2, continue looping through the actions that follow."

The script continues to do nothing but execute the actions in this inner loop until that condition becomes false. During the first iteration of this inner loop, the value of v is incremented by 1 (++v), giving it a value of 1. This variable's value is used several times in the lines of script that follow. Using ActionScript that should be familiar to you by now, the appropriate pictureID movie clip instance is duplicated and positioned. During the second iteration of this inner loop, the value of j is incremented by 1 (as shown in the loop's conditional statement), giving it a value of 1, which is still less than 2, so the actions within that loop are executed again.

This inner loop cannot perform a third iteration because j would be incremented again (++j), making it equal to 2 (a condition that exits the inner loop). As a result, the script revisits the outer loop. At that point, i (used by the outer loop) is incremented by 1 (++i), giving it a value of 1, which is still less than 2, so the actions in the outer loop are executed again. As a result, the value of j is reset to -1, and the actions in the inner loop are executed two more times.

The concept just described can be tricky; review the logic until you understand it thoroughly.

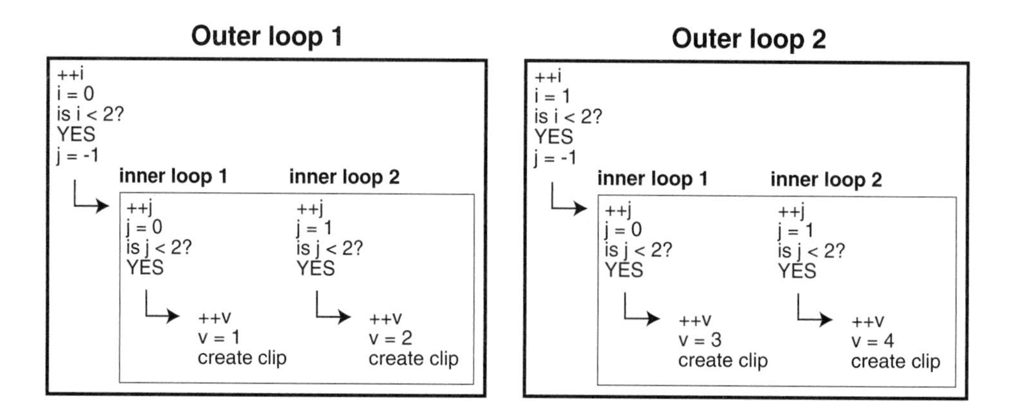

To achieve the effect of creating a two-by-two grid of movie clips (the proper spacing), you use this script:

```
_root[name]._x = xStart + i * xSpacing;
_root[name]._y = yStart + j * ySpacing;
```

The first line uses the current value of i to set the horizontal spacing. The second line uses the current value of j to set the vertical spacing when a movie clip is duplicated. You've already learned that with each outer loop iteration the inner loop performs two iterations. While i has a value of 0, the value of j is set to both 0 and 1 during execution of the inner loop, i is incremented to a value of 1, and the value of j is set to both 0 and 1. Because we know the values of xStart, xSpacing, yStart, and ySpacing, as well as how the values of i and j are incremented in the looping process, we can determine the spacing for each clip.

First instance duplicated:

```
_x = 190 + 0 * 160;// x set to 190
_y = 30 + 0 * 120;// y set to 30
```

NOTE *Remember that in a mathematical expression, multiplication always occurs before addition.*

Second instance duplicated:

```
_x = 190 + 0 * 160;// x set to 190
_y = 30 + 1 * 120;// y set to 150
```

Third instance duplicated:

```
_x = 190 + 1 * 160;// x set to 350
_y = 30 + 0 * 120;// y set to 30
```

Fourth instance duplicated:

```
_x = 190 + 1 * 160;// x set to 350
_y = 30 + 1 * 120;// y set to 150
```

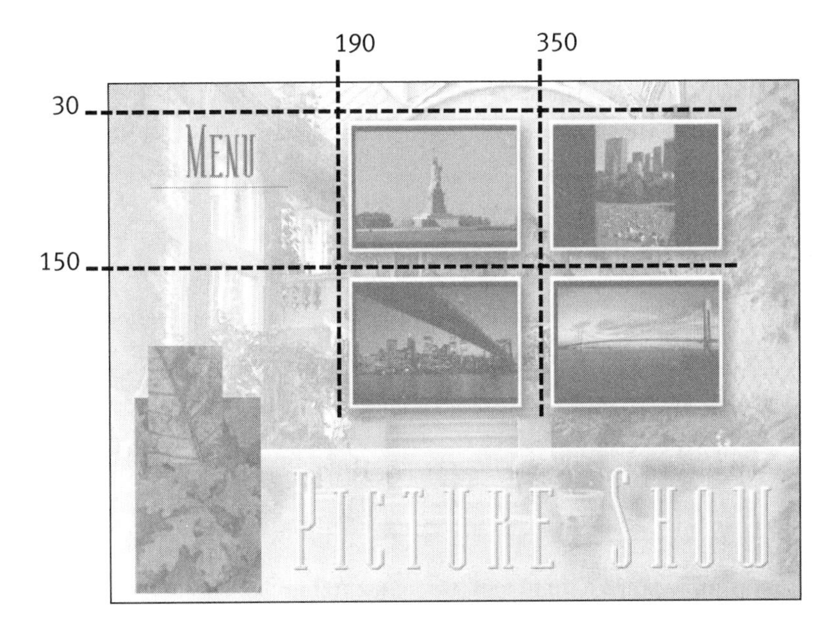

4) Add this action as the last line in the `itemClicked()` function definition:

```
removeButtons();
```

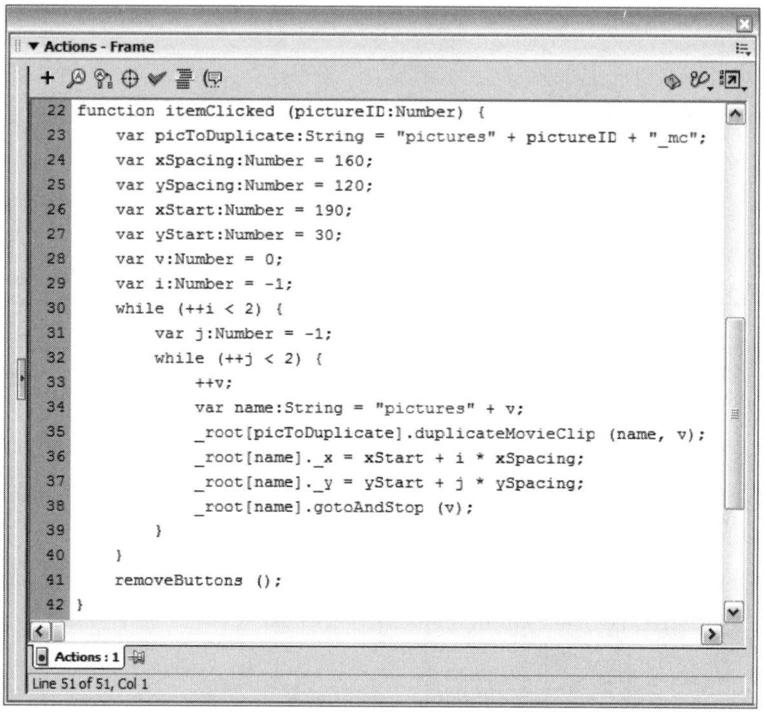

```
Actions - Frame
22 function itemClicked (pictureID:Number) {
23     var picToDuplicate:String = "pictures" + pictureID + "_mc";
24     var xSpacing:Number = 160;
25     var ySpacing:Number = 120;
26     var xStart:Number = 190;
27     var yStart:Number = 30;
28     var v:Number = 0;
29     var i:Number = -1;
30     while (++i < 2) {
31         var j:Number = -1;
32         while (++j < 2) {
33             ++v;
34             var name:String = "pictures" + v;
35             _root[picToDuplicate].duplicateMovieClip (name, v);
36             _root[name]._x = xStart + i * xSpacing;
37             _root[name]._y = yStart + j * ySpacing;
38             _root[name].gotoAndStop (v);
39         }
40     }
41     removeButtons ();
42 }
Actions : 1
Line 51 of 51, Col 1
```

This action calls a function named `removeButtons()`, which will remove the buttons in the drop-down list after a button has been clicked and the picture grid created. Let's create the function.

5) Add this code at end of the frame on the Actions layer:

```
function removeButtons() {
  var numberOfButtons:Number = buttonNames.length;
  var i:Number = -1;
  while (++i<numberOfButtons) {
    var name:String = "item" + i;
    dropDownList_mc[name].removeMovieClip();
  }
}
```

This function uses a simple `while` loop to loop through and remove all the buttons (which are actually the duplicate movie clip instances **item0**, **item1**, and **item2**) that make up the drop-down list choices under the Menu button. This loop works in similar fashion to the loop we used to create the duplicates that make up the list. Let's analyze this loop's syntax.

The value of numberOfButtons, which was also used in the populateList() function, is based on the length property of the buttonNames array. Because that array has three elements, the loop will perform three iterations. On each loop, the variable name is set based on the current value of i. The removeMovieClip() method is then used to remove the duplicate movie-clip instances referenced by the current value of name, thus removing the list of choices beneath the Menu button.

6) Choose Control > Test Movie to test your work.

Click the Menu button to display the list of choices. As you click any of the list buttons, the grid of images is created based on the value of pictureID that's passed to the itemClicked() function. Notice that the removeButtons() function removes the list choices.

7) Close the test movie and save your work as *pictureShow3.fla*.

In this exercise, you used nested loops to create a grid of images onscreen. While you could have dragged and placed four movie clip instances on the stage to accomplish the same goal, you used a nested loop to automate the entire process in such a way that, with a couple of minor adjustments, the script can create a grid of any size—perhaps as large as 100 by 100 images. Using loops—especially nested loops—in this fashion not only helps you to automate processes that you might otherwise perform manually in the authoring environment; it also enables your projects to scale up or down dynamically based on conditions that exist while the project plays.

LOOP EXCEPTIONS

In general, a loop continues to perform iterations until its condition is no longer true. You use two actions to change this behavior: continue and break.

With the continue action, you can stop the current iteration (that is, no further actions in that iteration will be executed) and jump straight to the next iteration in a loop. For example:

```
var total:Number = 0;
var i:Number = 0;
while (++i <= 20) {
  if (i == 10) {
    continue;
  }
  total += i;
}
```

The while statement in this script loops from 1 to 20, with each iteration adding the current value of i to a variable named total—until i equals 10. At that point, the continue action is invoked, which means that no more actions are executed on that iteration and the loop skips to the eleventh iteration. This would create the following set of numbers:

```
1 2 3 4 5 6 7 8 9 11 12 13 14 15 16 17 18 19 20
```

Notice that there is no number 10, indicating that no action occurred on the tenth loop.

The `break` action is used to exit a loop, even if the condition that keeps the loop working remains true. For example:

```
var total:Number = 0;
var i:Number = 0;
while (++i <= 20) {
  total += i;
  if (total >= 10) {
    break;
  }
}
```

This script increases the value of a variable named `total` by 1 with each iteration. When the value of `total` is 10 or greater—as checked by an `if` statement—a `break` action occurs and the `while` statement halts, even though it's set to loop 20 times.

In the following exercise, you'll use `continue` and `break` in a simple search routine.

1) Open *phoneNumberSearch1.fla* in the Lesson09/Assets folder.

This file contains two layers: Actions and Search Assets. The Actions layer will contain the search routine for this project. The Search Assets layer contains the text fields, button, and graphics for this exercise.

In this exercise, you'll produce a simple application that lets you enter a name in a search field to return the phone number for that individual. Two text fields are on the screen: **name_txt** will be used to enter the name to search; **result_txt** will display the search result. An invisible button over the Search button graphic has an instance name of **search_btn** that will be used to call a search function.

2) With the Actions panel open, select the first frame in the Actions layer and add the following script:

```
var info:Array = [["John","919-555-5698"],["Kelly","232-555-3333"],
⇒["Ross","434-555-5655"]];
```

This script creates a two-dimensional array called `info` containing three elements, each of which is its own array, or *sub-array*. The first element of each sub-array is a name, and the second element of each sub-array is a phone number.

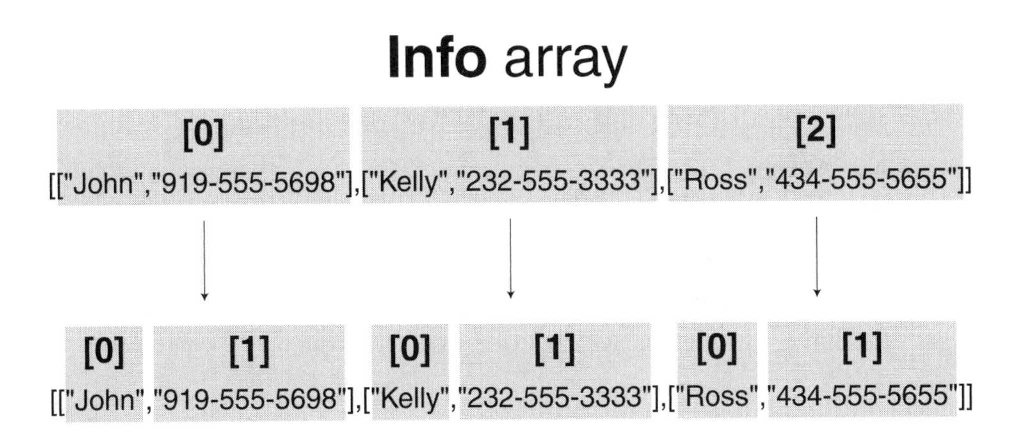

To access the first name in this array, you use `info[0][0]`; the first phone number would be accessed using `info[0][1]`. This syntax represents John's name and number. The syntax will play an important role in the search function we're about to script.

3) Add this function definition after the `info` array:

```
function search () {
  var matchFound:Boolean = false;
  var i:Number = -1;
  while (++i < info.length) {
  }
}
```

You've begun to define the function that will search the `info` array for a specific phone number. The first action in this function creates a variable called `matchFound` and assigns it an initial value of `false`. (We'll soon show you how this variable will be used.)

We've set up the `while` statement to loop once for every element in the `info` array.

4) Add this action to the `while` loop in the `search()` function:

```
if (info[i][0].toLowerCase() != name_txt.text.toLowerCase()) {
  continue;
}
result_txt.text = info[i][1];
matchFound = true;
break;
```

With each iteration of the loop, the `if` statement uses the current value of `i` to determine whether mismatches exist between names (made all lowercase) in the `info` array and the user-entered name (also forced to lowercase) in the **name_txt** text field.

When a mismatch is encountered, the `continue` action within the `if` statement is evoked and the script skips to the next loop. Using `toLowerCase()` to convert names to lowercase makes the search case insensitive.

If a name in the `info` array matches one in the **name_txt** text field, `continue` is not invoked and the actions *after* the `if` statement are executed. Using the value of `i` at the time a match was found, the first action sets the value of the variable **result_txt.text** to the matching phone number, sets `matchFound` to `true`, and executes the `break` action to halt the loop.

To understand better how this action works, imagine that someone has entered `Kelly` into the **name_txt** text field. The location of `Kelly` in the `info` array is as follows:

```
info[1][0]
```

On the first iteration of the loop, the value of `i` is `0`, which means that the `if` statement in the loop would look like this:

```
if (info[0][0].toLowerCase() != name_txt.text.toLowerCase()) {
  continue;
}
```

Here the statement asks whether `john` (the name at `info[0][0]`, made lowercase) is not equal to `kelly` (entered into the **name_txt** text field and made lowercase). Because `john` does not equal `kelly`, the `continue` action is invoked and the next loop begins. Because `i` is incremented by 1 with each loop, on the next iteration the `if` statement looks like this:

```
if (info[1][0].toLowerCase() != name_txt.text.toLowerCase()) {
  continue;
}
```

Here the statement asks whether `kelly` (the name at `info[1][0]`, made lowercase) is not equal to `kelly` (entered into the **name_txt** text field and made lowercase). Because `kelly` *does* equal `kelly`, the `continue` action is skipped and the next three actions are executed. The first action sets the value of **result_txt.text** to `info[i][1]`. Because `i` has a value of 1 when this action is executed, **result_txt.text** is set to `info[1][1]`—Kelly's phone number, which is now displayed. Next, `matchFound` is set to `true` and the `break` action exits the loop.

NOTE *Although the* `break` *action is not a necessity, it helps shorten search times. Think of how much time you would save by using a* `break` *action to avoid unnecessary loops in a 10,000-name array!*

5) Add this `if` statement as the last action in the `search()` function:

```
if (!matchFound) {
  result_txt.text = "No Match";
}
```

This statement, which is not part of the loop, checks whether `matchFound` still has a value of `false` (as it was set initially) once the loop is complete. If it does, the action in the `if` statement sets the value of **result_txt.text** to `No Match`. The syntax `!matchFound` is shorthand for `matchFound == false`.

6) Add this script at the end of the frame, after the `search()` function:

```
search_btn.onRelease = function() {
  search();
};
```

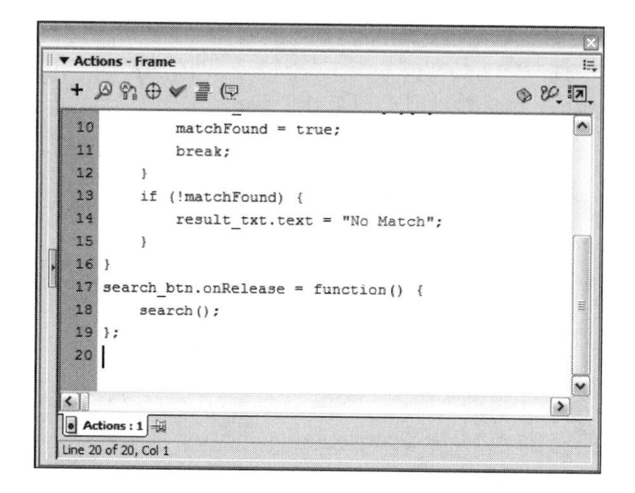

The script adds an `onRelease` event handler to the **search_btn** button. When the Search button is released, the `search()` function is executed.

7) Chose Control > Test Movie. Enter `John`, `Kelly`, or `Ross` in the search field and click the Search button. Then enter any other name and click the Search button.
A phone number should appear when a name is valid, and "No Match" should appear when no name is contained within the `info` array.

8) Close the test movie and save your work as *phoneNumberSearch2.fla*.
In this exercise, you used the loop exceptions `continue` and `break` to create a search routine. In practice, the `break` command is used more often than the `continue` command; this is because programmers often use `if` statements rather than `continue` to bypass actions in a loop.

WHAT YOU HAVE LEARNED

In this lesson, you have:

- Explored the usefulness of loops (pages 304–306)
- Learned about the three loop types available in ActionScript (pages 307–311)
- Applied `while` loops in several ways (pages 312–316)
- Created and used a nested loop (pages 316–323)
- Used the `continue` and `break` loop exceptions (pages 323–328)

scripting UI components

LESSON 10

Look at nearly any computer program, whether it's used for creating and managing a database or drawing illustrations, and you'll notice a number of interface elements common to those applications. You'll see similarities in buttons, scroll bars, drop-down boxes, sliders, and so on. These elements can be found in most applications because they are accepted and time-tested tools for allowing the user to interact with and receive information from the interface.

In most application development environments, such as Visual Studio .NET, the interface elements are pre-assembled, meaning that developers can simply drag an element such as a slider from a palette, drop it into the application being developed, and add some code to make the new element do something useful.

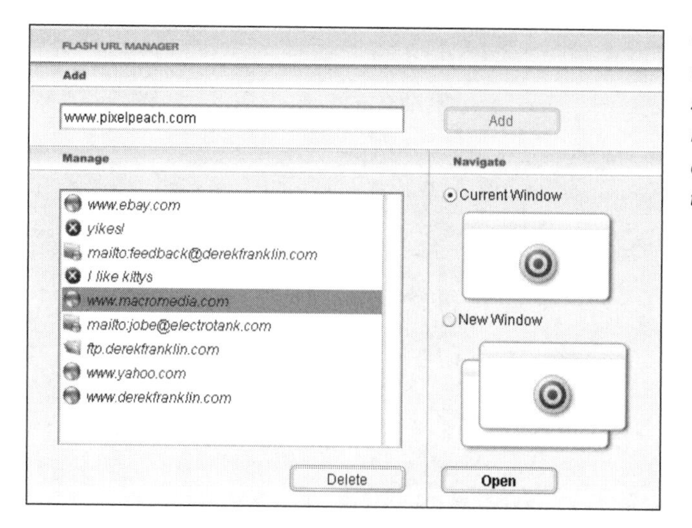

Using components, we'll create a fairly sophisticated URL manager that dynamically responds to user interaction.

Of course, developers could create their own interface elements from scratch; however, many of these prebuilt elements are not only highly functional, but contain a number of inherently powerful capabilities that can easily be accessed with a relatively minimal amount of programming.

The Flash authoring environment comes with its own prebuilt interface elements, called *components*. There are buttons, sliders, alert boxes, scrollable windows, menus, checkboxes, and more. Components allow you to quickly and easily drag and drop complex interactive elements into your project. After you have the interface elements where you want them, you can use ActionScript to control the elements in a number of useful ways.

In this lesson, we'll use components extensively to create an application with a highly interactive user interface. Creating this application from scratch would take many days. Using components and ActionScript, however, you can put together the application in a fraction of that time.

WHAT YOU WILL LEARN

In this lesson, you will:

- Learn how to set and get component property values
- Use component events to trigger scripts
- Use component methods to insert data dynamically
- Work with the FocusManager component to make a more usable application
- Style component instances individually and globally using ActionScript

APPROXIMATE TIME

This lesson takes approximately two hours to complete.

LESSON FILES

Starting File:

Lesson10/Assets/Components1.fla

Completed Project:

Components6.fla

COMPONENTS: A SCRIPTING PRIMER

Because the focus of this book is ActionScript, our discussion in this lesson largely centers on how to work with and use Flash components from a scripting standpoint. For a more thorough overview of components, consult the documentation that comes with Flash.

A *component* is usually nothing more than a movie clip with some built-in functionality. Components can be customized using ActionScript in two ways:

- You add components to a project *manually* by dragging them onto the stage within Flash's authoring environment, via the Property Inspector or Component Inspector.
- You add components to a project *dynamically* using ActionScript while the movie plays.

When a component is added by either technique, you're actually placing an instance of that component type/class into your project. For example, if you drag and drop a CheckBox component onto the stage in the authoring environment, that object is considered to be a CheckBox component instance. As when using other object instances, you assign names to component instances; the instance name can be used in your scripts to communicate with that component instance.

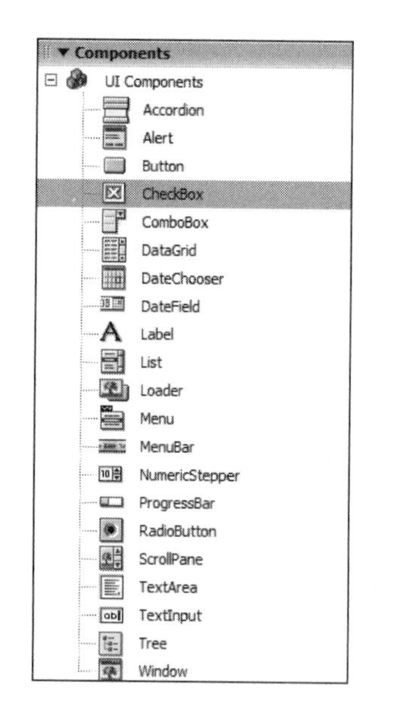

A number of *user interface components* ship with Flash. These components allow you to create forms and menus, or to display information and visual content in interactive ways.

Flash also ships with data components and media components. *Data components* provide a relatively easy way of working with the data in your application, especially sending and retrieving external data. *Media components* enable you to display and control the playback of media elements such as video and MP3 files. The primary focus of this lesson involves using and working with user interface components. You'll learn about media element component types in later lessons.

As you learn throughout this lesson, most components share some common functionalities and capabilities. As a result, the common ActionScript syntax works in the same way no matter what component instance you're scripting. At the same time, each type of component is built to be used for a specific purpose; thus, each type of component has some unique ActionScript commands.

Using ActionScript, you can do any of the following:

- Configure a component instance while your movie plays
- Tell the component instance to react to a specific event
- Retrieve data from a component instance
- Change the appearance of a component instance

In the exercises in this lesson, you'll implement each of these types of interactivity in the creation of a URL manager, which is used as a mini-database for Web, FTP, and email addresses. The result will be a highly interactive application, requiring relatively little scripting to make it work.

CONFIGURING COMPONENT PROPERTIES

As you're well aware by now, most graphical elements used in a Flash application have configurable *properties* that ActionScript can access and change while the application is running. For example, movie clip instances have properties that allow you to change their position, rotation, and transparency. Because components are usually nothing more than enhanced movie clips, it's obvious that they too have configurable properties that can be accessed and changed while a movie plays; however, due to their enhanced nature, working with component properties is slightly different from working with standard movie clip instance properties.

Component properties can be categorized into two groups: properties that are common to all component instances (to Macromedia-based components, at least), and properties that are unique to each type of component. Let's look at both.

NOTE *You may have installed some third-party components that don't abide by the following guidelines. This discussion focuses on the use and capabilities of the components that come pre-installed with Flash.*

Common Properties

In Lesson 7, "Creating Custom Classes," you learned about object-oriented programming. In this lesson, you put that information to use. How? Well, as already mentioned, most component instances have a set of common properties. This is because most components inherit properties from the UIComponent class, which itself inherits properties from the UIObject class. Both of these object classes are automatically and invisibly added to your project whenever you add a component instance. Let's break down this concept by looking at the Button component.

First, UIObject is an object class that defines a number of properties:

```
UIObject.bottom
UIObject.left
UIObject.right
UIObject.scaleX
UIObject.scaleY
UIObject.top
UIObject.visible
UIObject.width
UIObject.x
UIObject.y
```

The programming that gives these properties meaning exists within the UIObject class definition.

Next, the UIComponent class is set up to extend (inherit) all the functionalities of the UIObject class. This means that any properties of the UIObject class become available as properties of the UIComponent class. But the UIComponent class doesn't just inherit all of the properties of the UIObject class; it also defines some of its own:

```
UIComponent.enabled
UIComponent.tabIndex
```

As a final step, most component classes (CheckBox, Alert, RadioButton, and so on) inherit or extend the UIComponent class. This means that most component classes not only inherit the `enabled` and `tabIndex` properties of the UIComponent class, but also *all* of the properties of the UIObject class, because the UIComponent class extends the UIObject class. In the end, this means that most component instances you place in your project have the properties `x`, `y`, `visible`, `top`, `bottom`, `enabled`, `tabIndex`, and so on. Again, this entire inheritance process occurs invisibly whenever you place a component instance in a project.

Because most component instances share these common properties, it's easy to affect any component instance using a common syntax, as the following example demonstrates:

```
myButton_pb.enabled = false;
myRadioButton_rb.enabled = false;
myListBox_lb.enabled = false;
```

No matter what kind of component instance you're scripting—Button, RadioButton, or some other component instance—the `enabled` property is used in the same way and affects the component instance in the same manner across the board.

Component properties let you control various aspects of a component instance, including its size, position, and visibility; or they can be used to access property information pertaining to a particular component instance. For example, the following script assigns a value to `myVariable` based on the rightmost position of the component instance named **myButton_pb**:

```
var myVariable:Number = myButton_pb.right;
```

Component-Specific Properties

In addition to common properties, each component class has its own set of unique properties that allow you to work with an instance of that component class in specific ways. For example, the NumericStepper component class has properties named `maximum`, `minimum`, and `stepSize`. These properties have meaning only in the context of scripting NumericStepper instances. Attempting to use the `stepSize` property in relation to a RadioButton instance is an exercise in futility. It just won't do anything.

NOTE *There are too many component-specific properties to list here. For a complete listing of the properties of a component class, look up its entry in the ActionScript dictionary. Component-specific properties can also be found under each component listing in the Actions Toolbox section of the Actions panel.*

Using ActionScript in the following exercise, you'll set the initial property settings for most of the components in an application.

1) Open *Components1.fla* in the Lesson10/Assets folder.

This project contains three layers: Background, Components, and Actions. The Background layer contains all the non-component content in the project. This includes a static image of the URL manager's interface as well as two movie clip instances named **currentWin_mc** and **newWin_mc**. The Components layer contains all the components used in the project. A TextInput component named **inputURL_ti** accepts text input from the user; a List component instance named **listURL_lb** displays a list of items; three Button component instances named **addURL_pb**, **deleteURL_pb**, and **openURL_pb** work similarly to buttons; and a couple of RadioButton component instances named **currentWin_rb** and **newWin_rb** work in the same manner as HTML radio buttons.

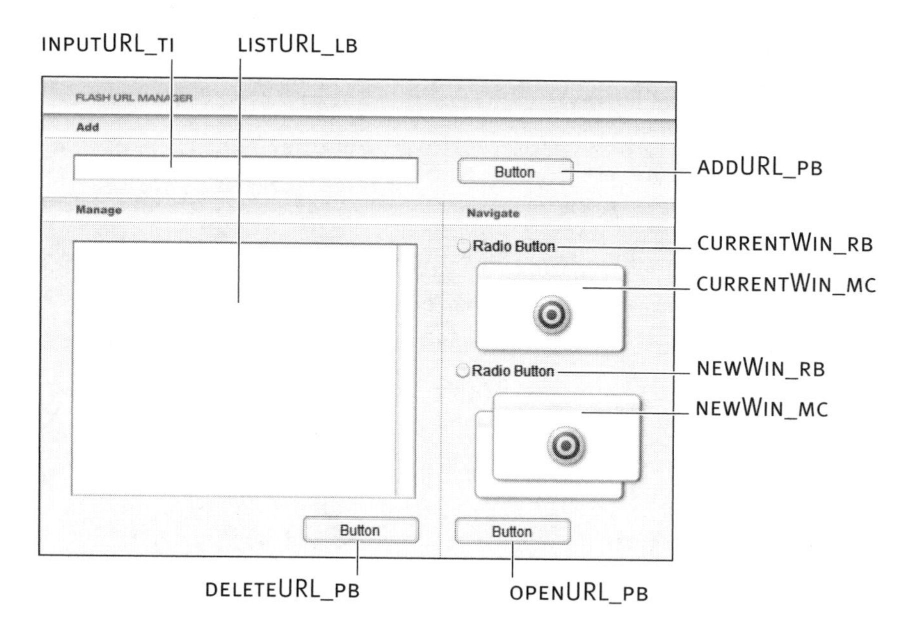

Although certain component instance properties can be configured within the authoring environment by using either the Component Inspector or the Property Inspector, the component instances in this project have only been given instance names. We'll use ActionScript to completely configure these instances, including their initial properties. Before you begin scripting, it's important for you to have a general idea of how this application will work.

When the application is finished and played within a browser window, the user can enter a URL (*www*, *ftp*, or *mailto*) into the **inputURL_ti** component instance and then click the **addURL_pb** component instance, which displays the URL in the **listURL_lb** component instance. All added URLs appear in the **listURL_lb** component instance. When the user selects a URL from the **listURL_lb** component instance, he or she has two choices: clicking the **openURL_pb** component instance opens the URL in either the current browser window or a new one (depending on whether the **currentWin_rb** or **newWin_rb** radio button is selected); clicking the **deleteURL_pb** component instance deletes the selected URL from the list. As the user interacts with the application, these various component instances are enabled and disabled dynamically, depending on the task the user is trying to accomplish. The finished application will have a few more capabilities, as you'll discover the further we progress.

To help you see how an unscripted version of the project looks and feels, let's do a quick test.

2) Choose Control > Test Movie.

Within the testing environment, notice that the application doesn't look any different now than it did in the authoring environment. All the Button component instances display the word *Button*, and each of the RadioButton instances displays the words *Radio Button*. If you try to interact with any of the elements, some of them glow green (dubbed `haloGreen` by the folks at Macromedia) when you move the pointer over the element or click it; otherwise, they don't do much. Over the next several exercises, this application will come to life in many ways. Along the way, you'll also be swapping the green glow effect for another effect.

We have a lot of work to do, so let's get started.

3) Close the test movie and return to the authoring environment. With the Actions panel open, select Frame 1 of the Actions layer and add the following script:

```
addURL_pb.label = "Add";
addURL_pb.enabled = false;
```

These two lines of script set the `label` and `enabled` properties of the **addURL_pb** Button component instance. The `label` property controls the text displayed on the button. Setting the `enabled` property to `false` *disables* the button. You can't interact with the button in this state; it appears dimmed, indicating to the user that the button is disabled, much like operating system interface elements appear in a disabled state.

The reason we're disabling this button initially is because it has no use until the user types a URL into the **inputURL_ti** TextInput component instance. When the movie first plays, that instance is devoid of any text; therefore, it makes sense that the **addURL_pb** instance should be disabled. Later, we'll add scripts that enable and disable this instance, depending on how the user interacts with the interface.

4) Add the following script at the end of the current script:

```
listURL_lb.enabled = false;
deleteURL_pb.label = "Delete";
deleteURL_pb.enabled = false;
openURL_pb.label = "Open";
openURL_pb.enabled = false;
```

These five lines of script do nearly the same thing as the two lines of script in Step 3 of this exercise. The first line disables the **listURL_lb** List component instance; the remaining four lines set the `label` values for and disable the **deleteURL_pb** and **openURL_pb** Button component instances, respectively.

5) Add the following script at the end of the current script:

```
newWin_rb.groupName = "windowOption";
currentWin_rb.groupName = "windowOption";
newWin_rb.label = "New Window";
newWin_rb.data = "_blank";
currentWin_rb.label = "Current Window";
currentWin_rb.data = "_self";
windowOption.enabled = false;
```

These seven lines of script set the initial properties of the two radio buttons named **newWin_rb** and **currentWin_rb**.

NOTE *You may have noticed that the script in Step 5 sets the New Window button before setting the Current Window button, yet they appear in the opposite order in the application, with the Current Window button on top. Scripting is an abstract process that really has little to do with the way things are positioned on the stage.*

The first two lines set the `groupName` property for each radio button instance. Radio buttons in most programming environments (including Flash) are designed to work within groups. Clicking a particular radio button in the group automatically deselects the previously selected button in the group, thus allowing only a single radio button in the group to be selected at any time. To facilitate this functionality, each radio button must be associated with a group. The `groupName` property sets the association. Both of our application's RadioButton component instances are assigned to the `windowOption` group. This group didn't exist before, and is created by using this script. As a result of associating the two RadioButton instances to the same group, only one can be selected at any time. The purpose of these instances is to allow the user to choose whether to open a URL in the current browser window or open a new window. This is important to remember as we discuss the remaining lines of the script.

NOTE *By default, all RadioButton instances added to a project belong to the same group (named radioGroup). Therefore, the RadioButton component instances in our project initially had the single-selection functionality that we just discussed.*

The next four lines set the `label` and `data` properties for the **newWin_rb** and **currentWin_rb** instances. Similar to the `label` property for Button component instances, the `label` property for RadioButton instances allows you to set the text that appears next to the instance. The `data` property lets you assign a value to the instance. This value is assigned to the group of which the instance is part whenever that instance is selected. This can be a tricky concept to understand, so let's look at it a bit more closely.

Remember that both of the RadioButton component instances are assigned to the `windowOption` group. Because the **newWin_rb** instance is given a `data` property value of `"_blank"`, selecting that instance assigns that value as the `windowOption` group value. Thus, the following script:

```
var myVariable:String = windowOption.getValue();
```

assigns a value of `"_blank"` to `myVariable`. The significance of this fact will be explained later in this lesson.

The last line in the script disables both the radio button instances. We could have disabled each instance individually using this syntax:

```
newWin_rb.enabled = false;
currentWin_rb.enabled = false;
```

but we can easily disable all instances belonging to our group with a single line of code because they're both part of the `windowOption` group.

As a result of the code we've added so far, all the component instances within our project, except for **inputURL_ti**, will initially be disabled. The only interface elements left to disable are the two movie clip instances named **newWin_mc** and **currentWin_mc**, which are graphical elements associated with our radio buttons. We want these movie clip instances to always appear in the same state (enabled or disabled) as our radio buttons. Because they're movie clip instances and not component instances, they don't have built-in `enabled` properties that can be set. We can get around this limitation, however, with a function.

6) Add the following function definition at the end of the current script:

```
function enableWindowGraphics(mode:Boolean){
  if(mode){
    currentWin_mc._alpha = 100;
    newWin_mc._alpha = 100;
  }else{
    currentWin_mc._alpha = 30;
    newWin_mc._alpha = 30;
  }
}
```

This function, named `enableWindowGraphics()`, accepts a single parameter value of `true` or `false`. A conditional statement within the function checks this value when the function is called and makes the movie clip instances completely opaque if the function is true, but nearly transparent if it's false (which will cause the movie clip instances to appear dimmed, similar to a disabled component instance). This function is an acceptable substitute for the missing inherent `enable` property.

7) Add the following function call at the end of the current script:

```
enableWindowGraphics(false);
```

Actions - Frame

```
1  addURL_pb.label = "Add";
2  addURL_pb.enabled = false;
3  listURL_lb.enabled = false;
4  deleteURL_pb.label = "Delete";
5  deleteURL_pb.enabled = false;
6  openURL_pb.label = "Open";
7  openURL_pb.enabled = false;
8  newWin_rb.groupName = "windowOption";
9  currentWin_rb.groupName = "windowOption";
10 newWin_rb.label = "New Window";
11 newWin_rb.data = "_blank";
12 currentWin_rb.label = "Current Window";
13 currentWin_rb.data = "_self";
14 windowOption.enabled = false;
15 function enableWindowGraphics(mode:Boolean){
16     if(mode){
17         currentWin_mc._alpha = 100;
18         newWin_mc._alpha = 100;
19     }else{
20         currentWin_mc._alpha = 30;
21         newWin_mc._alpha = 30;
22     }
23 }
24 enableWindowGraphics(false);
```

Actions : 1

Line 24 of 24, Col 29

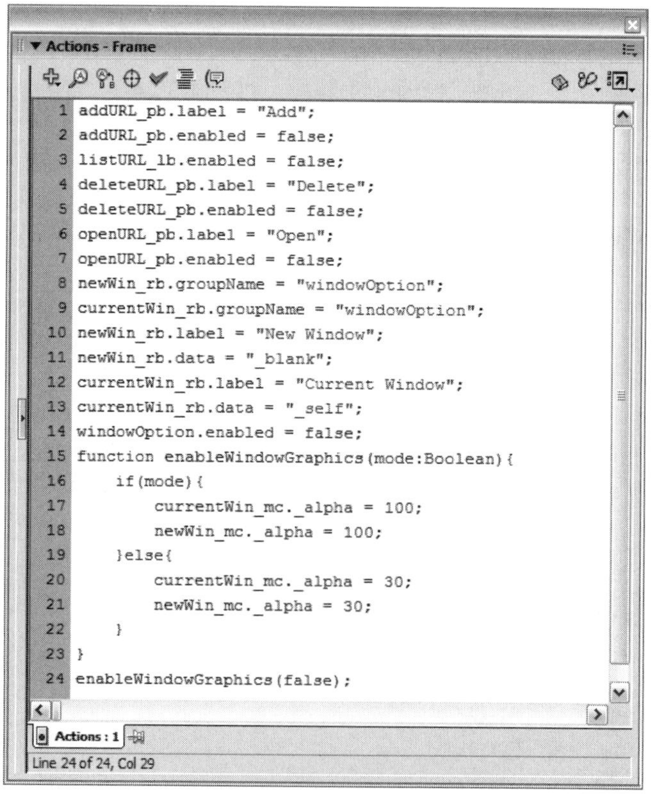

This function call will cause our two movie clip instances to initially appear disabled, similar to the component instances we scripted in Steps 3–5.

Let's test our project up to this point.

8) Choose Control > Test Movie.

Several things occur as soon as the movie begins to play. Most of the interface elements are disabled intitially, and the various component instances with `label` properties display the text labels we assigned to them.

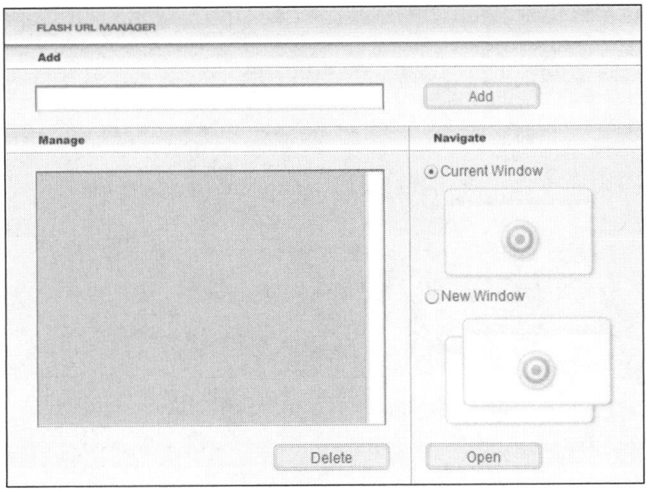

As you can see from this exercise, working with properties of component instances is simple and straightforward.

9) Close the test movie and save your file as *Components2.fla*.

We'll continue building on this file in the exercises that follow.

TRIGGERING SCRIPTS USING COMPONENT EVENTS

Users can interact with components in many ways. Depending on the component, users can type text into the component, click the component, select an item, and more. As with any interactivity such as this, it's important for your application to react according to what the user is doing. For example, if the user clicks a radio button, you might want your application to react to that selection by updating a variable's value, or you may want to change the appearance of your application's interface. Fortunately, most components have several built-in events that can be used to trigger a script's execution, providing you with the flexibility to easily create highly interactive applications.

Similar to component properties, component *events* can be categorized into two groups: events that are common to most component instances, and events that are unique to each type of component.

Common Events

As mentioned in our discussion of properties, most components inherit from the UIObject and UIComponent classes. Not only do those classes define properties that are available to most component instances; they also specify a number of events that, as a result of inheritance, are available to all component instances. Some of these common events include (but are not limited to) the following:

`move` - triggered when a component instance's x or y coordinates change

`focusIn` - triggered when a user interacts with a component instance in any way

`focusOut` - triggered when a user leaves a component instance and interacts with something else

Later in this lesson, you'll see how these events are used.

Component-Specific Events

In addition to the common events just discussed, most components have events relating to their specific functionality. Let's look at a couple of simple examples.

Button and RadioButton component instances react to `click` events, in addition to the common events previously discussed. A `click` event is fired when a Button component instance is pressed and released, or when a RadioButton instance is selected. When you think about it, these are not complex components; having such a simple event associated with them makes sense.

A component such as a ComboBox is a totally different story because it's designed to be interacted with in many ways. ComboBox component instances react to the following events:

`change` - triggered when the user selects a new item within the combobox

`close` - triggered when the drop-down box within the combobox begins to close

`open` - triggered when the drop-down box within the combobox is opened

`enter` - triggered when the user presses Enter after entering a value into the combobox

`scroll` - triggered when the list of items within the combobox is scrolled

`itemRollOver` - triggered when the user rolls the mouse over a list item

`itemRollOut` - triggered when the user rolls the mouse away from a list item

With such a wide range of available events, component instances become powerful tools in the creation of your applications.

NOTE *There are too many component-specific events to list here. For a complete listing of the events of a component class, look up its entry in the ActionScript dictionary. Component-specific events can be found under each component listing in the Actions Toolbox section of the Actions panel.*

HANDLING EVENTS

There are a couple of ways to use component events in your scripts. You can use the `on()` handler, and you can also create Listener objects, as you learned about in Lesson 2, "Using Event Handlers." Let's first look at using the `on()` handler.

The `on()` handler allows you to script events directly on a component instance, much in the same way that you add scripts directly to button and movie clip instances. For example, if you select a ComboBox instance and open the Actions panel, you can attach the following script to that instance:

```
on (open) {
  trace("A ComboBox instance has been opened");
}
on (scroll) {
  trace("A ComboBox instance has been scrolled");
}
```

If you use the term `this` in this type of script, it's a reference to the component instance to which the script is attached. Look at the following example:

```
on (focusOut) {
  this._alpha = 50;
}
```

Assuming that this script is attached to, say, a NumericStepper component instance, its transparency will be set to 50% when the `focusOut` event occurs.

The preferred way of handling component events is to use Listener objects. Let's convert our previous sample scripts to the Listener model syntax:

```
var myComboBoxListener:Object = new Object();
myComboBoxListener.open = function(){
  trace("A ComboBox instance has been opened");
}
myComboBoxListener.scroll = function(){
  trace("A ComboBox instance has been scrolled");
}
```

These several lines of code create an object named myComboBoxListener and then script it to react to the open and scroll events. Now we have to register this Listener object with a particular ComboBox component instance. If we have a ComboBox instance named **myCB_cb**, the syntax would look similar to the following:

```
myCB_cb.addEventListener("open", myComboBoxListener);
myCB_cb.addEventListener("scroll", myComboBoxListener);
```

When **myCB_cb** is opened or scrolled, the open or scroll function of our Listener object is fired.

NOTE *A single Listener object can be registered to listen to any number of component instance events.*

Another way of scripting for component events involves using functions as Listeners. For example, suppose you've created the following function:

```
function myFunction(eventObj:Object){
  trace ("I'm a Listener too!");
}
```

You could script this function to be called whenever a particular event was fired by a particular component instance:

```
myCB_cb.addEventListener("open", myFunction);
```

Whenever the **myCB_cb** component instance triggers an open event, myFunction() is called, and thus executed.

As mentioned in the discussion of the on() handler, use of the term this in either Listener object syntax or the syntax of functions that are used as Listener objects is a reference to the component instance that triggers the event.

You probably noticed within the parentheses of the myFunction Listener example the use of the syntax eventObj:Object.

When you use a Listener object or a function as a Listener, an *Event object* is passed to the specified handler script. This object usually contains two properties: type and target. The type property is a string reference to the event that was triggered; the target is a string reference to the target path of the component instance that fired the event. Using our previous ComboBox example, here's how an Event object is used.

Let's say we've defined a Listener function and registered it to listen for open events triggered by **myCB_cb**, as shown here:

```
function myFunction(eventObj:Object){
  trace(eventObj.target);
  trace(eventObj.type);
}
myCB_cb.addEventListener("open", myFunction);
```

If the **myCB_cb** instance triggers an open event, the Output panel will open and display the following:

```
_level0.myCB_cb
open
```

Information provided by the Event object can be used in a conditional statement within the function to take appropriate action, depending on the event that has been triggered and the instance that triggered it, as the following example shows:

```
function myFunction(eventObj:Object){
  if(eventObj.target == "_level0.myCB_cb"){
    //actions
  }else if(eventObj.name == "_level0.myRadioButton_rb"){
    //actions
  }
  if(eventObj.type == "click"){
    //actions
  }
}
```

As you can see, using the properties of the Event object allows you to set up a single function to handle several events from several different component instances.

NOTE *Some components, such as the MenuBar component, generate Event objects containing properties in addition to* `target` *and* `name`*. We'll discuss some of these properties in later lessons.*

In the following exercise, we'll create several Listener objects and script them to listen to various events that are triggered by components in our project.

1) Open *Components2.fla*.

This project continues from where we left off in the preceding exercise.

We'll add all the scripts for this exercise to Frame 1 of the timeline. The focus for this exercise is to create the framework for using component events via Listener objects. The Listener objects won't actually be scripted to do anything until the next exercise.

2) With the Actions panel open and Frame 1 selected, add the following script at the end of the current script:

```
var inputURL_tiListener:Object = new Object ();
inputURL_tiListener.focusIn = function () {
};
inputURL_ti.addEventListener ("focusIn", inputURL_tiListener);
```

The first line of this script creates an object named `inputURL_tiListener`. We'll use this object to listen for events generated by the TextInput component instance named **inputURL_ti**, which will be used in the application as an input field for new URLs.

The next two lines of script create a handler for the `focusIn` event. This handler will be scripted in the next exercise.

The last line of the script in this step registers the Listener object with the **inputURL_ti** instance. Anytime this instance generates the `focusIn` event, our Listener object will be notified and will execute its handler for that event.

3) Add the following script at the end of the current script:

```
var addURL_pbListener:Object = new Object ();
addURL_pbListener.click = function () {
};
addURL_pb.addEventListener ("click", addURL_pbListener);
```

This script creates a Listener object for the **addURL_pb** PushButton component instance, and sets it up to listen for any `click` events generated by that instance. The Listener object is registered with the **addURL_pb** instance.

4) Add the following script at the end of the current script:

```
var listURL_lbListener:Object = new Object ();
listURL_lbListener.focusIn = function () {
};
listURL_lb.addEventListener ("focusIn", listURL_lbListener);
var openURL_pbListener:Object = new Object ();
openURL_pbListener.click = function () {
};
openURL_pb.addEventListener ("click", openURL_pbListener);
var deleteURL_pbListener:Object = new Object ();
deleteURL_pbListener.click = function () {
};
deleteURL_pb.addEventListener ("click", deleteURL_pbListener);
```

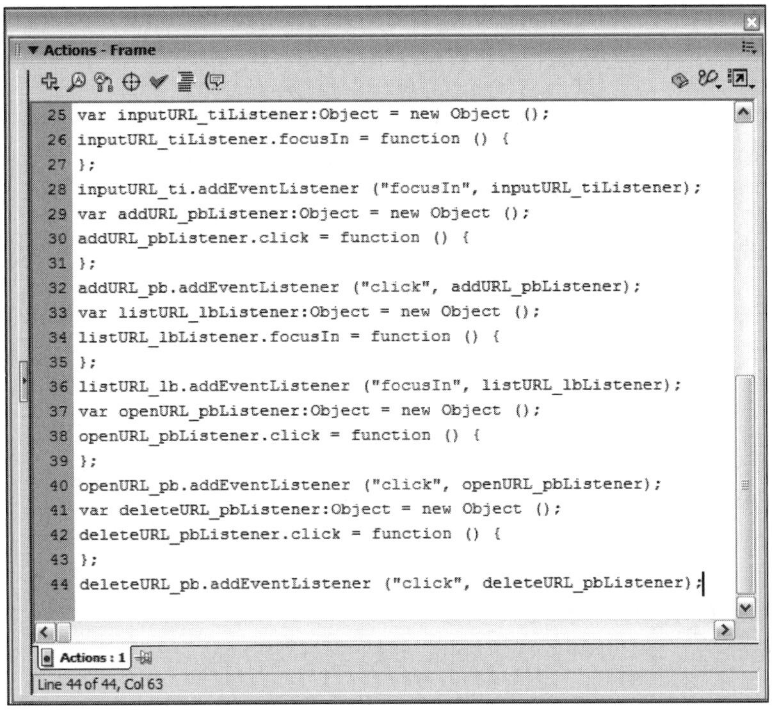

```
var inputURL_tiListener:Object = new Object ();
inputURL_tiListener.focusIn = function () {
};
inputURL_ti.addEventListener ("focusIn", inputURL_tiListener);
var addURL_pbListener:Object = new Object ();
addURL_pbListener.click = function () {
};
addURL_pb.addEventListener ("click", addURL_pbListener);
var listURL_lbListener:Object = new Object ();
listURL_lbListener.focusIn = function () {
};
listURL_lb.addEventListener ("focusIn", listURL_lbListener);
var openURL_pbListener:Object = new Object ();
openURL_pbListener.click = function () {
};
openURL_pb.addEventListener ("click", openURL_pbListener);
var deleteURL_pbListener:Object = new Object ();
deleteURL_pbListener.click = function () {
};
deleteURL_pb.addEventListener ("click", deleteURL_pbListener);
```

This creates three more Listener objects, which are registered to the **listURL_lb**, **openURL_pb**, and **deleteURL_pb** instances, respectively. Make a note of the events the objects are set up to handle, because these are important for the next exercise.

5) Save this file as *Components3.fla*.

In this exercise, we created five Listener objects and registered them to listen for events generated by various component instances in our project. At this point, the event handlers attached to our Listener objects are not scripted to do anything, but we'll take of that in the next exercise.

USING COMPONENT METHODS

As should be obvious by now, both the UIObject and UIComponent classes have methods that are inherited by all component instances. In addition, different component types have methods that are unique to themselves. For brevity, we'll only mention a few examples here before moving on to the exercise for this section.

COMMON METHODS

The following methods are common to all component instances:

`move(x, y)` moves a component instance to the specified x and y coordinates. For example: `myButton_pb.move(100, 200);`

`setSize(width, height)` resizes a component instance to the specified width and height values. For example: `myButton_pb.setSize(250, 150);`

`getFocus()` returns a value of the current object that has focus. For example, `var myVariable:String = myButton_pb.getFocus();` assigns `myVariable` a string value representing the name of the component instance that currently has focus.

`setFocus()` sets the focus to a particular component instance. For example, `myButton_pb.setFocus()` gives focus to the **myButton_pb** instance.

NOTE *For more information on what focus means and how it's used, see "Using the FocusManager Component" later in this lesson.*

There are other methods that are inherited by all instances, but these are the most common.

Component-Specific Methods

While most components have methods specific to themselves, most of these methods are used to do one of the following:

- Add something to a component instance, such as a piece of data or a graphic
- Get (return) information about a component instance; for example, what item is currently selected in a combobox
- Tell (set) the component instance to do something, such as scroll up or down, or highlight a specific piece of data
- Sort the component's data in a specific manner

NOTE *There are too many component-specific methods to list here. For a complete listing of the methods of a component class, look up its entry in the ActionScript dictionary. Component-specific methods can be found under each component listing in the Actions Toolbox section of the Actions panel.*

In the following exercise, we'll use component methods to dynamically insert, delete, and manipulate the data within our List component as well as to dynamically insert icon graphics. In addition, we'll use component methods to control and communicate with several other component instances.

1) Open *Components3.fla*.

In the preceding exercise, we set up the framework for using component events via Listener objects; however, we didn't script our Listener objects to do anything when events were triggered. In this exercise, we'll insert scripts that cause the application to perform an action when these events occur.

2) With the Actions panel open and Frame 1 selected, insert the following script just below `inputURL_tiListener.focusIn = function () {`**:**

```
deleteURL_pb.enabled = false;
openURL_pb.enabled = false;
windowOption.enabled = false;
enableWindowGraphics(false);
addURL_pb.enabled = true;
```

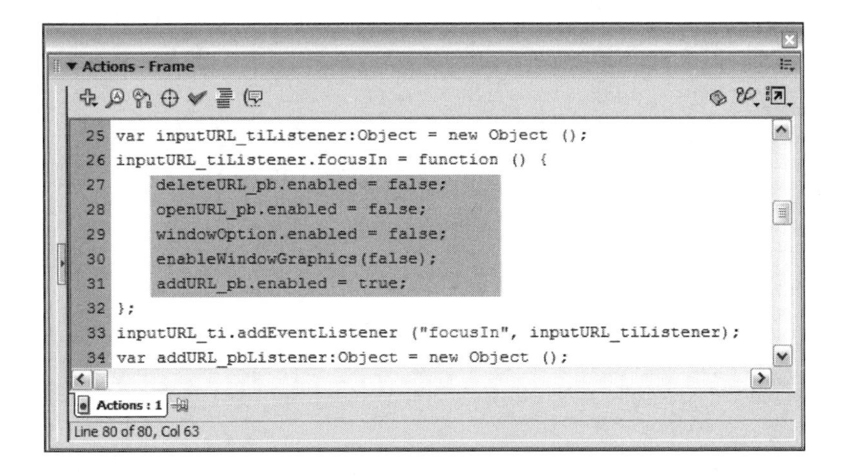

In the preceding exercise, we registered the `inputURL_tiListener` object to listen for the `focusIn` event in relation to the **inputURL_ti** component instance. The script we've just inserted tells the Listener object what to do when this event occurs in relation to that instance. When the user clicks inside the **inputURL_ti** instance (gives it focus), this script will execute.

The purpose of this script is to reset various elements to their initial state. The **deleteURL_pb** and **openURL_pb** Button instances are disabled, the radio buttons within the `windowOption` group are disabled, the `enableWindowGraphics()` function is called (making the graphics associated with the radio buttons transparent), and the **addURL_pb** instance is enabled.

We're resetting these various elements to their initial states. Other scripts we'll add shortly will change these states as the user interacts with the application; this script places these elements into the appropriate state for inputting a new URL. This will become clearer as we progress.

It's important to understand that the **addURL_pb** button is enabled (as shown in the last line of the script) when the **inputURL_ti** instance is given focus for inputting a new URL. This occurs because the two instances work in tandem. When typing a URL, the user adds it to the list by clicking the **addURL_pb** button, requiring that instance to be enabled. We'll script the functionality that adds the URL in a moment, but first let's take a look at some of the items in the library that play an important role in one of the following steps.

3) Choose Window > Library to open the Library panel.

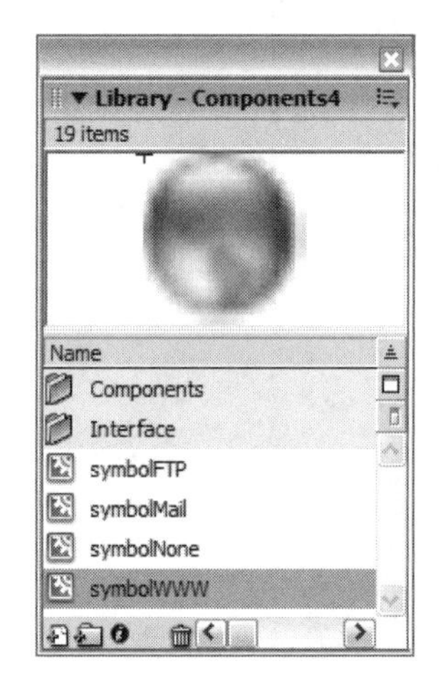

You'll find two folders within the library that contain movie elements, as well as four additional movie clips not contained within a folder. These movie clips represent icon graphics. Here's how they'll be used by our application.

When the user enters a URL containing *www*, not only will that URL be added to the **listURL_lb** instance, but our application will be scripted to detect that a *www* address has been entered. The appropriate icon graphic will be shown next to the URL in the list, which in this case would be the movie clip named *symbolWWW*. If the user enters a URL containing *ftp*, the *symbolFTP* movie clip will be used. Entering *mailto* causes *symbolMail* to be used. If none of the aforementioned URL types is entered, our app will assume that an errant URL has been added and the *symbolNone* movie clip will be shown next to that URL.

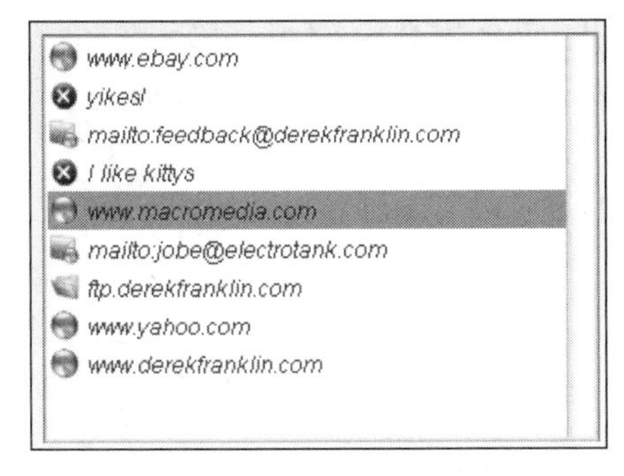

This functionality is made possible as the result of the capability of List component instances to dynamically attach icon graphics, which are nothing more than movie clips that have been given linkage identifier names. Let's look at how one of these movie clips is set up.

4) Right-click (Control-click on a Macintosh) the `symbolWWW` movie clip in the library and choose Linkage from the menu that appears.

This opens the Linkage Properties dialog box, which shows that this movie clip has been given a linkage name of `symbolWWW`. (Yes, it's the same name as the movie clip itself; it was done this way for simplicity.)

The remaining three movie clips have also been given identifier names representative of their movie clip names. Giving movie clips identifier names allows us to dynamically insert them into our project as it plays, something we'll script next.

5) Click OK to close the Linkage Properties dialog box. With the Actions panel open, insert the following script just below `addURL_pbListener.click = function () {`:

```
listURL_lb.enabled = true;
listURL_lb.addItemAt (0, inputURL_ti.text);
listURL_lb.selectedIndex = 0;
listURL_lb.iconFunction = function (item:Object):String {
  var tempString:String = item.label;
  if (tempString.indexOf ("www.") >= 0) {
    return "symbolWWW";
  } else if (tempString.indexOf ("mailto:") >= 0) {
    return "symbolMail";
  } else if (tempString.indexOf ("ftp.") >= 0) {
    return "symbolFTP";
  } else {
    return "symbolNone";
  }
};
inputURL_ti.text = "";
```

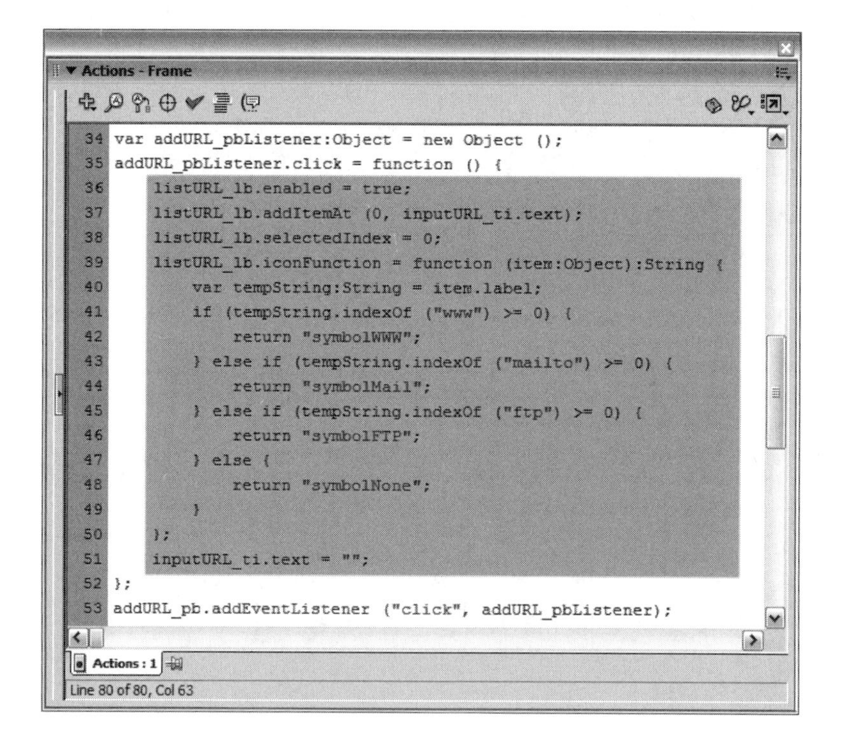

Because this script is inserted within the `click` handler of the `addURL_pbListener` object, it gets executed when the **addURL_pb** instance is clicked. Let's look at how this script works.

The first line enables the **listURL_lb** instance, just in case it has been disabled (such as when the application is initially opened). The next line of script uses the `addItemAt()` method, which is available to List component instances. This method adds an item (line of information) to the specified List component instance, which in this case is the one named **listURL_lb**.

NOTE *A disabled component cannot be manipulated by the user or via ActionScript.*

To understand how this method works, you need to understand that each item displayed in a List component instance is actually an object with two properties named `label` and `data`. The `label` property holds a value representing the text displayed for the item; the `data` property is a hidden value associated with that `label`. For example, if you had a List component that displayed computer parts, the `label` property could be used to hold a text description of the piece of hardware, while the associated `data` property could be used to hold the associated part number (hidden from the user) like this:

```
label: Monitor data: Mon359a4
label: Keyboard data: Key4e94f
```

and so on.

If the user later selected one of these items from the list, you could use a script to retrieve either the `label` or `data` value of the selected item. The `data` item is the preferred choice because it contains more specific information; the `label` property is used mostly for readability. With this understanding, let's look at the syntax for using the `addItemAt()` method:

```
nameOfListInstance.addItemAt(index, label, data);
```

The `index` parameter indicates where in the list to add the new item, with 0 being the top of the list. The `label` parameter represents the text you want to display for the new item. The `data` parameter represents any hidden value you would like to associate with the new item. The `data` parameter is optional, and omitting it will cause the `label` and `data` properties of the newly added item to contain the same value.

As you can see in the script we inserted, the method is set up to add a new item to index 0 (which, again, is the topmost position on the list), and the value assigned to the `label` property of this newly added item is the text currently displayed in the **inputURL_ti** instance (what the user has entered). Because we're not using the optional third parameter in the method call, the `label` and `data` properties contain the same value when the item is added to the list.

NOTE *Items shown in List component instances have index numbers (beginning with 0), indicating their position in the list. Thus, the first item in the list has an index of 0, the second has an index value of 1, and so on.*

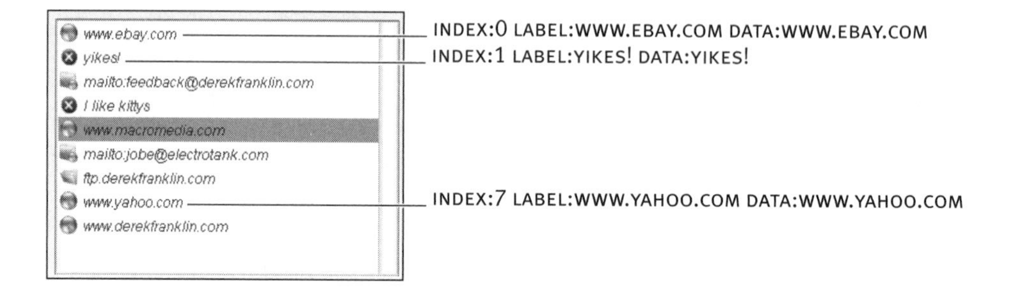

The third line of the script assigns a value to the `selectedIndex` property of the **listURL_lb** instance. This will set and highlight the item at index 0, which will always be any newly added item.

The next several lines of script set the `iconFunction` property of the **listURL_lb** instance. The value of this property specifies a function to execute when a new item is added to the list. This function is used to add an icon to the newly added item by returning a string value, representative of the identifier name of the icon to use (as discussed in Step 3). Let's look at how this function works.

When this function is executed, it's passed an object that we've named `item`. This object has two properties named `label` and `data`. The values of these properties are the same as the `label` and `data` properties as defined in the `addItemAt()` method call we just discussed. If our method call looked similar to this:

```
myList.addItemAt(0, "fruit", 47);
```

the object passed to `iconFunction` would have a `label` property value of `"fruit"` and a `data` property value of `47`. The value of one or both of these passed properties is used by the function to determine the name of the icon to attach.

The function's first action creates a variable named `tempString`. This variable is assigned a value based on the `label` property of the object passed to the function. If the user is adding the URL *www.derekfranklin.com*, for example, `tempString` will be assigned that URL as its value. Next, a series of conditional statements is used to determine whether the value contained in `tempString` includes *www.*, *mailto:*, *ftp.*, or none of these. As a result, the function will return a string value representing the linkage identifier name of the movie clip in the library to use.

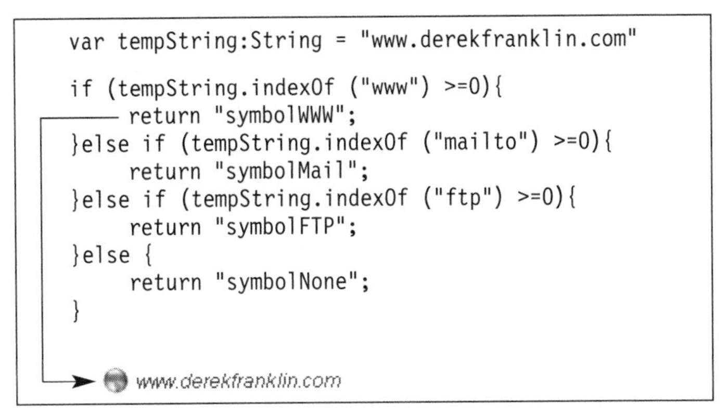

var tempString:String = "www.derekfranklin.com"
if (tempString.indexOf ("www") >=0){
return "symbolWWW";
}else if (tempString.indexOf ("mailto") >=0){
return "symbolMail";
}else if (tempString.indexOf ("ftp") >=0){
return "symbolFTP";
}else {
return "symbolNone";
}
www.derekfranklin.com

The last line in the script clears the **inputURL_ti** instance of the URL the user has entered, allowing the user to quickly add another URL.

Let's test our project.

6) Choose Control > Test Movie.

When the application appears, click inside the **inputURL_ti** instance. Notice that the **addURL_pb** instance immediately becomes enabled, as scripted in Step 2. Enter a URL and click the Add button to enable the **listURL_lb** URL and add it to the list. The URL is highlighted, the appropriate icon is attached, and the **inputURL_ti** instance is cleared of text and ready for the next entry, as we scripted in Step 5.

Let's return to the authoring environment to add a few more scripts.

7) Close the test movie to return to the authoring environment. With the Actions panel open and Frame 1 selected, insert the following script just below `listURL_lbListener.focusIn = function () {`**:**

```
addURL_pb.enabled = false;
deleteURL_pb.enabled = true;
openURL_pb.enabled = true;
windowOption.enabled = true;
enableWindowGraphics(true);
```

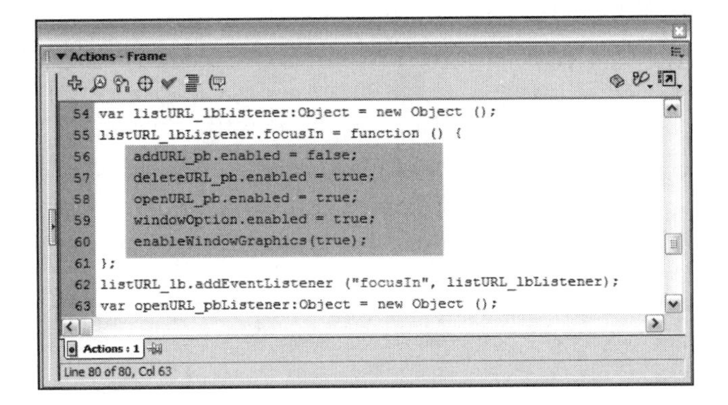

Because this script is inserted within the `focusIn` handler of the `listURL_lbListener` object, it gets executed when the **listURL_lb** instance is given focus (the user interacts with it). This script does nothing more than disable the **addURL_pb** instance, while enabling the other elements specified within the script. The bottom half of our app comes to life as a result. These elements are enabled because they have a purpose when the user gives focus to the **listURL_lb** instance (selects a URL from it).

Let's test this functionality.

8) Choose Control > Test Movie.

When the application appears, enter a URL and then click the Add button to add the URL to the list. Next, click the URL you just entered in the list. When you do, all the elements in the bottom half of the application become enabled as a result of the script we added in Step 7. These enabled elements don't do anything yet, but that will change in a moment. If you click inside the **inputURL_ti** instance at this point to add another URL, the script we added in Step 2 is executed, resulting in the Add button being enabled and the elements in the bottom half of the application becoming disabled.

This interactivity is all being managed through component events that make creating a responsive application simple and straightforward.

Let's return to the authoring environment to script the Delete and Open buttons and wrap up this exercise.

9) Close the test movie to return to the authoring environment. With the Actions panel open and Frame 1 selected, insert the following script just below `openURL_pbListener.click = function () {`**:**

```
getURL (listURL_lb.value, windowOption.getValue ());
```

Because this script is inserted within the `click` handler of the `openURL_pbListener` object, it gets executed when the **openURL_pb** instance is clicked. As you can see, the `getURL()` action is used to perform a single task—opening the specified URL.

Typically, the `getURL()` action is used in the following manner:

```
getURL("http://www.derekfranklin.com", "_blank");
```

The first parameter specifies the URL to open; the second specifies the HTML target. Our use of the `getURL()` action involves using two dynamic values in place of hard-coded values, as shown in this sample script.

The URL parameter of the `getURL()` action is determined by looking at the current `value` of the **listURL_lb** instance. This property reflects the currently selected item in the instance. If the currently selected item is *http://www.electrotank.com*, that's considered the `value` of the instance.

The value of the second parameter of the `getURL()` action is derived by getting the current value of the `windowOption` radio button group. You'll remember that in the first exercise of this lesson, we assigned `data` values to both of the radio button instances in our application, with the top radio button instance being given a `data` value of `_self` and the other instance a `data` value of `_blank`. We then assigned both of those radio buttons to the `windowOption` group. Depending on which radio button is currently selected when this `getURL()` action is executed, the method call of `windowOption.getValue()` will return a value of either `_self` or `_blank`. This determines whether the specified URL is opened in the current browser window or a new one.

NOTE *URLs entered containing* www *must be preceded by* http:// *for the* `getURL()` *action to work properly.*

10) Insert the following script just below `deleteURL_pbListener.click = function () {`**:**

```
listURL_lb.removeItemAt (listURL_lb.selectedIndex);
listURL_lb.selectedIndex = listURL_lb.length - 1;
if (listURL_lb.length <= 0) {
  deleteURL_pb.enabled = false;
  openURL_pb.enabled = false;
  windowOption.enabled = false;
  enableWindowGraphics(false);
  listURL_lb.enabled = false;
}
```

```
Actions - Frame
68 var deleteURL_pbListener:Object = new Object ();
69 deleteURL_pbListener.click = function () {
70     listURL_lb.removeItemAt (listURL_lb.selectedIndex);
71     listURL_lb.selectedIndex = listURL_lb.length - 1;
72     if (listURL_lb.length <= 0) {
73         deleteURL_pb.enabled = false;
74         openURL_pb.enabled = false;
75         windowOption.enabled = false;
76         enableWindowGraphics(false);
77         listURL_lb.enabled = false;
78     }
79 };
80 deleteURL_pb.addEventListener ("click", deleteURL_pbListener);
Actions : 1
Line 80 of 80, Col 63
```

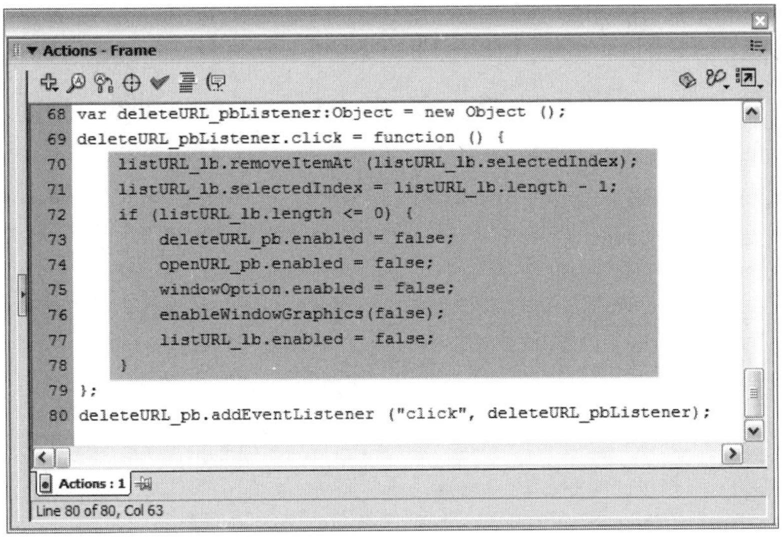

Because this script is inserted within the `click` handler of the `deleteURL_pbListener` object, it gets executed when the **deleteURL_pb** instance is clicked, and takes care of deleting items from the list.

The first line of the script uses the `removeItemAt()` method to remove an item from the list contained in the **listURL_lb** instance. This method accepts a single parameter, representing the index number of the item to be deleted. In our use of this method, this index value is dynamically determined by retrieving the index of the currently selected item in the list. If the currently selected item in the list is fourth from the top, it will have an index value of 3. As a result, item 3 on the list is deleted.

The next line of the script sets the `selectedIndex` property of the **listURL_lb** instance to select and highlight the last item in the list after a deletion occurs. The value of this property is dynamically assigned by determining the `length` of the **listURL_lb** (how many items it contains) minus 1. If the instance contains five items, for example, after the deleted item is removed the instance `length` property will be 5 and the item selected will have an index of 4. The extra step of subtracting 1 is done because although the `length` property is determined with a count starting at 1 (one item in the list means a `length` of 1), index values start from 0 (the first item in the list has an index of 0). This functionality is added simply from a usability standpoint, allowing the user to continue clicking the Delete button, removing the last item in the list automatically.

The last part of this script uses a conditional statement to react in the event that all items in the list have been deleted. If this occurs, the actions within the statement again disable the elements in the application used for managing and navigating URLs, because they have no meaning when no URLs exist.

Let's do one final test.

11) Choose Control > Test Movie.

When the application appears, add some URLs; then select a URL and either delete it or open it to see how the application handles these activities. Delete all the URLs from the list to see how the application reacts.

Component properties, events, and methods allow you to quickly create useful and responsive applications.

12) Close the test movie to return to the authoring environment. Save this file as *Components4.fla*.

In the sections that follow, we'll tweak the application's usability and appearance.

USING THE FOCUSMANAGER COMPONENT

One of the main goals of any good application is to make the user's experience as pleasant and straightforward as possible. A large part of accomplishing this goal involves anticipating the user's needs and making sure that your application allows users to accomplish tasks with minimal effort. For example, look at the process of doing a search on Google. When you navigate to Google's homepage, your cursor is automatically inserted in the Search box because they believe that your main purpose for visiting their site is to do a search. It's a simple thing, but it allows you to begin typing keywords as soon as the page loads, without having to first drag your mouse to place the cursor in the Search box manually.

What happens when you press Enter/Return? Because you've typed keywords into the Search box, pressing Enter/Return should submit your keywords to Google's search engine. Fortunately, it does. Imagine how awful it would be if pressing Enter/Return took you to their Help page. This would make using Google a real pain.

These kinds of simple anticipatory behaviors within an application are deliberately programmed by the developer as a way of making the application easier to use. Besides Google's homepage, you've probably experienced similar functionality in other applications—especially those with dialog boxes where pressing the Tab key allows you to quickly navigate from one field to the next.

Within Flash, these types of interactions are handled by the *FocusManager component*. Why is this component special? Because you never see it physically, unlike Button or CheckBox component instances. You can only see its effects—an invisible instance of the FocusManager component is automatically added to your project whenever you add a regular component instance. The FocusManager component takes care of managing focus-related tasks via ActionScript.

NOTE *Because the FocusManager component is invisible, it can't be configured using the Component Inspector or Property Inspector, as other component instances can. It can only be configured and worked with by using ActionScript.*

The term *focus* is simply a computer geek term meaning the object that's currently being manipulated. Type text into TextInput component instance, and it's said to have focus. Click a button; it has focus. Select a check box, and it has focus. Only a single item at a time in an application can have focus.

As you can see, what's considered as having focus in an application is constantly in flux. Normally, the user controls what has focus at any particular time due to the way he or she is interacting with the application. However, the FocusManager component gives you some control over the focus. Why would having control over the focus aspects of your application be helpful? Consider these scenarios.

SCENARIO 1

The user clicks a check box in your application, indicating that he or she wants to receive email about special offers. The FocusManager component allows you to automatically give focus to the TextInput instance, allowing the user to immediately begin typing an email address after selecting the check box—without having to manually move the cursor to the textbox. If the TextInput instance is named **myTextInput_ti**, it would be given focus using the following syntax:

```
focusManager.setFocus(myTextInput_ti);
```

SCENARIO 2

You want users to be able to press Enter/Return at any time, depending on the task they're trying to accomplish, and have Enter/Return simulate clicking the appropriate button. Because our sample application allows the user to enter an email address, chances are that there's a button on the interface that, when clicked, will submit the address. Instead of making the user click the button, you can set the FocusManager's `setDefaultButton` property like this:

```
focusManager.setDefaultButton = mySubmitButton_pb;
```

As a result, the `click` event for the Button component instance **mySubmitButton_pb** will be triggered when the Enter/Return button on the keyboard is pressed. Any objects registered to listen for this event will be notified that it has occurred, thus executing any scripts set up to execute as a result of the event.

In the following exercise, we'll use the functionality the FocusManager provides to make our application a bit more user-friendly in several ways, which we'll explain as we go along.

1) Open *Components4.fla*.

This project continues from where we left off in the preceding exercise. We'll insert several lines of code throughout the existing code on Frame 1.

2) With the Actions panel open and Frame 1 selected, insert the following line of script as the last line of the function that begins `inputURL_tiListener.focusIn = function () {`:

```
focusManager.defaultPushButton = addURL_pb;
```

Actions - Frame

```
24 enableWindowGraphics(false);
25 var inputURL_tiListener:Object = new Object ();
26 inputURL_tiListener.focusIn = function () {
27     deleteURL_pb.enabled = false;
28     openURL_pb.enabled = false;
29     windowOption.enabled = false;
30     enableWindowGraphics(false);
31     addURL_pb.enabled = true;
32     focusManager.defaultPushButton = addURL_pb;
33 };
34 inputURL_ti.addEventListener ("focusIn", inputURL_tiListener);
35 var addURL_pbListener:Object = new Object ();
36 addURL_pbListener.click = function () {
37     listURL_lb.enabled = true;
```

Actions : 1

Line 82 of 82, Col 63

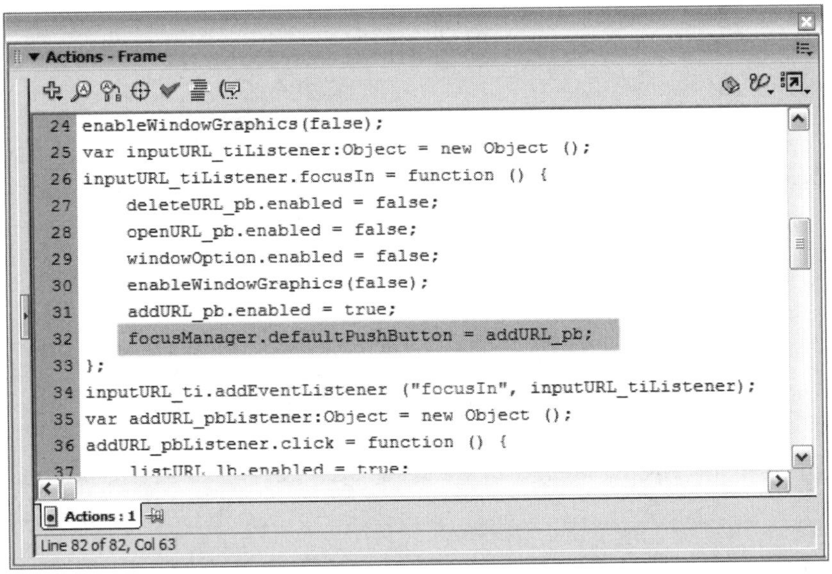

Remember that this function handles what happens when the **inputURL_ti** instance is given focus. As a result of placing this line of script within this function definition, when the **inputURL_ti** instance is given focus the **addURL_pb** button becomes the default button when the Enter/Return key is pressed. This means that pressing the Enter/Return key triggers a `click` event, just as if the **addURL_pb** were actually clicked. The Listener object we have set up to listen for this event is notified that the event has occurred, and takes action accordingly.

Let's do a test.

3) Choose Control > Test Movie.

When the application appears, click inside the **inputURL_ti** instance. As soon as you do, the Add button (**addURL_pb**) becomes highlighted, indicating that it's the default button. Type a URL, press the Return/Enter key, and you'll see that this has the same effect as manually clicking the Add button.

4) Close the test movie to return to the authoring environment. With the Actions panel open and Frame 1 selected, insert the following line of script as the last line *within* the conditional statement that's part of the function beginning `deleteURL_pbListener.click = function () {`**:**

```
focusManager.setFocus(inputURL_ti);
```

```
69 var deleteURL_pbListener:Object = new Object ();
70 deleteURL_pbListener.click = function () {
71     listURL_lb.removeItemAt (listURL_lb.selectedIndex);
72     listURL_lb.selectedIndex = listURL_lb.length - 1;
73     if (listURL_lb.length <= 0) {
74         deleteURL_pb.enabled = false;
75         openURL_pb.enabled = false;
76         windowOption.enabled = false;
77         enableWindowGraphics(false);
78         listURL_lb.enabled = false;
79         focusManager.setFocus(inputURL_ti);
80     }
81 };
82 deleteURL_pb.addEventListener ("click", deleteURL_pbListener);
```

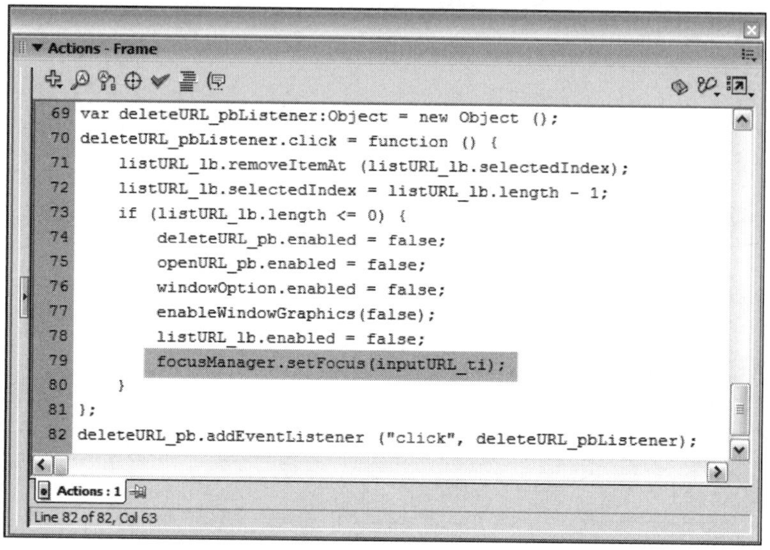

When the **deleteURL_pb** instance is clicked for the purpose of deleting a URL from the list, the function to which we added this line of script is executed. The conditional part of the statement is only executed when the *last* URL in the list is deleted. Because this line of script was inserted within that conditional statement, it also is executed only when the last URL is deleted from the list. When the last URL is deleted from the list, the **inputURL_ti** instance is given focus, allowing the user to immediately begin entering new URLs without manually placing the cursor first. This simple addition makes for a much more usable application.

5) Choose Control > Test Movie.

When the application appears, add some URLs; then begin deleting them. As soon as you delete the last one, the **inputURL_ti** instance is automatically given focus, allowing you to immediately add new URLs again.

TIP *The FocusManager component has additional functionality that can be explored by looking up its entry in the ActionScript dictionary.*

6) Close the test movie to return to the authoring environment. Save this file as *Components5.fla*.

Our application needs a bit of final visual tweaking, and we'll take care of this next.

CUSTOMIZING UI COMPONENTS WITH ACTIONSCRIPT

Let's face it—most coders couldn't care less about the design aspects of an application. They just want to see it work. However, there's no getting around the fact that in the real world, a great-looking application is just as important as a properly functioning one.

Because user interface components are visual elements, their appearance must fit in well with the overall design of your application. Fortunately, they have the built-in capability to be styled and customized in various ways using ActionScript. This allows you to easily change visual features such as colors, fonts, margins, and more.

NOTE *The look of components can also be changed in more dramatic ways by using Flash's drawing tools to tinker with the graphical elements that make up a component. Because the focus of this book is ActionScript, in this section we'll look only at visual aspects that can be changed using a script.*

Following are some of the visual aspects of components that can be changed:

```
borderColor
fontSize
fontStyle
fontWeight
marginLeft
marginRight
textAlign
textDecoration
```

For a complete listing and definitions of style properties that can be changed, look for "Supported Styles" in Flash's Help documentation.

Components can be styled on several different levels, including individually and globally. Components can also be styled as a class (such as RadioButton, CheckBox, or Button) so that all instances of that class share the same attributes. Although this strategy may be useful in some cases, individual and global styling are likely to be more commonly used, so we'll focus on those techniques.

When an individual component instance is styled a certain way, only that instance's appearance changes. When components are styled globally, all component instances are affected.

NOTE *Individual styling changes applied to an instance will override global styling changes in relation to that instance.*

To set a style property for an individual component instance such as `fontSize`, you use the following syntax:

```
myComponentInstance.setStyle("fontSize", 14);
```

To set its border color, you use the following syntax:

```
myComponentInstance.setStyle("borderColor", 0x006633);
```

When setting color styles, which would include any style property whose name ends with *Color*, there is the built-in capability to use color names instead of hexadecimal values:

```
myComponentInstance.setStyle("borderColor", "green");
```

TIP *Most common color names (black, red, green, blue, and so on) can be used. For greater versatility, use hex values. For more information about hex values, see Lesson 4, "Using Object Classes."*

Scripting global styling changes is similar to scripting individual components; however, instead of naming the individual component instance, you reference the global `style` object:

```
_global.style.setStyle("fontSize", 14);
```

This script will cause all component instances to use a font size of 14.

In the following exercise, we'll use both individual and global styling to give our application its final beautiful appearance.

1) Open *Components5.fla*.

This project continues from where we left off in the preceding exercise. We'll insert several lines of code at the end of the existing code on Frame 1.

2) With the Actions panel open and Frame 1 selected, add the following script at the end of the current script:

```
listURL_lb.setStyle("fontStyle", "italic");
listURL_lb.setStyle("color", 0x006699);
```

These two lines of script set the `fontStyle` and `color` properties of the **listURL_lb** instance. Setting the `fontStyle` property to `italic` causes text in the component to appear italicized; the `color` property determines the color of the text. Yes, it seems as though the property for changing the font color should be called `fontColor`, but it's not. It's simply `color`.

NOTE *For items in a List component instance, the `color` property refers to the color of text when the item is not selected.*

3) Add this script at the end of the current script:

```
deleteURL_pb.setStyle("color", 0x990000);
openURL_pb.setStyle("fontWeight", "bold");
```

The first line causes the text on the Delete button to appear red, as a proper Delete button should. The next line boldfaces the text on the Open button.

One more global change and our application will be finished.

4) Add the following line of script at the end of the current script:

```
_global.style.setStyle("themeColor", "haloOrange");
```

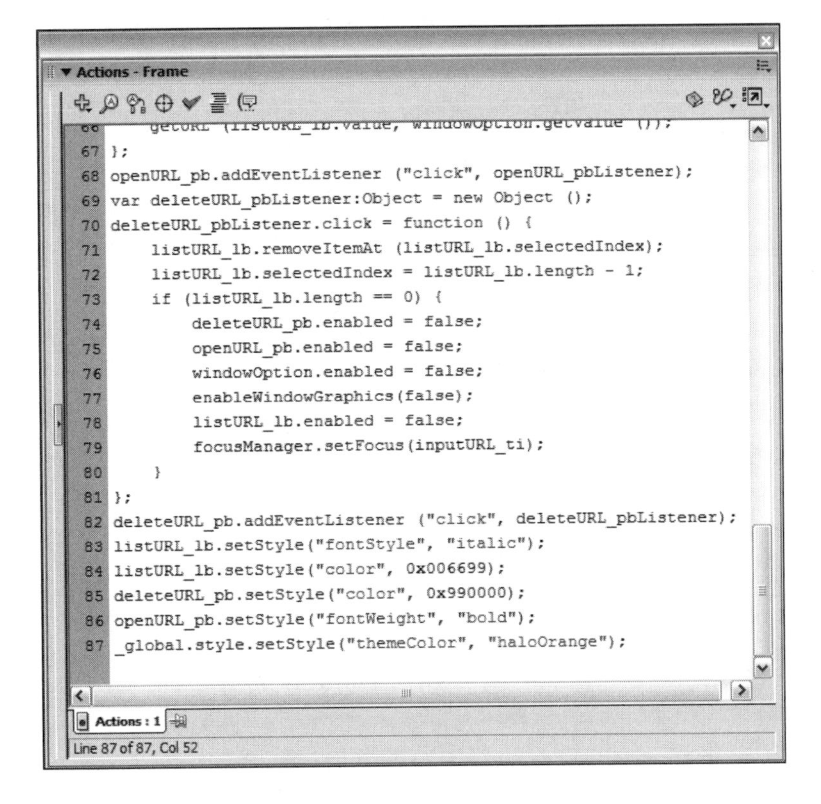

Actions - Frame
67 };
68 openURL_pb.addEventListener ("click", openURL_pbListener);
69 var deleteURL_pbListener:Object = new Object ();
70 deleteURL_pbListener.click = function () {
71 listURL_lb.removeItemAt (listURL_lb.selectedIndex);
72 listURL_lb.selectedIndex = listURL_lb.length - 1;
73 if (listURL_lb.length == 0) {
74 deleteURL_pb.enabled = false;
75 openURL_pb.enabled = false;
76 windowOption.enabled = false;
77 enableWindowGraphics(false);
78 listURL_lb.enabled = false;
79 focusManager.setFocus(inputURL_ti);
80 }
81 };
82 deleteURL_pb.addEventListener ("click", deleteURL_pbListener);
83 listURL_lb.setStyle("fontStyle", "italic");
84 listURL_lb.setStyle("color", 0x006699);
85 deleteURL_pb.setStyle("color", 0x990000);
86 openURL_pb.setStyle("fontWeight", "bold");
87 _global.style.setStyle("themeColor", "haloOrange");
Actions : 1
Line 87 of 87, Col 52

As you've probably noticed during the testing phases of this project, all the component instances are highlighted in a greenish tint whenever you interact with them. This tint is known as `haloGreen`. With this line of script, we've set the global `themeColor` property of all component instances to `haloOrange`, causing them to take on an orange tint when you interact with them.

TIP *A third possible value for this property is* `haloBlue`.

Time for one final test.

5) Choose Control > Test Movie.

When the application appears, you'll notice that the Add button glows orange when manipulated. Add some URLs. As you interact with the other elements, they also glow orange. In addition, the word Delete appears on the Delete button in red, and the word Open appears bold on the Open button. Items in the URL list appear italicized at all times, in addition to appearing blue when not selected.

This is just a small sampling of the dozens of style changes that can be made using ActionScript.

6) Close the test movie to return to the authoring environment. Save this file as *Components6.fla*.

This step completes this exercise and the lesson.

WHAT YOU HAVE LEARNED

In this lesson, you have:

- Learned how to set and get component property values (pages 330–341)
- Used component events to trigger scripts (pages 341–347)
- Used component methods to insert data dynamically (pages 347–358)
- Worked with the FocusManager component to make a more usable application (pages 359–363)
- Styled components instances individually and globally using ActionScript (page 363–366)

getting data in and out of flash

LESSON 11

One of Flash's most useful features is its capability to communicate with external sources, sending data to and receiving data from other locations. This makes Flash a powerful application development tool: it enables you to perform tasks such as load news dynamically, facilitate user login and registration, and build Flash chat applications.

In this lesson, we'll show you various ways in which Flash can send and receive data. You'll use this knowledge to build a simple Flash polling application that enables you to vote for a movie and displays the poll results, a journal that saves entries to your hard drive, and a Web services application that helps you to translate English text into several other languages.

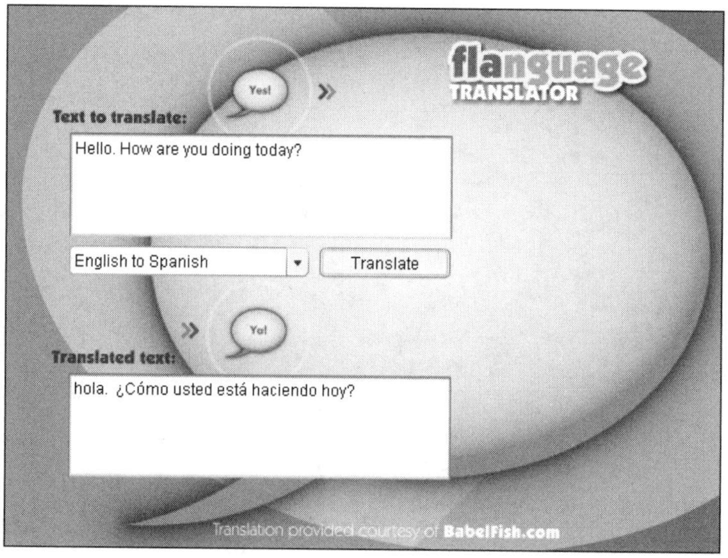

flanguage TRANSLATOR
Yes!
Text to translate:
Hello. How are you doing today?
English to Spanish
Translate
Yo!
Translated text:
hola. ¿Cómo usted está haciendo hoy?
Translation provided courtesy of BabelFish.com

You will build this language translator application, which demonstrates how easy it is to plug into a Web service to send data to and retrieve data from a third-party source.

WHAT YOU WILL LEARN

In this lesson, you will:

- Discover the data formats that Flash can load
- Learn about the objects designed for data transfer
- Send and receive data from a server
- Learn about policy files and how to use them
- Save data to your hard drive using shared objects
- Communicate with a Web service

APPROXIMATE TIME

This lesson takes approximately one and one half hours to complete.

LESSON FILES

Media Files:

Lesson11/Assets/Poll.asp
Lesson11/Assets/Poll.mdb

Starting Files:

Lesson11/Assets/poll1.fla
Lesson11/Assets/journal1.fla
Lesson11/Assets/Translator1.fla

Completed Projects:

poll2.fla
journal2.fla
Translator2.fla

UNDERSTANDING DATA SOURCES AND DATA FORMATS

A *data source* is a place from which Flash can load *external data* (that is, data not directly programmed into the movie). For example, Flash can load data from a simple text file, and that text file is considered a data source. *Data transfer* is the act of retrieving data from a source or sending data from Flash to another application. In this section, you'll learn about the different types of data sources as well as the Flash objects and methods used to communicate with these sources in the data transfer process.

Any data that you plan to load into Flash from an external source must be structured (formatted) in a specific way. Flash supports the following formats:

- **URL string.** In this type of name/value pair formatting, variables and their values are defined as a string of text. For example, the following text string:

  ```
  name=Jobe&website= http://www.electrotank.com&hairColor=brown
  ```

  defines three variables (`name`, `website`, `hairColor`) and their respective values (`Jobe`, `http://www.electrotank.com`, `brown`). After this text string has been loaded, Flash automatically breaks it into its respective variable names/values, making them available for use just as any other variables. An equals sign (=) is used to associate a variable name with its value and an ampersand (&) marks the end of one variable and the beginning of another. You will use this format in an exercise later in this lesson. The format supports an unlimited number of variables. Only simple variables can be stored in URL string format; data contained in objects, arrays, or any other data type is not supported by a string of text.

- **XML.** This popular formatting standard allows data to be stored in a logical structure. For example:

  ```
  <States>
    <State>
      <Name>North Carolina</Name>
      <Capital>Raleigh</Capital>
    </State>
    <State>
      <Name>Virginia</Name>
      <Capital>Richmond</Capital>
    </State>
  </States>
  ```

After an XML document is loaded into Flash, a script that you write is used to extract information from the XML document.

NOTE *See Lesson 12, "Using XML with Flash," for more information on the XML format.*

- **Shared objects.** These will be discussed later in this lesson; for now, understand that shared objects are similar to Flash cookies: shared objects allow you to store objects (data) locally on the user's hard drive. This means that after a user views and exits a Flash movie (as a projector or online), the data created while the movie was playing (user's name, last section visited, and so on) is saved. This data can be retrieved the next time the user plays the movie on the same computer. By using shared objects, you can store not only variables and their values, but *any* kind of data object, including arrays, XML objects—even custom objects. You can make this process of saving data transparent to users, or you can provide buttons for them to initiate the action. You can also have multiple shared-object data files on a single computer because each movie usually creates its own data file.

Now that you're familiar with the various data formats that Flash supports, let's review the sources from which Flash can load data:

- **Text files.** Flash can load text files (***.txt**) containing data formatted using the URL string format mentioned earlier in this lesson. Text files can be loaded using `loadVariables()` or the `load()` method of the LoadVars class, both of which we'll discuss later in this lesson. You can easily create these types of data sources using Windows Notepad or Apple Simple Text.
- **Server-side scripts.** Server-side scripts are placed on ASP, CFML, CGI, or JSP pages and executed by a server. Although invisible to the user, the scripted page actually generates formatted data (HTML, XML, and so on) that's sent back to the requesting source. For example, imagine visiting a page called **news.asp** that contains a server-side script, and probably no real content. The script, which is executed when a user visits the page, is used to dynamically generate and send to the user's browser an HTML-formatted page containing the latest news (probably extracted from a database). Server-side scripts can return data in both the XML and URL string formats. This means that by communicating with a page containing a server-side script, Flash can load dynamic data created on the fly.

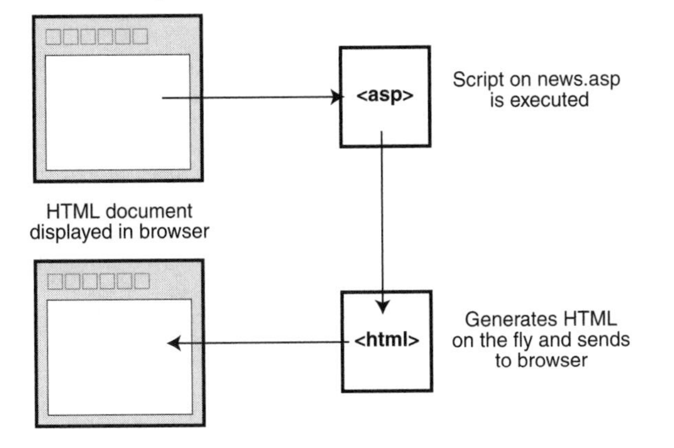

- **XML files.** An XML file is simply a text file that contains XML-formatted data; such files usually include an **xml** extension.
- **XML socket.** Socket servers are applications that run on a server and connect several simultaneous users to one another. Flash can send or receive information via the socket using the XML format. (You'll learn more about socket servers—including how to build a chat application with them—in Lesson 12, "Using XML with Flash.")
- **Shared objects.** As already mentioned, shared objects are used to create data files that store information on a user's hard drive. You can then retrieve these files for use with a movie, as you will see in the last exercise in this lesson.

GET VS. POST

There are two ways to transfer data between the server and Flash when working with server-side scripts: via GET or via POST. These two techniques for sending variables and their associated values are used in regular HTML pages and in Flash whenever data entered into a form is sent to a server to be processed. (We'll discuss the specific methods in the following exercises.)

When you send variables using GET, you're simply concatenating variable name/value pairs onto the URL itself. For example, if you wanted to use GET to send my name and email address to a script located on the **register.asp** page, you'd specify the URL as follows:

http://www.somedomain.com/register.asp?name=jobe&email=jobe@electrotank.com

The question mark (?) tells the script and server that everything that follows comprises variables. Although GET is easier to use than POST, it won't work for every situation because it has a 1024-character limit.

Now let's take a look at how POST is used. When variable data is sent using POST, that data is contained within the header of the HTTP request, which means you cannot see it being transferred. This gives you an added layer of security since the variables are not easily read. Because POST doesn't have a character limit, it provides a slightly more versatile way of sending variable data.

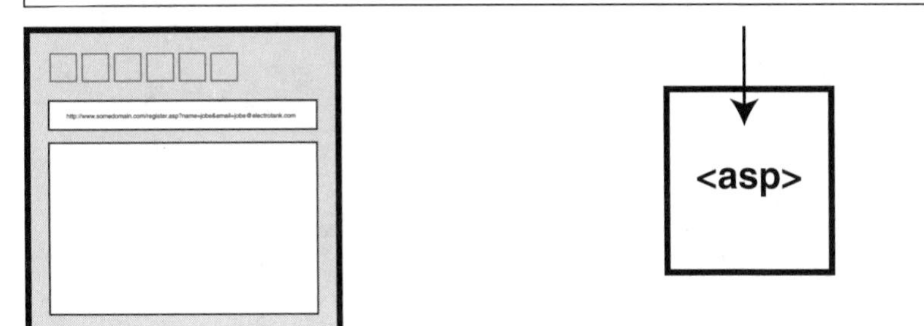

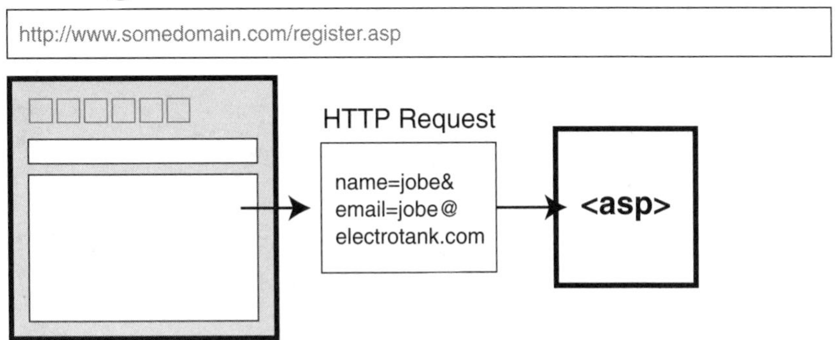

We'll return to the topic of GET and POST in the exercise that accompanies the next section, "Using the LoadVars Class."

NOTE *Because GET and POST are not always easily interchangeable, most server-side scripts are programmed to accept variables via either GET or POST, but usually not both.*

USING THE LOADVARS CLASS

You use the LoadVars class when working with data in the URL string format. This class enables you to load variable data from a text file, or to send and load variable data to and from a server-side script.

NOTE *While variable data contained in a text file can be loaded into Flash, Flash cannot save data to a text file directly; you must use a server-side script to do that.*

Creating a LoadVars object in Flash is simple. Look at the following example:

```
var container:LoadVars = new LoadVars();
```

This creates a new LoadVars object named `container`. To load variables from a URL into a LoadVars object, use the `load()` method:

```
container.load("http://www.myDomain.com/myFile.txt");
```

TIP *You can get the total number of bytes loaded so far or the total bytes that will be loaded by using the `getBytesLoaded()` and `getBytesTotal()` methods of the LoadVars object.*

When data has been loaded into a LoadVars object, you can access it by referencing the name of the particular LoadVars object that contains the data you want, followed by the variable name of that piece of data. For example, if you were to load the following string into a LoadVars object named `myData`:

```
name=Jobe&age=28&wife=Kelly
```

these variable values could be referenced as follows:

```
myData.name
myData.age
myData.wife
```

For example:

```
userAge = myData.age;
```

Here, `userAge` would have a value of `28`. In the same manner, a variable value in a LoadVars object can be set from within a script in Flash like this:

```
myData.age = 45;
```

A variable value inside a LoadVars object therefore can be set not only by loading external data into the object, but by setting the value internally (using a script inside the movie).

NOTE *When loading variables into a LoadVars object, Flash will overwrite existing variable values in the object or append new variable values.*

If you want to send the variables in a LoadVars object to a server-side script for processing, use the `send()` method. That syntax is as follows:

```
myLoadVarsObject.send("http://www.mydomain.com/process.asp");
```

No response is sent back to Flash when you use this method, so you would use it only to send variable data to the server for processing.

The sendAndLoad() method allows you to specify a LoadVars object whose contents you want to send, and the LoadVars object in which you want the response to load:

```
myLoadVarsObject.sendAndLoad("http://mydomain.com/process.asp",
⇒receivingLoadVarsObject);
```

In this case, the variables in myLoadVarsObject are sent to the specified URL for processing. The server sends data back to Flash, and that data is loaded into receivingLoadVarsObject. At that point, you can work with the receivingLoadVarsObject to extract the data that the server sent back. If you want to send variables in a LoadVars object and have that same object receive the data that the server sends back, simply use the load() method described in the following exercise.

Using the toString() method of the LoadVars class, you can create a URL-formatted string that represents the variables/values contained in the object.

myLoadVarsObject

name = "Jobe"
age = 25
email = "jobe@electrotank.com"

↓

myLoadVarsObject.toString()

↓

name=Jobe&age=25&email=jobe@electrotank.com

The LoadVars class has two properties: contentType and loaded. The contentType property can be changed before sending out variables, simply giving you the mime type specified in the HTTP header of the loaded document. The loaded property returns true if data has finished loading into the object, false if it has not, and undefined if a load() method has not yet been invoked.

There is only one event available to the LoadVars class: onLoad. Use this event to call a function when data has finished loading into the object. Each time data is loaded into the object, this event is fired again.

To load variables from a specified URL into a LoadVars object and then call a function when loading is complete, you must:

1) Define a function.

2) Create a new LoadVars object, using the new LoadVars constructor.

3) Specify the function to be called when the loading has completed.

4) Invoke the `load()` method of the LoadVars object.

For example:

```
function myFunction(){
  trace("Data is loaded");
}
var container:LoadVars = new LoadVars();
container.onLoad = myFunction;
container.load("http://www.somedomain.com/myFile.asp");
```

In this example, `myFunction()` is called when a string of data from the specified URL has been completely loaded into the `container` LoadVars object.

In the following exercise, you'll create a simple polling system using a LoadVars object. This object will send data to and load data from an ASP page in the URL string format. The ASP page contains a server-side script that enables it to read and write to a Microsoft Access database. When variable data is *sent* to the ASP page, the page interprets the data and updates the values in the database accordingly. When a LoadVars object requests that data be *loaded* into it from the ASP page, the page is set up so that it gets the data from the various fields in the database, encodes that data into the URL string format, and sends that data to the LoadVars object.

You will find this scripted page (**Poll.asp**) and the accompanying database (**Poll.mdb**) in the Lesson11/Assets folder on your CD-ROM. To complete this lesson successfully, you will need access to a Windows server running IIS so that the server-side script on the ASP page can be executed. Before you begin this exercise, upload **Poll.asp** and **Poll.mdb** to a Windows server and make a note of their location (URL).

1) Open *poll1.fla* in the Lesson 11/Assets folder.

We've already created the layers, frames, frame labels, and movie clips you'll need so that you can focus on the ActionScript.

With the timeline at Frame 1, you'll notice the text, "What was the best movie of 2003?" Below this text is some space and a Submit button. You will place four Radio Button components in the empty space between these two elements. These radio buttons will represent the selection method for your choice of the best movie of 2003. When a user presses the Submit button, the movie will execute a script, sending data to the server (based on which radio button is selected) and at the same time move the playhead to Frame 3, Waiting, where it will wait for a response from the server. When a response is received (data is loaded into a LoadVars object), the movie will move to the frame labeled Display. This frame will contain a script used to interpret the response from the server (data will be extracted from the LoadVars object). The data will be used to determine the percentage of the total number of votes that each of the four movies has received. Each movie's overall percentage value will then be displayed in a text field as well as graphically, using simple bar graphs.

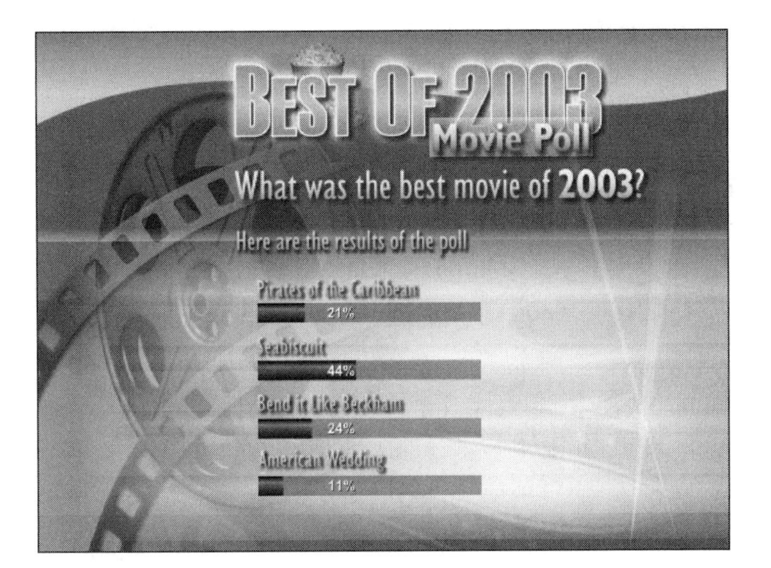

2) Move the playhead to Frame 1, and select the frame in the layer called Text and Buttons.

You will add four instances of the Radio Button component to this layer (beneath the question but above the Submit button).

3) Open the Components panel. Locate the Radio Button component and drag four instances of it onto the stage. Align these four components in a vertical column under the question on the screen.

You have just added four Radio Button components to the stage. If you select one of them and look at the Property Inspector, you'll see a list of the component's properties/parameters, all of which are editable.

NOTE *Although the Property Inspector lists what you see as parameters, from an ActionScript standpoint they represent properties of the component. Since this is an ActionScript book, we identify them as properties.*

The first property, `data`, should be blank. The `data` property associates a data value with the selected radio button instance. When the radio button instance is selected by the user as the movie plays, this value can be used by a script to perform a task based on that value.

The next property shown on the Property Inspector is `groupName`. As you learned in Lesson 10, "Scripting UI Components," radio button instances are designed to work in groups, allowing only a single radio button within a group to be selected at any time. This property setting enables you to assign the instance to a particular radio button group. You'll use the `radioGroup` default value for this property; therefore, the four radio button instances we've dragged onto the stage belong to the `radioGroup` group.

The `label` property represents the text displayed next to the radio button instance.

Next is the `labelPlacement` property. You can click the value of this property to display a drop-down list of label placement options. Each option specifies where the label text should be placed relative to the button itself. The default setting is `right`, which means that the text is shown to the right of the button.

The final property in the Property Inspector is `selected`. This is a Boolean value that determines whether a radio button should start off with a dot, indicating that the button is selected. By default, all radio button instances start with a `selected` value of `false`, meaning that the button is not selected. If you want one of your radio buttons to start off selected, you would change the value here to `true`.

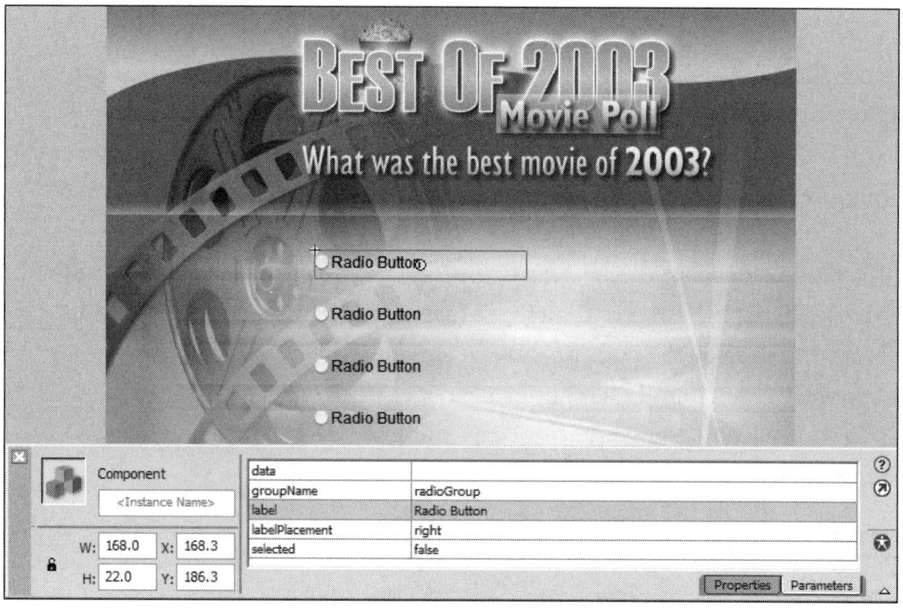

4) Select the top radio button and change its `label` property to `"Pirates of the Caribbean"`. Change the `label` properties of the next three radio buttons to `Seabiscuit`, `Bend it Like Beckham`, and `American Wedding`, respectively.

As you change the label names of the radio buttons (from top to bottom on the screen), you should see the text updated in the component itself.

NOTE *If the text in the component isn't updated, choose Control > Enable Live Preview.*

You may need to resize a couple of instances vertically to avoid truncating the appearance of the label text.

5) Change the `data` property of the four radio buttons to `1`, `2`, `3`, and `4`, from top to bottom.

When the movie is published and a radio button is selected, its `data` property value is set as the `data` value of the `radioGroup`. You retrieve this `data` value for use at any time by accessing the `selectedData` property of the RadioButtonGroup class. For example, if a radio button with a `data` property value of 3 was selected, and this radio button was part of a group of radio buttons with a group name of `radioGroup`, the following syntax would assign a value of 3 to `myValue`:

```
var myValue:Number = radioGroup.selectedData;
```

6) With the Actions panel open, select Frame 1 in the Actions layer and add `stop();`.

This `stop()` action prevents the movie from playing past Frame 1 until you instruct it to do so.

7) With Frame 1 still selected, add the following line of script:

```
var pollURL:String = "http://www.myDomain.com/poll.asp";
```

This creates a variable named `pollURL` and assigns it a value that represents the location (URL) of the **Poll.asp** page you uploaded to your server at the beginning of this exercise. (The URL shown should be replaced with the actual location where **Poll.asp** resides on your server.)

8) Add the following line of script:

```
var poll:LoadVars = new LoadVars();
```

This creates a new LoadVars object. With this object, we can load data from a remote location and make use of the convenient methods and properties described earlier in this lesson.

9) Define the `pollLoaded()` function by adding the following script at the end of the current script:

```
function pollLoaded() {
  gotoAndStop("Display");
}
```

This function is used to move the playhead to the frame labeled Display. (The next step explains when this function gets called.)

10) To associate the function we just defined with the `onLoad` event of the `poll` LoadVars object, add the following line of ActionScript:

```
poll.onLoad = pollLoaded;
```

This script says that when the last byte of data is completely loaded into the `poll` LoadVars object, the `pollLoaded()` function will be called; therefore, when the data has finished loading, the timeline will move to the frame labeled Display, as set up in Step 9. In a moment, we'll add a script at the Display label that will use the loaded data to display the results in several bar graphs.

11) Add the following function definition just below the last line of script:

```
function submitChoice() {
  var choice:Number = radioGroup.selectedData;
  poll.load(pollURL + "?choice=" + choice);
  gotoAndStop("Waiting");
}
```

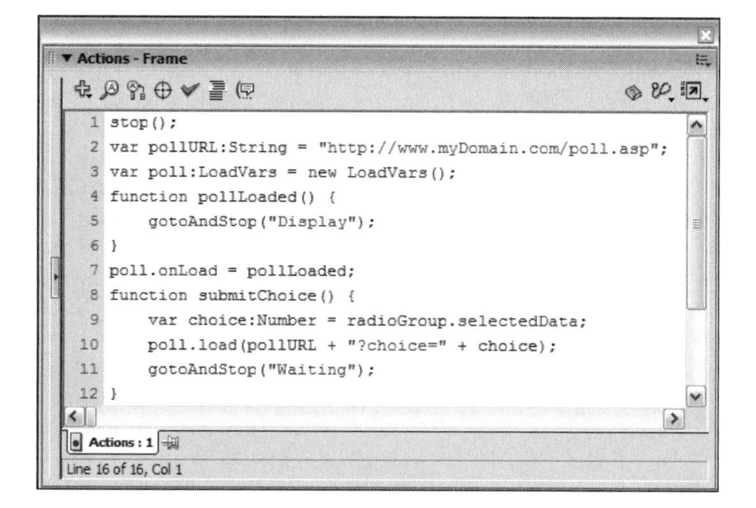

This function, which is used to submit the user's choice for best movie of 2003, is called when the Submit button is clicked.

The first line of the function definition creates a local variable named `choice`. This variable is assigned the current data value of the `radioGroup` group of radio buttons by accessing the `selectedData` property of the RadioButtonGroup class. If the user selected the second radio button, `choice` would have a value of `2`.

The next line of ActionScript invokes the `load()` method of the `poll` LoadVars object. Using an expression, the URL of the **Poll.asp** page is specified (`pollURL`), and the variable `choice` is added to the end of the string to send this to the server using the GET method of transferring variable data. If the user clicked the third radio button, this argument would look something like this:

```
"http://www.mydomain.com/poll.asp?choice=3"
```

Remember, everything after the question mark in the argument is a variable. In this case, we're sending a vote (`choice=3`) to the **Poll.asp** page. That page will then update the values in the database based on this vote and load the results into the `poll` LoadVars object. Those results are used in the actions described in Step 14.

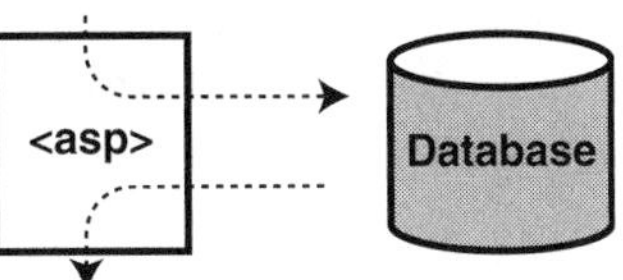

The final line of script in this function tells Flash to go to the frame labeled Waiting. The movie will stay on this frame until the data is loaded back into Flash from the server. At that point, the `pollLoaded()` function will be called (as described in Step 10), moving the timeline to the frame labeled Display.

12) Add the following `onRelease` event handler for the Submit button at the end of Frame 1:

```
submit_btn.onRelease = function() {
  submitChoice();
};
```

The `submitChoice()` function defined in Step 11 is executed when the Submit button is clicked.

13) Move the playhead to the frame labeled Display.

On this frame are four movie clip instances with horizontal bars—one bar graph for each movie on which the user is voting. All of these are instances of the same movie clip: their instance names are **barGraph1_mc**, **barGraph2_mc**, **barGraph3_mc**, and **barGraph4_mc**. Notice that all of these instance names include numbers. These numbers are used to associate one bar graph movie clip for each movie in the poll. Each of these instances also includes two text fields—**topPercent_txt** and **bottomPercent_txt**—that are used to display a textual representation of the percent. Both of these text fields display the same text; **bottomPercent_txt** is simply there to provide a slight shadow effect behind **topPercent_txt**. This movie clip also contains a horizontal bar with an instance name of **bar_mc**. It will be scaled horizontally based on the percentage value.

14) Select the frame in the Actions layer and add the following loop:

```
for (var i:Number = 1; i <= 4; ++i) {
  var graphName:String = "barGraph" + i + "_mc";
  var votes:Number = poll["item" + i + "total"];
  var totalVotes:Number = poll.totalVotes;
  var percent:Number = Math.round((votes / totalVotes) * 100);
  _root[graphName].bar_mc._xscale = percent;
}
```

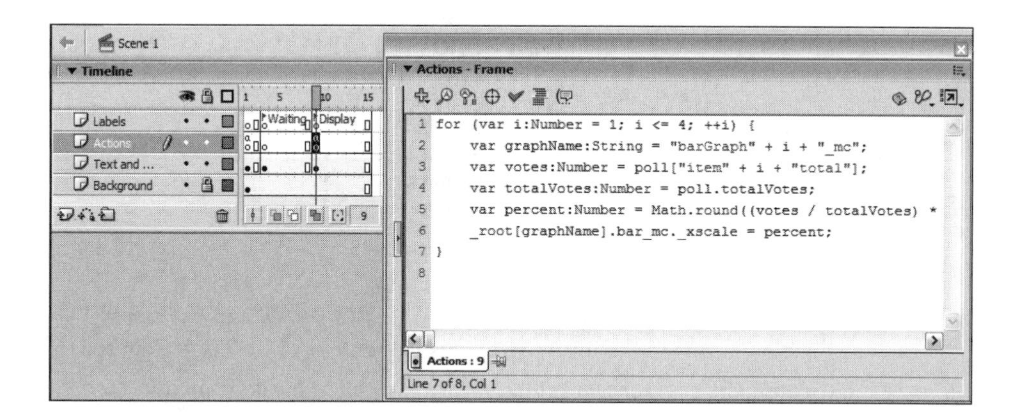

When the playhead has made it to this frame label (Display), the user has submitted his or her choice and the server has accepted it, added it to the current results, and loaded the resulting data into the `poll` LoadVars object. Remember that in Steps 9 and 10 we scripted our movie so that it would move to this frame label only after the resulting data from the server had been loaded completely into the `poll` LoadVars object. The script on this frame will now use that data. The variables loaded from the remote script into the LoadVars object are named `totalVotes`, `item1total`, `item2total`, `item3total`, and `item4total`. Obviously, `totalVotes` has a numeric value representing the total number of all votes submitted, and will be used to figure percentage values. The other variables hold the number of individual votes that each of the movies received. Because these variables have been loaded into the `poll` LoadVars object, you can access their values by using the following syntax:

```
poll.totalVotes
poll.item1total
poll.item2total
poll.item3total
poll.item4total
```

The loop calculates the percentage of votes received by each movie and scales the bar in the appropriate movie clip instance based on that number. The first line of script in the loop defines the variable `graphName`. Because the value of this variable is based on the concatenation of the string `"barGraph"` with the current value of `i` and the string `"_mc"`, it's actually a reference to the name of the movie clip instance that will be used during the current loop (**barGraph1_mc**, **barGraph2_mc**, and so on). Again, using the value of `i`, the next action in the loop sets a variable called `votes` equal to the total number of votes for the current item (`poll.item1total`, `poll.item2total`, and so on). A variable called `totalVotes` is then assigned a value that represents the total number of votes cast for all of the movies. Next, the `percent` variable is calculated by dividing the current item's number of votes by the total votes and multiplying by 100. This is rounded using the `Math.round()` method of the Math class. Finally, the **bar_mc** clip in the current movie clip (as referenced by the current value of `graphName`) is scaled to match the `percent` value. This loop will repeat these actions four times, scaling each of the bar graphs in the process.

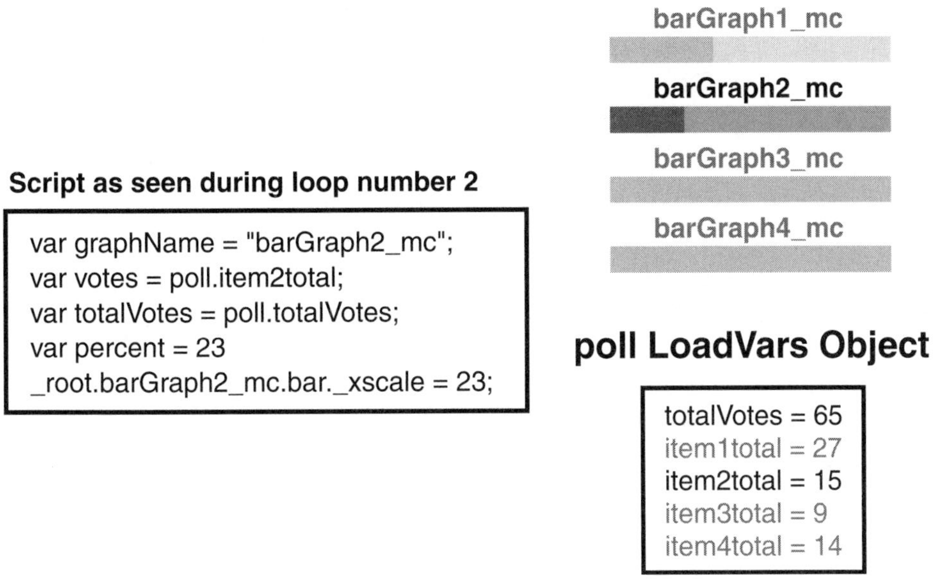

barGraph1_mc
barGraph2_mc
barGraph3_mc
barGraph4_mc

Script as seen during loop number 2

```
var graphName = "barGraph2_mc";
var votes = poll.item2total;
var totalVotes = poll.totalVotes;
var percent = 23
_root.barGraph2_mc.bar._xscale = 23;
```

poll LoadVars Object

```
totalVotes = 65
item1total = 27
item2total = 15
item3total = 9
item4total = 14
```

 *For more information about loops, see Lesson 9, "Automating Scripts with Loops."*

15) Add the following two lines of ActionScript at the end of but *within* the loop:

```
_root[graphName].topPercent_txt.text = percent + "%";
_root[graphName].bottomPercent_txt.text = percent + "%";
```

The text to be displayed in the **topPercent_txt** and **bottomPercent_txt** text fields, above the scaled **bar_mc** movie clip instance, is set using the value of the `percent` variable and concatenating `"%"` at the end.

16) Choose Control > Test Movie to test your work. Select a movie radio button and click the Submit button.

When you click the Submit button, your choice is sent to the **Poll.asp** page, which updates the database and returns the results of the poll to the `poll` LoadVars object. Your movie then moves to the frame labeled Display and shows you the results.

17) Close the test movie and save your work as *poll2.fla*.

You have just completed a basic application that uses the LoadVars class to talk to external scripts. You can now use this knowledge to build more complex and useful applications.

POLICY FILES

In this section, you will learn about the Flash player security restrictions as they apply to loading external data, and how the restrictions can be bypassed.

By default, an SWF can load external data only from the domain on which it resides. In other words, an SWF running within the Web page at *http://www.electrotank.com/addressbook.html* could not load the XML file at *http://www.derekfranklin.com/addresses.xml* because the running SWF and the file it's attempting to load are not on the same domain. However, the domain `derekfranklin.com` can give permission to SWF files that exist on `electrotank.com` by using a policy file, allowing those SWF files to load and use content from the `derekfranklin.com` domain. You will learn more about policy files later in this lesson, but before that you should understand what the Flash player considers to be a different domain.

The Flash player uses *exact domain matching* to determine whether a Flash file and external data source are on the same domain. A subdomain of a domain is not considered the same domain as its parent. For example, `store.electrotank.com` is not considered the same domain as games.electrotank.com, and www.electrotank.com is not the same as electrotank.com. If the two domain names don't look exactly alike, letter for letter, they're mismatched, and data exchange is not permitted without being granted access via a policy file.

A *policy file* is an XML-formatted file that sits in the root directory of a domain. When an SWF attempts to load data from another domain, the Flash player checks the destination domain for a policy file. If a policy file exists, the Flash player loads it and checks whether the origin domain is granted access. If the origin domain is granted access, the Flash player loads the requested data; otherwise, it doesn't.

NOTE *The loading of the policy file is transparent to the user. It happens in the background without any special ActionScript coding.*

The following is the format of a policy file:

```
<cross-domain-policy>
 <allow-access-from domain="www.derekfranklin.com" />
 <allow-access-from domain="www.electrotank.com" />
 <allow-access-from domain="63.74.114.215" />
</cross-domain-policy>
```

If the XML were saved to a file called **crossdomain.xml** and uploaded to the root directory of *http://www.gamebook.net*, Flash files on www.derekfranklin.com, www.electrotank.com, and the IP 63.74.114.215 would be granted access to load data from gamebook.net.

NOTE *A policy file for a domain must always be named* **crossdomain.xml** *and must exist in the root directory of the domain.*

The **crossdomain.xml** file would not grant access to an SWF file on store.electrotank.com because it doesn't exactly match the authorized domain.

The **crossdomain.xml** file supports wildcards. If you wanted your policy file to allow all subdomains of electrotank.com, you would use an asterisk in the policy file code as follows:

```
<cross-domain-policy>
  <allow-access-from domain="*.electrotank.com" />
</cross-domain-policy>
```

If you wanted to grant access to all domains everywhere, here is how you would set up the policy file:

```
<cross-domain-policy>
  <allow-access-from domain="*" />
</cross-domain-policy>
```

TIP *When you run a Flash movie from your own computer, as you have been doing with the exercises in this book, the domain restrictions just discussed do not apply. SWF files running on your computer can load a file from any domain in the world without having to be granted access from a* **crossdomain.xml** *file.*

USING SHARED OBJECTS

An SWF file can save data (variables as well as array, XML, and other data objects) to a user's hard drive using *shared objects*—similar to but more powerful than the cookies used by Web browsers. You can use shared objects to store information generated by the user while viewing your movie (name, last frame visited, music preference, and so on). Shared objects can be used by movies played in a Web browser as well as those turned into stand-alone projectors.

You can use shared objects with any of the following (for example):

- `XML.load`
- `XML.sendAndLoad`
- `LoadVars.load`
- `LoadVars.sendAndLoad`
- `LoadVariables`
- `LoadVariablesNum`
- `XMLSocket.connect`
- Importing a shared library

The following is an example of a script you might use to create a shared object:

```
var myObject:SharedObject = SharedObject.getLocal("stuff_I_saved");
```

If the shared object `stuff_I_saved` already exists on the user's hard drive, its data is loaded instantly into `myObject`. If `stuff_I_saved` does not yet exist, it's created and still referenced by `myObject`. In the latter case, `myObject` would be empty—that is, it would contain no data.

NOTE *If used as just mentioned, the* `getLocal()` *method will create a shared object if none exists, or will retrieve data from an existing shared object.*

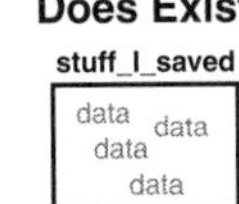

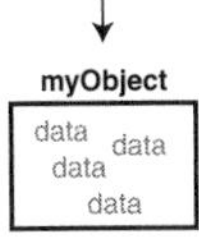

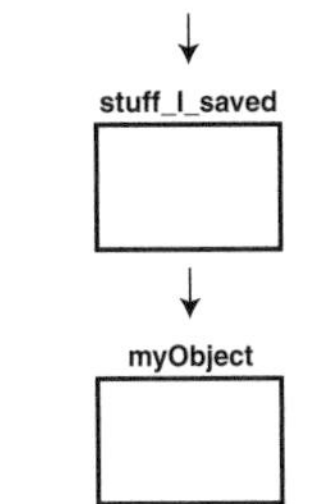

As you can see from the previous syntax, the shared object's name is actually `"stuff_I_saved"`; however, in ActionScript you can't reference the shared object directly using that name. Therefore, a reference to the shared object is created using `myObject`. This means that whenever you reference `myObject` in a script, you're actually referencing the shared object named `"stuff_I_saved"`—a tricky concept but essential to understanding how ActionScript deals with shared objects.

Data is saved to a shared object using the `data` property. Take a look at the following example:

```
myObject.data.userName = userName_txt.text;
```

This would save the `userName` variable (and its value, the text in the **userName_txt** text field) in the shared object. You can save entire objects as well. For example, if you wanted to save an array contained by your project, you would use the following syntax:

```
myObject.data.savedArray = nameOfArray;
```

A single shared object can contain multiple bits of data simultaneously:

```
myObject.data.savedArray = nameOfArrayObject;
myObject.data.savedXML = nameOfXMLObject;
myObject.data.userName = userName_txt.text;
```

A particular piece of data can be erased from a shared object using `null`, as in the following example:

```
myObject.data.userName = null;
```

If `userName` were a piece of data in the shared object, the preceding script would delete it.

You can delete an entire shared object by using the clear() method of the SharedObject class:

```
myObject.clear();
```

Extracting data from a shared object is similar to creating data in one:

```
userName_txt.text = myObject.data.userName;
```

In the **userName_txt** text field, the preceding script will display the value of userName in the shared object. If this variable doesn't exist in the shared object, the value displayed in the text field will be undefined.

When the SWF session ends (that is, the movie is closed or exited), all the information under the data property of your shared object is automatically written to the shared object file, ready to be retrieved using the getLocal() method described earlier. You can force a shared object to be written and saved at any time by using the flush() method. For example:

```
myObject.flush();
```

This line of ActionScript forces your shared object and all the data it contains to be saved. Because myObject references the shared object named "stuff_I_saved", this is the object that will actually be saved.

Flash stores all shared objects in a central location on the user's hard drive—the exact location depends on where the movie resides that created the shared objects.

On Windows XP, all shared objects are stored in the following general directory:

Documents and Settings\<username>\Application Data\Macromedia\Flash Player\

where <username> is the name of the user who was logged on when the shared object was created.

On a Mac, the location is as follows:

System Folder\Preferences\Macromedia\Flash Player\

TIP *Depending on the version of your operating system, the location of shared object files may vary somewhat. To locate shared object files on your machine, search for files with an* **.sol** *extension.*

These are both general paths—that is, when a movie creates a shared object, a new subdirectory is created at one of the previously mentioned locations. For example, if you were to view a movie at the following URL:

http://www.electrotank.com/fun/games/MiniGolf.swf

any shared object created by this movie would, by default, be saved at the following path on a Windows machine:

Documents and Settings\<username>\Application Data\Macromedia\Flash Player\electrotank.com\fun\games\MiniGolf

Notice how this subdirectory's path structure matches that of the URL.

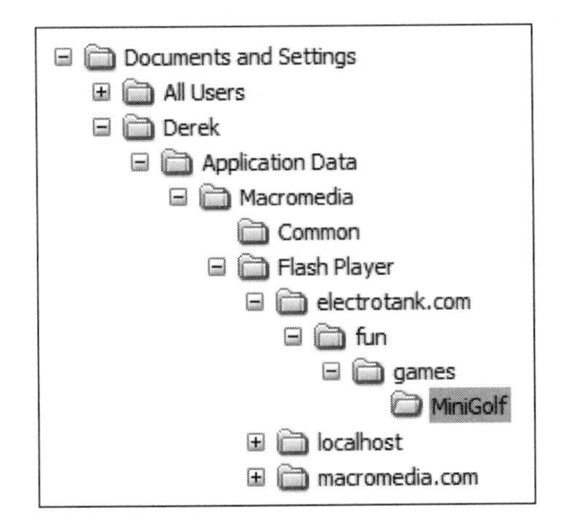

Because a movie played locally (such as a projector) doesn't exist at a URL, Flash will save shared objects that it creates to a localhost directory:

Documents and Settings\<username>\Application Data\Macromedia\Flash Player\localhost

All these directory paths are default paths where shared object data is stored. You actually have a lot of latitude as to where a shared object is stored or retrieved from within the general directory. Using the previous example, imagine playing a movie at the following URL:

http://www.electrotank.com/fun/games/MiniGolf.swf

This movie has the following shared object:

```
myScores = SharedObject.getLocal("scoreData");
```

This shared object is saved to the following path in Windows XP:

Documents and Settings\<username>\Application Data\Macromedia\Flash Player\electrotank.com\fun\games\MiniGolf\scoreData.sol

Flash will look for this same location again when the movie is played from that URL; however, the `getLocal()` method lets you add an optional directory path where the shared object should be saved. Assuming the movie at the aforementioned URL has this shared object declaration:

```
var myScores:SharedObject = SharedObject.getLocal("scoreData", "/fun");
```

the shared object would be saved to the following path:

Documents and Settings\<username>\Application Data\Macromedia\Flash Player\electrotank.com\fun\scoreData.sol

Armed with this knowledge, you can create movies at different locations that use the same shared object—useful if you want all the movies on your site to reference a "master" shared object containing information about the user. Simply save a shared object in the main (/) directory.

Be careful when using a single shared object across movies. Any one of the shared objects has the potential of overwriting the data it contains with new data.

A single movie can create, save, and load multiple shared objects simultaneously.

TIP *You can configure the amount of data that a given URL can store by using the Flash player. If you right-click the window of an open SWF and select Settings, you'll see the Local Storage controls. You can block any site from storing information on your machine.*

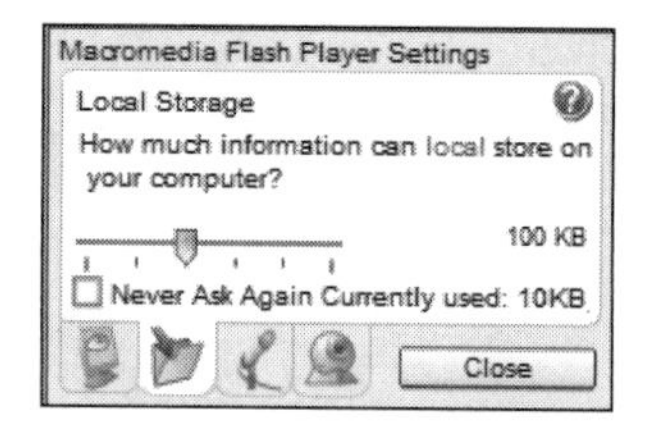

In this exercise, you'll create a journal that saves text entries in an array as a shared object.

1) Open *journal1.fla* in the Lesson11/Assets folder.

You will notice one frame with four layers, named according to their contents. The stage contains two text fields that will be used to display information. The large text field in the center, **journalBody_txt**, will be used for journal entries. The smaller text field at the bottom of the screen, **entryNumber_txt**, will be used to display the current journal entry number. The Buttons layer contains the Prev, Next, New, and Save buttons, which have instance names of **previous_btn**, **next_btn**, **new_btn**, and **save_btn**, respectively.

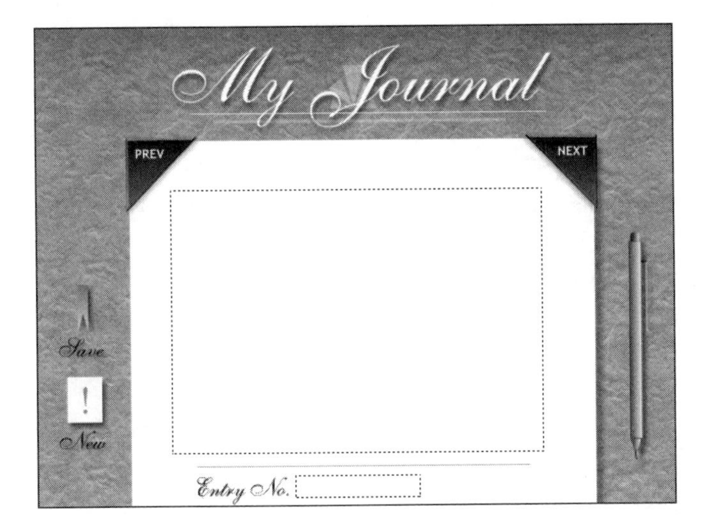

This application will allow you to start a new journal entry, save it, and browse through the entries you've created.

2) With the Actions panel open, select Frame 1 in the Actions layer and then add the following script:

```
var myJournal:SharedObject = SharedObject.getLocal("JournalObject");
```

This line of ActionScript creates a reference to the shared object `JournalObject`. This object can be read and modified using the `myJournal` reference set up here. When using `myJournal` in the following scripts, we're actually working with the shared object named `JournalObject`.

3) Add the following conditional statement just below the line of script you added in Step 2:

```
if (myJournal.data.journal == undefined) {
  myJournal.data.journal = [];
}
```

This statement looks in the shared object for an array named `journal`. If it doesn't find one (undefined), the action within the statement creates the `journal` array.

NOTE *If an array is created, it automatically becomes part of the shared object when the movie is exited or the shared object is saved using the* `flush()` *method.*

The `journal` array will appear undefined the first time the movie is played. Each subsequent time the movie is played, the array will exist and this action will be ignored.

TIP *It's a good idea to check for* undefined *data values in a shared object. This allows you to assign default values the first time a movie is played by the user.*

4) Add the following function definition at the end of the current script:

```
function displayEntry(num:Number) {
  var entry:String = myJournal.data.journal[num - 1];
  if (entry != undefined) {
    entryNumber_txt.text = num;
    journalBody_txt.text = entry;
  }
}
```

This function does two things: it sets the value of two text fields on the stage—**entryNumber_txt** and **journalBody_txt**—based on the value of `num`. Then, a conditional (`if`) statement is used to specify what should occur if the user has saved an entry in the journal.

As shown in Step 3, when the application is first used (as opposed to reopening it after adding an entry), an array named `journal` is created on the shared object. By default, a new array object always has a `length` of 1, indicating that it contains a single value at index 0, which is initially a value of undefined. The first time the application is used, `myJournal.data.journal[0]` contains a value of undefined. This value doesn't change until the user deliberately saves an entry into that index number.

In Step 5, we will script a call to this function:

```
displayEntry(myJournal.data.journal.length);
```

The first time the application is used, the `length` of the `journal` array will be 1; therefore, the function call will look like this:

```
displayEntry(1);
```

The first line in the displayEntry() function that we just defined uses the parameter value passed to it (in this case, 1) to set the value of entry. That line of script gets evaluated this way:

```
entry = myJournal.data.journal[1 - 1]
```

or, broken down further:

```
entry = myJournal.data.journal[0]
```

As already mentioned, if the user has never saved a journal entry at index 0 (such as the first time the application is used), entry is assigned a value of undefined; otherwise, it will contain the text of the first entry.

The conditional (if) statement looks at the value of entry, and performs an action only if the value of entry is *not* undefined. If entry has a value of undefined, the function does nothing and the **entryNumber_txt** and **journalBody_txt** text fields will be empty. This only occurs when the user has never saved a journal entry. After the user has saved at least one entry in the journal, the actions in the conditional statement are executed.

Assume that the user has saved nine entries and then reopens the application. In this circumstance, the displayEntry() function we just defined will be called and passed a parameter value of 9:

```
displayEntry(9)
```

NOTE *This function call is added and explained a bit more in the next step.*

As a result, the value of entry, within the function, is assigned a value representing the text of the ninth entry in the journal (which is actually stored in index 8 of the journal array, as explained later in this lesson). This will cause the actions in the conditional statement to execute because entry is no longer undefined. The first action displays the value of the number passed to the function in the **entryNumber_txt** text field, which in this case is 9. The second action displays the value of entry in the **journalBody_txt** text field.

The reason for subtracting 1 from the value of num, as shown in the first line of the function definition, is that the index (within the journal array) where each entry is saved is always one less than its actual entry number. Therefore, the fifth entry is saved in index 4, the sixth entry in index 5, and so on. The reason is that array indexes begin at 0, but we want our entry numbers to begin with 1; therefore, this conversion keeps them in sync. Several of the scripts that follow employ similar logic.

This script is probably the trickiest to understand of the entire project. Be sure to review it several times until you feel comfortable with how it works.

5) Add the following function call to the end of the current script:

```
displayEntry(myJournal.data.journal.length);
```

Because this function call exists on Frame 1, it's executed as soon as the movie plays. The `displayEntry()` function (which was defined in Step 4) is called and passed a value based on the `length` value of the `journal` array in the shared object. This will display the final entry that the user made before exiting the movie. For example, if the `journal` array has three entries, the `displayEntry()` function is passed a value of `3` and the third journal entry is displayed. If the `journal` array has just been created (as described in Step 3), it will contain a single, empty element; therefore, a length of `1` gets sent to the function.

6) Add the following function definition to handle saving data:

```
function save() {
  var num:Number = Number(entryNumber_txt.text) - 1;
  myJournal.data.journal[num] = journalBody_txt.text;
  myJournal.data.flush();
}
```

As mentioned earlier in this lesson, data is automatically saved to a shared object when a movie is exited. By using the `flush()` method, as shown here, you can save data at any time while the movie is playing. This function will be called when the Save button is clicked (see Step 11). Let's take a look at how this function works.

The first line in the function creates a variable named `num`. The value of this variable is set to the current value displayed in the **entryNumber_txt** text field, minus 1. The `Number()` function is used to make sure `num` contains a numerical value. The `num` value is used in the next line of the function to reference the appropriate array index of the current journal entry as it relates to the current entry number. As mentioned in Step 4, the number displayed in the **entryNumber_txt** text field is actually one more than the associated array index it references, which is why 1 is subtracted from the current entry value in the first line of script. (Keep reading. This will make more sense in a moment.)

The next line in this function definition uses the value of `num` to update the `journal` array with the text displayed in the **entryNumber_txt** text field. As always, the best way to understand this is by using a sample scenario. Imagine that the current entry number displayed in the **entryNumber_txt** text field is `9`. When this function is called, num would be set to a value of 8 (9 - 1). The second line in the function would be evaluated as follows:

```
myJournal.data.journal[8] = journalBody_txt.text;
```

This will place the text in the **journalBody_txt** text field into index 8 of the journal array. Note again that the current *entry number* is 9, but the currently referenced *index number* of the array is 8. (see Step 4 for more on this topic.) This line of script can affect the data in the array in two ways: if index 8 was previously empty (undefined), it will now contain text; if it previously included text, that text will be overwritten.

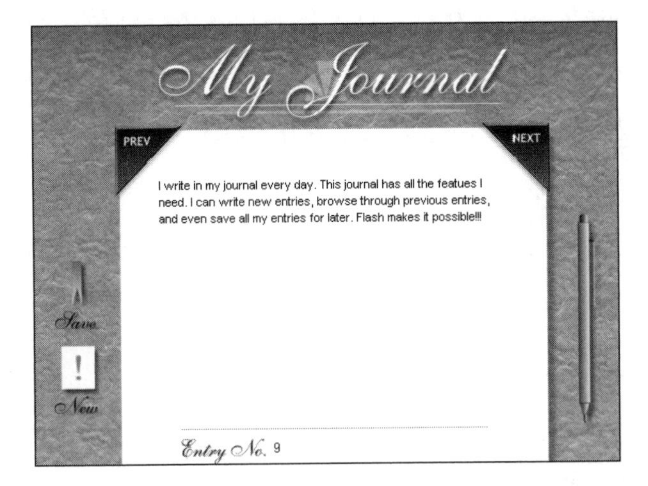

The last action in the function uses the flush() method to force the data and shared object to be saved to the user's hard drive. For our project, that will include all of the entries that exist in the journal array.

7) Add the following function definition to create a new journal entry:

```
function newEntry() {
  entryNumber_txt.text = myJournal.data.journal.length + 1;
  journalBody_txt.text = "";
  Selection.setFocus("journalBody_txt");
}
```

The first action in this function sets the current journal entry number (**entryNumber_txt** text field) to the length of the journal array, plus 1. If the journal array has two entries, it has a length of 2. Adding 1 will cause 3 to appear in the **entryNumber_txt** text field. This action causes all new entries to be inserted at the *end* of the array. The last two actions in this definition are used to empty the **journalBody_txt** text field and then to give it focus so that the user can immediately begin typing his or her entry. To better understand this, let's take a look at how this function works in harmony with the save() function discussed in the Step 6.

Assume that there are two entries in the journal array. This means that the array has entries at index positions 0 and 1 (important to remember), and that it has a length of 2. When the function in this step is executed, the **entryNumber_txt** text field displays 3 (the length of the journal array plus 1) and the **journalBody_txt** text field will be emptied. The user now types text into this text field and clicks the Save button, which calls the save() function defined in Step 6. At that point, the save() function subtracts 1 from whatever is displayed in the **entryNumber_txt** text field, which in turn saves the current text in the **journalBody_txt** text field to index position 2 of the journal array. The journal array now contains three entries at index positions 0, 1, and 2, and its length is 3. If the function is called again, the process begins again.

8) Add the following function definition, which will be used to display the next entry in the journal:

```
function nextEntry() {
  var num:Number = Number(entryNumber_txt.text) + 1;
  if (num > myJournal.data.journal.length) {
    num = myJournal.data.journal.length;
  }
  displayEntry(num);
}
```

When executed, this function displays the next journal entry in the array. It does this by assigning a value to num based on the current numerical value displayed in the **entryNumber_txt** text field, plus 1. This value represents the next journal entry to be displayed. To prevent our application from displaying an entry that doesn't exist, the value of num is compared against the total number of entries in the journal array (the length property of journal). If the value of num is greater (as the if statement determines), you're attempting to display a nonexistent entry. In that case, the action within the if statement resets the value of num to the length property value of the journal array, in effect causing the last entry in the array to be displayed instead. The final action in this function calls the displayEntry() function and passes it the value of num, enabling it to display the appropriate journal entry.

9) Create the following function to display previous journal entries:

```
function previousEntry() {
  var num:Number = Number(entryNumber_txt.text) - 1;
  if (num < 1) {
    num = 1;
  }
  displayEntry(num);
}
```

This function works similarly to the function described in Step 8. num is given a value representing the current entry number minus 1. The if statement prevents the application from displaying anything beyond journal entry 1. Here's how it works.

Suppose the user is currently viewing entry 6. When this function is called, num is assigned a value of 5 (6 - 1) and that value is checked to make sure it's not less than 1. Because it's more than 1, the action within the if statement is ignored, and the displayEntry() function is called and passed a value of 5, displaying journal entry 5.

If the user is viewing entry 1 when this function is called, num would initially be assigned a value of 0. The if statement would determine that this value is indeed less than 1 and change its value to 1. The displayEntry() function would then be passed a value of 1. Because entry 1 is already being displayed, it will appear as if nothing has changed onscreen. As mentioned, this mechanism prevents browsing past entry 1 because no entries exist at entry 0 or less.

10) Add the following onRelease **event handler for the *new_btn* instance:**

```
new_btn.onRelease = function() {
  newEntry();
};
```

When the user clicks the **new_btn** button instance, the newEntry() function is called, advancing the current entry number by 1 and clearing the **journalBody_txt** field so that new text can be entered.

11) Add the following onRelease **event handler for the *save_btn* instance:**

```
save_btn.onRelease = function() {
  save();
};
```

When the user clicks the **save_btn** button instance, the save() function is executed, at which point the current text in the **journalBody_txt** field either replaces an existing entry or is added as a new entry in the journal array (as described in Step 6).

12) Add the following onRelease **event handler for the *previous_btn* instance:**

```
previous_btn.onRelease = function() {
  previousEntry();
};
```

The call to the previousEntry() function changes the display to show the journal entry created before the current one that's displayed.

13) Finally, add the following `onRelease` event handler for the *next_btn* button instance:

```
next_btn.onRelease = function() {
  nextEntry();
};
```

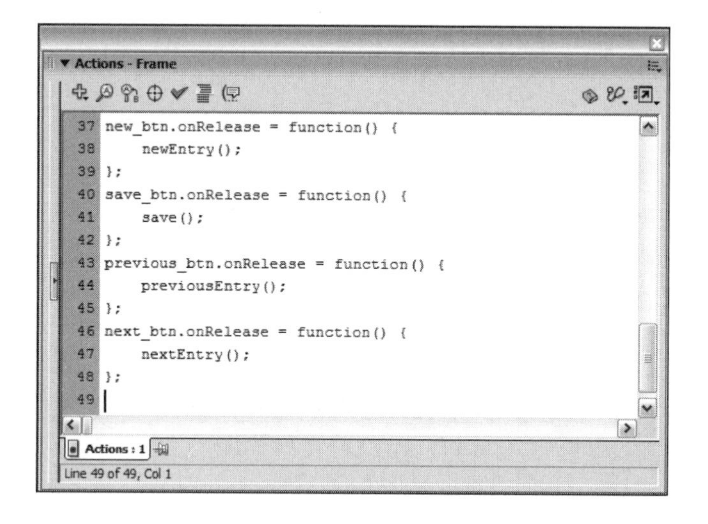

This ActionScript simply calls the `nextEntry()` function when the button is clicked. The screen is then updated to display the next entry in the list of journal entries.

14) Choose Control > Test Movie to test your work. Enter some text as a journal entry. Click the Save button to save the entry and then the New button to create a new journal entry. Click the Save button, and restart the movie.

When you restart your movie, the shared object will be loaded as described in Steps 2–3, and any data previously saved can be browsed using the Prev and Next buttons.

15) Close the test movie and save your work as *journal2.fla*.

Thus far in this lesson you have learned the basics of creating, retrieving, and saving shared objects.

You can also use shared objects to save any of the following (for example):

- User's name
- Last frame visited
- User's music preference
- Date of user's last visit
- User's ordering preferences
- Scores (for games)
- Appointments, addresses, lists
- Property values (`x`, `y`, `alpha`, `rotation`, and so on) of elements

USING THE WEBSERVICECONNECTOR COMPONENT

Through the use of the WebServiceConnector component, a Flash movie can connect to a Web service and load information from it. A *Web service* is a server-side application that accepts data, performs a service based on that data, and returns a result. For instance, a Web service might allow you to feed it a zip code and, as a result, return the weather in the specified area. Another Web service could find all the spelling mistakes in a string of text fed to it, correct the spelling errors, and return the modified text.

To send data to a Web service, the data must be formatted in XML. More precisely, the XML must meet the SOAP (Simple Object Access Protocol) standard. Fortunately, you don't need to learn this standard. The *WebServiceConnector component* handles the process of converting data to XML (the data you send to the Web service) in the appropriate format, sending it to the Web service as well as receiving and parsing the response. This means that you can communicate with Web services without having to worry about formatting the request properly or figuring out how to interpret the returned XML. The WebServiceConnector component handles everything.

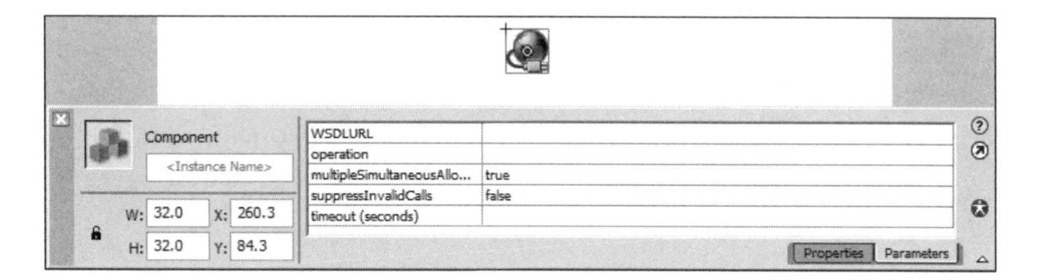

The WebServiceConnector component has five parameters:

- `WSDLURL`. This parameter is the URL for the file that defines the Web service operation. When this parameter is entered, the Flash authoring environment automatically attempts to load the destination file. This allows the authoring environment to display information related to the Web service in the Schema tab of the Component Inspector, which will be discussed later in this lesson.
- `operation`. After the file located at `WSDLURL` is loaded, the `operation` parameter allows you to select from a drop-down list the operation that you want to execute. Many Web services provide only one operation, such as `getPrice`, whereas other Web services may provide several types of operations, such as `SendICQmessage`, `SendMSNmessage`, and `SendAIMmessage`.

- `multipleSimultaneousAllowed`. This is a drop-down list in which you can choose `true` or `false`. The default value is `true`. If `true` is selected, the component makes Web requests to the Web service whenever it is asked to do so, even if it hasn't received a response from a previous request. If `false`, it won't make any more requests until a response to the current request has been received.
- `suppressInvalidCalls`. You can select either `true` or `false` from a drop-down list for this parameter. The WSDL file loaded via the `WSDLURL` parameter specifies what type of data is required to process the request. If `suppressInvalidCalls` is set to `true` and your Web services request doesn't contain the specified type of data, the request is not sent. If `suppressInvalidCalls` is set to `false`, the request is sent, no matter what type of data is entered.
- `timeout`. This parameter is optional. It expects either nothing or a number. If a number is entered, the WebServiceConnector component cancels the request for the service if a response is not received before the number of seconds in the `timeout` parameter is reached.

As mentioned a moment ago, the Schema tab of the Component Inspector is dynamically populated based on the file at the `WSDLURL` property and the value of the `operation` property. It defines what information you should send and what information you should expect as a result. For example, there is a Web service that will give you the physical distance between two zip codes. If you enter its `WSDLURL` into the component and select the `getDistance` operation, the Schema table updates to show the following image:

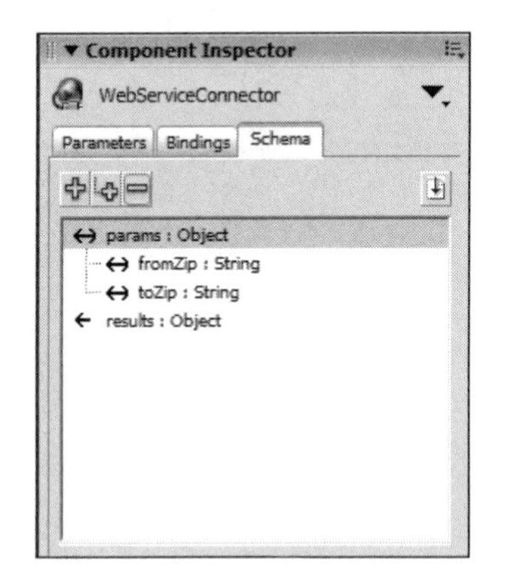

There are two main areas in the schema: `params` and `results`. The `params` property contains the variables that you should send with the Web service request, which in this case consist of two zip codes. The `results` property is usually just a string.

You use the params property on the Schema tab to learn what information you should send to the Web service. You then create an array in the component instance called params and assign it values in the order in which they appeared in the params property on the Schema tab. For example, if we gave the WebServiceConnector component an instance name of **zip_ws**, we would add the params array like this:

```
zip_ws.params = ["27609", "90210"];
```

The first zip code in the array corresponds to the first property in the Schema, fromZip. The second one corresponds to the second property in the Schema, toZip.

To get the component instance to perform the service request, you must invoke the trigger() method. For example:

```
zip_ws.trigger();
```

The trigger() method tells the component to take the params property, format a request, send the request, and wait for a response. The response fires an event called the results event. You must add a Listener to capture that event. For example:

```
function distanceReceived (ev:Object) {
  var distance:String = ev.target.results;
}
zip_ws.addEventListener("result", distanceReceived);
```

This code adds a Listener to the zip_ws WebServiceConnector component and calls the distanceReceived function when the results event is fired.

TIP http://www.xmethods.com *contains an extensive listing of Web services you can use in your applications.*

In the following exercise, you will get a chance to use everything introduced in this section. You will use a language translation Web service to create an application that enables you to translate English into a number of other languages.

NOTE *The WebServiceConnector component uses* XML.sendAndLoad *to communicate with the Web service; therefore, it is subject to the same security restrictions found when loading data onto one domain from another. For you to be able to use a Web service from an application sitting on a domain, the target domain (that is, where the Web service is located) must grant you access via its* **crossdomain.xml** *file.*

1) Open *Translator1.fla* in the Lesson11/Assets folder.

There are three layers on the main timeline: Actions, Assets, and Background. The Actions layer will contain the ActionScript that you will be adding to this project. On the Assets layer are a ComboBox component with an instance name of **language_cb**, two TextArea components named **input_ta** and **output_ta**, and a Button component named **translate_btn**.

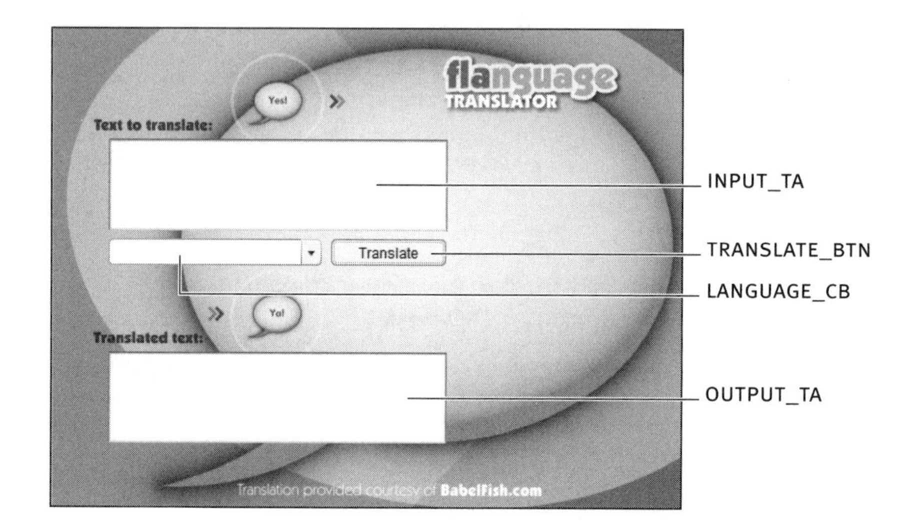

When this project is complete, you will be able to enter text in the **input_ta** TextArea component, select a translation language using the **language_cb** ComboBox component instance, and click the **translate_btn** Translate button. The Web service will then be sent a request containing the text to translate, as well as information about the selected language to translate it into. The Web service will translate the text and send the result back to the application, where it will be displayed in the **output_ta** TextArea component.

Communication with the Web service is handled by an instance of the WebServiceConnector component, which we'll add to our project next.

2) Open the Components panel and drag an instance of the WebServiceConnector component onto the stage. Place it to the left of the visible stage area so that it doesn't get in the way of the other assets.

You have now added an instance of the WebServiceConnector component to your project. Over the next few steps you will configure this component to do what you need.

3) Select the WebServiceConnector component and give it an instance name of *translator_ws*.

This name will be used in our scripts to communicate with the component.

4) With the component still selected, open the Component Inspector.

The Component Inspector should open showing three tabs: Parameters, Bindings, and Schema. In the steps that follow, you will work with the Parameters tabs and the Schema tabs.

5) On the Parameters tab of the Component Inspector, enter the following URL into the `WSDLURL` parameter:

```
http://www.xmethods.net/sd/2001/BabelFishService.wsdl
```

This is the URL for the WSDL file that defines exactly how the WebServiceConnector should talk to this particular Web service. In the WSDL file, the only data that interests us is the information regarding what data we need to send and what data we expect to be returned.

As soon as you enter the *http://www.xmethods.net/sd/2001/BabelFishService.wsdl* URL and deselect that particular parameter, the Flash authoring system loads that file into the authoring environment. When the file is loaded, you will be able to select a Web service operation from the `operation` parameter drop-down list shown on the Parameters tab. The Schema tab will update depending on the operation selected.

NOTE *You must be connected to the Internet to complete Step 5. Flash cannot load the WSDL file if you are not connected to the Internet.*

6) On the Parameters tab, click the `operation` drop-down list. Select BabelFish.

For this particular Web service, there is only one operation from which to choose.

You will not need to change any of the other parameters of this component instance.

7) Select the Schema tab in the Component Inspector. Notice that there are now two fields listed below `params` (`translationmode` and `sourcedata`).

The `params` object on the Schema tab defines what data should be sent to the Web service. From what we see here we determine that we need to send a string, `translationmode`, which represents the language of the text being sent as well as the language to which the text should be translated. In addition, we need to send a string, `sourcedata`, which represents the text to be translated.

While the Schema tab gives you some idea of what you're supposed to send, it doesn't tell you everything. For example, the `translationmode` string accepts strings such as `"en_fr"` (which stands for "English to French"). The only way you know this information is by actually reading about the Web service from wherever you found the Web service. For this example, the Web service was found through *Xmethods.com*. The listing for this Web service described exactly what the Web service does and exactly what the Web service needs to get the job done.

The following list shows just a few of the many acceptable `translationmode` string values:

- `en_fr`. English to French
- `en_de`. English to German
- `en_it`. English to Italian
- `en_es`. English to Spanish

The `sourcedata` string simply holds the text that you want to be translated.

In the next few steps, you will create an array called on the WebServiceConnector instance`params` , and will assign values. The `params` array holds the information that will be sent to the Web service.

You are now ready to ready to add the ActionScript needed to complete this project.

8) Select Frame 1 in the Actions layer and open the Actions panel. Add the following code:

```
language_cb.dataProvider = [{label:"English to French", data:"en_fr"},
⇒{label:"English to German", data:"en_de"},
⇒{label:"English to Italian", data:"en_it"},
⇒{label:"English to Spanish", data:"en_es"}];
```

You'll remember that **language_cb** is the name of the ComboBox component instance in our project. By setting the `dataProvider` property of the component instance equal to an array, we automatically populate the contents of the component. Each element in the array represents one item in the ComboBox and has two properties—`label` and `data`. When the Flash movie is published, the ComboBox shows the text entered in each of the `label` properties. When an item is selected, the value property of the ComboBox is set to the `data` property associated with the selected item.

If a user selects English to German, for example, the value of the ComboBox component instance is changed to `"en_de"`. This value will be used when the Translate button is clicked.

9) Add the following function to the frame:

```
function translationReceived(ev:Object) {
  var str = ev.target.results;
  output_ta.text = str;
}
```

In a moment, we will script our project to execute this function when a response from the Web service has been received. The `ev` parameter is a reference to the Event object created specifically for this event. (See Lesson 10, "Scripting UI Components," for more information about Event objects.)

The first line of this function creates a variable named `str`. This variable is assigned a value based on the `results` property of the Web services component in our project. This can be a tricky concept, so let's look at an example of how this will work.

As mentioned earlier, when a WebServiceConnector instance receives a response from the Web service with which it's communicating, that information is stored in the `results` property of the instance. Because receiving a response from the Web service executes this function, `ev.target` (as used in the function) is a reference to the **translator_ws** component instance in our project; therefore, `ev.target.results` is a reference to the information the Web service has sent back to our component instance. In the end, the value of `str` is the string value sent back from the Web service.

The second line in this function displays the value of `str` (the resulting translated text) in the **output_ta** component instance.

10) Add the following function, which asks the WebServiceConnector component instance to do its job:

```
function translate() {
  var direction:String = language_cb.value;
  var textToTranslate:String = input_ta.text;
  translator_ws.params = [direction, textToTranslate];
  translator_ws.addEventListener("result", translationReceived);
  translator_ws.trigger();
}
```

This function is executed when the Translate button is clicked (ActionScript to handle this action is added in the next step). A variable called `direction` is set. It gets its value from the `value` property of the **language_cb** ComboBox component instance. For example, if the user has selected English to French, `direction` is assigned a value of `"en_fr"`.

The next variable created is `textToTranslate`. This variable value is the text from the **input_ta** TextArea component.

The next line creates an array in the **translator_ws** instance called params. This array is used to store the data that will be sent to the Web service. Remember that the Schema tab listed the data to be sent to the Web service in this order: translationmode, sourcedata, with translationmode (the first parameter) representing a value such as "en_fr", and sourcedata (the second parameter) representing the text to translate. The names used for these parameters (as shown on the Schema tab) are really not as important as their order. In other words, the first parameter should hold a value representing how to translate the text, and the second parameter should hold the text to translate. The params array we've added to the **translator_ws** instance holds the data sent to the Web service, stored in the correct order.

The next line of the function registers the translationReceived() function (defined in Step 9) to listen for the results event in relation to the **translator_ws** instance. When the **translator_ws** instance receives a response from the Web service, the translationReceived() function is executed.

The last line of the function tells the **translator_ws** WebServiceConnector component instance to perform the request. This is done by invoking the trigger() method.

11) Add the following ActionScript to capture the click button event:

```
var buttonListenerObject:Object = new Object();
buttonListenerObject.click = function() {
  translate();
};
translate_btn.addEventListener("click", buttonListenerObject);
```

You should be familiar with this type of ActionScript by now. We create a Listener object for the button instance and then add a function called click to the Listener object. Finally, we register the Listener object to listen for that event when fired by the **translate_btn** instance.

In summary, when the **translate_btn** is clicked, the translate() function is called. translate() puts the data to be sent into the WebServiceConnector instance (by setting its params property), tells the instance to call the translationReceived() function when the results have been received, and finally triggers the connection process.

12) Add this final line of ActionScript to the frame:

```
input_ta.text = "Enter text here...";
```

This line of ActionScript forces the **input_ta** TextArea instance to show text when the application is launched. The user can remove this displayed text (by deleting or typing over the displayed text), and then enter new text.

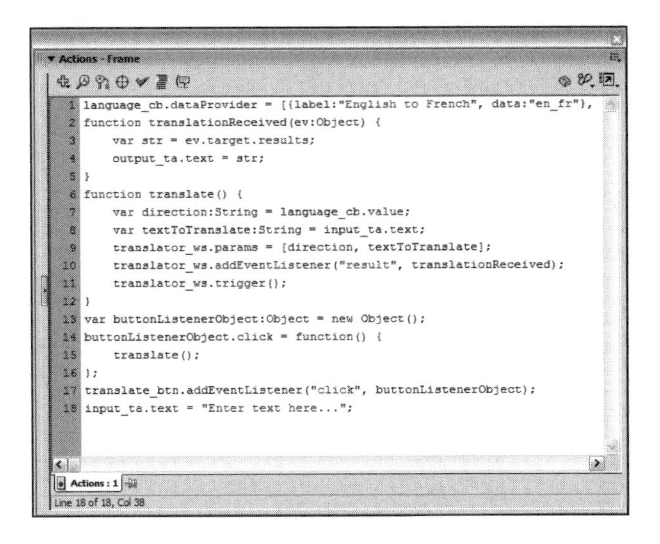

13) Choose Control > Test Movie to test your work. Enter some English text into the *input_ta* instance, choose the destination language from the drop-down list, and click the Translate button.

If you're connected to the Internet, your text should be translated and displayed in the **output_ta** component.

When you click the Translate button, the WebServiceConnector component formats a request for the Web service, sends the request, and waits for a response. When a response is received, the `results` event is fired and the text is displayed for the user to see.

14) Close the test movie and save your work as *Translator2.fla*.

You have successfully created an application that uses the WebServiceConnector component. Now that you know how to use this component, you can hook into any number of Web services to enhance the functionality of your projects.

WHAT YOU HAVE LEARNED

In this lesson, you have:

- Learned about the data formats that Flash can accept (pages 368–372)
- Discovered how GET and POST are used to transfer data (pages 372–373)
- Gained experience using the LoadVars object to communicate with a server-side script (pages 373–384)
- Learned about policy files and how they're used (pages 384–386)
- Saved and retrieved data locally using shared objects (pages 386–398)
- Created an language translation application using the WebServiceConnector component (pages 399–407)

using XML with flash

LESSON 12

Imagine what it would be like if every electrical appliance in your home had a different type of plug. Chances are you'd end up putting most of those gizmos back in the cupboard and doing the task manually. Or what if none of the screwdrivers or wrenches in your tool shed even came close to fitting the screws, nuts, and bolts that hold stuff together? Fortunately, neither scenario is likely because people figured out long ago that by creating products according to guidelines, or *rules of standardization*, they could have far more productive societies.

In essence, standards facilitate linkages between disparate items—battery and flashlight, Macromedia Flash and multi-user game server, and so on. And on the Web, where tons of data is transferred every second, having a standardized way of moving data among systems is essential. The powerful and easy-to-use XML has become one standard.

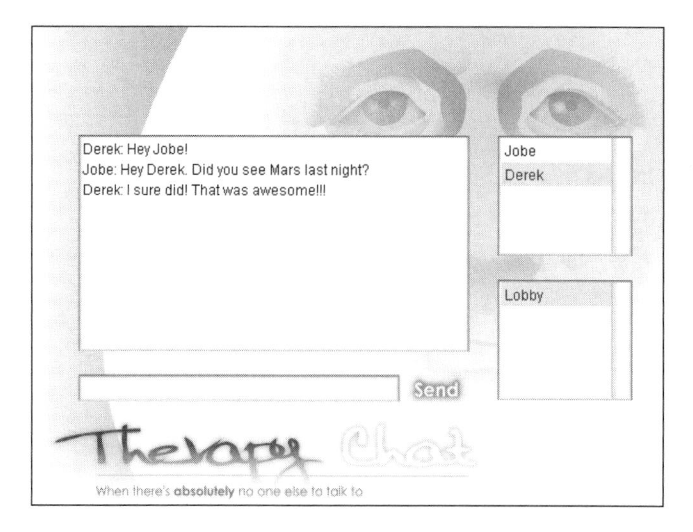

The simple chat application that you will script in this lesson shows you how to connect a Flash application to an XML socket server.

In this lesson, we'll introduce you to the XML format as well as show you how to use the XML class and the XMLSocket class in Flash. By lesson's end, you will have made Flash talk to ASP pages for user login and registration, and you will have created a very simple real-time chat application using a socket server.

WHAT YOU WILL LEARN

In this lesson, you will:

- Learn about the XML format
- Create new XML objects
- Learn how to parse an XML document
- Send and load XML from the server
- Use methods, properties, and events of the XML object
- Learn about the XMLSocket class and socket servers
- Build a simple real-time chat application

APPROXIMATE TIME

This lesson takes approximately one and one half hours to complete.

LESSON FILES

Media Files:

AddUser.asp
UserLogin.asp
XMLExample.mdb
InstallElectroServer.exe
ElectroServer.as
Wddx.as
WddxRecordset.as

Starting Files:

Lesson12/Assets/loginRegister1.fla
Lesson12/Assets/Chat1.fla

Completed Projects:

loginRegister2.fla
Chat2.fla

XML BASICS

Although the name *Extensible Markup Language* (XML) sounds a bit cryptic, don't worry: the format itself is actually quite easy to understand. In a nutshell, XML provides a way of formatting and structuring information so that receiving applications can easily interpret and use that data when it's moved from place to place. Although you may not realize it, you already have plenty of experience structuring and organizing information. Consider the following example.

Suppose you want to write a letter to a friend. You structure your thoughts (information) in a format you know your friend will recognize. You begin by writing words on a piece of paper, starting in the upper-left corner, and breaking your thoughts into paragraphs, sentences, and words. You could use images to convey your thoughts, or write your words in a circle, but that probably would confuse your friend. By writing your letter in a format familiar to your friend, you can be confident that your message will be conveyed—that is, you will have transferred your thoughts (data/information) to the letter's recipient.

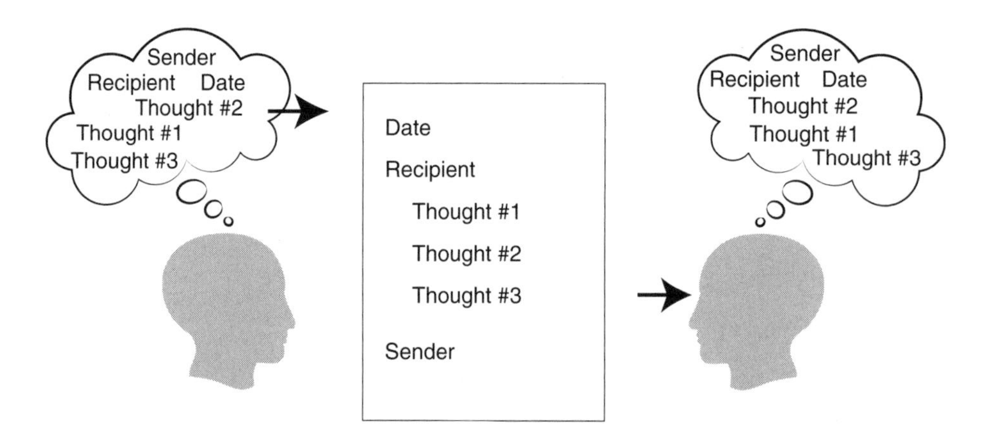

You can use XML in much the same way—as a format for conveying information. For example, if you want to send data out of Flash for processing by a Web server, you format that data as XML. The server then interprets the XML-formatted data and uses it in the manner intended. Without XML, you could send chunks of data to a server, but the server probably wouldn't know what to do with the first chunk or the second, or even how the first chunk related to the second. XML gives meaning to these disparate bits of data so the server can work with them in an organized and intelligent manner.

XML's simple syntax resembles HTML in that it employs tags, attributes, and values—but the similarity ends there. Where HTML uses predefined tags (for example, `<body>`, `<head>`, and `<html>`), in XML you create your own tags—that is, you don't pull them from an existing library of tag names. Look at the following simple XML document:

```
<MyFriends>
  <Name Gender="female">Kelly Makar</Name>
  <Name Gender="male">Mike Grundvig</Name>
  <Name Gender="male">Free Makar</Name>
</MyFriends>
```

Each complete tag (such as `<Name></Name>`) in XML is called a *node*, and any XML-formatted data is called an *XML document.* Each XML document can contain only one *root node*; the document just shown has a root node called `MyFriends`, which in turn has three *child nodes*. The first child node has a *node name* of `Name` and a *node value* of `Kelly Makar`. The word `Gender` in each child node is an *attribute*. Attributes are optional, and each node can have an unlimited number of attributes. You'll typically use attributes to store small bits of information that are not necessarily displayed onscreen—for example, a user identification number.

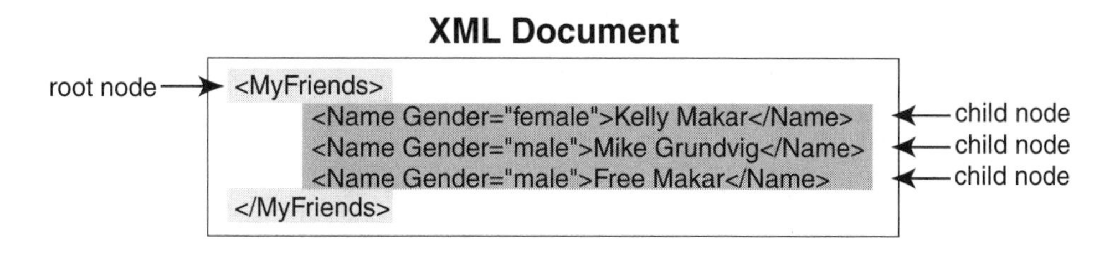

The tags in this example (which we made up and defined) give meaning to the bits of information shown (`Kelly Makar`, `Mike Grundvig`, and `Free Makar`).

The next XML document shows a more extended use of XML:

```
<AddressBook>
  <Person>
    <Name>Kelly Makar</Name>
    <Street>121 Baker Street</Street>
    <City>Some City</City>
    <State>North Carolina</State>
  </Person>
  <Person>
    <Name>Tripp Carter</Name>
    <Street>777 Another Street</Street>
    <City>Elizabeth City</City>
    <State>North Carolina</State>
  </Person>
</AddressBook>
```

This example shows how the data in an address book would be formatted as XML. If there were 600 people listed in the address book, the `Person` node would appear 600 times with the same structure.

So how do you create your own nodes and structure? How does the destination (ASP page, socket, and so on) know how the document is formatted? And how does it know what to do with each piece of information? The simple answer is that this intelligence has to be built into your destination. Thus, if you were planning to build an address book in Flash and wanted the information it contained to be saved in a database, you would send an XML-formatted version of that data to an ASP page (or another scripted page of choice), which would then *parse* that information and insert it into the appropriate fields in a database. The important thing to remember is that the ASP page must be designed to deal with data in this way. Because XML is typically used to transfer rather than store information, the address book data would be stored as disparate information in database fields, rather than stored as XML. When needed again, that information could be extracted from the database, formatted as XML by a scripted page, and sent along to Flash or any other application that requested it.

XML Document

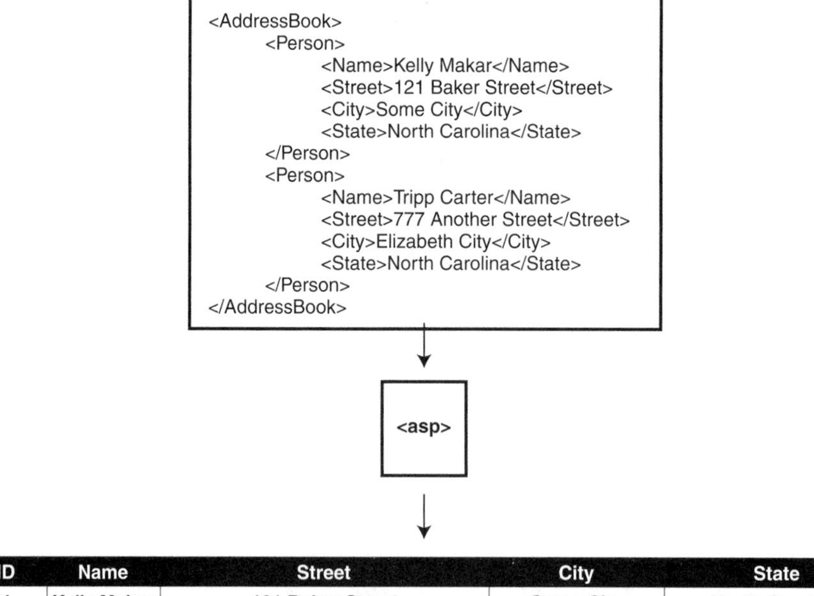
<AddressBook>
<Person>
<Name>Kelly Makar</Name>
<Street>121 Baker Street</Street>
<City>Some City</City>
<State>North Carolina</State>
</Person>
<Person>
<Name>Tripp Carter</Name>
<Street>777 Another Street</Street>
<City>Elizabeth City</City>
<State>North Carolina</State>
</Person>
</AddressBook>
<asp>

ID	Name	Street	City	State
1	Kelly Makar	121 Baker Street	Some City	North Carolina
2	Tripp Carter	777 Another Street	Elizabeth City	North Carolina

Web pages often use text files that contain XML-formatted information—for example, a static XML file for storing information about which ASP pages to call, or what port and IP to connect to when attempting to connect with a socket server.

Now that you know the basics of the XML format, here are some rules you need to follow when you begin using it:

- You cannot begin node names with the letters *XML*; many XML parsers break when they see XML at the beginning of a node name.
- You must properly terminate every node—for example, you would terminate `<Name>` with `</Name>`. The slash (/) inside the final tag indicates that a node is completed (terminated).
- You must URL-encode all special characters—which you can do by using the `escape()` function in Flash. Many parsers interpret certain unencoded characters as the start of a new node that is not terminated properly (because it wasn't a node in the first place). An XML document with non-terminated nodes won't pass through an XML parser completely. Attributes are less forgiving than text nodes because they can fail to pass through the parser on characters such as a carriage return or an ampersand. If you URL-encode the text, you won't experience this trouble.
- Most XML parsers are case sensitive, which means that all tags of the same type must have the same case. If you start a node with `<Name>` and terminate it with `</name>`, you're asking for trouble.
- You can have only one root node.

One more thing to note before you begin working with XML is that the clean XML structure shown in these examples is not necessary. The carriage returns and tabs are there to make it easier for *us* to read. These tabs and carriage returns are called *white space*, and you can add or delete white space without affecting the overall structure.

USING THE XML CLASS

It's time to start using some XML! Nearly everything you do with XML in Flash involves the XML class and falls into one of the following categories: formatting XML, parsing XML (extracting the information), loading XML, or sending XML. With the XML class, you can load XML from an external source such as a static file or a server-side script. After an XML document is loaded, you can access its information using the methods and properties of the XML class. You can also use the methods and properties of the XML class to create your own XML document. After this document is created, you can use it in a Flash movie or send it out to a server-side script. This section covers the ActionScript you need to accomplish these goals.

Formatting XML

The XML class in Flash has several methods, most of which you can use to create and format XML documents. The truth is, though, you're unlikely to employ them because they're difficult to use—and there's a better way. We'll show you how to create a string and then convert it into an XML object, a much easier (and more common) way of formatting XML objects.

To create an XML object in Flash, you must use the XML class constructor. Here's how you would create an empty XML object:

```
var myXML:XML = new XML();
```

To populate the object with XML-formatted data when it's created, you can pass (inside the parentheses of the constructor) the name of a variable that holds an XML-formatted string or another XML object.

Suppose you want to create the following XML document in Flash:

```
<MyFriends>
  <Name Gender="female">Kelly Makar</Name>
  <Name Gender="male">Free Makar</Name>
</MyFriends>
```

You would do two things:

1) Create the document as a string.

2) Convert the string to an XML object by using the XML class constructor `new XML()`.

Here's an example:

```
var myString:String = "<MyFriends>
⇒<Name Gender=\"female\">Kelly Makar</Name>
⇒<Name Gender=\"male\">Free Makar</Name></MyFriends>";
var myXML:XML = new XML(myString);
```

This code creates the XML document as a string and converts it to an XML object called `myXML`. This object can then be sent to the server using the send-related methods described later in this section of the lesson.

Parsing XML

The word *parse* simply means to analyze something or break it down into its parts. When someone speaks of writing a script to parse an XML document, they're talking about writing a script that extracts information from that XML document. The XML class has many properties to help you do this. We'll use the XML object just discussed, `myXML`, to illustrate the use of a few of the most common properties.

firstChild: This property points to the first node in the tree structure. For example:

```
myXML.firstChild.firstChild
```

returns

```
<Name Gender="female">Kelly Makar</Name>
```

The first child node of the XML document is the root node (MyFriends), and the root node's first child is Name, as shown.

childNodes: This property returns an array of the child nodes at any given point in the tree structure. For example:

```
var myArray:Array = myXML.firstChild.childNodes
```

Here, myArray contains two elements whose values are the same as those of the two Name nodes.

nextSibling: This property points to the next node in the same level of the tree structure. Thus,

```
myXML.firstChild.firstChild.nextSibling
```

returns:

```
<Name Gender="male">Free Makar</Name>
```

attributes: This property returns an associative array of attribute names. For example:

```
myXML.firstChild.firstChild.nextSibling.attributes.Gender
```

returns:

```
"male"
```

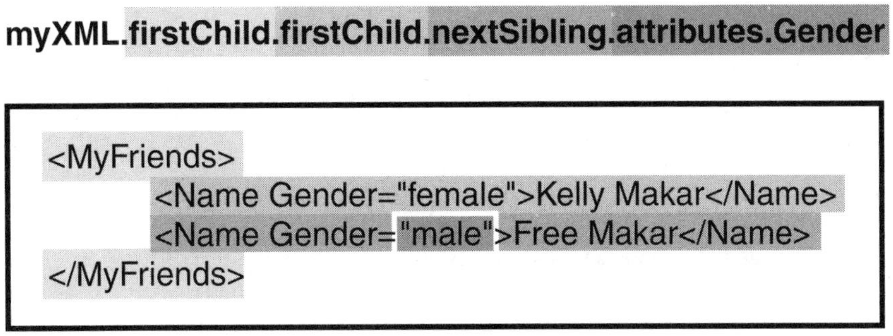

myXML.firstChild.firstChild.nextSibling.attributes.Gender

```
<MyFriends>
        <Name Gender="female">Kelly Makar</Name>
        <Name Gender="male">Free Makar</Name>
</MyFriends>
```

These examples represent the most commonly used properties of the XML object; others work in the same way, referencing different parts of the tree structure.

Loading XML

Typically, you'll only work with XML in Flash when you're loading or sending out the XML. To load XML from a remote source, do the following:

1) Create an XML object.

2) Use the `load()` method of the XML object to load XML-formatted data from an external source. For example:

```
var myXML:XML = new XML();
myXML.load("http://somedomain.com/info.xml");
```

Although in this example the document being loaded is a static XML file, it doesn't have to be. You can also point to an ASP page (or another scripted page) whose result is an XML document.

To determine when the XML has finished loading into an object, you use the `onLoad` event available to the XML object. You can define this event to call a function when the document is finished loading. Consider the following example:

```
function init () {
  //parse script here
}
var myXML:XML = new XML();
myXML.onLoad = init;
myXML.load("http://somedomain.com/info.xml");
```

As the next-to-last line shows, when the XML document is finished loading, the `init()` function will be called. In the `init()` function, you write special code to interpret the XML. For example, if you're expecting an XML-formatted address book, you write some special code to walk the XML nodes, pulling out the data within them. We'll show some simple parsing examples later in this lesson.

Sending XML

The XML class allows you to send XML to a URL. It also enables you to send XML and load the resulting document simultaneously.

To send XML to a URL, use the `send()` method and specify a destination URL:

```
var myXML:XML = new XML("<Message><Text>Hi!</Text></Message>");
myXML.send("http://somedomain.com/somedestination.asp");
```

To send XML and receive a response, all in one shot, use the `sendAndLoad()` method of the XML object. With this method, you must specify an XML object whose contents you want to send, a URL in which to send the XML document, and an XML object in which to receive the response. As with the load() example described earlier, you must define an onLoad event to handle the loaded XML. Here's an example:

```
var URL:String = "http://www.myDomain.com/UserLogin.asp";
function init () {
  trace(objToReceive);
}
var xmlToSend:String =
⇒"<Login><Username>Jobem</Username><Password>hayes</Password></Login>";
var objToSend:XML = new XML(xmlToSend);
var objToReceive:XML = new XML();
objToReceive.onLoad = init;
objToSend.sendAndLoad(URL, objToReceive);
```

This ActionScript creates an XML object (objToSend) containing login information and then sends that information to a URL, where it waits for a response from the destination. When the response is fully loaded into the receiving XML object (objToReceive), the init function is called.

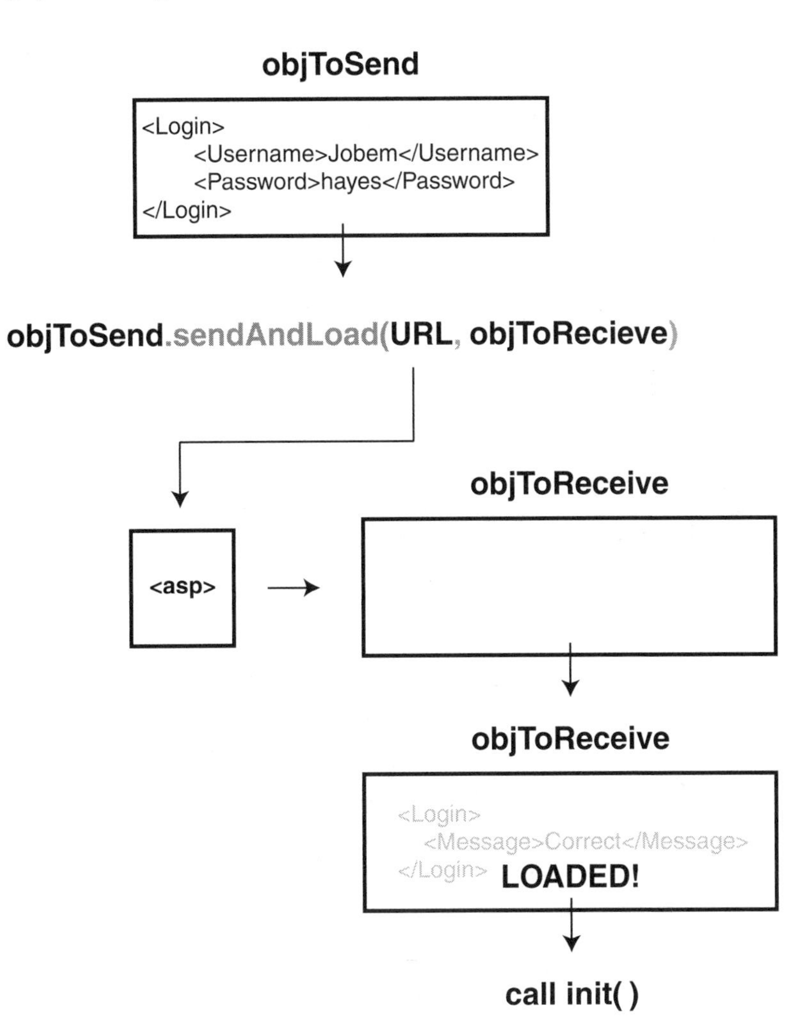

Now that you know a little bit about the XML format and the XML class, it's time to put that knowledge to use. In the following exercise, you'll format a few simple XML documents, perform some easy parsing, and use `sendAndLoad()` to create a simple Flash application that acts as a registration/login screen.

The Flash file used in this section communicates with ASP pages. To fully build and test this file, you'll need access to a server where you can run ASP scripts (this usually means a Windows server). To test the files in this exercise, you'll need to upload two ASP files (**AddUser.asp** and **UserLogin.asp**) and one Microsoft Access database file (**XMLExample.mdb**) to the same directory on a Windows server. These files can be found in the Lesson12/Assets folder.

NOTE *The ASP pages used in this lesson read and write to the database file. On most Windows servers, the permissions settings allow this exchange to take place. If you're having trouble getting the ASP files to perform correctly, ask your administrator or ISP to change the permissions settings to allow your ASP pages to access the database.*

We understand that not everyone reading this book has access to a Windows server. Because there are so many different server languages, it would be impossible to create supporting files for all of them. We chose ASP because of its ease of use and universality. Lack of a Windows server shouldn't diminish the value of the instructions that follow, however, because everything is explained in detail anyway.

The **AddUser.asp** page accepts an XML document structured as follows:

```
<Register>
  <Username>jobem</Username>
  <Email>jobe@electrotank.com</Email>
  <Password>secret</Password>
</Register>
```

If the user was registered properly, this page (**AddUser.asp**) returns the following result:

```
<Register>
  <Message>User Inserted</Message>
</Register>
```

If a user of the same name already exists, the ASP page returns this result instead:

```
<Register>
  <Message>User Exists</Message>
</Register>
```

The **UserLogin.asp** page accepts an XML document structured as follows:

```
<Login>
  <Username>jobem</Username>
  <Password>secretword</Password>
</Login>
```

If the information provided was correct, this page returns the following result:

```
<Login>
  <Message>Login Correct</Message>
</Login>
```

If the information provided was incorrect, the page returns this result instead:

```
<Login>
  <Message>Login Incorrect</Message>
</Login>
```

1) Open *loginRegister1.fla* in the Lesson12/Assets directory.

This file already includes all the frames, text fields, and buttons needed for this example. The file contains four layers: The Actions layer is where we'll write all the ActionScript; the Labels layer contains the frame labels we need; the Assets layer contains text fields (in the form of TextInput component instances) and buttons; and the Background layer contains the interface graphics.

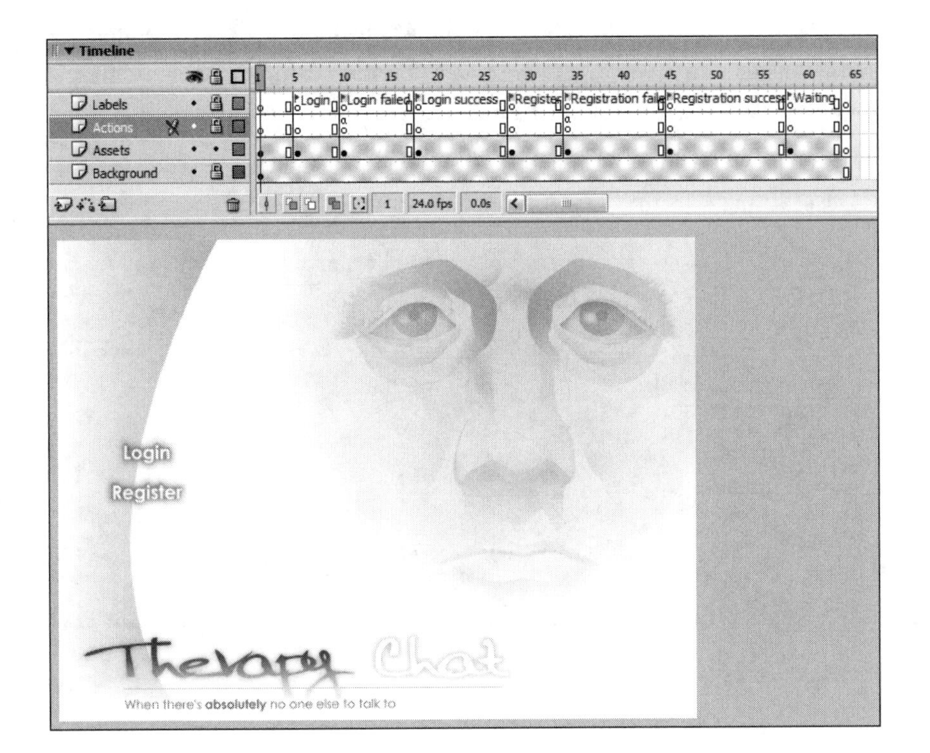

2) With the Actions panel open, select Frame 1 of the Actions layer and add a `stop()` action.

By placing a `stop()` action here, we prevent the movie from playing automatically.

3) Add the following script to the frame:

```
login_btn.onRelease = function() {
  _root.gotoAndStop("Login");
};
```

There is a button on the Assets layer on Frame 1 that has an instance name of **login_btn**. The script in this step assigns a function to the `onRelease` event handler for that button. The user clicks this button to go to the login frame, where he or she can log in.

4) After the *login_btn* event handler, add the following script:

```
register_btn.onRelease = function() {
  _root.gotoAndStop("Register");
};
```

This script adds an `onRelease` event handler to the **register_btn** button instance. The user clicks this button to go to the register frame to register a new account.

5) Move the playhead to the frame labeled Login. At this label are two TextInput component instances (*username_ti* and *password_ti*) and a button instance called *submit_btn* on the stage. With the Actions panel open, select the frame on the Actions layer at that label and add the following line of script:

```
var loginURL:String = "http://www.yourdomain.com/UserLogin.asp";
```

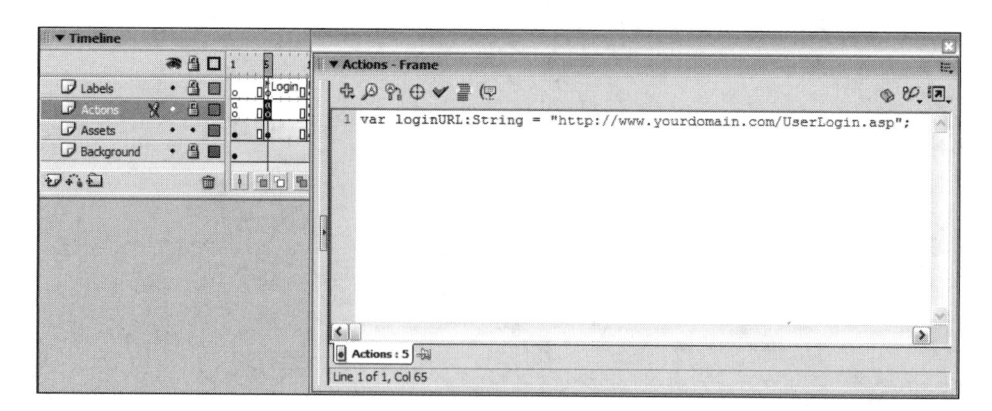

The variable `loginURL` points to the ASP page that accepts the login XML document (located at the domain where you uploaded it). The ASP page parses the document that you send and returns an answer to let you know whether the user provided the correct information. This URL should include the full path to the **UserLogin.asp** file that you uploaded.

6) With the same frame still selected, add the following script:

```
var objToReceive:XML;
submit_btn.onRelease = function() {
  var xmlToSend:String = "<Login><Username>" +
  ⇒username_ti.text + "</Username><Password>" + password_ti.text
  ⇒+ "</Password></Login>";
  var objToSend:XML = new XML(xmlToSend);
  objToReceive = new XML();
  objToReceive.onLoad = loginResponse;
  objToSend.sendAndLoad(loginURL, objToReceive);
  _root.gotoAndStop("Waiting");
};
```

The first line of this script creates a variable named `objToReceive`, which will eventually hold an XML object. Next, a function is defined. This function is called when the user clicks the Submit button, with an instance name of **submit_btn**. The function begins by using the values entered in the **username_ti** and **password_ti** TextInput component instances to format the XML that we're sending to the ASP page, and then places that formatted data into a string variable named `xmlToSend`.

Next, we create a new XML object named `objToSend` and pass it the XML-formatted string we just created. The reason for doing this is that the `sendAndLoad()` method only works with XML objects—we can't apply it to a string.

Next, we create a new object named `objToReceive`. This is the XML object into which the ASP page's response is loaded. Using the `onLoad` event, we tell the `objToReceive` object to call the `loginResponse()` function after the XML data has been loaded into it. We'll create the `loginResponse()` function in the next step.

The next action in the function invokes the `sendAndLoad()` method by specifying the object to send, the destination URL, and the object in which to load the response. Finally, the last action sends the timeline to a frame named Waiting. This frame informs the user that the information was sent but no response has been returned. The movie stops on this frame until it receives a response from the server.

You may wonder why `objToReceive` (which is used to receive incoming XML) was created *outside* the function definition, but `objToSend` (used to hold and then send outgoing XML) is created *within* the function definition. The reason is that any variables or objects created within the function itself (using the var keyword) are considered local to the function, and thus are deleted from memory as soon as the function has finished executing, which takes only a split second. While the sending of XML can be accomplished within the timeframe of the function's execution, it may take several seconds for the resulting XML to load into objToReceive, which is why that object must exist *after* the function has finished executing. If it was deleted when the function was finished executing, there would be no object into which to load the resulting XML.

7) Add the following function definition after the one you added in Step 6:

```
function loginResponse() {
  var response:String = objToReceive.firstChild.firstChild.firstChild.nodeValue;
  if (response == "Login Correct") {
    _root.gotoAndStop("Login Success");
  } else if (response == "Login Incorrect") {
    _root.gotoAndStop("Login Failed");
  }
}
```

The function in this step is called as soon as the last byte of XML is loaded into the XML object called objToReceive, as described in Step 6. The function in Step 7 parses the XML response from the server. The loginResponse() function creates a variable named response and sets its value based on the data extracted from the returned XML document. Remember that the response of the **UserLogin.asp** page is in this format:

```
<Login>
  <Message>Login Correct|Login Incorrect</Message>
</Login>
```

As a result, response will have a value of either Login Correct or Login Incorrect, depending on what's extracted from this XML document. An if statement then uses this value to send the timeline to the frame labeled either Login Success or Login Failed. This action moves from the Waiting frame, which is used as an interim location while waiting for a response from the server.

8) Move the playhead to the frame labeled Register. At this label are three TextInput component instances (*username_ti*, *email_ti*, and *password_ti*) and a button with an instance name of *submit_btn* on the stage. With the Actions panel open, select the frame on the Actions layer at that label and add the following line of script:

```
var registrationURL:String = "http://www.yourDomain.com/AddUser.asp";
```

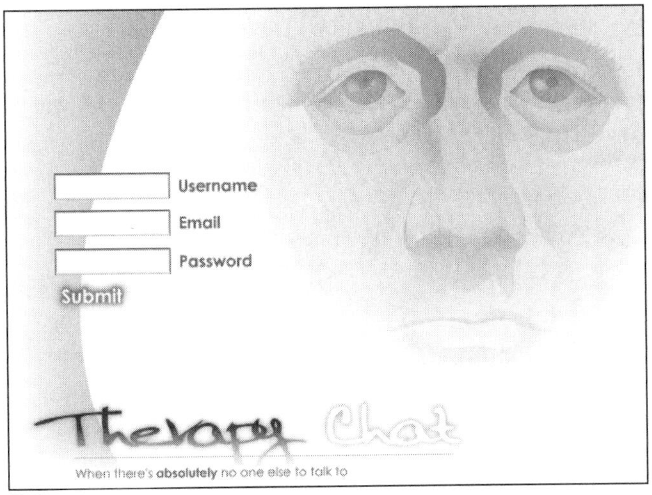

This is the ASP page that accepts the registration XML-formatted document. It will process the information and return a result. Be sure to enter the correct path to the file that you uploaded.

9) With the same frame still selected, add the following script:

```
var objToReceive:XML;
submit_btn.onRelease = function() {
  var XMLtoSend:String = "<Register><UserName>" + username_ti.text +
  ⇒"</UserName><Email>" + email_ti.text + "</Email><Password>" +
  ⇒password_ti.text + "</Password></Register>";
  var objToSend:XML = new XML(XMLtoSend);
  objToReceive = new XML();
  objToReceive.onLoad = registrationResponse;
  objToSend.sendAndLoad(registrationURL, objToReceive);
  _root.gotoAndStop("Waiting");
};
```

The ActionScript in this step is similar to that used in the Login frame label defined in Step 6—the only differences are in the format of the XML and some reference names. Notice that the XML document here contains three pieces of user information: **username_ti.text**, **email_ti.text**, and **password_ti.text**. This is the information entered into the TextInput instances by the user. The destination script will parse this document and extract the information.

When the user clicks the Submit button, the contents of the three text fields are used to format an XML document. That XML document is then sent to the **AddUser.asp** page to be parsed, and the relevant content is added to the database. The ASP page returns a response, which is captured by the function added in Step 10.

10) Add the following function definition after the one you added in Step 9:

```
function registrationResponse() {
  var response:String = objToReceive.firstChild.firstChild.firstChild.nodeValue;
  if (response == "User Inserted") {
    _root.gotoAndStop("Registration Success");
  } else if (response == "User Exists") {
    _root.gotoAndStop("Registration Failed");
  }
}
```

The function in this step is called when the last byte of information is loaded into `objToReceive`. This function is similar to the `loginResponse()` function defined in Step 7. Remember that the **AddUser.asp** page returns a document of this format:

```
<Register>
  <Message>User Inserted|User Exists</Message>
</Register>
```

As a result, `response` will have a value of either `User Inserted` or `User Exists`, depending on what is extracted from this XML document. An `if` statement then uses this value to send the timeline to the frame labeled Registration Success or the frame labeled Registration Failed.

11) Choose Control > Test Movie to test your work. Click the Register button and submit some information. Reopen the movie and then try to log in.

You have just created a simple application that illustrates some uses of the XML object. Test it a few times to make sure that you're comfortable with the ActionScript.

12) Close the test movie and save your work as *loginRegister2.fla*.

Now you're ready to start creating some advanced data-driven applications.

USING SOCKET SERVERS

A *socket server* is an application that can accept "socket" connections. Socket connections are persistent, which means that they let you remain connected to a server rather than making a connection just long enough to download information before disconnecting. Unlike a scripted page, a socket server is an application that's always running. It can accept simultaneous connections from multiple computers and exchange information among them. While you're connected to a socket server, you can send or receive information at any time. Using socket connections to continually transfer data to and from the server is how most chats and multiplayer games are created in Flash.

A key principle to understand about using socket connections with Flash is that you don't have to request information to get information—for example, in a chat application a message can be *pushed* into Flash at any time without Flash having to ask for it.

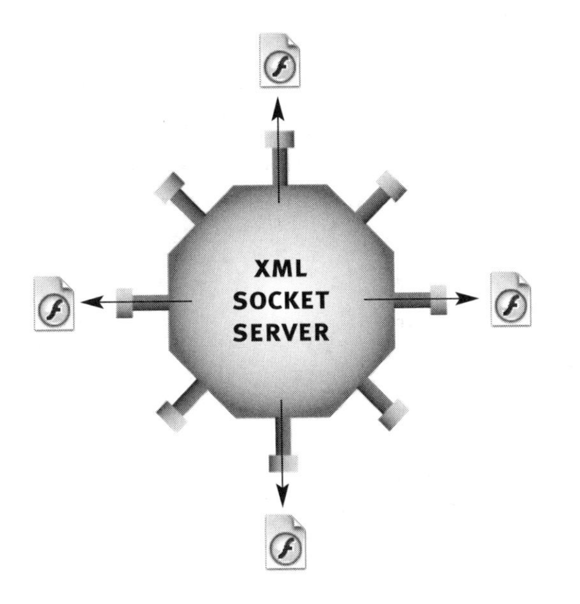

Introduction to the XMLSocket Class

This section provides a basic introduction to Flash's built-in XMLSocket class. This discussion is simply a guide to the use of this built-in class, so you can familiarize yourself with the general concepts needed for plugging your applications into nearly any socket server. The exercise that follows makes use of a special socket server that wraps most of the functionalities you're about to learn into a simple-to-use object. But more on this in a bit. Let's look at the inherent way Flash communicates with a socket server.

Before you can connect a Flash movie to a socket server, you must create a new XMLSocket object, using the constructor for the XMLSocket class. You can then use the methods of the object to connect to a server and exchange information. In this section, we'll show you how to create and use an XMLSocket object while also using the XML class methods and properties introduced earlier in this lesson.

To create a new XMLSocket object, you must use the constructor for XMLSocket. Here's an example:

```
var server:XMLSocket = new XMLSocket();
```

This line of ActionScript creates a new XMLSocket object named `server`. To connect the XMLSocket to a server, you simply employ the `connect()` method using the following syntax:

```
server.connect(hostName,port)
```

The `hostName` parameter is the IP address on which the socket server resides—usually a numeric sequence (for example, `65.134.12.2`). IP addresses such as `127.0.0.1` or `localhost` are valid references to your own computer. If you type *http://localhost* into your Web browser's address bar, it would try to connect to your computer as if it were a Web site. The `port` parameter refers to the port on which the server is listening. Flash can only connect to ports higher than 1024. For example:

```
var server:XMLSocket = new XMLSocket();
server.connect("localhost", 9999)
```

You can close a connection with a socket by using the `close()` method:

```
server.close();
```

To send information via the socket connection, simply use the `send()` method and pass in the object you want to send. For example:

```
server.send("<Text>Hi</Text>");
```

The XMLSocket class can respond to the following types of events:

- `onConnect`—This event fires when the connection is accepted or fails.
- `onXML`—This event fires when information arrives via the socket connection. This action lets you know that new information has arrived so that you can use it.
- `onClose`—This event fires when the connection with the socket is lost. This event will not fire as a result of purposely closing the connection from Flash using the `XMLSocket.close()` method.

As we did with the `onLoad` event in the XML class, we have to define these event handlers with the XMLSocket object that we create. For example:

```
function serverConnected (success:Boolean) {
  trace(success);
}
server.onConnect = serverConnected;
```

Here the `serverConnected()` function is called when the `onConnect` event is fired. The `success` parameter in the function definition has a value of `true` if the connection was successful and `false` if the connection was unsuccessful.

The onXML event is used as follows:

```
function xmlReceived (data:XML) {
  trace(data);
}
server.onXML = xmlReceived;
```

The xmlReceived() function is called each time information arrives via the socket. The data parameter contains the XML document pushed into Flash.

The onClose event handler can be defined and used as follows:

```
function socketClosed () {
  //notify the user
}
server.onClose = socketClosed;
```

You would typically use this type of event to let the user know that a connection has been lost.

ElectroServer 3

To utilize the functionality of any socket server, you can't just upload a script into the CGI-bin of your Web site or place it in a normal Web-accessible directory. Usually written in Java, C, C++, or Visual Basic, socket servers generally require root-level access to the Web server. This usually means that you must be running your own dedicated server in order to install and use a socket server. Fortunately, this isn't as scary as it sounds. As a matter of fact, you can set up a socket server on your own personal computer so that you can develop with it, which is a recommended and common practice when developing applications that use a socket server.

For the next exercise, we'll show you how to get a socket server up and running on your local machine so that you can go on to build a simple chat application that connects to the socket server. To test it, you'll need to use Windows 98, Windows 2000, Windows XP, or Windows ME.

The accompanying CD-ROM contains the installer for a Java-based socket server called ElectroServer 3. You need to have Java 2 Runtime Environment (JRE) version 1.4.1_02 or higher installed on your machine to run ElectroServer 3, as well as to test the chat program you build in the next section.

NOTE *ElectroServer 3 is supported by any operating system that supports the JRE. This includes Macintosh OS X and higher, Linux, UNIX, Windows, and so on. For non–Windows installation instructions for ElectroServer 3 and the JRE, see* http://www.electrotank.com/ElectroServer/.

The next exercise guides you through the steps to get ElectroServer 3 up and running on your Windows computer.

1) Download and install the JRE (for Windows) by going to *http://www.java.com*. This page will probably detect your operating system automatically. Click the download link. The Java software most likely will be installed automatically through the Web browser.

ElectroServer 3 will not run properly with a version of the JRE older than 1.4.1_02.

2) To install and start ElectroServer 3 on Windows, open the Lesson12/Assets directory. Double-click the file called *InstallElectroServer.exe* to install ElectroServer 3, and follow the series of prompts to completion. You don't need to change any of the default options during the installation process.

You have just installed ElectroServer 3, the socket server that we'll use in the next exercise to build a Flash chat. If you left the default options selected while installing ElectroServer 3, then it also installed several example files onto your hard drive.

3) To start ElectroServer 3, click Start > All Programs (or Program Files) > Electrotank > ElectroServer 3 > Start ElectroServer.

If you installed the JRE properly, ElectroServer 3 should have started without any problem.

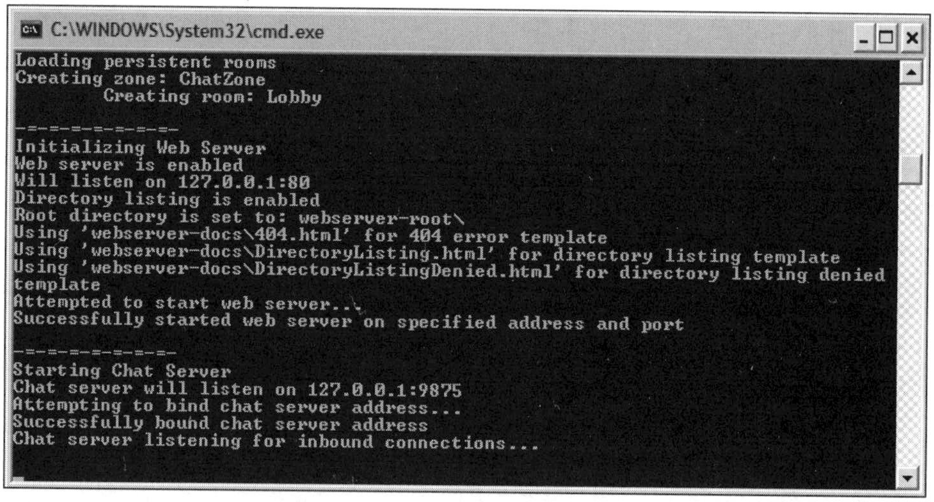

```
C:\WINDOWS\System32\cmd.exe
Loading persistent rooms
Creating zone: ChatZone
        Creating room: Lobby

-=-=-=-=-=-=-
Initializing Web Server
Web server is enabled
Will listen on 127.0.0.1:80
Directory listing is enabled
Root directory is set to: webserver-root\
Using 'webserver-docs\404.html' for 404 error template
Using 'webserver-docs\DirectoryListing.html' for directory listing template
Using 'webserver-docs\DirectoryListingDenied.html' for directory listing denied
template
Attempted to start web server...
Successfully started web server on specified address and port

-=-=-=-=-=-=-
Starting Chat Server
Chat server will listen on 127.0.0.1:9875
Attempting to bind chat server address...
Successfully bound chat server address
Chat server listening for inbound connections...
```

By default, ElectroServer 3 will connect to the `127.0.0.1` IP address, which is the IP address by which your computer refers to itself. Also, the default port on which ElectroServer 3 will exchange data is 9875. Both the IP and the port are configurable, but you won't need to change the settings for the chat exercise.

At least a dozen socket servers have been created for use with Flash. Among them, here are the most popular (not in order of popularity):

- ElectroServer 3 (*www.electrotank.com/ElectroServer/*) is a full-featured socket server that was created specifically to meet the needs of multi-user Flash game developers. As such, it has features (not seen in other socket servers) that appeal to Flash game programmers.
- Macromedia Flash Communication Server (*www.macromedia.com*) is not a socket server, although it's similar to one. It uses a proprietary data-exchange protocol developed by Macromedia. It can be used to accomplish tasks such as video and audio transfer (for video chatting).
- Unity (*www.moock.org/unity/*) is a general socket server that can be used to create any number of multi-user applications, including chat and games.

The ElectroServer Class

In the next exercise, you'll build a chat program that communicates with ElectroServer 3. When being developed, a socket server must be programmed to look for a certain protocol. XML is a protocol, but even deeper than that, the socket server must look for XML in a certain structure—a protocol within a protocol. For example, if you want to send an XML-formatted login request from Flash to ElectroServer 3, it must use this format:

```
<XmlDoc>
  <Action>Login</Action>
  <Parameters>
    <Name>myName</Name>
    <Password>myPassword</Password>
  </Parameters>
</XmlDoc>
```

ElectroServer 3 reads the Action node, and then knows what else to look for. When it sees that the Action is `Login`, it knows to expect a `Name` node and a `Password` node. You must use a specific XML protocol for every socket server. XML itself is a standard, but the structure of the XML is specific to the socket server being used.

Does this sound daunting? You can send or receive 100 or so different XML packets in ElectroServer 3 to accomplish tasks such as sending a message, creating a room, and so on. There is good news, though: the ElectroServer class is included with this lesson. The ElectroServer class internally handles all of the XML formats that need to be sent or received. You can talk to ElectroServer 3 easily through the ElectroServer class, without having to write a single line of XML.

NOTE *Within the directory of this project's lesson files is a file named* **ElectroServer.as**. *This file defines the ElectroServer class and its capabilities. During export or compiling of this movie, Flash uses the contents of this file to enable the exported movie to utilize the functionality of the ElectroServer class. It's important that this file (and its supporting files, named* **Wddx.as** *and* **WddxRecordset.as**) *exist in the same directory as the completed project file; otherwise, an error will occur when you export the movie.*

To send a chat message to the server, this is all you need to do:

```
ElectroServer.sendMessage("public", "Hello world!");
```

This line of ActionScript executes the `sendMessage` method of the ElectroServer class. The first parameter, `"public"`, tells the ElectroServer class to send a public message to the entire room. The second parameter is the message to send.

To send a private message to a user named Derek, you would use this line of ActionScript:

```
ElectroServer.sendMessage("private", "Hello Derek!", "Derek");
```

NOTE *Documentation for every method, property and event of the ElectroServer class can be found in a file named* **Class_Documentation.html** *in the directory Program Files\Electrotank\ElectroServer 3\Examples\Flash MX 2004 on your hard drive. To find the most up-to-date ElectroServer class and documentation, visit* `http://www.electrotank.com/ElectroServer/`. *You can also download the ElectroServer class as a Flash extension so that you can use the Actions panel to browse the ElectroServer class and access help on it, just as with all other Flash classes.*

It's time to build a simple chat application using ElectroServer 3. A few more basic concepts as well as specific methods and events of the ElectroServer class will be discussed as we go along.

1) Open *Chat1.fla* in the Lesson12/Assets folder.

The file contains four layers: the Actions layer, where we'll keep the ActionScript; the Labels layer, which contains the labels for the movie; the Assets layer, containing the text fields and buttons; and the Background layer, which contains the interface graphics.

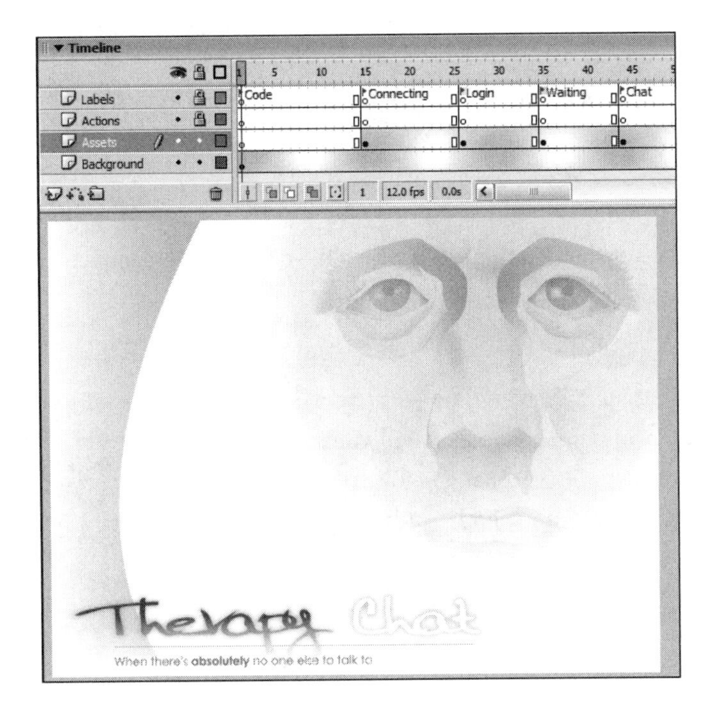

We'll begin by scripting the code to get a user connected to ElectroServer 3, logged in, and joined to a room. A *room* is nothing more than a collection of users. When a user sends a chat message, it's automatically sent to everyone in the room. ElectroServer 3, like most socket servers, supports multiple rooms. Many rooms can exists at once, each with users. A user can switch from one room to another, as you'll see later in this exercise.

After we've scripted our project to the point where a user can log in and join a room, we'll add the ActionScript needed to display the user list, room list, and allow the user to chat. All of this can be done in about 80 lines of code!

2) With the Actions panel open, select Frame 1 of the Actions layer and add the following script:

```
var es:ElectroServer = ElectroServer.getInstance();
```

The ElectroServer class is a *static class* (also known as a *singleton*), which means that only one instance of it can exist within your movie. To create this instance of the ElectroServer class, simply call the `getInstance()` method directly on the class, and it will return a reference to itself. The line of code in this step creates a variable named `es`, which is our reference to the instance of the ElectroServer class.

For the rest of this exercise, the ElectroServer class will be accessed by using the es reference created in this step.

NOTE *We're able to create an instance of the ElectroServer class only because of the* ***ElectroServer.as*** *file that exists in the same directory as this project file. This* ***.as*** *file is loaded during the process of exporting the project file SWF, enabling all the functionality of the ElectroServer class that we'll script in the following steps.*

3) Using the following code, set the IP and port to which the chat should connect:

```
es.setIP("127.0.0.1");
es.setPort(9875);
```

When you installed ElectroServer 3, it created default settings that it would use for its operation. Unless these settings are changed, when you start ElectroServer 3 it will bind to your local IP address (`127.0.0.1`) and listen on port 9875. The script above tells the ElectroServer class instance at which IP address to look for ElectroServer 3, and which port at that IP it should use.

The ElectroServer class will not attempt to connect to ElectroServer 3 until you invoke the `connect()` method. We'll do that later in the exercise.

4) With the same frame selected, add the following code to capture the connection response from ElectroServer 3:

```
es.onConnection = function(success:Boolean, error:String) {
  if (success) {
    gotoAndStop("Login");
  } else {
    msg_txt.text = error;
  }
};
```

In a moment, we'll create the script that connects our application to ElectroServer 3. When the connection happens, an `onConnection` event occurs, which is what this script handles. Two parameters are passed to the function when the `onConnection` event is fired: `success` and `error`.

The first parameter, `success`, is a Boolean value. If `true`, the connection was a success and the user is taken to the Login frame label to log in. If `false`, the connection failed. If the connection failed, the second parameter, `error`, is passed to the function. This parameter contains a string that explains what went wrong. When a failed connection occurs, the `else` part of the statement is executed. This part of the statement displays the error message in the text field named **msg_txt**. This text field exists at the

Connecting frame label on the timeline. To understand how this works, it's important to realize that one of the last scripts we will place on this frame (in Step 9) will move the timeline of our application to the Connecting frame label, where it will wait for a response from the server. If an error occurs, the part of our script that reads:

```
msg_txt.text = error
```

will display the error message in the **msg_txt** text field on the Connecting frame label because our application is paused at that label.

What can cause the connection to fail and what kind of error messages are generated? If the connection failed because the ElectroServer class could not find ElectroServer 3 (possibly due to a wrongly specified IP or port, firewall issues, or the fact that the server was not running), `error` will contain a string that reads, `Could not establish a server connection`. Otherwise, an error will be generated dynamically from the server. The server could deny a connection because it has reached its connection limit, which is 20 simultaneous users in the free license version.

Before proceeding further, take a look at the essential steps necessary for chatting using ElectroServer 3. The user must do the following successfully:

1) Connect to ElectroServer 3.

2) Log in to ElectroServer 3, which assigns you a username.

3) Join a room.

In Step 4, we've scripted what happens when the connection occurs. In the steps that follow, we'll script our application to take care of the login process as well as the process of joining a chat room.

5) Add the following script to capture the login response:

```
es.loggedIn = function(success:Boolean, error:String) {
  if (success) {
    joinRoom();
  } else {
    msg_txt.text = error;
  }
};
```

On the frame labeled Login, which will be covered later in this exercise, the user is allowed to enter a username and a room name, and click a button to send a login request to the server. The server will then send back a response either allowing or denying the login request. The `loggedIn` event is triggered when the server responds to a login request.

Similar to the `onConnection` event, the `loggedIn` event has two parameters: `success` and `error`. If `success` is `true`, the login attempt was successful and the `joinRoom()` function is called. If `success` is `false`, the login attempt was not successful and an error string is placed in the **msg_txt** field. A user might receive an error if attempting to log into the server with a username that's already being used.

6) Add the following function to handle joining a user to a room:

```
function joinRoom() {
  var roomOb:Object = new Object();
  roomOb.roomName = roomToJoin;
  es.createRoom(roomOb);
}
```

Before discussing this function, it's important to realize that on the frame labeled Login there are two TextInput component instances—**username_ti** and **room_ti**. The user will use these text input boxes to enter a username and the name of the chat room that he or she wants to join. A script we will be adding to that frame will take the room name that the user enters and convert it to a variable named `roomToJoin`, which is used by the function in this step (third line down). Now let's look at how this function works.

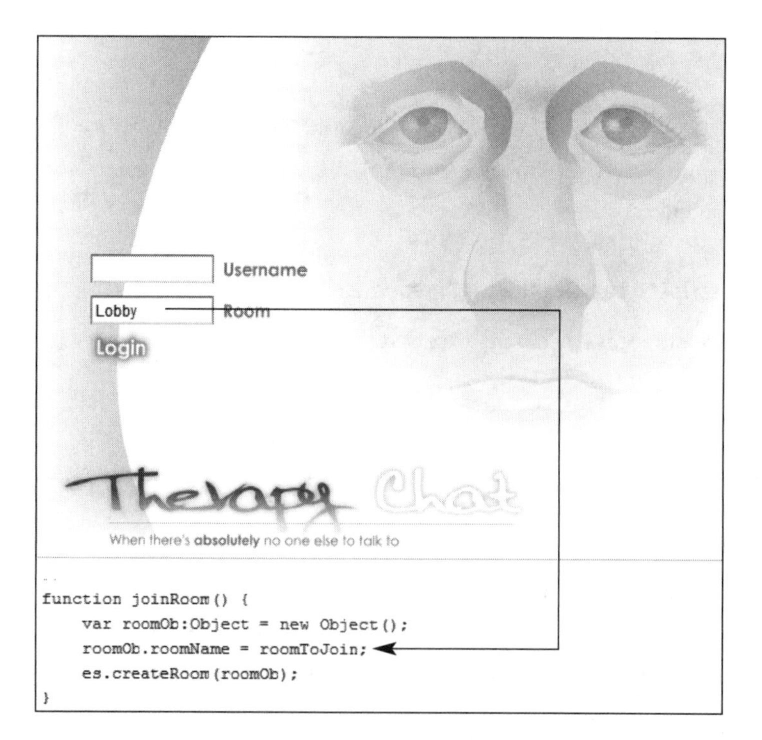

As shown in Step 5, when the login response from the server is a success, the `joinRoom()` function is called and the room that was specified by the user in the login screen is created. Here's how.

There are two methods of the ElectroServer class that are appropriate to mention here—createRoom() and joinRoom(). The joinRoom() method tells ElectroServer 3 that you want to join a specified room. Here's an example:

```
es.joinRoom("Sports");
```

If a room called Sports exists, you will join it. If it doesn't exist, an error will be returned by the server . This error is captured in the roomJoined event, which we'll script in the next step.

With the createRoom() method, you can create a room that doesn't yet exist. If you attempt to create a room that already exists, internally the ElectroServer class will capture the error and attempt to join you to that room instead.

Because the createRoom() function more easily facilitates joining a room, we use that in our function.

In the joinRoom() function—not to be confused with the joinRoom() method of ElectroServer 3—an object named roomOb is created and given a property named roomName. The value of roomName is the string that the user enters into the **room_ti** field on the Login frame. This object is then passed into the createRoom() method, which either creates the room (based on the properties of the passed-in object), if the user is the first person in that room, or joins the user to that room if it already exists.

It might seem like overkill to create an object just to store a single variable, the name of the room. This would be true if the name of the room were the only configurable property of a new room; however, many default properties of a room can be overridden if requested. For example, a room can be password protected, hidden from the room list, set to allow a maximum number of people, and much more. For simplicity, our room only needs to be given a name, so the roomOb object has a single property (roomName) attached to it.

NOTE *To learn about advanced properties, see the ElectroServer class documentation on the CD-ROM.*

7) To capture the ElectroServer 3 response to attempting to create/join a room, add the following code:

```
es.roomJoined = function(Results:Object) {
  if (Results.success) {
    gotoAndStop("Chat");
  } else {
    msg_txt.text = Results.error;
  }
};
```

In Step 6, you added the `joinRoom()` function, which requests that a room of a certain name be created. If that room doesn't exist, it's created, you're automatically joined to it, and the `roomJoined` event is fired. If the room already exists, internally the ElectroServer 3 class captures that error and attempts to join you to it, and the `roomJoined` event is fired. Here we've scripted what should occur when this event is fired.

An object is passed into the `roomJoined` event handler when it's triggered. This object contains two properties: `success` and `error`. If `success` is `true`, the user has successfully been joined to the room and is taken to the Chat label, which contains the elements that facilitate chatting. If there was an error joining the room, the error is shown in the **msg_txt** field (which exists on the Connecting label).

8) Add the following line of script at the end of the current script:

```
_global.style.setStyle("themeColor", 0xE5EEF4);
```

This line of script colors all of our component instances a light shade of blue to match the overall color of our design.

9) For the final action on this frame, add this line of script:

```
gotoAndStop("Connecting");
```

Actions - Frame

```
1  var es:ElectroServer = ElectroServer.getInstance();
2  es.setIP("127.0.0.1");
3  es.setPort(9875);
4  es.onConnection = function(success:Boolean, error:String) {
5      if (success) {
6          gotoAndStop("Login");
7      } else {
8          msg_txt.text = error;
9      }
10 };
11 es.loggedIn = function(success:Boolean, error:String) {
12     if (success) {
13         joinRoom();
14     } else {
15         msg_txt.text = error;
16     }
17 };
18 function joinRoom() {
19     var roomOb:Object = new Object();
20     roomOb.roomName = roomToJoin;
21     es.createRoom(roomOb);
22 }
23 es.roomJoined = function(Results:Object) {
24     if (Results.success) {
25         gotoAndStop("Chat");
26     } else {
27         msg_txt.text = Results.error;
28     }
29 };
30 _global.style.setStyle("themeColor", 0xE5EEF4);
31 gotoAndStop("Connecting");
```

Actions : 1

Line 31 of 31, Col 27

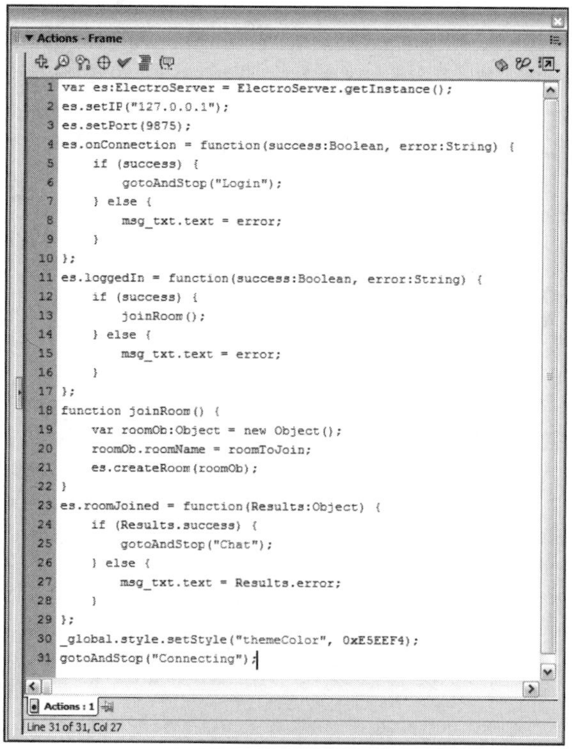

This step moves the timeline of our chat application to the Connecting frame label. In the next step, we'll add the code that asks the ElectroServer class to connect to ElectroServer 3.

10) On the frame labeled Connecting in the Actions layer, add the following two lines of script:

```
msg_txt.text = "Connecting..."
es.connect();
```

The first line of ActionScript populates the **msg_txt** text field with some text informing the user that the application is attempting to establish a connection. The next line calls the `connect()` method of the ElectroServer class. The `connect()` method takes the IP address and port (set in Step 3) and uses them to try to find ElectroServer 3 to establish a connection. The result is captured in the `onConnection` event (created in Step 4).

11) Move to the frame labeled Login. In the Actions layer, add the following variable declaration and button event handler:

```
var roomToJoin:String;
login_btn.onRelease = function() {
  var username:String = username_ti.text;
  roomToJoin = room_ti.text;
  if (username.length > 2 && username.length < 15) {
    es.login(username);
    gotoAndStop("Waiting");
  }
};
```

This frame includes two TextInput instances named **username_ti** and **room_ti**, and a button with an instance name of **login_btn**. When **login_btn** is clicked, the `onRelease` event handler shown here is called. It populates the variable `roomToJoin` with the contents the user entered into the **room_ti** instance (remember that the value of `roomToJoin` is used in the script added in Step 6). It also checks to make sure that the username entered is a reasonable size, over 2 characters but less than 15 characters. If the username has an acceptable length, the `login()` method of the ElectroServer class is called, passing in the username, and the application moves to the Waiting frame label.

Internally the ElectroServer class takes the username, formats an appropriate XML document, sends it to ElectroServer 3, and waits to hear a response. When a response is received, the `loggedIn` event (scripted in Step 5) is fired.

12) Add the following line of script to the Waiting frame in the Actions layer:

```
msg_txt.text = "Waiting…";
```

When the user clicks the login button on the Login frame, he or she is taken to the Waiting frame to wait for a response from the server, which will trigger the `loggedIn` event we scripted in Step 5. As shown in that script, if the `loggedIn` event captures an error, the **msg_txt** field will display that error; otherwise, the `joinRoom()` function is called to join the user to a room and, as a result, to take the user to the Chat frame label (as described in Steps 6 and 7). The elements enabling the user to chat are at this frame.

13) Move to the Chat frame.

This is the frame from which all users who have successfully connected to ElectroServer 3, logged in, and joined a room will chat. Notice that the TextArea component on the screen has an instance name of **chatBox_ta**, which will be used to display the chat messages. To the right of this instance are two List components with instance names of **roomListBox_lb** and **userListBox_lb**. As you can probably guess, the **roomListBox_lb** instance will be used to show the list of rooms that exist on the server, and **userListBox_lb** will display the list of users in your current room.

Below the **chatBox_ta** instance is a TextInput instance in which the user can type a chat message. It has an instance name of **msgBox_ti**. The button with the instance name **send_btn** is used to send a chat message.

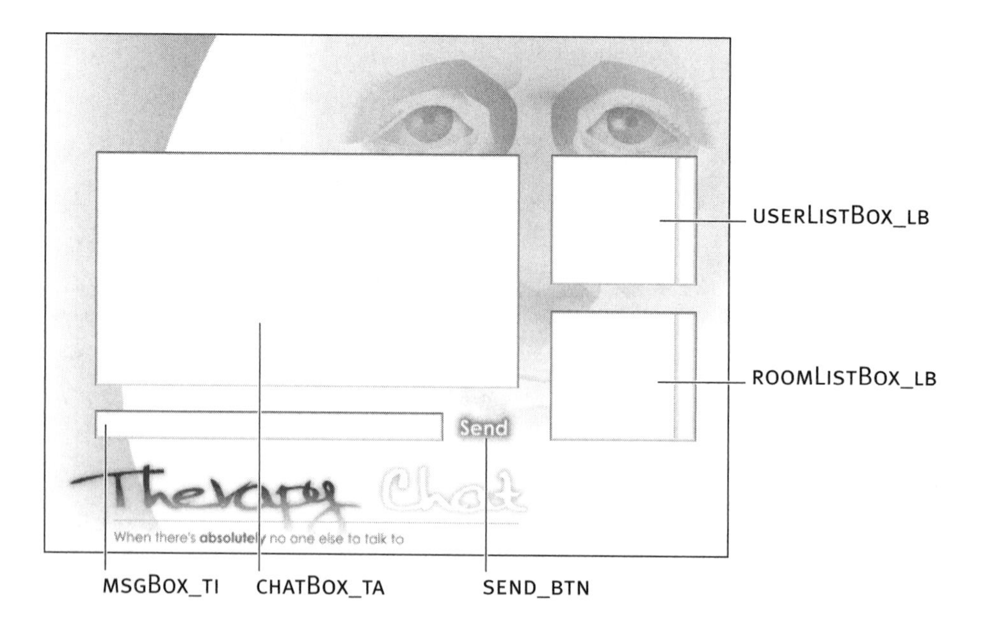

14) Select the frame on the Chat label in the Actions layer and open the Actions panel. Enter this button's `onRelease` event handler:

```
send_btn.onRelease = function() {
  var msg:String = msgBox_ti.text;
  if (msg.length > 0) {
    es.sendMessage("public", msg);
    msgBox_ti.text = "";
  }
};
```

This script is executed when the Send button is clicked. A variable called `msg` is created to store the contents of the **msgBox_ti** instance. If the length of the message to send is greater than 0, the `sendMessage()` method of the ElectroServer class is executed. The first parameter of this method, `"public"`, informs the ElectroServer class that the message is intended for everyone in the room. The second parameter contains the message to send. In addition to sending a message, the content of the **msgBox_ti** instance is erased so the user can type another message.

You have just created the script needed to send a chat message to everyone in the room.

15) Add the following event handler to capture the chat messages coming in from ElectroServer 3:

```
es.messageReceived = function(type:String, message:String, from:String) {
  chatBox_ta.text += from + ": " + message + newline;
  chatBox_ta.vPosition = chatBox_ta.maxVPosition;
};
```

This script assigns an event handler to the `messageReceived` event, which is triggered whenever an incoming message is received from the server. When this event is fired, it is passed three parameter values. The first parameter, `type`, can be a value of either `"public"` or `"private"`. In this exercise, all messages are public messages, so we don't need to worry about using that first parameter. However, in a full-featured chat front-end you would want to know whether an arriving message was public or private. If it's a private message, you might want Flash to play a sound or color code the text to give an indication to the person chatting that he or she just received a private message.

The second parameter, `message`, contains the chat message that has arrived. The final parameter, `from`, contains the username of the person who sent the message.

The first line of script inside the function adds a line of text to the **chatBox_ta** TextArea component. It starts with the name of the user who sent the message, adds a colon and the contents of the message, and finally adds a newline so the next message received will be on its own line.

Next, the script sets the scroll position of the text in the **chatBox_ta** component. In a chat application, incoming messages are typically appended to the bottom of the text field and the field is automatically scrolled to the bottom. This line of script sets the scroll position of the **chatBox_ta** instance to be the maximum scroll position possible.

16) To display the list of users in the room, the `userListUpdated` **event must be captured and used. Add the following script at the end of the current script:**

```
function showUsers() {
  var userlist:Array = es.getUserList();
  userListBox_lb.setDataProvider(userlist);
}
es.userListUpdated = showUsers;
showUsers();
```

First we create a function called `showUsers()`. This function grabs the most recent user list from the ElectroServer class using the `getUserList()` method and stores it as an array called `userlist`. As a result, the `userlist` array will contain one object for each user in the room. Each of these objects has a property named `label` that contains the username of the user that the object represents. If there are seven users in the room, the `getUserList()` method will return an array containing seven items; the array is stored in the array object named `userlist`.

The second line in the function takes the `userlist` array object and passes it into the `setDataProvider()` method of the **userListBox_lb** List component instance. The result is that the **userListBox_lb** is populated with a list of all of the usernames in the room.

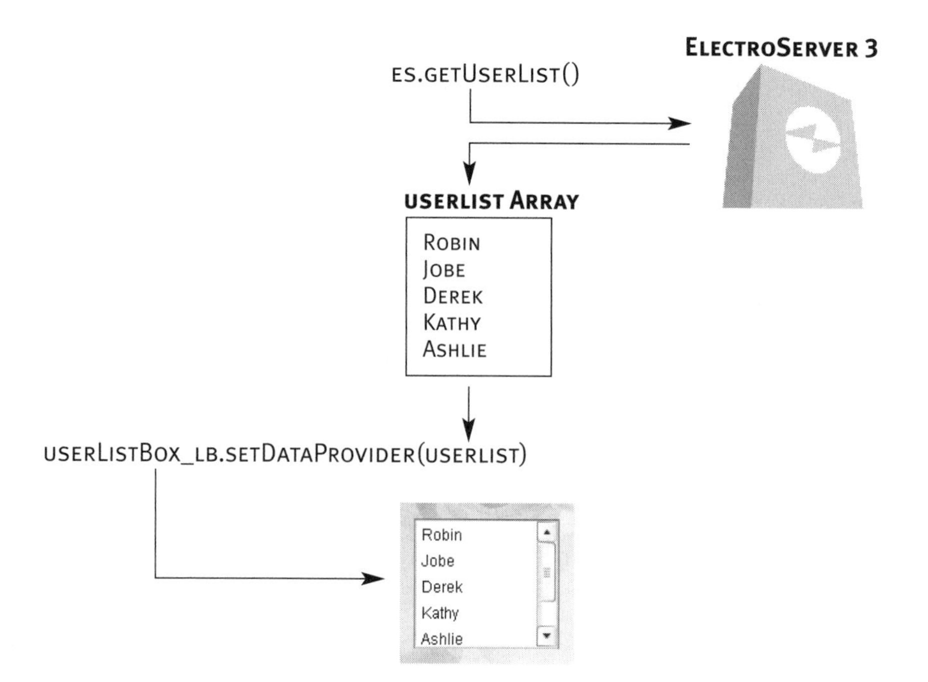

On the first line of script below the function definition, we assign the showUsers() function to the userListUpdated event. This event is triggered by the server automatically whenever the list of users in the room changes. Thus, whenever someone enters or leaves the chat room, the showUsers() function is called and the user list shown in the **userListBox_lb** instance is updated.

The last line of script calls the showUsers() function manually because when we first arrive at the Chat frame we want to display the current list of users. If we didn't call the showUsers() function manually, the current user list wouldn't display in the **userListBox_lb** instance until the next person came into the room or left the room, causing a userListUpdated event to fire.

17) To show the list of rooms, add the following code:

```
function showRooms() {
  var roomlist:Array = es.getRoomList();
  roomListBox_lb.setDataProvider(roomlist);
}
es.roomListUpdated = showRooms;
showRooms();
```

This script is almost identical to the script that captures and displays the user list. The showRooms() function grabs the room list (an array of objects, each representing one room) from the ElectroServer class and passes it into the setDataProvider() method of the **roomListBox_lb** List component instance.

The showRooms() function is then assigned as the event handler for the roomListUpdated event. Every time something about a room list changes, such as the number of people in a room or the addition/removal of a room, this event is fired.

Finally, the showRooms() function is manually called so that the current list of rooms can be displayed. After that it will be called only when the roomListUpdated event fires.

18) To allow a person to click the name of a room to join that room, add the following script:

```
var roomClickListenerObject:Object = new Object();
roomClickListenerObject.change = function(eventObject:Object) {
  var room:String = eventObject.target.value;
  es.joinRoom(room);
};
roomListBox_lb.addEventListener("change", roomClickListenerObject);
```

When a user arrives at the Chat frame, he or she will see the list of rooms in the **roomListBox_lb** instance. As the list of rooms changes, the box will update. The script that you just added gives the user the ability to click any room in the list and be joined to that room automatically.

We first create an object and then create a function called `change` on the object. Finally, we assign this object as an event listener to the **roomListBox_lb** component instance. The `change` event is fired whenever a user changes the selected room in the **roomListBox_lb** instance. Usually, this is accomplished by the user's clicking a room in the list, although it can also be accomplished using the keyboard.

When the `change` event is fired, an Event object is passed into the event handler. We extract the name of the item that was selected and give it a variable name of `room`. The value of that variable is then passed into the `joinRoom()` method to join the user to that room.

When a user joins a new room, he or she receives an updated user list, which is handled by code we have added to this frame. So, by simply clicking the name of a room, the user will be joined to that room and the list of users will change to display the list of users who are in that room.

19) Start ElectroServer 3.

The default IP and port for ElectroServer 3 are `127.0.0.1` and 9875. When you start ElectroServer 3, it will attempt to bind itself to your local IP and listen on the default port.

It's now time to test your chat application.

20) Choose File > Export > Movie to export this project to an *SWF* file in this lesson's directory on your hard drive. Navigate to that directory and double-click the exported *SWF*. Log in and send some chat messages.

You should see your chat messages appear in the **chatBox_ta** TextArea component. Try opening more than one copy of this SWF and log in with different usernames. You should be able to see all the users in the **userListBox_lb** List component.

Try to log in two users with the same username, to check that you receive an error. Log users into separate rooms and try to join a room by clicking the room name.

21) Close the test movie and save your work as *Chat2.fla*.

You've accomplished a lot in this exercise. You've created a basic chat application using the ElectroServer class, a little bit of ActionScript, and some components.

If you're interested in creating a more advanced chat room, look through the ElectroServer class documentation on the CD-ROM or download some source files from *http://www.electrotank.com/ElectroServer/*.

You can modify this chat to do any of the following:

- Enable password-protected rooms
- Allow private messaging
- Let a user create a new room from the Chat frame label
- Build in support for emoticons

WHAT YOU HAVE LEARNED

In this lesson, you have:

- Learned the basics of XML format (pages 408–413)
- Used several of the XML class methods and properties (pages 413–415)
- Created a simple Flash registration and login application (pages 416–424)
- Explored XML socket servers (pages 424–427)
- Built a real-time Flash chat application using the ElectroServer class (pages 427–443)

validating data

LESSON 13

Many applications collect information from users—phone numbers, email addresses, and so on—for later use, or to send to a database where the data can be stored and retrieved as needed. However, if an application trusted users to enter properly formatted, error-free information, the application probably wouldn't function properly—or your database would quickly fill with useless data. The fact is, users often enter data incorrectly, which is why it's a good idea to *validate* data before it's used or processed. Validating data usually entails writing a script to check the way data was entered against a set of guidelines or rules. If data-entry errors are found, the user can be prompted to reenter the data; or in some cases, the script can make the needed adjustments without further input from the user.

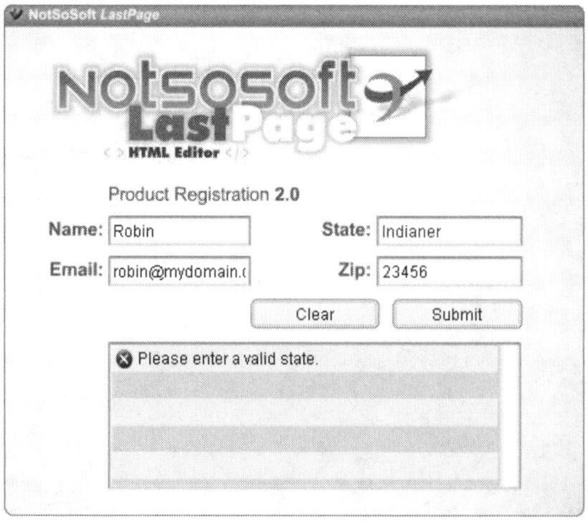

Our fictional product contains a product registration form that allows us to collect data from the user, validate it, and display any errors found.

In this lesson, we'll create an application that includes a form requiring user-input data that needs to be validated. After our application validates this information, the app will display a custom confirmation page and then send the data to a server for processing.

WHAT YOU WILL LEARN

In this lesson, you will:

- Learn why validation is important
- Define validation requirements
- Set up a mechanism to handle errors found in the validation process
- Create functions for validating strings, sequences, and numbers
- Send data from a validated form to a server for processing

APPROXIMATE TIME

This lesson takes approximately one and one half hours to complete.

LESSON FILES

Starting File:

Lesson13/Assets/validate1.fla

Completed Project:

validate7.fla

THE LOGIC BEHIND VALIDATING DATA

We validate things every day—from words in a sentence (to make sure they make sense) to change received from purchases. The concept of validation is a natural and easy one for us to understand. For example, examine the following (U.S.) phone number: 555-34567. Chances are you quickly recognized the phone number to be invalid. How? Your brain analyzed the phone number and noted that it contained eight digits. After comparing this fact to the rule that defines valid local phone numbers as those that include seven digits, your brain made a determination of true (the number was valid) or false (it was invalid). If you determine that the number is valid, you can place the phone call. If the number is invalid, however, your brain will log an error message—something similar to "That number is wrong. I need to get the correct number and then try to call."

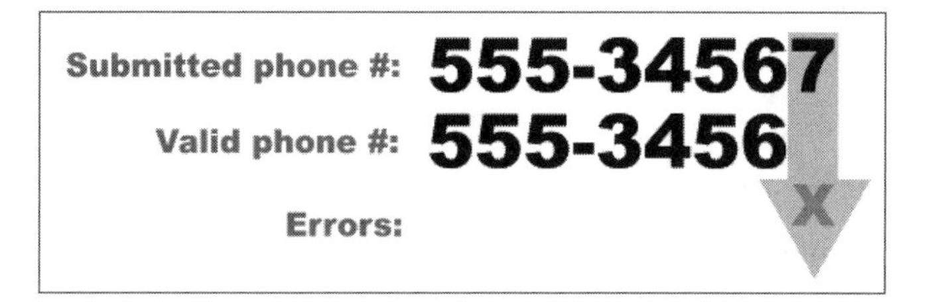

If we were to break down the validation process, it would look similar to the following:

1) Define criteria for valid data.

2) Analyze submitted data.

3) Compare this data against defined criteria.

4) Continue if data is valid; determine and note error if data is invalid; resolve and then try again.

In ActionScript, this process of analyzing information—comparing it to a set of rules and then determining the data's validity—is known as a *validation routine*. Just as your brain analyzes data instantaneously, an ActionScript validation routine takes a split second to complete.

You usually need to validate data within a Flash application whenever you require the user to enter information into an input text field—for example, on forms (name, address, phone number, and so on) and quizzes (to verify answers) and in e-commerce shopping carts (quantities, sizes, colors, and so on).

USING VALIDATION ROUTINES

You can think of a validation routine as a mini-scripting machine within your project that validates the data it receives and then acts accordingly, based on whether that data is valid or invalid. As such, most validation routines comprise functions composed primarily of conditional (`if`) statements.

It's typical to split validation routines into separate functions, one for each type of data to be validated, such as one function for validating strings, another for numbers, and so on. This allows you to script a function once and then use it anywhere in your project, as opposed to writing the validation routine repeatedly whenever a certain type of data needs to be validated.

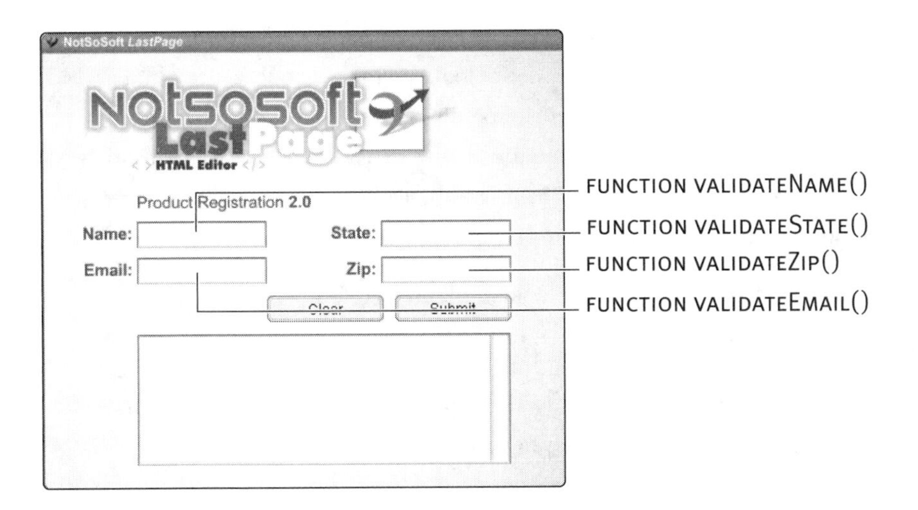

You can create two main types of validation routines (functions that validate data):

- Those that don't receive parameters but work in a specific way
- Those that receive parameters to provide additional functionality to your application

Let's take a look at each type.

With a validation routine that is not sent parameters, you define the function to work in a specific way, usually to validate a specific piece of data. Imagine you want to create a routine to validate a seven-digit telephone number that includes eight characters in all—seven digits and one hyphen (-) that the user enters into a text field named **telephone_txt**. The structure of that function would look similar to the following:

```
function validateTelephone () {
  if (telephone_txt.length == 8) {
    // number is valid, so do these specific actions
  } else {
    // number is invalid, so do these specific actions
  }
}
```

This routine can only validate the data in the **telephone_txt** text field because that's the field defined in the script. Let's now look at how versatile we can make this function by allowing it to accept a couple of parameters:

```
function validateTelephone (lookForAreaCode:Boolean, pNumber:String)
if (lookForAreaCode == true && pNumber.length == 12) {
    message_txt.text = "That is a valid 10-digit telephone number";
} else if (lookForAreaCode == false && pNumber.length == 8){
    message_txt.text = "That is a valid 7-digit telephone number";
  } else {
    message_txt.text = "That is not a valid telephone number";
  }
}
```

When called, this validation function receives two parameters: `lookForAreaCode`, a `true` or `false` value that indicates whether to look for an area code in the number to be validated, and a `pNumber` that represents the number to be validated. If `lookForAreaCode` is `true` when called, the number (`pNumber`) sent to the function is valid only if it contains 10 digits. If `lookForAreaCode` is `false`, the number sent to the function is valid only if it contains seven digits (and a hyphen).

A call to this validation routine would look similar to the following:

```
validateTelephone(true, 812-555-1234);
```

After processing this call, the function would display the following in the **message_txt** text field: "That is a valid 10-digit telephone number."

NOTE *You'll remember from previous lessons that the values sent to a function can actually be variables; therefore, you could use the validation function to validate the text in any text field by referencing that field's name and* `text` *property* (`textField_txt.text`) *in the second parameter of the function call.*

By creating a validation routine that accepts parameters and validates data accordingly, you increase the routine's usefulness because you can employ it to validate similar data in various ways.

Conditional statements play an important role in validating data because that process entails nothing more than evaluating various conditions to determine whether user-input data is valid. The rules that define valid data are considered *validation points.* To define validation points, you must consider the following:

- **Length.** Does the data contain the correct number of characters? A typical U.S. zip code, for example, contains five digits. If a user-entered zip code includes fewer than five digits, this is an error. Or imagine a name: because most names include more than one character, you would have an error if the length of the data entered were 1. (A length of 0 means nothing has been entered. If you require something to be entered, this would be an error.)

- **Value.** Is the value of the entered data more, less, or equal to what is considered valid? If you were asking for someone's age, you might define a lower limit of 18 and an upper limit of 100. If the value entered were more than 100 or less than 18, this would be an error.
- **Type.** Is the data entered a number when it should be a string, or vice versa? If the user specifies a garment size on an order, "pizza" would be an error when a number is required.
- **Sequence.** Is the data properly formatted? Some data needs to contain numbers, letters, and other characters, all placed in a specific sequence—for example, phone numbers (123-4567), dates (01/23/45), account numbers (1-2345-67-890), and so on. Missing or misplaced hyphens, slashes, or other characters represent errors.

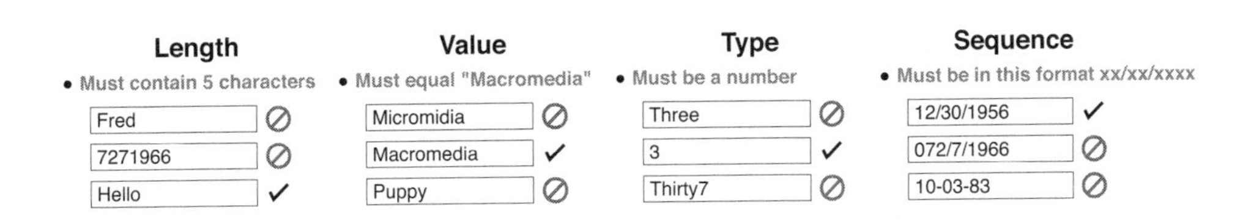

Most validation routines contain conditional statements that are used to validate data based on multiple validation points. We will use and discuss each of these validation points in more detail in the exercises that follow.

HANDLING ERRORS

Different projects require varying solutions for handling the errors that the validation process brings to light. In some cases, you may want to provide a graphical indicator such as a red *X* next to the field containing the error; in others, a text message may suffice.

The conditional statement within the validation routine usually determines how to handle any error that it detects. Take, for example, the following:

```
if (dataValid) {
  // perform these actions
} else {
  // Execute action to denote an error
}
```

Because error handling plays a major role in the validation process, you should think about how you want to handle errors in a particular project or situation before you script anything else.

In this exercise, we'll lay the foundation for the error-handling process in our project.

1) Open *validate1.fla* in the Lesson13/Assets folder.

This project contains two frame labels: Registration and Confirm. We'll work on the Confirm label in a later exercise; for now, we'll concentrate on the Registration label, which includes a form that the user must fill out, and thus data that needs to be validated. The timeline contains six layers named according to their content:

- The Background layer contains the project's static graphical content.
- The Text Components layer contains four TextInput component instances named **name_ti**, **email_ti**, **state_ti**, and **zip_ti**; and a List component instance named **errorLog_lb**. The TextInput instances allow the user to input name, email address, and so forth. The List component instance will be used to display any error messages generated during the form's validation process.
- The Button Components layer contains two button component instances named **clear_pb** and **submit_pb**—the former will be used to clear all form fields of data; the latter will be used to submit the form, thus initiating our application's form validation process.
- The Confirm Field layer contains a text field that we'll discuss in a later exercise.
- The Actions layer will contain all the scripts for this application.
- The Labels layer contains two frame labels (Registration and Confirm) to represent the application's two states: one containing the registration form, the other containing a "thank you" message. All of the scripting for this project will take place at the Registration label. In a later exercise, we'll script the application to move to the Confirm label when the user has completed the registration form accurately.

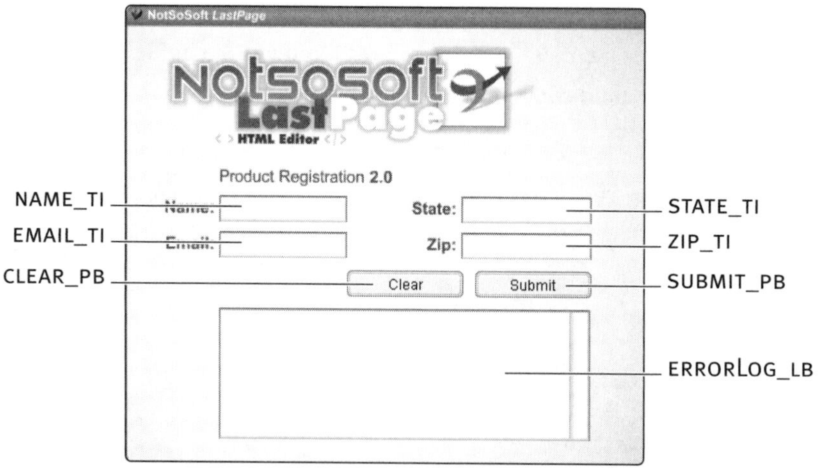

2) With the Actions panel open, select Frame 1 on the Actions layer and add the following script:

```
stop();
var errors:Array = new Array();
```

The first action prevents the timeline from moving beyond Frame 1 until we instruct it to do so.

The second action creates an array named `errors` that will hold error messages to be displayed as the result of the validation process. (We'll explain this in more detail as we move forward.)

3) Add the following function definition at the end of the current script:

```
function clearForm() {
  name_ti.text = "";
  email_ti.text = "";
  state_ti.text = "";
  zip_ti.text = "";
  errorLog_lb.removeAll();
  errors.length = 0;
  errorLog_lb.alternatingRowColors = null;
}
```

When called, this function resets the value of scene elements. First we remove any text that has been entered into the four TextInput instances. The next line uses the `removeAll()` method of the List component to remove any error messages displayed in the **errorLog_lb** instance. The next line removes any error messages stored in the `errors` array. The last line sets the `alternatingRowColors` property of the **errorLog_lb** instance to `null`. What does this do, and why are we doing it?

Setting the `alternatingRowColors` property of a List component instance allows you to configure the instance to display items shown in the list with alternating row colors. This is done by creating an array with two or more color values and then setting that array as the value of the `alternatingRowColors` property, such as the following:

```
var myArray:Array = new Array(0xFFCC00, 0xCC9900, 0x003366);
myList_lb.alternatingRowColor = myArray;
```

Later in this lesson we will script the **errorLog_lb** instance to display error messages using alternating row colors. When the form is cleared using this function, we want the **errorLog_lb** instance to revert back to its original all-white row colors. Setting the `alternatingRowColors` property to `null`, as this function does, takes care of that requirement.

VAR MYCOLORS:ARRAY = NEW ARRAY(0XCCCCCC, 0X999999);
ERRORLOG_LB.ALTERNATINGROWCOLORS = MYCOLORS;

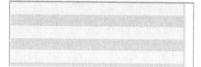

ERRORLOG_LB.ALTERNATINGROWCOLORS = NULL;

In the end, the scene will be reset to its original state.

4) With the Actions panel still open, add the following script:

```
clear_pb.addEventListener("click", clearForm);
```

This script calls the `clearForm()` function when the **clear_pb** instance is clicked.

5) Save this file as *validate2.fla*.

We'll build on this file throughout this lesson. The most important aspect of this exercise was the creation of the `errors` array, which will play a major role in the way our application handles any errors it detects in the validation process.

VALIDATING STRINGS

As mentioned earlier in this lesson, when validating different types of data (names, phone numbers, email addresses, and so on) it's best to break the process into specialized functions or validation routines. We will begin that process in this exercise.

The first type of data our form asks for is the user's name. For our form, the data entered must meet two requirements:

- **Length.** The name must be at least two characters long.
- **Type.** Text must be used; a number cannot be accepted as a valid name.

NOTE *We could define other validation points, such as a maximum length or even that the name begin with a D, but the ones we have chosen are sufficient for our purposes.*

In this exercise, we'll create a function for validating the name entered into our project's registration form.

1) Open *validate2.fla*.

We'll build on the project from the last exercise.

2) With the Actions panel open, select Frame 1 on the Actions layer and add the following function definition at the end of the current script:

```
function validateName() {
  if (name_ti.text.length < 2 || isNaN(name_ti.text) == false) {
    errors.push("Please enter a valid name.");
    name_ti.setStyle("color", 0x990000);
  }
}
```

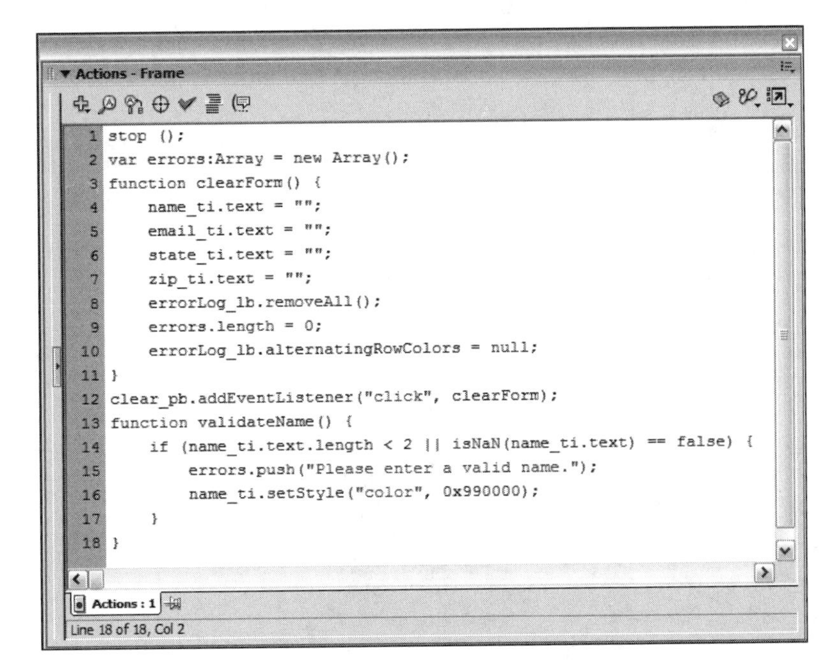

When called, this function checks the data entered in the **name_ti** instance for two conditions: length and type (the validation points we defined at the beginning of this exercise). The conditional statement here says that if the **name_ti** instance contains fewer than two characters or is a number (which would be considered an error), the string "Please enter a valid name" should be pushed into the `errors` array. In addition, we use the `setStyle()` method to change the color of text in the **name_ti** instance to red to make the location of the error a little more noticeable. Although we've used the `length` property in other scripts, some of this syntax is new and thus requires explanation.

One of the validation points we've defined for the **name_ti** instance is that a number entered into it would be considered an error (of course, a name containing a number, such as derek66, would be acceptable). To determine whether data is a number or text string, we would use the `isNaN()` function. This built-in function verifies that the argument passed to it (within the parentheses) is not a number (hence the name `isNaN`, or *is Not a Number*). Take a look at the following examples:

`isNaN("Box")` returns a value of `true` because the value of `"Box"` is a string, meaning it's true that it's not a number.

`isNaN(465)` returns a value of `false` because `465` is a number—that is, it's false to state that `465` is not a number.

Thus, `isNaN(name_ti.text) == false` is the same as saying, "If what **name_ti** contains is a number..."

If either of the conditions in the statement exists, data has been input improperly. As a result, the actions within the `if` statement are executed. The first action within the statement uses the `push()` method of the Array object to add an element to the end of the `errors` array. (This element is what's enclosed in the parentheses.) If you think of the `errors` array as a book, using the `push()` method is like adding a page to the end of the book, with the string within the parentheses representing the text on that page. The page number of this page would be its index position within the array.

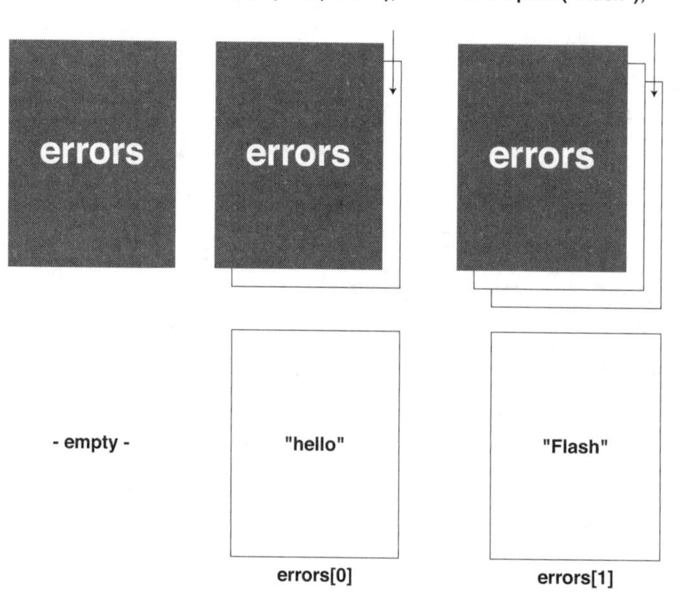

In the case of this function, if the data in the **name_ti** instance is invalid, the text "Please enter a valid name" is pushed into the `errors` array.

Next, we'll create a function to retrieve this error from the array (if **name_ti** doesn't contain a valid entry and an error is pushed into the array) and display it in the **errorLog_lb** List component instance.

3) With the Actions panel still open, add the following function definition at the end of the current script:

```
function validateForm() {
  errorLog_lb.removeAll();
  errors.length = 0;
  validateName();
  if (errors.length > 0) {
    errorLog_lb.defaultIcon = "errorIcon";
    var altColorArray:Array = new Array(0xF9F2F2, 0xECD9D9);
    errorLog_lb.alternatingRowColors = altColorArray;
    errorLog_lb.rollOverColor = 0xFFFFFF;
    errorLog_lb.selectionColor = 0xFFFFFF;
    errorLog_lb.dataProvider = errors;
  } else {
    gotoAndStop ("Confirm");
  }
}
```

In Step 2, we created a validation function to check the data entered into the **name_ti** instance. As we progress through this lesson, we'll create several more validation functions to validate the data entered into our other TextInput instances. The function created in this step—`validateForm()`—is really the mother of all these other functions; eventually it will be used to call all the individual validation functions and then finalize the validation process, including outputting error messages to the **errorLog_lb** List component instance. Take special note of the sequence of actions in this function: this flow plays an important role in how the function works.

The first two actions in this function clear the **errorLog_lb** instance of any displayed errors as well as any messages that may exist in the `errors` array. Obviously, the first time the form is validated, these actions are worthless because both begin empty. Any subsequent validation of the entered data will require that the **errorLog_lb** instance begin the validation process empty of any displayed items, and that any error messages in the `errors` array be erased.

The next line contains a function call to the `validateName()` function we defined in Step 2. This will cause that function to execute and validate the data in the **name_ti** instance. As a result, an error message is pushed into the `errors` array if data is invalid.

NOTE *We will add more function calls as we define them in the following exercises.*

The next action in this function is an `if` statement, which is evaluated only after the `validateName()` function has completed its job. This is where the sequence of actions becomes important. If an error message is pushed into the `errors` array as a result of calling the `validateName()` function, the `length` property of the `errors` array is changed to 1, indicating that it contains at least one error message. This `if` statement then looks at the `length` property of the `errors` array and acts accordingly. If the `length` property has a value greater than 0 (indicating error messages within the array), the resulting actions output those messages to the **errorLog_lb** List component instance. If `errors.length` is 0, this means there are no error messages and the data is valid; therefore, a `gotoAndStop()` action sends the timeline to the frame labeled Confirm.

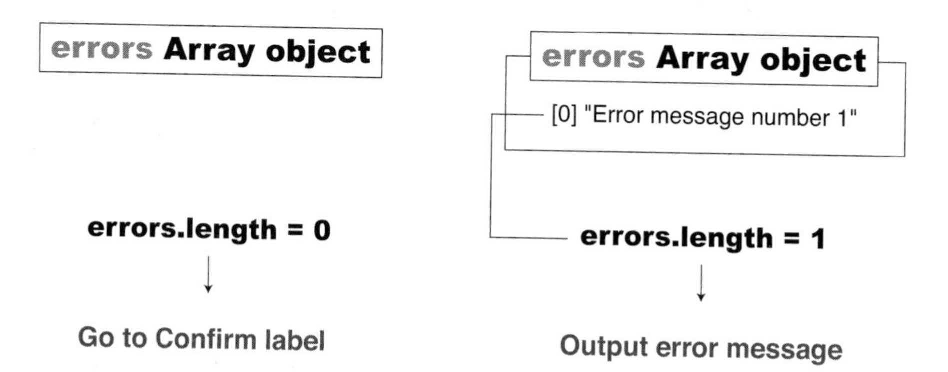

The actions used to output the error messages are fairly straightforward. The first action sets the `defaultIcon` property of the **errorLog_lb** instance. The value of this property is the identifier name of a movie clip in the library that will appear next to every item shown in the list. We've set the value of this property to `"errorIcon"`. This is the identifier name of a movie clip in the library that looks like a round circle with an *X* in the middle.

Linkage Properties
Identifier: errorIcon
AS 2.0 Class:
Linkage: Export for ActionScript
Export for runtime sharing
Import for runtime sharing
Export in first frame
URL:
OK
Cancel

Please enter a valid name.
@ missing in email or in the wrong place.
. missing in email or in the wrong place.
Email address not long enough.
Please enter a valid state.

The next two lines of script set the `alternatingRowColors` property of the **errorLog_lb** instance. As explained in Step 3 of the preceding exercise, an array is created that holds two or more color values (in this case, `altColorArray`). That array is then set as the `alternatingRowColors` property of the **errorLog_lb** instance. As a result, the rows in that instance will alternate between the colors listed in the `altColorArray` array.

The next two lines of the script set the color values used when items in the **errorLog_lb** instance are rolled over or selected.

Finally, the last line sets the `dataProvider` property of the **errorLog_lb** instance. As you can see, we've set the `errors` array as the value of this property. As a result, any error messages contained in that array will show up as individual items in the list.

4) With the Actions panel still open, add the following script at the end of the current script:

```
submit_pb.addEventListener("click", validateForm);
```

This script calls the `validateForm()` function when the **submit_pb** instance is clicked, causing the actions within that function to be executed when the button is released.

5) Choose Control > Test Movie to test the project up to this point.

Enter an invalid name into the **name_ti** instance to see what the validation process turns up. Click the Clear button to reset the scene's visual and data elements.

6) Close the test movie to return to the authoring environment, and save this file as *validate3.fla*.

We'll build on this file in the following exercise.

VALIDATING SEQUENCES

A *sequence* is a string of characters (letters, numbers, and special characters) placed in a specific order or formatted in a special way. Following are some sample sequences:

- Telephone number (xxx-xxxx)
- Credit card number (xxxx xxxx xxxx xxxx)
- Date (xx/xx/xxxx)
- URL (http://www.xxxxxx.xxx)

Although the characters within sequences may change, they must still follow certain formatting rules. Sequence validation is typically a bit more involved than other types of data validation primarily because there are numerous validation points to check. By breaking down the process, you can more readily understand how it works. The following are some validation points for a typical email address:

1) It cannot contain more than one @ symbol.
2) It must include at least one period (separating the actual domain name from the domain extension, such as in *mydomain.com* or *mydomain.net*).
3) The last period must fall somewhere after the @ symbol, but it can't be either of the last two characters.
4) The @ symbol cannot be the first or second character.
5) There must be at least two characters between the @ symbol and the first period that precedes it.
6) The email address must include at least eight characters (aa@bb.cc).

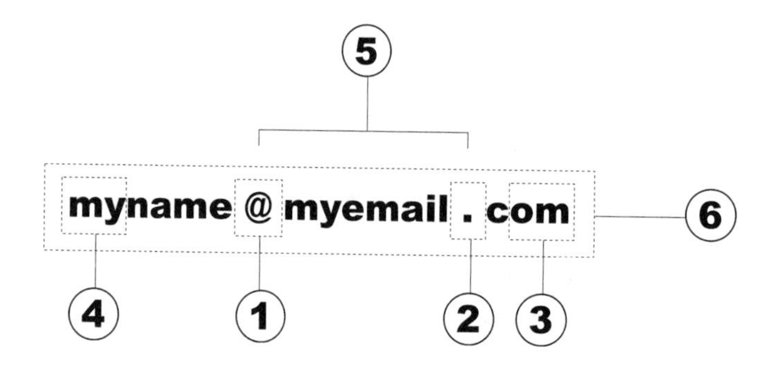

NOTE *If an email address has been checked for the six points listed above, you've performed a reasonable validation. Although we could add many more validation points (for example, characters following the last period must be* com, net, org, *or something similar), your code would become extremely long and you would need to update it frequently to keep pace with changing Internet standards. It's crucial to determine the most important validation points and check for them.*

In this exercise, we'll check only the following three validation points for text entered into the **email_ti** instance of our registration form:

- The @ symbol must be included somewhere after the second character.
- The email address must include a period at least two characters after the @ symbol.
- The email address must consist of at least eight characters.

TIP *Be sure to provide users with clear instructions about how to format data. It's common practice to provide an example of correctly formatted data either above or below the text box where it's to be entered, providing a quick reference for the user.*

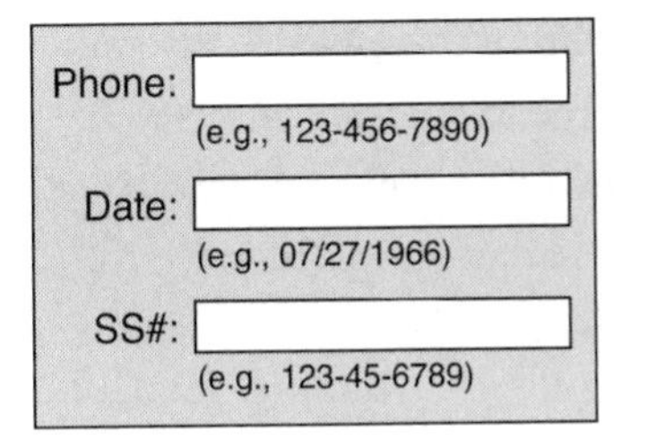

1) Open *validate3.fla*.

We will continue building on the project from the last exercise.

2) With the Actions panel open, select Frame 1 on the Actions layer and add the following function definition at the end of the current script:

```
function validateEmail() {
  if (email_ti.text.indexOf("@") < 2) {
    errors.push("@ missing in email or in the wrong place.");
    email_ti.setStyle("color", 0x990000);
  }
  if (email_ti.text.lastIndexOf(".") <= (email_ti.text.indexOf("@") + 2)) {
    errors.push(". missing in email or in the wrong place.");
    email_ti.setStyle("color", 0x990000);
  }
  if (email_ti.text.length < 8) {
    errors.push("Email address not long enough.");
    email_ti.setStyle("color", 0x990000);
  }
}
```

The `validateEmail()`function validates the text entered into the **email_ti** instance and is made up of three conditional statements, each of which checks one of the individual validation points we outlined at the beginning of this exercise. Because these are separate `if` statements, rather than `if/else`, `if/else if` groupings, all of them will be evaluated. Let's look at each one in depth. The first statement reads as follows:

```
if (email_ti.text.indexOf("@") < 2) {
  errors.push("@ missing in email or in the wrong place.");
  email_ti.setStyle("color", 0x990000);
}
```

You'll remember from Lesson 4, "Using Object Classes," that the `indexOf()` method returns the position (character number) where the value in the parentheses is first found in a string. Using this method, the statement above determines whether the first @ symbol appears before the third character in the **email_ti** instance. Because the first character in a string has an index number of 0, this statement evaluates to `true` and an error message is pushed into the `errors` array if the @ symbol is found at position 0 or 1. If the @ symbol doesn't occur anywhere within the **email_ti** instance, this statement returns a value of -1, which is still less than 2; this result causes the statement to evaluate to `true` and the error message to be pushed into the array. In addition to an error message being pushed into the errors array whenever this error occurs, the text in the **email_ti** is styled as red, which is helpful for emphasizing the location of the error.

TIP *Using the `indexOf()` method, you can also check for the existence of strings longer than one character. For example, you can check for `http://` in a string by using something similar to the following syntax: `string.indexOf("http://")`. The number returned is the character number of the first letter in the string.*

Let's look at the second statement in this function, which reads as follows:

```
if (email_ti.text.lastIndexOf(".") <= (email_ti.text.indexOf("@") + 2)) {
  errors.push(". missing in email or in the wrong place.");
  email_ti.setStyle("color", 0x990000);
}
```

This statement uses the `lastIndexOf()` method—similar to the `indexOf()` method except that it returns the character number of the last occurrence of the character in the parentheses. The following example returns 28:

```
email_ti.text = "derek.franklin@derekfranklin.com",
⇒email_ti.text.lastIndexOf(".")
```

Using this method, the statement looks at the position of the last period in relation to the @ symbol. If the period is less than two characters to the right of the @ symbol, this statement proves `true` and an error message is pushed into the `errors` array. Again, if this error occurs, the text in the **email_ti** instance is styled in red, indicating the location of the error.

m	y	e	m	a	i	l	@	d	.	c	o	m
0	1	2	3	4	5	6	7	8	9	10	11	12

```
if (email.text.lastIndexOf(".") <= (email.text.indexOf("@")+2))
```

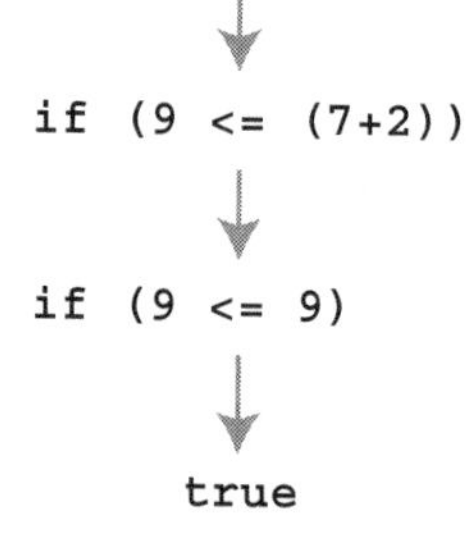

The third statement in this function is the easiest one to comprehend. It reads as follows:

```
if (email_ti.text.length < 8) {
    errors.push("Email address not long enough.");
    email_ti.setStyle("color", 0x990000);
}
```

As mentioned earlier in this lesson, the smallest reasonable email address is *aa@bb.cc*—eight characters, including the @ symbol and the period. If the `length` of the text entered into the **email_ti** instance is fewer than eight characters, an error message stating the email address is too short is pushed into the `error` array and the text in the **email_ti** instance is styled as red.

After all of these statements have been evaluated, you may find that the information entered into the **email_ti** instance is invalid on all counts. In this case, three different error messages would be pushed into the `errors` array.

3) Add the following function call just below the `validateName()` function call in the `validateForm()` function definition:

```
validateEmail();
```

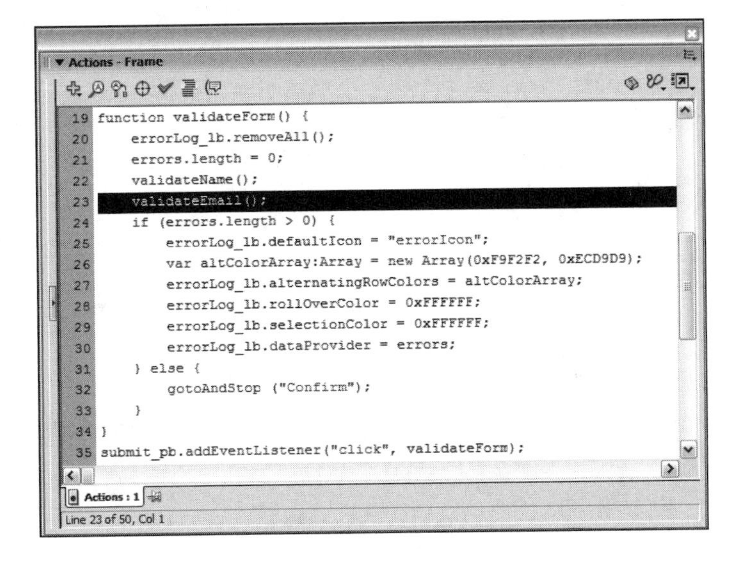

This is a call to the function we just defined. Placing this function call here adds email validation capability to the main `validateForm()` function. This function call is placed just above the statement that checks the length of the `errors` array because the `validateEmail()` function is able to push error messages into the array, thus affecting its length and the way the statement is evaluated. In the end, if either the `validateName()` or `validateEmail()` function finds errors, the corresponding messages will be displayed in the **errorLog_lb** instance.

NOTE *The Submit button in our scene already calls the* `validateForm()` *function when clicked; therefore, any new functionality we add to that function (as we have just done) is automatically executed when the button is released.*

4) Choose Control > Test Movie to test the project up to this point.

Enter an invalid email address into the **email_ti** instance or an invalid name into the **name_ti** instance to see what the validation process turns up. Clicking the Clear button resets the visual and data elements in the scene.

5) Close the test movie to return to the authoring environment, and save this file as *validate4.fla*.

We will build on this file in the following exercise.

VALIDATING AGAINST A LIST OF CHOICES

There are times when a value entered into a form must match one of several choices. For example, if a form asks the user to enter a specific color—red, yellow, or blue—and the user accidentally enters *rod* or *yullow* instead, it's important to be able to detect that error when validating the form.

If you're going to compare data entered against a list of choices, obviously you must define that list first. In ActionScript, an array can include a list of choices. The validation process is simply a matter of comparing the entered data against the values in the array to see if there's a match.

In this exercise, we'll create another validation routine—this one to compare what's entered in the **state_ti** instance against an array of state names.

TIP *It's best to have users do as little manual data entry as possible. Instead of requiring the user to input data that matches one of several choices, you would be better off providing a drop-down list from which the user could choose a value—a method that eliminates the need for data validation. In some applications, however, this is impossible—for example, in a quiz application that contains a list of answers you don't want users to be able to access. In such cases, there's no way to avoid manual validation.*

Method 1

State: Indianer

Method 2

State: Indiana
Illinois
Kentucky

1) Open *validate4.fla*.

We will continue building on the project from the last exercise.

2) With the Actions panel open, select Frame 1 on the Actions layer and add the following function definition at the end of the current script:

```
function validateState() {
  var states:Array = ["California", "Indiana", "North Carolina", "Oklahoma"];
  var matchFound:Boolean = false;
  for (var i = 0; i <= states.length; ++i) {
    if (state_ti.text == states[i]) {
      matchFound = true;
      break;
    }
  }
  if (!matchFound) {
    errors.push("Please enter a valid state.");
    state_ti.setStyle("color", 0x990000);
  }
}
```

The `validateState()` function validates the data entered into the **state_ti** instance.

The first action in this function creates an array named `states`, which will hold all of the possible choices. To keep this as short as possible, we've included only four state names, although you could easily add all 50.

The next action creates a variable named `matchFound` and assigns it an initial value of `false`. The importance of this variable will become evident in a moment.

The next several lines in this function are part of a looping statement, which is used to loop through all the values in the `states` array, comparing each to the value entered in the **state_ti** instance. If a match is found, `matchFound` is set to `true`. If no match is found, the value of this variable remains `false` (its initial state), indicating an error.

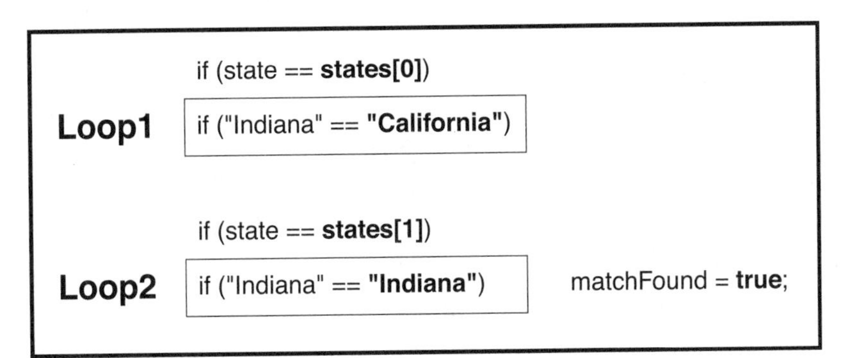

The last part of the function contains an `if` statement that's executed after the looping statement has completed its job. It says that if `matchFound` is `false` (which it will be if no match is found), an appropriate error message should be pushed into the `errors` array and the **state_ti** instance's text should be styled as red (as in the other functions we've created thus far).

3) Add the following function call just below the `validateEmail()` function call in the `validateForm()` function definition:

```
validateState();
```

This is a call to the `validateState()` function we just defined. Placing this function call here adds state-name validation capability to the main `validateForm()` function. This function call is placed just above the conditional statement that checks the `length` of the `errors` array because that function is able to push error messages into the array, thus affecting its length and the way the statement is evaluated. In the end, if `validateName()`, `validateEmail()`, or `validateState()` finds errors, the corresponding messages will be displayed in the **errorLog_lb** List component instance.

4) Choose Control > Test Movie to test your project thus far.

Enter an invalid state name (anything other than the four state names in the array) into the **state_ti** instance to see what the validation process turns up. Click the Clear button to reset the visual and data elements in the scene.

5) Close the test movie to return to the authoring environment, and save this file as *validate5.fla*.

We will build on this file in the following exercise.

VALIDATING NUMBERS

Validating numbers is not much different from validating strings, which we've already discussed.

In this exercise, we'll create one last validation function to validate the data entered into the **zip_ti** instance. To be a valid five-digit zip code, the entered data must meet the following two requirements:

- **Length.** The data must include exactly five characters.
- **Type.** The data must contain numbers; text is invalid.

TIP *When validating numbers, you may need to call for the number entered to be more or less in value than another number—which by now you should be able to do easily!*

1) Open *validate5.fla*.

We will continue building on the project from the last exercise.

2) With the Actions panel open, select Frame 1 on the Actions layer and add the following function definition at the end of the current script:

```
function validateZip() {
  if (zip_ti.text.length != 5 || isNaN(zip_ti.text) == true) {
    errors.push("Please enter a valid zip.");
    zip_ti.setStyle("color", 0x990000);
  }
}
```

When called, this function checks that the data entered into the **zip_ti** instance meets two conditions regarding length and type—the validation points we defined at the beginning of this exercise. The conditional statement here states that if the **zip_ti** instance does not contain five characters, or if it consists of text (rather than numbers), the text in the **zip_ti** instance should be styled as red and the following text string should be pushed into the `errors` array: "Please enter a valid zip."

NOTE *If you need to refresh your understanding of* `isNaN()`*, review the information in the "Validating Strings" exercise earlier in this lesson.*

3) Add the following function call just below the `validateState()` **function call in the** `validateForm()` **function:**

```
validateZip();
```

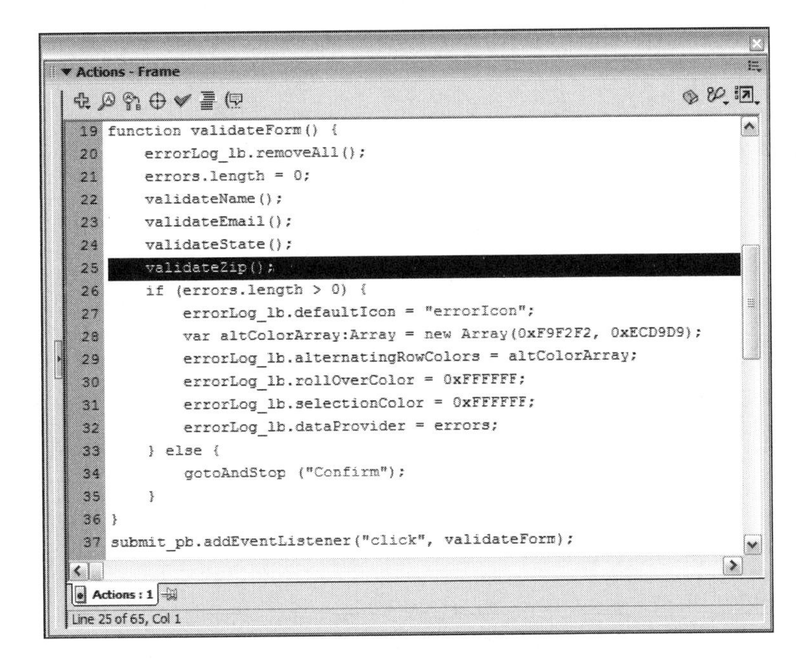

This is a call to the function we just defined. Placing this function call here adds zip code validation capability to the main `validateForm()` function. This function call is placed just above the statement that checks the length of the `errors` array because that function is able to push error messages into the array, thus affecting its length and the way this statement is evaluated. In the end, if `validateName()`, `validateEmail()`, `validateState()`, or `validateZip()` finds errors, the corresponding messages will be displayed in the **errorLog_lb** instance.

4) Choose Control > Test Movie to test the project up to this point.

Enter an invalid zip code in the **zip_ti** instance to see what the validation process turns up. Clicking the Clear button resets the visual and data elements in the scene.

As you've probably noticed when testing the application, the text in the TextInput instances remains red from the point at which an error is found in a particular instance until the application is shut down or moves to the Confirm label as the result of an error-free form submission. In addition, the `haloGreen` color used by the components just doesn't suit our design.

In the next couple of steps, we'll add some cosmetic improvements to our application so that a TextInput instance that contains red text (as the result of an error found there) is updated to contain black text whenever the user subsequently clicks inside the text box. We'll also change the theme color of components to a light blue.

5) Close the test movie to return to the authoring environment. With the Actions panel open, select Frame 1 of the Actions layer and add the following script:

```
function resetColor(eventObj:Object){
  eventObj.target.setStyle("color", 0x000000);
}
name_ti.addEventListener("focusIn", resetColor);
email_ti.addEventListener("focusIn", resetColor);
state_ti.addEventListener("focusIn", resetColor);
zip_ti.addEventListener("focusIn", resetColor);
```

The first part of the script contains a function named `resetColor()`. The remaining lines set up the TextInput instances in our application to call the `resetColor()` function when any of the text boxes is given focus.

As you learned in Lesson 10, "Scripting UI Components," when a function is called as the result of being registered as an event listener, the function is passed an Event object containing two properties: `target` and `type`. The `target` property identifies the target path of the component instance that calls the function. As a result of this script, when the user clicks in the **email_ti** instance, it is given focus and the `resetColor()` function is called. The single action inside the function uses the `target` property of the Event object (which in this case would have a value of _level0.email_ti) to reference the component instance that calls the function, and the setStyle() method to set that instance's text color to black.

6) Add the following script at the end of the current script:

```
_global.style.setStyle("themeColor", 0xBDDDEB);
```

This sets the overall theme color of all component instances in our application to light blue.

7) Choose Control > Test Movie to test our cosmetic improvements to the project.

As you interact with the interface, you'll see how the last two scripts we added improve the overall look of our application.

8) Close the test movie to return to the authoring environment, and save this file as *validate6.fla*.

We'll build on this file in the following exercise.

PROCESSING VALIDATED DATA

The last task for our application is to send all the validated data to a server for processing. We'll use a LoadVars object to accomplish this goal.

1) Open *validate6.fla*.

We'll continue building on the project from the preceding exercise.

2) With the Actions panel open, select Frame 1 of the Actions layer and add the following script at the top of the current script, just below the stop() action:

```
var registrationData:LoadVars = new LoadVars();
```

This creates a new LoadVars object named registrationData. In the next step we will add a script that places our validated data into this object and sends it to the server.

3) Add the following script to the else leg of the validateForm() function:

```
registrationData.name = name_ti.text;
registrationData.email = email_ti.text;
registrationData.state = state_ti.text;
registrationData.zip = zip_ti.text;
registrationData.sendAndLoad("http://www.myDomain.com/registration.php",
⇒registrationData, "POST");
```

When all the data entered into the form is valid, the actions in the `else` part of the `validateForm()` function—including this section of script—are executed.

The first four lines of the script place the data in the various TextInput instances into the `registrationData` object. The last line sends this data to a server-side script.

NOTE *For the last line of script, you should insert the URL to a script on your server for processing the data. Or, if you simply want to do a final test of your code, use this URL:* http://www.derekfranklin.com/cftemplates/notsosoft.cfm. *The ColdFusion page at this URL will send you email containing the validated data.*

The `else` part of this script already had an action that would send the application to the Confirm label automatically when all the data entered was valid. Because the application is now set up to send data to a server, let's change this functionality a bit so that the application only moves to that frame label after a response has been received from the server, indicating that the submitted data has been received and processed.

4) Remove the line of script in the `else` leg of the `validateForm()` function that reads `gotoAndStop("Confirm")` and insert the following script just above the `sendAndLoad()` method call:

```
registrationData.onLoad = function(){
  gotoAndStop("Confirm");
}
```

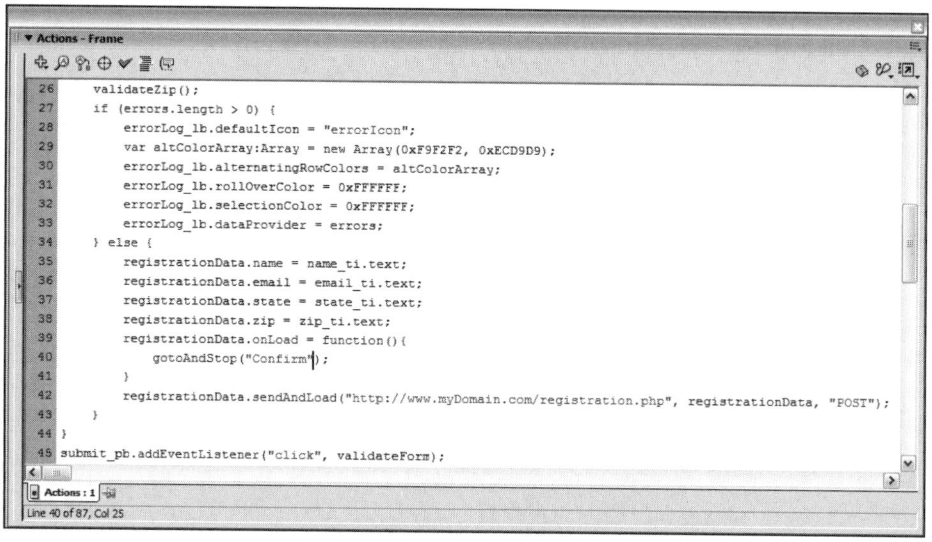

```
Actions - Frame
26      validateZip();
27      if (errors.length > 0) {
28          errorLog_lb.defaultIcon = "errorIcon";
29          var altColorArray:Array = new Array(0xF9F2F2, 0xECD9D9);
30          errorLog_lb.alternatingRowColors = altColorArray;
31          errorLog_lb.rollOverColor = 0xFFFFFF;
32          errorLog_lb.selectionColor = 0xFFFFFF;
33          errorLog_lb.dataProvider = errors;
34      } else {
35          registrationData.name = name_ti.text;
36          registrationData.email = email_ti.text;
37          registrationData.state = state_ti.text;
38          registrationData.zip = zip_ti.text;
39          registrationData.onLoad = function(){
40              gotoAndStop("Confirm");
41          }
42          registrationData.sendAndLoad("http://www.myDomain.com/registration.php", registrationData, "POST");
43      }
44  }
45  submit_pb.addEventListener("click", validateForm);
Actions : 1
Line 40 of 87, Col 25
```

This script will move the application to the Confirm label when a server response has been sent back to the `registrationData` object. Let's do one final test.

NOTE *Before testing, make sure that the URL specified in the* `sendAndLoad()` *method discussed in Step 3 contains a server-side script for handling the incoming data.*

5) Choose Control > Test Movie.

If you enter valid data into the form fields and click the Submit button, the application should send the data to the specified server-side script for processing, and eventually move the application's timeline to the Confirm label after a response has been received from the server.

6) Close the test movie to return to the authoring environment, and save this file as *validate7.fla*.

This step completes the exercise and this lesson. The great thing about the way we've set up this project's validation process is that it's dynamic. To analyze additional rules or validation points for any of the text fields, all you have to do is add more conditional statements to the appropriate function. The validation process can grow as your needs grow.

WHAT YOU HAVE LEARNED

In this lesson, you have:

- Learned why validation is important (pages 444–446)
- Defined validation requirements and used them to create conditional statements (pages 447–449)
- Set up a mechanism to handle errors detected in the validation process (pages 449–452)
- Created several functions for validating strings, sequences, and numbers (pages 452–467)
- Sent data from a validated form to a server for processing (pages 467–469)

working with text fields

LESSON 14

Although it's best known for animated and interactive content, Flash also provides a number of powerful capabilities for working with text. This is important because most of us learn and are informed by means of text-based content.

Flash allows you dynamically create text fields, set their various properties using ActionScript, and load and style the content within them. This gives you extensive control over the text content in your movie. In this lesson, we'll explore most of Flash's text capabilities.

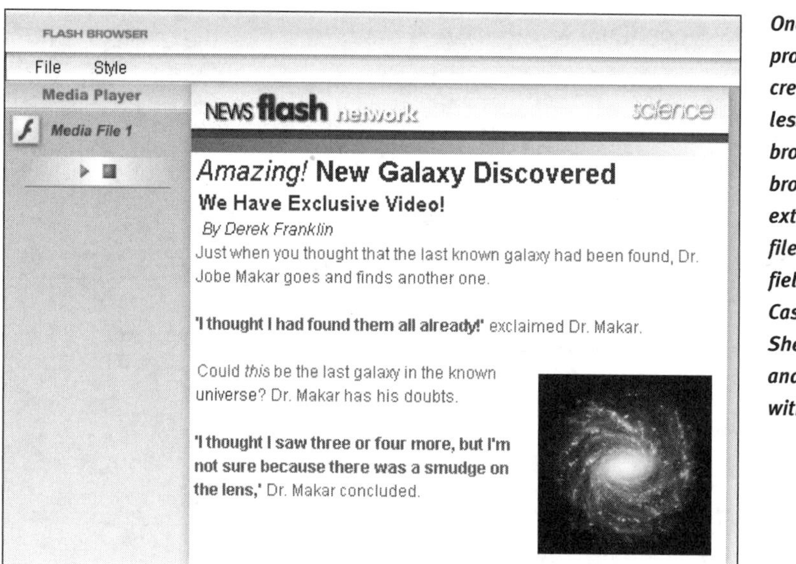

One of the projects you'll create in this lesson is a Flash browser. This browser loads external HTML files into a text field and uses Cascading Style Sheets to format and style the text within the field.

WHAT YOU WILL LEARN

In this lesson, you will:

- Create text fields dynamically
- Format text using TextFormat objects
- Use the MenuBar component to add a menu to an application
- Use Cascading Style Sheets to easily format text within a text field

APPROXIMATE TIME

This lesson takes approximately two hours to complete.

LESSON FILES

Media Files:

Lesson14/Media/home.htm
Lesson14/Media/science.htm
Lesson14/Media/header_home.jpg
Lesson14/Media/header_science.jpg
Lesson14/Media/morning.swf
Lesson14/Media/galaxy.swf
Lesson14/Media/external.css

Starting Files:

Lesson14/Assets/flashWriter1.fla
Lesson14/Assets/flashBrowser1.fla

Completed Projects:

flashWriter3.fla
flashBrowser3.fla

DYNAMICALLY CREATING AND CONFIGURING TEXT FIELDS

Although you're presented with a variety of options when creating and configuring text fields in the authoring environment, being able to create text fields on the fly—*while* your movie is running—gives you even greater control over the way your project handles text. Let's take a look at the dynamic creation process.

To create a text field using ActionScript, you use the `createTextField()` method, as follows:

```
createTextField(instanceName, depth, x, y, width, height);
```

Now note the following example, which uses the `createTextField()` method to create a text field:

```
createTextField("myField_txt", 10, 20, 50, 200, 30);
```

This script creates a text field named **myField_txt**, with its initial `depth`, `x`, `y`, `width`, and `height` properties set as shown.

Every text field, whether placed on the stage while authoring the movie or created dynamically, is considered an instance of the TextField class. As such, text fields can be treated in several ways similarly to movie clip instances. Individual text fields are given instance names from the Property Inspector (or when created dynamically, as shown in the preceding code). When targeting a text field instance with a script, you use its target path, which includes its instance name.

You may not be able to tell by looking at the Actions toolbox in the Actions panel, but several methods—similar to Movie Clip object methods—are available to text field instances. For example, this script makes the **myField_txt** text field draggable:

```
startDrag("myField_txt", true);
```

Unlike movie clips, text fields are not timelines; therefore, certain methods such as `prevFrame()`, `attachMovie()`, `loadMovie()`, and so on have no meaning when used in the context of a text field instance.

Text field instances have several properties similar to those of movie clips. For example,

```
myField_txt._alpha = 50;
```

makes the **myField_txt** text field 50 percent transparent. With a little bit of experimentation, you'll be able to see which methods and properties are shared by movie clip and text field instances.

In addition to the properties and methods discussed thus far, text fields have numerous unique methods and properties for manipulating and controlling text *within* the text field (rather than the text field itself, as previously discussed). Several of these methods are employed to format text-field text using TextFormat and Cascading Style Sheet (CSS) objects—we'll save our discussion of those for the later sections of this lesson. In the meantime, let's look at a couple of useful methods that *don't* pertain to formatting.

To remove a text field instance that was created dynamically, use the `removeTextField()` method in the following manner:

```
myField_txt.removeTextField();
```

This script removes the text field named **myField_txt**.

NOTE *Only text fields created dynamically can be removed using this method. Text fields placed on the stage while authoring your movie cannot be removed in this way.*

Two of the most common actions you can perform in conjunction with text fields are adding and deleting text—both of which can use the `replaceSel()` method. You can invoke this method to replace the currently selected text with anything you define.

In the following example, assume that the **myField_txt** text field contains the text, "I love my dog and cat very much!" Then assume that the "dog and cat" portion of the text has been selected. You can use the `replaceSel()` method, as shown in the following code, to replace that text:

```
myField_txt.replaceSel("bird and snake");
```

The **myField_txt** text field now reads, "I love my bird and snake very much!"

The value placed within the `replaceSel()` method when it's invoked can be a string of text, an empty string (`""`), or even a variable.

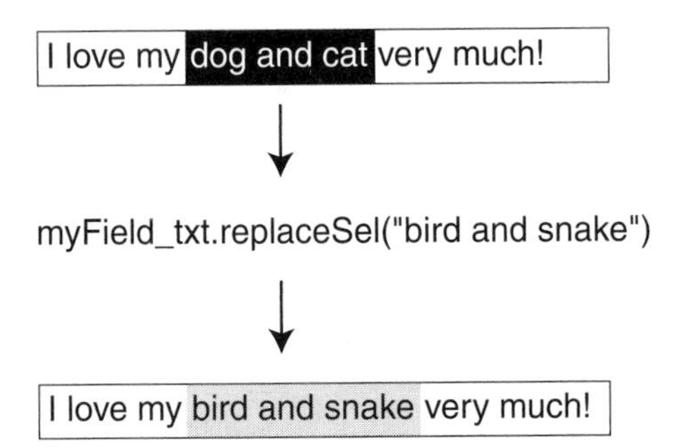

As mentioned earlier in this lesson, text fields have numerous properties that you can configure using ActionScript while the movie is playing. These properties affect not only the way the field looks and reacts to text, but how it functions. Some of these properties are familiar because we've already used and discussed them; others don't warrant much discussion because they do the same thing as the corresponding properties that you set with the Property Inspector when creating a text field in the authoring environment. For example, consider the `selectable` property. You would use the following syntax to make the text in the **myField_txt** text field instance selectable:

```
myField_txt.selectable = true;
```

Now let's review some of the less obvious properties of text field instances:

- `autoSize`. This property determines whether a text field expands and contracts its borders automatically to accommodate the amount of text it contains. A text field's width and height are normally set using static (unchanging) values. The `AutoSize` property allows a text field's size to be dynamic—that is, determined by the text that's typed into it.
- `borderColor`. This property represents the color of the border around a text field. You can set it using a hex value:

  ```
  myField_txt.borderColor = 0x336699;
  ```

  Setting the border color has no visible effect unless the border itself is visible:

  ```
  myField_txt.border = true;
  ```

  The same logic applies to the `background` and `backgroundColor` properties.
- `bottomScroll`. This read-only property represents the line number of the bottom-most visible line of text in a text field.

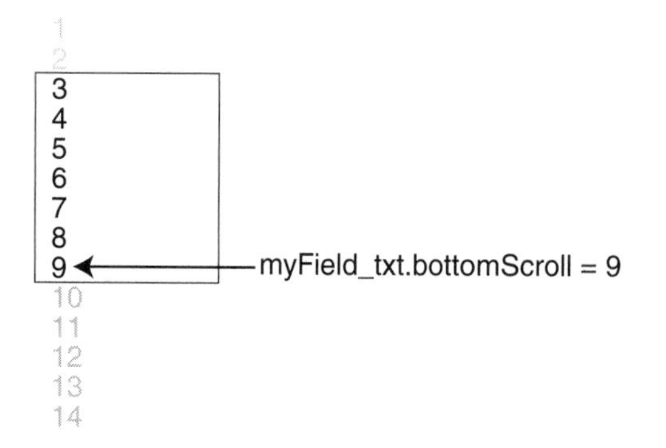

- `hscroll`. This property is a numeric value representing in points the current horizontal scrolling position. If the `hscroll` property of a text field is set to anything greater than 0, all the text is shifted to the left. With a setting of 10, for example, the text is left-shifted by 10 points. This property cannot be set to a value higher than the `maxhscroll` property value for the same field and is only useful if word wrapping is disabled in the text field, thus requiring horizontal scrolling to see text that exists beyond the right boundary of the field.

- `maxhscroll`. This read-only property represents the maximum amount that text can be scrolled horizontally.

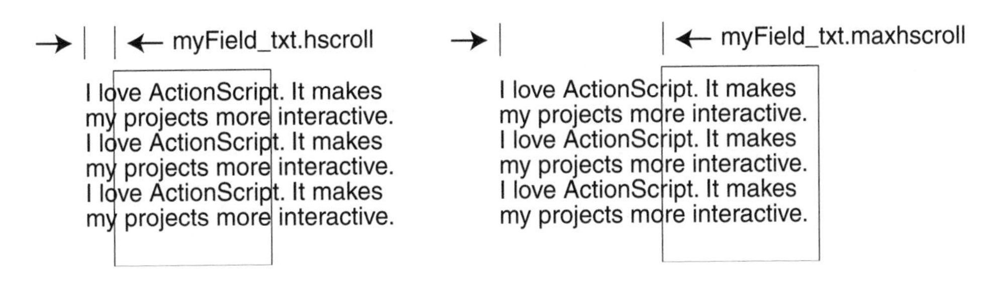

- `maxscroll`. This read-only property represents the highest line number to which text can be scrolled vertically in a field. To understand this property better, imagine that a particular text field contains 14 lines of text, but can display only 7 lines at a time. Because you don't want the user to be able to scroll beyond line 14, you would set the `maxscroll` property value to 8—a value that can change if lines are added.

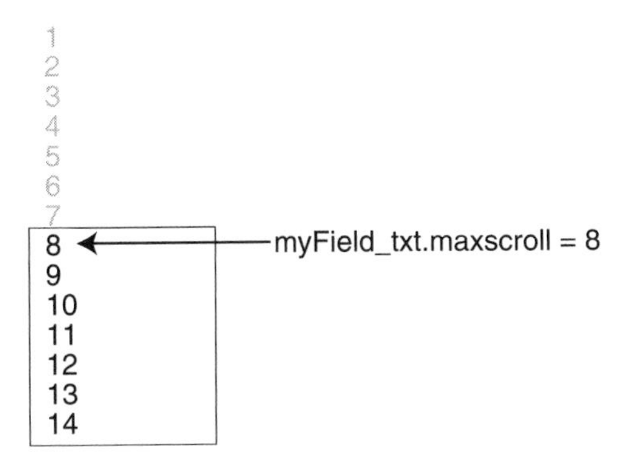

- `restrict`. This property determines which characters can be entered into the field. A value of `null` or `""` indicates that any character can be entered into the field:

  ```
  myfield_txt.restrict = null;
  ```

  A specified string of text means that only characters included in that string can be entered into the field:

  ```
  myField_txt.restrict = "meatloaf";
  ```

  A range of characters can be indicated using a hyphen:

  ```
  myField_txt.restrict = "A-Z 0-9 a-z";
  ```

Using the caret symbol (^), you can specify a range of characters to accept, with exceptions. For example:

```
myField_txt.restrict = "0-9^567";
```

This range allows 0, 1, 2, 3, 4, 8, and 9, but not 5, 6, or 7. To include all characters with some exceptions, use the caret in the following manner:

```
myField_txt.restrict = "^bug";
```

In this example, all characters except *b*, *u*, and *g* are allowed. The `restrict` property applies only to text entered by the user; ActionScript can place any text in the field regardless of this property's setting.

- `scroll`. This property represents the number of the top line displayed in the text field. For example, if you want to scroll the text in a field so that the fourth line is the highest displayed in the field, use the following syntax:

  ```
  myField_txt.scroll = 4;
  ```

  This property's value cannot exceed the `maxscroll` property value for the same field.

- `tabEnabled`. This property determines whether the field is included for selection when using the Tab key to select elements in the scene. A value of `true` or `undefined` includes the field. A value of `false` causes the field to be skipped.

- `tabIndex`. If a field's `tabEnabled` property is set to `true` or `undefined` (allowing the field to be included in tab selecting), the `tabIndex` property value indicates the field's selection position in the process.

- `textHeight`. This read-only property determines the height of text in a field—not the height of the field itself, which can differ from the height of the text.

- `textWidth`. This read-only property represents the width of text in a field—not the width of the field itself.

- `type`. This property determines whether the field is an input or dynamic text field. For example, this script makes **myField_txt** an input text field:

  ```
  myField_txt.type = "input";
  ```

- `variable`. This property represents the name of the variable associated with the text field. As mentioned earlier, associating a variable with a text field causes that variable's value to be displayed in the field. You can change this property at any time to display a different variable's value.

Most of these property values can be set or retrieved for use in other scripts.

When a text field is created, it has the following default property settings:

```
type = "dynamic";
border = false;
background = false;
password = false;
multiline = false;
html = false;
embedFonts = false;
variable = null;
maxChars = null;
```

In the following exercise, we'll dynamically create, configure, and control a couple of text fields as we build an interactive typing application.

1) Open *flashWriter1.fla* in the Lesson14/Assets folder.

This project contains five layers named according to their content. The Background layer contains the scene's graphical content, with the exception of the buttons (named **style1_btn**, **style2_btn**, **style3_btn**, and **style4_btn**) that reside on the Buttons layer. The Components layer contains the **applyToAll_cb** Checkbox component that appears at the upper-left of the stage. The Box layer contains the movie clip instance named **box_mc**, just to the left of the stage; it looks like a transparent white box with a white border. Other than some ActionScript, which will be placed on Frame 1 of the Actions layer, the white box is the only element in the scene used in this exercise. The buttons and Checkbox component will be used and scripted in the next exercise.

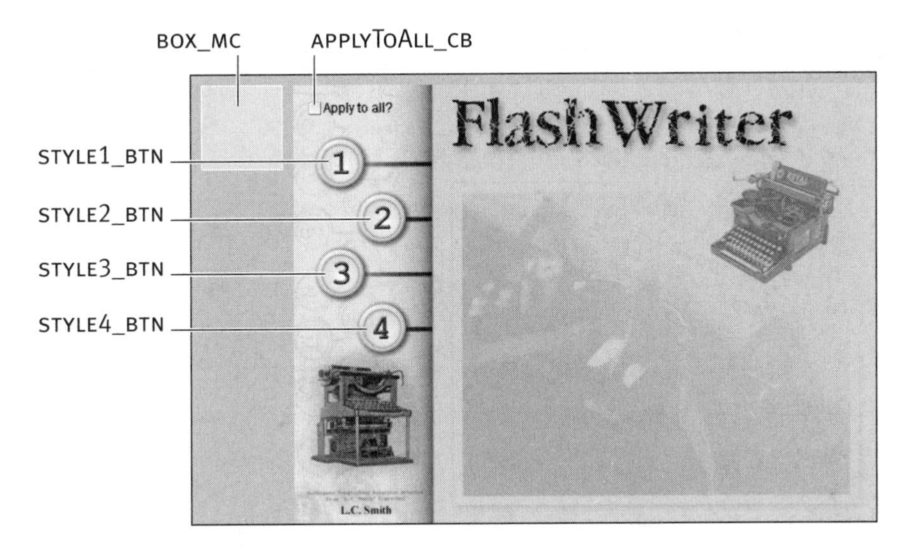

The goal of this exercise is to dynamically create a couple of text fields as the movie plays. One field is larger than the other and is used for entering text. The smaller one is used to keep a running total of the number of characters (including spaces) in the larger field. Both fields move from left to right as text is typed into the larger field. Because transparent backgrounds behind text fields are not inherently possible, the white box (which is semitransparent) mimics the movement and size of the larger text field to act as its background.

2) With the Actions panel open, select Frame 1 of the Actions layer and add the following script:

```
createTextField("movingField_txt", 10, 150, 80, 200, 20);
with (movingField_txt){
  autoSize = true;
  html= true;
  multiline = true;
  text = "Enter text here";
  type = "input";
  wordWrap = true;
}
```

The first line of script creates a text field named **movingField_txt**, placed initially at x/y positions of 150 and 80, respectively, and with a width of 200 and a height of 20. Using a `with` statement that references **movingField_txt**, the initial property settings are configured for this field. Initially, this field (which is set to autosize text as it's entered), displays the text `Enter text here`. Notice that **movingField_txt** has been set up as an input text field and can wrap lines of text. It's the larger of the two text fields that this project contains.

TIP *A `with` statement provides a quick and easy way to address an object (text field, movie clip, and so on) when several lines of script need to reference the object.*

3) Add the following script at the end of the current script:

```
createTextField("statusField_txt", 20, 150, 80, 100, 20);
with (statusField_txt){
  autoSize = true;
  background = true;
  html = true;
  multiline = false;
  selectable = false;
  text = "0";
  type = "dynamic";
  wordWrap = false;
}
```

The first line of script creates a text field named **statusField_txt**, placed initially at x/y positions of 150 and 80, respectively, and with a width of 100 and a height of 20. Using a `with` statement that references the newly created **statusField_txt**, the initial property settings are configured for this field. The field, which is set up to autosize, initially displays the text 0. **statusField_txt** has been set up as a dynamic text field and cannot wrap lines of text. As the smaller of the two text fields, it mimics the larger field's movement. Next, let's script a function for **statusField_txt**.

4) Add the following function definition at the end of the current script:

```
function updateStatus(){
  statusField_txt._x = movingField_txt._x;
  statusField_txt._y = (movingField_txt._y + movingField_txt._height) + 10;
  statusField_txt.text = movingField_txt.length;
}
```

In a moment we'll script the **movingField_txt** to move as text is typed into it.

The `updateStatus()` function accomplishes two things when called: it keeps **statusField_txt** at a specific relative distance from the **movingField_txt** text field as the latter field moves, and updates the text displayed in the **statusField_txt** text field.

The function begins by setting the x position of the **statusField_txt** to match that of **movingField_txt**. The next line places the top of **statusField_txt** (its y position) 10 pixels below **movingField_txt**. It does this by adding the **movingField_txt** y position to its height (which gives us the coordinate of its bottom boundary) and then adding 10 to that result.

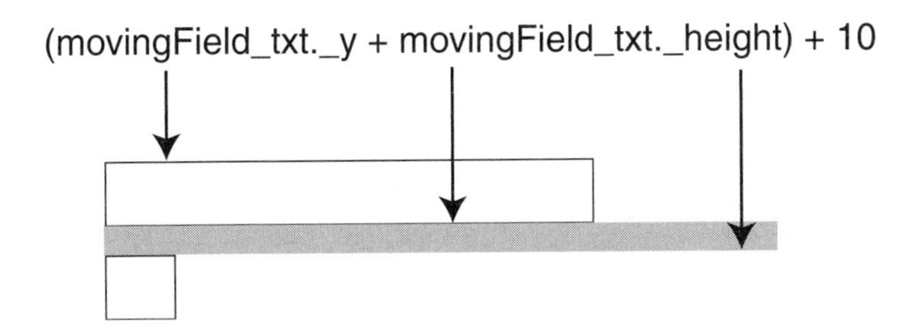
(movingField_txt._y + movingField_txt._height) + 10

The last action updates the text in **statusField_txt** to indicate the number of characters in **movingField_txt**. In a moment, we'll script this function to be called every time text is added to or removed from **movingField_txt**.

5) Add the following function definition at the end of the current script:

```
function reshapeBox(){
  with(box_mc){
    _x = movingField_txt._x;
    _y = movingField_txt._y;
    _width = movingField_txt._width;
    _height = movingField_txt._height;
  }
}
```

When called, this function causes the **box_mc** movie clip instance to mimic the position and size of the **movingField_txt** text field, using familiar actions. As with the function defined in Step 4, we'll soon script this function to be called every time text is added to or removed from **movingField_txt**, making the **box_mc** movie clip instance act as the background for that text field.

6) Add the following function calls at the end of the current script:

```
updateStatus();
reshapeBox();
```

These two lines of script call the functions we just defined so that the **statusField_txt** text field and the **box_mc** movie clip instance can be configured (as defined in the function definitions) as soon as the movie begins to play. These same functions will eventually be scripted to be called repeatedly.

7) Add the following script at the end of the current script:

```
movingField_txt.onChanged = function(){
  movingField_txt._x += 4;
  if (movingField_txt._x + movingField_txt._width > 500){
    movingField_txt._x = 150;
  }
  reshapeBox();
  updateStatus();
}
```

This section of script uses the `onChanged` event handler method (available to text field instances) to deal with what happens each time text is added to or removed from the **movingField_txt** text field.

The function first moves **movingField_txt** four pixels from its current position, causing the text field to move to the right each time a character is added to or deleted from the field. The `if` statement prevents the field from moving off the stage when it moves to the right. It does this by comparing the right side of the field's position (achieved by adding the x position to the width of the field) with the value `500`—the farthest right we want to allow the field to move. If the right side of the field exceeds this amount, the field is set back to its starting x position of `150`.

The last two lines call the functions we defined earlier, updating the **statusField_txt** text field and **box_mc** movie clip instance immediately each time text is added to or removed from the **movingField_txt** text field.

8) Choose Control > Test Movie to view the project up to this point.

As soon as the movie begins to play, two text fields are created and their properties set. The **statusField_txt** text field appears below the **movingField_txt** text field, and the **box_mc** movie clip instance has the same position and size as the **movingField_txt** text field. As text is typed into the **movingField_txt** text field, it moves to the right; **statusField_txt** follows the movement of **movingField_txt**, but displaying the current number of characters in the **movingField_txt** text field. After **movingField_txt** moves too far to the right, it's moved back to its original position.

9) Close the test movie and save your work as *flashWriter2.fla*.

We'll continue building on this file in the next exercise.

As you've seen, creating and controlling text fields dynamically is a straightforward process that enables you to add a new dimension of interactivity to your projects.

USING TEXTFORMAT OBJECTS

Using HTML tags in strings of text (as in Lesson 12, "Using XML with Flash") is not the only way to style text dynamically: *TextFormat objects* provide all the formatting power of HTML—and more!

As nothing more than special objects containing formatting properties for character and paragraph styles, TextFormat objects offer functionality similar to that of Cascading Style Sheets (CSS). After a TextFormat object has been defined, that object is then "applied" to a text field or section of text in a field, causing the affected text to take on the formatting style described by the object. A TextFormat object can be created and defined in one of two ways. Look at the following syntax:

```
var myStyle:TextFormat = new TextFormat(nameOfFont, size, color, bold, italic);
```

In this syntax, a TextFormat object is created and its formatting settings configured simultaneously. Here's an example:

```
var myStyle:TextFormat = new TextFormat("Arial", 12, 0x336699, true, true);
```

TIP *You can configure many additional formatting settings by using the constructor function.*

The preceding syntax creates a TextFormat object named `myStyle`. This object represents a format that uses the Arial font at a point size of 12, using the color blue, and in bold italic. If you create the same TextFormat object using the alternative syntax, here's how it would look:

```
var myStyle:TextFormat = new TextFormat();
with(myStyle){
  font = "Arial";
  size = 12;
  color = 0x336699;
  bold = true;
  italic = true;
}
```

The preceding syntax uses a `with` statement to configure various formatting properties of the newly created object. Either way works, but the latter syntax is generally easier to read and use.

After you've created a TextFormat object, you can apply it to all or just a portion of the current text in the field, or to any new text entered into the field.

To apply a TextFormat object to all the text in a text field, use the following syntax:

```
myField_txt.setTextFormat(myStyle);
```

This script causes all text in the **myField_txt** text field to be displayed in the formatting style described by the `myStyle` TextFormat object. If the text had previously been styled using a different TextFormat object, that style is overwritten with the newly applied style.

To apply a TextFormat object to a single character in a text field, use the following syntax:

```
myField_txt.setTextFormat(27, myStyle);
```

This script causes the character at index position 27 to take on the style defined by the `myStyle` TextFormat object.

To style a range of characters in a field, use the following syntax:

```
myField_txt.setTextFormat(27, 50, myStyle);
```

This script causes the characters between index positions 27 and 50 to take on the formatting style described by the `mySty1e` TextFormat object.

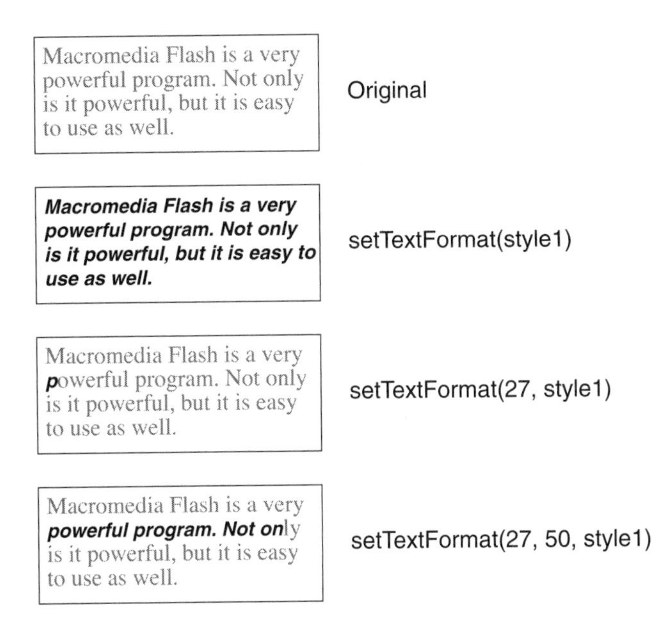
Macromedia Flash is a very powerful program. Not only is it powerful, but it is easy to use as well.
Original
Macromedia Flash is a very powerful program. Not only is it powerful, but it is easy to use as well.
setTextFormat(style1)
Macromedia Flash is a very powerful program. Not only is it powerful, but it is easy to use as well.
setTextFormat(27, style1)
Macromedia Flash is a very powerful program. Not only is it powerful, but it is easy to use as well.
setTextFormat(27, 50, style1)

If you want the *current* text in the field to maintain its formatting while styling any *new* text entered into the field, use the `setNewTextFormat()` method. Look at the following syntax:

```
myField_txt.setNewTextFormat(myStyle);
```

Using this script, nothing in the **myField_txt** text field changes initially; however, any new text entered into it (either by the user or via ActionScript) takes on the character and paragraph formatting defined by the `myStyle` TextFormat object.

NOTE *This rule applies to new text entered at the end of any text currently in the field. If the insertion point is moved somewhere in the middle of the text, that text takes on the same formatting as the character just to the right of the insertion point.*

At some point, you may need to know what formatting has been applied to a specific character or an entire text field (that is, which TextFormat objects have been applied), so that you can copy and apply that formatting elsewhere. You can get this information by using the `getTextFormat()` and `getNewTextFormat()` methods. To understand how these methods work, keep in mind that when you apply a TextFormat object to text in a field, Flash keeps a record of it, so to speak. For example, consider the following script, which assigns the `myStyle` TextFormat object to the **myField_txt** text field:

```
myField_txt.setTextFormat(myStyle);
```

Later, if you wanted another text field to be styled in the same way but weren't sure what style had been applied, you could use the following script to find out:

```
var newStyle:TextFormat = myField_txt.getTextFormat();
```

This script creates a new TextFormat object named `newStyle` that's automatically defined with the same formatting and character settings as the TextFormat object currently applied to **myField_txt**. The `newStyle` TextFormat object can then be applied to text fields. Just as the `setTextFormat()` method allows you to apply a format to a specific character or range of characters (as opposed to an entire field), the `getTextFormat()` method allows you to retrieve formatting data that has been applied at a specific character index or to a range of characters. Look at the following example:

```
var newStyle:TextFormat = myField_txt.getTextFormat(27);
```

This script creates a new TextFormat object named `newStyle` that's automatically defined with the same formatting and character settings as the TextFormat object currently applied to the character at index position 27. If you want to retrieve the formatting that's applied to *new* text entered into a field, as set with the `setNewTextFormat()` method, use the following syntax:

```
var otherStyle:TextFormat = myField.getNewTextFormat();
```

This script creates a TextFormat object named `otherStyle` that's automatically defined with the same formatting and character settings as the TextFormat object currently applied to *new* text entered into the **myField_txt** text field.

TextFormat objects have numerous properties that can be set to describe the formatting that the object represents. Many properties are self-explanatory, including `align`, `bold`, `color`, `leftMargin`, `rightMargin`, and so on. You may not be as familiar with the following properties:

- `font`. This property represents the font face used by the object, using a string value such as `"Arial"` or `"Times New Roman"`. Using the `getFontList()` method of the Text Field object in conjunction with this property, you can apply virtually any font face the user currently has installed on his or her machine. (We'll demonstrate the use of this property in the following exercise.)
- `tabStops`. This property represents the distance (in points) that the caret moves within a field when the Tab key is pressed. This property's value is set by referencing the name of an array that contains positive numbers. For example, the following script creates an array with five numbers:

```
var myTabStops:Array = [4, 20, 36, 52, 70];
```

To use the values in this array to set the tabStops property of the style1 TextFormat object, you would use the following syntax:

```
style1.tabStops = mytabStops;
```

Any field using this TextFormat object will tab at 4, 20, 36, 52, and 70 points.

- target. Used in conjunction with the url property, this property represents the window in which a URL opens when requested. This is similar to the target setting used with HTML.
- url. This property represents a URL to which the text formatted as a TextFormat object is hyperlinked. This is a string value such as "http://www.macromedia.com".

In the following exercise, we'll access your computer's fonts to create TextFormat objects and apply them in various ways to the **movingField_txt** text field that we created earlier.

1) Open flash*Writer2.fla*.

We'll continue building on the file you used in the preceding exercise. In this exercise, you'll add script to Frame 1 of the Actions layer, script the buttons, and use the Checkbox component to facilitate part of the project's functionality.

2) With the Property Inspector open, select the Checkbox component.

The most important fact to know about this component is that its instance is **applyToAll_cb**. Knowing this, we can use the value property available to Checkbox components to determine whether the check box is currently checked (true) or not (false), and then act accordingly. For example, if the check box is currently checked, the following script places a value of true into the currentValue variable:

```
var currentValue:Boolean = applyToAll_cb.value;
```

3) With the Actions panel open, select Frame 1 of the Actions layer and add the following script at the end of the current script:

```
var myFonts:Array = TextField.getFontList();
```

This script creates an array named myFonts, which contains the names (as string values) of all fonts on the Flash Player host system (including fonts in the SWF file and any loaded asset SWF files). For example, after running the script on my machine, myFonts[3] has a value of "Arial". You can work with this array in the same manner as with any other array. The various values in this array randomly set font face styles for several TextFormat objects we'll create.

NOTE *When using the getFontList() method, you don't reference a particular text field instance name (as you might expect). Instead, you simply use TextField.*

4) Add the following lines of script at the end of the current script:

```
var styleStatus:TextFormat = new TextFormat()
with(styleStatus){
  font = myFonts[random(myFonts.length)];
  color = 0x858273;
  size = 16;
  bold = true;
}
```

The first line of this script creates a new TextFormat object named `styleStatus`. In a moment, you'll see how this object dictates the appearance of the text in the **statusField_txt** text field. The `with` statement defines several of the object's formatting parameters. Although most of the settings are fairly easy to understand, let's take a look at the line that sets the `font` property. The value of this property is set based on a random index value of the `myFonts` array. The expression uses the length of the `myFonts` array to generate a random number from all possible index values in the array. Thus, if the array has a length of `200`, the number generated is between 0 and 199. That random number is then used to set the index value of one of the font names in the `myFonts` array. For example, if the number generated is `37`, the expression would be evaluated as follows:

```
font = myFonts[37];
```

If the string value at that index is `"DiscoMonkey"`, that's the name of the font face assigned to this TextFormat object.

To apply the formatting of this new TextFormat object to the **statusField_txt** text field, we need to use the `setTextFormat()` method, which we'll do in the following step.

5) Modify the `updateStatus()` **function definition as shown:**

```
function updateStatus(){
  statusField_txt._x = movingField_txt._x;
  statusField_txt._y = (movingField_txt._y + movingField_txt._height) + 10;
  statusField_txt.text = movingField_txt.length;
  statusField._txt.setTextFormat(styleStatus);
}
```

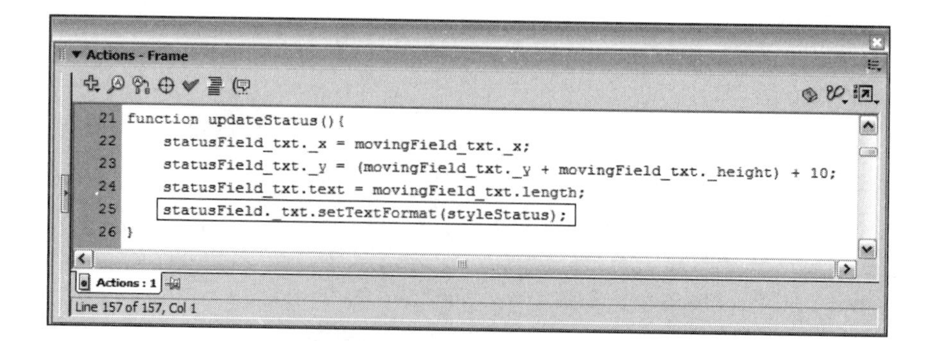

Note the last line of script that we added to this function definition: Remember that this function updates the position and text displayed in the **statusField_txt** text field. Here, we're using the `setTextFormat()` method to set the format of the **statusField_txt** text field to that described by the `styleStatus` TextFormat object. Because we've placed this line of script in the function definition, any changes to the format description of the `styleStatus` object will be reflected in **statusField_txt** when the function is called.

6) Add the following script at the end of the current script on Frame 1:

```
var style1:TextFormat = new TextFormat()
with(style1){
  align = "left";
  bold = false;
  color = 0x1A1917;
  font = myFonts[random(myFonts.length)];
  indent = 0;
  italic = true;
  leading = 0;
  leftMargin = 20;
  rightMargin = 20;
  size = 20;
  target = null;
  underline = false;
  url = null;
}
```

This script creates another TextFormat object named `style1`. The `with` statement defines the formatting properties of that object. Note that the properties `bold`, `indent`, `leading`, `target`, `underline`, and `url` are set to `false`, `0`, or `null`, in essence indicating that this TextFormat object should not use these properties.

Although the TextFormat object could be defined even if we removed these lines of script, we've set them as shown for a reason. Assume you applied a TextFormat object (whose `bold` property was set to `true`) to a text field. The text in that field would appear in bold—simple enough. Now suppose you apply a different TextFormat object (whose `bold` property was not explicitly set) to that same field. In this case, the text in that field would still appear bold, although it would take on the other characteristics of the newly applied TextFormat object. For a formatting characteristic to change when applying a *new* TextFormat object, that new object must specifically define a different value; otherwise, the old value (and its effect) remains. This same principle applies when using the `setNewTextFormat()` method; therefore, it's good practice to always define *something* for property values so that you get the results you intended.

7) Add the following script at the end of the current script on Frame 1:

```
var style2:TextFormat = new TextFormat()
with(style2){
  align = "center";
  bold = false;
  color = 0xCC0000;
  font = myFonts[random(myFonts.length)];
  indent = 0;
  italic = false;
  leading = 15;
  leftMargin = 0;
  rightMargin = 0;
  size = 14;
  target = null;
  underline = false;
  url = null;
}
```

This script creates another TextFormat object named `style2`.

NOTE *The accompanying source file for this exercise has defined two additional TextFormat objects—`style3` and `style4`. To avoid redundancy (because these objects are similar to the ones already defined) as well as to save trees, we're not including the syntax for these two objects here.*

We've now defined all the TextFormat objects for the project. Before we put them to use, however, we need to tweak the script's flow in Frame 1 just a bit.

8) Move the `updateStatus()` and `reshapeBox()` function calls from just above where it says `movingField_txt.onChanged = function(){` to the end of the script on Frame 1.

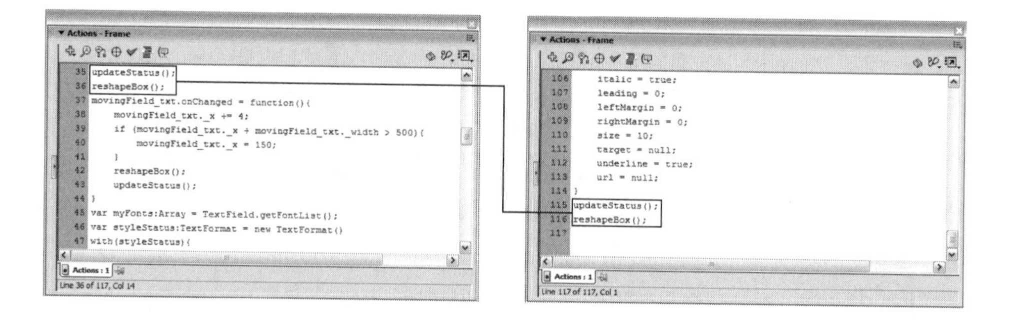

As always, it's a good idea to put all initial function calls at the end of a script, but there's an especially good reason now. Remember that in Step 5 we modified the `updateStatus()` function to include a line of script that uses the `styleStatus` TextFormat object. If we had left that function call where it was, the `updateStatus()` function would have been called a split second before the script that creates and defines the `styleStatus` TextFormat object. This would have resulted in a minor bug because you can't use something before it's created. By moving the function calls to the end of the script, we've ensured that all objects are created and defined *first*.

The last action we need to perform is scripting the buttons.

9) Add the following event handler at the end of the current script:

```
style1_btn.onRelease = function(){
  if (applyToAll_cb.value){
    movingField_txt.setTextFormat(style1);
    movingField_txt.setNewTextFormat(style1);
  }else{
    movingField_txt.setNewTextFormat(style1);
  }
  updateStatus();
  reshapeBox();
}
```

This step adds an `onRelease` event handler to the **style1_btn** instance. This handler takes one of two actions, depending on whether the Checkbox component (named **applyToAll_cb**) is checked or unchecked when the button is clicked. The `if` statement says that if its value is `true` (the checkbox is checked), we want to apply the `style1` TextFormat object to all currently displayed text in the **movingField_txt** text field (`setTextFormat()`), as well as any new text entered into that field (`setNewTextFormat()`). This action causes all text in that field to immediately reflect the new formatting style. If the checkbox's value is `false` (`else`), the `style1` TextFormat is applied only to *new* text entered. After either of these sets of actions has executed, the `updateStatus()` and `reshapeBox()` functions are called to handle any changes that need to be made to the **statusField_txt** text field and the **box_mc** movie clip instance as a result of the new formatting.

10) Place three similar scripts below the current script, changing `style1` to read `style2`, `style3`, and `style4`, respectively.

11) Choose Control > Text Movie to test the project.

When the movie appears, test the various buttons in conjunction with the check box to see the effect that it has on the text in the **movingField_txt** text field. All the functionality from the preceding exercise should be retained as well.

12) Close the test movie and save your work as *flashWriter3.fla*.

This completes the exercise. As you've learned, TextFormat objects provide a lot of power and flexibility for formatting text. But the formatting fun doesn't end there. No, as you'll learn later in this lesson, Flash provides a means to tap into one of the most popular means of formatting text—Cascading Style Sheets.

LOADING AND COMMUNICATING WITH INLINE IMAGES AND SWFS

What text can't be spruced up and enhanced with a splash of graphical content in the form of an image, or even a Flash movie? Although placing text and graphical content together was certainly possible with previous versions of Flash, there wasn't a way of embedding an image or Flash movie within the text so that text flowed around it. Flash MX 2004 changes all that with built-in support of the HTML image tag (`<img>`) within text fields.

When a text field has been set to accept and interpret HTML, using the `<img>` tag embeds the specified graphic at the location you choose within the text. Let's look at a simple example:

```
var myText:String = "<p><b>Hello!</b><img src='myDog.jpg' width='100'
⇒height='100'> Do you like this picture of my doggie?</p>";
```

This script creates a string using some simple HTML tags. The next step is to render this HTML snippet in a text field, which is done with the following bit of code:

```
myTextField_txt.htmlText = myText;
```

This line sets the `htmlText` property of the **myTextField_txt** text field to the string that was just created. As a result, the text field displays the text, formatted as shown, and loads the specified JPG image between the first bit of text and the last.

For a text field to have the capability to render HTML loaded into it, its `html` property must be set to `true`. This can be accomplished by selecting the text field in the authoring environment and clicking the Render Text as HTML button on the Property Inspector, or via ActionScript:

```
myTextField_txt.html = true
```

NOTE *Currently, Flash can load only non-progressive JPG images. Progressive JPGs, GIFs, and PNGs are not supported.*

If you thought loading a JPG was great, it gets even better because Flash can also load SWFs into a text field in the same way, using the <img> tag. Look at this revised example:

```
var myText:String = "<p><b>Hello!</b><img src='myDogMovie.swf'
⇒id='myDogMovie_mc' width='100' height='100'> Do you like this picture
⇒of my doggie?</p>";
myTextField_txt.htmlText = myText;
```

NOTE *For an SWF to render properly in the* `<img>` *tag, its registration point must be at 0,0.*

This has an effect similar to that of the previously discussed script, except that the revised HTML string loads **myDogMovie.swf**. You can interact with this movie just as if you had viewed it separately.

TIP *The* `<img>` *tag can also be used to embed movie clips from the library. Simply reference the clip's identifier name in the* `src` *attribute.*

But it gets even better! Notice within the <img> tag the use of an attribute named `id`. This attribute provides an instance name to the loaded SWF, enabling other elements within your movie to communicate with that loaded SWF. Its full target path is the name of the text field into which it's loaded, followed by its ID/instance name:

```
myTextField_txt.myDogMovie_mc
```

Other supported attributes of the <img> tag include `width`, `height`, `hspace`, `vspace`, and `align`.

NOTE *The* `align` *attribute only supports a* `"left"` *or* `"right"` *value. The default value is* `"left"`.

In the following exercise, you'll begin scripting a Flash-based HTML browser. The browser has the capability to load external HTML pages, and display images and SWFs within those pages. You'll also create a simple media player that plays SWFs embedded within the HTML. Finally, you'll use the MenuBar component to add a menu bar at the top of the application window.

1) Open *flashBrowser1.fla* in the Lesson14/Assets folder.

This project contains six layers—Background, Media Player, MenuBar, Titlebar, Content Window, and Actions. Our project's static graphics are on the Background layer. There are two button instances on the Media Player menu, named **play1_btn** and **stop1_btn**. These are used as playback controls for SWFs loaded in using the <img> tag. The MenuBar layer contains an instance of the MenuBar component named **mainMenu**. This menu will contain two menu buttons: File and Style. The File menu allows users to select HTML pages to open; the Style menu allows them to select a style for the various text elements in the loaded HTML page (the latter functionality is explored more in the next lesson). The Titlebar layer contains a graphical bar that spans the top of the application. This is for design purposes only. The Content Window layer contains a text field instance named **window_txt**. This field acts as our browser's main window. HTML content (including embedded images and SWFs) is loaded into this field. As always, the Actions layer will contain all the script for this project.

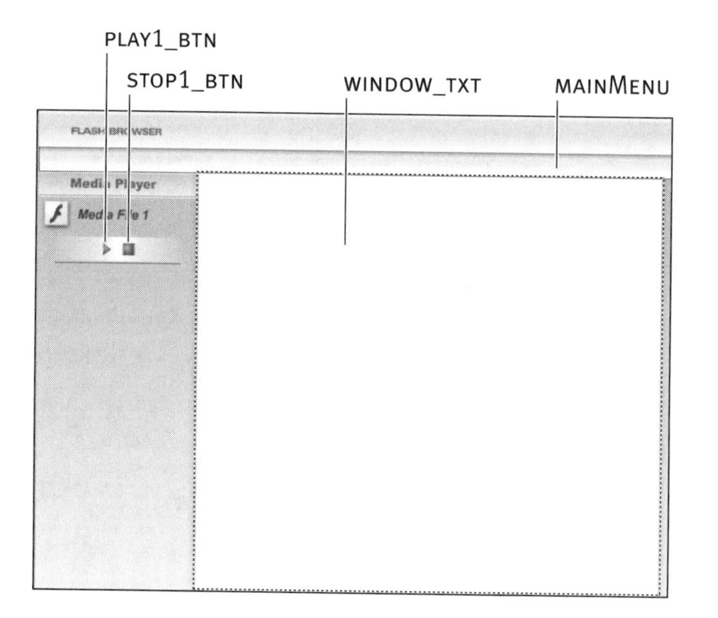

This project uses several external files that have already been created. Before we begin scripting, let's review those files and what they contain.

2) Using your operating system's directory-exploring application, navigate to the Lesson14/Assets directory and locate the following files:

- **home.htm**
- **science.htm**
- **header_home.jpg**
- **header_science.jpg**
- **morning.swf**
- **galaxy.swf**

The first two files on this list are the HTML files that the project will open. The **home.htm** file contains `<img>` tags that embed the **header_home.jpg** and **morning.swf** files; the **science.htm** file embeds the two remaining files.

To help you get a sense of the structure of one of these HTML files, let's open it.

3) Using your favorite HTML editor, open *home.htm*.

As you can see, this is a simple document. Unlike most HTML documents, however, it begins and ends with a `<body>` tag. Within the `<body>` tag, several other tags are used, most of which are explained in the next exercise. The only tag we're concerned with for now is the `<img>` tag, which is used twice in this document. The first use of this tag appears at the top of the document:

```
<img src='header_home.jpg' width='400' height='50' hspace='0' vspace='0'/>
```

This embeds **header_home.jpg** at the top of the page. The next use of the tag looks like this:

```
<img src='morning.swf' width='150' height='90' id='media1_mc' align='left'
⇒hspace='10' vspace='12'/>
```

This line embeds the **morning.swf** movie. Be aware that we've given this SWF an `id` of `media1_mc`. This plays an important role in our browser's media player functionality, which we'll discuss shortly.

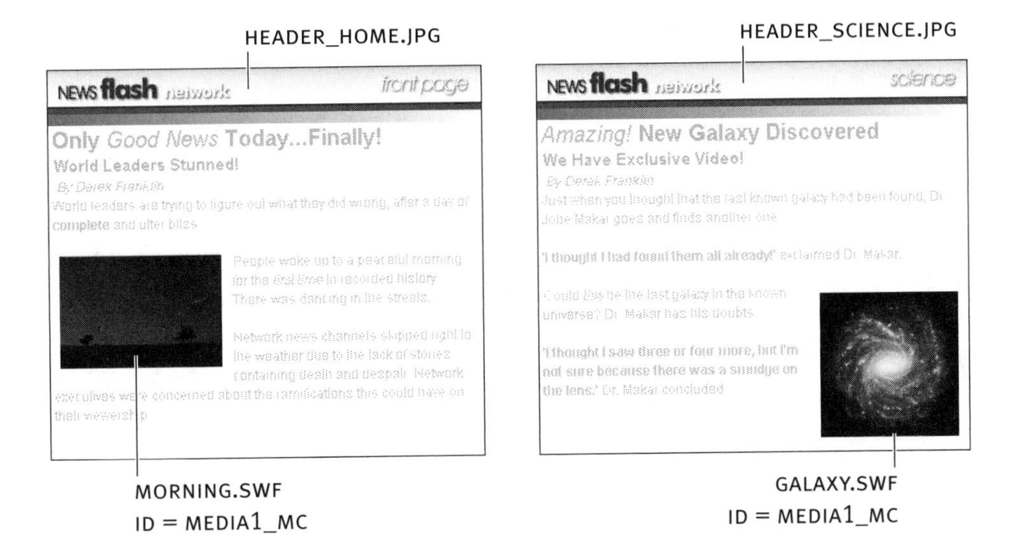

If you opened **science.htm**, you'd see that it's set up in a similar way. It contains an `<img>` tag at the top of the document that embeds the **header_science.jpg** image, and another `<img>` tag that embeds **galaxy.swf**. In that file, the embedded SWF has *also*

been given an id of media1_mc (same as the SWF embedded in **home.htm**). This ensures that no matter which of the two pages is currently loaded in the browser, there will be an embedded SWF with an id of media1_mc. This structure enables a single Play button on our media player to play the SWF in the currently loaded HTML page.

Now that you're familiar with the external files for the project, let's return to Flash and begin scripting, starting with creating the browser's menu bar.

4) Return to Flash. With the Actions panel open, select Frame 1 of the Actions layer and add the following script:

```
var fileMenu:MovieClip = mainMenu.addMenu("File");
fileMenu.addMenuItem({label:"Front Page", instanceName:"page1"});
fileMenu.addMenuItem({label:"Science", instanceName:"page2"});
```

The first task in scripting our menu bar (named **mainMenu**) is to add menu items to it. This includes main menu items, such as the File, Edit, and View menu items that you see in most applications, and submenu items that appear on the main menus.

Our menu will have two main menu items named File and Style, and each of these will have two submenu items. The submenu items on the File menu allow users to select an external HTML page to load (**home.htm** or **science.htm**); the submenu items on the Style menu allow users to choose a style for the text in the loaded document. We'll discuss this technique in the next exercise.

The first line in our script creates the File main menu item for the **mainMenu** instance. This menu item is given a variable name of fileMenu. The next two lines populate this menu with two submenu items. Each of these submenu items is given a label and an instanceName property. The label property represents the text that appears for the item; the instanceName property is used to reference this menu item in other scripts. You'll see this in action later in this lesson.

5) Add the following script:

```
var styleMenu:MovieClip = mainMenu.addMenu("Style");
styleMenu.addMenuItem({label:"Style 1", instanceName:"style1"});
styleMenu.addMenuItem({label:"Style 2", instanceName:"style2"});
```

These three lines of script create the Style main menu item as well as its two submenu items, which have instance names of `style1` and `style2`.

6) Style the menu by adding the following script:

```
mainMenu.setStyle("themeColor", 0xF3F3F3);
```

This step changes the color of the menu to light gray, which is more in line with our browser's design.

Let's look at the results of our scripting so far.

7) Choose Control >Test Movie.

When the movie appears, it contains the two main menu items we added (File and Style). Clicking one of these items reveals a submenu containing the items we added. Next, we need to script the application to do something when one of these menu choices is selected.

8) Close the test movie to return to the authoring environment. With the Actions panel open, select Frame 1 of the Actions layer and add the following script at the end of the current script:

```
var mainMenuListener:Object = new Object();
mainMenuListener.change = function(eventObj:Object){
  var menu = eventObj.menu;
  var item = eventObj.menuItem;
  if(item == menu.page1){
    loadPage("home.htm");
  }else if(item == menu.page2){
    loadPage("science.htm");
  }else if(item == menu.style1){
    setCSS("internal");
  }else if(item == menu.style2){
    setCSS("external");
  }
}
fileMenu.addEventListener("change", mainMenuListener);
styleMenu.addEventListener("change", mainMenuListener);
```

When the user selects a menu choice from the menu bar, a `change` event is fired. The first several lines of this script creates a Listener object (named `mainMenuListener`) for reacting to the `change` event; the last two lines of the script register the Listener object to listen for that event from the File menu and the Style menu.

NOTE *Individual main menu items fire separate* `change` *events when one of their submenus items is selected. This fact allows you to create separate Listener objects for each item. In our application, a single Listener object works fine, so we've registered the single Listener object to listen for this event from both the File and Style menus.*

When the event is fired, the `change` handler on the `mainMenuListener` is executed. The handler is passed an Event object when this occurs. This Event object contains information about the menu item that triggered the event. An `if` statement within the handler is used to evaluate the information within that Event object so that the handler can take the appropriate action.

`eventObj.menu` is a reference to the main menu whose submenu was selected; `eventObj.menuItem` is a reference to the submenu item. The first two lines of the event handler assign these values to the `menu` and `item` variables, respectively. This step makes it easier to reference those values later in the script. To understand how the `if` statement uses these values in its execution, let's look at an example.

Assume that the user has selected the Style 2 submenu choice from the Style menu. When this occurs, the `menu` and `item` variables within the event handler are assigned these values:

```
menu //_level0.depthChild1
item //<menuitem instanceName="style2" label="Style 2" />
```

Although it may not be obvious, `_level0.depthChild1` (the value assigned to `menu`) is the ActionScript target path to the Style menu (the File menu's target path is `_level0.depthChild0` because it appears first on the menu bar).

The `item` variable contains the `label` and `instanceName` information about the selected submenu item. This is the same information we set for the menu item when it was created in Step 5.

The final piece of the puzzle is realizing that after the value of `menu` has been assigned to `_level0.depthChild1`, this script:

```
menu.style2
```

returns this value:

```
<menuitem instanceName="style2" label="Style 2" />
```

Notice that this is the same value as the `item` variable:

```
item // <menuitem instanceName="style2" label="Style 2" />
```

By looking for equality between these two values, the `if` statement is able to determine which menu item has been selected.

Because our entire menu bar only has four submenu items, the `if` statement within the event handler only does four evaluations. The first evaluation states that if the `page1` menu item (Front Page item on the File menu) has been selected, the script calls the `loadPage()` function (which we have yet to create) and passes it a value of `"home.htm"`. If the `page2` menu item is selected (Science on the File menu), the `loadPage()` function is called and passed a value of `"science.htm"`. If the `style1` menu item (Style 1 item on the Style menu) is selected, the script calls the `setCSS()` function (which we still have to create) and passes it a value of `"internal"`. Finally, if the `style2` menu item (Style 2 item on the Style menu) is selected, the script calls the `setCSS()` function and passes it a value of `"external"`.

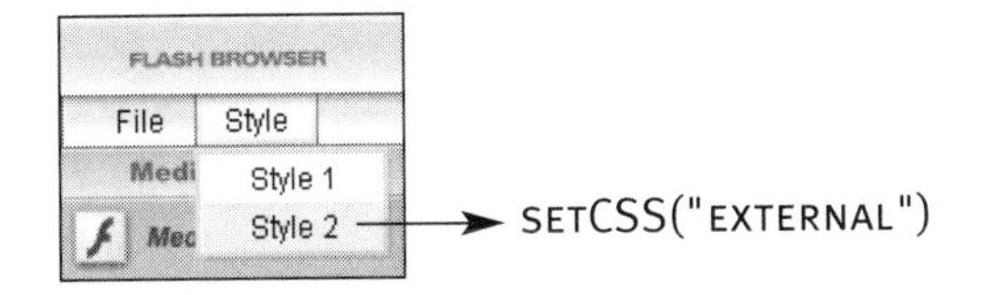

In the end, when one of the items from the File menu is selected, the `loadPage()` function is called. When one of the items from the Style menu is selected, the `setCSS()` function is called.

We'll create the `loadPage()` function next, and leave the creation of the `setCSS()` function for the next exercise.

9) Add the following function definition at the end of the current script:

```
function loadPage(page:String){
  var pageLoader = new XML();
  pageLoader.ignoreWhite = true;
  pageLoader.onLoad = function(){
    window_txt.htmlText = this;
  }
  pageLoader.load(page);
}
```

This step creates the `loadPage()` function, which accepts a single parameter named `page`. This function loads one of the external HTML pages into the **window_txt** text field.

The function begins by creating an XML object named pageLoader. Although XML objects were designed primarily to handle XML, they do have some usefulness when loading HTML content (which is similar to XML).

The next line within the function tells Flash to ignore any useless whitespace that the loaded file contains.

The next part of the script uses an onLoad event handler to tell the pageLoader object what to do when the external document has finished loading. In this case, the content within the pageLoader object (this) is displayed in the **window_txt** text field as HTML-based text.

The final line in the function begins the loading process. Here, the passed-in value of page is used to determine what external document to load.

10) Add the following event handlers at the end of the current script:

```
play1_btn.onRelease = function(){
  window_txt.media1_mc.play();
}
stop1_btn.onRelease = function(){
  window_txt.media1_mc.stop();
}
```

These two event handlers are used to control that SWF file by telling it when to play and when to stop. As we discussed in Step 3, both of our external HTML files contain an SWF that has been embedded in the file and given an ID/instance name of **media1_mc**. When either one of these instances appears within the **window_txt** text field, the target path becomes the following:

```
window_txt.media1_mc
```

Let's test our project.

11) Choose Control >Test Movie.

When the movie appears, select either Front Page or Science from the File menu. When you do, either the **home.htm** or **science.htm** file is loaded into the **window_txt** text field. Although the content of the page may look completely disorganized (something we'll fix in the next exercise), you can see the JPG image and an SWF movie. Press the media player's Play button to begin playback of the embedded SWF. If you select a different page from the File menu, the media player works on the SWF embedded in that page as well.

12) Close the test movie and save your work as ***flashBrowser2.fla***.

We'll continue building on this file in the next exercise.

FORMATTING TEXT FIELDS WITH CASCADING STYLE SHEETS

Cascading Style Sheets (CSS) have become an essential tool in the creation of modern Web pages because of the extensive formatting capabilities they provide. With Flash MX 2004, text fields now have access (albeit somewhat limited) to that same power.

NOTE *This lesson is not intended to be an extensive overview of Cascading Style Sheets, but rather a simple introduction.*

A Cascading Style Sheet is a set of rules that describe how various elements are styled and formatted in a tag-based document. Although this might sound complicated, it's actually very simple. As always, the best learning tool is an example.

Imagine you have an HTML document structured like this:

```
<greeting>Hello!</greeting>
<message>I hope to see you soon.</message>
<signature>Derek</signature>
```

This document doesn't contain any of the normal HTML tags. Instead, it contains text placed between custom tags that we made up. This is the first part of the Cascading Style Sheet equation; next, we create our style sheet to describe the formatting that each of these tags represents:

```
//this is our cascading style sheet
greeting {
  color: #663399;
  font-family: Arial, Helvetica, sans-serif;
  font-size: 16px;
  font-weight: bold;
  display: block;
}
message {
  color: #FF3300;
  font-size: 12px;
  font-weight: normal;
  display: block;
}
signature {
  color: #990000;
  font-size: 14px;
  font-weight: italic;
  display: block;
}
```

This style sheet contains three rules: `greeting`, `message`, and `signature`. The formatting of each rule is defined within the curly braces. Each line within the curly braces represents a formatting property (`color`, `font-family`, `font-size`, and so on) followed by a colon (:), followed by the value of the property, followed by a semicolon (;).

When this style sheet is applied to our HTML document, text between specific tags takes on the formatting of that tag as defined in the style sheet; therefore, the text "Hello!" appears in a purple, bold, 16-pixel, sans-serif font.

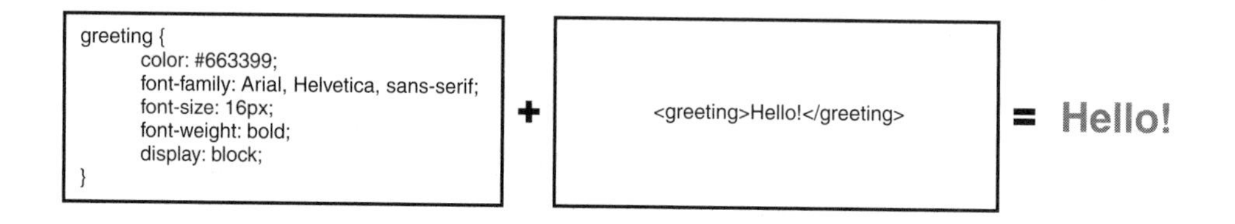

There are major benefits to using style sheets. Formatting your document is a breeze because the styling of elements requires the use of a single tag, as opposed to a bunch of nested tags. Another benefit is that if you have several hundred or even thousand HTML documents that get their styling via a style sheet, updating the rules in that single style sheet automatically updates the formatting of all those documents.

Although the standard that defines modern Cascading Style Sheet usage allows for some extensive formatting capabilities, Flash's implementation of Cascading Style Sheet functionality is somewhat limited. We'll discuss this in a moment, but now let's look at how Cascading Style Sheets are used in Flash.

Cascading Style Sheets can be used in Flash to define how text displayed in a dynamic text field should be formatted. The CSS can be defined internally within a movie using ActionScript, or can exist externally from Flash in a text document with a **.css** file extension. Creating and using Cascading Style Sheets within Flash requires use of the StyleSheet object. The syntax used to define the rules in the style sheet varies depending on whether the style sheet is internal or external. To help bring this all together, let's look at an example:

```
var myStyleSheet:TextField.StyleSheet = new TextField.StyleSheet();
```

This line creates a StyleSheet object named `myStyleSheet`. The `setStyle()` method is used to define rules for this object within Flash:

```
mySty1eSheet.setStyle("greeting", {
  color: '#663399',
  fontFamily: 'Arial, Helvetica, sans-serif',
  fontSize: '16',
  fontWeight: 'bold',
  display: 'block'
});
```

This syntax creates a `greeting` rule (similar to the one discussed earlier) within the `myStyleSheet` object. However, there are some syntactical differences between this definition and the one shown earlier. The syntax shown earlier represents the standard syntactical structure of a Cascading Style Sheet (including external style sheets that would be loaded into Flash). The syntax shown above for defining a style is unique to ActionScript, and should only be used when defining rules using the `setStyle()` method.

The main differences to note here are that the style is defined within parentheses; the style's name is within quotes, followed by a comma; property values are between single quotes (`''`), property settings are terminated by commas instead of semicolons; and the last property definition (in this case, `display`) is not terminated by anything. Another subtle difference is the fact that standard style sheet syntax defines property names using hyphens (`font-family`, `font-weight`, and so on), but internally these same properties are defined by removing the hyphen and using an uppercase character instead (`fontFamily`, `fontWeight`, and so on).

Externally defined rule

```
greeting {
	color: #663399;
	font-family: Arial, Helvetica, sans-serif;
	font-size: 16px;
	font-weight: bold;
	display: block;
}
```

Internally defined rule

```
myStyleSheet.setStyle("greeting", {
	color: '#663399',
	fontFamily: 'Arial, Helvetica, sans-serif',
	fontSize: '16',
	fontWeight: 'bold',
	display: 'block'
});
```

To apply this style sheet to a text field, you simply set that text field's `styleSheet` property like this:

```
myTextField_txt.styleSheet = myStyleSheet;
```

Now, whenever any text loaded into that field makes use of the `<greeting>` tag, that text is styled according to the greeting rule:

```
myTextField_txt.htmlText = "<greeting>Hello!</greeting>";
```

NOTE *Although it should be obvious, a text field must be set to render HTML for style sheets to work in that field.*

Using external **.css** files is a bit different, yet still requires the use of a StyleSheet object. Let's look at another example (which assumes that there is an external **.css** file named **myCSS.css** containing style rules):

```
var myStyleSheet:TextField.StyleSheet = new TextField.StyleSheet();
myStyleSheet.onLoad = function(){
  myTextField_txt.styleSheet = myStyleSheet;
}
myStyleSheet.load("myCSS.css");
```

The first line of this script creates a StyleSheet object for holding the external style sheet rules. The next several lines assign that object an `onLoad` event handler so that when the external style sheet has completely loaded into it, that object is set as the `styleSheet` property of the **myTextField_txt** text field. The last line begins the loading of the external CSS file.

As mentioned earlier, Flash's implementation of Cascading Style Sheets is somewhat limited. It offers support for the following style properties (shown using their standard HTML names followed by their ActionScript names):

- `color` (`color`)
- `display` (`display`)
- `font-family` (`fontFamily`)
- `font-size` (`fontSize`)
- `font-style` (`fontStyle`)
- `font-weight` (`fontWeight`)
- `margin-left` (`marginLeft`)
- `margin-right` (`marginRight`)
- `text-align` (`textAlign`)
- `text-decoration` (`textDecoration`)
- `text-indent` (`textIndent`)

NOTE *For a complete listing of acceptable values for these properties, consult the ActionScript dictionary.*

In the following exercise, we set up our Flash browser so the user can change the formatting of the loaded HTML pages via submenu choices on the Style menu. The exercise uses both internally and externally defined style rules. The externally defined rules are contained in an external **.css** file that will be loaded as needed.

1) Open *flashBrowser2.fla*.

Because this exercise is a continuation of the preceding one, you should be familiar with the elements within the project, including the MenuBar component instance and the text field named **window_txt** where the external HTML files are loaded. In this exercise, we'll simply add ActionScript to Frame 1 of the Actions layer.

2) Using your operating system's directory-exploring application, navigate to the Lesson14/Assets directory and locate the following files:

- **home.htm**
- **science.htm**
- **external.css**

The first two files are the HTML documents that our browser is already set up to load. The other file is an external **.css** file, which our application will load and use.

3) Using your favorite HTML editor, open *home.htm*.

We opened and looked at this document in the preceding exercise, but with a different purpose. This time, notice how various portions of text are placed between tags that we defined. A total of seven custom tags are used, including these:

- `<headline>`
- `<headlineemphasis>`
- `<subheadline>`
- `<author>`

In addition, the text includes a hyperlink (`<a>`). This is not a custom tag, but rather a normal HTML tag; you'll soon see how style sheet formatting can be applied even to standard HTML tags.

```
<body>
<img src='header_home.jpg' width='400' height='50' hspace='0' vspace='0'/><br><br><br>
<headline>Only <headlineemphasis>Good News</headlineemphasis> Today...Finally!</headline>
<subheadline>World Leaders Stunned!</subheadline>
<author>By Derek Franklin</author>
<mainbody>World leaders are trying to figure out what they did wrong, after a day of <bodybold>complete</bodybold>
<img src='morning.swf' width='150' height='90' id='media1_mc' align='left' hspace='10' vspace='12'/>People woke up
Network news channels skipped right to the weather due to the lack of stories containing death and despair. Networ
</body>
```

NOTE *The* **science.htm** *file uses the same tags.*

Let's look at the **external.css** file.

4) Using your favorite text editor (or HTML editor, if it supports displaying CSS files), open *external.css*.

Using standard CSS syntax, this file contains rules for every one of the custom tags contained in our HTML files.

You are now armed with enough information to complete the browser project.

```
headline {
    color: #333333;
    font-family: Arial, Helvetica, sans-serif;
    font-size: 20;
    font-weight: normal;
    margin-left: 4;
    display: block
}
headlineemphasis {
    color: #8F1D03;
    font-weight: bold;
    font-style:normal;
    display: inline
}
subheadline {
    color: #FF7F00;
    font-family: Arial, Helvetica, sans-serif;
    font-size: 15;
    font-weight: bold;
    font-style: italic;
    margin-left: 6;
    display: block
}
author {
    color: #808080;
    font-family: Arial, Helvetica, sans-serif;
    font-size: 12;
    font-weight: bold;
    font-style: normal;
    margin-left: 12;
    display: block
}
```

5) Return to Flash. With the Actions panel open, select Frame 1 of the Actions layer and add the following script at the end of the current script:

```
var windowCSS:TextField.StyleSheet = new TextField.StyleSheet();
```

This step creates the `windowCSS` StyleSheet object, which handles the application's style sheet needs.

6) Add the following function definition:

```
function setCSS(cssStyle:String){
  if(cssStyle == "internal"){
  }else{
  }
}
```

This step is the beginning of the setCSS() function. We'll add script to this function over the next couple of steps. Before we do that, however, it's important to remember that our application was set up in the preceding exercise to call this function when either the Style 1 or Style 2 submenu choice was selected from the Style menu. At the time we coded that functionality, we specified that this function would be passed a value of "internal" if Style 1 was selected, but a value of "external" if Style 2 was selected. The if statement within the function evaluates this passed-in value and causes the function to react accordingly.

Over the next couple of steps, we'll use this if statement to tell the function to use internal style rules when "internal" is passed, but load an external CSS file and use those style rules if "external" is passed.

7) Add the following script within the if leg of the conditional statement:

```
with(windowCSS){
  setStyle("headline", {
  color: '#333333',
    fontFamily: 'Arial, Helvetica, sans-serif',
    fontSize: '20',
    fontWeight: 'bold',
    marginLeft: '4',
    display: 'block'
  });
  setStyle("headlineemphasis", {
    color: '#8F1D03',
    fontWeight: 'normal',
    fontStyle:'italic',
    display: 'inline'
  });
  setStyle("subheadline", {
    color: '#333333',
    fontFamily: 'Arial, Helvetica, sans-serif',
    fontSize: '15',
    fontWeight: 'bold',
    marginLeft: '6',
    display: 'block'
  });
  setStyle("author", {
    color: '#8F1D03',
    fontFamily: 'Arial, Helvetica, sans-serif',
    fontSize: '12',
    fontWeight: 'normal',
    fontStyle:'italic',
    marginLeft: '8',
    display: 'block'
  });
```

continues on next page

```
    setStyle("mainbody", {
      color: '#666666',
      fontFamily: 'Arial, Helvetica, sans-serif',
      fontSize: '12',
      fontWeight: 'normal',
      marginLeft: '4',
      marginRight: '6',
      display: 'block'
    });
    setStyle("bodybold", {
      fontWeight: 'bold',
      display: 'inline'
    });
    setStyle("bodyitalics", {
      fontStyle: 'italic',
      display: 'inline'
    });
    setStyle("a:link", {
      color: '#00389E'
    });
    setStyle("a:hover", {
      textDecoration: 'underline'
    });
  }
  window_txt.styleSheet = windowCSS;
```

Although this script is lengthy, it's actually quite simple. When the function is passed the value `"internal"`, this section of script is executed. The first part of the script uses a `with` statement to create the styles in the `windowCSS` StyleSheet object for all the custom tags that our HTML document uses. The last line of the script applies the `windowCSS` StyleSheet object to the **window_txt** text field, causing text within that field to take on the formatting shown here.

There are a couple of important points to mention about these styles before we move on. Note that some styles have been defined using a `display` property of `block`; others have this property set as `inline`. (This is also true of the external **.css** file.) A rule where the `display` property has been set to `block` indicates that Flash should automatically place a line break before and after the section of text styled with that rule. Consider this as having the same effect as the paragraph (`<p>`) HTML tag. A value of `inline` indicates that content formatted with that rule should appear on the same line as preceding and following content. This is similar to the effect of bold (`<b>`) or italic (`<i>`) tags in HTML. Flash also supports a value of `none` for this property. This setting hides any content styled with that rule. Switching this property value from `none` to `block` or `inline` within the style sheet is an easy way to turn certain sections of content on and off.

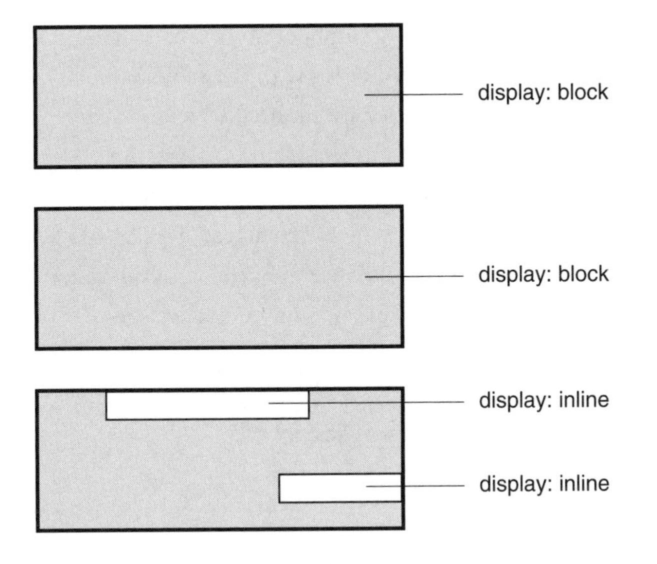

Finally, the last two style sets refer to hyperlinks—how they're normally styled, and how a link looks when the user mouses over the link. Yes, you can also define how content formatted with built-in HTML tags looks. For example, to define the appearance of text within an HTML paragraph tag, you use the following syntax:

```
myStyleSheet.setStyle("p", {
  //property settings
});
```

8) Add the following script within the `else` leg of the conditional statement:

```
windowCSS.onLoad = function(){
  window_txt.styleSheet = windowCSS;
}
windowCSS.load("external.css");
```

This script takes care of what occurs when the function is passed a value of `"external"`. When this happens, an `onLoad` event is assigned to the `windowCSS` StyleSheet object, which states that when the external **.css** file has finished loading into the `windowCSS` object, that object will be set as the `styleSheet` property of **window_txt**. This action causes the rules defined in the external style sheet to be applied to the HTML document currently loaded into **window_txt**.

The last line begins loading the external style sheet into `windowCSS`.

When we load an external style sheet into the same StyleSheet object that had internally defined styles (as discussed in Step 7), only styles with the same name in both definitions are updated. For example, in Step 7 we internally created a style named `subheadline` and defined its properties. If the externally loaded **.css** file defines a property with the same name, the external definition of the rule overwrites the internally defined rule when that file is loaded. If the external **.css** file has no rule named `subheadline`, however, the formatting of the internal version of the rule remains intact. The same logic is true conversely: internally defined styles can overwrite externally loaded styles.

9) Add the following two lines at the end of the current script:

```
setCSS("internal");
loadPage("home.htm");
```

Our application is currently set up to load and style content only when a menu choice is selected, meaning that the content window of the browser is blank on loading. These two lines fix that problem by calling the `setCSS()` and `loadPage()` functions immediately when the application loads.

It's time to do a final test.

10) Choose Control >Test Movie.

When the movie appears, the **home.htm** page is loaded into the **window_txt** text field and is formatted using the internally defined style rules, as discussed in Step 7. If you select Style 2 from the Style menu, the external CSS file is loaded into the application, and the styles defined in it are used as discussed in Step 8.

11) Close the test movie and save your work as *flashBrowser3.fla*.

This lesson taught you the extreme versatility of text fields and how they can be created, controlled, and configured dynamically to enhance your projects in many ways.

WHAT YOU HAVE LEARNED

In this lesson, you have:

- Dynamically created, configured, and controlled several text fields (pages 470–481)
- Used TextFormat objects to style the text in a field dynamically (pages 481–490)
- Used the MenuBar component to add a menu to an application (pages 490–499)
- Used Cascading Style Sheets to format text within a text field (pages 499–508)

controlling movie clips dynamically

LESSON 15

In earlier lessons, you learned how to use frame, clip, and button events to make things happen—often to manipulate a movie clip instance. In this lesson, you'll learn how to manipulate movie clip instances—duplicating, attaching, coloring, scaling, and positioning them—based on *dynamic input*. We'll also show you how to control movie clip instances based on the feedback of a clicked button, as well as introduce you to Flash's drawing methods. By the end of the lesson, you will have created a simple drawing application and a dynamically generated scrolling list.

You will create this drawing application in this lesson to learn about the various ways in which you can control movie clip instances dynamically.

WHAT YOU WILL LEARN

In this lesson, you will:

- Duplicate and attach movie clip instances
- Create continuous-feedback buttons to move a movie clip instance
- Draw lines and filled shapes dynamically
- Change the stacking order of movie clip instances dynamically
- Script drag-and-drop functionality
- Remove movie clip instances dynamically

APPROXIMATE TIME

This lesson takes approximately one hour to complete.

LESSON FILES

Starting Files:

Lesson15/Assets/scrollingList1.fla
Lesson15/Assets/draw1.fla

Completed Projects:

scrollingList3.fla
draw5.fla

CREATING MOVIE CLIP INSTANCES DYNAMICALLY

You can create a movie clip instance dynamically by using one of the following methods of the Movie Clip class:

- `duplicateMovieClip()`: This method duplicates an existing movie clip instance on the stage to create a new instance of that movie clip.
- `attachMovie()`: This method creates a new instance of a movie clip directly from the library.
- `createEmptyMovieClip()`: This method creates an empty movie clip instance—that is, one that contains no data or graphical content.

You'll use each of these methods in the course of working through the exercises in this lesson.

USING `duplicateMovieClip()`

Although we introduced the `duplicateMovieClip` method in Lesson 9, "Automating Scripts with Loops," we didn't cover it in detail. Now you get to learn everything you need to know about this powerful method.

Using the `duplicateMovieClip()` method, you can direct Flash to duplicate a movie clip instance that's currently on the stage and give it a new instance name. If the movie clip instance is not on the stage—that is, it's in a previous frame or in a frame not yet visited—Flash cannot duplicate it. In addition, the movie clip instance can only be duplicated into the same timeline as the original, and it will exist in the same relative hierarchical position as the original.

NOTE *To dynamically create a movie clip instance that also allows dynamic timeline insertion, you would use `attachMovie()`, which we'll discuss later in this lesson.*

When a movie clip instance is duplicated, the duplicate inherits all of the instance's current physical properties. A duplicated movie clip instance inherits the following properties from the original:

- Position
- Scale
- Alpha
- Rotation
- Color
- Clip events attached to the movie clip instance

A duplicated movie clip doesn't inherit the following:

- Variables, arrays, objects
- Name
- Visibility
- Current frame

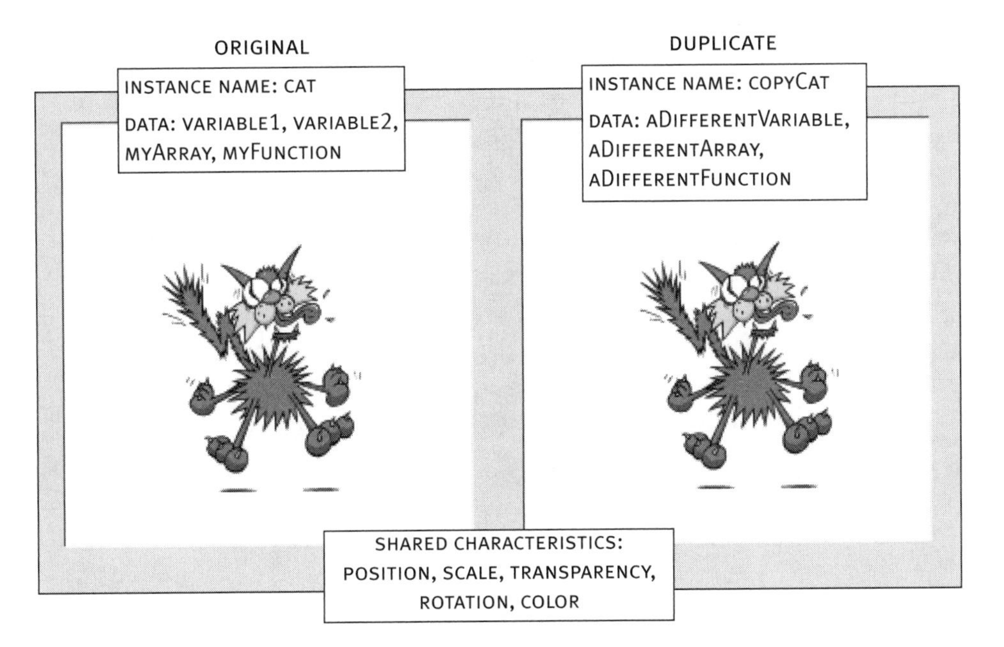

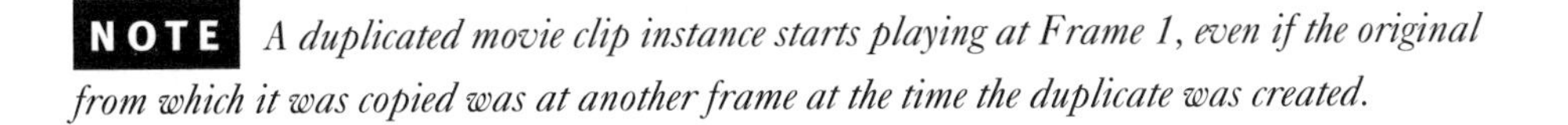

NOTE *A duplicated movie clip instance starts playing at Frame 1, even if the original from which it was copied was at another frame at the time the duplicate was created.*

Following is the syntax for duplicating a movie clip instance:

```
myClip.duplicateMovieClip(name, depth, object);
```

This line of ActionScript starts with the instance name (target path) of the movie clip to be duplicated. It then invokes the `duplicateMovieClip()` method of the Movie Clip class to create a new instance with the value of `name` at `depth`. The `object` parameter is optional. For example:

```
var name:String = "ball2_mc";
var depth:Number = 100;
ball_mc.duplicateMovieClip(name, depth);
```

These three lines of ActionScript duplicate the **ball_mc** movie clip instance, name the new instance **ball2_mc**, and place it at a depth of 100.

When we talk about *depth*, we're referring to the stacking order of movie clip instances in a particular timeline. If two movie clip instances overlap in Flash, one must appear to be above the other, with the top instance having a higher depth. Every movie clip instance has a unique depth in relation to other objects on the stage. When a movie clip instance is duplicated, you can assign it a numeric depth of any positive integer. The higher the integer, the higher the depth in that timeline. Although you may not be aware of it, any movie clip instances that you manually place in a particular timeline while authoring a movie are placed at a depth starting from –16384. This means that if a dynamically created instance is placed in a timeline at a depth of 1, it will appear above any manually placed instances.

Each timeline has its own range of depths, from –16384 to 1048575. These depths are relative to the depth of the parent timeline. In other words, instance1 contains child instances at levels on its timeline from –16384 to 1048575. But instance1 is below instance2, so that even the highest-placed child instance in the timeline of instance1 is still lower than the lowest-placed child instance in instance2.

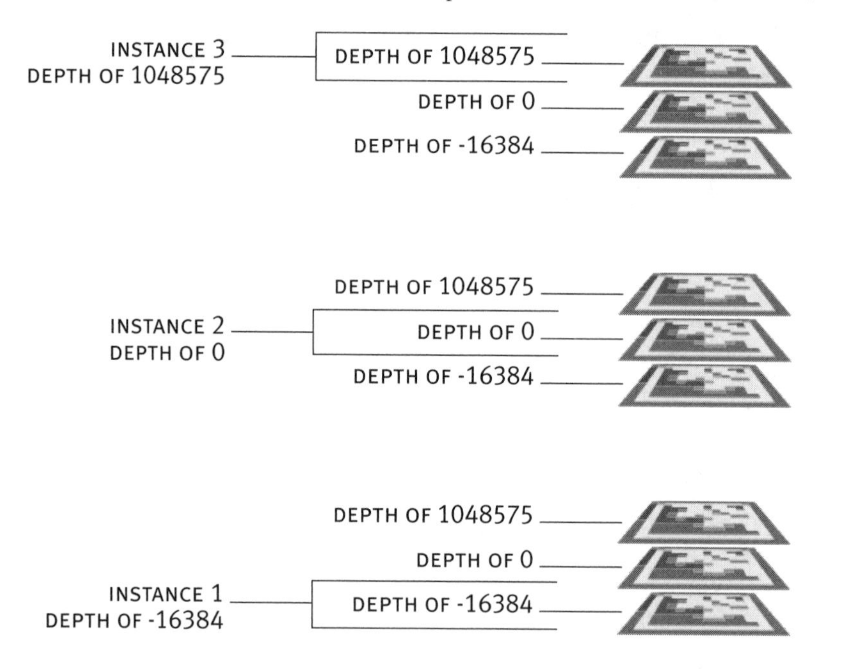

NOTE *A depth can contain only one movie clip instance at a time. If you duplicate a movie clip instance into a depth that already contains another movie clip instance, you will destroy the movie clip instance that's already there.*

Movie clip instances can be placed in a total of 1064960 (–16384 to 1048575) depths in a single timeline. Every timeline in a movie has its own set of depths that don't interfere with any other timelines. This means, for example, that you can duplicate instances into a depth of 10 in as many timelines as you like.

The third parameter in the `duplicateMovieClip()` method, `object`, is optional but useful. The properties of any object specified in that parameter are used to populate the newly duplicated movie clip instance. If the parameter is left blank, it's ignored. To extend the previous example, look at the following:

```
var myObject:Object = new Object();
myObject.ballColor = "red"
var name:String = "ball2_mc";
var depth:Number = 100;
ball_mc.duplicateMovieClip(name, depth, myObject);
```

When **ball_mc** is duplicated, the duplicate, named **ball2_mc**, will contain all of the properties of the `myObject` object. In this case, a variable named `ballColor` with a value of `"red"` is created in the new instance.

TIP *To copy the variables from the original instance into the duplicate, use the instance name of the original as the initializing object. For example:*

```
ball_mc.duplicateMovieClip(name, depth, ball_mc);
```

USING attachMovie()

Using `attachMovie()`, you can actually pull a movie clip out of the library dynamically and attach an instance of it to any timeline currently available on the stage—in essence, adding the content of the attached movie clip instance to the content of the movie. The attached movie becomes a child of the timeline to which it's attached. As such, the attached child movie takes on any graphical transformations performed on its parent (size, rotation, transparency, and so on) yet remains separate with respect to data, visibility, current frame, and so on. For more information on parent/child relationships in ActionScript, see Lesson 3, "Understanding Target Paths."

FACE_MC.ATTACHMOVIE("GLASSES", "MYGLASSES_MC", 1)

FACE_MC.ATTACHMOVIE("MOUTH", "MYMOUTH_MC", 2)

TRANSFORMATIONS TO FACE (SIZE, ROTATION)

So what are the main differences between the `attachMovie()` method and the `duplicateMovieClip()` method? As mentioned earlier, you can use `attachMovie()` to attach a movie clip instance from the library to any timeline currently in the scene. Because this method attaches clip instances from the library (and the library contains all your movie clips), the attached instance doesn't have to be on stage when you attach it. With `duplicateMovieClip()`, on the other hand, an instance of the movie clip that you want to duplicate must exist on the stage at the time the method is used. What's more, you must place the duplicate inside the same timeline as the original—you can't duplicate it to another timeline. In addition, if the instance you're duplicating has any attached clip events (`data`, `enterframe`, `mouseDown`, and so on), the duplicate will automatically inherit those same clip events. Although there are ways to add clip events to an attached movie clip instance, the process is not as straightforward as in the duplication process.

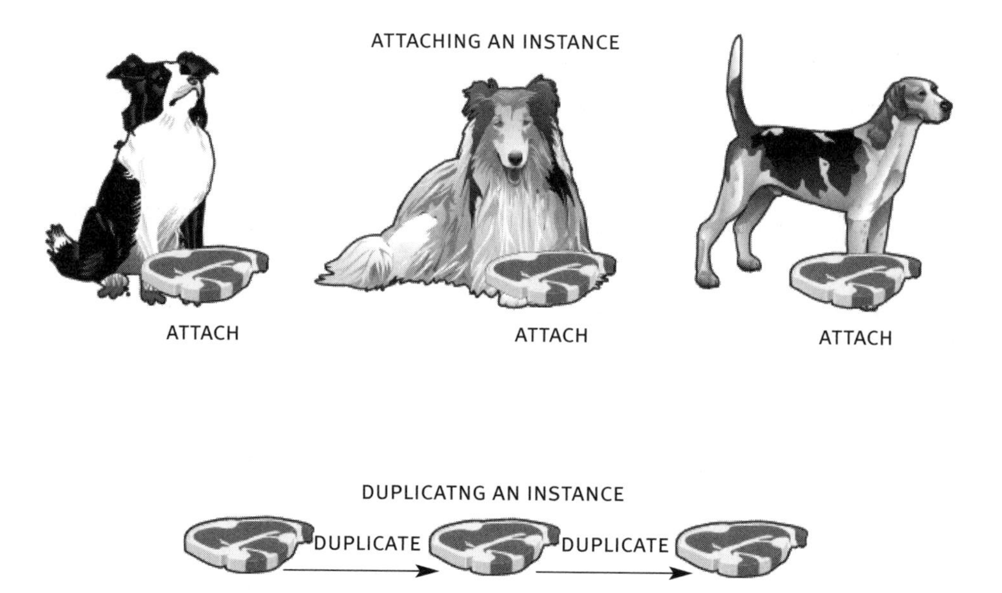

In the simplest terms, attaching movie clip instances allows you to add virtually any timeline to any other timeline. Duplicating movies, in contrast, enables you to make nearly exact replicas of movie clip instances for inclusion in the same timeline as the original.

There are several steps you'll need to follow to use the `attachMovie()` method in a project, the first of which is to specify, in the library, which movie clips you want to make available for attaching. This is called *linkage*. Linkage may not seem to be the best term to describe identifying movie clips in the library that can be attached; however, the term also pertains to sharing libraries in which assets in one SWF library are *linked*, or shared, by another SWF. When specifying movie clips to make available for attaching, or when sharing assets between two SWFs, the movie clips involved must be given identifier names. Macromedia therefore considers as linkage any process that involves giving a movie clip in the library an identifier name.

To add the most common type of linkage to a movie clip, follow these steps:

1) Open the library.

2) Right-click the movie clip of interest.

3) Select Linkage.

4) Select the Export for ActionScript check box.

5) Enter the identifier name. (The identifier is how you will refer to this library-based movie clip with ActionScript.)

TIP *You can also set the linkage when creating a movie clip in the Convert to Symbol dialog box by clicking the Advanced button.*

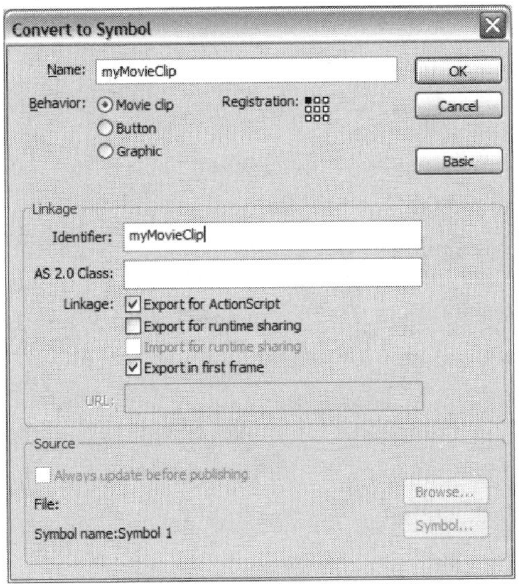

When setting linkage, there is an option to note: Export in First Frame is checked by default. This option is used to determine when a linked (or attachable) movie clip is downloaded when your project is viewed over the Web. If this box is checked, that movie clip will be downloaded before Frame 1 of your movie so that the clip's content is available before your first opportunity to attach it (that is, Frame 1). If you're using large movie clips (for example, clips that contain many other movie clips or sounds), Flash may appear to hang. Don't worry: it's just preloading the contents of all linked movie clips. If you uncheck the Export in First Frame option, the movie clip will not be preloaded before the first frame as just described. If you choose this option, you must place an instance of that movie clip on the stage at some point before it can be attached, so that Flash knows when to load it. After it's instantiated (seen or placed in your movie) on some frame, you can attach it anywhere. For example, if there's an action on Frame 25 that attaches the movie clip, an instance of that clip must have been placed on Frame 24 or lower for the `attachMovie()` action to work. Any frames after Frame 24 can attach the instance because it has been loaded into memory.

NOTE *There's an AS 2.0 Class field in the Convert to Symbol box. If you enter a class name in this field, every instance of the movie clip will inherit the methods and properties of that class, essentially creating a super movie clip. If the specified class file has a* `run()` *method, for example, every instance of this class will have that method as well.*

Here's the syntax to attach an instance of a movie clip in the library to a timeline:

```
path.attachMovie(identifier, newName, depth, object)
```

NOTE *As with* `duplicateMovieClip()`*, the optional* `object` *option populates the newly created clip with the properties and variables of an object.*

For example:

```
_root.wall_mc.attachMovie("paint", "paint2_mc", 10)
```

This script attaches the **paint** movie clip in the library to the **_root.wall_mc** movie clip instance. The newly attached movie is given an instance name of **paint2_mc** and placed on a depth of 10. Because an attached movie becomes a child of the movie clip instance to which it's attached, the newly attached instance will have a target path of `_root.wall_mc.paint2_mc`.

TIP *The easiest way to dynamically assign a clip event to an attached or duplicated movie is to define the assignment immediately after the attachment or duplication action, as the following example shows:*

```
_root.attachMovie("box", "dynamicBox_mc", 1);
dynamicBox_mc.onEnterFrame = function (){
  dynamicBox_mc._rotation += 15;
}
```

In this example, an instance of the movie clip named `"box"` *(its identifier name in the library) is dynamically attached to the* `_root` *timeline. The attached instance is given a name of* **dynamicBox_mc**. *On the next few lines after the* `attach` *action, a clip event is assigned to this newly attached instance.*

USING createEmptyMovieClip()

Using the createEmptyMovieClip() method, you can dynamically create a new instance of an empty movie clip instance in any timeline. You might do this for the following reasons:

- With this method, after you've created an empty instance, you can attach other movie clip instances to it—useful for dynamically generating a list of movie clip instances for use as menu choices. After you create this type of "main" movie clip instance, you can move the group around as a whole rather than move each menu item individually.
- You can create an empty movie clip instance and then dynamically load in music or an image.
- You can use an empty movie clip instance as a storage area for lines, fills, and gradient fills created using Flash's drawing capabilities.

Here's the syntax for creating an empty movie clip instance in a timeline:

```
path.createEmptyMovieClip(name, depth);
```

For example:

```
_root.createEmptyMovieClip("box_mc", 1);
```

The first parameter is the instance name that you want to assign to the empty movie clip instance you create; the second parameter is the depth at which you want to place that movie clip instance. If you were to test this action, you wouldn't get a visual result because you're creating an empty movie clip instance. Later in this lesson you'll learn how to use createEmptyMovieClip() to hold drawn lines.

USING attachMovie()

With attachMovie(), you can create a new instance of a movie clip in the library. In this exercise, you'll begin a project that when complete will be a scrolling list of items. You will create the items in the list by attaching movie clip instances dynamically.

1) Open *scrollingList1.fla* in the Lesson15/Assets folder.

There are three layers on the main timeline: Actions, Window, and Background. The Background layer contains the main graphics for the project, the Actions layer contains most of the project's ActionScript, and the Window layer contains a movie clip instance called **display_mc**.

Inside the **display_mc** timeline are four layers: Mask, Fields, Scroll Buttons, and Window Graphics. The Window Graphics layer contains the border and background graphics of the window. The Scroll Buttons layer contains two button instances,

down_btn and **up_btn**, that you will work with in the next exercise. The Fields layer contains an empty movie clip instance called **list_mc**, which will contain instances that are dynamically created using `attachMovie()`. These attached instances will appear as items on a list, one on top of the other. When the **list_mc** movie clip instance is filled with these attached instances, it will become quite long. Thus, **list_mc** is masked by a rectangular shape in the Mask layer (of its own timeline) so that only the area of **list_mc** over the window graphics will be visible.

CONFIGURATION

RESULT

LIST_MC DISPLAY_MC

2) Open the library and locate the movie clip named *list info bar*. Right-click it (Control-click on a Mac) and select Linkage from the menu that appears. Select Export for ActionScript in the Linkage Properties dialog box that appears and enter `infoBar` into the Identifier field. Click OK to close the dialog box.

This movie clip is now available for use with the `attachMovie()` method.

One instance of this movie clip will be attached to the **list_mc** instance for every line of information in the scrolling list (16 lines, 16 attachments). Inside this attached movie clip are two dynamic text field instances, **moonName_txt** and **moonNum_txt**, which will be used in the attached instances to display the various names of the moons as well as associated moon numbers.

MOONNUM_TXT MOONNAME_TXT

3) Select Frame 1 in the Actions layer on the main timeline. Open the Actions panel and enter the following script:

```
var list:Array = ["Adrastea", "Amalthea", "Ananke", "Callisto",
⇒"Carme", "Elara", "Europa", "Ganymede", "Himalia", "Io",
⇒"Leda", "Lysithea", "Metis", "Pasiphae", "Sinope", "Thebe"];
```

The goal of this exercise is to create a list of items by attaching movie clip instances. To this end, we've created an array of names: the 16 most well-known moons of Jupiter. For each name in this array, an instance of the movie clip in the library to which we previously gave an identifier name will be attached to the **list_mc** instance.

Now it's time to begin defining the function that will be used to create the list of movie clip instances.

4) With Frame 1 still selected, add the following script:

```
function buildList () {
  var spacing:Number = 30;
}
```

The `buildList()` function will ultimately contain all of the ActionScript needed to attach, position, and populate the entire list with movie clip instances. To position the vertical list properly, a variable called `spacing` is created and given a value of 30, which will be used to set the vertical (y) distance between the center of one attached movie clip instance and the center of the one placed below it.

5) To attach and position the list items, add the following script to the `buildList()` **function definition, just under the** `spacing` **variable:**

```
for (var i = 0; i < list.length; ++i) {
  var name:String = "infoBar" + i + "_mc";
  var y:Number = i * spacing;
  display_mc.list_mc.attachMovie("infoBar", name, i);
  display_mc.list_mc[name]._y = y;
  display_mc.list_mc[name].moonName_txt.text = list[i];
  display_mc.list_mc[name].moonNum_txt.text = i + 1;
}
```

This part of the function uses a `for` loop to loop through every element in the `list` array. For each element in the array, the loop attaches an instance of the **infoBar** movie clip to the **list_mc** instance to build the list.

The first action in the loop creates a variable called `name` whose value is set using an expression that concatenates the string `"infoBar"` with the current value of `i` and `"_mc"` concatenated on the end. Because the value of `i` is incremented with each loop, the value of `name` will be `"infoBar0_mc"`, `"infoBar1_mc"`, `"infoBar2_mc"`, and so on, with each successive iteration of the loop. Further down in the loop, the current value of `name` is used to assign a name to each successive attached instance of **infoBar**. Next in the loop, a variable called `y` is created to store the intended y position of the movie clip instance that's being attached. The value of this variable is based on an expression that multiplies the current value of `i` by the value of `spacing`. Because the value of `i` increases with each iteration, so does the value of `y`. This results in successive attached instances being placed in a y position below the previous one created.

The last four actions in the loop attach and populate (with data) the dynamic text fields in each attached instance. An attached instance of the **infoBar** movie clip is created with an instance name and depth based on the current value of `name` and `i`, respectively. This attached instance's y position is then set based on the current value of the variable named `y`. Because each attached instance contains the same graphical elements as the original, each has two text fields: **moonName_txt** and **moonNum_txt**. The last two actions in the loop populate those fields with the appropriate data. Using the current value of `i`, the text value of **moonName_txt** in the attached instance is set to the appropriate string value in the `list` array. Because the value of `i` is incremented with each loop, the **moonName_txt** text field in each successively attached instance will display the successive string elements (moon names) in the `list` array. The **moonNum_txt** text field in each attached instance is set to a numerical value of `i` plus 1. This will result in numerical values of `1`, `2`, `3`, and so on appearing in the **moonNum_txt** text fields of successive attached instances.

After this loop has been completed, each element in the `list` array has an attached movie clip instance that's populated with information and appears in an ordered vertical fashion.

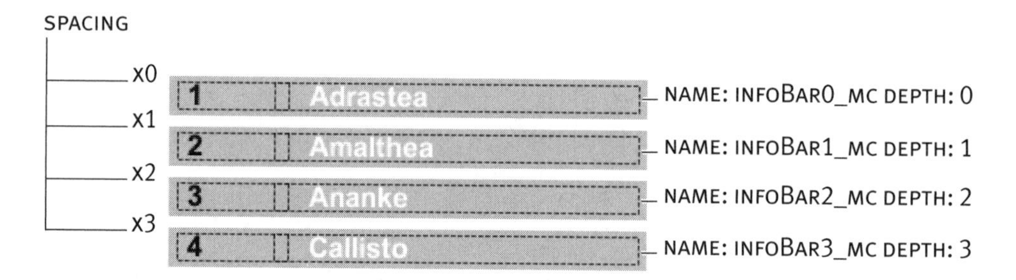

6) To execute the function, add the following line at the end of the current script on Frame 1 (below the function definition):

```
buildList();
```

```
1  var list:Array = ["Adrastea", "Amalthea", "Ananke", "Callisto"
2  function buildList() {
3      var spacing:Number = 30;
4      for (var i = 0; i < list.length; ++i) {
5          var name:String = "infoBar" + i + "_mc";
6          var y:Number = i * spacing;
7          display_mc.list_mc.attachMovie("infoBar", name, i);
8          display_mc.list_mc[name]._y = y;
9          display_mc.list_mc[name].moonName_txt.text = list[i];
10         display_mc.list_mc[name].moonNum_txt.text = i + 1;
11     }
12 }
13 buildList();
```

After the function has been defined in Frame 1 of the movie, this line of script will execute all the actions we set up in the previous steps.

7) Choose Control > Test Movie to test what you've created.

When the movie initializes, your list of items will appear. Remember: because you've used a mask to limit the number of items that can be displayed simultaneously, you'll see only a partial list.

The list will not scroll yet. That is functionality that you still need to add.

8) Close the test movie and save your work as *scrollingList2.fla*.

You've completed the hardest part of this lesson: you've written ActionScript that dynamically attaches instances of a movie clip from the library to build a list of items. In the next exercise, you'll be working with the same file to make the window scrollable.

BUILDING CONTINUOUS-FEEDBACK BUTTONS

It's sometimes useful to have actions executed continually while a button is being clicked. A button set up to enable continuous execution is known as a *continuous-feedback button*—and a scroll button (the focus of this exercise) is a perfect example.

If you wanted to scroll through a list of information in a window, you would quickly become frustrated if you had to click a button every time you wanted to make the information scroll up or down. Far less frustrating is a button that needs to be clicked just once to scroll continuously until the button is released. In Flash, you can create this type of functionality by using the `onEnterFrame` clip event with a button, as we'll soon demonstrate.

In this exercise, you'll add scrolling buttons to the list you built in the previous exercises.

1) Open *scrollingList2.fla*.

In this exercise, you'll add ActionScript to Frame 1 of the Actions layer in the main timeline, to the scroll buttons themselves, and to the clips that contain the scroll buttons. You'll build the function that performs the actual scrolling; then you'll add the commands to the required areas so that the function is called.

Remember that there's a movie clip instance called **list_mc** inside the **display_mc** clip. All the attached **infoBar** movie clip instances that we create will exist inside the **list_mc** instance. We'll set up our scrolling function to move the **list_mc** movie clip instance up and down to achieve the effect of scrolling through the list of items.

NOTE *When we use the term* scrolling *in this exercise, we're talking about increasing or decreasing the _y property value of the* **list_mc** *movie clip instance to move it up or down onscreen.*

2) With the Actions panel open, select Frame 1 of the Actions layer and then add the following line of script just below the line that creates the `list` array:

```
var startingY:Number = display_mc.list_mc._y;
```

With scrolling, you must establish maximum and minimum vertical locations (y) to which the list can scroll: these represent the boundaries for scrolling (or continued vertical movement). In any application where scrolling is allowed, you're prevented from scrolling beyond the top or bottom borders of the document. The preceding line of script is used to establish the edge of one of these vertical boundaries: the movie clip instance **list_mc**, which will contain the list of attached instances, should not continue scrolling if its y position exceeds the starting y position. In a moment, we'll use the value of the `startingY` variable to control scrolling.

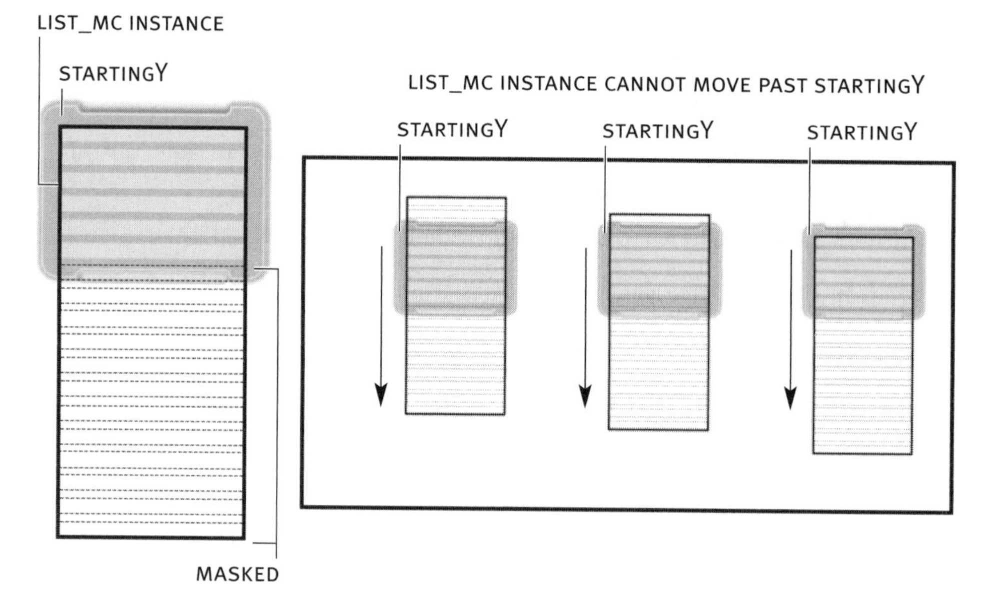

3) To set part of the other scrolling boundary, add the following line to Frame 1, just below the line of script you added in Step 2:

```
var bottom:Number = 120;
```

As mentioned in Step 2, the highest possible y value that the **list_mc** movie clip instance can scroll to is its starting position. The `bottom` variable defined in this step will be used as an offset to the upward extreme of scrolling so that the bottom of the list doesn't go all the way to the top of the window. The reasons for using this variable will become more obvious in coming steps.

4) Define the following variable just after the line of script added in Step 3:

```
var direction:String;
```

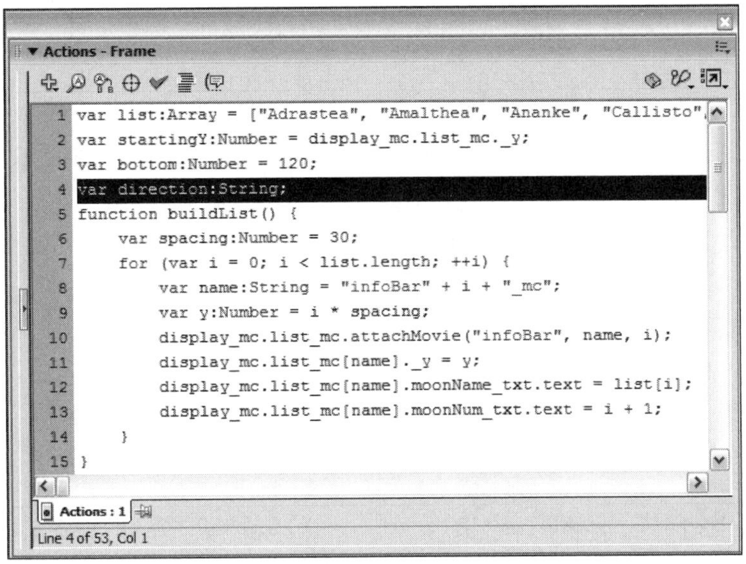

```
Actions - Frame
1  var list:Array = ["Adrastea", "Amalthea", "Ananke", "Callisto",
2  var startingY:Number = display_mc.list_mc._y;
3  var bottom:Number = 120;
4  var direction:String;
5  function buildList() {
6      var spacing:Number = 30;
7      for (var i = 0; i < list.length; ++i) {
8          var name:String = "infoBar" + i + "_mc";
9          var y:Number = i * spacing;
10         display_mc.list_mc.attachMovie("infoBar", name, i);
11         display_mc.list_mc[name]._y = y;
12         display_mc.list_mc[name].moonName_txt.text = list[i];
13         display_mc.list_mc[name].moonNum_txt.text = i + 1;
14     }
15 }
Actions : 1
Line 4 of 53, Col 1
```

The function that handles scrolling, which you'll start setting up in the next step, will scroll the list either up or down based on the value of the `direction` variable. This variable will be set from one of two separate button events that will be created later in this exercise.

5) Start defining the function that will be used to scroll the movie clip instance. To do this, add the following ActionScript to Frame 1, just below the `buildList()` function definition:

```
function scroll () {
  var speed:Number = 10;
}
```

Soon, we'll set up our project to call this function via an `onEnterFrame` clip event on the main timeline if one of two scrolling buttons is being clicked. One of the scroll buttons will be used to scroll up; the other will be used to scroll down.

The variable `speed` is just that—the scrolling speed. When the scroll button is held down, the **list_mc** instance will scroll up or down by the value of `speed` in every frame.

 *There's nothing magic about the number 10; you can adjust it to anything that looks good.*

6) Add the following `if/else if` **statement inside the function definition, just below** `var speed:Number = 10;`**:**

```
if (direction == "up") {
} else if (direction == "down") {
}
```

The `direction` variable is used to store a string value of `"up"` or `"down"`. The conditional statement in this step determines how the `scroll()` function works, based on that value. Over the next few steps, you'll be adding actions to this conditional statement so that if the intended scrolling direction is up, a certain list of actions will be performed; if the scrolling direction is down, another set of actions will be performed.

7) Nest the following `if/else` **statement in the** `"up"` **leg of the** `if/else if` **statement you just entered in Step 6:**

```
if (display_mc.list_mc._y - speed + display_mc.list_mc._height >
⇒(startingY + bottom)) {
  display_mc.list_mc._y -= speed;
} else {
  display_mc.list_mc._y = (startingY + bottom) - display_mc.list_mc._height;
}
```

Because this statement is nested within the `"up"` leg of the previous statement, it's evaluated if the value of `direction` is up.

The first part of the expression in the statement is used to determine what the bottom position of the **list_mc** instance would be if it were to move 10 pixels upward. The expression does this by looking at the **list_mc** instance's current y position and then subtracting the value of `speed` and adding the height of the instance. That bottom position of the instance is then compared against one of the scrolling boundaries, as established by adding the value of `bottom` to the value of `startingY`. If moving the **list_mc** instance up doesn't cause the bottom of the instance to exceed the boundary, the first action in the statement is executed and the list is moved up. If moving the instance up would make it exceed the boundary, however, the `else` part of the statement would be executed, simply snapping its vertical position to the maximum allowable.

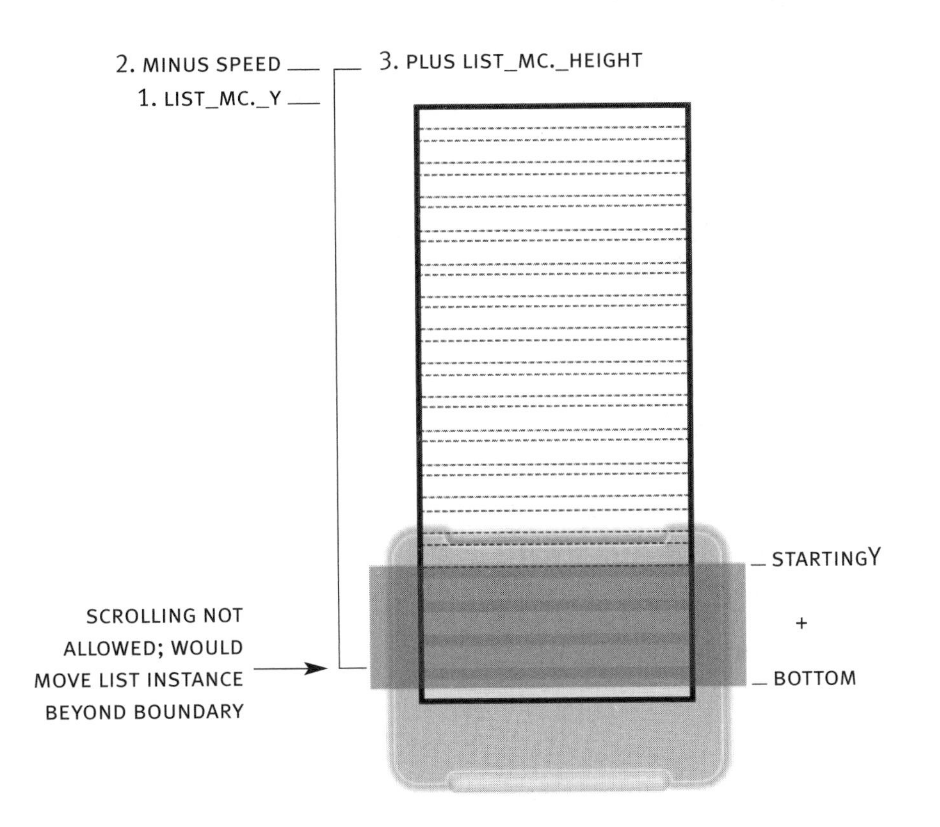

If you're confused, don't worry: Let's look at an example to see how this technique works. For this demonstration, we'll assume the following values:

```
var speed:Number = 10
var startingY:Number = 100
var bottom:Number = 120
display_mc.list_mc._height = 400 //vertical height of the list instance
display_mc.list_mc._y = -165 //current vertical position of the list instance
```

Using these values, the expression in the `if` statement is evaluated as follows:

```
if (-165 - 10 + 400 > (100 + 120))
```

which further evaluates to:

```
if (225 > 220)
```

In this case, 225 is greater than 220, so the following action is executed:

```
display_mc.list_mc._y -= speed;
```

This moves the **list_mc** instance up 10 pixels, and its y position now equals –175. If the statement were evaluated again, it would look like this:

```
if (-175 - 10 + 400 > (100 + 120))
```

which further evaluates to:

```
if (215 > 220)
```

In this case, 215 is less than 220, so the following action (the `else` part of the statement) is executed:

```
display_mc.list_mc._y = (startingY + bottom) - display_mc.list_mc._height;
```

Here, the **list_mc** instance's y position is set based on the value of the expression to the right of the equals sign. Using the values established for this example, this expression would be evaluated as follows:

```
(startingY + bottom) - display_mc.list_mc._height
```

which further evaluates to:

```
(100 + 120) - 400
```

which further evaluates to:

```
220 - 400
```

which further evaluates to:

```
-180
```

This means that the **list_mc** instance would be snapped into a vertical position of –180, placing the bottom of the instance at the edge of the upper scrolling boundary. This statement is set up so that the bottom of the **list_mc** instance never scrolls beyond this point.

NOTE *This can be a tricky concept: You may want to review this information several times.*

Next, let's set up the function to handle downward scrolling.

8) Nest this `if/else` statement in the `"down"` portion of the outer `if/else if` statement:

```
if (display_mc.list_mc._y + speed < startingY) {
  display_mc.list_mc._y += speed;
} else {
  display_mc.list_mc._y = startingY;
}
```

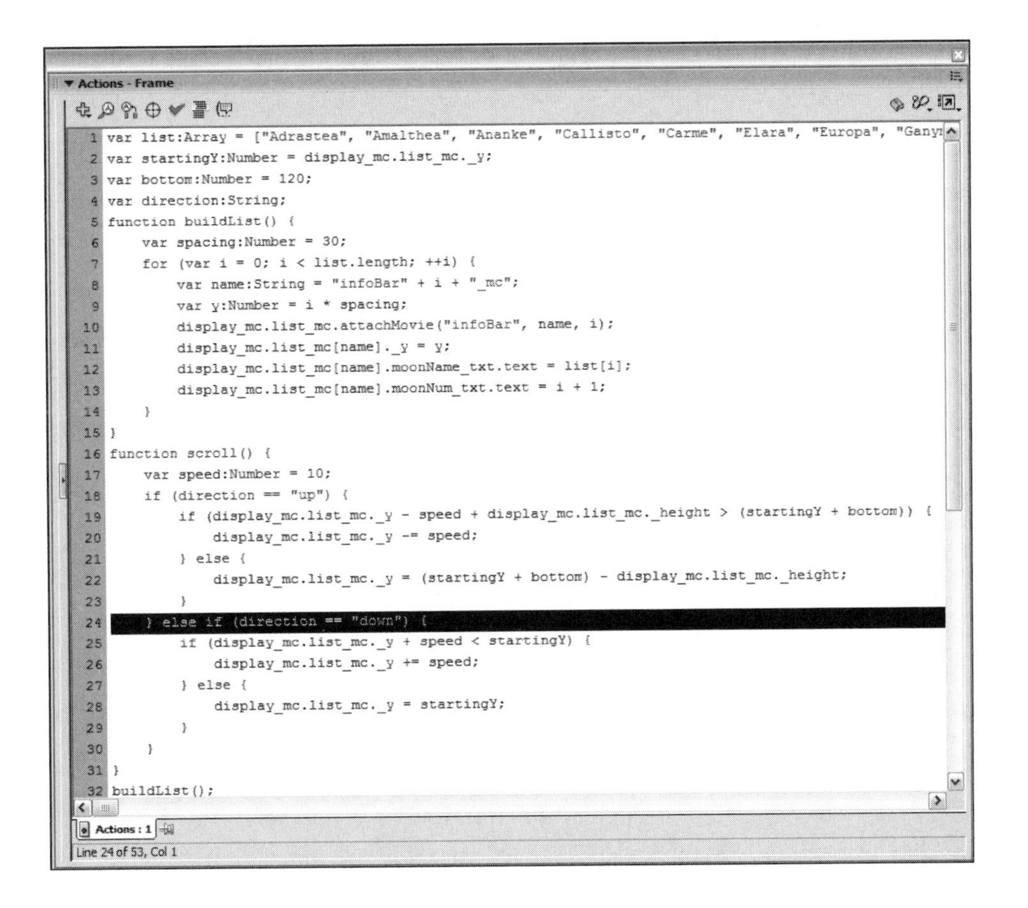

This part of the statement serves to scroll the movie clip instance downward. Similar to the statement in Step 7, this statement looks to see whether moving the **list_mc** instance down by the value of speed:

```
display_mc.list_mc._y + speed
```

will keep the instance within the lower scrolling boundary (startingY). If so, the first action in the statement is executed, moving the instance down; otherwise (else), if moving the instance by the value of speed causes it to exceed the lower boundary, the action within the else part of the statement is executed, snapping the instance into vertical alignment with the lower boundary.

Now that you've defined this function, it's time to begin working with the scroll buttons.

9) At the end of the current script on Frame 1, add the following line of script to initialize the `scrollButtonPressed` **variable:**

```
var scrollButtonPressed:Boolean = false;
```

The variable scrollButtonPressed can have a value of either true or false. In future steps you'll add button events that will serve to toggle the value of scrollButtonPressed between true and false. When true, the scroll function will be called repeatedly by an onEnterFrame event.

10) Add the following script at the bottom of the frame:

```
display_mc.down_btn.onPress = function() {
  scrollButtonPressed = true;
  direction = "down";
};
display_mc.down_btn.onRelease = function() {
  scrollButtonPressed = false;
};
```

The **display_mc** movie clip contains two buttons that you will use to control the scrolling. Their instance names are **down_btn** and **up_btn**. In this step you are adding onPress and onRelease button events to the **down_btn** button instance.

When the **down_btn** button is pressed, the variable scrollButtonPressed is set to true and the variable direction is given a value of "down". The onEnterFrame event (not yet added) will call the scroll() function when it sees that scrollButtonPressed has a value of true. The scroll() function will in turn use the value of the direction variable to determine whether to scroll the **list_mc** movie clip up or down, as described in Steps 7 and 8.

11) Add the following button events for the *up_btn* button instance:

```
display_mc.up_btn.onPress = function() {
  scrollButtonPressed = true;
  direction = "up";
};
display_mc.up_btn.onRelease = function() {
  scrollButtonPressed = false;
};
```

This script acts similar to the script added in Step 10. When the **up_btn** button instance is clicked, the scrollButtonPressed variable is set to true so that the onEnterFrame event can continually call the scroll() function. In addition, the value of direction is set to "up". As mentioned in Step 10, an onEnterFrame event we will add in the next step will call the scroll() function whenever scrollButtonPressed is true. This, accompanied by the fact that the value of direction is set to "up", will cause our list of items to scroll upward continuously when this button is clicked.

When the button is released, the scrollButtonPressed variable is set back to false to stop the scrolling.

12) Add the following `onEnterFrame` event:

```
this.onEnterFrame = function() {
  if (scrollButtonPressed) {
    scroll();
  }
};
```

This script defines an `onEnterFrame` event for the `_root` timeline. It's executed once every frame (24 times a second). When it's executing, if the value of `scrollButtonPressed` is `true`, the `scroll` function is called. The `scroll` function will then scroll the **list_mc** movie clip based on the current value of `direction`.

13) Choose Control > Test Movie to test this movie.

Give your buttons a try to test your ActionScript. You can click and hold a button down to make scrolling occur. When the **list_mc** movie clip instance reaches its upper or lower maximum, it will stop scrolling.

14) Close the test movie and save your work as *scrollingList3.fla*.

You've now created the ActionScript required to scroll a list of dynamic items between upper and lower boundaries using continuous-feedback buttons.

USING ACTIONSCRIPT TO DRAW LINES DYNAMICALLY

Using ActionScript, you can dynamically draw lines in a movie as it plays—a capability that comes with a number of drawing methods available to the Movie Clip class.

Using these drawing methods, you can:

- Draw a line from the current drawing position to a point you specify
- Move the current drawing position without drawing
- Specify the line style for a timeline
- Fill a shape with a color
- Fill a shape with a gradient
- Curve a line between two points
- Clear a timeline of drawn lines and gradients

In this section, we'll show you how to draw lines, move the drawing position, set the line style, and clear a movie clip instance. In the next section, we'll briefly touch on using flat and gradient fills. Although we won't cover the `curveTo()` method (which allows you to dynamically draw curved lines), you should understand enough about Flash drawing fundamentals by the end of the lesson that you'll be able to implement it in your own drawing applications.

USING lineStyle()

Before drawing any lines in a timeline, you must set the line style for that timeline. Flash uses this setting to determine line thickness, color, and alpha.

Here's the syntax:

```
path.lineStyle(thickness, color, alpha)
```

`thickness` must be a value between 0 and 255 (with a `thickness` of `0` representing a hairline). `color` must be a hex color value. `alpha` represents the transparency level for a line, where 0 is transparent and 100 is opaque. Look at the following example:

```
_root.myClip_mc.lineStyle(10, 0x009900, 100);
```

This line of ActionScript sets the line style in **myClip_mc** so that all lines drawn will be green and opaque, and have a thickness of 10.

USING moveTo()

All movie clip instances have a drawing position that indicates the coordinate at which a line would start—in other words, the beginning point of a line. (You use `lineTo()` to draw the line, as described in the next section.) When a movie clip instance is created, the drawing position is set as x = 0 and y = 0; however, you can move the drawing position at any time using `moveTo()`. When a line is drawn, the drawing position is updated to the endpoint of the drawn line.

The following is the syntax for using `moveTo()`:

```
path.moveTo(x, y);
```

All you need to do is specify the x and y positions of your drawing position. For example:

```
_root.myClip_mc.lineStyle(10,0x009900,100);
_root.myClip_mc.moveTo(100,100);
```

This ActionScript sets the line style and then moves the drawing position.

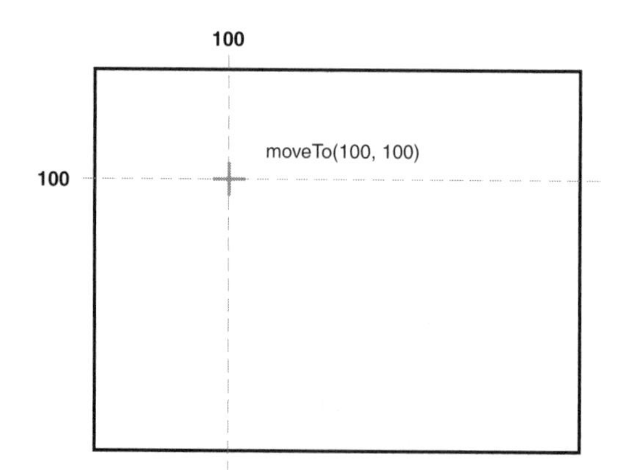

USING `lineTo()`

The `lineTo()` drawing method of the Movie Clip class simply draws a line of the destination timeline's `lineStyle` format from the drawing position to the end position specified in the method.

Following is the syntax for `lineTo()`:

```
myClip_mc.lineTo(x,y);
```

The `x` and `y` parameters specify the end point of the line to be drawn.

NOTE *After the line is drawn, the* `moveTo()` *position is updated to the end point of the line.*

The following example shows how you would use the methods we've described to draw a line:

```
_root.createEmptyMovieClip("canvas_mc",1);
_root.canvas_mc.lineStyle(2,0x009900,100);
_root.canvas_mc.moveTo(100,100);
_root.canvas_mc.lineTo(200,150);
```

This ActionScript draws a line between the points `(100,100)` and `(200,150)`.

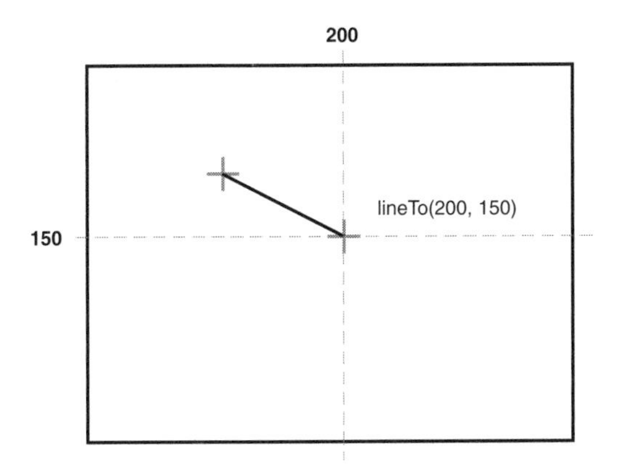

USING THE DRAWING METHODS

In this exercise, you'll use the drawing methods of the Movie Clip class to start a simple drawing application.

1) Open *draw1.fla* in the Lesson15/Assets folder.

The main timeline includes five layers, named according to their contents. The Background layer contains the project's main graphics. The Canvas layer contains a movie clip instance, **canvas_mc**, which will be used to define an allowable area in which to draw. The Icon layer contains the movie clip instance with an insect, just to the left of the stage. This instance is named **icon_mc**; in a later exercise, we'll duplicate it to provide the user with several icons to drag onto **canvas_mc** to draw over. The Windows layer contains two instances, **window1_mc** and **window2_mc**, which appear to the right of **canvas_mc** and will be addressed in a later exercise. Finally, the Actions layer will be used to store most of the ActionScript used in the final version of this project.

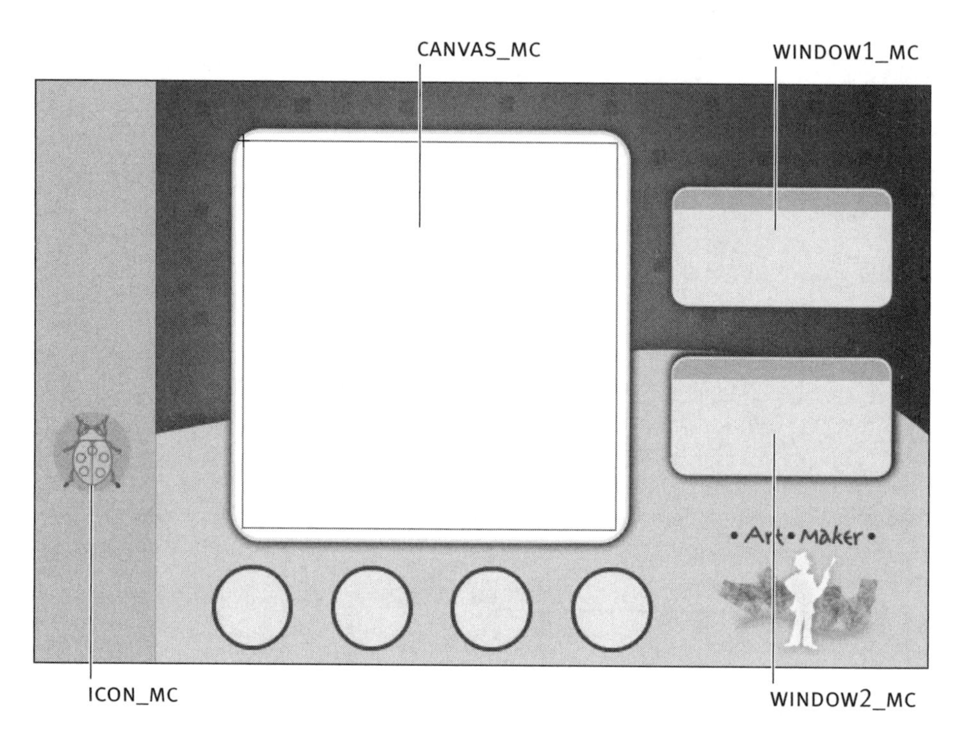

The main focus of this exercise is creating ActionScript that will enable you to draw on the canvas. You will use clip events in concert with the `hitTest()` method to determine whether the mouse button is pressed while the mouse pointer is over the **canvas_mc** instance; you will then use the `onMouseMove` clip event to draw. Every time the `onMouseMove` event is fired, the mouse's positions are recorded and a line is drawn between its last and current position, resulting in a drawing.

2) With the Actions panel open, select Frame 1 of the Actions layer on the main timeline and add the following script:

```
var down:Boolean = false;
```

This line of script creates a variable named `down` that will be used to store the current state of the mouse. Using the `onMouseDown` and `onMouseUp` events, this variable's value is set to `true` or `false` (pressed down or not). When `down` is `true`, the application will draw lines every time the mouse moves. When `down` is `false`, no lines are drawn.

3) Add the following onMouseDown **clip event at the end of the current script:**

```
_root.onMouseDown = function() {
  if (_root.canvas_mc.hitTest(_root._xmouse, _root._ymouse)) {
    var x:Number = _root._xmouse;
    var y:Number = _root._ymouse;
    _root.holder_mc.moveTo(x, y);
    down = true;
  }
};
```

On onMouseDown, we use a conditional statement to determine whether the mouse pointer is over the **canvas_mc** movie clip instance when the mouse button is pressed. If it is, several things occur. The current x and y positions of the mouse are recorded as the values of the x and y variables, respectively. These values are then used in a moveTo() action to move the beginning drawing position of a clip named **holder_mc** to the current coordinates of the mouse. The **holder_mc** clip is an empty movie clip instance that will be created dynamically (as scripted in Step 5). This instance will contain all the drawn lines. The last action in this script sets the down state variable to true, indicating that the mouse button is pressed.

4) Add the following onMouseUp **event at the end of the current script:**

```
_root.onMouseUp = function() {
  down = false;
};
```

When the mouse button is released, we set the value of down to false. When down is false, no lines are drawn.

5) Add the following two lines of script at the end of the current script:

```
var currentColor:String = "7F6696";
_root.createEmptyMovieClip("holder_mc", 100);
```

In our application, as lines are drawn, their color will be based on the current value of currentColor. The value entered in the script represents the initial value of currentColor—that is, its value when the project first plays. In the next exercise, you'll change this variable's value dynamically based on button actions in one of the window's movie clip instances, enabling coloring of lines using different colors.

The next line of this script creates an empty movie clip instance, **holder_mc**. As mentioned earlier, this clip will contain all the lines that are drawn. It's given a depth of 100 so that drawn lines will appear above any icons dragged onto the **canvas_mc** movie clip instance.

6) Start defining the `draw()` **function by adding the following lines at the end of the current script:**

```
function draw() {
  _root.holder_mc.lineStyle(0, parseInt(currentColor, 16), 100);
  var x:Number = _root._xmouse;
  var y:Number = _root._ymouse;
  _root.holder_mc.lineTo(x, y);
}
```

This function will eventually be called by the `onMouseMove` clip event, which we'll script in the next step. When called, the first thing it does is set the line style for the lines to be drawn. The lines drawn will be hairlines (`thickness` of `0`); their color will be based on the `currentColor` variable; and their alpha setting will be `100`. The last three lines of this script are used to complete the drawing of a line. A line is drawn from the current drawing position as set with `moveTo()` when the `onMouseDown` event occurs (as scripted earlier), to the current mouse position (`x` and `y` values in this script) using `lineTo()`.

7) Add the following `onMouseMove` **clip event at the end of the current script:**

```
_root.onMouseMove = function() {
  updateAfterEvent();
  if (down && _root.canvas_mc.hitTest(_root._xmouse, _root._ymouse)) {
    draw();
  }
};
```

The `onMouseMove` event is fired whenever the mouse changes positions. The `updateAfterEvent()` function is a predefined Flash function that tells Flash to update the stage after this event is fired—that is, don't wait until the next frame. The `if` statement checks that the `down` variable state is `true` and that the mouse pointer is indeed over the **canvas_mc** movie clip instance. If both are `true`, the `draw()` function is called. Calling the function repeatedly with this event will emulate the effect of drawing while the mouse button is pressed and the mouse pointer is over the **canvas_mc** movie clip instance. The `if` statement prevents the `draw()` function from being called if the mouse button is up or the mouse pointer moves outside the boundary of the **canvas_mc** movie clip instance.

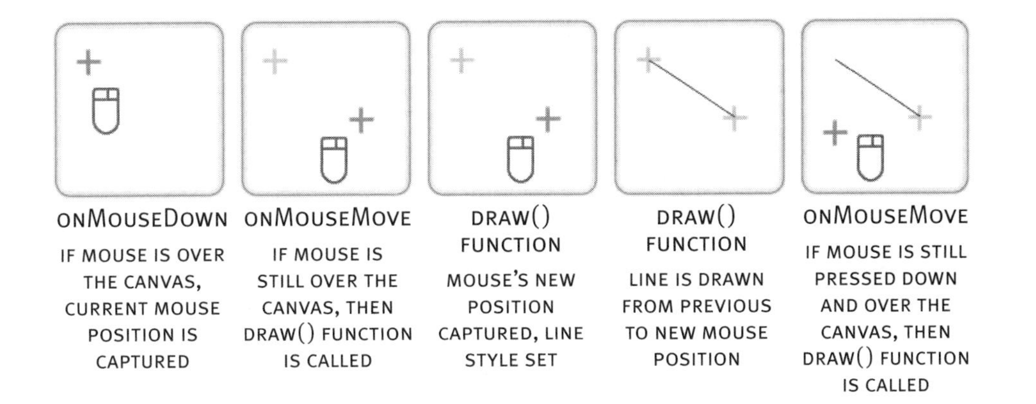
ONMOUSEDOWN
IF MOUSE IS OVER THE CANVAS, CURRENT MOUSE POSITION IS CAPTURED
ONMOUSEMOVE
IF MOUSE IS STILL OVER THE CANVAS, THEN DRAW() FUNCTION IS CALLED
DRAW() FUNCTION
MOUSE'S NEW POSITION CAPTURED, LINE STYLE SET
DRAW() FUNCTION
LINE IS DRAWN FROM PREVIOUS TO NEW MOUSE POSITION
ONMOUSEMOVE
IF MOUSE IS STILL PRESSED DOWN AND OVER THE CANVAS, THEN DRAW() FUNCTION IS CALLED

8) Choose Control > Test Movie. Start drawing.

When your mouse button is pressed while the mouse pointer is over the canvas, the `down` variable is set to `true`. This means that when the mouse is moved, lines are drawn. If the mouse pointer leaves the canvas area, drawing ceases.

9) Close the test movie and save your work as *draw2.fla*.

Now you're ready to make the windows to the right of the canvas active and add the drag-and-drop functionality that will allow you to add icons to the canvas.

CREATING FILLED SHAPES DYNAMICALLY

Even though we're not going to devote an exercise to the topic, drawing filled shapes is still worth discussing.

By building on the syntax you've used thus far in this lesson, you can use the drawing methods to create a shape and then fill it with a single color (a *flat fill*) or a gradient (a *gradient fill*).

To create a flat fill, you must let Flash know that the shape you're about to draw will be filled. You do this by employing the following method:

```
path.beginFill(color,alpha)
```

The path points to the timeline where the lines will exist. The `color` parameter accepts a hex color value. The `alpha` parameter accepts a number between 0 and 100 to set the alpha level of the fill. To let Flash know when you're finished drawing a shape, use the following method:

```
path.endFill()
```

The following example shows how this method is used:

```
_root.createEmptyMovieClip("box_mc",1);
with (_root.box_mc) {
  lineStyle(0,0x000000,100);
  beginFill(0x990000,100);
  moveTo(0,0);
  lineTo(100,0);
  lineTo(100,100);
  lineTo(0,100);
  lineTo(0,0);
  endFill();
}
```

This ActionScript does the following:

1) Creates an empty movie clip instance.

2) Sets the line style.

3) Initiates the fill.

4) Draws a shape.

5) Ends the fill.

It's important to note that when creating a filled shape, the starting point of the shape, as defined by `moveTo()`, must also be the ending point of the shape, as defined by the last `lineTo()`.

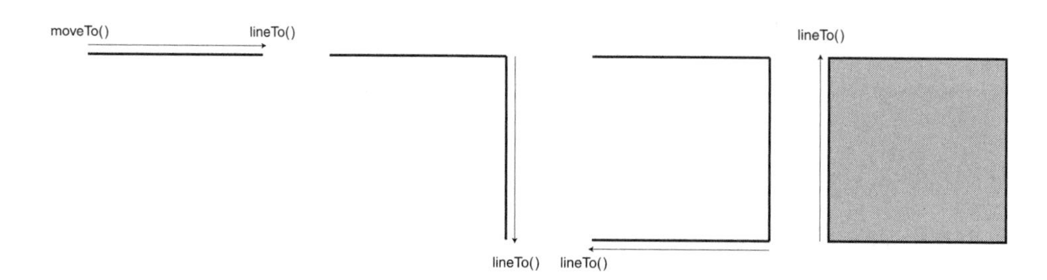

Creating a gradient fill is a little more difficult than creating a flat fill. You must first tell Flash that the shape you're about to draw is to be filled with a gradient. The syntax is as follows:

```
path.beginGradientFill(type, colors, alphas, ratios, matrix)
```

- The `type` parameter accepts the string `linear` or `radial`.
- The `colors` parameter is an array of hex color values that you want to use in your gradient. This array can contain two or more elements.
- The `alphas` parameter is an array of alpha values to be applied to each respective color. This array should have the same number of elements as the `colors` array.

- The `ratios` parameter is an array of elements that contain values between 0 and 255. These values determine the color distribution.
- The `matrix` parameter of the `beginGradientFill()` method contains values that are used to move, skew, and rotate the gradient.

There are two ways to configure the `matrix` object, the more common of which contains the following properties:

- `matrixType` is a variable with a value of `"box"`. You must set it so that Flash knows which type of matrix you're using.
- `x` is the x position at which to start the gradient. Flash uses the upper-left corner of the overall gradient to place this gradient.
- `y` is the y position at which to start the gradient. Flash uses the upper-left corner of the overall gradient to place this gradient.
- `w` is the width of the gradient.
- `h` is the height of the gradient.
- `r` is the rotation of the gradient (in radians).

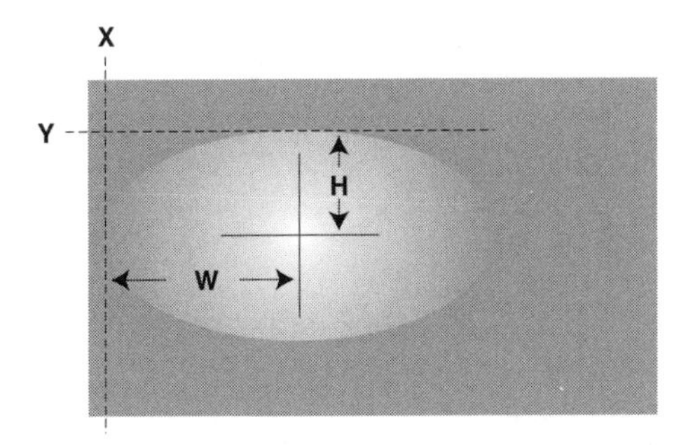

Following is an example of the syntax used to create a gradient-filled shape:

```
_root.createEmptyMovieClip("holder_mc", 1);
with (_root.holder_mc) {
  lineStyle(0, 0x000000, 0);
  rotation = 90 * (Math.PI/180);
  colors = [ 0x6666FF, 0xFF6600 ];
  alphas = [ 100, 100 ];
  ratios = [ 0, 255 ];
  matrix = { matrixType:"box", x:0, y:150, w:200, h:100, r:rotation };
  beginGradientFill( "linear", colors, alphas, ratios, matrix );
  moveTo(0,0);
  lineTo(550,0);
  lineTo(550,300);
  lineTo(0,300);
  lineTo(0,0);
  endFill();
}
```

This example creates a square and fills it with a gradient. The lines of the square have an alpha of 0 so you can't see them.

You'll probably need to test beginGradientFill() a few times to feel comfortable using it.

Z-SORTING MOVIE CLIP INSTANCES

Changing the depth of movie clip instances is known as *z-sorting*. The letter *z* is used in the name because changing the depth gives the effect of a third dimension in Flash: z (in addition to x and y). You can use duplicateMovieClip() or attachMovie() to set the depth of movie clip instances when you create them, or you can change the depth dynamically using the swapDepths() method of the Movie Clip class. With swapDepths() you can exchange the depth of any two movie clip instances or move an instance to a specified depth.

Here's the syntax for swapping the depths of two movie clip instances:

```
movieClip1_mc.swapDepths(movieclip2_mc);
```

If **movieClip2_mc** is above **movieClip1_mc**, this script swaps their depths, causing **movieClip1_mc** to appear above **movieClip2_mc**.

Here's the syntax for sending any movie clip instance—even one created using duplicateMovieClip() or attachMovie()—to a specific depth:

```
movieClip1_mc.swapDepths(anyDepth);
```

The anyDepth parameter is an integer. The swapDepths() method is easy to use and can add a nice effect to applications and games.

There are two more Movie Clip class methods that can assist you with z-sorting: getDepth() and getNextHighestDepth(). The getDepth() method returns the numeric depth of a movie clip. For example:

```
var mc_depth:Number = myClip_mc.getDepth();
```

The getNextHighestDepth() method returns the highest unused depth that has no other depths above it filled. For example, imagine that you had a movie clip with an instance name of **holder_mc** and you attached a movie clip at depth 2050 inside it. This ActionScript:

```
var nextDepth:Number = holder_mc.getNextHighestDepth();
```

creates a variable named nextDepth with a value of 2051.

These methods, both new in ActionScript 2.0, make managing the depth of dynamically added instances much simpler than before.

In this exercise, you'll make the two windows in the drawing application draggable, use `swapDepths()` to bring the window of interest to the top of the stack, and add actions to some of the buttons.

1) Open *draw2.fla*.

This is the file as you left it at the end of the preceding exercise. In this exercise, you'll add more ActionScript to Frame 1 in the Actions layer on the main timeline and work with the window clips.

2) With the Actions panel open, select Frame 1 of the Actions layer and add these two lines of script at the end of the current script:

```
window1_mc.gotoAndStop("color");
window2_mc.gotoAndStop("admin");
```

window1_mc and **window2_mc** are instances of the same movie clip—they just have different instance names. The ActionScript in this step is used to direct these instances to the frames labeled *color* and *admin*, respectively.

The *color* frame label contains several buttons that will be used to change the drawing color. (You will soon add the ActionScript to handle this task.) The *admin* frame contains two buttons—one to clear the canvas and one to print what's on the canvas. You will not add the ActionScript for the buttons on the *admin* frame until the last exercise in this lesson.

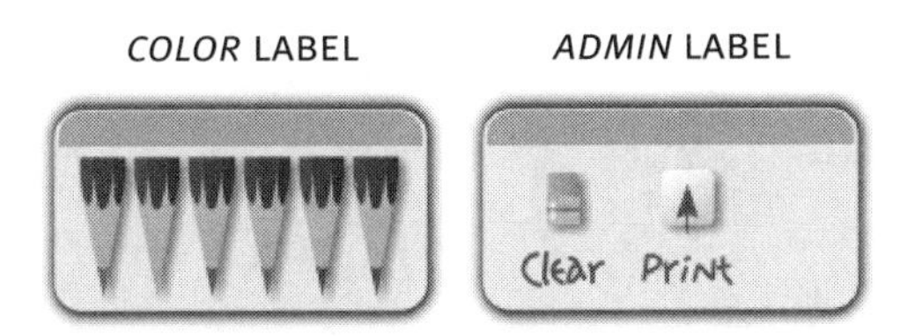

3) Double-click *window1_mc* and move to the *color* frame label. Select the frame in the Actions layer and add the following script:

```
var colors:Array = ["7F6696", "FAC81C", "E72638", "1091CB", "1FA900",
"BC0077"];
for (var i:Number = 1; i <= 6; ++i) {
  var temp_btn = this["pencil" + i + "_btn"];
  temp_btn.color_index = i - 1;
  temp_btn.onRelease = function() {
    changeColor(this.color_index);
  };
}
```

This frame has six button instances—**pencil1_btn** through **pencil6_btn**. This script is used to set up their functionality.

The first line creates an array. Each element in the array is a string that stores a color. Notice that there are a total of six color values, each of which will eventually be associated with a button.

The `for` loop adds an `onRelease` event handler to each of the six buttons. It also stores a variable on each button called `color_index`. The `color_index` variable is a number that corresponds to a position in the `colors` array. For example, the button instance **pencil1_btn** will be assigned a `color_index` value of `0`, and **pencil6_btn** will get a `color_index` value of `5`.

The `onRelease` event handler added to each button instance calls a function (not yet added) called `changeColor()` and passes in the `color_index` of the button instance that calls the function. The `changeColor()` function will use the value of `color_index` to grab a color from the `colors` array, and use that color to change the drawing color.

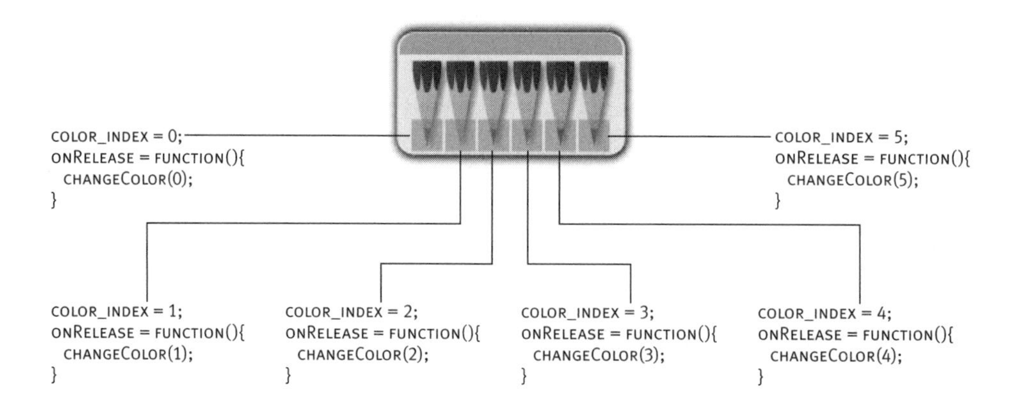
COLOR_INDEX = 0;
ONRELEASE = FUNCTION(){
CHANGECOLOR(0);
}
COLOR_INDEX = 5;
ONRELEASE = FUNCTION(){
CHANGECOLOR(5);
}
COLOR_INDEX = 1;
ONRELEASE = FUNCTION(){
CHANGECOLOR(1);
}
COLOR_INDEX = 2;
ONRELEASE = FUNCTION(){
CHANGECOLOR(2);
}
COLOR_INDEX = 3;
ONRELEASE = FUNCTION(){
CHANGECOLOR(3);
}
COLOR_INDEX = 4;
ONRELEASE = FUNCTION(){
CHANGECOLOR(4);
}

4) Add the following `changeColor()` **function to this frame:**

```
function changeColor(color_index:Number) {
  _root.currentColor = colors[color_index];
}
```

This function is called when any of the six button instances is released. It changes the value of the variable called `currentColor` on the `_root` timeline to that of one of the color values in the colors array, depending on which button is clicked. Every time the `draw()` function is called, it uses the value of `currentColor` to color the line that it's drawing. By changing the value of the `currentColor` variable, you're changing the color of the lines that will be drawn.

5) Move the current movie clip timeline to Frame 1. With the Actions panel open and the Actions layer selected, add the following script below the `stop()` action that's already there:

```
drag_btn.onPress = function() {
  startDrag(this._parent);
  _root.swap(this._parent);
};
drag_btn.onRelease = function() {
  stopDrag();
};
```

The yellow button at the top of this movie clip has an instance name of **drag_btn**. This script tells the button what to do when it's pressed or released.

When pressed, two things occur. The `startDrag()` method begins dragging the button's parent, which is the window movie clip the button is part of. The second action calls a function (not yet written) on the `_root` timeline called `swap()`, the purpose of which is to change the z-order of the window to bring it to the front of the stack. When the function is called, it's passed a reference to the button's parent, which once again is the window movie clip the button is part of. Because our project contains two instances of this movie clip—**window1_mc** and **window2_mc**—the actions on this button will work as follows: when the button is clicked in the **window1_mc** instance, that instance becomes draggable and a reference of the instance is passed to the `swap()` function. When the button in **window2_mc** is clicked, that instance becomes draggable and a reference of that instance is sent to the `swap()` function.

6) Return to the main timeline. With the Actions panel still open, select Frame 1 of the Actions layer and add the following line of script at the end of the current script:

```
var topClip:MovieClip = window1_mc;
```

We will be using the `swapDepths()` method to swap the depths of the **window1_mc** and **window2_mc** movie clip instances. The `topClip` variable is used to store the reference of the instance, which is currently at the higher depth. When the movie is exported, **window1_mc** is at a higher depth, so that's how we initialize this variable's value.

7) Add the following function definition to the frame:

```
function swap(clip:MovieClip) {
  clip.swapDepths(topClip);
  topClip = clip;
}
```

This function accepts a parameter named `clip`. This parameter is a reference to the movie clip that's requesting to be forced to the top depth (as discussed in Step 5). The first line of this function swaps the depths of the movie clip reference passed in, clip, and the one currently stored as the top clip, topClip. If both clip and topClip are references to the same movie clip, the function changes nothing. The last line of the function changes the value of topClip to store a reference to the clip that was just forced to the top.

When the Flash movie first starts, topClip points to **window1_mc**. If the **drag_btn** button instance in **window2_mc** is pressed, the swap function is called and **window1_mc** and **window2_mc** exchange depths.

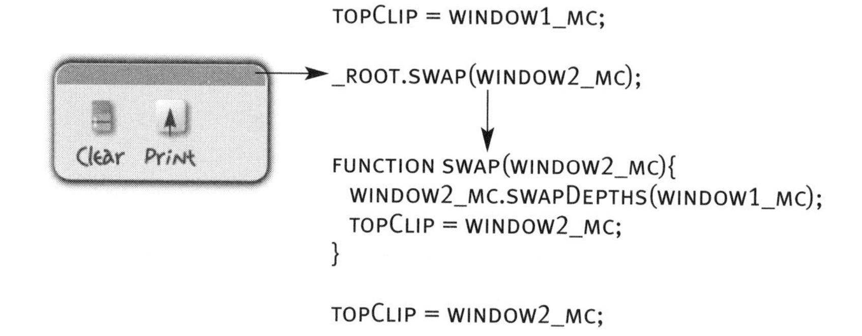
TOPCLIP = WINDOW1_MC;
_ROOT.SWAP(WINDOW2_MC);
FUNCTION SWAP(WINDOW2_MC){
WINDOW2_MC.SWAPDEPTHS(WINDOW1_MC);
TOPCLIP = WINDOW2_MC;
}
TOPCLIP = WINDOW2_MC;
Clear
Print

8) Choose Control > Test Movie to test the movie. Click the windows and drag them around. Change the color of the lines.

When you click the button at the top of one of the windows, its depth is set to the highest in the stacking order and a drag is initiated.

The only thing that happens when you click the color buttons is that the value of the currentColor variable on the _root timeline changes, allowing you to draw lines of different colors.

9) Close the test movie and save your work as *draw3.fla*.

You've now used swapDepths() to bring the window of interest to the front of the window stack—but you're not finished yet! You still need to script the functionality to clear the canvas and add drag-and-drop functionality to the icons.

DRAGGING AND DROPPING MOVIE CLIP INSTANCES

In user interfaces, it's sometimes useful to add *drag-and-drop* behaviors to movie clip instances—a term that refers to the process of clicking and dragging movie clip instances around the stage, so that when they're released (dropped), they'll perform a set of actions determined by the location where they're dropped. The easiest way to conceptualize this type of behavior is by thinking of the trashcan icon on your computer desktop: If you drag a file over the trashcan and let go of it, that file is deleted; however, if you're not over the trashcan when you let go, you've simply moved the file icon.

The most common way to create drag-and-drop items in Flash is by using _droptarget or hitTest(). Accessing the _droptarget property of a movie will return the path in slash syntax to the highest movie clip instance that the currently dragged movie clip instance is over. Using the hitTest() method, you can determine whether the bounding box of one instance is touching the bounding box of another and take action accordingly. For more on this topic, see Lesson 8, "Using Conditional Logic." The hitTest() method is used more frequently because it's more versatile than the _droptarget property.

In this exercise, you'll extend your project to dynamically create a row of icons—simple graphical movie clip instances—that can be dragged and dropped onto the **canvas_mc** movie clip instance using hitTest(). When dropped, a copy of the movie clip instance will be created using duplicateMovieClip() and the original will be sent back to its initial position.

1) Open *draw3.fla*.

This file is as you left it at the end of the preceding exercise. You will continue to add ActionScript to the _root timeline in this exercise. You'll create a function that creates the row of icons below the **canvas_mc** movie clip instance. Then you'll add the ActionScript that makes them draggable and the ActionScript that detects whether they were dropped onto **canvas_mc**.

2) With the Actions panel open, select Frame 1 of the Actions layer and add the following function:

```
function buildIconList() {
  var spacing:Number = 85;
  var iconY:Number = 360;
  var iconX:Number = 70;
  for (var i = 0; i < _root.icon_mc._totalframes; ++i) {
    var newName:String = "icon_mc" + i;
    var clip:MovieClip = _root.icon_mc.duplicateMovieClip(newName, 10000 + i);
    clip.gotoAndStop(i + 1);
    clip._x = iconX + i * spacing;
    clip._y = iconY;
    clip.homeX = clip._x;
        clip.homeY = clip._y;
    clip.icon_btn.onPress = function() {
      startDrag(this._parent);
    };
    clip.icon_btn.onRelease = function() {
      stopDrag();
      _root.iconReleased(this._parent);
    };
  }
}
```

Although this function is fairly large, there's nothing here that you haven't seen before. The **icon_mc** movie clip instance contains a certain number of frames on its timeline, each of which includes a different icon graphic. This script duplicates the **icon_mc** clip once for every frame in that movie clip. It sends each duplicated movie clip instance to a unique frame and aligns it along the bottom of the screen. The result is a row of icons at the bottom of the screen. You can add or remove icons (that is, add or remove frames) in the **icon_mc** movie clip instance, and this loop will adapt based on the `_totalframes` property used in the `for` loop. The `spacing` variable represents the vertical space between the duplicated icons. `iconY` and `iconX` represent the coordinates of the first duplicate.

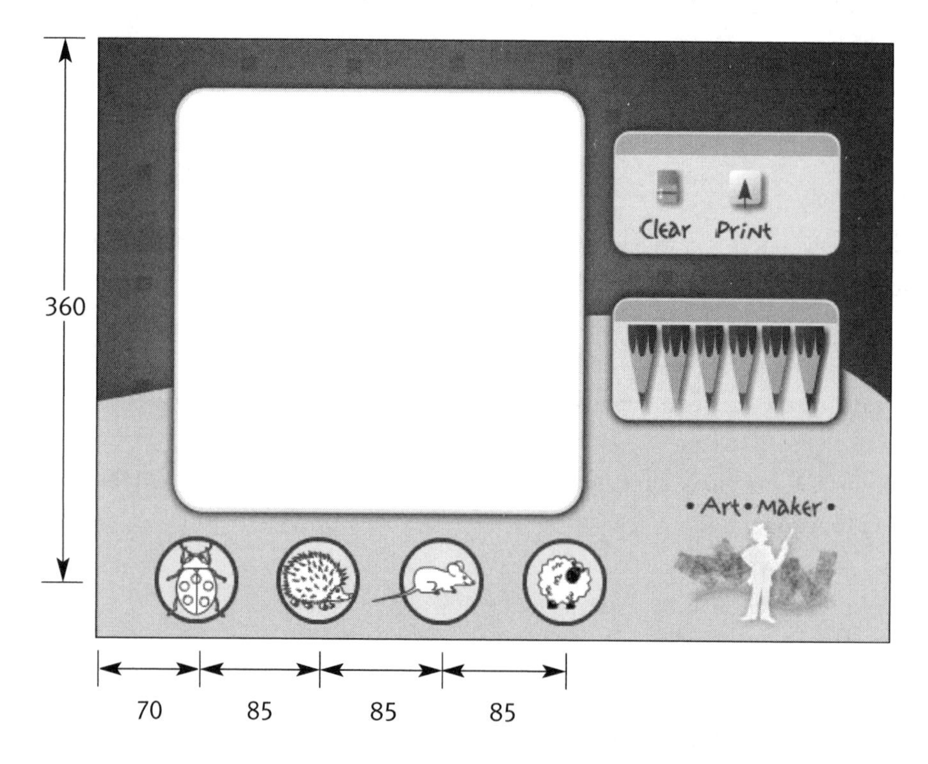

Each new movie clip instance stores the variables `homeX` and `homeY`. Those variables represent the position on the stage where the movie clip instance is initially placed when created and where it snaps back to after being dragged and dropped.

The **icon_mc** movie clip instance as well as its duplicates contains a button instance with a name of **icon_btn**. The last section of this function adds `onPress` and `onRelease` event handlers to that button instance inside each of the duplicates. The `onPress` event handler tells the movie clip instance that's holding the button to begin dragging when the button is clicked. The `onRelease` event handler tells the movie clip instance to stop being dragged, and calls the `iconReleased()` function when the button is released. The `iconReleased()` function, which will be defined in a moment, checks whether the movie clip instance was dragged onto the canvas. If so, the function creates a duplicate of that instance on top of the canvas and then places the original instance back at its original position. For the `iconReleased()` function to know which icon instance to duplicate, it's passed a reference of the instance that was just dragged and dropped.

3) Add this code at the bottom of the frame:

```
buildIconList();
```

This will call the function you created in Step 2 to create the icon list.

4) Add the following function at the end of Frame 1:

```
function iconReleased(icon:MovieClip) {
  if (_root.canvas_mc.hitTest(_root._xmouse, _root._ymouse)) {
    ++iconDepth;
    var newName:String = "object" + iconDepth + "_mc";
    var clip:MovieClip = icon.duplicateMovieClip(newName,iconDepth);
    clip.gotoAndStop(icon._currentFrame);
    clip.icon_btn.enabled = false;
    clip._xscale = 250;
    clip._yscale = 250;
  }
  icon._x = icon.homeX;
  icon._y = icon.homeY;
}
```

This function is set up to receive one parameter, which is identified as `icon`. This parameter is a reference to the icon movie clip instance that has just been dragged and dropped. The value of this parameter plays an important role in how the rest of the function works.

A conditional statement checks whether the mouse pointer is over the **canvas_mc** movie clip instance when the function is called, indicating that the icon has actually been dropped *on* the canvas. If the mouse pointer is over **canvas_mc**, a copy of the movie clip instance that's dragged and dropped is created using `duplicateMovieClip()`. The name given to the duplicate is derived by concatenating `"object"` with the current value of `iconDepth` (which is defined in the next step, and is incremented with each new duplicate created) and adding `"_mc"` to the end. Based on this functionality, the current value of `iconDepth` will always reflect the number of duplicate icons that have been dragged and dropped onto the canvas—an important thing to remember for the next exercise.

After it's created, the duplicate is sent to the same frame as the original instance so that the same icon that was dragged appears on the canvas. The next action is used to disable the invisible button inside the duplicate named **icon_btn**. In addition, the duplicate is scaled vertically and horizontally by 250 percent so that it will appear on the canvas as a larger representation of the icon instance from which it was created.

NOTE *A duplicated instance inherits the exact x and y positions of the original at the time of its duplication; therefore, unless you use a simple script to move it, a duplicate—upon its creation—is placed right on top of the original. This means you won't be able to tell that a duplicate has been created because nothing will have changed visually.*

The last two lines of ActionScript in this function send the dragged movie clip instance back to its original position, based on the values of `homeX` and `homeY` on its timeline. Notice that these actions are placed outside the conditional statement, meaning that they're executed regardless of whether the statement proves `true` and a duplicate is created. If the user tries to drop an icon anywhere other than on top of the **canvas_mc** movie clip instance, no duplicate will be created, and the icon will simply snap back to its original position below the canvas.

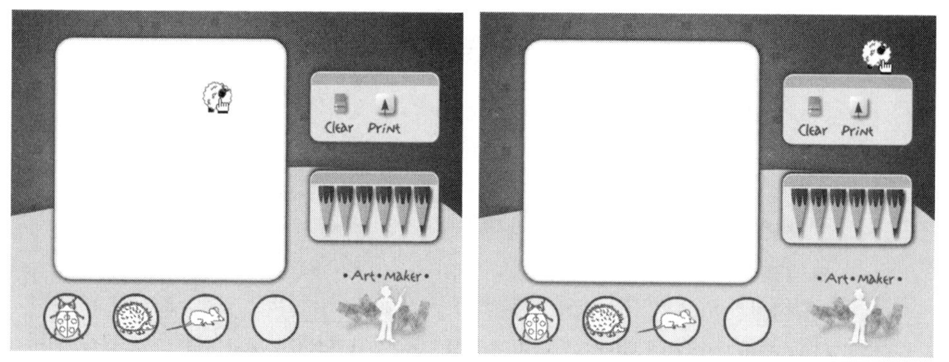
IF DROPPED OVER THE CANVAS, DUPLICATE WILL BE CREATED
IF DROPPED OUTSIDE THE CANVAS, DUPLICATE WILL *NOT* BE CREATED
Clear
Print
• Art • Maker •

5) Add the following variable at the top of Frame 1:

```
var iconDepth:Number = 0;
```

This variable is used to store the number of icons duplicated onto the canvas as well as to assign a unique depth to a duplicated icon and give it a unique name. `iconDepth` was used for these purposes in Step 4. It's defined outside of a function because it needs to exist for as long as the application is running.

6) Choose Control > Test Movie to test your work. Drag the icons onto the canvas.

If you drag an icon and drop it anywhere other than on the **canvas_mc** instance, it will return to its original location, unduplicated. If you release the icon over the **canvas_mc** movie clip instance, a duplicate will be created and the original will be sent back to its starting position.

7) Close the test movie and save your work as *draw4.fla*.

You've now created a simple, medium-sized drawing application. By applying the concepts you've learned here, you can create an application that includes many more features than this one.

REMOVING DYNAMICALLY CREATED CONTENT

You can easily remove dynamically drawn lines from a timeline using the `clear()` method. Here's the syntax:

```
path.clear();
```

Movie clip instances that are created using `duplicateMovieClip()` or `attachMovie()`, such as icons that are dragged and dropped onto **canvas_mc**, can be removed using a method of the Movie Clip class called `removeMovieClip()`.

NOTE *You can't use this method to remove movie clip instances that were not created using ActionScript—that is, instances that you've actually dragged from the library and placed on the stage.*

Removing movie clip instances can be useful for dynamically clearing the stage content, freeing system resources, reinitializing applications, or adding functionality to some applications. The syntax is simple:

```
someMovieClip.removeMovieClip()
```

In this exercise, you'll create a function that will clear the canvas of all dynamically drawn lines as well as instances of the **icon_mc** movie clip instance that might be dragged and dropped onto **canvas_mc**.

1) Open *draw4.fla*.

This is the file as you left it at the end of the preceding exercise. In this exercise, you'll add a function to Frame 1 in the Actions layer of the main timeline that will clear the canvas of any content, and you'll add a script to the Clear button in the **window2_mc** movie clip instance that calls this function.

2) With the Actions panel open, select Frame 1 of the Actions layer and add the following function definition at the end of the current script:

```
function clearContent() {
  _root.holder_mc.clear();
  for (var i = 0; i <= iconDepth; ++i) {
    var name:String = "object" + i + "_mc";
    _root[name].removeMovieClip();
  }
  iconDepth = 0;
}
```

The first action in this function clears all dynamically drawn lines from the **holder_mc** movie clip instance, using the `clear()` method. A simple `for` loop is then used to remove any instances of the **icon_mc** movie clip instance that have been dragged and dropped onto the canvas. Because the value of `iconDepth` is incremented with each **icon_mc** instance that's dragged, dropped, and duplicated, as shown in the `buildIconList()` function definition scripted in the preceding exercise, its value always represents the number of **icon_mc** instances that have been duplicated and placed on the canvas. This value is thus used in the loop to set how many iterations the removal loop should perform. After the loop finishes removing all the dragged and dropped **icon_mc** instances, the value of `iconDepth` is set to `0` so that the next time an **icon_mc** instance is dragged and dropped onto the canvas, naming of the duplicated instances can once again begin with `0`.

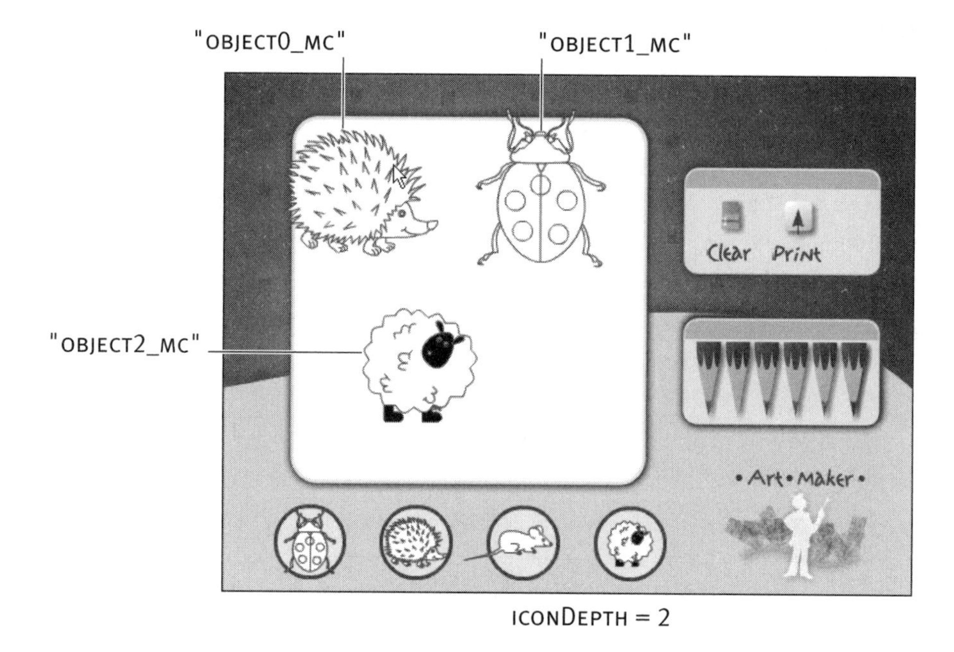

3) Double-click the *window2_mc* instance to edit it in place. Move the playhead to the *admin* frame label. Select the frame on the Actions layer and add the following script:

```
clear_btn.onRelease = function() {
  _root.clearContent();
};
```

This frame contains two buttons: **clear_btn** and **print_btn**. The script added in this step defines an `onRelease` event handler for the **clear_btn** button instance. When clicked, the `clearContent()` function on the main timeline is called, clearing the canvas of content.

4) On the same frame, add the following script for the *print_btn* button instance:

```
print_btn.onRelease = function() {
  printAsBitmap("_root", "bmovie");
};
```

When the **print_btn** button is released, the graphical content of the _root timeline, as well as of any of its child movies (essentially, everything you see, including dynamically created instances), will be printed as a bitmap graphic at actual size.

NOTE *This script demonstrates how dynamically created instances can be printed as easily as anything else. Had we wanted to get a bit more sophisticated, we might have opted to print only what was drawn on the canvas itself; however, this would require some different syntax in our various functions, and printing options are not the focus of this exercise. You'll see more on printing in Lesson 21, "Printing and Context Menus."*

5) Choose Control > Test Movie to test the movie. Draw a few lines and then click the Clear button.

When you click the Clear button, the `clearContent()` function is executed and the `for` loop iterates through and deletes every created movie clip instance.

6) Close this movie and save your work as *draw5.fla*.

This completes the exercise and the lesson. As you have learned, the dynamic removal of content is even easier than its creation; however, knowing how to do both allows your projects to scale and change in many ways based on user input and interaction.

WHAT YOU HAVE LEARNED

In this lesson, you have:

- Duplicated and attached movie clip instances dynamically (pages 510–523)
- Created a scrolling window that uses continuous-feedback buttons (pages 523–531)
- Drawn lines using Flash's drawing methods and techniques (pages 531–537)
- Learned how to fill shapes with colors and gradients (pages 537–540)
- Changed the z-order of instances dynamically (pages 540–544)
- Created drag-and-drop movie clip instances (pages 544–549)
- Removed movie clip instances and drawn lines dynamically (pages 549–551)

time- and frame-based dynamism

LESSON 16

Your Macromedia Flash movie doesn't need to depend on user actions (such as moving the mouse or pressing a button) to trigger a response; it can also respond to the passage of time and frames—elements that can be set in motion independently of the user. By combining these elements with user interaction, you can create even more powerful and interactive projects. In this lesson, we'll show you how time and frames work in Flash. We'll then demonstrate how you can enhance your projects by making them more dynamic.

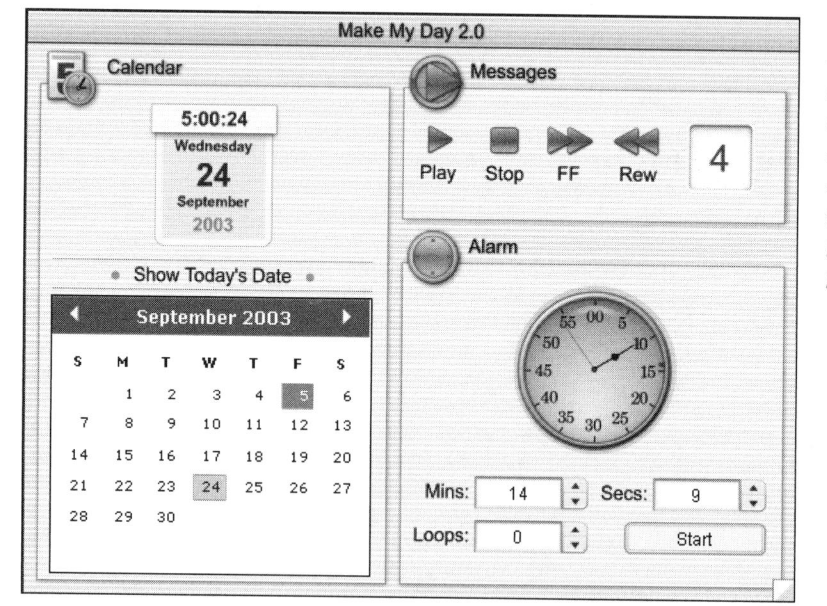

The Make My Day project includes a number of dynamic elements that we'll build in this lesson.

WHAT YOU WILL LEARN

In this lesson, you will:

- Learn how to use the element of time in Flash projects
- Create and use a Date object to display the current date and time
- Use the DateChooser component to navigate and display date-related information
- Use the `getTimer()` function to create a Flash-based timer and alarm so you can track the progression of time in a Flash project
- Control a timeline dynamically using play, stop, fast forward, and rewind controls
- Create a percentage-based preloader

APPROXIMATE TIME

This lesson takes approximately one and one half hours to complete.

LESSON FILES

Starting Files:

Lesson16/Assets/makeMyDay1.fla
Lesson16/Assets/preloader1.fla

Completed Projects:

makeMyDay4.fla
preloader2.fla

Bonus File:

preloaderBytes.fla

THE USE OF TIME IN FLASH

Flash uses several techniques to measure the passage of time in projects. The following are the most common strategies:

- **Date class.** A prebuilt class in Flash, useful for interactivity that depends on dates, days, months, and years.
- getTimer(). A special Flash function useful for measuring the passage of time in milliseconds.
- **Frames.** Representing divisions of time as they relate to animation, sounds, and other interactivity on timelines. Frames provide the most common way of measuring the passage of time in Flash. The movement of one frame to the next (or previous) frame represents the movement of time in a project, either forward or backward. As the timeline moves forward, a progression of events occurs—a streaming sound plays, for example, or a character moves across the stage.

After you understand these elements, you'll be able to make your projects do the following:

- Play forward or backward, depending on user interaction
- React based on the current date, time, or frame number
- Display percentage-based information and download status

There's also a special ActionScript tool—setInterval()—that allows a function to be called at a regular specified interval (measured in milliseconds). Consider the following example:

```
function rotateClip() {
  myMovieClip_mc._rotation += 10;
}
setInterval(rotateClip, 1500);
```

The first three lines of the script define the function that will be used. Next, the setInterval() action is set up to call the rotateClip() function every 1.5 seconds (1,000 milliseconds equals 1 second).

If you want to pass arguments to the called function, simply add them to the setInterval() action:

```
setInterval (updateMessageFunction, 20000, "Hello", arg2, arg3)
```

A setInterval() action can be turned on and off by assigning a variable name, as in the following example:

```
var myInterval:Object = setInterval(rotateClip, 1500);
```

This example assigns the name `myInterval` to the `setInterval()` action. To remove the functionality of the `setInterval()` action, use the following syntax:

```
clearInterval(myInterval);
```

Using the syntax shown, you can initiate the `setInterval()` action at any time, calling any function.

WORKING WITH DATES IN FLASH

It's useful in Flash to be able to access date information—to display the date, make a movie do specific things on certain dates, create countdown timers, or display the day of the week for a particular date in history, to name just a few examples.

To use dates in Flash, you create an instance of the Date class by using the following syntax:

```
var myDate:Date = new Date(year, month, date);
```

This syntax creates a new Date object named `myDate`. The parameters in parentheses associate the Date object with a specific date. For example:

```
var myDate:Date = new Date(66, 6, 27);
```

This example creates a Date object associated with July 27, 1966. The first parameter represents the year, the second represents the month, and the third represents the date. You may wonder why July, which we consider the seventh month in the year, is actually defined as the sixth month in the script above. In ActionScript, both months and days of the week are referenced by numbers, beginning with 0; therefore, January is the "zero" month, February is the first month, March is the second month, and so on—up to December, which is the eleventh month. Likewise, days of the week begin with Sunday as the "zero" day, Monday the first day, and so on. The following exercise demonstrates the usefulness of this numbering system.

NOTE *Dates and years are recognized by their true values; therefore, 66 refers to 1966, while 27 refers to the 27th day in the month.*

When referencing years between 1900 and 1999, the `year` *parameter needs only two digits—the last two digits of the specified year (99 for 1999, 66 for 1966, and so on). Years outside these boundaries must be specified using all four digits (2007 for 2007, 2001 for 2001, and so on).*

TIP *You can add parameters for the hour, minute, second, and millisecond if the application requires that precision.*

To create a Date object that references the current point in time (as indicated by the user's system clock), you can leave the parameter settings blank:

```
var myDate:Date = new Date();
```

After you've created the Date object, you can use Date class methods to retrieve all sorts of information about that date. For example, the preceding line of script would create a Date object that references today's date. To discover the current month, use the following syntax:

```
var currentMonth:Number = myDate.getMonth();
```

If the current month is August, for example, `currentMonth` would have a value of `7` after executing.

To find out the current day of the week, use the following syntax:

```
var currentDay:Number = myDate.getDay();
```

If the current day is Thursday (as set on the computer executing the script), `currentDay` would have a value of `4` after executing.

Other methods of the Date class allow you to retrieve information about the current hour, minute, and second, as defined by the user's computer clock. These methods include the following:

```
myDate.getHours();
myDate.getMinutes();
myDate.getSeconds();
```

This functionality can be useful for displaying the current time in an application—something we'll demonstrate later in this lesson.

 *Your project can contain multiple Date objects, each used for a different purpose.*

Using the DateChooser Component

The DateChooser component provides an easily recognizable visual interface for displaying date-related information; in fact, it looks like a calendar. When placed in a project, the DateChooser component initially displays and highlights the current date according to the computer's system clock; but the DateChooser component does more than provide a pretty face for displaying the current date. It's also an interface for allowing the user to navigate dates. Dates can be selected by clicking them, and months can be navigated by clicking the left arrow icon (to move back one month) or the right arrow icon (to move forward one month).

September 2003

S	M	T	W	T	F	S
	1	2	3	4	5	6
7	8	9	10	11	12	13
14	15	16	17	18	19	20
21	22	23	24	25	26	27
28	29	30				

With ActionScript, a DateChooser component instance can be moved instantly to a specific date, or information about a date that the user has manually highlighted can be retrieved and used in an application. Both of these tasks are made possible via the `selectedDate` property of DateChooser instances. This property's functionality relies on the use of Date objects, as discussed previously. Let's look at a couple of examples.

Suppose there's a DateChooser component instance named **calendar_dc** in your application. To tell this instance to move ahead to and display February 21, 2018, you use syntax like the following:

```
var my25thAnniversary:Date = new Date(2018, 1, 21);
calendar_dc.selectedDate = my25thAnniversary;
```

The first line creates a Date object named `my25thAnniversary`, and the next line uses that Date object to set the value of the `selectedDate` property.

Here's a shorthand way of doing the same thing:

```
calendar_dc.selectedDate = new Date(2018, 1, 21);
```

When retrieving the current value of the `selectedDate` property, the component instance returns a Date object. The following example creates a Date object named `displayedDate`:

```
var displayedDate:Date = calendar_dc.selectedDate;
```

The date referenced by this object is the currently selected date in the **calendar_dc** component instance. Using methods of the Date class, you can retrieve information from this Date object (such as the selected day, month, and year), so that the application knows and can react to the date the user has selected.

In the following exercise, you'll create a highly interactive calendar application using Date objects, the `setInterval()` function, and an instance of the DateChooser component.

1) Open *makeMyDay1.fla* in the Lesson16/Assets folder.

This project contains three distinct sections: Calendar, Alarm, and Messages. In this exercise, we'll concentrate on making the Calendar section functional. The remaining sections are for later exercises.

The Calendar section consists of five text fields, a button, and a DateChooser component instance. The five text fields are shown in the following list (from top to bottom). These settings will be used to display various portions of the date dynamically:

- **time_txt.** Displays the current time in hours, minutes, and seconds. The result is updated for every second that time ticks away.
- **calendarDay_txt.** Displays the current day of the week (for example, `Saturday`).
- **calendarDate_txt.** Displays the current day of the month (for example, `27`).
- **calendarMonth_txt.** Displays the current month (for example, `April`).
- **calendarYear_txt.** Displays the current year (for example, `2004`).

The button is named **showToday_btn** and the DateChooser component instance is named **calendar_dc**.

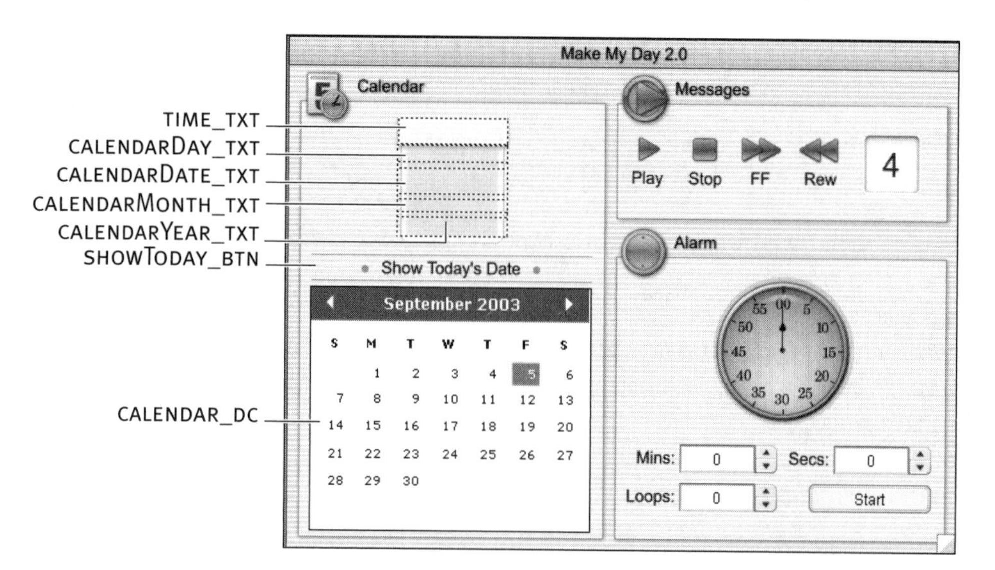

When the application is opened and played initially, the text fields display the current date and time information. As the user interacts with the **calendar_dc** instance, the date information in the text fields is updated accordingly. Clicking the **showToday_btn** instance resets the **calendar_dc** instance and text field instances to display information related to today's date.

All the elements for this exercise reside on the Calendar Assets layer. Nearly all of the ActionScript for this project will be placed on Frame 1 of the Actions layer.

Our first task is to script the functionality for updating the time display, which shows the current hour, minute, and second as determined by the user's system clock. First we'll create a function that captures and displays the most up-to-date time information from the operating system; then we'll use the `setInterval()` action to call this function once every second.

2) With the Actions panel open, select Frame 1 on the Actions layer and add the following script:

```
function updateTime(){
}
```

In the next several steps, we'll add script to the `updateTime()` function that enables it to capture and display the current time.

3) Insert the following line of script within the `updateTime()` function:

```
var currentTime = new Date();
```

This step creates a new Date object named `currentTime`. Because we haven't specified any date parameters within the parentheses, this Date object stores/references the current time on the user's computer—that is, the exact time when the function is executed. The next several lines of script will extract the hour, minute, and second data within the object.

This Date object only needs to exist for the duration of this function's execution (as we'll demonstrate shortly); therefore, it has been declared as a local variable. Of course, if we needed it to exist beyond that point, we would have used strict typing syntax instead:

```
var currentTime:Date = new Date();
```

4) **Insert the following script after the script added in Step 3:**

```
var hour = currentTime.getHours();
var minute = currentTime.getMinutes();
var second = currentTime.getSeconds();
```

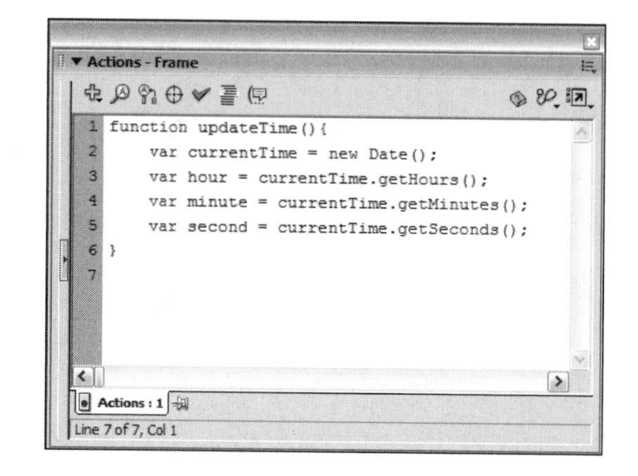

Actions - Frame
function updateTime() {
var currentTime = new Date();
var hour = currentTime.getHours();
var minute = currentTime.getMinutes();
var second = currentTime.getSeconds();
}
Actions : 1
Line 7 of 7, Col 1

These three lines of script create three variables named `hour`, `minute`, `second`. The values of these variables are determined by using various methods of the Date class:

- The `getHours()` method extracts the current hour from the `currentTime` Date object and assigns that value to the `hour` variable. The `getHours()` method always returns an hourly value based on what's commonly referred to as *military time*, where the 24 hours in a day are specified in a range from `0` to `23`.
- The `getMinutes()` method extracts minute data from the `currentTime` Date object and assigns that value to the `minute` variable. The value returned by this method can be anything from `0` (indicating the top of the hour) to `59`.
- The `getSeconds()` method is similar to the `getMinutes()` method. It returns a value between `0` and `59` (seconds); our script assigns that value to the `second` variable.

To help understand this functionality, let's look at an example. Suppose the current time on your computer is 4:04:07 p.m. If you execute the `updateTime()` function now, `hour` would be assigned a value of `16`, `minute` a value of `4`, and `second` a value of `7`.

Although these values are accurate, there's an inherent formatting problem when displaying them in Flash: most clocks display time in the hour:minute:second format. If you plug in the current values of `hour`, `minute`, and `second`, the result is 16:4:7, which isn't easily understood to mean 4:04:07. The next task for our `updateTime()` function is to convert these raw time values into readable values that make sense to the general public. Hour values need to be converted to the 12-hour format; minute and second values need to add a beginning zero (0) if the value is less than 10.

5) Insert the following script after the script added in Step 4:

```
var convertHour;
if (hour >= 13){
  convertHour = hour - 12;
}else if(hour == 0){
  convertHour = 12;
}else{
  convertHour = hour;
}
```

These eight lines of script convert the value of the `hour` variable from a military-time value into the more widely accepted 12-hour format. The converted value is stored in a variable named `convertHour`, which is created on the first line of the script. The conversion occurs as a result of the conditional statement. Here's the logic that went into putting it together.

As we mentioned earlier, the `getHours()` method always returns a value between 0 and 23, representing the hours between 12 a.m. and 11 p.m. 12 a.m. is represented by a value of `0` and 11 p.m. by a value of `23`. Between 1 p.m. and 11 p.m., the `hour` variable would hold a value between 13 and 23. To reformat this value into the 12-hour format, we simply need to subtract 12 from it, which results in a new value between 1 and 11. Perfect! The first part of the conditional statement essentially says, "If `hour` has a value equal to or greater than 13, assign `convertHour` the result of subtracting 12 from `hour`." If `hour` has a value less than 13, this part of the statement is skipped and the next part evaluated.

The next part of the conditional statement handles what happens when `hour` has a value of `0` (representing 12 a.m.). In this case, `convertHour` is given a value of `12`, which is an appropriate representation of 12 a.m. in the 12-hour format. If neither of the preceding conditions is true, the value of `hour` is already appropriate for the 12-hour format (3 a.m. is represented as 3, 10 a.m. as 10, and so on). In such a scenario, the value of `hour` is simply assigned to the value of `convertHour`. In the end, `convertHour` always has a value between 1 and 12.

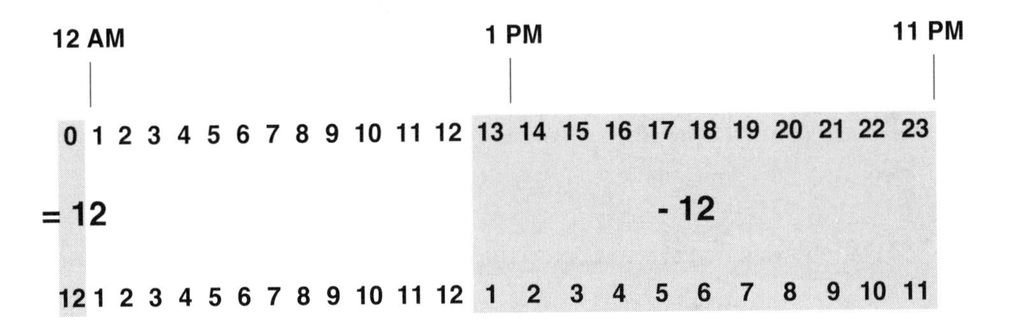

6) Insert the following line after the conditional statement added in Step 5:

```
var convertMinute = (minute < 10) ? "0" + minute : minute;
```

This line of script adds "0" to minute values less than 10, so that numbers such as 2, 5, and 9 appear as 02, 05, and 09, respectively. Here we've used the ternary operator (?) to assign a converted minute value to the convertMinute variable. Because we haven't used the ternary operator that often, let's look at how it's used here.

The expression to the right of the equals sign could be read this way:

```
(evaluate this expression) ? do this if true: do this if false;
```

Our expression states: "If minute has a value less than 10, place a zero (0) in front of that value and assign the result to convertMinute. If the value of minute is greater than 10, assign the value of minute to convertMinute without doing anything." In the end, convertMinute has a value between 00 and 59.

7) Insert the following line after the script added in Step 6:

```
var convertSecond = (second < 10) ? "0" + second : second;
```

This line of script adds "0" to second values less than 10, in the same manner as the line of script discussed in Step 6.

Using our example of 4:04:07, after the conversion process convertHour has a value of 4, convertMinute a value of 04, and convertSecond a value of 07.

The last step we need to take is to string these values together, insert a colon (:) between them, and display the result in the **time_txt** text field.

8) Insert the following script after the script added in Step 7:

```
var timeString = convertHour + ":" + convertMinute + ":" + convertSecond;
time_txt.text = timeString;
```

The first line of this script creates a variable named timeString that holds the concatenated values of convertHour, convertMinute, and convertSecond, separated by colons. The next line displays the resulting value of timeString in the **time_txt** text field.

This step completes the construction of the updateTime() function. The only thing left to do is get the application to call this function repeatedly, once every second.

9) Add the following line of script below the updateTime() function definition:

```
setInterval(updateTime, 1000);
```

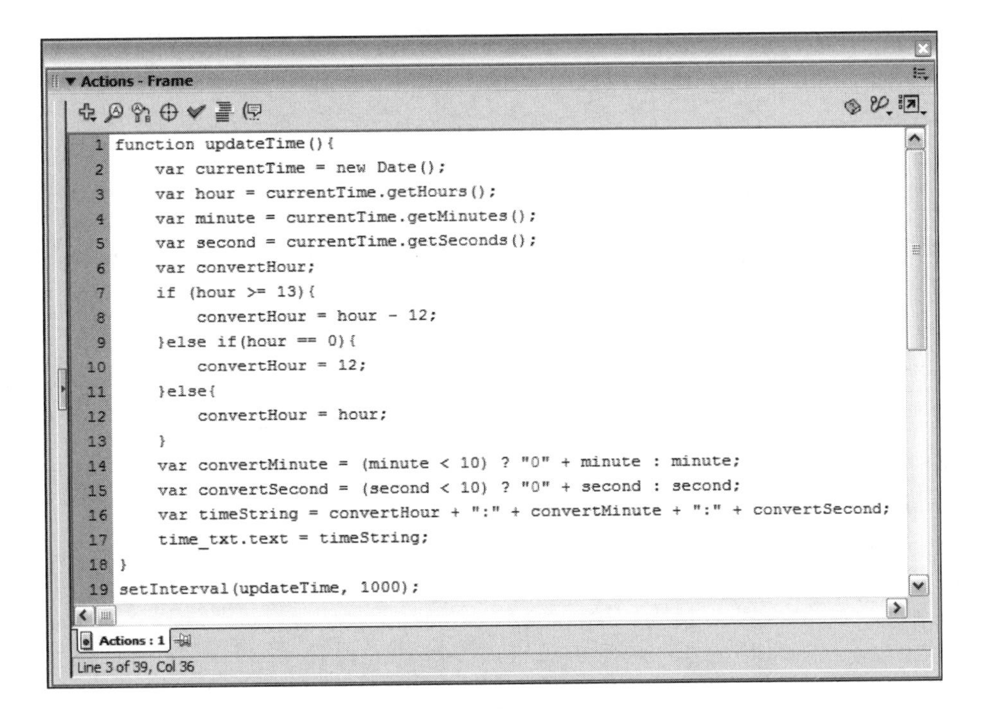
Actions - Frame
function updateTime(){
var currentTime = new Date();
var hour = currentTime.getHours();
var minute = currentTime.getMinutes();
var second = currentTime.getSeconds();
var convertHour;
if (hour >= 13){
convertHour = hour - 12;
}else if(hour == 0){
convertHour = 12;
}else{
convertHour = hour;
}
var convertMinute = (minute < 10) ? "0" + minute : minute;
var convertSecond = (second < 10) ? "0" + second : second;
var timeString = convertHour + ":" + convertMinute + ":" + convertSecond;
time_txt.text = timeString;
}
setInterval(updateTime, 1000);
Actions : 1
Line 3 of 39, Col 36

This `setInterval()` action calls the `updateTime()` function once every second (1,000 milliseconds). Each time the `updateTime()` function is called, the current time data stored in the `currentTime` Date object is updated, extracted, converted, and displayed. The end result is an up-to-the-second time display. Let's check it out.

10) Choose Control > Test Movie.

As soon as the movie begins to play, the current time is displayed in the **time_txt** text field.

We still have a bit more work to do in this exercise.

11) Close the test movie to return to the authoring environment. With the Actions panel open and Frame 1 of the Actions layer selected, add the following script:

```
function updateDate(eventObj:Object){
}
calendar_dc.addEventListener("change", updateDate);
```

The `updateDate()` function eventually will contain script telling the function how to display day, date, month, and year information in the text fields named **calendarDay_txt**, **calendarMonth_txt**, **calendarDate_txt**, and **calendarYear_txt**, respectively. The third line of the script above shows that we've set up the application to call the `updateDate()` function when the user selects a date (firing a `change` event) from the **calendar_dc** instance.

In addition to being called as a result of the `change` event, this function will be called under two other circumstances (which we have yet to script):

- When the application first opens
- When the **showToday_btn** instance is clicked

The function will display today's date information when the application is first opened and when the **showToday_btn** instance is pressed, but it will show the information for *any* date selected by the user when the user interacts with the **calendar_dc** instance. How will it know which of these actions to perform?

When called as a result of the user's interacting with the **calendar_dc** instance, the function is sent an Event object, as discussed in Lesson 10, "Scripting UI Components." Under the other two circumstances when the function is called, no Event is passed. The existence (or nonexistence) of this Event object is checked when the function is executed, allowing the function to react appropriately. This principle will become clearer in a moment.

12) Insert the following script within the `updateDate()` function:

```
if(eventObj.target.selectedDate != undefined){
  var calendarDate = calendar_dc.selectedDate;
}else{
  var calendarDate = new Date();
}
```

This conditional statement helps the function determine what date information to display. The end result of this statement is a Date object named `calendarDate` that contains either today's date information or information related to the currently selected date in the **calendar_dc** instance. Let's look at how it works.

When the function is called as a result of the user's interacting with the **calendar_dc** instance, an Event object is sent to the function; the Event object contains a `target` property value of `calendar_dc`. The following expression:

```
eventObj.target.selectedDate != undefined
```

looks for the existence of a `selectedDate` property on `eventObj.target`, or the **calendar_dc** instance. When the function is called as a result of the user's interacting with the **calendar_dc** instance, this expression evaluates to `true`. When this function is called at any other time, no Event object is passed to the function, and the expression evaluates to `false`.

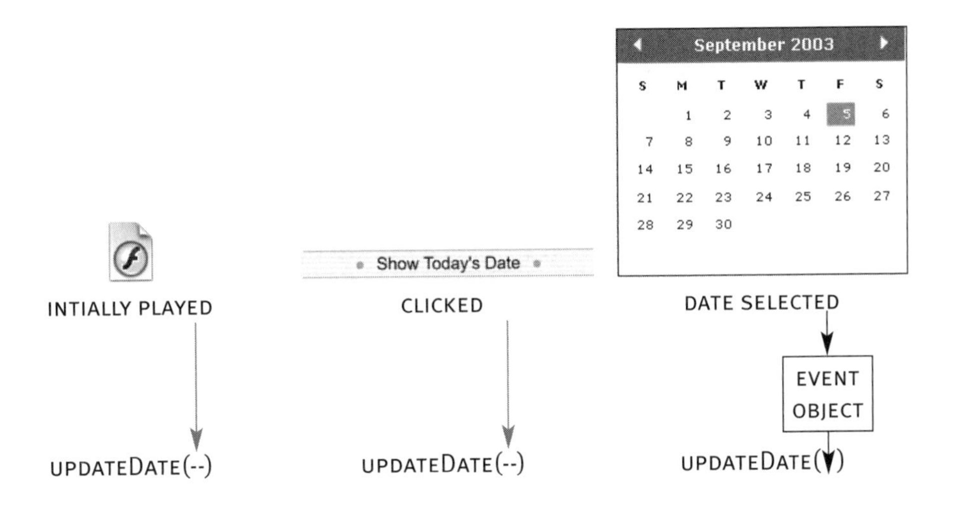

When the expression evaluates to `true`, the value of `calendar_dc.selectedDate` is assigned to `calendarDate`, placing a Date object representing the currently selected date into `calendarDate`. If the currently selected date in the **calendar_dc** instance is July, 27, 2008, for example, the following line of script:

```
var calendarDate = calendar_dc.selectedDate;
```

is essentially the same as this one:

```
var calendarDate = new Date(2008, 6, 27);
```

The `else` part of the statement in Step 12 is executed when the function is called by any means other than the user's interacting with the **calendar_dc** instance. When this occurs, a Date object representative of today's date is placed into `calendarDate`.

The information contained in the `calendarDate` Date object plays a significant role in how the rest of the function works. The remainder of the function deals with extracting date information from the `calendarDate` Date object and displaying it in the appropriate text fields.

13) Insert the following lines of script after the conditional statement added in Step 12:

```
var nameOfDays = ["Sunday", "Monday", "Tuesday", "Wednesday", "Thursday",
⇒"Friday", "Saturday"];
var nameOfMonths = ["January", "February", "March", "April", "May", "June",
⇒"July", "August", "September", "October", "November", "December"];
```

The script creates two arrays: `nameOfDays` and `nameOfMonths`. Each array contains several string values representing the names of days and months, respectively. These arrays are necessary because ActionScript doesn't assign names to months and days of the week. Instead, it references with a number the aspects of dates that we normally associate with a name. The trick to making this part of the project work is associating the proper name (based on its index value in the array) with the numbers ActionScript returns as the current day and month, respectively.

14) Insert the following line of script after the script added in Step 13:

```
calendarDay_txt.text = nameOfDays[calendarDate.getDay()];
```

This action sets the information displayed in the **calendarDay_txt** text field. Here's how it works.

The `getDay()` method (inside the brackets) determines the day of the week for the `calendarDate` Date object. This method returns a value between 0 and 6, with `0` representing Sunday and `6` representing Saturday. If this method determines that the day of the week is `3`, for example, that value is inserted into the brackets within the expression, making it look like this:

```
calendarDay_txt.text = nameOfDays[3];
```

At this point, **calendarDay_txt** displays the value residing at index position 3 of the `nameOfDays` array: the string value `"Wednesday"`. Knowing that the `getDay()` method returns a value between 0 and 6, we created an array (in Step 13) with the names of the days at corresponding array index positions of 0 through 6. When the script is executed, the appropriate day name is used based on the numerical value returned by the `getDay()` method.

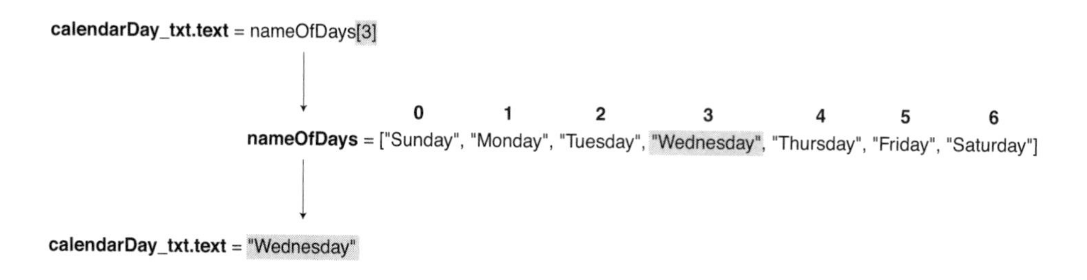

15) Insert the following line of script after the line added in Step 14:

```
calendarMonth_txt.text = nameOfMonths[calendarDate.getMonth()];
```

This action sets the information displayed in the **calendarMonth_txt** text field. It works like the action in Step 14, except that the `getMonth()` method returns a numerical value between 0 and 11 (for January through December). The `nameOfMonths` array from Step 13 has appropriate string values at corresponding index positions.

16) Insert the following line of script after the line added in Step 15:

```
calendarDate_txt.text = calendarDate.getDate();
```

This action sets the information displayed in the **calendarDate_txt** text field. It uses the `getDate()` method, which returns a numerical value between 1 and 31, depending on the date associated with the Date object. Because we want to use the numerical value returned in this circumstance, we don't need to use an array to convert the information to a string value (as discussed in the previous two steps).

17) Insert the following line of script after the line added in Step 16:

```
calendarYear_txt.text = calendarDate.getFullYear();
```

This action sets the information displayed in the **calendarYear_txt** text field. It uses the `getFullYear()` method, which returns a numerical value representing the full year of the date associated with the Date object (for example, 2003). Because we want to use the numerical value returned in this circumstance, we don't need to use an array to convert it to a string value.

This completes the function definition. As scripted in Step 11, this function is called when the user interacts with the **calendar_dc** instance (the `change` event). We still have to add several lines of script to call the function when the application is first opened or when the **showToday_btn** instance is clicked.

18) Add the following script after the line `calendar_dc.addEventListener("change", updateDate);`**:**

```
updateDate();
showToday_btn.onRelease = function(){
  calendar_dc.selectedDate = new Date();
  updateDate();
}
```

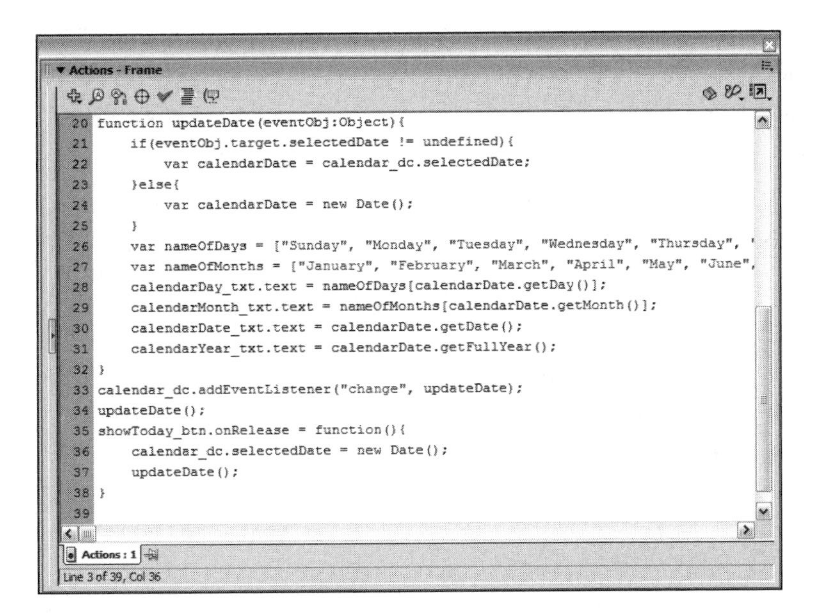

The first line here calls the `updateDate()` function when the application is opened. The remaining lines assign an `onRelease` event handler to the **showToday_btn** instance. When this event is triggered, the script uses a new Date object representative of today to set the `selectedDate` property of the **calendar_dc** instance. This causes today's date to be displayed in the instance, no matter what date the user has navigated to. The second line within the event handler calls the `updateDate()` function.

Remember that neither of the two calls to the `updateDate()` function shown here sends an Event object to the function. As a result, the function is programmed to display today's date information automatically.

19) Choose Control > Test Movie to view the project to his point.

As soon as the movie appears, the text fields in the calendar section of the screen are populated with the appropriate data, displaying the full date. As you select dates from the **calendar_dc** instance, the date information is updated accordingly. Clicking the **showToday_btn** instance moves the **calendar_dc** instance to today's date and updates the displayed date information accordingly.

20) Close the test movie and save the project as *makeMyDay2.fla*.

We'll continue building on this file in the exercises that follow.

DETERMINING THE PASSAGE OF TIME

The `getTimer()` function returns (in milliseconds) the length of time elapsed since the movie was first opened and played; therefore, if the movie has been open for six seconds, the following script:

```
var playBackTime:Number = getTimer();
```

would assign `playBackTime` a value of `6000` (1,000 milliseconds for each second). This is an accurate and precise representation of time based on the user's system clock and is not dependent on the movie's frame rate, the user's processor speed, or whether the movie is playing. This is also a universal value, which means that it represents the playback of the movie as a whole; you cannot track the length of time for which individual timelines have been present.

By setting a variable's value based on the value returned by the `getTimer()` function and comparing that value to the value returned by the function at a later point in time, you can evaluate the amount of time (too much or too little) that has passed within that span, and take appropriate action. To better understand this principle, consider the following example:

```
// Button A functionality
var startTime:Number;
buttonA_btn.onRelease = function() {
  startTime = getTimer();
}
// Button B functionality
var nowTime:Number;
buttonB_btn.onRelease = function() {
  nowTime = getTimer();
  if (nowTime - startTime < 1000) {
    message_txt.text = "You press buttons pretty quickly";
  } else {
    message_txt.text = "You're pretty slow";
  }
}
```

Here, the action on one button (**buttonA_btn**) establishes a starting point by capturing the time when the button is pressed and released. When **buttonB_btn** is pressed and released, the time is captured again. A conditional statement is then used to determine whether the amount of time between these two button presses was more or less than a second—and then acts accordingly. Similarly, by using the following script, you can facilitate double-clicking functionality for a button—that is, the script takes action only if separate clicks occur within a half-second of each other.

```
var lastClick:Number;
myButton_btn.onRelease = function(){
  if(getTimer() - lastClick < 500) {
    // Actions
  }
lastClick = getTimer();
}
```

By integrating the `getTimer()` function with the `onEnterFrame` event and some conditional statements, you can create a mechanism that triggers actions at specific times, independently of the timeline and with much greater accuracy. Look at the following example:

```
slideShow.onEnterFrame = function() {
  if (getTimer() > 5000) {
    // Actions
  }
  if (getTimer() > 10000) {
    // Actions
  }
  if (getTimer() > 15000) {
    // Actions
  }
}
```

This script triggers actions every five seconds while the movie plays. This is often the most accurate way of executing actions at specific points in time during a movie's playback.

In the following exercise, we'll use the `getTimer()` function to create a timer/alarm.

1) Open *makeMyDay2.fla*.

We'll continue building on the project from the preceding exercise. This time around, however, we'll work on the Alarm section of the application. This section of the project contains three NumericStepper component instances named **minutes**, **seconds**, and **loops**, which control when the alarm goes off as well as how many times the alarm sound plays.

Next to these NumericStepper instances is a Button component instance named **start_btn** that starts the timer/alarm.

Above these elements is a movie clip instance named **clock_mc**, which includes several moving elements (just like a real timer). Let's take a look at those.

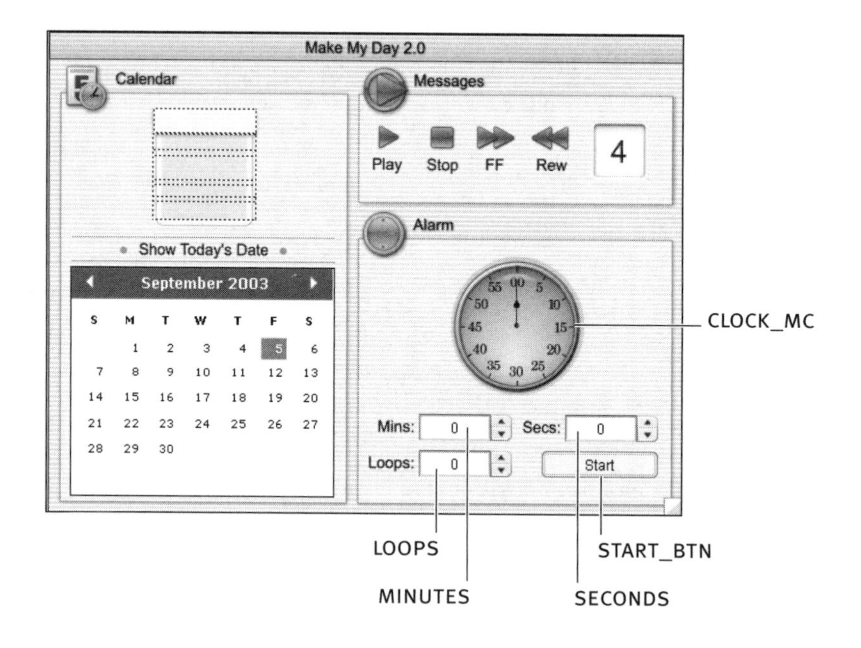

2) Double-click the *clock_mc* movie clip instance to edit it in place.

This timeline contains two layers: the Graphic layer contains the main clock graphic, and the Hands layer contains three movie clip instances that represent various indicators on the clock face. The **secondHand_mc** movie clip represents the clock's second hand, which rotates and simulates a tick each second the timer is on. Just below this instance is a movie clip instance named **minuteHand_mc**, which also rotates—but at 1/10 the speed of the second hand (just as on a real clock). The third movie clip instance appears as a small red tick mark at the top of the clock. Named **alarmHand_mc**, this instance rotates when the timer is started, to indicate when the alarm is set to go off.

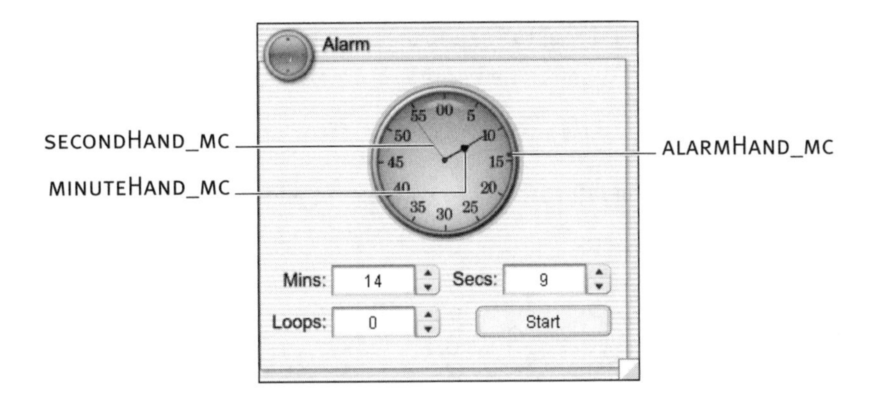

The functionality of the Alarm section of the application will be handled by two main functions: one for starting the alarm timer, and another for stopping the timer and playing the alarm sound. All the script for this exercise will be placed on Frame 1 of the application.

3) Return to the main timeline. With the Actions panel open, select Frame 1 of the Actions layer and add the following script at the end of the current script:

```
start_btn.onRelease = function (){
  alarmOn();
}
```

This step attaches an `onRelease` event handler to the **start_btn** instance. When this event is triggered, the `alarmOn()` function (which we have yet to script) is called. This function turns on the timer and activates the alarm.

4) Add the following script at the end of the current script:

```
var startingTime:Number;
function alarmOn(){
}
```

The first line creates a variable named `startingTime`, which eventually will hold a numeric value representing the split second when the timer is started. The remaining two lines are the beginning of the `alarmOn()` function. As described in Step 3, this function is called when the **start_btn** instance is clicked.

5) Insert the following line of script within the `alarmOn()` function:

```
startingTime = getTimer();
```

When this function is executed, the `startingTime` variable's value is set to a numerical value representing the length of time (in milliseconds) that has elapsed since the movie was first opened and played. Capturing the exact time at which the timer was started is critical to making the Alarm section of the project work properly—we'll explain why in a moment.

6) Insert the following event handler after the line of script added in Step 5:

```
clock_mc.onEnterFrame = function() {
}
```

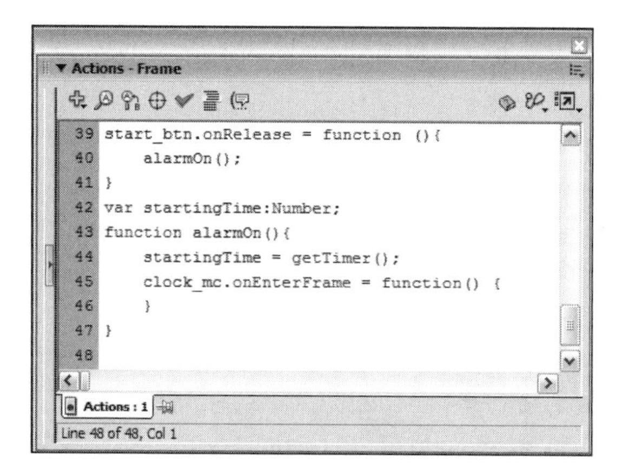

As a result of the `alarmOn()` function being called, this `onEnterFrame` event handler gets attached to the **clock_mc** instance. In the next few steps, we'll add several lines of script within this event handler, which will execute every time the `onEnterFrame` event occurs (24 times a second).

7) Add the following line of script within the `onEnterFrame` event handler:

```
var totalTimeToAlarm = (minutes.value * 60) + seconds.value;
```

Remember that our scene contains one NumericStepper component instance for entering minutes (named **minutes**) and another for entering seconds (named **seconds**). Used together, they determine how much time should elapse before the alarm goes off. The line of script in this step converts the minutes entered to seconds and then adds that figure to the seconds entered, to come up with the total time (in seconds) that must elapse before the alarm sounds.

Before we explain how the expression is evaluated, note that it makes reference to a `value` property in relation to both the **minutes** and **seconds** NumericStepper instances. This property simply represents the current numeric value displayed in the instance.

Using parentheses in the expression, we've sectioned it off into two parts: `(minutes.value * 60)` is added to `seconds.value` to determine the value of `totalTimeToAlarm`. To understand how this expression works, let's look at an example. Assume that the user has entered a value of 5 into the **minutes** instance and 37 into the **seconds** instance. Using these values, the expression would initially look like this:

```
(5 * 60) + 37
```

Because there are 60 seconds in a minute, you can get the seconds equivalent of the minutes entered by multiplying the value entered for **minutes** by 60. In this case, the result is 300. This value is then added to the actual seconds entered to give a final total of 337 (seconds), which is assigned to `totalTimeToAlarm`. Eventually our script will compare this value with the number of seconds that have passed since the timer was started. After the passing seconds exceed the value of `totalTimeToAlarm`, the script knows that it's time to sound the alarm—more on this topic in a bit.

NOTE *Although the timer would work just fine if the value of `totalTimeToAlarm` was set just once, by placing this line of script within the `onEnterFrame` event handler we enable the variable's value to be updated 24 times a second (the frame rate of the movie) if necessary. This allows the user to reset the minute and second settings of the timer dynamically—that is, while the timer is on—and update the value of `totalTimeToAlarm` automatically, affecting when the alarm sounds.*

8) Add the following line of script after the line you added in Step 7:

```
var secondsElapsed = Math.round((getTimer() - startingTime) / 1000);
```

It's critical that our script track the amount of time that has elapsed since the user clicked the Start button and activated the timer. That's what this line of script does. Understanding the precedence in this expression, we know that it's evaluated in the following manner:

Using the `getTimer()` function, the current time (which is checked 24 times a second) is subtracted from the value of `startingTime`:

```
getTimer() - startingTime
```

Remember that the value of `startingTime` is set to the current time at the point when the Start button is clicked and the `alarmOn()` function is called. By constantly checking and subtracting the current time from that value, the script can determine how many milliseconds have elapsed between the current time and the time the Start button was pressed. As we mentioned earlier, this part of the expression results in a millisecond value, such as 29349. If you divide this value by 1,000, as the next part of the expression does (`/ 1000`), you get a result of 29.349—equal to 29.349 actual seconds. The last part of the expression rounds the value:

```
Math.round()
```

In the end, `secondsElapsed` would be assigned a value of `29`. Remember, however, that this value continues to increment as long as the script executes because the difference between the current time and the time the Start button was pressed continues to increase. Also, because the `Math.round()` method is used in the expression, its value increments only in whole numbers—29, 30, 31, and so on. This provides us with the amount of time that has elapsed—accurate to 1/24 of a second because that's how often the line of script is executed.

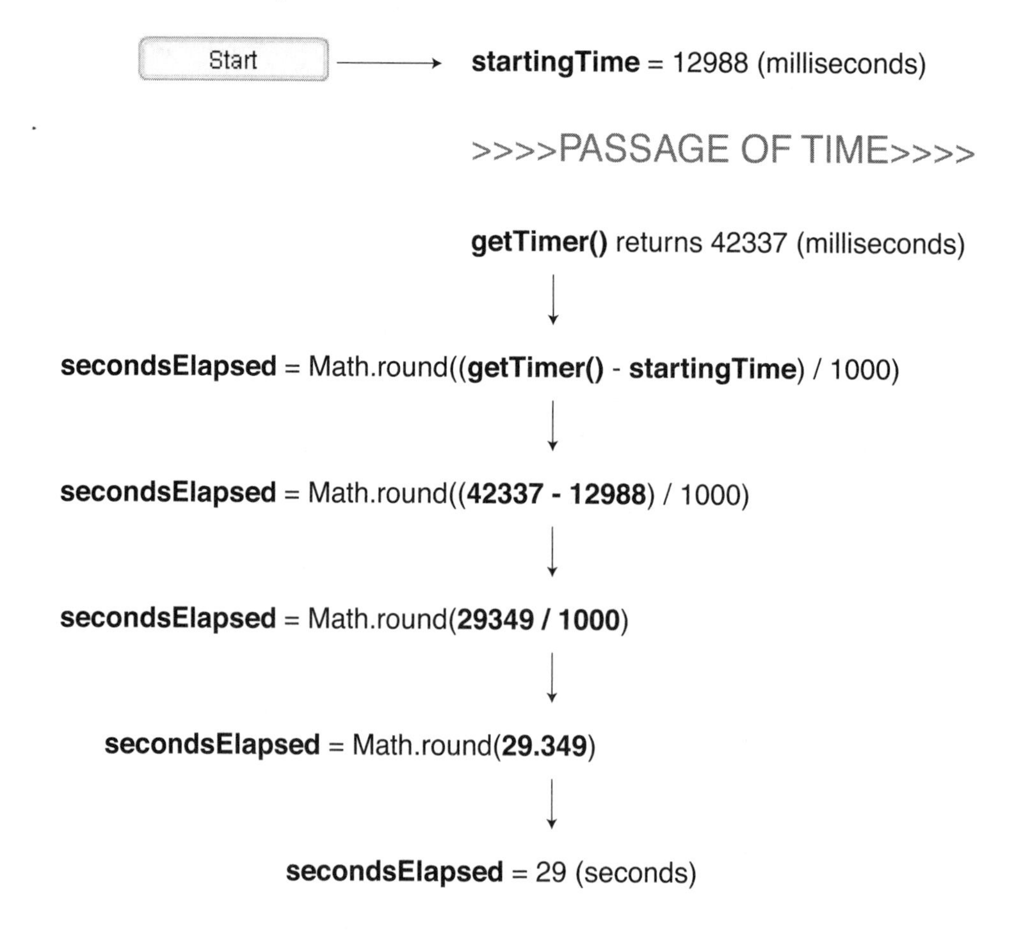
Start
startingTime = 12988 (milliseconds)
>>>>PASSAGE OF TIME>>>>
getTimer() returns 42337 (milliseconds)
secondsElapsed = Math.round((getTimer() - startingTime) / 1000)
secondsElapsed = Math.round((42337 - 12988) / 1000)
secondsElapsed = Math.round(29349 / 1000)
secondsElapsed = Math.round(29.349)
secondsElapsed = 29 (seconds)

At this point, we have two variable values that will facilitate the rest of the actions in this script.

9) Add the following line of script just below the one added in Step 8:

```
clock_mc.alarmHand_mc._rotation = totalTimeToAlarm / 10;
```

Remember that **alarmHand_mc** is the instance name of the hand (red tick mark) inside the **clock_mc** movie clip instance that indicates (on the clock's face) when the alarm is set to go off. This line of script sets the **alarmHand_mc** rotation so that it can perform this functionality. For example, if the alarm is set to go off in 20 minutes, the **alarmHand_mc** instance needs to be rotated so that the red tick mark in the instance appears at the 20-minute mark on the clock's face. Let's look at how this expression accomplishes that goal.

A full circular rotation is 360 degrees. By breaking this rotation into the 60 points on a clock's face that represent minutes, we can determine that each minute needs to represent a rotation of 6 degrees (6 × 60 = 360); therefore, to move the **alarmHand_mc** movie clip instance to the 20-minute point, it must be rotated 120 degrees (6 degrees per minute × 20 minutes). Using the expression that sets the value of `totalTimeToAlarm` (as shown in Step 7), 20 minutes would be converted to 1,200 seconds. The script in Step 9 then divides this value by 10, resulting in rotating **alarmHand_mc** by 120 degrees—where it must be to indicate that the alarm will go off in 20 minutes.

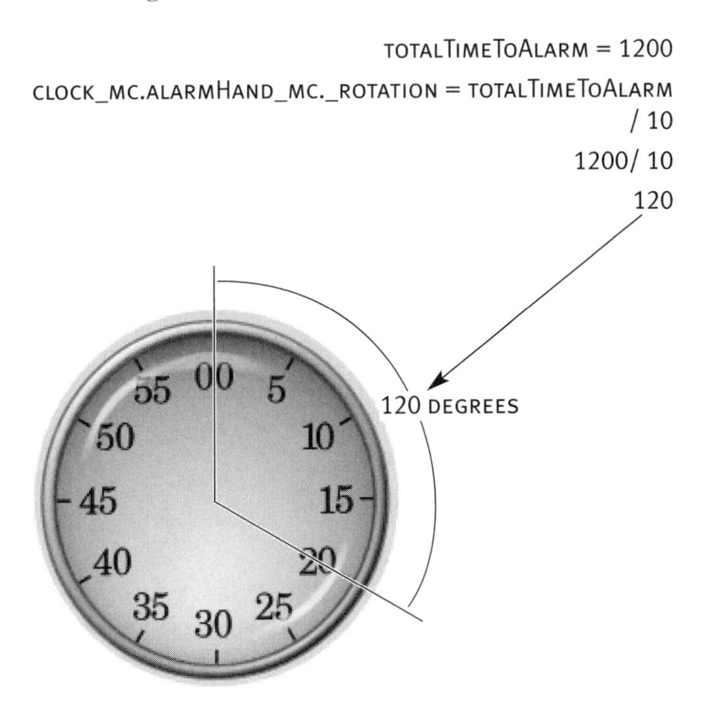

NOTE *Because the minute and second values that the user sets can be changed while the timer is on, and this script uses that total time to rotate this instance, changing those values changes the rotation to reflect the updated values.*

10) Add the following lines of script after the line added in Step 9:

```
clock_mc.secondHand_mc._rotation = secondsElapsed * 6;
clock_mc.minuteHand_mc._rotation = secondsElapsed / 10;
```

These two lines rotate the **secondHand_mc** and **minuteHand_mc** movie clip instances (inside **clock_mc**), based on the continually updated value of `secondsElapsed`. The logic that makes this occur is again based on the fact that a full circular rotation is 360 degrees, and the clock face is split into 60 graduations (both minutes and seconds) of 6 degrees each. For each second that elapses, the second hand needs to move 6 degrees, representing one second. Knowing this, the first action in Step 10 sets the rotation of the **secondHand_mc** movie clip instance to the value of `secondsElapsed` multiplied by 6. At one second it's rotated 6 degrees, at two seconds 12 degrees, and so on, making it appear to tick like a real clock.

The minute hand functionality requires a slightly different approach. The minute hand on a clock usually rotates at 1/60 the pace of the second hand. For example, if 60 seconds have ticked away, the second hand has made a full rotation. At this point, the minute hand should have rotated just 6 degrees on the clock face, indicating that one minute has passed. Knowing this, the second action in Step 10 sets the rotation of the **minuteHand_mc** movie clip instance based on the value of `secondsElapsed` divided by 10. Thus, if 60 seconds pass, this expression evaluates to a value of `6`, which is the amount that **minuteHand_mc** has rotated.

In the end, the **secondHand_mc** movie clip instance is rotated six times the value of `secondsElapsed`, while the **minuteHand_mc** instance is rotated 1/10 that same value. The **minuteHand_mc** instance rotates 1/60 as much as the **secondHand_mc** instance, just like on a real clock.

Because the value of `secondsElapsed` is constantly being updated, both of these hands are in constant motion while the timer (the entire script we've been working on) is turned on.

11) Add the following conditional statement after the actions added in Step 10:

```
if (secondsElapsed >= totalTimeToAlarm) {
  activateAlarm();
}
```

This conditional statement, which is executed 24 times a second like all the other actions in the `onEnterFrame` event handler, compares the value of `secondsElapsed` to the value of `totalTimeToAlarm`. When both have the same value (indicating that it's time for the alarm to sound), this statement becomes `true` and the action within the statement is executed, calling the `activateAlarm()` function, which in turn causes the actions of the `activateAlarm()` function to be executed. This function is defined next.

The `alarmOn()` function definition is now complete!

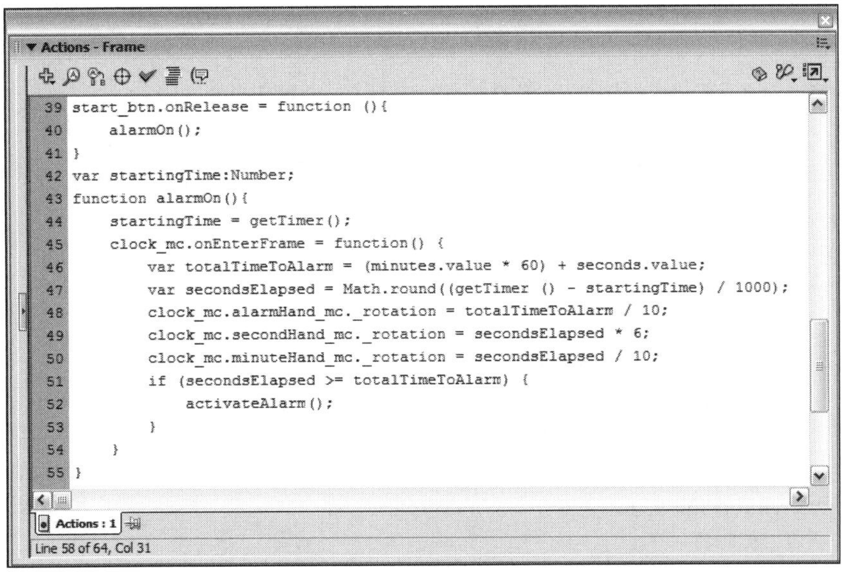

```
▼ Actions - Frame
39 start_btn.onRelease = function (){
40     alarmOn();
41 }
42 var startingTime:Number;
43 function alarmOn(){
44     startingTime = getTimer();
45     clock_mc.onEnterFrame = function() {
46         var totalTimeToAlarm = (minutes.value * 60) + seconds.value;
47         var secondsElapsed = Math.round((getTimer () - startingTime) / 1000);
48         clock_mc.alarmHand_mc._rotation = totalTimeToAlarm / 10;
49         clock_mc.secondHand_mc._rotation = secondsElapsed * 6;
50         clock_mc.minuteHand_mc._rotation = secondsElapsed / 10;
51         if (secondsElapsed >= totalTimeToAlarm) {
52             activateAlarm();
53         }
54     }
55 }
Actions : 1
Line 58 of 64, Col 31
```

12) Add the following script just below the current script:

```
var alarmSound:Sound = new Sound();
function activateAlarm() {
  delete clock_mc.onEnterFrame;
  clock_mc.secondHand_mc._rotation = 0;
  clock_mc.minuteHand_mc._rotation = 0;
  clock_mc.alarmHand_mc._rotation = 0;
  alarmSound.attachSound("alarm");
  alarmSound.start(0, loops.value);
}
```

The first line creates a Sound object named `alarmSound`, which eventually will contain the alarm sound to be played. The remaining lines define the `activateAlarm()` function.

The first thing the function does is delete the `onEnterFrame` event handler attached to the **clock_mc** instance when the `alarmOn()` function was called. This action causes the timer to stop functioning. The next three actions in the function reset the rotation of the various hands on the clock to their starting positions. The next action attaches the sound named **alarm** in the library to the `alarmSound` Sound object. The last action uses the `start()` method to play that sound. The first parameter of the method determines how many seconds into the sound it should begin to play; the second parameter determines how many times the sound should loop. Because we want the sound to start playing at its beginning, we set the first parameter to `0`. The value of the second parameter is set based on what the user inputs into the **loops** NumericStepper instance.

13) Choose Control > Test Movie to view the project to this point.

When the movie appears, use the NumericStepper instances to input time values for the timer; then click the Start button. The various hands on the clock should go into action. When the alarm time is reached, the timer turns off, its hands are reset, and the alarm sounds and continues to loop based on the value entered into the **loops** instance.

14) Close the test movie and save the project as *makeMyDay3.fla*.

As you've seen in this lesson, the `getTimer()` function plays a vital role in interactivity that requires an accurate measurement of time to function properly.

We'll continue building on this file in the next exercise.

CONTROLLING THE PLAYBACK SPEED AND DIRECTION OF A TIMELINE

Normally, a movie's timeline plays in a forward direction at a pace dictated by the fps (frames per second) setting in the Movie Properties dialog box. However, *you* can control the direction in which the timeline moves as well as its speed by using ActionScript. In fact, by combining scripting elements (which control direction) with the `onEnterFrame` event, you can gain incredible control over the project's timeline.

The first two scripting elements we'll discuss are the `nextFrame()` and `prevFrame()` methods of the MovieClip class. You use these methods to move a timeline to the next or previous frame by employing the following syntax:

```
myButton_btn.onRelease = function(){
  myMovieClip_mc.nextFrame();
}
```

or

```
myButton_btn.onRelease = function(){
  myMovieClip_mc.prevFrame();
}
```

By assigning these event handlers to buttons, you can create navigation controls that automatically advance or rewind a timeline one frame at a time with each click of the button.

Even more powerful is a timeline's `_currentframe` property (a read-only property): its value represents the frame number at which the playhead currently resides. For example, if the main movie is being played, the following script places the numerical value of the playhead's current frame position into a variable named `whereAreWe`:

```
var whereAreWe:Number = _root._currentframe;
```

WHEREAREWE = 45

You can also use this property in conjunction with a conditional statement to determine when the playhead is within a specific range of frames and make it act accordingly:

```
_root.onEnterFrame = function() {
  if(this._currentframe >= 50 && _this.currentframe <= 100)
    // Perform these actions
  }
}
```

In this script, the actions within the conditional statement are executed only when the playhead on the main timeline is between Frames 50 and 100.

Using the `_currentframe` property in conjunction with a `gotoAndPlay()` action allows you to control the direction as well as the pace in which the timeline moves. In the following example, the playhead on the main timeline advances 10 frames from its current position:

```
_root.gotoAndPlay (_currentframe +10);
```

In the same way, you can use the following script to make the timeline move backward 10 frames:

```
_root.gotoAndPlay (_currentframe -10);
```

As the following exercise demonstrates, by using the `onEnterFrame` event to execute a line of script such as the one above, you can create fast forward and rewind buttons to control a timeline's playback.

1) Open *makeMyDay3.fla*.

We'll continue to build on the project from the preceding exercise; most of the work for this exercise focuses on the Messages section of the application. In this area are four buttons named **play_btn**, **stop_btn**, **ff_btn**, and **rew_btn**, and a graphically empty movie clip named **messages_mc**. The four buttons eventually will be scripted to control the **messages_mc** timeline. Let's take a closer look at that timeline.

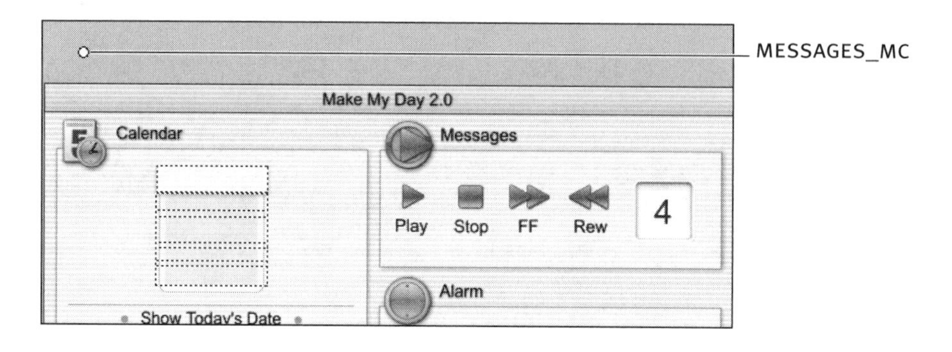

2) Double-click the *messages_mc* movie clip instance to edit it in place.

This movie clip's timeline contains two layers, Sound Clips and Actions. Frame 1 of the Actions layer contains a `stop()` action to prevent the timeline from moving forward until we instruct it to do so. The Sound Clips layer has a series of streaming sound clips that stretches across 700 frames. (Dragging the playhead plays the various clips.) In this exercise, we'll set up the buttons on the main timeline that the user can employ to navigate this timeline forward and backward.

3) Return to the main timeline. With the Actions panel open, select Frame 1 of the Actions layer and add the following script at the end of the current script:

```
var fastSound:Sound = new Sound(messages_mc);
function handleMessages(action:String){
}
```

The first line of the script creates a Sound object named `fastSound`. This Sound object eventually will be scripted to play a fast-forwarding sound when the **messages_mc** timeline is fast-forwarded or rewound.

The remaining lines of the script are the beginnings of the `handleMessages()` function. This function accepts a single parameter named `action`, which contains a string value of `"play"`, `"stop"`, `"ff"`, or `"rew"`. This parameter value tells the function whether it should play, stop, fast-forward, or rewind the **messages_mc** timeline. As we'll describe shortly, this function will be called and passed various parameter values when you interact with one of the playback control buttons.

4) Insert the following conditional statement within the `handleMessage()` **function definition:**

```
if(action == "play"){
  fastSound.stop()
  delete messages_mc.onEnterFrame;
  messages_mc.play();
}else if(action == "stop"){
  fastSound.stop();
  delete messages_mc.onEnterFrame;
  messages_mc.stop();
}else{
  fastSound.attachSound("rewind");
  fastSound.start(0, 50);
  if(action == "ff"){
    messages_mc.onEnterFrame = function(){
      this.gotoAndStop(this._currentframe + 3);
    }
  }else{
    messages_mc.onEnterFrame = function(){
      this.gotoAndStop (this._currentframe - 10);
    }
  }
}
```

Actions - Frame

```
65 var fastSound:Sound = new Sound(messages_mc);
66 function handleMessages(action:String){
67     if(action == "play"){
68         fastSound.stop()
69         delete messages_mc.onEnterFrame;
70         messages_mc.play();
71     }else if(action == "stop"){
72         fastSound.stop();
73         delete messages_mc.onEnterFrame;
74         messages_mc.stop();
75     }else{
76         fastSound.attachSound("rewind");
77         fastSound.start(0, 50);
78         if(action == "ff"){
79             messages_mc.onEnterFrame = function(){
80                 this.gotoAndStop(this._currentframe + 3);
81             }
82         }else{
83             messages_mc.onEnterFrame = function(){
84                 this.gotoAndStop (this._currentframe - 10);
85             }
86         }
87     }
88 }
```

Actions : 1

Line 106 of 106, Col 2

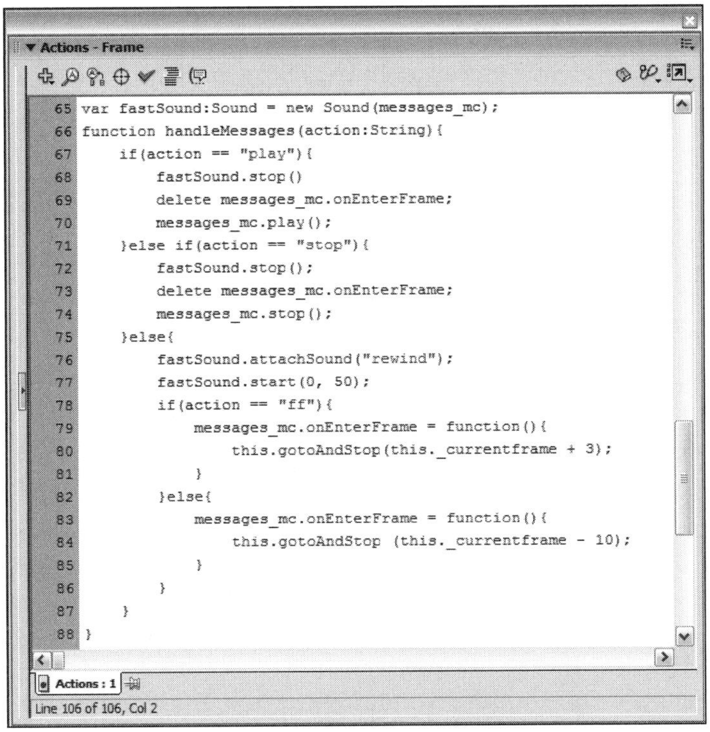

Before we discuss how the first part of the conditional statement works, you should be aware of two events that occur later in the statement when the function is passed a value of `"ff"` or `"rew"`. In either of those circumstances, a fast-forwarding sound is attached to the `fastSound` Sound object and played, and the functionality for carrying out either the fast-forwarding or rewinding of the **messages_mc** timeline is accomplished via an `onEnterFrame` that gets attached to the **messages_mc** instance. With that in mind, let's look at the conditional statement one section at a time.

If the `handleMessages()` function is passed a value of `"play"`, the first part of this conditional statement is executed. It uses the `stop()` method of the Sound class to tell the `fastSound` Sound object to quit playing, deletes the `onEnterFrame` event handler from the **messages_mc** movie clip instance (to prevent that timeline from continuing to fast-forward or rewind), and tells the **messages_mc** instance to `play()`.

If the function is passed a value of `"stop"`, the second part of the conditional statement is executed. This part of the statement does almost the same thing as the first, except that the `stop()` command stops the **messages_mc** timeline from playing.

If the `handleMessages()` function is not passed either a value of `"play"` or `"stop"`, the last part of the conditional statement (`else`) is executed. If this part of the statement is executed, the function has been passed a value of `"ff"` or `"rew"`. This part of the conditional statement has a nested `if/else` statement. Because the task of fast-forwarding and rewinding have both common and unique functionalities, this structure allows us to handle this circumstance in the most efficient manner. Here's how.

Whenever the **messages_mc** timeline is either fast-forwarded or rewound as a result of this function's being passed a value of `"ff"` or `"rew"`, the application should attach the sound named **rewind** in the library to the `fastSound` Sound object and then play it. The first two lines of script within the `else` part of the statement handle this common functionality in either case. Following that, the value of `action` is further evaluated. If `action` has a value of `"ff"`, an `onEnterFrame` event handler is attached to the **messages_mc** instance. This event handler advances the **messages_mc** timeline to its current frame, plus 3. Because the `onEnterFrame` event executes this script 24 times a second, the movie's timeline moves forward rapidly. If `action` has a value of `"rew"`, the actions in the nested `else` statement are executed. This is much like the script we just discussed, except that it moves the **messages_mc** timeline *backward* 10 frames with every `onEnterFrame` event, moving the timeline in reverse very rapidly.

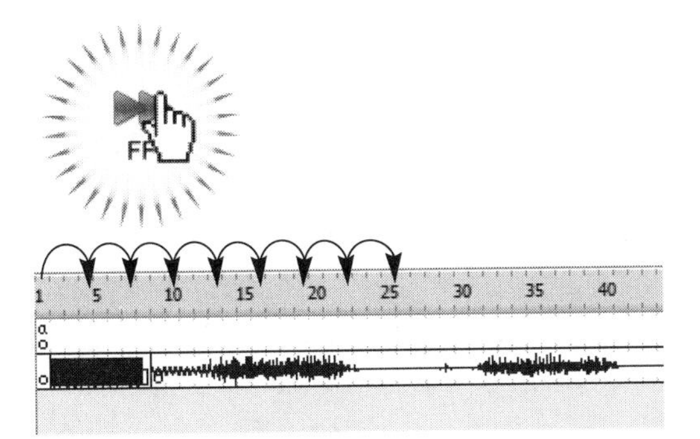

To reiterate a point made earlier, fast-forwarding or rewinding continue until the `onEnterFrame` event is deleted from the **messages_mc** instance. This occurs when the `handleMessages()` function is passed a value of `"play"` or `"stop"`.

The `handleMessages()` function is complete. The only thing left to do is to set up our button instances to call this function and pass it the appropriate values.

5) Add the following script at the end of the current script:

```
play_btn.onRelease = function(){
  handleMessages("play");
}
stop_btn.onRelease = function(){
  handleMessages("stop");
}
ff_btn.onPress = function(){
  handleMessages("ff");
}
ff_btn.onRelease = function(){
  handleMessages("play");
}
rew_btn.onPress = function(){
  handleMessages("rew");
}
rew_btn.onRelease = function(){
  handleMessages("play");
}
```

These lines of script assign event handlers to the various playback control buttons. How this works should be obvious to you by now. The only thing to be aware of is that both the **ff_btn** and **rew_btn** instances have an `onPress` and an `onRelease` event assigned. This allows those buttons to fast-forward or rewind when pressed, but to automatically initiate normal playback when released.

It's time to test the final result.

10) Choose Control > Test Movie to view the project to this point.

When the movie appears, use the various buttons to control the playback of the **messages_mc** movie clip instance. Clicking the FF button moves that timeline forward quickly; clicking the Rew button moves it backward quickly (as is evident from the points where the various sound clips in the instance are heard).

11) Close the test movie and save the project as *makeMyDay4.fla*.

Playback control buttons such as the ones we set up here have a wide range of uses—not just for streaming sounds (as demonstrated) but for any kind of project whose timeline contains hundreds of frames of content. By making use of these buttons, you enable users to control the way they view your projects—a powerful capability.

TRACKING PLAYBACK AND DOWNLOADING PROGRESSION

The number of frames in a movie and the file size of their contents determine the movie's overall length and size—a fact made evident by looking at the main timeline where these factors represent the length and size of the entire SWF. The total number of frames in a movie is a represented by the `_totalframes` property. If the main timeline has 400 frames that span several scenes, the following script sets the value of `myVariable` to 400:

```
var myVariable:Number = _root._totalframes;
```

You can use this property in scripts to determine the overall length of the movie (based in frames).

NOTE *Because it's a read-only property, the value of `_totalframes` is set automatically by Flash (based on the number of frames on a timeline). Not only does it not make sense to attempt to reset this value—it's not even possible!*

If you know the value of `_totalframes`, you can use it in conjunction with other movie properties to make comparisons during downloading and playback. For example, by comparing the value of the `_currentframe` property with the value of the `_totalframes` property, you can determine how much longer the movie will play:

```
var framesLeft:Number = _root._totalframes - _root._currentframe;
message_txt.text = "There are " + framesLeft + " to go.";
```

Because Flash is based on streaming technology, the process of downloading and viewing an SWF from a Web site actually occurs one frame at a time. Another property, `_framesloaded`, provides the total number of frames that have been downloaded. The value of this property can be compared to the `_totalframes` property to provide information about the progress of the download. In the following exercise, we'll demonstrate this principle by creating a progress bar (known as a *preloader*) that shows the percentage of frames that have been downloaded.

1) Open *preloader1.fla* in the Lesson16/Assets folder.

This project contains two scenes: Preloader and Content. The Content scene simply contains several layers of graphics and animation that demonstrate how the preloader works. The Content scene also contains a frame label named Start that plays an important role in the end result of the project. All of our work in this exercise takes place in the Preloader scene, which contains three layers: Background, Preloader, and Actions. The Background layer contains a square with a radial gradient. The Actions layer contains a `stop()` action to prevent the timeline from moving forward until we instruct it to do so. The Preloader scene contains two elements—a text label containing the text `"now loading..."` and a movie clip instance named **preloader_mc**, which includes the elements that show the downloading progress. We'll add script to this instance's timeline, so let's take a closer look at it.

2) Double-click the *preloader_mc* movie clip instance to edit it in place.

This movie clip's timeline consists of four layers named according to their contents. The most important aspects of this timeline are the text field named **info_txt**, which resides on the Text layer, and the tweened animation on the Amount layer. The text field dynamically displays the percentage of frames that have downloaded. The tweened animation represents a 100-frame progress bar that begins at 0 percent and ends at 100 percent. Among other things, our script moves this movie's timeline to the appropriate frame number based on the percentage of frames that have been downloaded, and the progress bar moves accordingly.

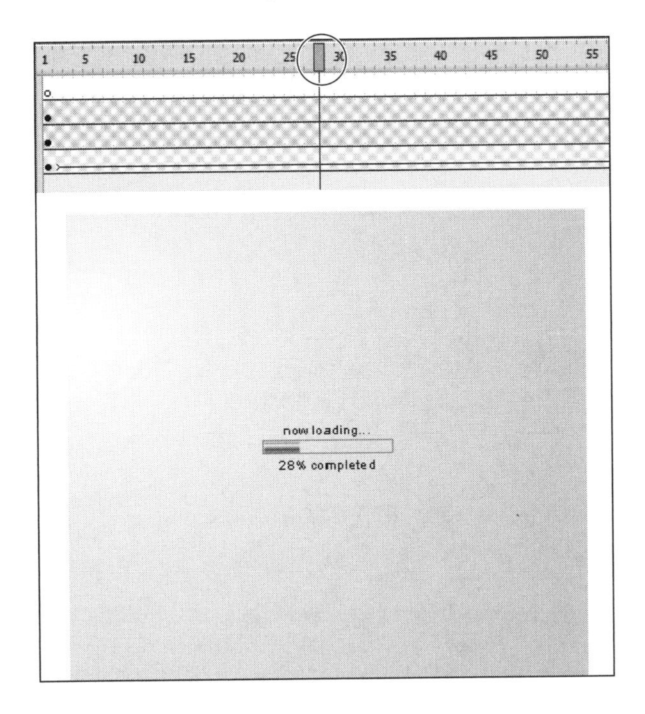

3) With the Actions panel open, select Frame 1 of the Actions layer and add the following script:

```
stop();
onEnterFrame = function() {
  var framesLoaded = (Math.ceil (( _parent._framesloaded /
  ⇒_parent._totalframes) * 100));
  gotoAndStop (framesLoaded);
  info_txt.text = framesLoaded + "% completed";
  if (framesLoaded >= 90) {
    _root.gotoAndPlay ("Start");
  }
}
```

The first action prevents the timeline from moving forward until we tell it to do so.

The second line attaches an `onEnterFrame` event handler to the preloader clip. As a result, the script within the event handler is executed 24 times a second, which means that it instantly reacts to the current downloading conditions to display the most accurate representation of the process.

This script determines a percentage value for the number of frames that have downloaded. It then rounds up that number and assigns the resulting value to the `framesLoaded` variable. Using precedence, the expression employed to do this work is evaluated in the following manner:

```
_parent._framesloaded /_parent._totalframes
```

With this part of the expression, the number of frames on the main timeline that have loaded is divided by the total number of frames *on* the main timeline.

NOTE *Because this script is within the preloader movie clip instance and the instance resides on the main timeline, the use of* `_parent` *as the target path is a reference to the main timeline. This setup allows the preloader clip to be used (and function properly) without modification in any project.*

For demonstration purposes, let's assume that the movie has 735 frames, 259 of which have loaded. The expression would look like this:

```
259 / 735
```

This would result in a value of .3523. The next part of the expression multiplies that result by 100:

```
* 100
```

This would result in a value of 35.23. Finally, using the `Math.ceil()` method, this value is rounded up to the next whole number, `36`—and thus `framesLoaded` is assigned a value of `36`. Remember that because this script is executed 24 times per second, the value of `framesLoaded` increases as the movie is downloaded.

```
Math.ceil ((259 /  735) * 100)
              ↓
  Math.ceil (.3523 * 100)
              ↓
  Math.ceil (35.23)
              ↓
             36
```

TIP *The `_framesloaded` and `_totalframes` properties used in this script can be replaced with the `getBytesLoaded()` and `getByteTotals()` methods of the MovieClip class if you want to make this preloader react to bytes loaded (rather than just frames). This is sometimes the preferred method of scripting a preloader because a frame is not considered loaded (and thus the preloader doesn't advance) until all the data that it contains is loaded. The preloader may appear stalled if the frames loaded contain numerous bytes of data. In contrast, looking at the bytes loaded causes the preloader to move forward more smoothly because changes in byte data happen more frequently (as each byte of data is downloaded). See the bonus file on the CD that demonstrates this principle.*

The next action in the script sends the preloader instance to the appropriate frame, based on the value of `framesLoaded`. Because the current movie contains the tweened animation of the progress bar moving from left to right, this action controls the movement of that bar. As the value of `framesLoaded` increases, so does the appearance of progress on the progress bar.

The next action sets what's displayed in the **info_txt** text field. Here, the value of `framesLoaded` is concatenated with the string `"% completed"`. If `framesLoaded` has a value of `36`, for example, the result is `"36% completed"`.

The last part of the script contains a conditional statement used to determine when the preloader's work is complete. It says that when the value of `framesLoaded` is equal to or more than 90, the main timeline should be moved to the frame labeled Start and played from there.

NOTE *The value of 90 in this conditional statement could easily be changed to any value to specify when the preloader's work is finished and the movie can begin to play.*

4) Choose Control > Test Movie to view the project to this point. When the test movie appears, choose View > Download Settings > 56K; then choose View > Simulate Download.

This setting provides a fairly accurate simulation of how the preloader will look and function when the movie is being downloaded over a 56K modem. As the movie loads, the percentage of the movie downloaded changes repeatedly. The progress bar reflects the ongoing status of the downloading process. As explained in Step 3, after 90 percent of the movie's frames have downloaded, the timeline moves to the Content scene and the movie plays from there.

5) Close the test movie and save the project as *preloader2.fla*.

This step completes the exercise and this lesson.

WHAT YOU HAVE LEARNED

In this lesson, you have:

- Learned how you can use time in Flash projects (pages 552–555)
- Created and used a Date object to display the current date (page 555–556)
- Used the DateChooser component to navigate and display date-related information (pages 557–568)
- Used the `getTimer()` function to create a Flash-based timer and alarm to track progression of time (pages 568–578)
- Controlled a timeline dynamically using play, stop, fast forward, and rewind controls (pages 578–584)
- Created a percentage-based preloader using the `_framesloaded` and `_totalframes` properties (pages 584–588)

scripting for sound

LESSON 17

Few things enhance the way we experience something more than sound. Not only does sound provoke an almost instantaneous emotional response, it also provides dimension. When standing in the middle of a crowded room, you can close your eyes and easily determine the relative position of people and clattering items just by listening. In a Flash presentation you can employ sound to provide your user with context as well as to create an engaging experience.

Flash's sound controls will make this basketball sound like the real thing.

A thorough understanding of how to control sound dynamically is key to creating everything from games to custom MP3 players. In this lesson, we'll demonstrate Flash's versatile sound controls by emulating a bouncing basketball inside an arena. The user can drag the ball within a predefined area of the screen. As the ball is dragged, the volume and panning of the bounce will be controlled dynamically to indicate its current location. You'll also see how Flash enables you to add and control sounds in your movie without placing them on the timeline.

WHAT YOU WILL LEARN

In this lesson, you will:

- Explore the uses of sound with ActionScript
- Learn how to create a Sound object
- Drag an object within a visual boundary
- Control the volume of a Sound object
- Control the panning of a Sound object
- Add sounds to your movie by using the `attachSound()` method
- Start, stop, and loop sounds dynamically

APPROXIMATE TIME

This lesson takes approximately one and one half hours to complete.

LESSON FILES

Starting File:

Lesson17/Assets/basketball1.fla

Completed Project:

basketball6.fla

CONTROLLING SOUND WITH ACTIONSCRIPT

Although most of us can enjoy listening to music without thinking too much about what we're hearing, the vibrations that make up even the most elementary sounds are actually far from simple—a fact made evident by the processing-power requirements of most audio-editing programs. Despite the complexity of even the simplest audio clip, however, sounds can be broken down into three basic characteristics:

- **Length.** A sound's *length* can provide sensory cues about size (the short chirp of a small-car horn compared to the roar of a semi-truck's horn) and urgency (the tinkle of a viciously shaken dinner bell compared to the long bong of a lazy Sunday church bell).
- **Volume.** A sound's *volume* provides clues about distance. Louder sounds give the feeling of closeness, whereas quiet sounds imply distance. A sound that gradually goes from quiet to loud or vice versa creates a sense of movement.
- **Panning.** *Panning* represents the position of the sound from left to right or right to left. Like volume, panning allows you to determine the relative position of the element making the sound. If you were to close your eyes at a tennis match, you could accurately determine the position of the ball (left or right of the net) simply by the "pop" of the ball being smacked by the racket.

With Flash, you can control sound characteristics simply by editing sound instances on the timeline—a solution that works well for presentations that don't require audience or user participation. However, if you want to give your user control—allowing the user to move and slide things around—you need a more dynamic solution. Fortunately, you can easily emulate and control all of these sound characteristics via ActionScript.

CREATING A SOUND OBJECT

To control sounds dynamically, you must use *Sound objects*. One of the most important points to realize about Sound objects is that you associate each one with a particular timeline in your movie at the time you create the sound. To dynamically control sound on the root timeline, you would need to create a Sound object and associate it with the root timeline. To dynamically control sound in a movie clip instance, you would have to create a Sound object associated with that timeline. Sound objects are also used to control sounds in movies loaded into levels. Because Flash projects can contain multiple timelines, projects can contain several Sound objects, each controlling the sound in a different timeline.

NOTE *Although a particular timeline may contain several layers of sounds, it should be understood that when a Sound object is created and associated with a particular timeline, all sounds in that timeline will be controlled equally using that single Sound object. Setting the volume of that timeline's Sound object to 50 will relatively decrease all sounds on all layers of that timeline by 50 percent.*

The syntax used to create Sound objects is quite simple:

```
var soundObjectName:Sound = new Sound (Target);
```

Let's break it down:

- `soundObjectName` denotes the name of your new Sound object. You can assign any name you want; just make sure the name describes the sounds that it controls and that you follow the same rules for naming your Sound object as you would for naming variables: no spaces, punctuation marks, or numbers as the first character of the name.
- The syntax `new Sound` is ActionScript's way of creating a new Sound object.
- `(Target)` is where you indicate to the timeline which target path will be associated with this Sound object.

After you've created a timeline-associated Sound object, you control that timeline's sound (for example, volume and panning) by referencing in your scripts the name of the Sound object, *not* the target path or instance name of the timeline.

Let's look at a real example. To create a Sound object to control the sound in a movie clip instance named **myMovieClip_mc**, you would use the following syntax:

```
var mySound:Sound= new Sound ("myMovieClip_mc");
```

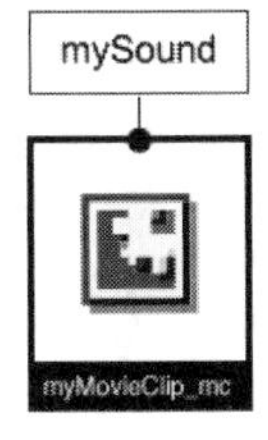

After you've created a Sound object associated with the movie clip instance **myMovieClip_mc**, you would use the `setVolume()` method of the Sound class to dynamically adjust the volume to 50 percent, as the following syntax shows:

```
mySound.setVolume (50);
```

As mentioned earlier, the goal of this lesson's project is to simulate the sound of a basketball bouncing around the court. In the exercise that follows, we'll create a Sound object—the first step in producing that bouncing ball.

1) Open *basketball1.fla* in the Lesson17/Assets folder.

This file contains six layers—Background, Ball, Ball Score, Score Fields, Watermark, and Actions:

- The Background layer contains the background graphics.
- The Ball layer contains the basketball graphic, which is a movie clip instance appropriately named **basketball_mc**. We'll be looking at this instance's timeline in a moment because it plays a part in the functionality of our project.
- The Ball Score layer contains a movie clip named **score_mc** (placed in front of the goal) that will be used to simulate the ball swishing into the goal. We'll be working with this instance later in the lesson.
- The Score Fields layer contains a couple of text field instances named **indiana_txt** and **northCarolina_txt** that will eventually be used to display scores. We'll discuss these in a later exercise as well.
- The Watermark layer contains a see-through graphic that appears on the lower-right portion of the stage, simply to give our project a realistic "television station" feel.
- The Actions layer will contain most of the scripts for this project.

2) Double-click the *basketball_mc* movie clip instance to open its timeline.

This movie clip contains three layers: Shadow, Graphic, and Sound. The Shadow and Graphic layers contain a couple of tweens to emulate the look and movement of a bouncing basketball. The Sound layer simply contains a "bounce" sound on Frame 5. This sound plays at the same time the bouncing ball appears to hit the floor.

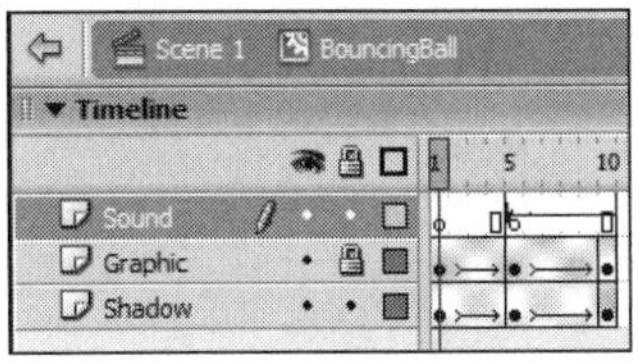

Because the movie clip's timeline doesn't include a `stop()` action, playback will continue to loop, giving the effect of a continuously bouncing ball.

3) Choose Edit > Edit Document to return to the main timeline.

Now it's time to create a Sound object associated with the **basketball_mc** movie clip instance. This object will allow us to control the volume and panning of the bounce sound as the user drags the ball around the court.

4) With the Actions panel open, select Frame 1 of the Actions layer and add the following script:

```
var bounce:Sound = new Sound(basketball_mc);
```

The only function of this line of script is to create a new Sound object named `bounce` that's associated with the **basketball_mc** timeline. Because the bouncing sound is part of this timeline, we'll be able to dynamically control the volume and panning of that sound by controlling the `bounce` Sound object.

5) Choose Control > Test Movie to see the movie play.

In its current state, our project doesn't appear very dynamic. You can't drag the ball around, and the bouncing sound maintains a consistent volume and pan throughout. We'll remedy this situation as we progress through this lesson. The important point to realize is that as soon as the movie begins to play, a Sound object is created. The bounce inside the **basketball_mc** instance won't sound different until we modify our new Sound object.

6) Close the testing environment to return to the authoring environment. Save the current file as *basketball2.fla*.

We'll build on this file as we progress through this lesson.

DRAGGING A MOVIE CLIP INSTANCE WITHIN A BOUNDARY

Being able to drag the ball movie clip instance around the screen is critical to our project's interactivity. The ball's position onscreen will determine the volume and panning of the bouncing sound. If we were to allow users to freely drag the **basketball_mc** movie clip instance onscreen, however, our scene would not be realistic because the user could drag and bounce the ball over the crowd, the backboard, and so forth. Obviously, we need to restrict dragging to the area denoted by the court.

There are several ways of scripting so that an object can be dragged only within a certain area. In this exercise, you'll learn how to control the draggable area by tracking the mouse's movement and allowing dragging to occur only when the mouse pointer is within a certain area onscreen.

1) Open *basketball2.fla*.

Continue using the file you were working with at the end of the preceding exercise.

Before you continue, it's important to think through the problem at hand; that is, how to drag the ball movie clip instance in sync with the mouse movement, and how to constrain that dragging to a specific area onscreen.

The first objective is to establish the draggable area, or *boundary*, of our screen. In Flash, you define a boundary by determining four coordinates: top, bottom, left, and right. Our script will use these coordinates to restrict movement within that area. For this exercise, the coordinates that represent the four sides of our boundary will be as follows:

Top boundary = 220

Bottom boundary = 360

Left boundary = 60

Right boundary = 490

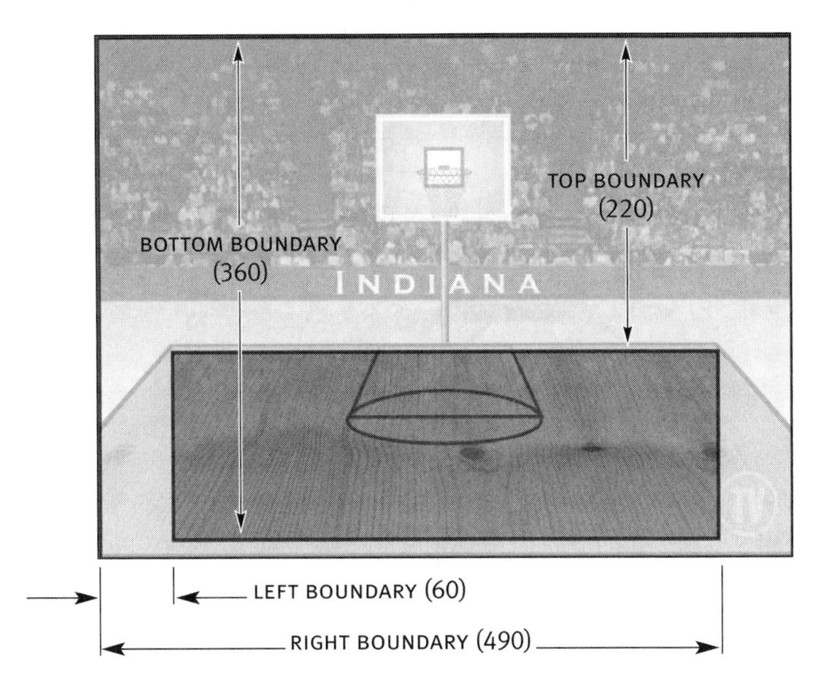

As shown by the arrows, all coordinates are based on the distance of that side from the top and left sides of the stage.

TIP *An easy and visual method of determining boundary coordinates is to draw a simple box on the stage. Resize it and position it in the area that will serve as the boundary in the scene. Select the box and then open the Info panel. Using the information in the X, Y, W, and H boxes, you can determine the four coordinates of your boundary: Y is the top boundary, X is the left boundary, Y + H is the bottom boundary, and X + W is the right boundary. After you've determined the four coordinates of your boundary, delete the box. There are other, more dynamic ways of setting a border, but this technique is the most straightforward.*

Because we want the basketball to move only when the mouse pointer is within the boundary, in scripting terms we need to check for a condition before the ball can be dragged. Logically, this might be translated as follows: *If the mouse pointer's position is within the coordinates of the boundary, drag the* **basketball_mc** *movie clip instance; otherwise, stop dragging.*

We'll need to instruct the script to check for this condition on a regular basis because the mouse is in frequent motion. Using the `onMouseMove` event handler, we can check for this condition each time the mouse is moved. This will allow our script to act instantly to enable or prevent the **basketball_mc** movie clip instance from being dragged.

We now have all the information necessary to proceed.

2) With the Actions panel open, select Frame 1 of the Actions layer. After the line of script from the preceding exercise creating the bounce Sound object, add the following lines of script:

```
var leftBoundary:Number = 60;
var rightBoundary:Number = 490;
var topBoundary:Number = 220;
var bottomBoundary:Number = 360;
```

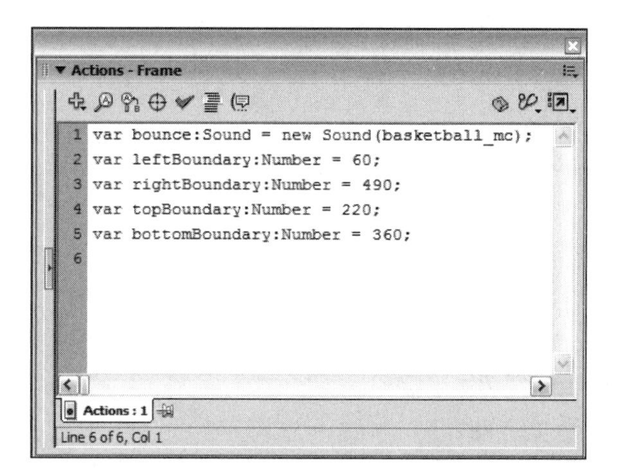

These variables contain the x and y coordinates of our boundary.

Next, we'll add an `if` statement that constantly checks the position of the mouse and allows the ball to be dragged only if the mouse pointer is within the boundary we just defined.

3) Add the following lines at the end of the current script:

```
this.onMouseMove = function() {
  if (_xmouse > leftBoundary && _ymouse > topBoundary &&
  ⇒_xmouse < rightBoundary && _ymouse < bottomBoundary) {
    basketball_mc.startDrag(true);
  } else {
    stopDrag();
  }
}
```

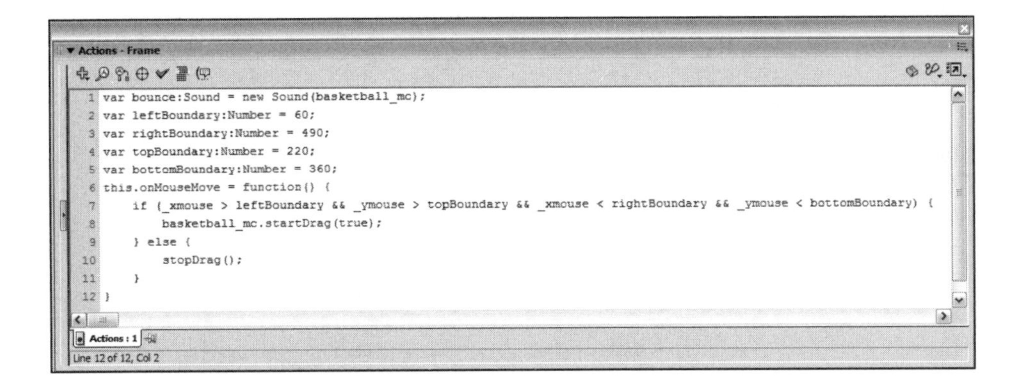

Using an `onMouseMove` event handler, the `if` statement is analyzed each time the mouse is moved.

With this `if` statement, we're checking to determine that four conditions are true. If they are, dragging will commence; if not, dragging will cease. We're checking the current horizontal and vertical positions of the mouse pointer (`_xmouse` and `_ymouse`, respectively) to see how they compare to the boundaries we defined earlier.

Let's look at a couple of possible scenarios to understand the logic behind this `if` statement. Suppose that during playback of the movie, the mouse pointer is moved to where its horizontal position (`_xmouse`) is 347 and its vertical position (`_ymouse`) is 285. By plugging in these values as well as the values that define our boundaries, the `if` statement would look similar to the following:

```
if (347 > 60 and 347 < 490 and 285 > 220 and 285 < 390)
```

In this circumstance, the `if` statement would evaluate to `true` because all the conditions are true—347 is greater than 60 and less than 490, and 285 is greater than 220 and less than 390. In this scenario, dragging is allowed.

Let's look at one more scenario. Suppose that during playback of the movie, the mouse pointer is moved to a horizontal position of 42 and a vertical position of 370. If we plug in these values, the `if` statement looks like this:

```
if (42 > 60 and 42 < 490 and 370 > 220 and 370 < 390)
```

In this circumstance, the `if` statement evaluates to `false` because not all the conditions are true—42 is *not* greater than 60 (the first condition in the statement).

When the `if` statement evaluates to `true`, the `startDrag()` action is triggered and the **basketball_mc** instance becomes draggable. The `true` parameter value used in this action causes the center of the **basketball_mc** movie clip instance to be locked to the vertical and horizontal positions of the mouse pointer.

TIP *The `startDrag()` action is not the only way to drag a movie clip instance. In our script, we could replace this action with the following:*

```
basketball_mc._x = ._xmouse;
basketball_mc._y = ._ymouse;
```

*These two lines would cause the x and y coordinates of the **basketball_mc** movie clip instance to mimic the x and y coordinates of the mouse pointer, so it appears to be dragged. The advantage of this technique is that it allows you to drag multiple movie clip instances simultaneously. In contrast, the `startDrag()` action allows only one movie clip instance at a time to be dragged. In our script, this is sufficient because the basketball is the only item that needs to be draggable.*

When the `if` statement evaluates to `false`, the `stopDrag()` action is triggered, causing the ball to stop being dragged. Because this `if` statement is evaluated with each movement of the mouse, the dragging process can be stopped and started frequently, depending on the current position of the mouse pointer.

4) Choose Control > Test Movie to see how the movie operates.

In the testing environment, move your mouse around the court. When the mouse pointer is moved within the boundary we defined, dragging will occur, causing the ball to appear as if it's bouncing around the court. Move the mouse pointer outside this boundary, and dragging stops.

5) Close the testing environment to return to the authoring environment. Save the current file as *basketball3.fla*.

CONTROLLING VOLUME

Everything we've done to this point has been in preparation for the next several exercises. Although controlling the volume of a movie clip instance with an attached Sound object is a straightforward task, we plan to take an extremely dynamic approach to the process.

Remember in the first exercise of this lesson that we created a Sound object named `bounce` and associated it with the **basketball_mc** movie clip instance. This movie clip instance contains a bouncing sound that plays when the ball appears to hit the floor. To adjust the volume of this Sound object, you would use the following syntax:

```
bounce.setVolume(70);
```

This line of script uses the `setVolume()` method to set the volume of the `bounce` Sound object to 70 percent. Because this particular Sound object is associated with the **basketball_mc** movie clip instance, the volume of all sounds on that timeline will be adjusted accordingly. Volume can be set anywhere from `0` (muted) to `100` (100 percent).

Because ActionScript is such a dynamic scripting language, we can also use a variable name to set the volume rather than hard-coding it as demonstrated previously. If the value of the variable changes, so does the amount of the volume adjustment. Take a look at the following example:

```
bounce.setVolume(myVariable);
```

This line of script adjusts the volume of the `bounce` Sound object to the current value of `myVariable`. As the value of `myVariable` changes, so does the volume of the `bounce` Sound object. We'll use this dynamic approach for this exercise.

The project's background was designed to provide a sense of depth, with the bottom of the basketball court sounding close to the user and the top of the court seeming distant. The court itself is a close visual representation of the boundary we scripted in the preceding exercise. With this fact in mind, our goal is simple: we want to set the volume of the `bounce` Sound object based on the vertical position of the ball within the boundary. When the ball is at the top of the boundary, the bouncing sound will be at 50 percent volume, giving a sense of distance. As the ball moves toward the bottom of the boundary, the bouncing sound should get louder (to a maximum of 100 percent) so that the ball sounds as if it's getting progressively closer.

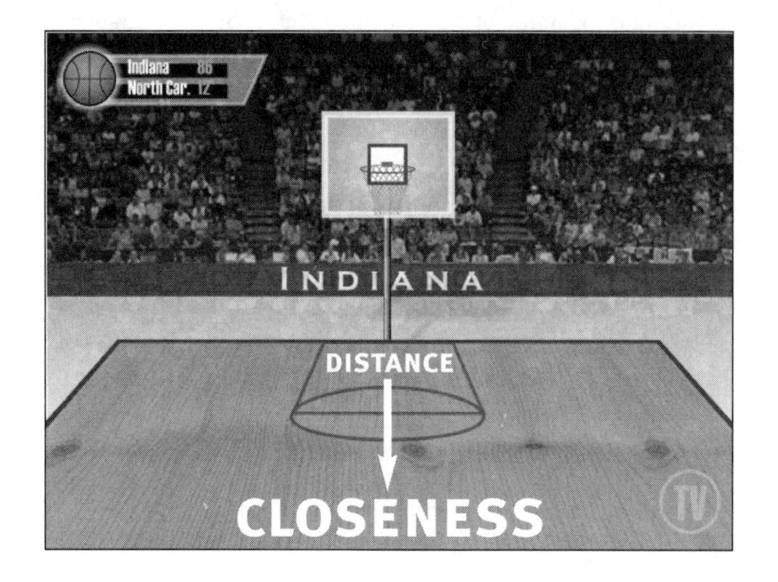

To achieve this objective, we need to do a couple of tasks. We want to create a variable and constantly update its value to a number between 50 and 100. We'll determine this value by figuring the vertical distance (as a percentage value) between the mouse pointer and the top side of our boundary in relation to the overall vertical size of the boundary. Sound confusing? Let's review the formula for figuring percentages and take a look at a sample scenario. Here's the formula we'll be using:

1) Determine the overall height of the area.

2) Determine the height of the portion for which the percentage must be figured.

3) Divide the size of the portion by the overall size and then multiply by 100.

Remember that the top boundary in our script is 220 and the bottom boundary is 360. With the first part of the formula above, we determine the overall height of the area—that is, the vertical size of the boundary—by subtracting 220 (the top boundary) from 360 (the bottom boundary). This gives us a value of 140 (360 – 220). Next, we need to determine the height of the portion for which the percentage must be figured. Suppose the mouse pointer has a vertical position of 310. We subtract 220 (the top boundary) from 310 (the current position of the mouse pointer). This gives us a value of 90 (310 – 220), which means that the mouse pointer is currently 90 pixels from the top boundary. Finally, we divide the size of the portion (90) by the overall vertical size of the boundary (140) and then multiply that result by 100. Mathematically, our equation would look like this:

(90 / 140) * 100 = x

(.6428) * 100 = x

x = 64.28 or 64.28%

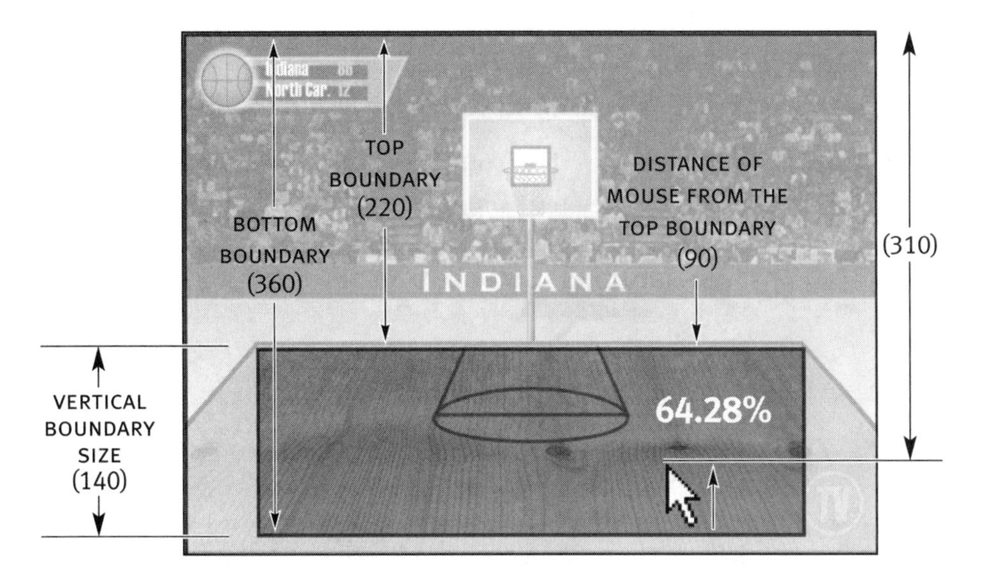

If x were a variable in our movie, we could set the volume of our bounce Sound object to the value of this variable by using the following syntax:

```
bounce.setVolume (x)
```

Because the value of x is currently 64.28, the volume of the bounce Sound object is set to that value; however, because the mouse is constantly moving, the value of x is always changing—as is the volume of the bounce.

We have one more mathematical issue to deal with. Using our current percentage-generating equation, we have a percentage range between 0 and 100, with 0 indicating that the mouse is at the top of the boundary and 100 indicating that it's at the bottom. We want a percentage range between 50 and100, where 50 is generated when the mouse is at the top of the boundary and 100 when it's at the bottom. We can easily accomplish this goal by dividing the percentage value generated (0 to 100) by 2 and then adding 50. For example, suppose the percentage value is 50:

50 / 2 = 25

25 + 50 = 75

Using the conversion formula, you can see how a value of 50 (normally midway between 0 and 100) is converted to 75 (midway between 50 and 100). Let's look at one more example:

20 / 2 = 10

10 + 50 = 60

A value of 20 is one-fifth the value between 0 and 100, and the converted value of 60 is one-fifth the value between 50 and 100.

At this point, the overall logic we'll use to accomplish volume control looks like this:

1) Each time the mouse is moved, if the mouse pointer is within the boundary, determine the vertical distance of the mouse pointer (as a percentage between 0 and 100) from the top boundary.

2) Divide this value by 2 and then add 50.

3) Plug this value into a variable.

4) Use this variable's value to set the volume of the `bounce` Sound object.

Now let's add this functionality to our movie.

1) Open *basketball3.fla*.

Continue using the file you were working with at the end of the preceding exercise.

2) With the Actions panel open, select Frame 1 of the Actions layer. After the four lines of script defining the sides of the boundary (following the line `var bottomBoundary:Number = 360;`), insert the following line of script:

```
var boundaryHeight:Number = bottomBoundary - topBoundary;
```

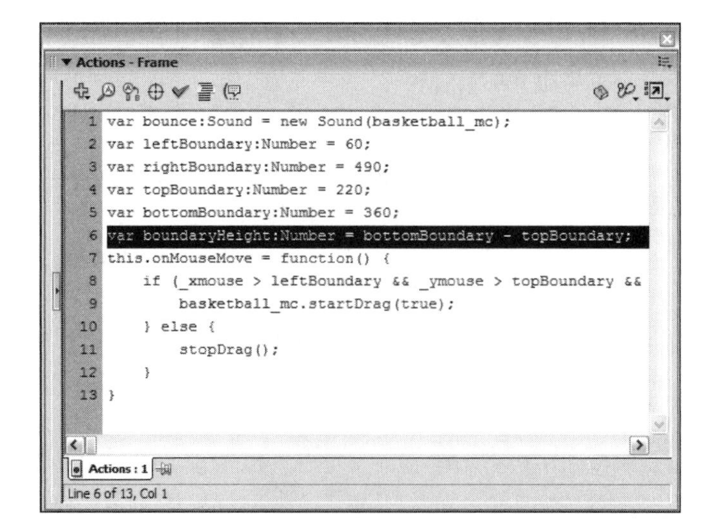

This step creates a variable named boundaryHeight and assigns it the value of bottomBoundary - topBoundary. The two lines of script directly above this line indicate that bottomBoundary = 360 and topBoundary = 220. Written out, this line of script would look like this:

boundaryHeight = 360 – 220

or

boundaryHeight = 140

This value represents the vertical size of our boundary and will be used to determine percentage values as described previously.

TIP *Although we could have directly assigned a value of 140 to the* boundaryHeight *variable, using an expression is much more dynamic. This way, if you ever change the value of* topBoundary *or* bottomBoundary, *the value of* boundaryHeight *would automatically be updated. A well-thought-out script contains few hard-coded variables; be conscious of where you can use expressions.*

3) Insert the following line of script after the basketball_mc.startDrag (true) **action:**

```
var topToBottomPercent = ((((_ymouse - topBoundary) / boundaryHeight) *
⇒100) / 2) + 50;
```

Actions - Frame

```
1  var bounce:Sound = new Sound(basketball_mc);
2  var leftBoundary:Number = 60;
3  var rightBoundary:Number = 490;
4  var topBoundary:Number = 220;
5  var bottomBoundary:Number = 360;
6  var boundaryHeight:Number = bottomBoundary - topBoundary;
7  this.onMouseMove = function() {
8      if (_xmouse > leftBoundary && _ymouse > topBoundary && _xmouse < rightBoundary && _ymouse < bottomBoundary) {
9          basketball_mc.startDrag(true);
10         var topToBottomPercent = ((((_ymouse - topBoundary) / boundaryHeight) * 100) / 2) + 50;
11     } else {
12         stopDrag();
13     }
14 }
```

Actions : 1

Line 10 of 14, Col 90

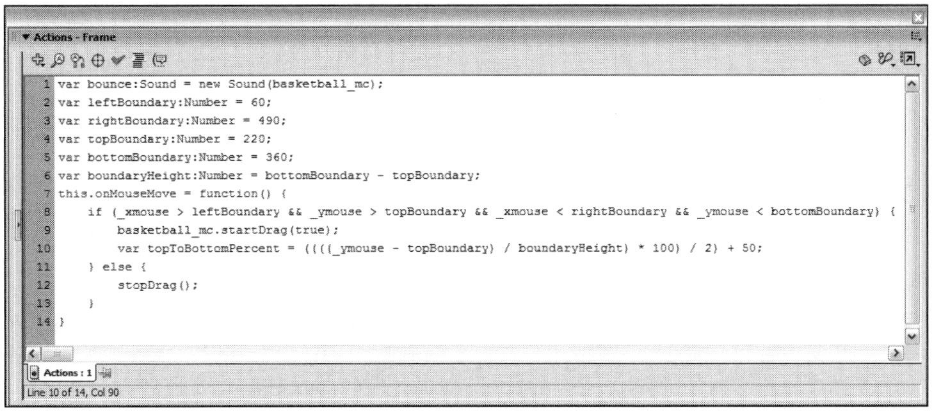

This line creates the variable topToBottomPercent and assigns it a value based on an expression. This expression is the mathematical representation of the percentage formula we discussed earlier. Three dynamic values are needed for this expression to be evaluated: _ymouse (the vertical position of the mouse pointer), topBoundary (which currently equals 220), and boundaryHeight (which currently equals 140). The multiple parentheses denote the order in which each part of the expression is evaluated. The following steps demonstrate how this expression is evaluated:

1) Evaluate _ymouse - topBoundary.

2) Divide the result by boundaryHeight.

3) Multiply by 100.

4) Divide by 2.

5) Add 50.

There are two unique aspects of the location of this line of script, which is nested within the onMouseMove event handler. The expression that determines the value of topToBottomPercent is evaluated almost every time the mouse is moved; therefore, the value of the variable is constantly changing based on the current position of the mouse pointer. We say *almost* because this line of script is also nested within the if statement that checks whether the mouse is within the boundary. This variable's value is set/updated only when the mouse is within the boundary. Because this variable's value will soon be used to set the volume of the bounce Sound object, you should understand that nesting it within the if statement prevents changes to the volume of the sound whenever the mouse pointer is outside the boundary.

4) Add the following line of script after the line added in Step 3:

```
bounce.setVolume(topToBottomPercent);
```

This line simply sets the volume of the bounce Sound object based on the current value of the topToBottomPercent variable. Because the value of this variable is being updated constantly, the volume of the bounce Sound object will be updated as well.

This line is nested within the onMouseMove event handler as well as in the if statement that looks for movement within the boundary, so the volume of the bounce Sound object is updated each time the mouse pointer is moved within the boundary.

5) Add the following lines of script after the line added in Step 4:

```
basketball_mc._xscale = topToBottomPercent;
basketball_mc._yscale = topToBottomPercent;
```

These two lines of script add a bonus effect to our project. Using the current value of the `topToBottomPercent` variable, these lines adjust the `_xscale` and `_yscale` properties of the **basketball_mc** movie clip instance. The ball is scaled in size at the same time that the volume of the `bounce` Sound object is set. In other words, while the volume is being adjusted to provide an auditory sense of the ball's movement, the ball's size is being comparably adjusted visually to give the project a greater sense of reality. Because these lines are nested within the `onMouseMove` event handler as well as in the `if` statement that looks for movement within the boundary, the size of the ball movie clip instance is updated each time the mouse pointer is moved within the boundary.

6) Choose Control > Test Movie.

In the testing environment, move your mouse pointer around the court. As the ball is dragged upward, its size and bounce volume decrease, making the ball seem to move away. As the ball is dragged downward, its size and bounce volume increase, making the ball seem to move closer.

7) Close the testing environment to return to the authoring environment. Save the current file as *basketball4.fla*.

CONTROLLING PANNING

Although the volume of a sound gives a sense of distance, panning helps determine its left/right position. Similar to setting the volume of a Sound object, setting a Sound object's panning is straightforward, as the following example demonstrates:

```
bounce.setPan (100);
```

This code causes the `bounce` sound to play out of the right speaker only. You can set a Sound object's panning anywhere between `-100` (left speaker only) and `100` (right speaker only), with a setting of `0` causing the sound to play equally out of both speakers.

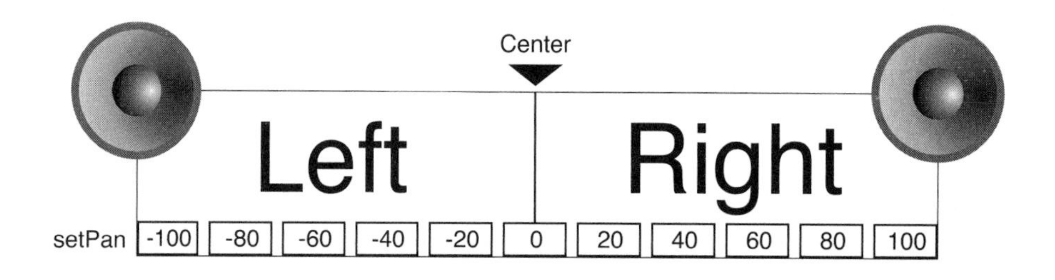

As with the `setVolume()` method, the `setPan()` method can use the value of a variable to set a Sound object's panning more dynamically, as the following example demonstrates:

```
bounce.setPan (myVariable);
```

We'll use a variable to set the pan of the `bounce` Sound object. As in the preceding exercise, this variable will contain a percentage value between `-100` and `100` (encompassing the entire spectrum of panning values). We'll base the pan setting of the `bounce` Sound object on the horizontal distance of the mouse pointer from the center point in either the left or right quadrant.

To make this technique work, we must do the following:

1) Determine the horizontal size of the draggable boundary and then split it in two, essentially breaking the boundary into two "quadrants," left and right.

2) Establish the position of the horizontal center.

3) Determine the mouse pointer's current horizontal position (at the exact center or in the left or right quadrant) each time it's moved.

If the mouse pointer is at the exact center point, the pan is set to 0. If the mouse is left of the center point (in the left quadrant), the pan is set to a value between -100 and 0. This value represents the horizontal distance (percentage-based) of the mouse pointer from the center point in relation to the overall size of the quadrant. Likewise, if the mouse pointer is right of the center point (in the right quadrant), the pan is set to a value between 0 and 100, which represents the horizontal distance (percentage-based) of the mouse pointer from the center point in relation to the overall size of the quadrant.

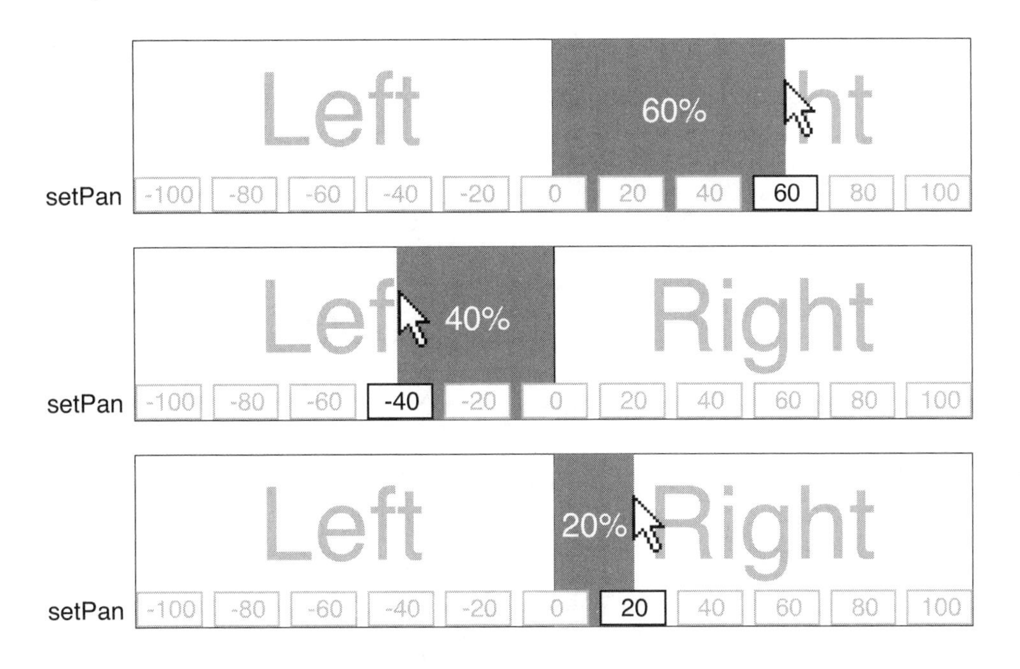

Don't worry if you're confused. We've already discussed most of the principles for translating this logic into ActionScript; we just need to adapt them a bit.

1) Open *basketball4.fla*.

Continue using the file you were working with at the end of the preceding exercise.

2) With the Actions panel open, select Frame 1 of the Actions layer. After the line of script `var boundaryHeight:Number = bottomBoundary - topBoundary`**, insert the following line of script:**

```
var boundaryWidth:Number = rightBoundary - leftBoundary;
```

This line creates a variable named `boundaryWidth` and assigns it the value of `rightBoundary - leftBoundary`. The lines of script directly above this one indicate that `rightBoundary = 490` and `leftBoundary = 60`. This is how the line of script looks when written out:

`boundaryWidth` = 490 – 60

or

`boundaryWidth` = 430

This value represents the horizontal size of the boundary and will be used to determine the size of the left and right quadrants of the boundary.

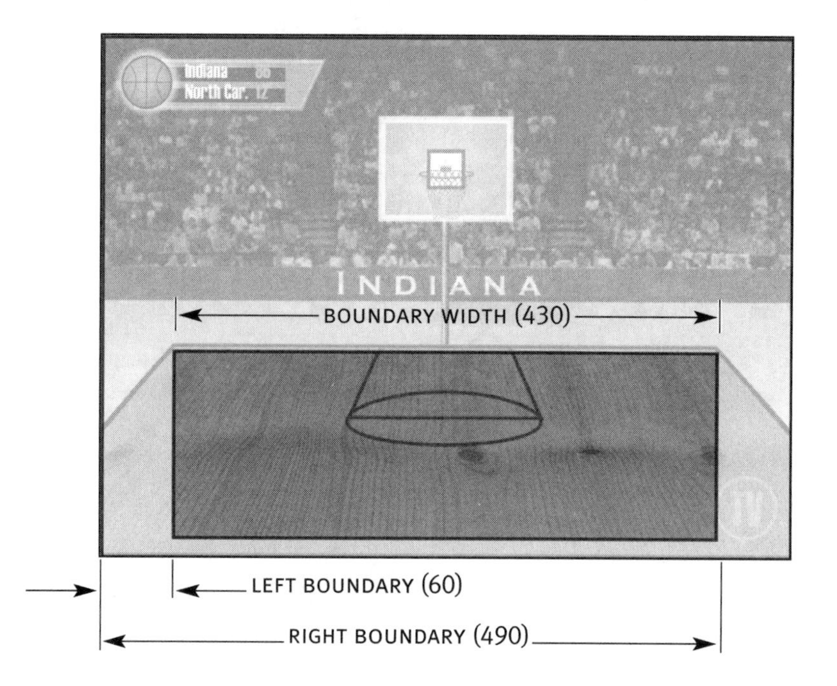

3) Add the following line of script after the line added in Step 2:

```
var quadrantSize:Number = boundaryWidth / 2;
```

This step creates a variable named `quadrantSize` and assigns it a value based on the value of `boundaryWidth / 2`. At this point, `boundaryWidth` has a value of 430. This line of script written out would look like this:

`quadrantSize` = 430 / 2

or

`quadrantSize` = 215

You need to know the size of these quadrants to determine what percentage values to use for setting the pan of the bounce Sound object.

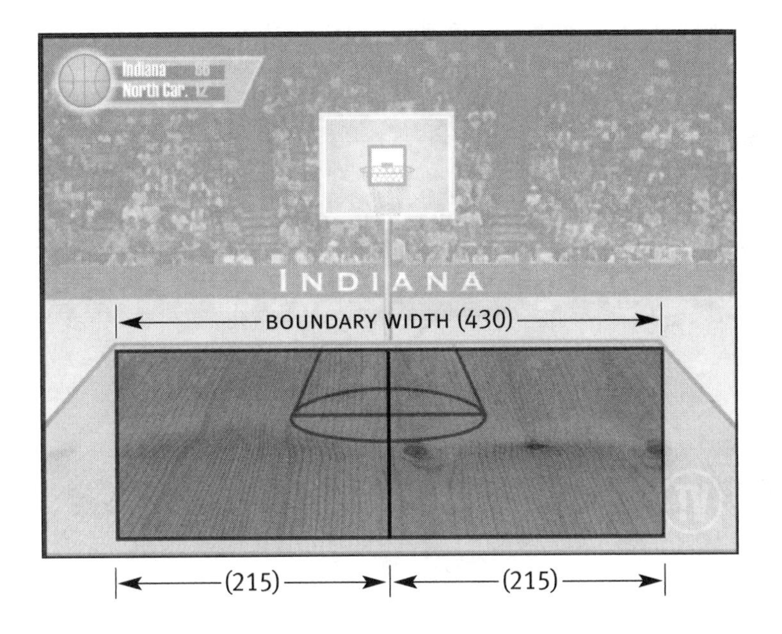

4) Add the following line of script after the line added in Step 3:

```
var centerPoint:Number = rightBoundary - quadrantSize;
```

This step creates a variable named centerPoint and assigns it the value of rightBoundary - quadrantSize. At this point, rightBoundary has a value of 490 and quadrantSize has a value of 215. Here's how this line of script would look when written out:

centerPoint = 490 – 215

or

centerPoint = 275

This value denotes the horizontal location of the center point of the boundary—the place where the left and right quadrants meet. This variable plays a critical role in the panning process because it allows us to determine which quadrant the mouse pointer is in—and thus whether the bounce Sound object should be panned left or right. If the mouse pointer's horizontal position (_xmouse) is greater than centerPoint (275), we know that the mouse pointer is in the right quadrant; if it's less than 275, we know the mouse pointer is in the left quadrant.

5) After the line `basketball_mc._yscale = topToBottomPercent;` **in the script (within the** `onMouseEvent` **handler), insert the following lines of script:**

```
var panAmount = ((_xmouse - centerPoint) / quadrantSize) * 100;
bounce.setPan(panAmount);
```

Actions - Frame

```
var bounce:Sound = new Sound(basketball_mc);
var leftBoundary:Number = 60;
var rightBoundary:Number = 490;
var topBoundary:Number = 220;
var bottomBoundary:Number = 360;
var boundaryHeight:Number = bottomBoundary - topBoundary;
var boundaryWidth:Number = rightBoundary - leftBoundary;
var quadrantSize:Number = boundaryWidth / 2;
var centerPoint:Number = rightBoundary - quadrantSize;
this.onMouseMove = function() {
    if (_xmouse > leftBoundary && _ymouse > topBoundary && _xmouse < rightBoundary && _ymouse < bottomBoundary) {
        basketball_mc.startDrag(true);
        var topToBottomPercent = ((((_ymouse - topBoundary) / boundaryHeight) * 100) / 2) + 50;
        bounce.setVolume(topToBottomPercent);
        basketball_mc._xscale = topToBottomPercent;
        basketball_mc._yscale = topToBottomPercent;
        var panAmount = ((_xmouse - centerPoint) / quadrantSize) * 100;
        bounce.setPan(panAmount);
    } else {
        stopDrag();
    }
}
```

Actions : 1

Line 17 of 22, Col 1

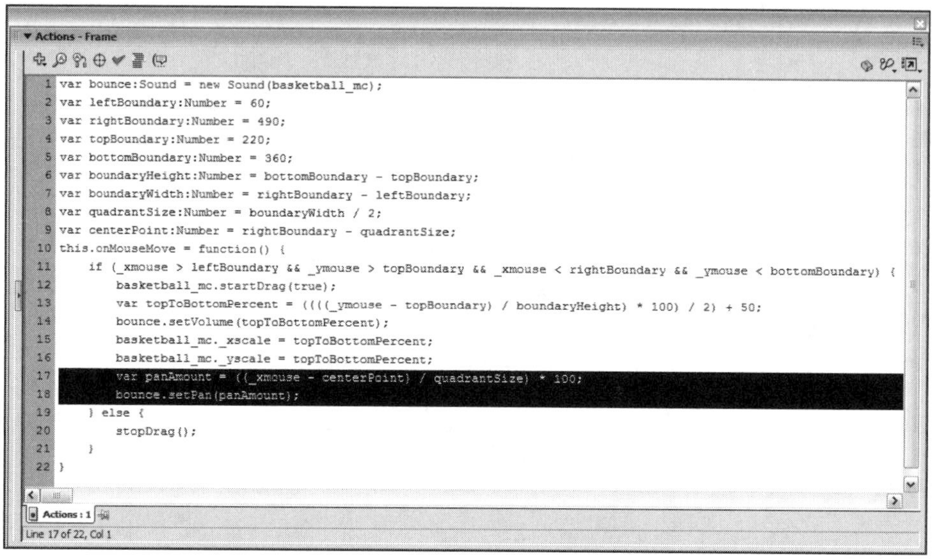

The variable `panAmount` is created in the first line. The expression that sets the value of `panAmount` is based on the percentage-generating equation we used to set the volume. After the value of `panAmount` has been established, this variable is used to set the pan for the `bounce` Sound object. The expression is set up to generate a value between `100` and `-100` for `panAmount`.

To help you understand how this section of script works, we'll look at a couple of scenarios. Let's assume that the mouse pointer's horizontal position (`_xmouse`) is 374 when the expression that sets the value of `panAmount` is evaluated. By plugging in the values for `centerPoint` (275) and `quadrantSize` (215), we can break down this expression in the following way:

`panAmount` = ((374 – 275) / 215) * 100

or

`panAmount` = (99 / 215) * 100

or

`panAmount` = .4604 * 100

or

`panAmount` = 46.04

After the value of panAmount has been determined, the next line of script sets the pan of the bounce Sound object based on the value that the expression assigned to the panAmount variable. At this point, the value of panAmount is 46.04. Setting the pan to this amount will cause it to sound 46.04 percent louder in the right speaker than in the left, indicating that the ball is on the right side of the basketball court. Visually, the ball will appear on the right side of the court as well, because the mouse pointer's horizontal position (374) is greater than that of centerPoint (275), indicating that the mouse pointer (and thus the **basketball_mc** movie clip instance) is 99 pixels (374 – 275) to the right of the center point.

Now let's look at another scenario. Assume that the mouse pointer's horizontal position is 158. Plugging all the necessary values into our expression, we can break it down as follows:

panAmount = ((158 – 275) / 215) * 100

or

panAmount = (–117 / 215) * 100

or

panAmount = –.5442 * 100

or

panAmount = –54.42

In this scenario, panAmount is set to a negative number (–54.42). This is the result of subtracting 275 from 158 at the beginning of the expression. Because 158 – 275 = –117 (a negative number), the expression evaluates to a negative value—ideal because we need a negative value to pan our sound to the left. After the value of panAmount has been determined, the next line of script sets the pan of the bounce Sound object based on the value that the expression assigned to the panAmount variable (–54.42). This causes the bounce to sound 54.42 percent louder in the left speaker than in the right, indicating that the ball is on the left side of the basketball court. Visually, the ball will appear on the left side of the court as well, because the mouse pointer's horizontal position (158) is less than that of centerPoint (275), indicating that the mouse pointer (and thus the **basketball_mc** movie clip instance) is –117 pixels (158 – 275) to the left of the center point.

If the mouse pointer's horizontal position is equal to that of `centerPoint` (275), the expression sets the value of `panAmount` to `0`, causing sound to come out equally from the left and right speakers. This in turn indicates that the ball is in the center of the court.

Because the two lines of script in this step are nested within the `onMouseMove` event handler as well as in the `if` statement that looks for movement within the boundary, the sound is panned each time the mouse pointer is moved within the boundary.

6) Choose Control > Test Movie to see how the movie operates.

In the testing environment, move your mouse pointer around the court. As you drag the ball, not only does the bounce's volume change, so does the location of the sound—moving from left to right and vice versa.

7) Close the testing environment to return to the authoring environment. Save the current file as *basketball5.fla*.

ATTACHING SOUNDS AND CONTROLLING SOUND PLAYBACK

In non-dynamic projects, sounds are placed directly on and controlled from the timeline. If you want a sound to play in your movie, you must drag it from the library onto the timeline and then indicate when and how long it should play, as well as how many times it should loop on playback. Although this may be a fine way of developing projects for some, we're ActionScripters—we want control! That's why in this exercise we show you how to leave those sounds in the library and call on them only when you need them. Using other methods available to Sound objects, you'll learn how to add sounds and control their playback on the fly.

When you create a Sound object in Flash, one of the most powerful things you can do with it is attach a sound—in essence, pulling a sound from the library that can be played or halted anytime you want. To do this, you must assign identifier names to all the sounds in the library. After these sounds have identifier names, you can attach them to Sound objects and control their playback and even their volume and panning, as we discussed earlier in this lesson.

For example, let's assume that there's a music soundtrack in the project library with an identifier name of rockMusic. Using the following code, you could dynamically employ this sound in your project and control its playback:

```
var music:Sound = new Sound();
music.attachSound("rockMusic");
music.start(0, 5);
```

When executed, the first line of this script creates a new Sound object named `music`. The next line attaches the rockMusic sound (in the library) to this Sound object. The third line starts the playback of this Sound object, which in effect starts the playback of the rockMusic soundtrack because it's attached to this Sound object. The `0` in this action denotes how many seconds into the sound to start playback. For example, if the rockMusic soundtrack includes a guitar solo that begins playing 20 seconds into the soundtrack, setting this value to `20` would cause the sound to begin playback at the guitar solo rather than at the sound's beginning. The second value in this action, which we've set to `5`, denotes how many times to loop the sound's playback. In this case, our soundtrack will play five times before stopping.

TIP *You can set all of these values using variables or expressions—opening a world of possibilities.*

In the following exercise, we show you how to attach a random sound from the library to a Sound object, and trigger its playback whenever the mouse button is pressed. We'll also set up our script so that pressing any key halts the sound's playback.

1) Open *basketball5.fla*.

Continue using the file you were working with at the end of the preceding exercise.

The Ball Score and Score Fields layers of our project contain assets we'll use in this exercise. The Ball Score layer contains a movie clip instance named **score_mc** above the basketball goal. This instance contains two frames labeled Empty and Score. At the Empty frame label, the instance is, well, empty. This is its state when it first appears in the project. At the Score label is a short animation used to simulate the basketball going through the net, as if a score has been made. A script we'll be adding shortly will play this animation in various circumstances.

The Score Field*s* layer contains two text fields named **indiana_txt** and **northCarolina_txt**. These fields will be used to display updated scores under various circumstances. (This will become clear shortly.)

Before we begin scripting, we need to look at some of the assets in the library.

2) Choose Window > Library to open the Library panel.

The library contains a folder called Dynamic Sounds where you'll find four sounds that have been imported into this project. These sounds exist only within the library; they have not been placed on our project's timeline yet.

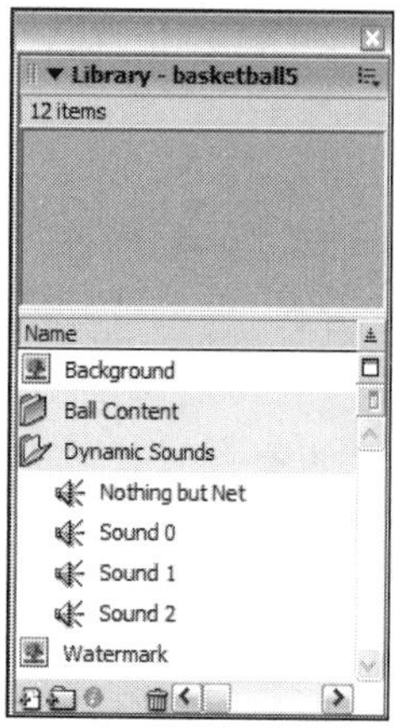

3) Click on Sound 0 to select it. From the Option menu in the library, choose Linkage.

The Linkage Properties dialog box appears. This is where you assign an identifier name to the sound.

4) Choose Export for ActionScript from the Linkage options, and give this Sound an identifier name of Sound0.

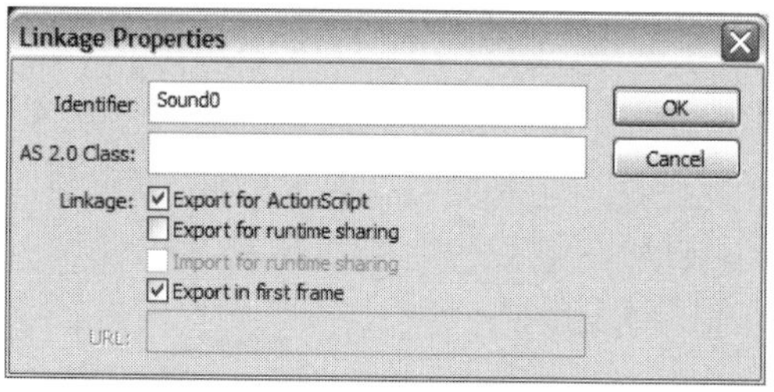

The reason we've used an identifier name ending in a number is that our script generates a random number between 0 and 2: when 0 is generated, Sound0 plays; when 1 is generated, Sound1 plays; when 2 is generated, Sound2 plays. The number at the end of the identifier name is therefore crucial.

After you've assigned an identifier name to the sound, click OK.

5) Repeat steps 3 and 4 for Sound 1 and Sound 2 in the library. Give Sound 1 an identifier name of Sound1 and Sound 2 an identifier name of Sound2.

NOTE *Library item names can contain space; identifier names cannot. When assigning identifier names, follow the naming rules that apply to variables.*

At this point, you have given three of the sounds in the Dynamic Sounds folder identifier names of Sound0, Sound1, and Sound2. The other sound, named Nothing but Net, has already been given an identifier of Net. This sound will be used in a moment to simulate the sound that a basketball net makes when a ball swishes through it.

6) With the Actions panel open, select Frame 1 of the Actions layer. After the line of script that creates the `bounce` **Sound object, insert the following line of script:**

```
var dynaSounds:Sound = new Sound();
```

This step creates a new Sound object called `dynaSounds`. This Sound object will eventually be used to randomly play one of the sounds in the library (`Sound0`, `Sound1`, or `Sound2`).

Notice that when we created this Sound object, we didn't associate it with a timeline. This means that our new Sound object will be associated with the entire project—a "'universal" Sound object, so to speak.

7) Add the following line after the script added in Step 6:

```
var netSound:Sound = new Sound ();
```

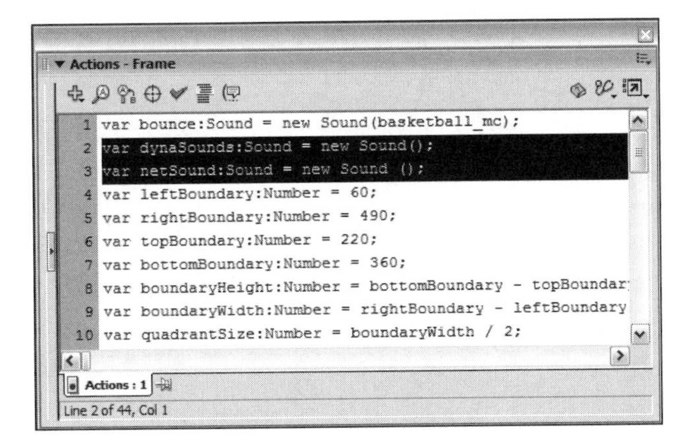

This line creates another Sound object named netSound that will be used to play the sound in the library with an identifier of Net.

8) Add the following lines at the end of the current script:

```
this.onMouseDown = function() {
  var randomSound = random(3);
  dynaSounds.attachSound("Sound" + randomSound);
  dynaSounds.start(0, 1);
}
```

This onMouseDown event handler causes these lines of script to be triggered whenever the mouse is clicked anywhere on the stage. The expression random(3); generates one of three values between 0 and 2 and assigns this value to the randomSound variable. The next line attaches a sound from the library to the dynaSounds Sound object, based on the current value of randomSound. If the current value of randomSound is 2, this would be the same as writing the following line of script:

```
dynaSounds.attachSound("Sound2");
```

With each click of the mouse, a new number is generated, and the sound attached to this Sound object can change. The last line of the script plays the current sound attached to this Sound object. For the two parameters of this action, 0 causes the sound to play back from the beginning; the second parameter value of 1 causes the sound to play back once.

9) Insert the following conditional statement within the onMouseDown **event handler, just after** dynaSounds.start(0, 1);**:**

```
if(randomSound == 0){
  northCarolina_txt.text = Number(northCarolina_txt.text) + 2;
  netSound.attachSound("Net");
  netSound.start(0, 1);
  score_mc.gotoAndPlay("Score");
}else if(randomSound == 1){
  indiana_txt.text = Number(indiana_txt.text) + 2;
  netSound.attachSound("Net");
  netSound.start(0, 1);
  score_mc.gotoAndPlay("Score");
}
```

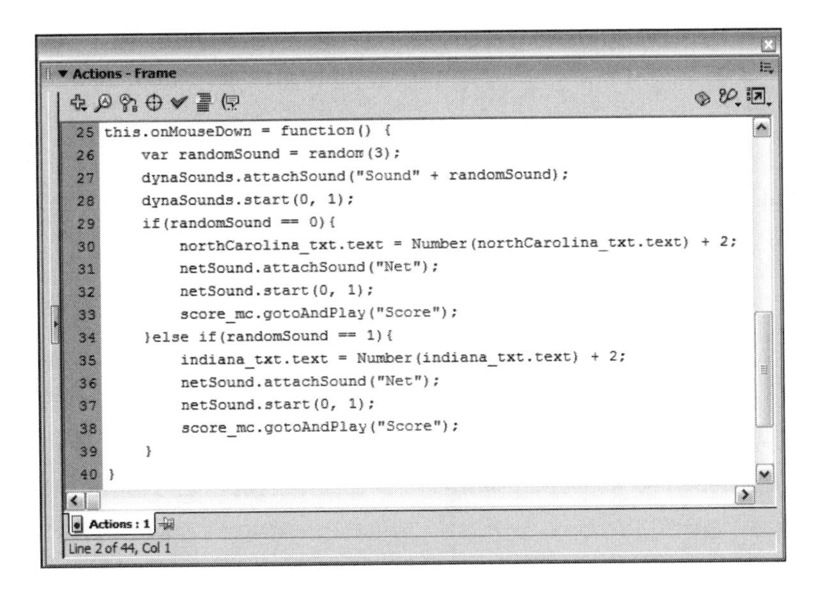
Actions - Frame
this.onMouseDown = function() {
var randomSound = random(3);
dynaSounds.attachSound("Sound" + randomSound);
dynaSounds.start(0, 1);
if(randomSound == 0){
northCarolina_txt.text = Number(northCarolina_txt.text) + 2;
netSound.attachSound("Net");
netSound.start(0, 1);
score_mc.gotoAndPlay("Score");
}else if(randomSound == 1){
indiana_txt.text = Number(indiana_txt.text) + 2;
netSound.attachSound("Net");
netSound.start(0, 1);
score_mc.gotoAndPlay("Score");
}
}
Actions : 1
Line 2 of 44, Col 1

Because this conditional statement was placed within the `onMouseDown` event handler, it's evaluated every time the mouse button is pressed, and one of the sounds in the library is randomly played (as discussed in Step 8).

Before we explain what this conditional statement does, it's important that you realize how the three sounds in the library sound. The sound with an identifier of Sound0 is a clip of a booing crowd. Sound1 is a crowd cheering! Sound2 is a referee's whistle. Because this project was built with the Indiana basketball fan in mind, whenever Sound0 (booing) is attached to the `dynaSounds` Sound object, we want team North Carolina to score two points, the cumulative total of which will be displayed in the **northCarolina_txt** text field instance in the upper-left corner of the stage. Whenever Sound1 is attached (cheering), team Indiana is given two points, displayed in the **indiana_txt** text field. When Sound2 is attached, neither team gets a point.

So how do we know which sound is being attached with each mouse click? Simple—by evaluating the value of `randomSound`, which is what the conditional statement does. If it has a value of `0`, Sound0 has been attached and team North Carolina has scored. If it has a value of `1`, Sound1 has been attached and team Indiana has scored.

With that in mind, the conditional statement says that if `randomSound` has a value of `0`, update the value shown in the **northCarolina_txt** text field to its current value plus 2, attach the sound in the library with the identifier of Net to the `netSound` Sound object, play that sound, and send the **score_mc** instance to the frame labeled Score. All this transpires to give the realistic feel of team North Carolina scoring a point (which will happen very rarely!).

If randomSound has a value of 1, the second part of the conditional statement is executed, which essentially performs the same actions as the first part, except that team Indiana's score is updated.

10) Add the following lines at the end of the current script (below the onMouseDown event handler):

```
this.onKeyDown = function() {
  dynaSounds.stop();
}
Key.addListener(this);
```

The onKeyDown event handler causes this line of script to be triggered whenever a key is pressed. When this action is executed, playback of the dynaSounds Sound object is stopped, regardless of where it is in its playback. The last line causes the Key object to listen for this event.

11) Choose Control > Test Movie to see how the movie operates.

In the testing environment, clicking the mouse causes a random sound from the library to play. The sound stops if you press a key while the sound is playing.

12) Close the testing environment to return to the authoring environment. Save the current file as *basketball6.fla*.

This step completes the project! You should now be able to see how dynamic sound control enables you to add realism to your projects—and in the process makes them more memorable and enjoyable. You can do all kinds of things with sounds, including loading them from an external source, which we'll describe in Lesson 18, "Loading External Assets."

WHAT YOU HAVE LEARNED

In this lesson, you have:

- Learned why and how you create Sound objects (pages 590–595)
- Controlled an object's movement within a visual boundary (pages 596–600)
- Controlled the volume of a Sound object based on the vertical position of the mouse pointer (pages 601–607)
- Controlled the panning of a Sound object based on the horizontal position of the mouse (pages 608–614)
- Added random sounds to your project and controlled the playback, looping, and stopping of sounds dynamically (pages 614–620)

loading external assets

LESSON 18

One of Flash's greatest strengths is that it allows you to load all of a project's media assets dynamically—bitmaps, sounds, videos, even other movies—from external sources. As a result, a greater range of content can exist externally from the movie (such as on a Web server) and be loaded into the movie on an as-needed basis. This means that you can deliver more dynamic content than ever before because the content of your movie is not restricted to what's placed in it at the time it was authored.

In this lesson, we'll show you how the various types of media are loaded into a running movie, as well as how to work with and manipulate this external content once it has been loaded. As a result, you'll be able to greatly expand the content used in your own projects without significantly increasing the time it takes for your user to download and view it.

Loading external video clips is one of the powerful capabilities of Flash that we'll explore in this lesson.

WHAT YOU WILL LEARN

In this lesson, you will:

- Create a scalable slideshow presentation using external assets
- Create a rotating Flash banner system by loading external movies into a level
- Control a movie from its own timeline and another timeline
- Dynamically load MP3s into a project while it plays
- Script an MP3 playback progress bar
- Load MP3 files based on XML files and display ID3 tag data from the MP3s
- Load an external video into a Media component and trigger actions

APPROXIMATE TIME

This lesson takes approximately two hours to complete.

LESSON FILES

Media Files:

Lesson18/Media/background0.swf
Lesson18/Media/background1.swf
Lesson18/Media/background2.swf
Lesson18/Media/banner0.swf
Lesson18/Media/banner1.swf
Lesson18/Media/banner2.swf
Lesson18/Media/image0.jpg
Lesson18/Media/image1.jpg
Lesson18/Media/image2.jpg
Lesson18/Media/music0.mp3
Lesson18/Media/music1.mp3
Lesson18/Media/music2.mp3
Lesson18/Media/Agent00.mp3
Lesson18/Media/HardCope.mp3
Lesson18/Media/LoungeJam.mp3
Lesson18/Media/Prosonica.mp3
Lesson18/Media/playlist.xml
Lesson18/Media/bluezone.flv
Lesson18/Media/cue0.jpg
Lesson18/Media/cue1.jpg
Lesson18/Media/cue2.jpg
Lesson18/Media/cue3.jpg
Lesson18/Media/cue4.jpg
Lesson18/Media/cue5.jpg
Lesson18/Media/cue6.jpg

Starting Files:

Lesson18/Assets/virtualaquarium1.fla
Lesson18/Assets/mp3Player1.fla
Lesson18/Assets/video1.fla

Completed Projects:

virtualaquarium8.fla
mp3Player2.fla
video2.fla

THE INS AND OUTS OF LOADING EXTERNAL ASSETS

When you load external assets into a movie, you're loading a media file (such as an MP3 file, a JPG graphic, a video, or even another SWF) into a Flash movie *as it plays*. In other words, you're *adding* assets to your movie. In fact, you can create a Flash movie that contains nothing but script set up to load text, animations, graphics, and sounds from external assets. Media that's loaded dynamically in this fashion can exist on a Web server or on a disk or CD if your project is distributed as a projector; therefore, a single project can load media from several sources simultaneously. All that's usually required is the directory path to the files. It's that simple! No special server technologies required. Sometimes, as is the case when loading media files from a disk or CD, not even a server is needed.

By loading external assets (rather than placing all of your project's media in a single SWF), your project benefits in a number of ways:

- **Your movie downloads faster over the Web.** Imagine that you have a site containing four sections—Home, Services, Products, and Contact—each of which has its own graphic and soundtrack. Together, the graphic and soundtrack add 100 KB to each section—a total of 400 KB if you place everything in a single SWF. For users connecting via 56 Kbps modems, your site will take nearly two minutes to download—a sure way to turn viewers away. You're better off loading each section's graphic/soundtrack on an as-needed basis, or only when a user navigates to that section—the approach that most HTML-based sites take.
- **You can view multiple movies in the player window without navigating to different HTML pages.** When using a browser to navigate Web sites, you don't need to close one window and then open another just to move from page to page. Instead, the browser remains open while the window's content changes as pages are loaded and unloaded. The same thing happens when external movies are loaded into Flash's player window: The player window simply acts as a container whose contents (a Flash movie) change without the user having to close the movie window or navigate to a different HTML page.

- **Your project becomes modular—and thus easy to update and reuse.** When you begin using assets loaded from external sources in your project, Flash movies become nothing more than interactive modules that you can load (plug into) your project at will. Any revisions to a particular module will appear automatically in any other project that contains it. Think again of a standard Web site: Even though each graphic (for example, a logo) usually resides in a single location on the server, multiple pages can contain that logo simply by referencing its directory path on the server—so you don't need to create a separate logo graphic for each page. You can reuse that graphic on any number of pages, and all of the pages on which it appears will reflect those changes anytime you update that graphic. The same holds true for externally loaded content in your Flash projects—a benefit that cannot be overemphasized because it's much easier to individually edit several smaller, externally loaded files than to open a complex project with numerous scenes, layers, tweens, movie clip instances, and scripting every time you need to make a change.
- **Your project becomes more dynamic, offering each user a unique experience.** By loading external assets, you can provide the user with a much more dynamic experience, employing a wider range of content that loads based on time of day, month, user input, or even a randomly generated number.

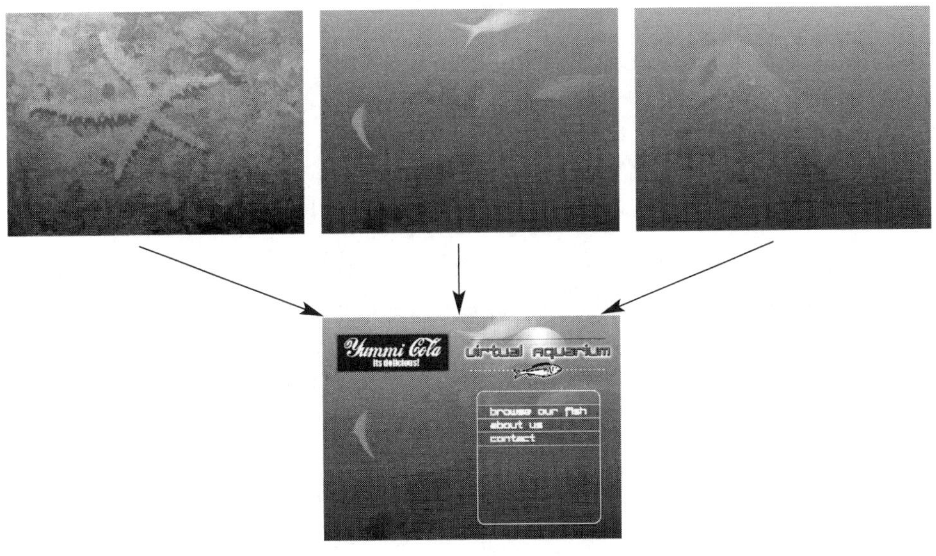

Although it would be next to impossible to create a single SWF that could display appropriate content based on so many variables, using externally loaded assets makes this type of dynamic functionality a breeze.

You can load external assets by using `loadMovie()` or `loadMovieNum()` for external SWF or JPG files, or `loadSound()` for external MP3s. Video assets can be loaded using an instance of the `netStream()` class; however, the Media components provide a much easier interface for getting video (and MP3) content into your project, as we'll discuss later in this lesson.

In the following exercises, you'll learn how to load a variety of external file types, and how to control these assets using ActionScript.

LOADING MOVIES INTO TARGETS

When loading media from an external source, you must assign a place for the media to reside within your main movie, which we'll call the *receiving* movie. For externally loaded SWFs and JPGs, that location can be either a target or a level.

NOTE *Loading an MP3 file is a different process; you can't load MP3s into a target or level. Later in this lesson, we'll discuss the processes for loading MP3s and for loading a movie into a level.*

A *target* is simply an existing movie clip instance within the receiving movie. In fact, every movie clip instance in the receiving movie is a potential target for externally loaded SWFs or JPGs.

The syntax for loading a movie into a target looks like this:

```
loadMovie ("myExternalMovie_mc.swf", "_root.myPlaceholderClip_mc");
```

This action loads `myExternalMovie_mc.swf` into the movie clip instance with the target path of **_root.myPlaceholderClip_mc**, thereby replacing the current timeline at that target path with the one that's loaded into it. When loading external media, you can think of a movie clip instance as nothing more than a shell containing timelines—one timeline that's placed there when the movie was authored (which happens automatically when a movie clip instance is placed on the stage), and one timeline that's loaded dynamically as the movie plays.

TIP *The directory path to the external asset can be written as an absolute or relative URL, depending on where the file exists.*

When loading an external asset into a target, it's important to remember the following rules:

- The registration point of the externally loaded asset will match the registration point of the target/instance into which you load the asset.
- If the target/instance that an external asset is loaded into has been transformed in any way (for example, rotated), the loaded asset will take on those transformations.
- After an externally loaded asset has been loaded into a target, you can control the asset via ActionScript, using the target path to the instance into which the asset was loaded. In other words, the externally loaded asset *becomes* that instance. For example, if an external movie is loaded into an instance with a target path of **_root.myPlaceholderClip_mc**, you can control the externally loaded asset by referencing that target path.

NOTE *For more information about target paths, see Lesson 3, "Understanding Target Paths."*

An external SWF loaded into a target can be as simple as an animated banner or as complex as an entire Flash production.

1) Open *virtualaquarium1.fla* in the Lesson18/Assets folder.

This file (which we'll build on throughout this lesson) contains no actions, and the frame and movie clip structure have already been created so that we can focus on the ActionScript involved. Although the file looks uninspiring now, it will contain several pieces of externally loaded content when the lesson is complete.

This file is made up of nine layers:

- The bottom layer, Loaded Background, contains two elements: a text field at the lower left of the screen says `"loading background..."`, and an empty movie clip instance (with no graphical content) named **background_mc** is placed at an x,y position of 0,0. Soon, this movie clip instance will contain our project's background, which will be loaded from an external source.
- The second layer, Banner Back, contains a movie clip instance of a white box (named **bannerBack_mc**) that says `"loading banner..."`, as well as a button instance named **bannerControl_btn**. We'll use these features in a later exercise.
- The third layer, Next-Prev Buttons, contains two arrow buttons named **next_btn** and **prev_btn**, which we'll set up in the next exercise.
- The fourth layer, Panel, contains a bitmap of a gray panel box.

- The fifth layer, Placeholder, contains another empty movie clip instance named **placeholder_mc** (which will be used in the following exercise), as well as a movie clip instance named **maskClip_mc** that resembles a big black square just to the left of the stage.
- The layer above the Placeholder layer, called Paneltop, contains a dynamic text field named **title_txt** as well as a bitmap of a black rectangle, which sits at the upper-right corner of the gray panel.
- The Progressbar layer contains a movie clip instance named **progress_mc** that we'll use in a later exercise.
- The Logo layer contains a bitmap of our logo.
- The Actions layer will contain all of the actions that make this project work.

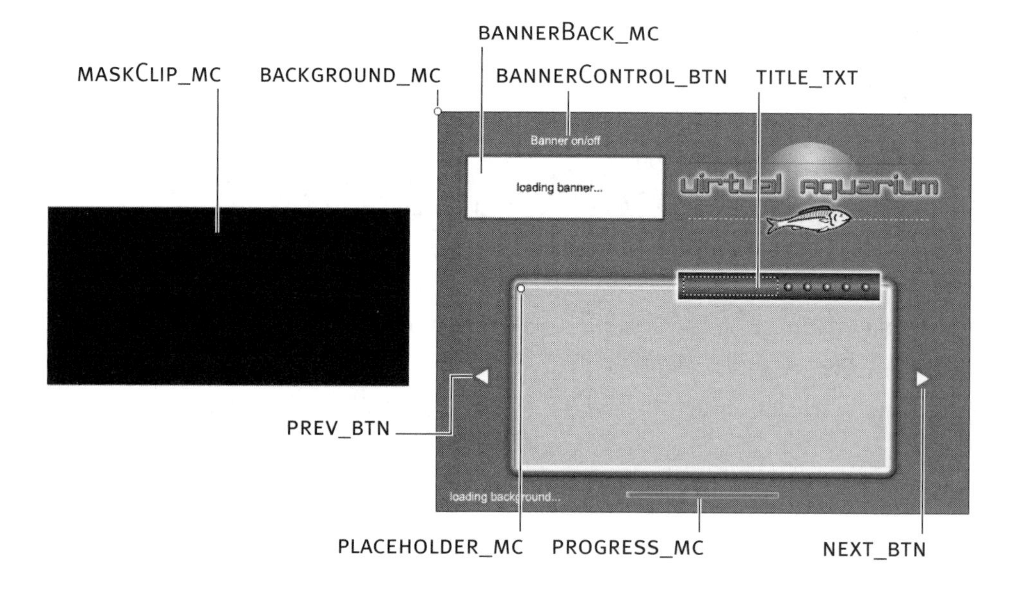

In a moment, we'll begin scripting the project to randomly load one of three SWFs into this instance. Before we do that, though, let's take a quick look at the external assets we'll load into the project in the next several exercises.

2) Using your operating system's directory-exploring application, navigate to the Lesson18/Assets directory.

In this directory are the files that will eventually be loaded dynamically into this project: **background0.swf**, **background1.swf**, **background2.swf**, **banner0.swf**, **banner1.swf**, **banner2.swf**, **image0.jpg**, **image1.jpg**, **image2.jpg**, **music0.mp3**, **music1.mp3**, and **music2.mp3**.

In this lesson, we'll work with **background0.swf**, **background1.swf**, and **background2.swf**: simple animated movies that represent our project's background (the dimensions of which are 550 pixels wide by 400 pixels high, the same as those of the receiving movie). You can double-click these files to view them in the Flash player.

Keep the directory window open and available as we progress through the following exercises, as we'll reference it again.

3) Return to Flash. With the Actions panel open, select Frame 1 of the Actions layer and add the following script:

```
var backgrounds:Array = new Array ("background0.swf", "background1.swf",
⇒"background2.swf");
```

This step creates a new array named backgrounds, which holds the paths to our external background movies.

Now let's create a function that randomly loads one of these background movies into our project.

4) Add the following function definition below the script you added in Step 3:

```
function randomBackground() {
  var randomNumber = random (backgrounds.length);
  loadMovie (backgrounds[randomNumber], "background_mc");
}
```

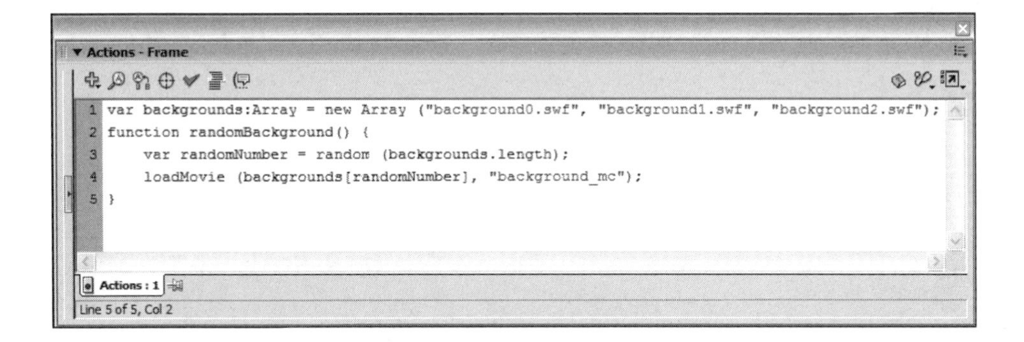

Let's look at how the randomBackground() function works. The function begins by generating a random number based on the number of elements in the backgrounds array. The length of the array is analyzed to determine the range of possible random numbers to generate. Because the backgrounds array has three elements, one of three possible numbers (0, 1, or 2) will be generated and set as the value of randomNumber. The next line of the function uses the value of this variable to determine which background movie to load. If the number 1 was generated and set as the value of randomNumber, the loadMovie() action would look like this:

```
loadMovie (backgrounds[1], "background_mc");
```

Because the value of element 1 of the backgrounds array is "background1.swf", this line could be broken down further:

```
loadMovie ("background1.swf", "background_mc");
```

In this scenario, the external movie named **background1.swf** would be loaded into the movie clip instance with a target path of **background_mc**. The movie at this target path is the empty movie clip instance in the upper-left portion of the stage. Because the externally loaded background movie and the receiving movie share the same dimensions (550 pixels wide by 400 pixels high), the externally loaded background movie covers the entire stage.

5) Add the following function call after the function definition added in Step 4:

```
randomBackground();
```

Because this function call resides on Frame 1 of the movie, it will be executed as soon as the movie begins to play.

NOTE *Depending on its file size, an externally loaded movie (like any other movie) may require a preloader, which you would construct and program as a regular preloader. For more information on how to create a preloader, see Lesson 16, "Time- and Frame-Based Dynamism."*

6) Choose Control > Test Movie.

As soon as the movie begins playing, one of the three background movies is loaded into the project.

The **background_mc** movie clip instance (into which our external background is loaded) resides on the bottom layer of the scene; the rest of the scene's content resides above **background_mc**. When the external movie is loaded into the instance, the loaded content appears at that same depth. In other words, it's on the bottom layer, with the rest of the scene's content above it.

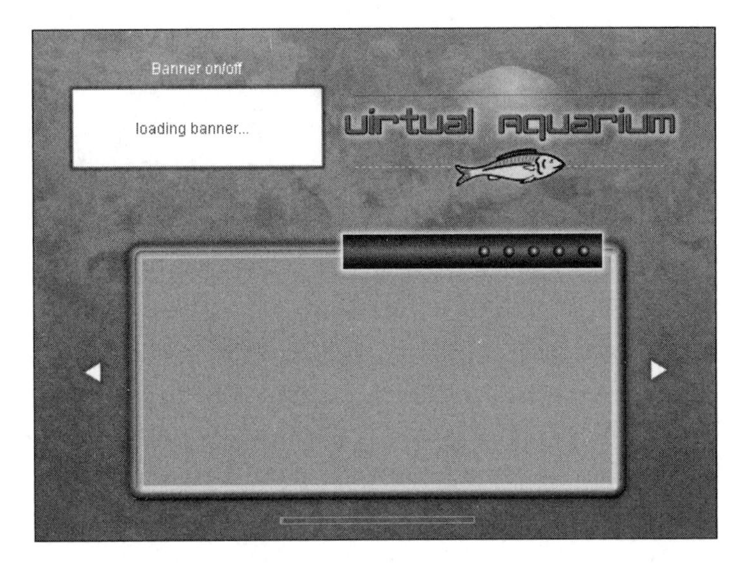

Using the technique described in this exercise, you could construct dozens or even hundreds of background movies, although only one would be loaded when the movie plays. In this way, you can create a dynamic project without increasing download or viewing time.

TIP *With ActionScript, you could use a variation of this technique to determine the current date and then load an external background based on time of day, day of week, or month.*

7) Close the test movie. Save the file as *virtualaquarium2.fla*.

This completes the exercise. We'll build on this file in the following exercises.

Although our project is set up to randomly load a background movie into a target, a typical Web site might use a navigation bar that loads content movies into a target. In other words, clicking a button named Products might load **products.swf** into a target named **content_mc**. There are many variations to this concept.

LOADING JPGS DYNAMICALLY

Now that you've learned how to load an external movie into a project, the process of dynamically loading a JPG should be easy—it's almost identical to that of loading an external SWF. As demonstrated in the preceding exercise, the `loadMovie()` action loads an external SWF into a target. You'll use the same action to load an external JPG—but with a twist. Look at the following syntax:

```
loadMovie("myBitmap.jpg", "myClip_mc");
```

This `loadMovie()` action identifies a JPG as the external asset to load. Here, **myBitmap.jpg** is loaded into the **myClip_mc** target. After a JPG is loaded into a movie in this fashion, Flash sees it as a movie clip instance, which means that you can control it via ActionScript—rotating, resizing, or making it transparent as with any other clip.

In this exercise, we'll build slideshow functionality into our project to demonstrate how we can load JPGs into a target on an as-needed basis.

1) Open *virtualaquarium2.fla*.

We'll continue working with this file from the preceding exercise.

Note the empty movie clip instance on the Placeholder layer (the small white circle in the panel graphic's upper-left corner). Called **placeholder_mc**, this is the movie clip instance into which our external JPGs will be loaded. Also note the text field with the name **title_txt**, at the top of the panel; we'll use that in our exercise as well.

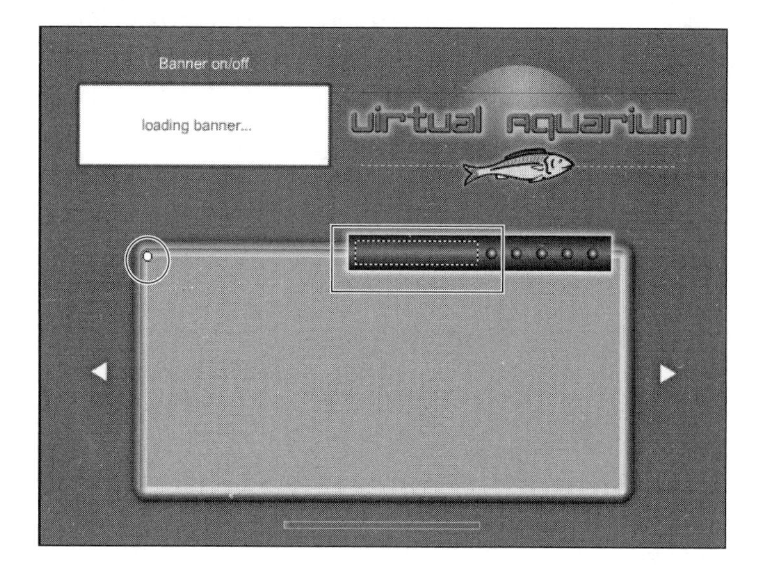

Before we begin scripting, let's review the contents of the directory containing our externally loaded assets.

2) Using your operating system's directory-exploring application, navigate to the Lesson18/Assets directory and locate the image files named *image0.jpg*, *image1.jpg*, and *image2.jpg*.

Each of these images is 378 pixels wide by 178 pixels high—the size at which the image will be loaded into the receiving movie. After the images are loaded, however,

Flash will recognize them as movie clip instances and can thus resize and transform them in any number of ways, as we'll demonstrate in the next exercise.

IMAGE0.JPG

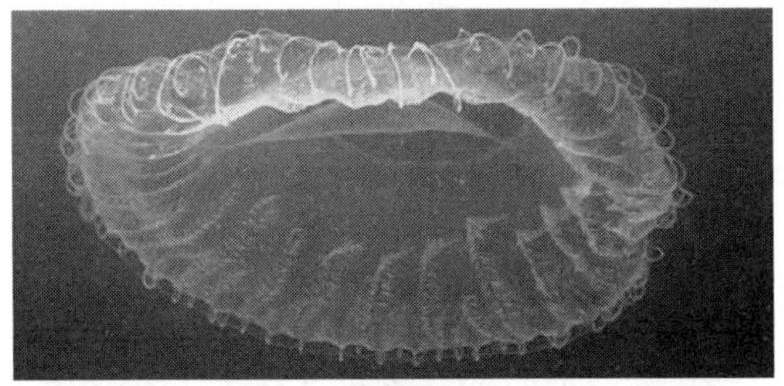

IMAGE1.JPG

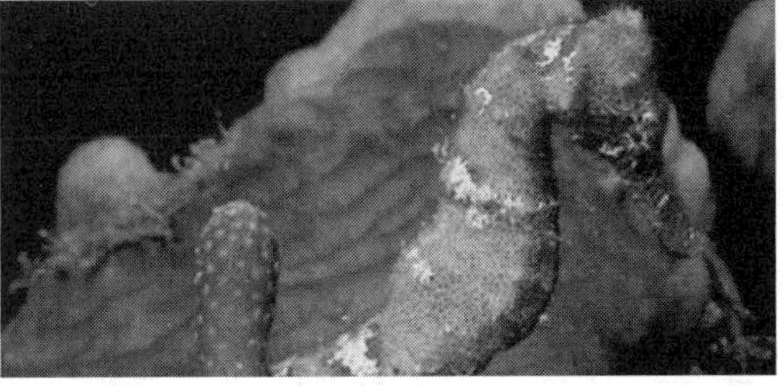

IMAGE2.JPG

NOTE *Only standard JPG files are supported. Progressive JPG files are not supported.*

3) Return to Flash. With the Actions panel open, select Frame 1 of the Actions layer and add the following line of script just below the `backgrounds` **array from the preceding exercise:**

```
var slides:Array = new Array(["Shark", "image0.jpg"], ["Jellyfish",
⇒"image1.jpg"], ["Seahorse", "image2.jpg"]);
```

This step creates a new two-dimensional array named `slides`. As you learned in Lesson 6, "Creating and Manipulating Data," this is an array in which each element contains more than one item. The first part of each element is simply a string description of the image; the second parameter represents the directory path to that image.

Now let's create a function to load these images into our project, with the functionality of a slideshow.

4) Add the following script just below the `randomBackground()` function call:

```
var currentSlide:Number;
function changeSlide(number:Number){
  if (number >= 0 && number < slides.length){
    currentSlide = number;
    title_txt.text = slides[number][0];
    loadMovie (slides[number][1], "placeholder_mc");
  }
}
```

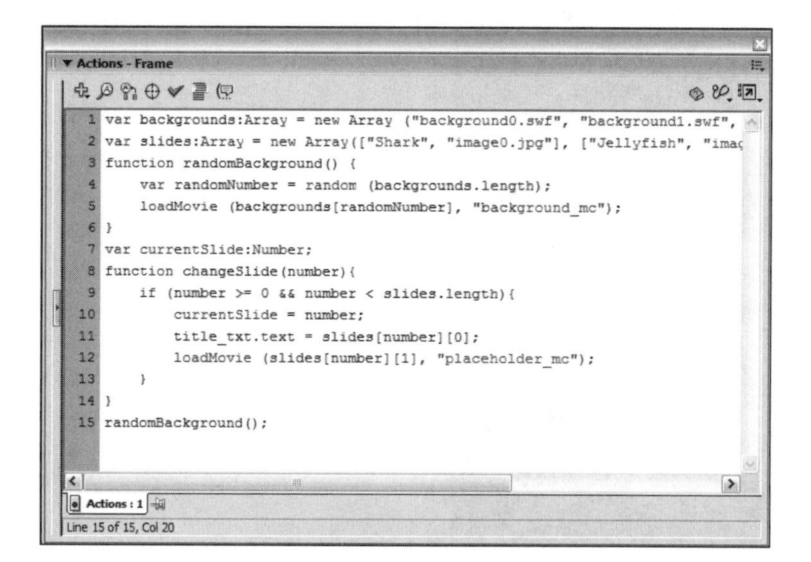

The first line creates a variable named `currentSlide`, which will track the currently visible slide. This variable is created outside the function because it needs to exist as long as the application is running. Upcoming steps will discuss how this variable is used.

The next part of the script creates a function named `changeSlide()`. Let's look at how this function works.

Notice that the function is passed a parameter named `number`—a numerical value that the function will use to determine which image to load. The `if` statement at the beginning of the function definition dictates that the function executes only when a number within a certain range is passed to the function. The lower end of this range is `0`, and the upper end depends on the number of elements in the `slides` array. Thus, the `if` statement basically states that if `number` is greater than or equal to 0 and less than the length of the `slides` array (which is `3` because the array contains three elements), the actions in the function should be executed. Under these circumstances, the function executes only if `number` is `0`, `1`, or `2`. (In a moment, you'll begin to understand why we've set up the function this way.)

The first action in the function sets the value of `currentSlide` to the value of the `number` parameter passed to the function. This variable's value will be used a bit later, when executing actions on our two arrow buttons.

The next line in our script sets the value of the text field **title_txt** to the value of `slides[number][0]`. The last line in the function uses a `loadMovie()` action to load one of our external JPG images into the instance named **placeholder_mc**, which is on the root timeline. To make sense of this function, let's look at a couple of scenarios:

If the value `1` is passed to this function, the `if` statement determines that to be an acceptable value, and the actions in the function are executed—in which case, they're evaluated as follows:

```
currentSlide = 1;
title_txt.text = slides[1][0];
loadMovie (slides[1][1], "placeholder_mc");
```

Because the last two actions in the function reference elements in the `slides` array, you can further break down those actions:

```
currentSlide = 1;
title_txt.text = "Jellyfish";
loadMovie ("image1.jpg", "placeholder_mc");
```

The result is that **image1.jpg** is loaded into the instance named **placeholder_mc** and the text string `"Jellyfish"` appears above the panel in the **title_txt** text field.

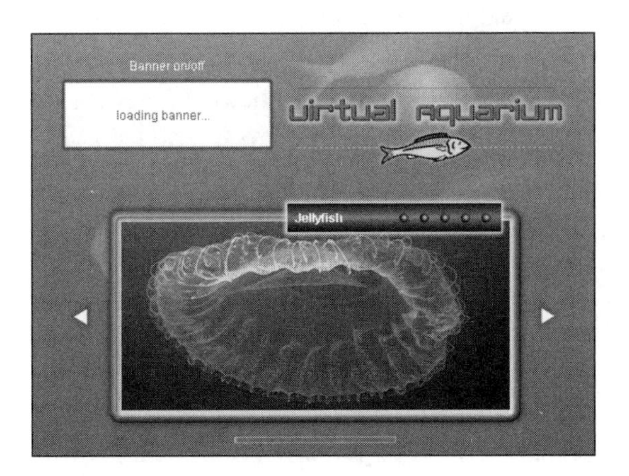

Let's consider one more scenario. If the value `3` is passed, the `if` statement prevents the function from executing—and prevents our project from attempting to load content that doesn't exist (as defined in the `slides` array). In other words, the `slides`

array doesn't contain an element at index number 3; therefore, the function wouldn't work properly if it executed. Obviously, we could increase the number of elements in the `slides` array, and the upper limit accepted by the `if` statement would dynamically increase to match.

5) Add the following function call just below the `randomBackground()` function call:

```
changeSlide(0);
```

This line of script calls the `changeSlide()` function, passes that function a value of `0`, and as a result displays the initial image when the movie is initially played. Note that this initial function call sets the value of `currentSlide` to `0`, as defined in the `changeSlide()` function definition—an important point to keep in mind as you progress through the next couple of steps.

6) Add the following event handler at the end of the current script:

```
prev_btn.onRelease = function(){
  changeSlide(currentSlide - 1);
}
```

When the **prev_btn** instance is clicked, this script calls the `changeSlide()` function defined in Step 4. The parameter value passed to the function depends on how `currentSlide - 1` is evaluated. When the movie initially plays, the `changeSlide()` function is called and passed a value of `0`, as scripted in Step 5. Consequently, `currentSlide` is initially set to `0`. Clicking the **prev_btn** instance just after the movie begins to play results in calling the `changeSlide()` function and passing a value of `-1` (the result of subtracting 1 from the value of `currentSlide`). The `if` statement in the `changeSlide()` function then evaluates that value (`-1`) and prevents the function from executing (Step 4 explains why). As a result, this button does nothing until `currentSlide` has a value greater than 0. In other words, this button cannot navigate the slideshow beyond the initial image. The other arrow button (**next_btn**) increases the value, as shown in the next step.

7) Add the following event handler after the script added in Step 6:

```
next_btn.onRelease = function(){
  changeSlide(currentSlide + 1);
}
```

This script adds an `onRelease` event handler to the **next_btn** instance, similar to the one in Step 6 but with one exception: the parameter value passed to the `changeSlide()` function depends on how `currentSlide + 1` is evaluated. If `currentSlide` has a value of `0` when this button is clicked (after the movie begins playing), the `changeSlide()`

function receives 1 (the result of adding 1 to the value of `currentSlide`). Remember that this value is evaluated by the `if` statement in the function. In this case, because the number is between 0 and 2, the `if` statement allows the continued execution of the function, which loads the appropriate JPG as described in Step 4. As the image is loading, the `changeSlide()` function updates the value of `currentSlide` based on the value passed to the function (1 in this case) so that the **prev_btn** and **next_btn** buttons we just scripted can act based on this value when subsequently clicked.

The **next_btn** button instance cannot navigate the slideshow beyond the last image, because after `currentSlide` has the value 2, clicking this button again would send the `changeSlide()` function a value of 3 (which the `if` statement in that function would analyze, and then would prevent the function from executing).

In tandem, these two buttons advance and rewind the slideshow—though only within the limits described.

8) Choose Control > Test Movie.

As soon as the movie begins playing, the image of a shark appears and the **title_txt** text field above the panel displays the text string `"Shark"`. The upper-left corner of the image is placed at the registration point of the empty movie clip into which it was loaded.

Click the **prev_btn** instance and nothing happens. Click the **next_btn** instance once, and the next JPG image loads; click it again and another JPG loads. However, if you click this button a third time, nothing happens because you've reached the upper limit of how far this button can advance. The **prev_btn** button instance has a similar restriction in the opposite direction.

To add slides to this project, you simply add the appropriate data to the `slides` array and place the JPG files in the directory. The movie would then accommodate the new images automatically. This means that you can add hundreds of images without affecting the file size of the main movie. Because the images are external, you can easily bring them into a photo editor, update or change them, and then resave them, and your changes will be reflected the next time the project is played.

TIP *To remove a movie that has been loaded into an instance, so that the instance becomes empty, use the following syntax:*

```
unloadMovie("nameOfInstance")
```

9) Close the test movie and save the file as *virtualaquarium3.fla*.

This step completes the exercise. We'll build on this file in the following exercises.

CREATING AN INTERACTIVE PLACEHOLDER

A *placeholder* is nothing more than a movie clip instance (empty or otherwise) into which external content can be loaded (also known as a *target*). Creating an *interactive* placeholder involves giving that placeholder the capability of interactivity when an event of some sort occurs. The great thing about loading external content into an instance that has been scripted in such a way is that even though the instance's *content* will change, its scripted *functionality* can remain the same. Look at the following example:

```
this.onMouseDown = function(){
  placeholder_mc._rotation += 30;
}
```

If you attach this script to the main timeline, the **placeholder_mc** instance rotates 30 degrees each time the mouse is clicked. This instance can be thought of as an interactive placeholder because any external movie or JPG loaded into it will also rotate when the mouse is clicked. The only thing that changes is the instance's content.

There are many ways to create interactive placeholder movie clip instances with a minimum of scripting. The following exercise shows an example.

1) Open *virtualaquarium3.fla*.

When we worked with this file in the preceding exercise, we set the movie to dynamically load JPGs into the movie clip instance named **placeholder_mc**. In this exercise, we'll add ActionScript to make the loaded content draggable and to scale it 150 percent when the mouse button is pressed. The ActionScript will also ensure that when the mouse button is released, dragging ceases and the content is scaled back to 100 percent. In the process of setting up this functionality, we'll use the black rectangle (a movie clip instance named **maskClip_mc**) on the left of the stage as a dynamic mask.

Let's get started.

2) With the Actions panel open, select Frame 1 of the Actions layer and add the following script at the end of the current script:

```
var placeholderStartX:Number = placeholder_mc._x;
var placeholderStartY:Number = placeholder_mc._y;
```

This script creates two variables whose values represent the initial x and y positions of the **placeholder_mc** movie clip instance, into which our JPGs are loaded. The importance of these values will become evident in a moment.

TIP *We could have opened the Property inspector, selected the instance, copied the x and y values shown there, and set* `placeholderStartX` *and* `placeholderStartY` *accordingly, but the method shown in Step 2 is much more dynamic. It allows the values to change automatically if the instance is moved to a new point on the stage during development.*

3) Add the following script below the script you just added in Step 2:

```
this.onMouseDown = function(){
  if (placeholder_mc.hitTest(_xmouse, _ymouse)){
    maskClip_mc._x = placeholderStartX;
    maskClip_mc._y = placeholderStartY;
    placeholder_mc.setMask(maskClip_mc);
    placeholder_mc._xscale = 150;
    placeholder_mc._yscale = 150;
    startDrag(placeholder_mc, false);
  }
}
```

This step attaches an `onMouseDown` event handler to the main timeline, causing the script to execute whenever the mouse button is pressed. An `if` statement determines whether the mouse pointer is over the **placeholder_mc** instance when the mouse is pressed. If so, the remaining actions are executed. In other words, because our JPG images are being loaded into this instance, these actions execute only if the mouse button is pressed while the pointer is on top of the image.

The first two actions within the `if` statement dynamically position the black rectangle **maskClip_mc** movie clip instance so that its x and y values equal `placeholderStartX` and `placeholderStartY`, respectively. This action places the **maskClip_mc** instance directly over the **placeholder_mc** instance during this script's execution.

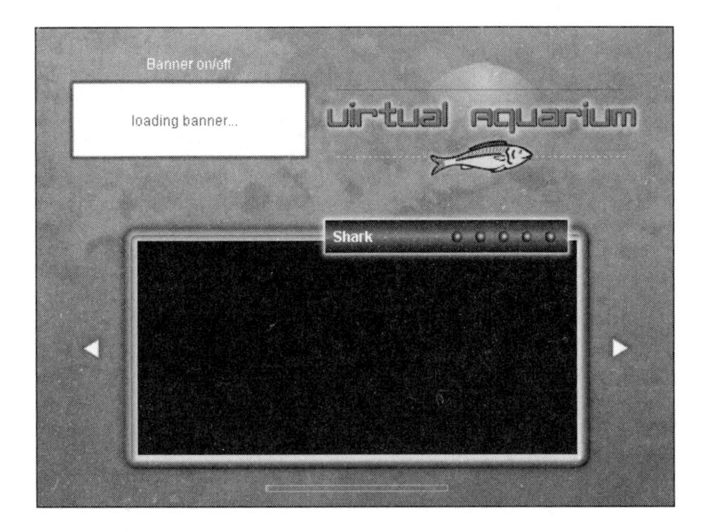

The next action dynamically sets the **maskClip_mc** instance to mask the **placeholder_mc** instance's content—necessary because the next two lines in the script scale the size of **placeholder_mc** by 150 percent. By masking the **placeholder_mc** contents, those contents appear to remain within the panel window even though **placeholder_mc** becomes larger.

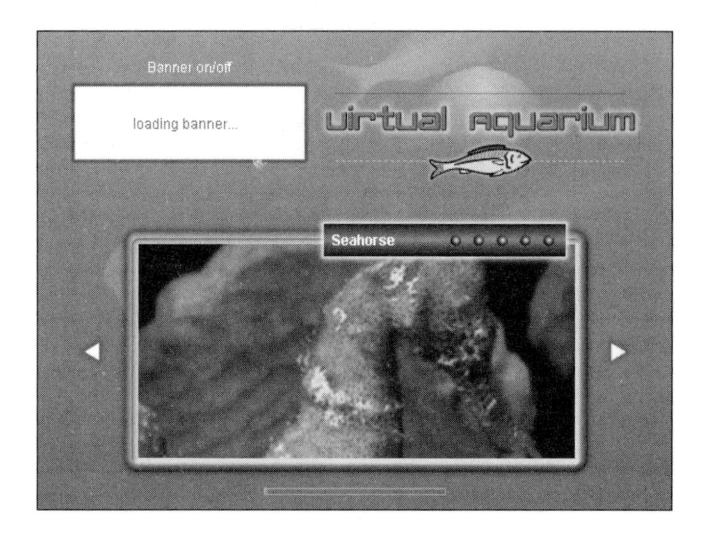

The last action in the event handler makes the **placeholder_mc** movie clip instance draggable.

4) Add the following event handler below the script you just added in Step 3:

```
this.onMouseUp = function(){
  stopDrag();
  with(placeholder_mc){
    setMask(null);
    _xscale = 100;
    _yscale = 100;
    _x = placeholderStartX;
    _y = placeholderStartY;
  }
}
```

This script—executed when the mouse button is released—simply reverses the actions that occur when the mouse button is pressed. The script first stops the dragging process; then the next several lines use a `with` statement to perform a set of actions in relation to the **placeholder_mc** instance. The first action removes the mask from the instance.

NOTE *Using `null` removes the mask effect completely.*

The next two actions scale the instance back to its original size. Because this instance was draggable, the last two actions perform the necessary task of resetting it to its original position.

5) Choose Control > Test Movie.

As soon as the movie begins to play, click and drag the image of the shark. When the mouse button is pressed, the image becomes larger and draggable, and the dynamic mask we set up takes effect. Release the mouse button, and you'll see **maskClip_mc**. The reason for this is that when our script removed the masking effect, we didn't compensate for the fact that **maskClip_mc** would become visible again as a normal clip. Obviously, this isn't what we want, but there's an easy fix.

6) Return to the authoring environment. With the Actions panel open, select Frame 1 of the Actions layer and attach this script:

```
maskClip_mc._visible = false;
```

This line of script makes the instance invisible as soon as it loads, and it remains this way because our movie doesn't contain an action to change it. Because the instance is invisible, it won't interfere with viewing the images in the **placeholder_mc** instance, even when the masking effect is disabled.

7) Choose Control > Test Movie.

As soon as the movie begins to play, click and drag the image of the shark. With the mouse button pressed, the image becomes larger and draggable, and the dynamic mask we set up takes effect. Release the mouse button, and the image appears as it did originally. This time, **maskClip_mc** no longer appears, because it's invisible.

Load a new image, using the right-arrow button. Click that newly loaded image, and you'll find that it has retained its original functionality. The image's functionality resides not within the loaded asset, but in the instance into which the asset is loaded (**placeholder_mc**); although the loaded content may change, the instance and its functionality remain the same.

8) Close the test movie and save the file as *virtualaquarium4.fla*.

This step completes this exercise. We'll continue to build on this file in the following exercises.

LOADING MOVIES INTO LEVELS

Thus far, we've loaded external content into an existing movie clip instance; however, you can also load external movies and JPGs into *levels*. You can think of levels as layers of movies (SWFs) that exist within the Flash player window, all at the same time. For example, when you view an HTML page containing a Flash movie, a Flash player window is created and the initial movie (as identified in the `<object>` and `<embed>` tags) is loaded into the player. That movie is loaded into a *z-plane* (a term signifying depth) within the player window known as *Level 0*. You can load additional SWFs into higher levels in the player window.

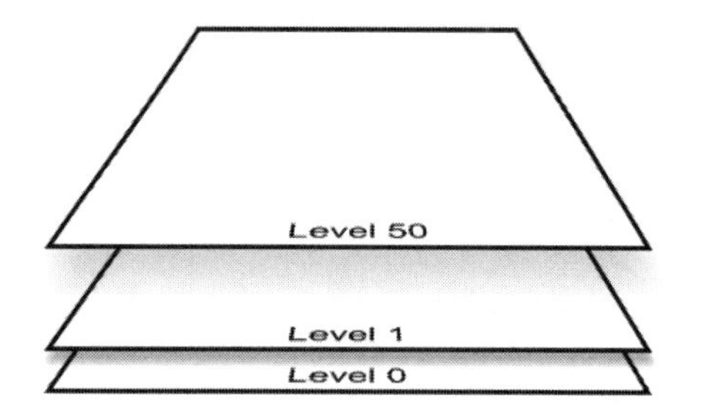

You load SWFs into higher levels by employing a variant of the `loadMovie()` action:

```
loadMovieNum("myExternalMovie.swf", 1);
```

There are two differences between this code and the code used to load an external asset into a target/instance: the action is now named `loadMovieNum()` rather than `loadMovie()`, and instead of identifying a *target* for the external asset, we've identified a *level number*. This action loads **myExternalMovie.swf** into Level 1 of the Flash player window.

It's important to keep the following rules in mind when loading a movie into a level:

- Only one SWF (or JPG) can occupy a level at any time.
- You don't have to load movies (or JPGs) into sequential levels. (For example, you can load a movie into Level 50 even if Levels 1 through 49 are empty.)
- The content of movies on higher levels appears above the content from levels below it. In other words, the content of a movie on Level 10 appears above all content on Levels 9 and lower.
- The frame rate of the movie loaded into Level 0 takes precedence, dictating the rate at which all movies in the Flash player window will play. For example, if the movie on Level 0 is set to play at 24 frames per second, and an external movie with a frame rate of 12 fps is loaded into a target or level, the externally loaded movie's frame rate speeds up to match that of the movie on Level 0. Be sure to set similar frame rates when authoring your various movies; otherwise, you may get unexpected results in the final product.

- If you load a movie into Level 0, every level in the Flash Player is automatically unloaded (removed), and Level 0 is replaced with the new file.

In the following exercise, we'll enable our project to randomly load banner movies into levels.

1) Open *virtualaquarium4.fla.*

We'll continue working with the file from the preceding exercise, adding script to Frame 1. Because we'll be loading our banner movies into levels as opposed to targets, you don't need to use any of the elements in the current scene to make the process work. A rectangular graphic (with an instance name of **bannerBack_mc**) has been added to the scene for design purposes.

Before going any further, let's review the contents of the directory that contains our externally loaded assets.

2) Using your operating system's directory-exploring application, navigate to the Lesson18/Assets directory and locate the movies named *banner0.swf, banner1.swf,* and *banner2.swf.*

Our project will be set up to randomly load one of these simple animated movies (each of which is 200 pixels wide by 60 pixels high) into a level.

3) Return to Flash. With the Actions panel open, select Frame 1 of the Actions layer and add the following line of script below the script for the `slides` array:

```
var banners:Array = new Array("banner0.swf", "banner1.swf", "banner2.swf");
```

This script creates a new array named `banners`, which holds the paths to our external banner movies.

Now let's create a function that will randomly load one of these banner movies into our project.

4) Add the following function definition at the end of the current script on Frame 1:

```
function randomBanner() {
  var randomNumber = random (banners.length);
  loadMovieNum (banners[randomNumber], 1);
}
```

The `randomBanner()` function works much like the `randomBackground()` function we set up in the first exercise in this lesson. Notice the slightly different name of the action that executes the loading function—`loadMovieNum()`. Also note that we've indicated it should load the movie into Level 1. Each time this function is called, a random banner is loaded into Level 1, replacing the banner that's already there.

5) Add the following function call below the function definition you added in Step 4:

```
randomBanner();
```

This function call loads the initial banner when the movie begins playing. Next, to make better use of the function, we'll use a `setInterval()` action to call this function automatically on a regular basis.

6) Add the following line of script below the `randomBanner()` function call:

```
setInterval(randomBanner, 10000);
```

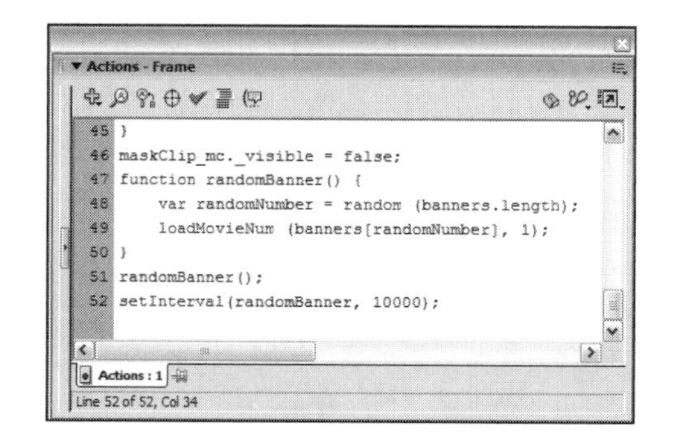

Using the `setInterval()` action, we've scripted the `randomBanner()` function to execute every 10,000 milliseconds (once every 10 seconds). This will provide our project with rotating banner functionality.

7) Choose Control > Test Movie.

As soon as the movie begins to play, a random banner is loaded into the project. The main movie is loaded into Level 0 automatically while the banner is set to load into Level 1—which means that it's loaded above everything else in the project. If you replay the movie, chances are that a different banner will load. There's a problem, though. The banner's position on the stage isn't correct; it should appear above the white rectangular box.

By default, the banner movie's upper-left corner (its registration point) loads at a position of 0x and 0y in relation to the registration point of the movie on Level 0. In essence, the upper-left corner of the loaded movie is automatically aligned to the upper-left corner of the movie on Level 0. This is true of any movie loaded into any level. However, because our banner movie is only 200 pixels wide by 60 pixels high, a spacing discrepancy exists when it's loaded into a movie that's 550 pixels wide by 400 pixels high. When the banner movie is loaded, it needs to be repositioned directly above the white rectangle on the stage—something we'll correct in the next exercise.

8) Close the test movie and save the file as *virtualaquarium5.fla*.

This step completes this exercise. We'll continue to build on this file in the following exercises.

CONTROLLING A MOVIE ON A LEVEL

You can control a movie loaded into a level from another timeline or from within the movie itself. The target path to a movie loaded into a level is simply its level number. For example, if you've loaded a movie into level 5, you would use the following syntax to make it rotate from any other timeline currently in the player window:

```
_level5._rotation = 45;
```

Straightforward and simple. It's also easy to place an action on Frame 1 of a loaded movie so that it takes some action immediately upon loading. We'll look at both approaches in the following exercise, in which we'll script our banner movies to reposition themselves correctly upon loading, as well as create a banner On/Off button.

1) Open *virtualaquarium5.fla*.

We'll continue working with this file from the preceding exercise. The white rectangle on the stage is a movie clip instance named **bannerBack_mc**. The location of this instance's registration point (upper-left corner of the instance) will be pivotal in a script that repositions the banner movies when they're loaded into Level 1. Because this repositioning script will reside within the banner movies, we need to open the banner movie's authoring files.

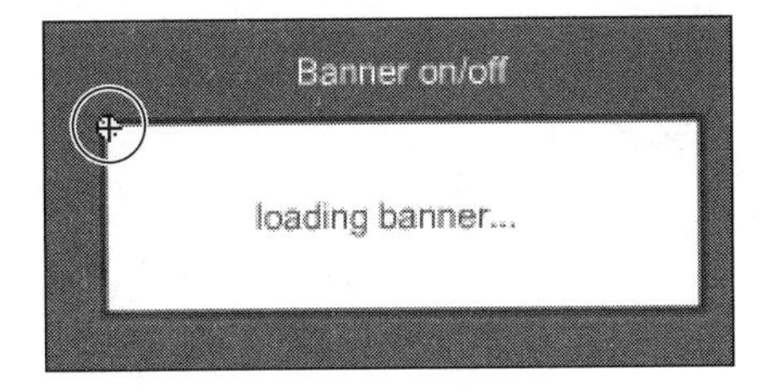

2) Choose File › Open. Navigate to the Lesson18/Assets folder, locate the file named *banner0.fla*, and open it in Flash.

This simple animated movie is made up of five layers, the top of which is named Actions. We'll place a two-line script on Frame 1 so that as soon as the banner movie is loaded, the script is executed.

3) With the Actions panel open, select Frame 1 of the Actions layer and add the following script:

```
_x = _level0.bannerBack_mc._x;
_y = _level0.bannerBack_mc._y;
```

These two lines of script set the x and y properties of this movie to match the x and y properties of the **bannerBack_mc** movie clip instance on Level 0. This technique causes the banner movie to load exactly on top of the **bannerBack_mc** instance, even if **bannerBack_mc** is eventually moved from its current location.

4) Add the script from Step 3 to Frame 1 of the other banner movies (*banner1.fla* and *banner2.fla*); then re-export the three movies as *banner0.swf*, *banner1.swf*, and *banner2.swf*, respectively.

5) Return to *virtualaquarium5.fla*. Choose Control › Test Movie.

Again, a random banner is loaded; however, this time it loads at the proper location. If you wait 10 seconds, a different banner may load, also at the proper location in relation to **bannerBack_mc**.

This is the best approach for triggering an action to occur as soon as the movie loads.

6) Close the test movie to return to the authoring file (*virtualaquarium5.fla*).

The banner movie loaded into Level 1 can easily be controlled from this movie as well. We'll script a button to demonstrate this principle.

7) With the Actions panel open, select Frame 1 of the Actions layer and add the following script at the end of the current script:

```
bannerControl_btn.onRelease = function() {
  _level1._visible = !_level1._visible;
  bannerBack_mc._visible = !bannerBack_mc._visible;
}
```

This script adds an `onRelease` event handler to the **bannerControl_btn** instance. This step creates a toggling functionality that makes both the banner movie loaded into Level 1 and the **bannerBack_mc** movie clip instance either visible or invisible, depending on the current state of the instance when the instance is clicked. Using the NOT (`!`) operator provides a quick and easy way to reverse Boolean values of any kind.

8) Choose Control > Test Movie.

Click the On/Off button several times to test its functionality. Wait 10 seconds for the banner to change. The button continues to work because it's set up to control the movie loaded into Level 1 rather than a particular banner movie.

9) Close the test movie. Save the file as *virtualaquarium6.fla*.

This step completes the exercise. We'll continue to build on this file in the following exercises.

It's important to note that security issues can arise when loading files from different domains into a single player window (the Flash player considers a subdomain as a different domain). There are a few restrictions to keep in mind. For example, if a movie at *www.derekfranklin.com/derekMovie.swf* is being played and contains an action to load a movie located at *www.electrotank.com/jobeMovie.swf* into Level 5, these two movies initially won't be able to exchange data via ActionScript because they were loaded from different domains. A permission setting for allowing movies loaded from different domains to access each other's data can be used to override this restriction. In this scenario, if **derekMovie.swf** contains the following setting (placed on Frame 1):

```
System.security.allowDomain("www.electrotank.com")
```

then **jobeMovie.swf** (loaded from *electrotank.com*) will have access to the data in **derekMovie.swf**.

If **jobeMovie.swf** contains this setting:

```
System.security.allowDomain("www.derekfranklin.com")
```

then **derekMovie.swf** (loaded from *derekfranklin.com*) will have access to the data in **jobeMovie.swf**.

To this point in the lesson, we've concentrated on loading and controlling graphical content; however, a good Flash developer knows that graphics are just part of any great multimedia project. You also need sound, but sound contributes significantly to file size, which means that smart sound management is key. In the next two exercises, we'll show you how to use audio efficiently in your projects.

LOADING MP3S DYNAMICALLY

MP3s are everywhere these days—a popularity that can be attributed to the fact that they provide an acceptable way of delivering audio (especially music) over the Web in a low-bandwidth world. Although MP3s are much more compact than standard, noncompressed audio files, a single MP3 of any length (let alone several MP3s) can still balloon a movie's file size to an unacceptable level.

Flash helps to alleviate this problem by providing the capability to *dynamically* load MP3 files into movies. As you'll soon see, loading an external MP3 into our project is a bit different from loading an external movie or JPG—but almost as easy.

If you want to load an MP3 into Flash, the first thing you need to do is create a place where you can load the file. This requires a Sound object:

```
var myFavMP3:Sound = new Sound();
```

After you've created a Sound object, simply use the `loadSound()` method to load an external MP3 into that object:

```
myFavMP3.loadSound("mySong.mp3", true);
```

This script loads the external MP3 file named **mySong.mp3** into the `myFavMP3` Sound object. After the MP3 has been loaded, you can control volume, panning, and other characteristics (see Lesson 17, "Scripting for Sound"). Notice that the `loadSound()` method has two parameters. The first parameter identifies the path to the external MP3; the other parameter determines whether the loaded file will be streamed (`true`) or considered an event sound (`false`). If this parameter is set to `true`, the externally loaded file begins playing as soon as a sufficient amount of the file has been downloaded. If set to `false`, the `start()` method must be invoked before the file will play:

```
myFavMP3.start();
```

NOTE *If the file is loaded as an event sound, it won't play—even if you invoke the* `start()` *method—until the complete file has been downloaded.*

In this exercise, we'll make it possible for each loaded image in the slideshow to have an associated music track that's loaded externally.

1) Open *virtualaquarium6.fla*.

We'll simply add some script to Frame 1 of this file from the preceding exercise.

Before going any further, let's review the contents of the directory that holds our externally loaded assets.

2) Navigate to the Lesson18/Assets directory and locate the files *music0.mp3*, *music1.mp3*, and *music2.mp3*.

3) Return to Flash. With the Actions panel open, select Frame 1 of the Actions layer and modify the `slides` array:

```
slides = new Array(["Shark", "image0.jpg", "music0.mp3"],
⇒["Jellyfish", "image1.jpg", "music1.mp3"],
⇒["Seahorse", "image2.jpg", "music2.mp3"]);
```

Here, the path/name of an MP3 file has been added to each element in the array.

Next, we'll alter the `changeSlide()` function defined in an earlier exercise, to make use of this new data.

4) Insert the following line of script above the `changeSlide()` function definition:

```
var slideSound:Sound = new Sound();
```

In the next step, we'll add script to the `changeSlide()` function that makes use of this Sound object. As we've mentioned before, the Sound object is created outside the function because it needs to exist beyond the execution of the function.

5) Add the following lines of script at the end of (but within) the `if` statement of the `changeSlide()` function definition:

```
slideSound.stop();
slideSound = new Sound();
slideSound.loadSound(slides[number][2], true);
```

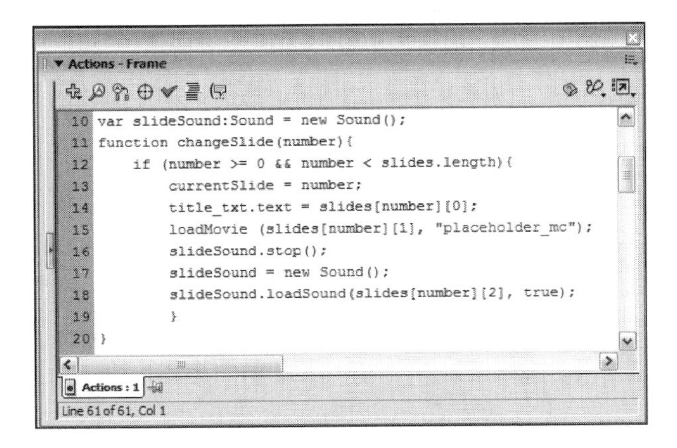

Actions - Frame
10 var slideSound:Sound = new Sound();
11 function changeSlide(number){
12 if (number >= 0 && number < slides.length){
13 currentSlide = number;
14 title_txt.text = slides[number][0];
15 loadMovie (slides[number][1], "placeholder_mc");
16 slideSound.stop();
17 slideSound = new Sound();
18 slideSound.loadSound(slides[number][2], true);
19 }
20 }
Actions : 1
Line 61 of 61, Col 1

Recall that the `changeSlide()` function is set up to load a new JPG image when called. The image that's loaded depends on the number passed to the function when the function is called. This number's value is evaluated and used to pull specific values from the `slides` array. By adding the MP3 files' path to the `slides` array and including the three lines of script above, we've extended the capability of this function so that when it's called and an image is loaded, the associated MP3 file will be loaded as well.

The first action stops the `slideSound` Sound object from playing—an action that's ignored the first time the function is called because no sound is playing initially. This `stop()` action ensures that when a new sound is loaded into the `slideSound` Sound object, the old sound stops playing. This strategy prevents one sound from "walking over" another.

The next line re-creates/reinitializes the `slideSound` Sound object just before a new sound is loaded into it. This lets the new sound load in a fresh instance of the `slideSound` object. The reason for this step will be explained in the next exercise.

Using the `loadSound()` action, the next line loads the external MP3 into the `slideSound` Sound object. In the first parameter of this action, the value of `number` is evaluated to determine which MP3 file to load, as defined in the `slides` array. The second parameter indicates that the loaded file is set to stream; therefore, the file will begin playing as soon as sufficient data has been downloaded.

Because we've simply altered the way this function works and we previously scripted a call to it, the sound should load and play as soon as the movie begins playing.

6) Choose Control > Test Movie.

As soon as the movie plays, the image in the panel is loaded and the associated music file is loaded and begins to play. If you advance the slideshow by clicking the right-arrow button, not only does the image change but a new sound file is loaded and plays.

7) Close the test movie and save the file as *virtualaquarium7.fla*.

This step completes the exercise. We'll continue to build on this file in the following exercises.

REACTING TO DYNAMICALLY LOADED MP3S

Want to trigger a set of actions to execute when a sound has finished playing? Want to know a sound's duration (play length) or current position (playback position)? Flash provides you with precisely this type of dynamic control when using loaded MP3s (or even internally attached sounds).

NOTE *Lesson 17, "Scripting for Sound," discussed many of the ways that you can control sounds dynamically.*

It's often useful to know when a sound will finish playing. Consider a presentation in which the next screen of info should be displayed only after the voiceover has finished explaining the current screen. Or a music jukebox that automatically loads the next song when the current one has finished playing. You can easily achieve this type of functionality by using the `onSoundComplete` event handler:

```
mySoundObject.onSoundComplete = function(){
  //actions go here...
}
```

Using this syntax, you would define a series of actions to be triggered when the sound in the Sound object finishes playing. The Sound class also provides two other events, `onLoad` and `onID3`, which we'll discuss in the next exercise.

NOTE *A Sound object must exist in your movie before you can define an* `onSoundComplete` *event handler to it. If you delete or re-create the Sound object, you must redefine the* `onSoundComplete` *event. In other words, you can't attach an event to an object that doesn't exist, and after an object has been deleted or re-created, the attached event ceases to exist as well.*

Every Sound object has a `duration` property, representing the sound's length (in milliseconds). Accessing this property's value is accomplished in the following manner:

```
var soundDuration:Number = mySoundObject.duration;
```

This script sets the value of `soundDuration` to the duration of the sound currently in the referenced Sound object. If the sound is 5.5 seconds long, the value of `soundDuration` is set to `5500` (1,000 × 5.5). This property exists for loaded sounds as well as sounds attached to the Sound object by using `attachSound()`.

You can determine how far a sound has progressed in its playback by using the following syntax:

```
var soundPosition:Number = mySoundObject.position;
```

If the sound in the referenced Sound object has been playing for three seconds, `soundPosition` is set to a value of 3000 (1,000 × 3).

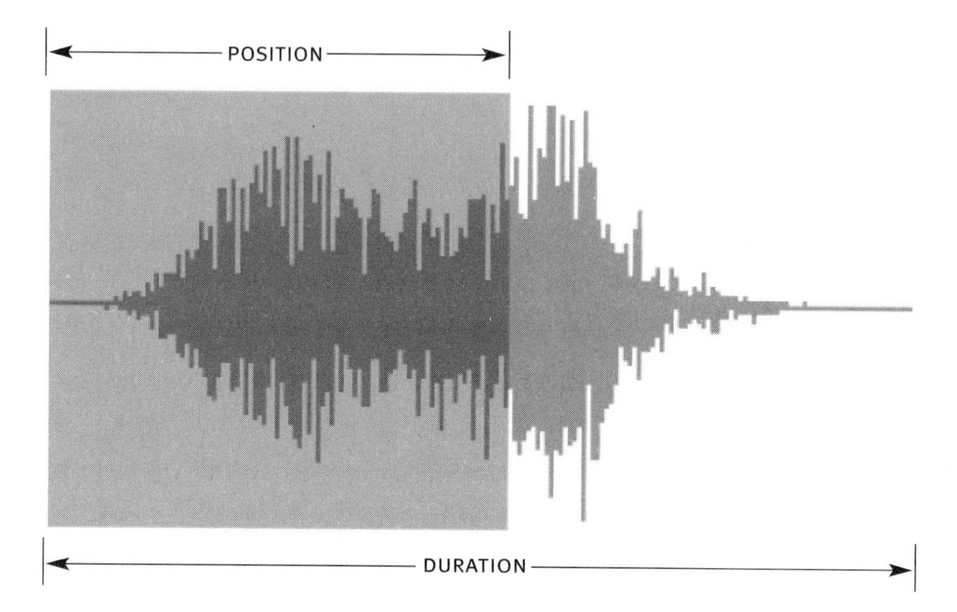

In the following exercise, we'll use the `onSoundComplete` event to trigger a function. We'll also employ the `duration` and `position` properties of the Sound object to create a playback progress bar.

1) Open *virtualaquarium7.fla*.

We'll add some script to Frame 1 of this file from the preceding exercise, as well as add a simple script to the **progress_mc** movie clip instance (which is below the panel graphic).

2) With the Actions panel open, select Frame 1 of the Actions layer and add the following lines of script at the end of (but within) the `if` statement of the `changeSlide()` function definition:

```
slideSound.onSoundComplete = function(){
  changeSlide(currentSlide + 1);
}
```

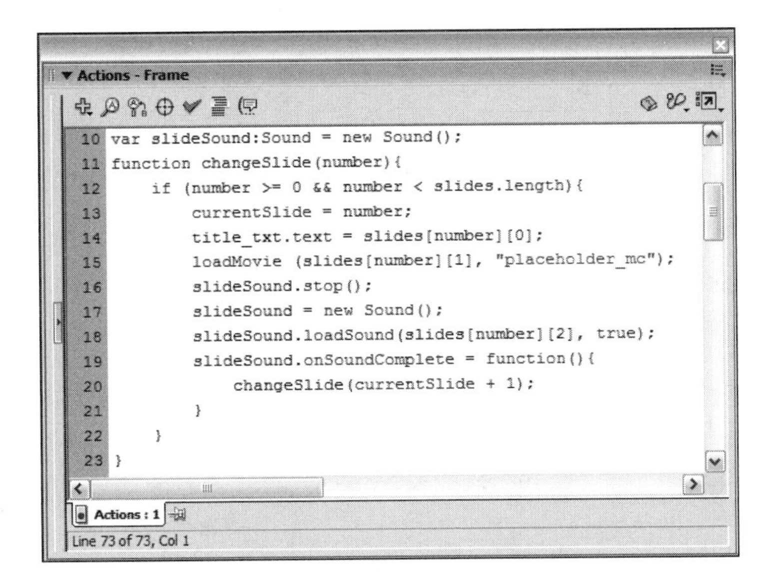
Actions - Frame
10 var slideSound:Sound = new Sound();
11 function changeSlide(number){
12 if (number >= 0 && number < slides.length){
13 currentSlide = number;
14 title_txt.text = slides[number][0];
15 loadMovie (slides[number][1], "placeholder_mc");
16 slideSound.stop();
17 slideSound = new Sound();
18 slideSound.loadSound(slides[number][2], true);
19 slideSound.onSoundComplete = function(){
20 changeSlide(currentSlide + 1);
21 }
22 }
23 }
Actions : 1
Line 73 of 73, Col 1

This script defines what should occur when the sound loaded into the `slideSound` Sound object has finished playing. A call is made to the `changeSlide()` function. This call acts as an automatic advancing mechanism for the slideshow: As soon as a sound has finished playing, the next image and sound are loaded as a result of the function call to the `changeSlide()` function.

In the preceding exercise, we discussed how our `slideSound` Sound object is re-created/reinitialized each time before a new sound is loaded into it. Every time this occurs, the event handler is removed from the Sound object instance as well. By placing this script just a few lines after the Sound object's reinitialization, we reattach this `onSoundComplete` event handler to the Sound object.

Let's look at the structure of the playback progress bar before we script it.

3) Double-click the *progress_mc* movie clip instance to edit it in place.

This movie clip is made up of three layers. We're most interested in the bottom layer, named *bar*, which contains a 100-frame tween. If you drag the playhead, you'll see that this tween is set up to emulate a progress bar with a range of 0 to 100 percent. In a moment, we'll add a script to move this timeline to the appropriate frame based on the percentage of the sound file that has played. In other words, if 47 percent of the sound file has played, this clip will be at Frame 47, showing the appropriate progress.

4) Return to the main timeline. With the Actions panel open, select Frame 1 of the Actions layer and add the following script at the end of the current script:

```
progress_mc.onEnterFrame = function(){
  var progressAmount = Math.round(((slideSound.position /
  ⇒slideSound.duration) * 100));
  this.gotoAndStop(progressAmount);
  if (progressAmount == 100){
    this._visible = false;
  }else{
    this._visible = true;
  }
}
```

This script attaches an event handler to the **progress_mc** instance. For each `onEnterFrame` event, the value of `progressAmount` is updated to a percentage value between 0 and 100. This percentage value is determined by evaluating the current `position` and `duration` values of the `slideSound` Sound object and then rounding the result. This value is next used to move the instance's timeline to the appropriate frame. Together, these actions emulate the functionality of a progress bar.

The `if/else` statement makes the progress bar invisible when `progressAmount` has a value of 100, as when the last image/sound has been shown/played. The progress bar will be visible anytime this value is less than 100 (whenever a sound is still playing).

5) Choose Control > Test Movie.

If you let the project play by itself, after the first loaded sound finishes playing, the project automatically advances to the next image/sound and then repeats this process. Notice that the progress bar tracks the playback of the sound as well.

After the third image/sound has loaded and finished playing, the presentation stops and the progress bar disappears because there is no more content to load, as defined in the `slides` array. Only by pressing the left-arrow button can you bring the presentation to life again.

6) Close the test movie and save the file as *virtualaquarium8.fla*.

This step completes the exercise, and we're finally done with this application!

You've created a fairly sophisticated project that loads external assets and can be scaled easily to include an almost limitless amount of external content. By loading content into a movie as it plays, you need never worry about huge files or stale content again.

EXTRACTING ID3 DATA FROM AN MP3 FILE

Do you think an MP3 file holds nothing but code for playing back an audio file? Think again. Most people are unaware that hidden in most MP3 files are *ID3 tags*. These tags, known as *metadata*, contain information such as the following about the MP3 file:

- Name of the song
- Artist
- Genre
- Year the song was recorded
- Album from which the song came
- Lyrics
- Comments

Most modern MP3 players can read, display, and react to this included data when playing a file. Thankfully, ActionScript also provides access to this information when using MP3 files in your projects. This fact allows you to create sophisticated audio applications.

NOTE *Not all MP3s contain ID3 tags.*

When an MP3 is loaded into or attached to a Sound object, that file's ID3 tag information can be read by accessing the Sound object's `ID3` property. For example, the `ID3` tag representing a song name is `TIT2`. To extract this data from the MP3 file loaded into a Sound object named `music`, you would use the following syntax:

```
var songName_txt.text = music.ID3.TIT2;
```

Other common ID3 tags include `TALB` (album), `TPE1` (artist), `TYER` (year of recording), `TRCK` (track), and `COMM` (comment).

TIP *For more information about ID3 tags, consult the ActionScript dictionary or visit* www.id3.org. *Many ID3 tag editors are available to help you add your own ID3 tags to MP3 files. A search on* www.google.com *will return a number of possibilities.*

In the following exercise, you'll create an MP3 player that loads MP3 files based on data in an XML file. The MP3 files contain ID3 tag data that will be extracted and displayed on the user interface.

1) Open *mp3Player1.fla* in the Lesson18/Assets folder.

This project contains five layers named Background, Text Fields, Buttons, Components, and Actions. Our project's static graphics are on the Background layer. There are five text fields on the Text Fields layer: **song_txt**, **artist_txt**, **year_txt**, **URL_txt**, and **comments_txt**. These fields will eventually be used to display extracted ID3 tag data. The Buttons layer contains two button instances named **play_btn** and **stop_btn**. Obviously, these will be used as playback controls for the currently selected MP3 file. The Components layer contains a List component instance named **playlist_lb**, which will be used to display a list of available MP3 files loaded in from an external XML file (we'll discuss this in a moment). The Actions layer will contain all the script for this project.

This project will work by loading a list of MP3 files from an external XML file and displaying the list in the **playlist_lb** instance. When the user selects an MP3 file from the list and clicks the **play_btn** instance, that MP3 file not only plays, but its ID3 tag data is extracted and displayed in the text fields on the Text Fields layer.

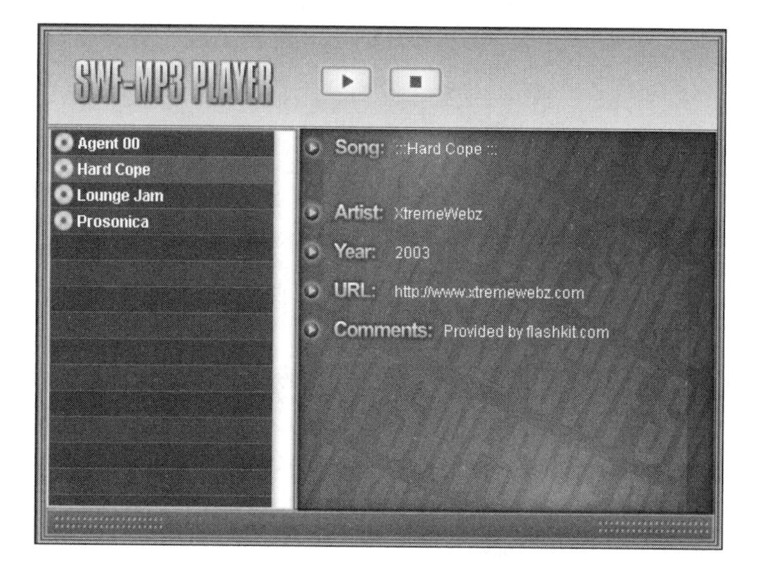

Before we begin scripting, let's review the external files that this project will use.

2) Using your operating system's directory-exploring application, navigate to the Lesson18/Assets directory and locate the files *Agent00.mp3*, *HardCope.mp3*, *LoungeJam.mp3*, *Prosonica.mp3*, and *playlist.xml*.

There's nothing special about the MP3 files other than the fact that each contains several ID3 tags. We'll access these files in our project.

The **playlist.xml** file contains basic information about these four files in a simple structure:

```
<Playlist>
  <Song URL="Agent00.mp3">Agent 00</Song>
  <Song URL="HardCope.mp3">Hard Cope</Song>
  <Song URL="LoungeJam.mp3">Lounge Jam</Song>
  <Song URL="Prosonica.mp3">Prosonica</Song>
</Playlist>
```

The only items identified in this file are the name and the filename (in the form of a `URL` attribute) for each song. This data will eventually be loaded into the **playlist_lb** List component instance.

By placing the information about our MP3 files in this XML file, we can add and delete songs simply by editing this file, and our MP3 player will compensate automatically, as you'll soon see.

3) Return to Flash. With the Actions panel open, select Frame 1 of the Actions layer and add the following script:

```
var playlistXML:XML = new XML();
playlistXML.ignoreWhite = true;
var music:Sound = new Sound();
var currentSong:String;
```

Because our project will load the **playlist.xml** file, the first line of this script creates a new XML object named `playlistXML` for holding the incoming file. The next line tells that XML object to ignore any spaces within the loaded XML document because keeping these spaces could prevent our script from accurately locating data within the file.

The next line creates a Sound object named `music` into which we'll load our external MP3 files, one at a time, as they're selected and played by the user.

The last line creates a variable named `currentSong` to store the filename of the last selected song from the **playlist_lb** instance. The reason for this variable is that selecting a song from the list won't cause it to load and play automatically. This occurs only after the Play button is clicked. This variable is necessary to store the filename of the last selected MP3 from the list until the Play button is clicked and the file is loaded. This principle will become clearer in a moment.

4) Add the following script below the current script:

```
playlistXML.onLoad = function(){
  var tempArray = new Array();
  for(var i = 0; i < this.firstChild.childNodes.length; ++i){
    tempArray[i] = new Object();
    tempArray[i].label = this.firstChild.childNodes[i].firstChild.nodeValue;
    tempArray[i].data = this.firstChild.childNodes[i].attributes.URL;
  }
  playlist_lb.dataProvider = tempArray;
}
playlistXML.load("playlist.xml");
```

The last line shown here loads the **playlist.xml** file into the `playlistXML` object. Before that action occurs, however, the first part of the script creates an `onLoad` event handler so that the object knows what to do with the data after loading it. Let's look at this event handler in detail.

It's important to remember that the data loaded in from this XML file contains the name of each song, such as `Agent 00`, and the filename of the song, such as `Agent00.mp3` (go back to Step 2 if you need to review this info). Our goal is to transfer these two pieces of data for each song in the XML file into a list item for the **playlist_lb** instance, where the name of the song represents the `label` property for the item, and the filename represents the `data` property. Because our XML file contains four songs, our **playlist_lb** instance will eventually contain four items, each with a `label` and a `data` property. Remember that the `label` property for an item represents the text shown (this will be the song's name) for the item; the `data` property represents a hidden value that can be accessed and used when the item (the song's filename) is selected from the list.

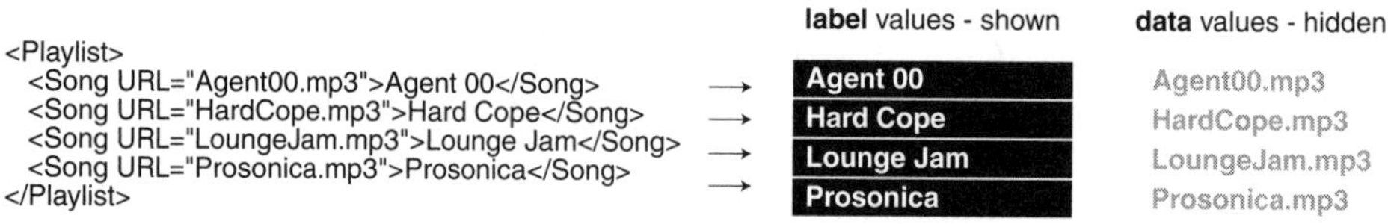

```
<Playlist>
  <Song URL="Agent00.mp3">Agent 00</Song>
  <Song URL="HardCope.mp3">Hard Cope</Song>
  <Song URL="LoungeJam.mp3">Lounge Jam</Song>
  <Song URL="Prosonica.mp3">Prosonica</Song>
</Playlist>
```

label values - shown	**data** values - hidden
Agent 00	Agent00.mp3
Hard Cope	HardCope.mp3
Lounge Jam	LoungeJam.mp3
Prosonica	Prosonica.mp3

To get this data from our XML file into the **playlist_lb** instance, we need to take the loaded XML data, place it into indexed positions of an array, and set that array as the data provider for the **playlist_lb** instance. As a result, our loaded XML data appears in the **playlist_lb** instance.

The first step in this transfer process is to create an Array object, as shown in the first line of the event handler. The next line uses a `for` loop to populate the array with data from the loaded XML file. Here's how it works.

The loop is set up to iterate while i (which is initially set to 0) is less than this.firstChild.childNodes.length. The term this refers to the loaded XML document. firstChild refers to the root node of the file. In this case, the root node is as follows:

```
<Playlist>
</Playlist>
```

childNodes is an array representing any child nodes within the root node. Because our XML document lists four songs within the root node (firstChild), childNodes has a length of 4; therefore, our for loop will iterate four times. Adding songs to or deleting songs from the XML file will change this value, and thus the number of iterations that the loop makes.

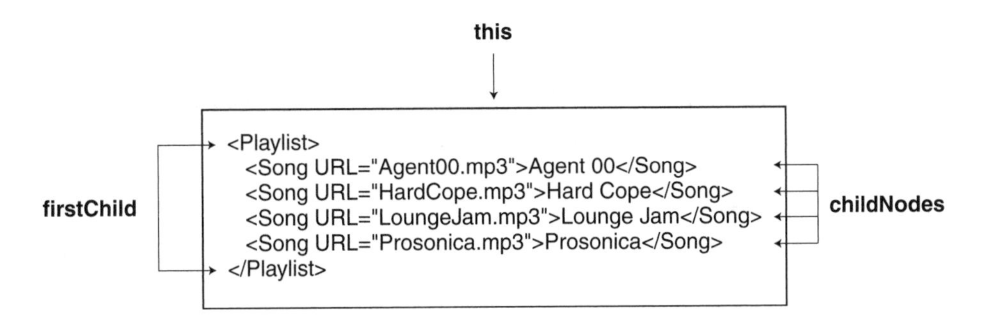

With each iteration, an object is created in the current index position of the tempArray array (i). That object is next assigned label and data property values, based on values extracted from the XML object. To understand this better, let's look at an example of what happens during an iteration.

Let's assume that the loop is about to begin its third iteration and thus i has a value of 2. This would cause the script within the loop to be evaluated this way:

```
tempArray[2] = new Object();
tempArray[2].label = this.firstChild.childNodes[2].firstChild.nodeValue;
tempArray[2].data = this.firstChild.childNodes[2].attributes.URL;
```

This shows that a new object is created in index position 2 of the tempArray array. Next, that object is given a label property. The value of that property is based on the following expression:

```
this.firstChild.childNodes[2].firstChild.nodeValue;
```

As discussed earlier, this.firstChild.childNodes is an array containing the four <Song> nodes in our XML file. The <Song> node at index position 2 of this array is the following:

```
<Song URL="LoungeJam.mp3">Lounge Jam</Song>
```

The remaining part of the expression that sets the `label` value, `.firstChild.nodeValue`, is a reference to the listed song name within that node (`Lounge Jam`); therefore:

```
tempArray[2].label = "Lounge Jam";
```

this.firstChild.childNodes[2].firstChild.nodeValue

```
<Playlist>
  <Song URL="Agent00.mp3">Agent 00</Song>
  <Song URL="HardCope.mp3">Hard Cope</Song>
  <Song URL="LoungeJam.mp3">Lounge Jam</Song>
  <Song URL="Prosonica.mp3">Prosonica</Song>
</Playlist>
```

The value of the `data` property of the object is set almost the same way, except that it extracts the `URL` attribute of the currently referenced `<Song>` node; therefore:

```
tempArray[2].data = "LoungeJam.mp3";
```

By the time the loop is finished, there will be four objects in the `tempArray`, each with `label` and `data` properties representative of song names and song filenames, as just described.

The last action within the `onLoad` event handler sets `tempArray` as the data provider for the **playlist_lb** instance. The objects within the array are used to populate the list with items.

Let's test our work up to this point.

5) Choose Control > Test Movie.

As soon as the movie appears, you should see the songs contained in the external XML file loaded into the **playlist_lb** instance. Clicking a song name in the list doesn't do anything yet, but we'll change that situation in the next several steps, as well as improve the look of the List component instance so that it matches our project's design.

6) Close the test movie to return to Flash. With the Actions panel open, select Frame 1 of the Actions layer, and add the following script at the end of the current script:

```
var playlist_lbListener:Object = new Object();
playlist_lbListener.change = function(){
  currentSong = playlist_lb.selectedItem.data;
}
playlist_lb.addEventListener("change", playlist_lbListener);
```

When the user selects a song from the list, we need to store the filename for that song in the currentSong variable. The first line in this step creates a new Listener object named playList_lbListener. The next several lines assign this Listener object a change event handler. The last line registers the Listener object to listen for that event from the **playlist_lb** instance.

When fired, the change event handler sets the value of currentSong to the data property of the currently selected item in the **playlist_lb** instance. As discussed in Step 4, the data property for each item of the list contains the filename of that song. When the Play button is clicked, this value is used to load and play a song. Let's set up that functionality next.

7) Add the following event handler at the end of the current script:

```
play_btn.onRelease = function(){
  music.stop();
  music = new Sound();
  music.onID3 = function(){
    song_txt.text = this.id3.TIT2;
    artist_txt.text = this.id3.TPE1;
    year_txt.text = this.id3.TYER;
    URL_txt.htmlText = "<a href=\"" + this.id3.WXXX + "\">" +
    ⇒this.id3.WXXX + "</a>";
    comments_txt.text = this.id3.COMM;
  }
  music.loadSound(currentSong, true);
}
```

This script defines what happens when the **play_btn** instance is clicked. The script handles loading the external MP3 currently stored in the currentSong variable into the music Sound object, as well the displaying the ID3 tag data contained in that file.

If the music Sound object is playing, the first line stops it, to prevent two sounds from playing at the same time. The next line of the script reinitializes/re-creates a new instance of the music Sound object. The next several lines use the onID3 event to define what should happen when ID3 tag data has been loaded in from the external MP3 file. This data is usually at the beginning of the file, so this event should fire soon after the loading of the file begins. This event handler contains five lines of script for displaying ID3 tag data in the various text fields in our project. Be aware that the **URL_txt** text field will actually contain a clickable link based on the URL provided in the WXXX tag of the loaded file.

The last line within the onRelease event handler takes care of loading the selected MP3 file, as defined by the current value of the currentSong variable. As always, the onID3 event handler is defined before the file is actually loaded, so that the Sound object knows ahead of time how to react to incoming ID3 data.

7) Add the following event handler at the end of the current script:

```
stop_btn.onRelease = function(){
  music.stop();
}
```

When the **stop_btn** instance is clicked, the `music` Sound object is stopped.

The last thing we need to take care of is the restyling of our **playlist_lb** instance so that it more closely resembles our project's overall design.

8) Add the following script at the end of the current script:

```
with(playlist_lb){
  setStyle("defaultIcon", "CDIcon");
  setStyle("alternatingRowColors", [0x4E535C, 0x565B65]);
  setStyle("color", 0xFFFFFF);
  setStyle("fontWeight", "bold");
  setStyle("rollOverColor", 0x6C7380);
  setStyle("selectionColor", 0x6C7380);
  setStyle("textRollOverColor", 0xFFFFFF);
  setStyle("textSelectedColor", 0xFFFFFF);
  setStyle("textIndent", 2);
}
```

Most of this script's functionality should be familiar to you by now. A `with` statement efficiently sets several style properties of the **playlist_lb** instance. The main style change is the first set, named `defaultIcon`. This style change displays the movie clip identified as CDIcon from the library next to each item listed in the instance.

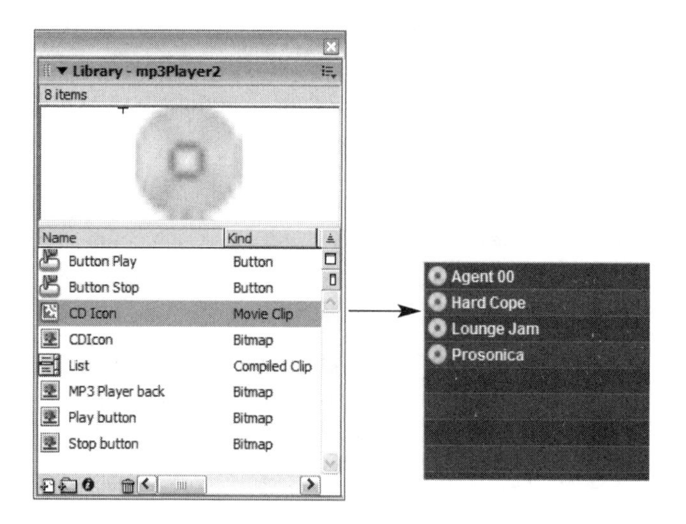

Let's do one final test.

9) Choose Control > Test Movie.

As soon as the movie appears, select a song from the **playlist_lb** instance and then click the Play button. The music file loads, plays, and its embedded ID3 tag data is displayed in the appropriate text fields. Select a different song from the list, click the Play button again, and the interface is updated. Because this application uses an XML document to define available songs, editing that file's data will automatically be reflected in the application when the file is run again.

10) Close the test movie to return to Flash. Save this file as *mp3Player2.fla*.

As you've learned in this exercise, creating a sophisticated, scalable, SWF-based MP3 player is not difficult. At this point in the book, you're armed to add more features such as volume and panning controls, or anything else a good MP3 player application might need.

LOADING AND CONTROLLING EXTERNAL VIDEO

With the growing popularity of broadband, the use of video in applications continues to escalate. Fortunately for us, so do Flash's capabilities for loading and playing video.

The previous version of Flash (Flash MX) could load and play external video clips, but only with the assistance of Flash Communication Server. It was possible to embed video clips within the SWF, but this tended to make the file size rather large. Not only does Flash MX 2004 not need Flash Communication Server when using external video, but it provides some excellent tools in the form of Media components. These tools make the process of using video in your applications much easier.

External video clips have some great advantages over embedded clips:

- The clip can be edited separately from the SWFs that use it.
- The clip can be progressively downloaded as it plays, making it unnecessary for the entire clip to load before it can be viewed.
- The clip can play at a different frame rate than the SWF in which it's loaded, ensuring that the video clip always plays at the intended frame rate.

To use an external video clip in a Flash project, it must first be converted to the **.flv** (Flash Video) file format. Flash has the built-in capability to import most video formats (including AVI and QuickTime), which can then be exported to the FLV format for use as an externally loaded clip. Although this is a sufficient means for creating FLV files, you may want to create, edit, and eventually export a video from your favorite video-editing application, such as Adobe Premiere. Fortunately, Flash MX 2004 Professional ships with the Flash Video Exporter. After installation, the Exporter allows you to export FLV files directly from your favorite video-editing application. (For more information about importing and creating **FLV** files, consult your Flash documentation.)

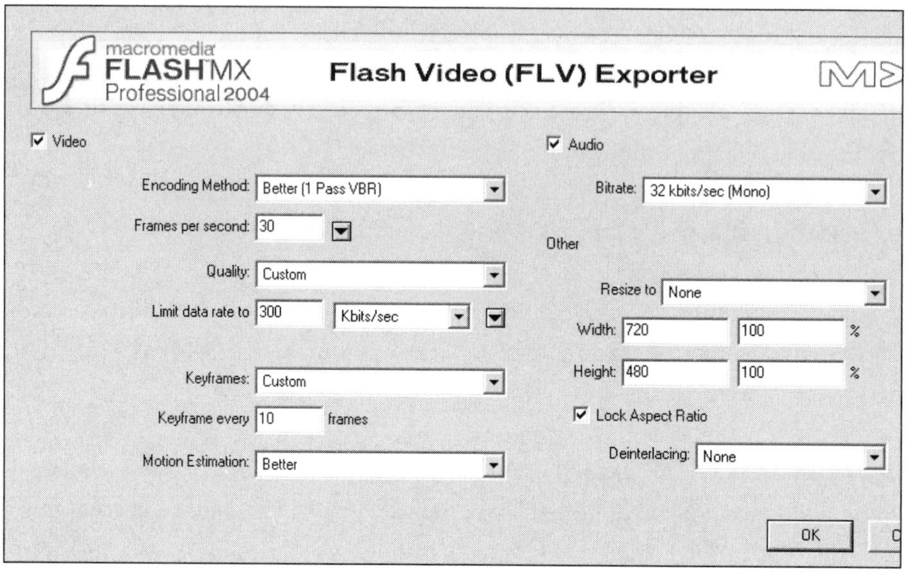

TIP *Sorenson Media's excellent application called Sorenson Squeeze was built for the purpose of creating FLV files from many video file formats. For more information about this useful tool, visit* www.sorenson.com.

After you have a usable FLV file, you need to know how to load it into Flash as well as how to control it and communicate with it. The direct way is by creating an instance of the Video class and then loading video into that object via instances of the NetConnection and NetStream classes. If that sounds like too much work, you're absolutely right. A more elegant solution is to use the incredibly versatile and powerful Media components that ship with Flash MX 2004 Professional. These components allow you to work with the Media class to handle the most demanding video-related tasks, including the use of cue points.

The Media components come in three forms:

- **MediaDisplay.** This component is used as a container for loading and playing either external FLV or MP3 files. Graphical playback controls are not provided with this component, but the loaded file can be controlled using methods of the component, including `play()` and `stop()`, or by setting property values such as `volume`. This component is useful for inserting media into your project without the added intrusion of playback controls.

- **MediaController.** This component complements the MediaDisplay component by providing playback controls for controlling media loaded into a MediaDisplay instance. Media is never loaded into or played by the MediaController; the MediaController is used only for controlling playback in a MediaPlayback or MediaDisplay instance. This component allows you to place media in one location on the screen, via the MediaDisplay component, and control it from another location on the screen. Associating an instance of the MediaController component (named **controller**) with an instance of MediaDisplay component (named **display**) is as simple as this:

  ```
  controller.associateDisplay(display);
  ```

- **MediaPlayback.** This component contains the combined functionality of both the MediaDisplay and MediaController components.

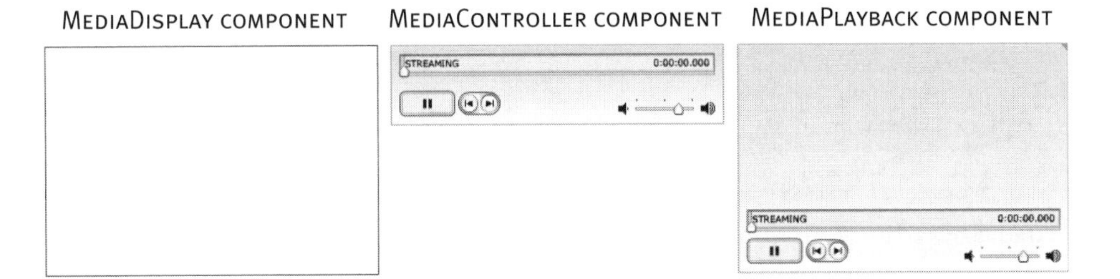

Although the Component Inspector provides a visual way of configuring Media component instances, there are a number of properties, methods, and events that can be used to configure and control Media component instances via ActionScript. All these components inherit functionality from the Media class, which means that instances of the components can be controlled and configured using common commands. Let's look at what you can do with Media component instances.

One of the most important tasks a Media component instance can perform is to load media. This can be done using the `setMedia()` method:

```
myMediaComponent.setMedia("myVideo.flv", "FLV");
```

This line loads **myVideo.flv** into the Media component instance named **myMediaComponent**. Because Media components can also load MP3 files, the second parameter of the `setMedia()` method is used to define the media type. Loading an MP3 file into the same instance would look like this:

```
myMediaComponent.setMedia("mySong.mp3", "MP3");
```

NOTE *Media cannot be loaded into instances of the MediaController component.*

After media has been loaded into an instance, its playback can be controlled via ActionScript using the `play()`, `pause()` and `stop()` methods. Here's an example of the `play()` method:

```
myMediaComponent.play();
```

NOTE *Of course, the playback of media is also controlled automatically via playback controls when using the MediaController and MediaPlayback instances.*

Media component instances generate various events, allowing your application to react to such actions as a click of the Play button, the end of playback, or a volume adjustment by the user. Reacting to these events requires Listener objects. For example:

```
var myListener:Object = new Object()
myListener.volume = function(){
  //actions
}
myMediaComponent.addEventListener("volume", myListener);
```

Here, `myListener` is set up to react to volume changes in the **myMediaComponent** instance.

Media component instances can generate unique events in response to *cue points*. Cue points are used to mark points of time during a media file's playback. When playback reaches a point in time marked as a cue point, the component instance playing the media fires a `cuePoint` event. This event can be captured by a Listener, which can be scripted to react to that particular cue point. For example:

```
myMediaComponent.addCuePoint("liftoff", 54);
myListener.cuePoint = function(eventObj:Object){
  //actions
}
myMediaComponent.addEventListener("cuePoint", myListener);
```

This script adds a cue point named `liftoff` to the **myMediaComponent** instance. This cue point is fired 54 seconds into the playback of the loaded media. The Event object sent to the `cuePoint` event handler when the event is fired contains the name of the cue point (`"liftoff"`) so that the event handler can be scripted to take action based on that specific cue point's being reached.

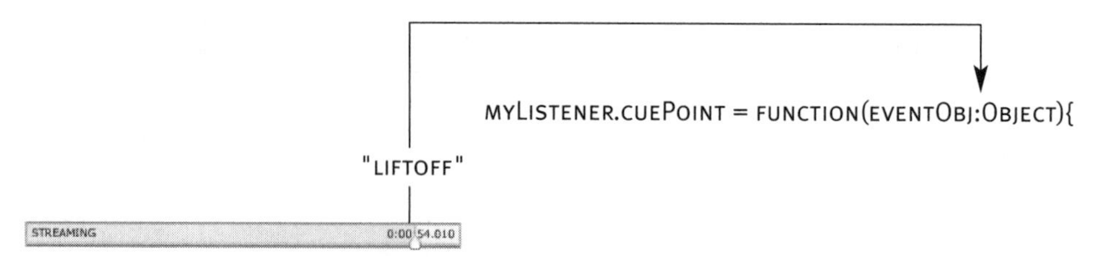

In this exercise, you'll use an instance of the MediaPlayback component to load and play an external video file. You'll add cue points so that the application can react to specific points during the video's playback.

1) Open *video1.fla* in the Lesson18/Assets folder.

This project contains four layers named Background, Boxes, Media Component, and Actions. Our project's static graphics are on the Background layer. There are two elements of interest on the Boxes layer: a movie clip named **cueBox_mc** and a text field named **cue_txt**. Our application will eventually load a JPG into the **cueBox_mc** instance in response to a specific cue point's being reached. The **cue_txt** text field will display text associated with that loaded JPG.

The Media Component layer holds an instance of the MediaPlayback component named **display**. We'll load and play back our video clip within this instance.

The Actions layer will contain all the script for this project.

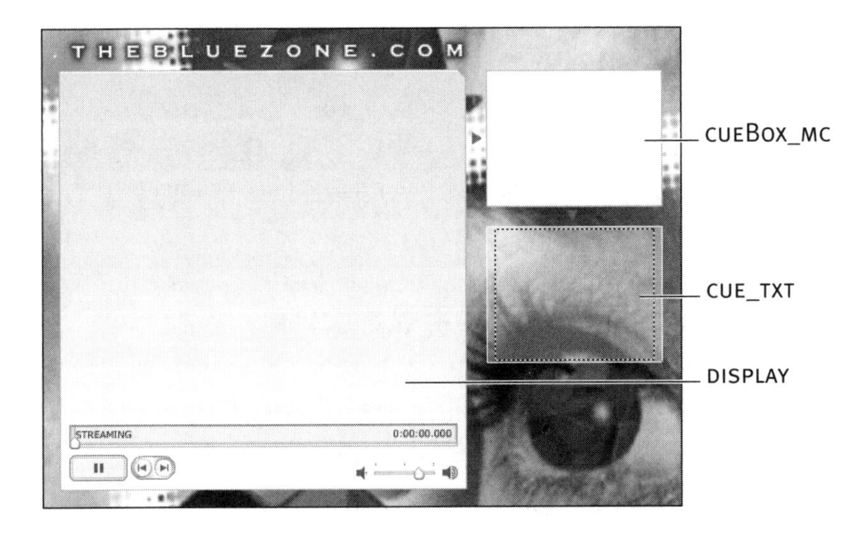

As with the other projects in this lesson, we'll start by reviewing the external files that this project will use.

2) Using your operating system's directory-exploring application, navigate to the Lesson18/Assets directory and locate *bluezone.flv*, *cue0.jpg*, *cue1.jpg*, *cue2.jpg*, *cue3.jpg*, *cue4.jpg*, *cue5.jpg* and *cue6.jpg*.

The **bluezone.flv** file is the external Flash video file that our application will load. The other files represent snapshots of various points in the video file's playback. Our application will eventually load each of these snapshots, using cue point functionality.

NOTE *The video file for this project was graciously provided by Brooks Patton, who helped co-author two of Derek Franklin's first Flash books. He brilliantly wrote, produced, and directed this commercial, which Derek feels is one of the best he's ever seen. Thanks, Brooks!*

3) Return to Flash. With the Actions panel open, select Frame 1 of the Actions layer and add the following script:

```
display.autoPlay = true;
display.activePlayControl = true;
display.controllerPolicy = "on";
display.totalTime = 60;
```

These four lines of script tell the **display** instance how it should be configured before we load any media into it.

The first line tells the instance to immediately begin playback of the loaded media file. The next line tells the instance to show the Play button in an active state, indicating that the media file is playing. You would think this would happen automatically with the `autoPlay` property set to `true`, but it doesn't. If `autoPlay` is set to `false`, `activePlayControl` must also be `false`.

The next line indicates that the component's playback controls should always be visible. By default, this property is set to `"auto"`, which causes the playback controls to slide into visibility whenever the user mouses over the playback control area.

The last line indicates to the component instance that the media to be loaded is 60 seconds long. We specify this setting so the playback slider/indicator can accurately reflect the playback progress of the loaded file. Again, you would think that this would be known automatically by the instance, but it's not.

STREAMING 0:00:18.874

NOTE *The `totalTime` property doesn't need to be set in order for the rest of the functionalities of the component instance to work properly.*

Before we script the **display** instance to load the video file, let's set it up to open a URL when playback of the loaded file is complete.

4) Add the following script:

```
var displayListener:Object = new Object();
displayListener.complete = function(){
  getURL("http://www.thebluezone.com");
}
display.addEventListener("complete", displayListener);
```

Here we've created the `displayListener` object and scripted it to open a URL in response to the firing of a `complete` event. We've also registered this object to listen for this event from the **display** instance. When the loaded video file has completely played, *www.thebluezone.com* opens in a browser window.

5) Add the following script to load the external video:

```
display.setMedia("bluezone.flv", "FLV");
```

This loads **bluezone.flv** into the **display** instance.

Let's do a test.

6) Choose Control > Test Movie.

As soon as the movie appears, the external video file is loaded and begins to play. You can interact with any of the playback controls to see the effect they have on the video's playback. As you've seen, using a Media component instance makes adding external video to your project a breeze.

Let's return to the authoring environment to add several cue points.

7) Close the test movie to return to Flash. With the Actions panel open, select Frame 1 of the Actions layer and insert the following script, just below the line `display.addEventListener("complete", displayListener);`**:**

```
display.addCuePoint("0", 1);
display.addCuePoint("1", 8);
display.addCuePoint("2", 14);
display.addCuePoint("3", 31);
display.addCuePoint("4", 35);
display.addCuePoint("5", 53);
display.addCuePoint("6", 56);
```

This script creates seven cue points in the **display** instance. The first cue point is named "0" and is set to trigger one second into the media's playback. The next cue point is named "1" and is set to trigger eight seconds into the media's playback. The remaining cue points are self-explanatory. The name of the cue points can be any string value you choose. We've named them for specific reasons, which we'll explain in a moment.

NOTE *If you load a different media file into the display instance, these cue points still exist. Because these cue points may not be appropriate for the newly loaded file, you can use the* `removeAllCuePoints()` *method to delete them all quickly:*

```
display.removeAllCuePoints()
```

8) Insert the following script just below `display.addCuePoint("6", 56);`**:**

```
var cueTextArray:Array = new Array();
cueTextArray[0] = "Potential Fluffy victim";
cueTextArray[1] = "Sweet, innocent Fluffy appears";
cueTextArray[2] = "Fluffy is crammed into dial-up pipe";
cueTextArray[3] = "Fluffy enters The Blue Zone";
cueTextArray[4] = "Fluffy's revenge!";
cueTextArray[5] = "Faceful of Fluffy";
cueTextArray[6] = "Blue Zone information";
```

This script creates an array named `cueTextArray`, which is then filled with short snippets of text. Each of these snippets is displayed in the **cue_txt** text field when its corresponding cue point has been reached. It should be noted that the index position of each snippet relates to the name of a cue point added in the preceding step (the cue point named "0" relates to the snippet in index position 0 of this array).

It's time to bring together our cue points, the text snippets in `cueTextArray`, and our external JPGs to complete the functionality of this project.

9) Insert the following script just below the closing brace of the `displayListener.complete` **event handler:**

```
displayListener.cuePoint = function(eventObj:Object){
  var index = Number(eventObj.target.name);
  loadMovie("cue" + index + ".jpg", "cueBox_mc");
  cue_txt.text = cueTextArray[index];
}
display.addEventListener("cuePoint", displayListener);
```

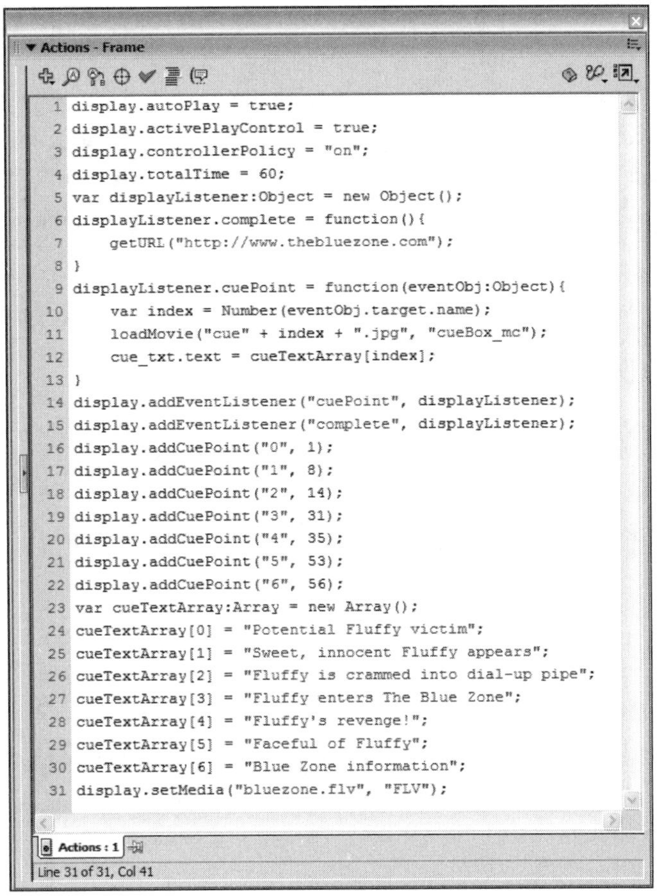

Actions - Frame

```
1 display.autoPlay = true;
2 display.activePlayControl = true;
3 display.controllerPolicy = "on";
4 display.totalTime = 60;
5 var displayListener:Object = new Object();
6 displayListener.complete = function(){
7     getURL("http://www.thebluezone.com");
8 }
9 displayListener.cuePoint = function(eventObj:Object){
10     var index = Number(eventObj.target.name);
11     loadMovie("cue" + index + ".jpg", "cueBox_mc");
12     cue_txt.text = cueTextArray[index];
13 }
14 display.addEventListener("cuePoint", displayListener);
15 display.addEventListener("complete", displayListener);
16 display.addCuePoint("0", 1);
17 display.addCuePoint("1", 8);
18 display.addCuePoint("2", 14);
19 display.addCuePoint("3", 31);
20 display.addCuePoint("4", 35);
21 display.addCuePoint("5", 53);
22 display.addCuePoint("6", 56);
23 var cueTextArray:Array = new Array();
24 cueTextArray[0] = "Potential Fluffy victim";
25 cueTextArray[1] = "Sweet, innocent Fluffy appears";
26 cueTextArray[2] = "Fluffy is crammed into dial-up pipe";
27 cueTextArray[3] = "Fluffy enters The Blue Zone";
28 cueTextArray[4] = "Fluffy's revenge!";
29 cueTextArray[5] = "Faceful of Fluffy";
30 cueTextArray[6] = "Blue Zone information";
31 display.setMedia("bluezone.flv", "FLV");
```

Actions : 1

Line 31 of 31, Col 41

The first part of this script creates a `cuePoint` event handler on the `displayListener` object, and the last line of the script registers that object to listen for that event from the **display** instance. Because we added seven cue points to the display instance in Step 7, this event handler will be triggered seven times by the time the video has played through. Let's look at how the event handler works.

The event handler is passed an Event object when the event is fired. This Event object contains the name and time of the cue point that fired the event. The name of the cue point is accessible using this syntax:

```
eventObj.target.name
```

and the time of the cue point with the following syntax:

```
eventObj.target.time
```

When our third cue point is fired, the event objects will have the following values:

```
eventObj.target.name// has a value of "2"
eventObj.target.time// has a value of 14
```

All we're really interested in is the `name` property of the cue point that triggered the event. The first line within the event handler converts this value to a number and assigns it to the `index` variable. The remaining two lines in the event handler use this value. A `loadMovie()` action loads one of the external JPG images into the **cueBox_mc** instance. Which JPG is loaded depends on the value of `index`. When the first cue point is reached, **cue0.jpg** is loaded; when the next cue point is reached, **cue1.jpg** is loaded; and so on.

The last line in the event handler displays one of the text snippets in the `cueTextArray` in the **cue_txt** instance. Again, the snippet displayed depends on the current value of `index`.

When the cue point named `"0"` is fired, **cue0.jpg** is loaded and the text snippet at index position 0 of the `cueTextArray` is displayed; when the cue point named `"1"` is fired, **cue1.jpg** is loaded and the text snippet at index position 1 of the `cueTextArray` is displayed, and so on.

Our scripting is complete, and now it's time to do one final test.

10) Choose Control > Test Movie.

When the movie appears and the video begins to play, simply sit and watch as cue points are reached and the `cuePoint` event handler does its job. Utilizing this event is a great way to synchronize other elements in your movie to the playback of a video, or even an MP3 file.

11) Close the test movie to return to Flash, and save this file as *video2.fla*.

This step completes the exercise and this lesson. As you've learned, Flash provides many tools and a lot of flexibility when your project calls for the use of external media assets.

WHAT YOU HAVE LEARNED

In this lesson, you have:

- Created a scalable slideshow presentation using external assets (pages 622–641)
- Created a rotating Flash banner system by loading external movies into a level (pages 642–645)
- Controlled a movie from its own timeline and another timeline (pages 645–647)
- Dynamically loaded MP3s into a project while it plays (pages 648–650)
- Scripted an MP3 playback progress bar (pages 651–654)
- Displayed ID3 tag data from loaded MP3s (pages 655–663)
- Loaded an external video into a Media component and created cue points to trigger actions (pages 663–672)

testing and debugging

LESSON 19

In computer-driven interactive content, errors in code are referred to as *bugs*—and they can be as ugly and bothersome as their name implies. Although your project is probably not as complex as a major piece of software, you're still likely to discover some glitches. If you don't want to scare off your audience, you'll need to exterminate these bugs.

One of the keys to becoming a Flash master is understanding the need for testing and debugging. It doesn't matter how good your project is: if you don't test and debug it, you're putting your reputation (not to mention your neck) on the line. But testing is about more than simply eliminating mistakes; it's also about optimizing your movie so that it plays back in the most efficient manner. Luckily, the powerful testing tools in Macromedia Flash make this process quick and easy.

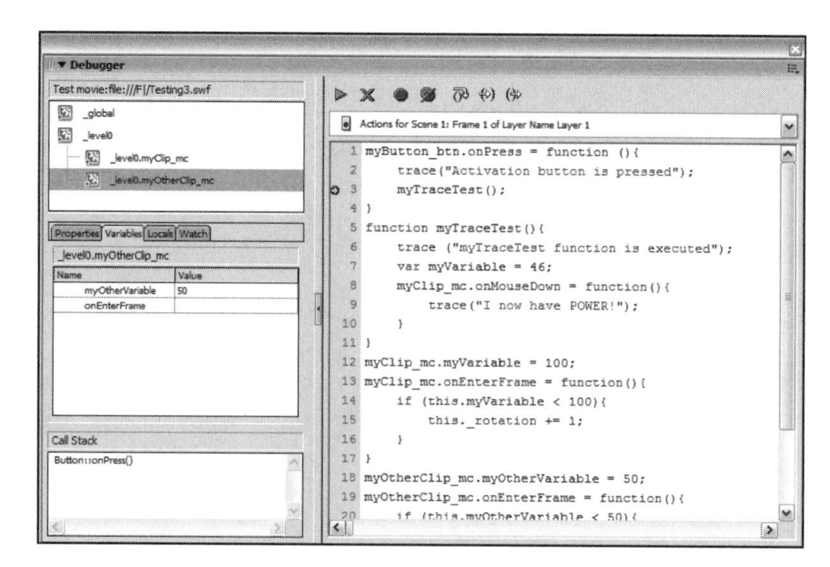

The Debugger plays an essential role in finding and eliminating bugs in your projects. This lesson shows you how to use the Debugger.

WHAT YOU WILL LEARN

In this lesson, you will:

- Learn how to avoid common scripting mistakes
- Learn how auto-generated messages from Flash can help you locate and squash compile-time bugs
- Find run-time bugs by using the `trace()` action
- Use Flash's built-in Debugger tool
- Set and use breakpoints to control the execution of scripts in a project
- Learn how to debug a movie playing in a browser window

APPROXIMATE TIME

This lesson takes approximately 45 minutes to complete.

LESSON FILES

Starting File:

Lesson19/Assets/Testing1.fla

Completed Project:

Testing3.fla

ELIMINATING BUGS BEFORE THEY HATCH

Writing code is not something you want to do while half asleep. As you've probably experienced, Flash is unforgiving when it interprets the script you add to a project. Seemingly tiny errors such as a faulty line of script or even a misspelled word can have a damaging domino effect on the rest of the code in your project. These minor problems are experienced by scripters of all skill levels. Most problems can usually be solved by a tap on the Backspace key. But if errors are hidden deep inside your code, you'll find yourself staring at it for hours, pulling out your hair, and yelling at your dog (maybe even pulling out your dog's hair if things get really out of control). Sometimes the simplest problem can be the largest contributor to a stressful development cycle.

One of the best ways to avoid many problems is to be aware of what they are. The following list shows some of the more common mistakes that all scripters make:

- **Omitting quotation marks in strings.** Strings of text should always be identified with quotes.
- **Misnaming variables, functions, and objects.** As your project grows, you'll need to keep track of more named items. It's a good idea to adopt a common naming convention, based on your preferences. Some scripters use all lowercase letters and underscores to name variables, such as `my_variable` and `my_other_variable`, and in-fix notation (where the first letter of the first word is lowercase, while the first letter in subsequent words is uppercase) for function names such as `myFunction()` and `myOtherFunction()`. Other scripters avoid using plural names completely; they don't have to remember whether an element's name has an *s* at the end. Whatever naming conventions you adopt, consistency is the key. Remember that ActionScript is case-sensitive, so `userName` and `username` are not the same.
- **Omitting quotation marks when comparing string values.** When writing a conditional statement, the concept of using quotes to identify strings sometimes gets lost in our brains as we type. If a conditional statement is not doing what it should, suspect missing quotation marks.
- **Forgetting case when comparing string values.** This is an easy mistake to commit. Remember, `"this string"` is not equal to `"This String"`. Case must be considered when comparing string values.
- **Confusing = and ==.** A single equals sign assigns a value (this = that). A double equals sign compares values (does this == that?).
- **Missing or mismatched curly braces around blocks of code.** Make sure that the end of a code block has as many closing curly braces (}) as the beginning of the block has opening braces ({).
- **Omitting the `return` statement in a function.** If a function is meant to return a value, it will be worthless (broken) without a `return` statement.

MAXIMIZING THE TESTING AND DEBUGGING PROCESS

There's no denying that testing and debugging is part of every programmer's life, but that doesn't mean that it has to be an awful and overwhelming experience. Before we discuss some of the tools that Flash provides to test and debug a project, here are some general guidelines to follow as you build your project:

- **Plan.** Don't approach a project until you've created a basic outline of how it should work. You can't reach your end goal if you don't know your final destination.
- **Test everything.** Never assume that something works—even if it seems a trivial part of your project. All it takes is one mistake to bring your movie to a screeching halt.
- **Test often.** Don't wait until your project is nearing completion—test at every opportunity. It's much easier to isolate problems if you know your movie was working five minutes ago.
- **Fix bugs in an orderly fashion.** Don't attempt to fix a bunch of bugs at the same time. It's best to fix one or two problems at a time and then test after each. After all, you don't want to create any new bugs in the process.
- **Avoid quick fixes.** Maybe you're aware that a bug exists, but you're not sure why. In an effort to save time, you may decide to attempt a quick fix or workaround, rather than tracking down the problem. This kind of coding always costs more time in the long run. Take the necessary time to track down the culprit.
- **Comment your code.** It's a fact of life: many beginning coders just don't like using comments in their code. They feel that it slows them down, and wastes time. Well, it may seem like a waste of time to comment a project when you first begin coding it. After all, you can typically figure out what your code is doing by simply glancing at it. Start adding several hundred or even several thousand lines of code, however, and your attitude will quickly change. Comments provide the means for you to detail in human terms what a particular piece of code is doing. This can be a great help as the number of lines of code in your project increases. A useful technique is to comment before you start writing any code. This forces you to think about the problem (breaking it down into commented steps) before diving into it.
- **Know when to step away.** Few things are as frustrating as knowing that something *should* work, but yet it doesn't. In an attempt to resolve these problems, it's easy to lose track of time, forget to eat, or even forget that you have friends and family. Instead of doing all this forgetting, step away for awhile, refresh yourself, and return to the bug-squashing process a little later. Sometimes, all it takes to locate a nagging problem is to recharge your batteries.

Okay, so you've approached your project with a well-defined plan, used comments and a standard naming convention, and double-checked all your code—but you still have a project that's just not working properly. What can you do? The remainder of this lesson will deal with that question.

FIXING COMPILE-TIME BUGS

When you export or test a movie, Flash's compiler analyzes all the code in the project. If a syntactical error is found in the code (a curly brace is missing, a colon is used instead of a semicolon at the end of a line of script, and so on), the Output panel automatically opens and displays a detailed listing of the error(s).

These auto-generated error messages include the scene name, layer name, frame number, and line number of the faulty code. They also include a simple explanation about what's causing the error in addition to the faulty code. All this information helps you easily fix compile-time errors because you simply return to the authoring environment, locate the faulty code, and edit the syntax appropriately.

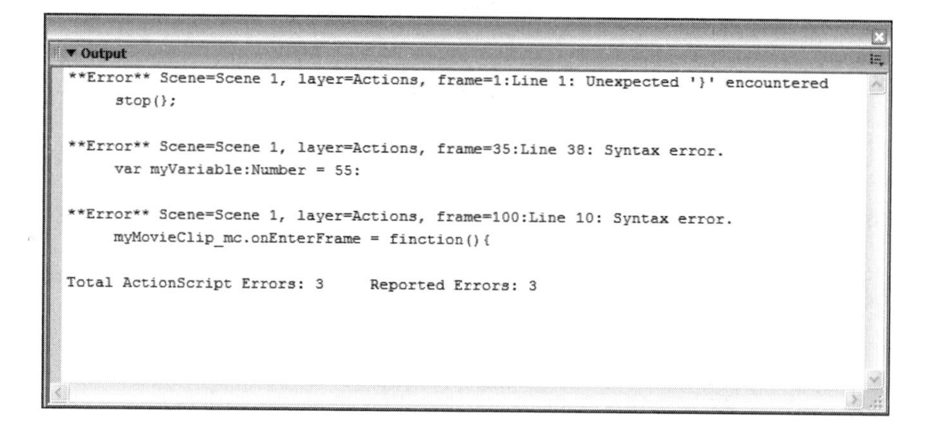

When you receive a compile-time error(s) as a result of an attempt to export your movie to an SWF (either by directly exporting it or by using the Control > Test Movie command), Flash's compiler analyzes the code in the *entire* project (all timelines, scenes, and frames). As a result, the Output panel may display errors that exist in more than one location in the project. Although this information is helpful in certain circumstances, large projects can take several seconds to compile; therefore, constant testing can eat up substantial time. In addition, viewing multiple batches of errors at once in the Output panel can get confusing. The Check Syntax button on the Actions panel can help alleviate both problems.

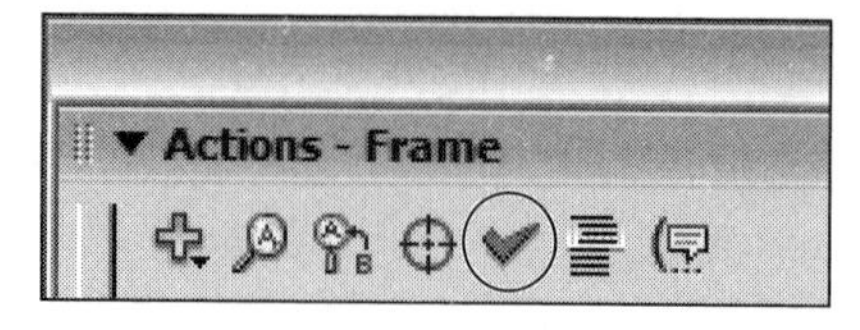

Clicking the Check Syntax button saves time because Flash simply analyzes the code without spending the extra processing time needed to compile the entire movie into a compact SWF. This technique helps eliminate confusion because only the code currently displayed in the Actions window is analyzed. Any errors detected can be edited without jumping around to different locations in your project.

FINDING AND FIXING RUN-TIME BUGS

You've made it through the process of exporting an application without a compile-time error. So far, so good. But as you begin to work with the exported application, you discover that it's just not working properly. Perhaps displayed data is not correct, text and graphics onscreen are not positioned correctly, or when you press a button that's supposed to send information to the server, nothing (or the wrong thing) happens. These kinds of bugs are known as *run-time bugs* because they're not obvious until the application is run and put through the ringer.

Run-time bugs typically result from spelling or logic errors, such as mistakenly referring to a movie clip instance named **miMovie_mc** instead of **myMovie_mc**, or using a less-than operator (<) rather than the intended greater-than operator (>) in a conditional statement. Or a function might contain a script that's logically but not syntactically faulty, so that when executed the function has a very bad effect on the rest of the application.

Unfortunately, information about these kinds of bugs doesn't automatically show up in the Output window; a bit of sleuthing and logical deduction is required to find and eliminate such errors.

Fortunately, Flash provides several tools to help you perform various deductive reasoning tasks with your project while it plays. The two most widely used tools are the `trace()` action and the Debugger. We'll look at both of these tools in the following sections.

USING THE `trace()` ACTION

The `trace()` action allows you to output a custom message to the Output panel in response to a script's execution. This is useful to get a behind-the-scenes look at how a script is functioning—primarily to test interactivity and to output custom messages that tell you what's happening with the data in a movie at any point in time. Consider the following simple example.

Imagine you want to place the following script on Frame 10 of your movie:

```
trace ("The movie is currently on Frame " + _currentframe);
```

When the movie is played in the testing environment and reaches Frame 10, the Output panel will automatically open and display the following message:

```
"The movie is currently on Frame 10"
```

This example is not meant to demonstrate the true power of the `trace()` action, but simply to illustrate its use. The `trace()` action can be useful in finding bugs because it allows you to track down the error by means of deduction, as the following exercise shows.

1) Choose File > New. From the New Document dialog box that appears, select Flash Document to start a new Flash project.

Because the end result of this project is to teach how custom messages are output in the Output panel and not so much to see the onscreen results of ActionScript, we won't use a prebuilt project file. Nevertheless, we'll need a simple movie clip and button instance to work with. Let's create those.

2) Select the Oval tool and draw a small circle anywhere on the stage.

The size and appearance of the circle are not important for this exercise.

3) With the circle selected, press F8 on your keyboard to open the Convert to Symbol dialog box. Give this symbol any name you choose, select the Button behavior, and click OK.

This step converts the circle to a button.

4) With the Property Inspector open, select the button instance and give it an instance name of *myButton_btn*.

Next we'll create a movie clip instance.

5) Select the Rectangle tool and draw a small square on the stage.

Again, the way it looks is not important.

6) With the square still selected, press F8. Give this symbol any name you choose, but select the Movie Clip behavior. Click OK.

This step converts the square to a movie clip.

7) With the Property Inspector open, select the square movie clip instance and give it an instance name of *myClip_mc*.

Now we'll do some scripting.

8) With the Actions panel open, select Layer 1 and add the following script:

```
myButton_btn.onPress = function(){
  trace("Activation button is pressed");
  myTraceTest();
}
```

This script is executed when the **myButton_btn** is clicked. The script performs two functions. First it uses a `trace()` action to output a message to the Output panel indicating that the button has been pressed; then the script calls a function we have yet to define, named `myTraceTest()`. Let's define that function next.

9) Add the following function definition at the end of the current script:

```
function myTraceTest(){
  trace ("myTraceTest function is executed");
  myClop_mc.onMouseDown = function(){
    trace("I now have POWER!");
  }
}
```

This function uses a `trace()` action to send a message to the Output panel indicating that the function has been executed. The next few lines are *intended* to assign an `onMouseDown` event handler method to the **myClip_mc** movie clip instance, so that another custom trace message is sent to the Output panel whenever the mouse button is pressed. This event handler is not assigned to the clip until the function has been executed, which occurs only after the **myButton_btn** instance has been pressed. As we mentioned, that's what this part of the script is *intended* to do; however, note that there's an error in our script. We've intentionally misspelled **myClip_mc** as **myClop_mc**.

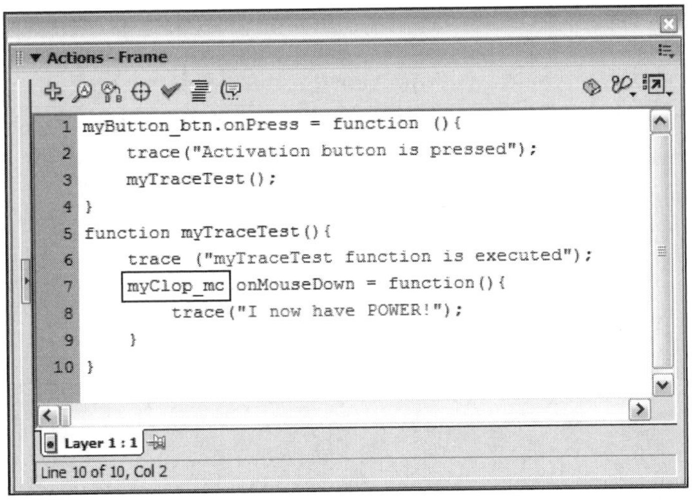

Actions - Frame

```
1  myButton_btn.onPress = function (){
2      trace("Activation button is pressed");
3      myTraceTest();
4  }
5  function myTraceTest(){
6      trace ("myTraceTest function is executed");
7      myClop_mc onMouseDown = function(){
8          trace("I now have POWER!");
9      }
10 }
```

Layer 1 : 1

Line 10 of 10, Col 2

Let's test the project.

10) Choose Control > Test Movie.

In the testing environment, click the **myButton_btn** instance. The Output panel will open and display the following message:

```
Activation button is pressed
myTraceTest function is executed
```

This message indicates that the button worked, and that the function call the button made to `myTraceTest()` was executed. So far, so good. Because the function executed, **myClip_mc** would have been assigned an `onMouseDown` event handler method, allowing the user to click anywhere on the stage to see the trace message, "I now have POWER!" displayed in the Output panel. When you click, though, nothing happens. Interesting. Using our `trace()` actions, we can deduce that the script on the button was executed, and the function was executed, but something went wrong with the part of the script that assigns the `onMouseDown` event handler to **myClip_mc**. We know where to look for a bug!

Sure, we gave it away in Step 9, when we told you that the event handler method assignment had a spelling error. But even without this help you could have quickly deduced that something was wrong with that section of code by simply realizing that everything leading up to the event handler assignment worked as designed, as indicated by the `trace()` messages we used. `trace()` messages are very useful in tracking down bugs.

11) Close the test movie to return to the authoring environment. Select Frame 1, open the Actions panel, and fix the spelling error in the function definition by changing *myClop_mc* to *myClip_mc*. Choose Control > Test Movie.

In the testing environment, click the **myButton_btn** instance. The Output panel will open and display this message:

```
Activation button is pressed
myTraceTest function is executed
```

This indicates that the button worked, and that the function call the button made to `myTraceTest()` was executed.

Now click anywhere on the stage. The message "I now have POWER!" will appear in the Output window, indicating that the entire project is now working as it should.

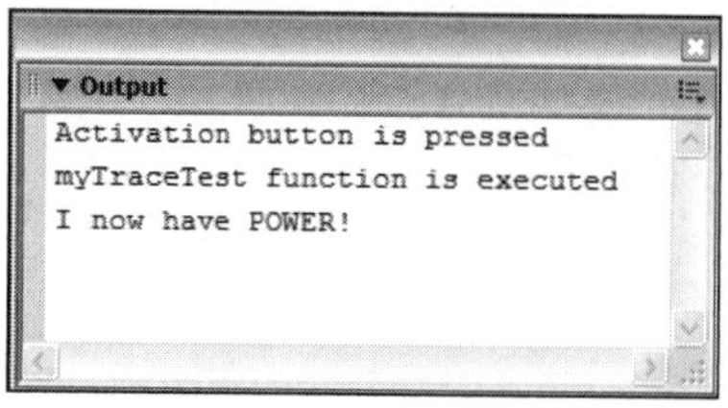

```
▼ Output
Activation button is pressed
myTraceTest function is executed
I now have POWER!
```

12) Close the test movie, return to the authoring environment, and save this file as *Testing1.fla*.

We will build on this file in the next section.

This has been a simple demonstration of the `trace()` action. You can see how strategically placed `trace()` actions can help you to follow the execution of a script, and thus deduce where an error might exist. This feature lets you focus your bug-sleuthing efforts on a particular section of code.

The `trace()` action can be used to inform you when a function has been executed:

```
function myFunction(){
  trace("myFunction has been called");
}
```

or what parameter values were passed to the function when it was called:

```
function myFunction(name:String, age:Number){
  trace("myFunction has been called and passed values of " + name +
  ⇒" and " + age);
}
```

or how conditional statements are evaluated:

```
if (age < 100){
  trace("age is less than 100");
}else if (age > 100){
  trace("age is greater than 100");
}else{
  trace("age is exactly 100");
}
```

and so on.

These little hints throughout your code can provide insight into how things are working behind the scenes.

TIP *`trace()` actions can be turned on or off individually by commenting the action, as in the following example:*

```
//trace("Let me speak my peace!")
```

This strategy can be helpful if you're using several `trace()` actions in your code, but you only want to focus on the output of an individual `trace()` action.

Using the Debugger

Normally, you can't see either the data in variables or the values associated with movie properties while your movie is playing; however, this data plays a crucial role in determining how your interactive movie looks and works. Visual bugs are easy to spot, but bugs in ActionScripts can be trickier to track down and correct. Not only is the data usually invisible; it can also be changing constantly. This is where Flash's Debugger comes in: with the Debugger, you can view the real-time values of variables and properties while a movie is playing, as well as change values at will to see how such alterations will affect the flow of an individual script or the movie as a whole. In addition, the Debugger allows you to control script execution line by line. You can start and pause a script at different points of its execution, which lets you slow to a crawl something that normally takes milliseconds to complete. This functionality enables you to assess how a particular script is affecting the movie as it executes. By taking control of the movie's logic in this manner, you can often quickly pinpoint problems in your scripts.

Before learning how to use the Debugger, it's a good idea to become familiar with its interface, which is made up of the following elements:

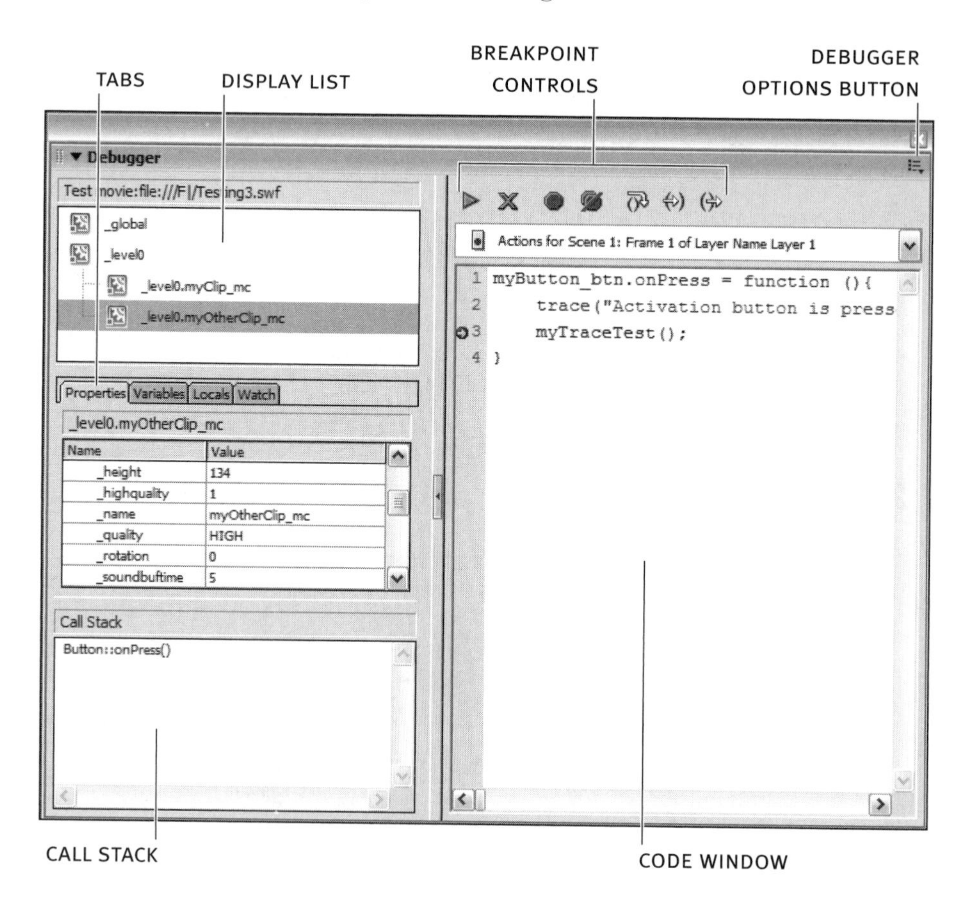

- **Display list.** The Display list shows the hierarchical structure of the movies in the movie (Flash player) window, including the main movie, movie clips, and any movies that have been loaded. This list is updated in real time as various clips and loaded movies are added and removed from the Player window as the movie plays. Selecting a movie in the Display list causes the Properties and Variable tabs to reflect that movie's current properties and variables.
- **Properties tab.** Clicking this tab displays the names and current property values of the movie selected in the Display list. Some of the properties here are dimmed, meaning that you can view but not change them. If you double-click a value that's not dimmed, you can change that value and immediately see the effect of that change in the movie while it plays. Because the movie may contain scripts with conditional statements based on the current value of a specific property of a particular movie, you can make sure that these conditional statements are working properly by changing a property value on this tab. Keep in mind, however, that you can't use expressions when entering new property values from the Debugger: New values can be strings (remember to use quotes), numbers, or a Boolean (true or false).
- **Variables tab.** Clicking this tab displays the names and current values of the variables included in the movie that's selected in the Display list. Double-clicking a value allows you to change it and view the immediate results of that change in the movie. Because variables provide the foundation of most ActionScripts, using the Debugger to change individual values can help you track down the problems that might occur when a movie is fed a certain piece of data. Although you can see the values of Object and Array variables on this tab, you can't change them, nor can you use expressions when entering new variable values from the Debugger. New values can be strings (remember to use quotes), numbers, or a Boolean (true or false).
- **Locals tab.** This tab contains a list of local (temporary) variables that are used within a function when that function block is being stepped through using breakpoints. Breakpoints are explained in greater detail in the exercise for this section.
- **Watch list tab.** The Watch list tab contains a list of variables that you've designated to be "watched," meaning that their values are constantly monitored on this tab. You can add variables from multiple movies to this list so that you can manage all of them from a single tab.
- **Call Stack.** When a script calls a function—and even when a function calls another function that may call yet another function (enough already!)—this pane displays a hierarchical list of those calls. This list helps you determine the path the project takes to perform a certain task, enabling you to possibly optimize your code a bit so that it requires fewer steps to perform a task, with the end goal of helping it run faster.

- **Breakpoint controls.** These buttons control the execution of scripts when using *breakpoints* (markers in a script that indicate a pause in the script's execution). These buttons are discussed in more detail in the exercise for this section.
- **Code window.** This window displays individual scripts within your project, similar to the code window in the Actions panel. The window is updated to display a script when a breakpoint is encountered within that script, although you can specifically select a script to display by using the drop-down menu above the code window.
- **Debugger Options button.** Clicking this button displays a menu of commands pertaining to the Debugger. The menu also contains commands for controlling playback and view quality of the movie being debugged.

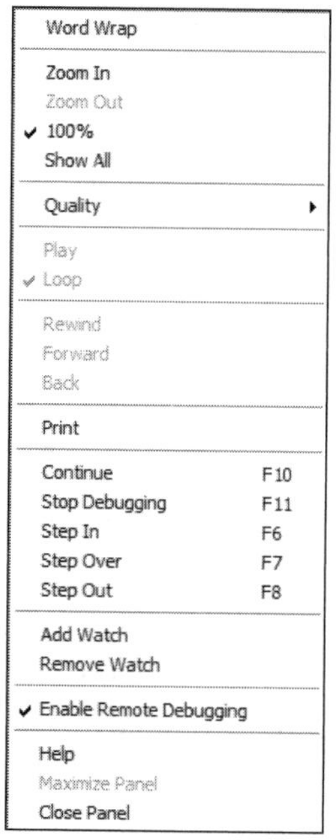

Word Wrap
Zoom In
Zoom Out
✔ 100%
Show All
Quality ▸
Play
✔ Loop
Rewind
Forward
Back
Print
Continue F10
Stop Debugging F11
Step In F6
Step Over F7
Step Out F8
Add Watch
Remove Watch
✔ Enable Remote Debugging
Help
Maximize Panel
Close Panel

Because each project is totally unique, it would be impossible to address every conceivable way in which the Debugger could be used to track down and eliminate bugs. In the following exercise, we'll attempt to give you an overall feel for the process, so that you know how to insert and use breakpoints, see and work with your project's invisible data, and understand the usefulness of the Debugger's features.

1) Open *Testing1.fla*.

This is the file you created in the preceding exercise. We'll add a movie clip instance as well as a few additional scripts to test the features of the Debugger.

2) While pressing the Control key (Windows) or Command key (Macintosh), click and drag the square movie clip instance (named *myClip_mc*) to create a duplicate.

Place this duplicate anywhere on the stage.

3) Select the duplicate and give it an instance name of *myOtherClip_mc*.

Next we'll add event handlers to the two square movie clip instances.

4) With the Actions panel open, select Frame 1 of Layer 1 and add the following script:

```
myClip_mc.myVariable = 100;
myClip_mc.onEnterFrame = function(){
  if (this.myVariable < 100){
    this._rotation += 1;
  }
}
```

A variable named `myVariable` is created on the **myClip_mc** timeline and assigned a value of 100. Then an `onEnterFrame` event handler is set up to constantly check the value of that variable. The `if` statement specifies that if the variable's value ever drops below 100, the clip will start rotating. Let's add a similar script to the duplicate clip.

5) Add the following script at the end of the current script:

```
myOtherClip_mc.myOtherVariable = 50;
myOtherClip_mc.onEnterFrame = function(){
  if (this.myOtherVariable < 50){
    this._rotation += 1;
  }
}
```

This script has similar functionality to the one in Step 4, with a couple of minor exceptions. The name of the variable is `myOtherVariable`, and the variable is assigned to the **myOtherClip_mc** timeline with an initial value of 50. When this variable's value drops below 50, **myOtherClip_mc** will start rotating.

Let's test this new functionality and see how the Debugger can help control these values to affect the movie as it plays.

6) Choose Control > Debug Movie.

This step opens the movie in the testing environment, with the Debugger panel open. Initially, the movie is paused because Flash assumes that you want absolute control over when the movie begins playing and the debugging process begins—especially when using breakpoints. Click the Continue button on the Debugger.

The Display list contains a hierarchical structure of timelines in the current frame, including the main timeline. Clicking one of the movie clip icons makes that movie's properties and variables the focus of the Properties and Variables tabs, respectively. Let's look at some properties.

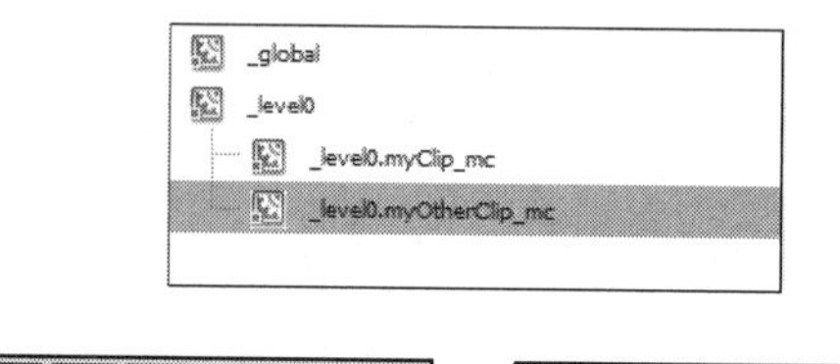

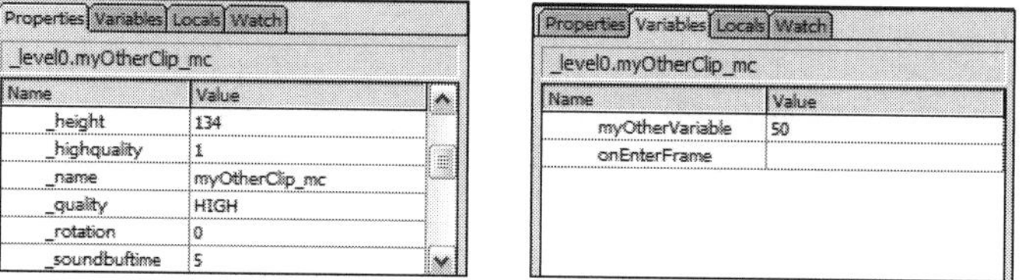

NOTE *Although* `_global` *is shown as a timeline in the Display list, it's actually a global object within the movie, which is available to all timelines. It's shown as a timeline for the sake of congruency.*

7) Click the *myClip_mc* instance in the Display list; then click the Properties tab to view the various properties of *myClip_mc*.

Notice that some properties (and their values) are dimmed. This is because they're read-only properties; their values cannot be set, only viewed. All other property values can be set by you as the movie plays. Setting and viewing property values in this manner, while the movie plays, can help you to discover bugs in scripts that use these values in some way. Being able to target and set a specific property value can help you see how a project will react to that change (if the project is scripted to do something in response to that change). Let's change a property value to see how this works.

8) Scroll to the `_yscale` property at the bottom of the Properties tab. Double-click its value; then enter `150` and press Enter/Return.

The vertical size of **myClip_mc** changes immediately in the testing environment. This is a simple demonstration of how you can control properties of timelines with the Debugger. Not only do the values change, but you can see the results of the change. Having control over the property values of timelines allows you to test how an application will react to changes in a timeline's position, size, rotation, and so on.

Let's look at variable values next.

9) Click the Variables tab.

Because **myClip_mc** is still selected in the Display list, the Variables tab displays any variables within that timeline. Remember that we created a variable named `myVariable` on this timeline. That variable and its initial value of `100` appear on this tab. This value is editable while the movie plays. We created a script that would rotate **myClip_mc** if this variable's value ever dropped below 100. Let's edit the value to see what happens.

10) Double-click the `myVariable` value; then enter `99` and press Enter/Return.

myClip_mc immediately begins rotating. Resetting this value to 100 or above stops the movie from rotating. Because variable values are an integral part of how most scripts work (or don't work), being able to view and set values by using the Variables tab will enable you to quickly test the effect of setting different values.

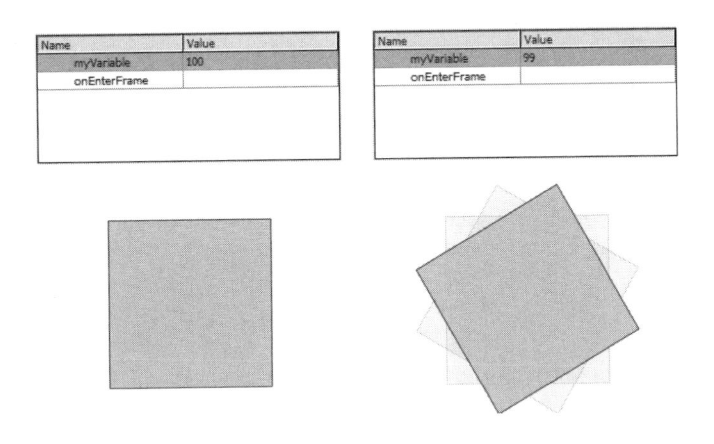

11) In the Display list window, click the *myOtherClip_mc* icon.

The Variables tab should still be open; it displays the variables inside the newly selected timeline. There is only one variable (`myOtherVariable`) in this timeline, with an initial value of `50`. If you change this value to less than 50, **myOtherClip_mc** will begin rotating. Do this if you want to test the result.

If you wanted to update values frequently in the Display list for debugging purposes, it could easily become a major hassle to constantly switch among timelines. This is where *watches* can help, as shown in the following steps.

12) Right-click (Windows) or Control-click (Macintosh) the variable name on the Variables tab and choose Watch from the menu that appears.

This step sets up watching for `myOtherVariable`; an icon appears next to the variable's name indicating that it's being watched.

13) In the Display list, click the *myClip_mc* icon. On the Variables tab, right-click (Windows) or Control-click (Macintosh) the variable name and choose Watch from the menu that appears.

This step makes `myVariable` watched.

14) Click the Watch tab.

This tab shows the two variables from the two different timelines. This demonstrates the main purpose of the Watch tab—enabling you to work with variables from multiple timelines without having to constantly switch among them via the Display list. Variable values here can be changed in the same manner as discussed in the previous few steps.

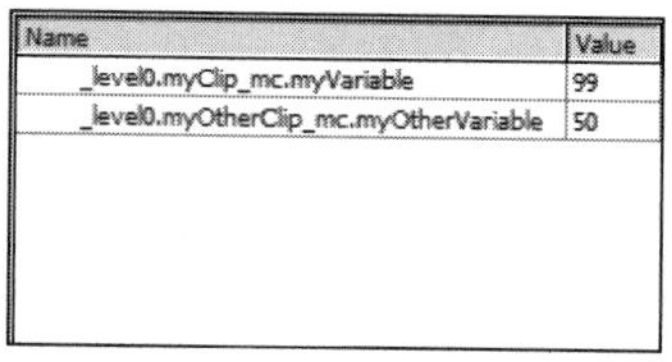

Name	Value
_level0.myClip_mc.myVariable	99
_level0.myOtherClip_mc.myOtherVariable	50

To remove a variable from the Watch list, right-click (Windows) or Control-click (Macintosh) its name on the Watch tab and choose Remove from the menu that appears.

15) Close the test movie to return to the authoring environment. Save this file as *Testing2.fla*.

We will use this file again in the next exercise.

As this exercise has shown, the Debugger gives you a deep look into an application—its timelines, variable values, and property values. You can test different scenarios to see how the application reacts to data you input. You can change values as well as watch those values to make sure that the application is manipulating variable and property values correctly under various circumstances.

SETTING AND USING BREAKPOINTS

Watching and changing property and variable values are only part of the debugging process. Next, we'll look at how setting breakpoints and stepping through your code using the Breakpoint controls on the Debugger panel can also help you locate problems in scripts.

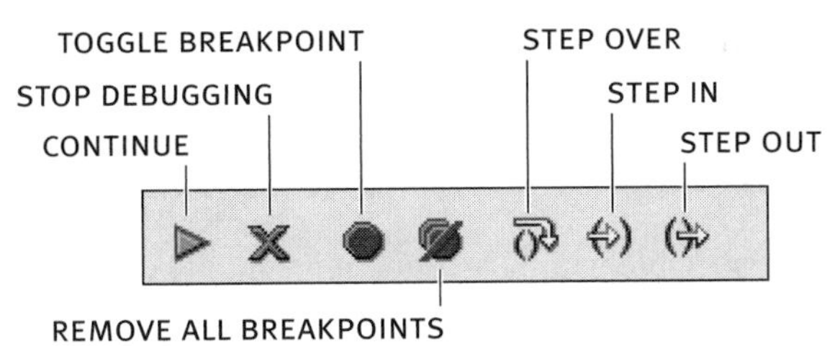

1) Open *Testing2.fla*.

In this exercise, we'll add a single line of script to the file from the preceding exercise, after which we'll begin working with the Debugger again. Make sure that the View Line Numbers option is turned on for the Actions window.

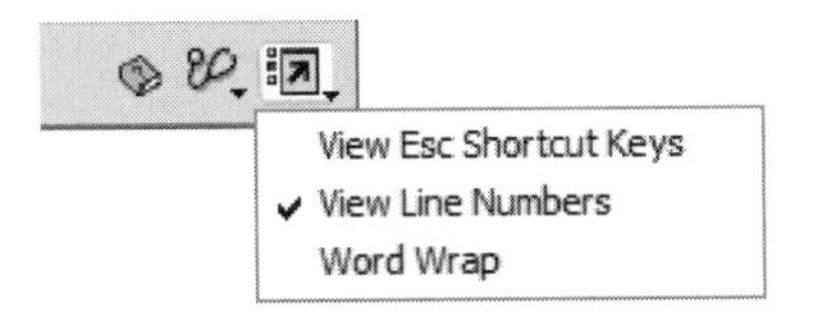

2) With the Actions panel open, select Frame 1 of Layer 1 and add a breakpoint to line 3 by clicking the number 3 in the left margin of the Actions window.

A small red dot appears to the left of the line of script, indicating that a breakpoint has been placed there. When this script is executed (as a result of the button's being clicked), script execution will pause just before line 3, which contains a call to the `myTraceTest()` function. Line 2, which sends a trace message to the Output panel, will still be executed.

```
Actions - Frame
1  myButton_btn.onPress = function (){
2      trace("Activation button is pressed");
3      myTraceTest();
4  }
5  function myTraceTest(){
6      trace ("myTraceTest function is executed");
7      myClip_mc.onMouseDown = function(){
8          trace("I now have POWER!");
9      }
10 }
11 myClip_mc.myVariable = 100;
12 myClip_mc.onEnterFrame = function(){
13     if (this.myVariable < 100){
14         this._rotation += 1;
15     }
16 }
17 myOtherClip_mc.myOtherVariable = 50;
18 myOtherClip_mc.onEnterFrame = function(){
19     if (this.myOtherVariable < 50){
20         this._rotation += 1;
21     }
22 }
Layer 1 : 1
Line 3 of 23, Col 1
```

3) Insert the following line of script on line 7, after the line `trace ("myTraceTest function is executed");`**:**

```
var myVariable = 46;
```

This step creates a local variable within the function named `myVariable`. The variable and its value have no real meaning within our project; we've simply created it to demonstrate the functionality of the Debugger, as you'll see in a moment.

4) Choose Control > Debug Movie.

This step opens the movie in the testing environment with the Debugger open. As mentioned earlier, the movie will be paused initially.

5) Click the Continue button on the Debugger panel.

This action begins playback of the movie.

6) Click the circle button.

Remember that in Step 2 of this exercise, we placed a breakpoint on line 3 of the script, within the `onPress` event handler of this button instance. When the button is clicked, the script begins to execute but pauses at line 3. A small arrow appears within the breakpoint dot on line 3 to indicate that the script's execution is paused at that point. Line 2 has a `trace()` action that sends a message to the Output panel, so that window opens and displays the message. Without the breakpoint, this script would have called the `myTraceTest()` function, but setting the breakpoint caused the script to pause before calling the function. The break in the script's execution allows you to get a snapshot look at property and variable values before the script continues to execute—to make sure that everything looks the way it should—or to enter property and variable values manually before progressing. Either way, this feature gives you complete control over the testing process, allowing you to test or try to break your program in every way imaginable.

TIP *You can place multiple breakpoints in scripts from the Debugger panel. To set or remove a breakpoint on a particular script, select the script from the drop-down list of scripts above the code window, and click the left margin of the line where you want to place or remove a breakpoint. If you want to remove all breakpoints within your movie at once, click the Remove All Breakpoints button on the Debugger panel.*

Now that the script is paused before calling the `myTraceTest()` function, you can proceed in several ways:

- If you click the Continue button, the script continues executing until another breakpoint is encountered or the script has completed execution.
- If you click the Step Over button, the script executes the current line but pauses execution again at the next line (unless you're already at the end of the script).
- If you click the Step In button, the `myTraceTest()` function is called but *stepped into*, meaning that execution pauses on the second line of the function. (The first line contains the opening structure of the function, which simply names the function; there's no reason to pause execution there.)

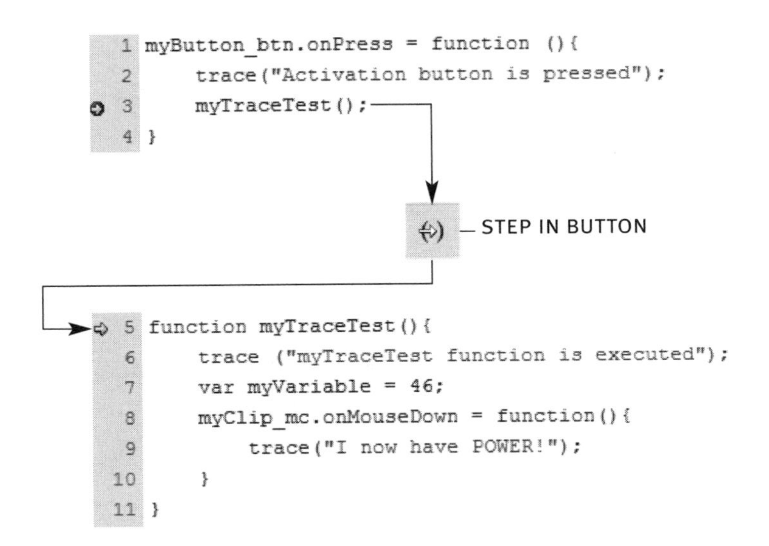

1 myButton_btn.onPress = function (){
2 trace("Activation button is pressed");
3 myTraceTest();
4 }
STEP IN BUTTON
5 function myTraceTest(){
6 trace ("myTraceTest function is executed");
7 var myVariable = 46;
8 myClip_mc.onMouseDown = function(){
9 trace("I now have POWER!");
10 }
11 }

We're going to take the third approach to demonstrate a few other facets of the Debugger.

7) Click the Step In button on the Debugger panel.

Two actions occur when you click the Step In button: the function is called, but paused at its second line (first line of executable ActionScript), and the name of the function—`myTraceTest()`—appears in the Call Stack section of the Debugger panel, indicating that the current script has made a call to this function. If `myTraceTest()` made a call to another function somewhere during its execution (it doesn't), that function's name would appear below the `myTraceTest()` function in the Call Stack window, indicating the overall path or flow that the script takes to complete its task. As mentioned earlier, observing this flow can provide hints as to where a project's code might be optimized.

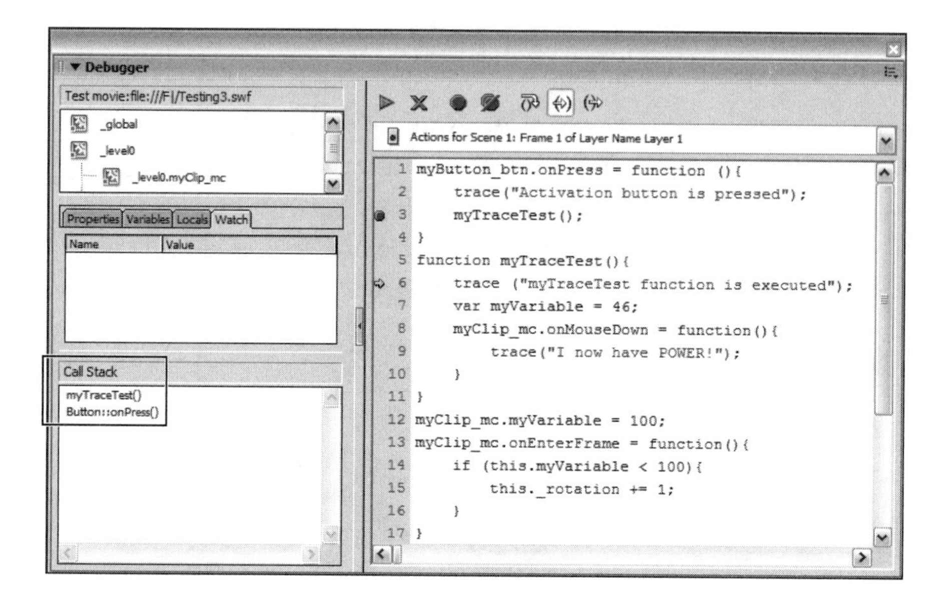

NOTE *Anonymous functions called as event handlers appear in this window when executed; therefore, the execution of the* `onPress` *event handler on the* ***myButton_btn*** *instance is visible in the Call Stack window.*

Let's return our attention to the script paused in the code window. You can click the Continue button to continue executing the function until another breakpoint is encountered or the function (and the script that called it) has been completely executed; you can click the Step Over button to execute the current line of the script, but pause at the one that follows; or you can click the Step Out button to step out of the function and return to the execution of the main script. We're going to use the Step Over button to demonstrate one more aspect of the Debugger panel: the ability to view (and possibly change) local variables that are created as a function executes.

8) Click the Locals tab on the Debugger panel.

This tab needs to be open as we proceed.

9) Click the Step Over button twice.

The first use of the Step Over button executes the `trace()` action within the function. As a result, a message appears in the Output panel.

With the second click of the Step Over button, the next line in the function definition is executed, which creates a local variable named `myVariable` and assigns it a value of `46`. After this variable is created, it appears on the Locals tab. This variable's value can be changed by double-clicking its current value and entering a new one. This feature allows you to control local variable values that a function uses in its execution, providing another means of testing scripts—in this case, functions.

10) Close the test movie and save this file as *Testing3.fla*.

This completes the debugging session. As you've learned, using breakpoints and stepping through code line by line allows you to follow the execution of the code step by step. If the code contains an error, debugging enables you to see the moment (as well as the code) where things go awry.

REMOTE DEBUGGING

Our focus to this point has been the debugging of a movie that's played within the testing environment. But Flash allows you to also debug a movie on the Web, a process known as *remote debugging.*

By default, SWF files on the Web cannot be debugged—the assumption is that you don't necessarily want people to know how your movie is assembled, which the debugging process completely reveals. To allow your movie to be debugged remotely, you must take three steps:

1) Set up the SWF file to permit debugging.
2) Publish the movie. This step generates not only an SWF file, but an SWD file, which works in tandem with the SWF file to allow debugging. Without this file, debugging is impossible (more on this in a moment).
3) Have Flash (the authoring tool) running when you view the SWF you're debugging.

The following exercise steps you through the process.

NOTE *For remote debugging to work, you must have the Debug version of the Flash player installed. (By default, this player is not installed.) Instructions for installing the Debug version are located in Macromedia\Flash MX 2004\Players\Readme.htm. The Debug version of the player is like the regular (release) version, but a bit larger in size due to extra code that helps facilitate remote debugging. If you're having trouble with remote debugging, double-check that you have the Debug version installed.*

1) Open the Flash document you want to make available for remote debugging.

Use the **Testing3.fla** file from the preceding exercise, or another FLA of your choice.

2) In the authoring environment, choose File > Publish Settings.

This action opens the Publish Settings dialog box.

3) On the Formats tab in the Publish Settings dialog box, select the Flash and HTML format types; then click the Flash tab.

These settings will cause Flash to create an HTML page and embed the selected Flash movie within the page.

4) On the Flash tab, select the Debugging Permitted option.

This step makes the Password field editable.

5) To set a password that must be entered before debugging the movie, enter a password into the Password box.

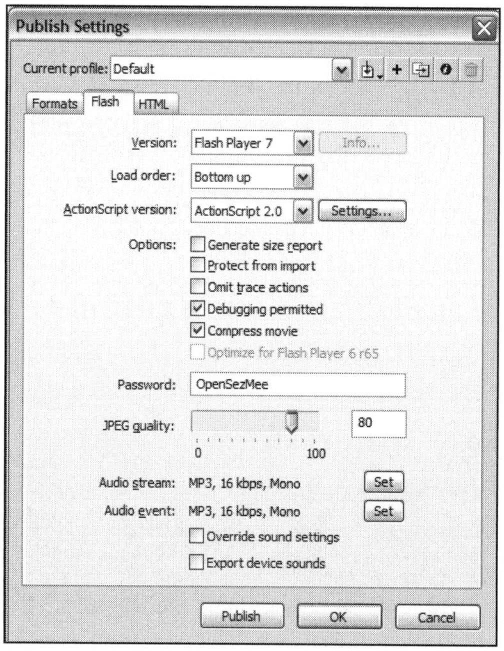

If you leave the Password field blank, you can debug the movie without first providing a password; however, you'll probably want to use a password, so that only those you authorize can view the code in the movie.

6) Publish the movie.

Flash creates HTML, SWF, and SWD files. As we mentioned earlier, the SWD file is a special Flash-created file that enables the movie to be debugged.

7) Upload all three of these files to your server.

All three files must be placed in the same directory.

8) In Flash, choose Window > Development Panels > Debugger to open the Debugger panel. Click the Debugger panel's Options button and select Enable Remote Debugging from the menu that appears.

The Debugger is now enabled for remote debugging.

9) Using your browser, navigate to the URL of the HTML file containing your SWF.

This action opens the Remote Debugging dialog box, which asks you to indicate the location where Flash (the authoring tool) is running.

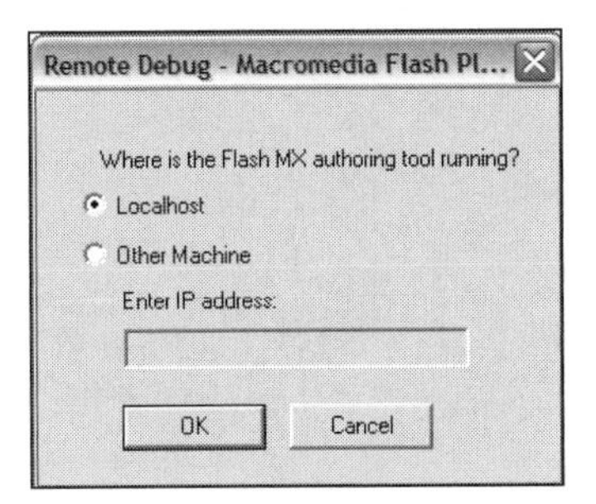

10) Because Flash is most likely running on your own computer, select the Localhost option and then click OK.

If you set the file to require a password before it can be debugged (as described in Step 5), a box will appear asking you for that password.

11) Enter the password, if one is required.

The movie opens, the Debugger becomes active, and you can now debug the movie as discussed in the previous sections.

TIP *If you want to disable debugging of the remote file completely so that the SWF file simply plays when opened, either move or delete the associated SWD file that was created and uploaded to the server as described in Steps 6 and 7. This file contains the functionality that enables debugging. Without it, debugging is impossible.*

This step completes the exercise and this lesson.

WHAT YOU HAVE LEARNED

In this lesson, you have:

- Learned how to avoid common scripting mistakes (pages 674–677)
- Experimented with auto-generated messages from Flash that help you squash compile-time bugs (pages 678–679)
- Located run-time bugs by using the `trace()` action (pages 679–683)
- Debugged scripts with Flash's built-in Debugger tool (pages 684–690)
- Set and used breakpoints to control the execution of scripts in a project (pages 690–695)
- Learned how to debug a movie remotely (pages 695–698)

maximum-strength swfs

LESSON 20

Over the last several years, Flash has gained the respect of programmers as a tool to develop applications. The majority of these applications are used in Web browsers and loaded over the Internet. There are a few amazing software packages designed to assist you in creating Flash applications designed to run outside the browser as a standalone executable file (on Windows). These programs let you add functionality to your Flash applications that you couldn't get from authoring the file from within Flash. In this lesson, you'll learn about some of these programs, and experience working with one of them.

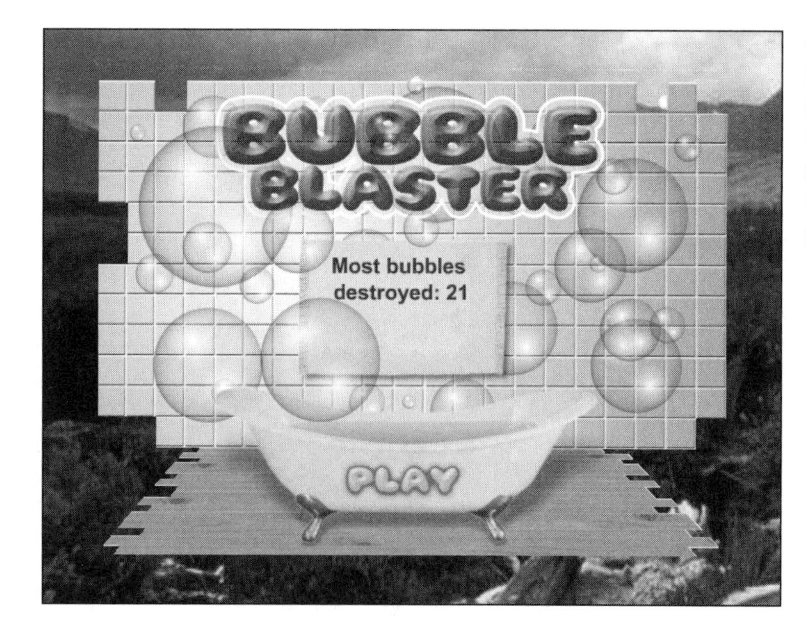

In this lesson, you'll use a third-party tool to create a Flash game with a uniquely shaped playback window.

WHAT YOU WILL LEARN

In this lesson, you will:

- Use FSCommands to extend the functionality of a Flash application
- Enhance a Flash executable file by using a third-party tool
- Configure movie functionality using HTML and FlashVars

APPROXIMATE TIME

This lesson takes approximately one and one half hours to complete.

LESSON FILES

Media Files:

Lesson20/Media/background.gif
Lesson20/Media/bullet.gif
Lesson20/Media/contactus.gif
Lesson20/Media/leftsidebar.gif
Lesson20/Media/placeholder.gif
Lesson20/Media/resources.gif
Lesson20/Media/resourcesdivider.gif
Lesson20/Media/welcomeheader.gif
Lesson20/Media/whatsnew.gif
Lesson20/Media/mask.bmp
Lesson20/Media/highest_score.txt

Starting Files:

Lesson20/Assets/Game1.fla
Lesson20/Assets/NavBar1.fla
Lesson20/Assets/home1.htm
Lesson20/Assets/news1.htm
Lesson20/Assets/contact1.htm

Completed Projects:

Game1.exe
Game1.swf
Game2.fla
NavBar1.swf
NavBar2.fla
home2.htm
news2.htm
contact2.htm

UNDERSTANDING AND USING `fscommand()`

`fscommand()` is a function that enables a Flash movie to communicate with the application that's currently holding the movie. The following are examples of applications that hold (*host*) Flash movies:

- Standalone Flash player
- Web browser
- Executable that displays the Flash movie, such as those created by third-party tools discussed later in this lesson; or executables created using C++, Visual Basic, and so on

It's simple to use an FSCommand from within Flash. The `fscommand()` function accepts two parameters: a command name, and optional extra information. The extra information is used as a parameter of the command:

```
fscommand("command_name", "optional extra stuff");
```

When Flash executes an `fscommand()`, the host application receives notification that a command has been sent to it. The name of the command is sent, as well as any optional parameter data. The host application must be programmed to deal with these incoming commands; it looks at the name of the incoming command and reacts accordingly, using any optional parameter data to complete the task. This functionality will become clearer as we progress in this lesson.

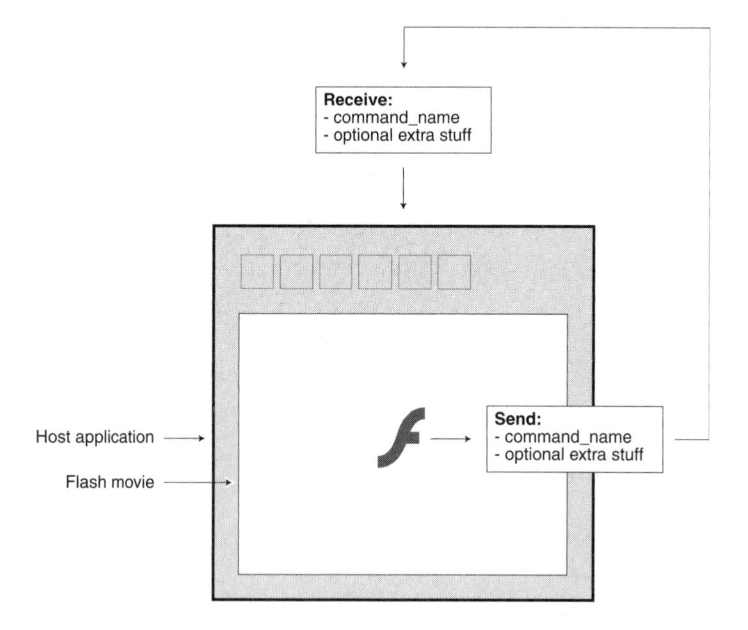

Let's explore in detail some of the previously mentioned uses of the `fscommand()` function.

Controlling the Standalone Flash Player (Projectors)

Using the Publish settings in Flash, you can publish a Flash movie as a *projector*. A projector file typically contains your movie as well as the Flash player. Opening the file causes your movie to play in its own application window (the Flash player/Projector window). The `fscommand()` function can be used in your movie so that it can communicate with the projector in various ways. There are six built-in FSCommands that the standalone player can execute:

```
fscommand("quit")
```

This command closes the standalone player window.

```
fscommand("fullscreen", true)
```

or

```
fscommand("fullscreen", false)
```

This command forces the standalone player to play at full screen (if `true`) or at the defined movie size (if `false`).

```
fscommand("allowscale", true)
```

or

```
fscommand("allowscale", false)
```

This command determines what happens if the user resizes the projector window while your movie is playing. If `true`, the movie is scaled to fit 100% in the resized standalone player window. If `false`, the player window is still resizable, but the movie playing inside it remains at its original size.

```
fscommand("showmenu", true)
```

or

```
fscommand("showmenu", false)
```

Right-clicking (Control-clicking on a Macintosh) a movie playing in the standalone player opens a context menu. The minimal version of this menu is shown if this `fscommand()` parameter is set to `false`. The full menu is shown if `true`.

```
fscommand("exec", fileName)
```

This command executes (opens) another application (such as an .EXE file on Windows). The parameter is the filename of the application to open. Applications opened using this command must reside in a folder named *fscommand*. This folder must reside in the same directory as the projector.

```
fscommand("trapallkeys", true)
```

or

```
fscommand("trapallkeys", false)
```

If `true`, all key events are sent to the Flash player. If `false`, certain key events such as accelerator keypresses are not sent.

Any of these commands can be executed from within your movie using syntax similar to the following:

```
myButton_btn.onRelease = function(){
  fscommand("quit");
}
```

Standalone FSCommands have no effect on Flash movies played outside the standalone player.

Executing AppleScripts with FSCommands

AppleScript is a built-in scripting language for the Macintosh operating system. AppleScripts (files containing AppleScript code) are used to tell the operating system to perform tasks such as these:

- Batch processing
- File conversion and manipulation
- Performing tasks at specified times

One of the more powerful aspects of using the `exec` FSCommand in a Macintosh-based projector is its capability to execute an AppleScript. Let's look at a simple example.

NOTE *This is not intended to be extensive instruction on how to create AppleScripts, but rather a simple demonstration of how AppleScripts can be executed via Flash. For more information on AppleScript, visit* http://www.apple.com/applescript/.

The following AppleScript opens the file named **catalog.pdf** on the My CD disk:

```
tell application "Finder"
activate
select file "catalog.pdf" of disk "My CD"
open selection
end tell
```

To execute this AppleScript from Flash, you name it (for example, launchCatalog), save it in the *fscommand* folder, and create a script within your Flash movie similar to the following:

```
myButton_btn.onRelease = function(){
  fscommand("exec", "launchCatalog");
}
```

When **myButton_btn** is clicked, the launchCatalog AppleScript is executed, and **catalog.pdf** opens.

Communicating with a Web Browser

When a Flash movie is embedded in an HTML page and the page is viewed in a Web browser, the `fscommand()` function enables the Flash movie to communicate with the browser via JavaScript. This feature allows you to do tasks such as open alert boxes, resize the browser, and other JavaScript activities.

NOTE *Because the success of this communication depends on the specific browser and version, some Flash developers limit their use of the* `fscommand()` *function. For more information about using the FSCommand to communicate with a browser, visit* www.macromedia.com.

Creating an Enhanced Executable (Projector)

Several companies make software to extend the functionality of a Flash movie. Most of these products take an SWF file and wrap it within a powerful executable shell. This shell can be considered a high-tech "box" that contains your SWF. The box has been programmed with the capability to perform all sorts of tasks that a typical SWF can't do. The SWF controls this powerful box by sending specialized FSCommands to it. Think of the SWF as the interface and brains of the resulting application, and the box (executable) as the facilitator. These are a few of the most popular products that extend Flash:

- **Flash Studio Pro**—Multidmedia (MDM) Limited (*www.multidmedia.com*)
- **SWF Studio**—Northcode (*www.northcode.com*)
- **Screenweaver**—Rubberduck (*www.screenweaver.com*)

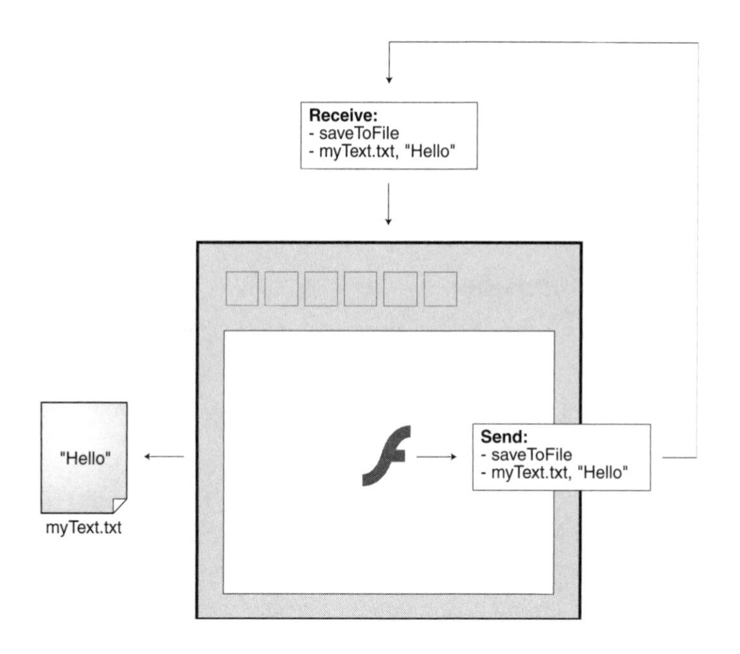

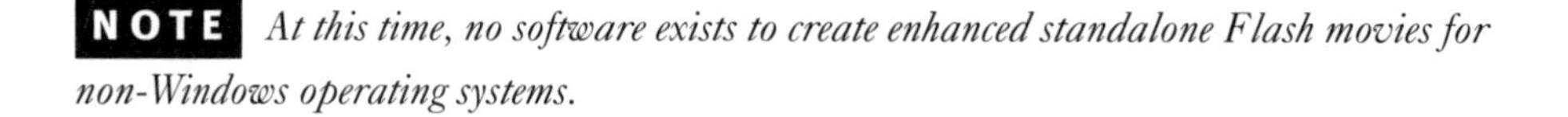

NOTE *At this time, no software exists to create enhanced standalone Flash movies for non-Windows operating systems.*

These applications extend Flash's capabilities with hundreds of commands. Typically, you open the application (such as Flash Studio Pro), locate the SWF file that makes use of special FSCommands, adjust a few settings, and click the GO button, which creates an .EXE file. When opened, this file contains and plays your SWF movie, and is sent commands by your movie. The end result is a powerful Flash movie.

NOTE *Flash Studio Pro and SWF Studio extend Flash by means of FSCommands; Screenweaver takes an approach that's more similar to typical ActionScript syntax.*

The following are a few of the tasks that can be accomplished with FSCommands through the use of a third-party tool:

- Create or remove text files or directories
- Upload and download files from the Internet
- FTP files from the Internet
- Force the computer to display the Flash content in DirectX mode
- Open a file browse pop-up window to allow a user to locate a file or location
- Save a screenshot of the Flash content or a specific area within the Flash content
- Set the desktop wallpaper on the user's computer

Although most of the extended functionality that you gain from these software products comes from executing FSCommands, several configurable options can be set directly from the software's interface (to be applied to the executable file that's created):

- Disable right-click
- Remove window borders
- Make the window always run on top of all other windows
- Assign a custom icon to the executable
- Include additional files in the executable

USING FLASH STUDIO PRO

In the following exercise, you'll create an enhanced standalone Flash application using Flash Studio Pro and FSCommands.

Before proceeding, you need to install the Flash Studio Pro trial version (Windows only) on your computer by following these steps:

1) Locate the file **flashstudiopro_trial_setup.exe** on the CD-ROM for this book and double-click the file to open it.
2) Follow the installer's instructions to install Flash Studio Pro.
3) After installation, launch the application.

When launching Flash Studio Pro for the first time, you get a Flash Studio Pro tips pop-up window. Close that window. You can control a variety of Flash Studio Pro settings (see figure). The following is a brief overview of the available options and settings:

TAB	DESCRIPTION
Input File	Flash Studio Pro creates an executable file that holds at least one SWF file. On this tab, you specify the location on your hard drive for that SWF file.
Style	On this tab, you can change visual properties of the file and the window in which it launches. This includes properties such as the window title, the window borders, and the icon used for the executable file.
Size/Position	Here you can specify the size of the window and where on the screen it should position itself when launched.
Mouse/Keyboard	On this tab, you can define how you want the window to respond to certain keypresses and mouse interactions. For example, you can set the right-click to be, ignored or to drag the window.
Flash	This tab allows you to specify a few playback options for the Flash file, such as quality and background color. Also, you can select the option to include the Flash Player OCX with your executable file.
Files	Flash Studio Pro gives you the option to include files, such as extra SWF files or text files, in the final executable. You can specify on this tab which files to include.
Output File	On this tab, you specify certain properties of the executable file, such as its name, output directory, compression, and even an expiration date.
Batch	You can specify multiple SWF files and convert them to executable files. All SWF file names entered in this tab are processed with the same options.

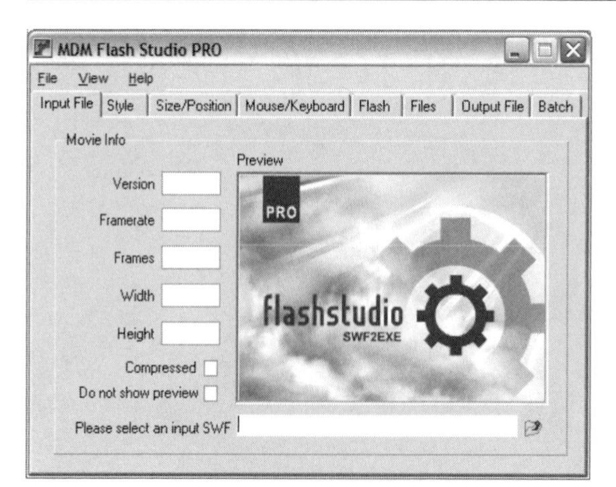

Now that you're acquainted with Flash Studio Pro's interface, let's use it to create an enhanced Flash game. This game creates a text file (used for holding a high score), shakes the projector window, and even talks to you!

1) Open *Game1.fla* in the Lesson20/Assets directory.

Notice that there are five layers—Background, Assets, Top Bubbles, Actions, and Labels—as well as three frame labels (which we'll discuss in a moment). The Labels layer contains no content. It's just used to place empty frames that are given a frame label. The Background layer contains the project's background graphics. The Assets layer contains most of the remaining visual elements for the game, except for a bitmap of some bubbles on the Top Bubbles layer (this graphic was added to give the game some depth). As usual, the Actions layer will contain the ActionScript used in this project.

The game that you're going to build is very simple. You move a ship left and right using the Left Arrow and Right Arrow keys. You can fire a projectile upward from the ship, using the Spacebar. Bubbles appear from the left side of the screen and move to the right. The goal is to destroy as many bubbles as you can within a certain time limit. When finished, your score is saved to a text file if you have attained a new high score.

The Initial frame label will contain script to load the current high score data from a text file. Also on this label is a button that we'll use to begin gameplay. When the user clicks the button, the timeline moves to the Game label, which contains the script and assets for playing the game. After the game's time limit has been exceeded, the timeline moves to the Game Over label, where the current score is saved to a text file if the score is higher than the previously saved high score.

Other than the specific FSCommands used in this exercise, all the ActionScript used in this project should be familiar from earlier lessons. There are functions, arrays, duplicated movie clips, and the `hitTest()` function. Instead of dissecting each script line by line, we'll focus more on what a group of code accomplishes, and in some cases how it relates to the use of FSCommands.

Before we begin scripting, you should be aware of two important assets you'll use in the exercise, both of which are contained in the Lesson20/Assets directory. Both of these assets must be in the same directory as the final project file. The first asset is a text file named **highest_score.txt**. This file contains the variable declaration `score=0`. We'll explain this in a moment. The second asset is a file named **mask.bmp**, which is a black-and-white bitmap image that acts as a mask for the game application's window.

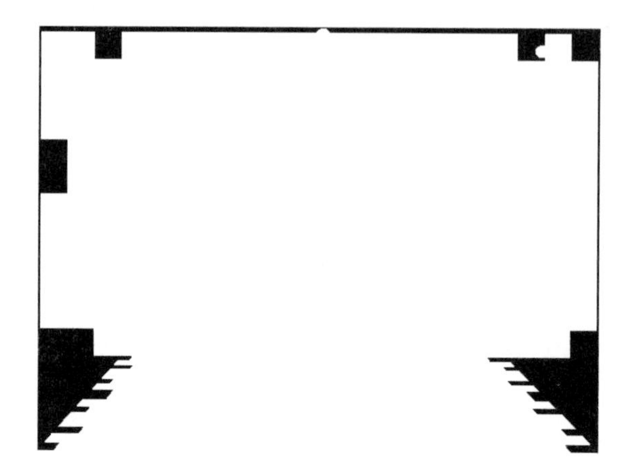

2) Move the playhead to the Initial frame label.

This frame contains two important assets—a text field named **score_txt** that displays the current high score, and a button instance named **play_btn** that moves the timeline to the Game frame label. We'll script both of these elements in a moment.

3) With the Actions panel open, select the frame in the Actions layer (at the Initial frame label) and add the following script:

```
var mask:String = "mask.bmp";
fscommand("flashstudio.maskon", "mask");
```

These actions execute an `fscommand()` when the resulting **SWF** is wrapped in a Flash Studio Pro executable file, sending the executable a command that it has been programmed to act upon. In this case, the command tells the executable file to apply the specified bitmap file as a mask to the playback window. The end result is an executable file in the shape defined by the black-and-white image of the bitmap. The command specified here is `flashstudio.maskon`. (All Flash Studio Pro FSCommands start with `flashstudio`, so the command is actually just `maskon`.) The second parameter of the command specifies the path to the bitmap to be used as a mask. As you can see, we've referenced the value `"mask"`, which actually refers to the value contained in the `mask` variable (`mask.bmp`). Although variables within Flash are not referenced in scripts by using quotes, they are when using Flash Studio Pro commands. This functionality may seem strange at first, but you'll quickly become accustomed to it.

NOTE *To reference the path of the bitmap directly, the syntax would look like this:*

```
fscommand("flashstudio.maskon", "\"mask.bmp\"");
```

4) Add the following script to load and display the previously saved high score:

```
var highscore:Number;
function scoreLoaded() {
  score_txt.text = "Most bubbles destroyed: "+ lv.score;
  highscore = Number(lv.score);
}
var lv:LoadVars = new LoadVars();
lv.onLoad = scoreLoaded;
lv.load("highest_score.txt");
```

This script creates an instance of the LoadVars class and loads the contents of the **highest_score.txt** text file into it. When the text file is loaded, the string `"Most bubbles destroyed: 37"` is displayed in the **score_txt** text field. The number of bubbles destroyed varies depending on the current value of `score` in the loaded text file.

The first line of the script in this step declares `highscore` as a variable on the main timeline. In the `scoreLoaded()` function, when the text file is loaded the value of `score` in the file sets `highscore`'s initial value. The `highscore` variable is declared on the main timeline because we need to keep it around for the duration of gameplay. At the end of the game, the current score is compared to this value to determine whether a new text file containing the updated high score should be created.

5) Add the following script for the Play button:

```
play_btn.onRelease = function() {
  gotoAndStop("Game");
};
stop();
```

When the **play_btn** button instance is clicked, the timeline moves to the Game frame label.

The final action list keeps the movie from playing automatically when the application is opened.

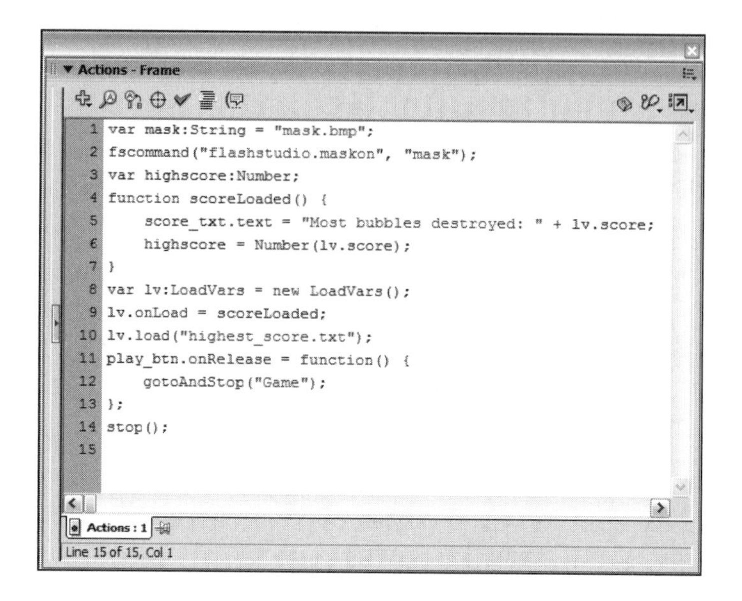
Actions - Frame
var mask:String = "mask.bmp";
fscommand("flashstudio.maskon", "mask");
var highscore:Number;
function scoreLoaded() {
score_txt.text = "Most bubbles destroyed: " + lv.score;
highscore = Number(lv.score);
}
var lv:LoadVars = new LoadVars();
lv.onLoad = scoreLoaded;
lv.load("highest_score.txt");
play_btn.onRelease = function() {
gotoAndStop("Game");
};
stop();
Actions : 1
Line 15 of 15, Col 1

6) Move the playhead to the Game frame label.

This frame contains three movie clip instances: **bubble_mc**, **ship_mc**, and **projectile_mc**. The ship is controlled with the arrow keys, allowing it to move left or right depending on which arrow key is pressed. The **bubble_mc** clip is duplicated at certain times, with the duplicates acting as potential targets. The **projectile_mc** clip is duplicated when the Spacebar is pressed. These duplicates are used to shoot down (pop) bubbles as they move across the screen.

7) With the Actions panel open, select the Actions layer at the Game frame label and add the following actions:

```
var ship_speed:Number = 2;
var projectile_speed:Number = 4;
var bubble_speed:Number = 3;
var projectiles:Array = new Array();
var bubbles:Array = new Array();
var hits:Number = 0;
var depth:Number = 0;
var game_length:Number = 60 * 1000;
var shooting:Boolean = false;
```

The ship, projectiles, and bubbles all move at their own speeds. A `speed` value is the amount that the object can move (in pixels) during one frame. The variables `ship_speed`, `bubble_speed`, and `projectile_speed` define these speeds.

Arrays of projectiles and bubbles are also created, named projectiles and bubbles, respectively. These arrays store and keep track of bubbles and projectiles that are created and used during gameplay. Using arrays makes it easy to loop through the existing projectiles and bubbles to check for collisions or to remove them all from the screen.

The hits variable stores the number of bubbles destroyed. The depth variable stores the current highest unused depth. The game_length variable stores the amount of time that the game lasts, in milliseconds (we set it to last 60 seconds). The shooting variable stores a value of false. These variables will be discussed later.

8) Add the following onEnterFrame event at the end of the current script:

```
this.onEnterFrame = function() {
  generateBubbles();
  captureKeyPresses();
  moveProjectiles();
  moveBubbles();
  detectCollisions();
};
```

This onEnterFrame event executes these five functions (none of which have been created yet) for every frame:

- generateBubbles() creates a new bubble at a random time.
- captureKeyPresses() checks whether the arrow keys or Spacebar have been pressed. Depending on which key is pressed, this function moves the ship left or right, or fires a projectile.
- moveProjectiles() moves fired projectiles upward.
- moveBubbles() moves bubbles to the right.
- detectCollisions() loops through the projectiles and bubbles looking for collisions.

Let's add these functions next and briefly discuss how they work.

9) Add the generateBubbles() function at the end of the current script:

```
function generateBubbles() {
  if (random(50) == 0) {
    ++depth;
    var name:String = "bubble" + depth;
    var clip:MovieClip = bubble_mc.duplicateMovieClip(name,depth);
    bubbles.push(clip);
    clip._xscale = clip._yscale = 50 + random(50);
  }
}
```

If random(50) evaluates to 0, a new bubble is created. Statistically this should occur once every 50 frames. When a new bubble movie clip instance is created, a reference to it is stored in the bubbles array. The generated bubble instance is given a random size by setting its _xscale and_yscale properties to values between 50 and 100.

10) Create the captureKeyPresses() **function:**

```
function captureKeyPresses() {
  if (Key.isDown(Key.LEFT) && ship_mc._x > 185) {
    ship_mc._x -= ship_speed;
  } else if (Key.isDown(Key.RIGHT) && ship_mc._x < 370) {
    ship_mc._x += ship_speed;
  }
  if (Key.isDown(Key.SPACE) && !shooting) {
    shooting = true;
    shoot();
  } else if (!Key.isDown(Key.SPACE)) {
    shooting = false;
  }
}
```

If the Left Arrow or Right Arrow key is pressed and **ship_mc** is within a horizontal boundary of 185 on the left and 370 on the right, the **ship_mc** instance is moved the amount of ship_speed in the appropriate direction. The boundary exists to prevent the instance from moving beyond the area of water in the tub.

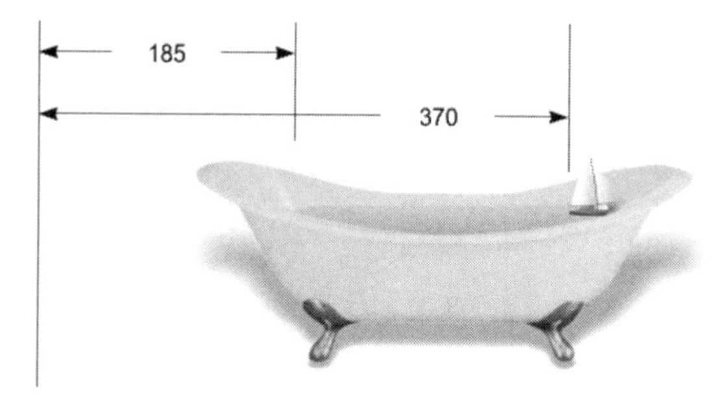

If the Spacebar is pressed and the value of the shooting variable is false, the shoot() function is called and shooting is set to true. If the Spacebar is not pressed, shooting is set to false again. This ensures that the game player has to press the Spacebar once for every shot. Without this condition, the game player could hold down the Spacebar to have a continuous barrage of shots fired. That's not fair to the bubbles!

11) Add the `shoot()` **function at the end of the current script:**

```
function shoot() {
  ++depth;
  var name:String = "projectile" + depth;
  var clip:MovieClip = projectile_mc.duplicateMovieClip(name, depth);
  clip._x = ship_mc._x;
  clip._y = ship_mc._y;
  projectiles.push(clip);
}
```

This function is called when the Spacebar is pressed. It creates a new projectile, positions it on top of the **ship_mc** movie clip instance (so it appears that the projectile is being fired from the ship), and adds a reference to the new projectile in the `projectiles` array.

12) Now create the `moveProjectiles()` **function:**

```
function moveProjectiles() {
  for (var i:Number = projectiles.length - 1; i >= 0; --i) {
    var clip:MovieClip = projectiles[i];
    clip._y -= projectile_speed;
    if (clip._y < 40) {
      clip.removeMovieClip();
      projectiles.splice(i, 1);
    }
  }
}
```

At this point in the book, you're used to seeing `for` loops; however, this is the first time that we've used a `for` loop to count backward. This function serves two purposes: moving any projectiles that have been created as a result of the user pressing the Spacebar, and removing the projectiles if they get too high on the screen.

This loop processes every projectile instance referenced in `projectiles` array. With every iteration, each instance referenced in the array is moved up on the screen by the amount of `projectile_speed`. If the y position of the currently referenced movie clip instance goes past 40, the instance is removed. The instance is removed in two steps: it's physically removed from the screen by using the `removeMovieClip()` method; then the reference to the instance in the `projectiles` array is deleted, using the `splice()` method of the Array class.

You may wonder why this particular loop call requires `i` to be counted backward (`--i`). Think of the references to projectile instances in the `projectiles` array as a stack of nine books, with the book at the bottom of the stack having an index value of 0, and the topmost book having an index value of 8. Now suppose you're given the task of removing the books at positions 1 and 4. If you remove the book at index 1, the remaining books on top of that book drop down one position; the book that was formerly at position 2 is now at position 1, the book that was at position 3 is now at position 2, and so on. This creates a problem when you remove the book at position 4, because it has been dropped to position 3. Removing the book at position 4 actually results in removing the book that was formerly at position 5. The book that was originally at index 4 is skipped altogether.

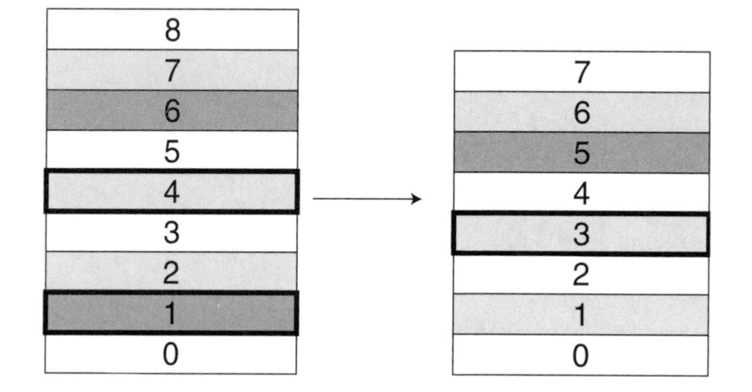

The same kind of logic problem would exist in our loop if we removed items by starting at index 0 and working our way up. By working backward, we eliminate this problem. Here's how.

Returning to the book illustration, if book 4 is removed first, books 5 through 8 are all dropped one position. But that's okay because you're working backward; the book at position 1 is still at position 1. When the time comes to remove it, it's right where it needs to be. Our backward loop solves this problem in the same way when removing projectiles.

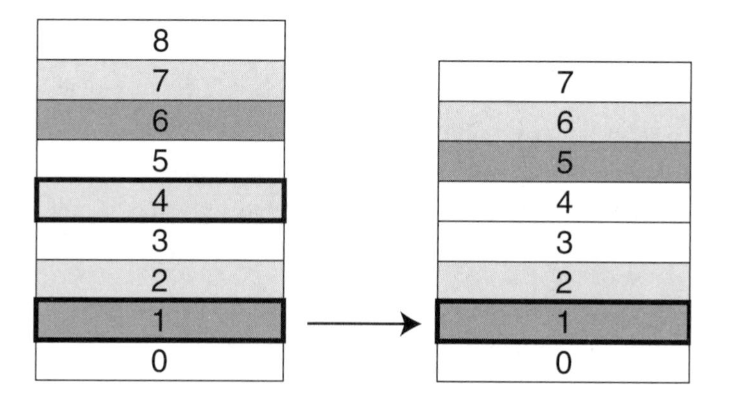

13) Create the `moveBubbles()` **function:**

```
function moveBubbles() {
  for (var i:Number = bubbles.length - 1; i >= 0;  --i) {
    var clip:MovieClip = bubbles[i];
    clip._x += bubble_speed;
    if (clip._x > 550) {
      clip.removeMovieClip();
      bubbles.splice(i, 1);
    }
  }
}
```

This function works like `moveProjectiles()`, except that it handles the movement and deletion of bubble instances. These are moved to the right at the rate of `bubble_speed`, and removed when they've breached the rightmost boundary of the project.

14) Next, create the `detectCollisions()` **function:**

```
function detectCollisions() {
  for (var i:Number = projectiles.length - 1; i >= 0;  --i) {
    var projectile_clip:MovieClip = projectiles[i];
    for (var j:Number = bubbles.length - 1; j >= 0;  --j) {
      var bubble_clip:MovieClip = bubbles[j];
      if (projectile_clip.hitTest(bubble_clip)) {
        ++hits;
        projectile_clip.removeMovieClip();
        projectiles.splice(i, 1);
        bubbles.splice(j, 1);
        bubble_clip.play();
        fscommand("flashstudio.shake", "\"5\"");
      }
    }
  }
}
```

This function has a nested loop. For every projectile in the `projectile` array, the entire `bubble` array is looped through and a `hitTest()` is performed. If `hitTest()` returns a value of `true`, a collision has occurred between the projectile being tested and a bubble instance.

If a collision is detected, the `hits` variable is incremented, the projectile is removed, and the bubble is removed from the `bubbles` array. The bubble is told to play a "bursting" animation. The final frame in the **bubbles_mc** movie clip has an action assigned, `this.removeMovieClip()`, that removes the bubble clip as soon as the bubble has burst.

The final action that occurs if a collision is detected is the execution of the FSCommand. `shake`. The `shake` command tells the executable to shake the playback window the number of times listed as the second parameter. When a collision is detected, the playback window shakes five times.

15) Create the `gameOver()` function to handle ending the game:

```
function gameOver() {
  clearInterval(gameID);
  for (var i:Number = projectiles.length - 1; i >= 0;  --i) {
    var clip:MovieClip = projectiles[i];
    clip.removeMovieClip();
    projectiles.splice(i, 1);
  }
  for (var i:Number = bubbles.length - 1; i >= 0;  --i) {
    var clip:MovieClip = bubbles[i];
    clip.removeMovieClip();
    bubbles.splice(i, 1);
  }
  gotoAndPlay("Game Over");
}
var gameID:Number = setInterval(gameOver, game_length);
```

The last line of script shown here uses `setInterval()` to tell the `gameOver()` function to execute after the game has been played for one minute, which is the length of time specified in the `game_length` variable created in Step 7.

When executed, the `gameOver()` function takes four actions: It first clears the interval so that the `gameOver()` function is not called again in another 60 seconds. Then it uses a couple of looping statements to loop through and remove any outstanding projectile and bubble instances. Finally, it sends the movie to the Game Over frame label.

16) Move the playhead to the Game Over frame label.

This frame contains the text showing that the game has ended. There is also a button named **playagain_btn** that moves the timeline back to the Initial frame so that the game can be played again.

No ActionScript will actually be assigned to this frame; rather, it will be assigned to the next frame because of the FSCommands used. Typically, when these FSCommands are placed on a frame, they're executed *before* the visual content of the frame is rendered. Therefore, execution of FSCommands on the Game Over frame label technically occurs while the user still sees the content of the Game label (albeit just for a split second). By putting these commands on the next frame, we let the visual content of the Game Over frame label render on the screen first, before the execution of the commands.

17) Select the frame in the Actions layer directly after the Game Over frame label and add the following script:

```
if (hits != 1) {
  var message:String = "Game Over! You destroyed "+ hits + "bubbles!";
} else {
  var message:String = "Game Over! You destroyed " + hits + "bubble!";
}
fscommand("flashstudio.say", "message");
```

Both Windows 2000 and Windows XP come with a speech pack built in, allowing them to render strings of text to voice. This script formats a dynamic message and has Windows play the message using the `flashstudio.say` command. The second parameter of this command specifies a variable whose value is the text to speak.

NOTE *If you're testing the game on a Windows 98 or Windows 95 machine (which doesn't have a built-in speech engine), don't include this portion of script, or you'll get an error at the end of the game.*

18) Add the following script to handle saving a high score:

```
if (hits > highscore) {
  var saveTo:String = "highest_score.txt";
  var saveContent:String = "score=" + hits;
  fscommand("flashstudio.savetofile", "saveTo, saveContent");
}
```

At the end of the game, this conditional statement compares the value of `hits` (the number of bubbles hit) with the value of `highscore` (which is the current high score, as discussed in Step 4). If `hits` has a greater value, a new high score has been achieved and needs to be saved. The `savetofile` command saves the new score to a text file, which is loaded at the beginning of the next game.

The `savetofile` command accepts two parameter values, separated by commas. The first line within the conditional creates a variable named `saveTo`, which represents the name of the target text file. The second line creates a variable named `saveContent`, which contains the text that will be saved. The value of this variable is created by adding the string `"score="` to the value of `hits`. If `hits` has a value of `53`, for example, the text `score=53` is written to the **highest_score.txt** file, overwriting any existing text in the file.

19) Add the following button event handler and `stop()` action at the end of the current script:

```
playagain_btn.onRelease = function() {
  gotoAndStop("Initial");
};
stop();
```

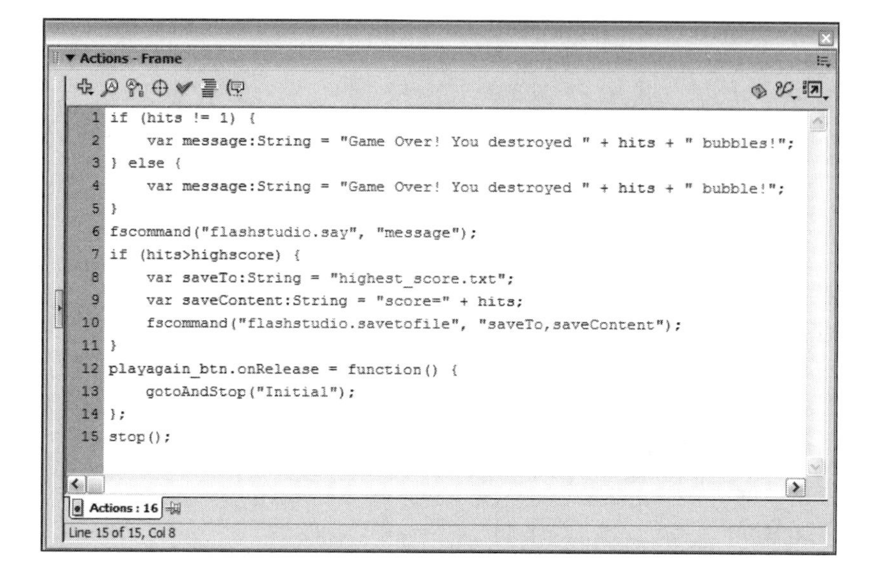

When the **playagain_btn** button instance is clicked, the user returns to the Initial frame label, where the high score is reloaded and the game can be replayed. A `stop()` action is added here to keep the movie from playing.

The scripting of our file is complete. The last tasks are creating an SWF file and then wrapping that file in an executable generated by Flash Studio Pro.

20) Choose File > Publish to create an *SWF* file.

Next you will be using Flash Studio Pro to create an executable file.

This step assumes that the default publish settings are used.

21) With Flash Studio Pro open, select the Input File tab. At the bottom of the tab is the option Please Select an Input SWF. Use this option to browse to and select the *Game1.swf* file on your hard drive.

Obviously, this is where you select the file that you want to convert into a Flash Studio Pro executable.

22) Click the Style tab. In the lower-left corner of the tab, click the No Border radio button.

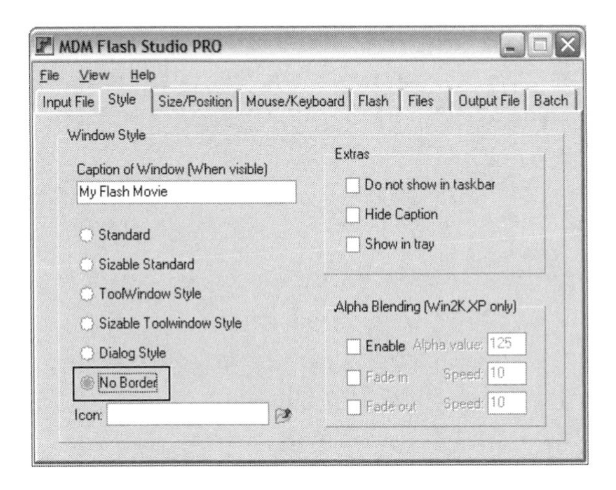

This option setting is necessary for the bitmap mask to fit the movie properly.

23) Click the Output File tab. At the bottom of the tab is the option Please Select the Output File. Use this option to select the name and directory for the output file. This should be the default directory that contains the mask image and *highest_score.txt* file. Click the GO button to generate an executable file.

A progress bar appears as Flash Studio Pro creates an executable file. When complete, a dialog box asks whether you want to launch the file. Select Cancel.

24) Check your working directory for a file named *Game1.exe*. Double-click this file to launch your game!

Immediately upon launching, the game's playback window is masked based on the all-white portions of the **mask.bmp** image. The Initial frame label is shown first, and the current high score (which is 0) is loaded. Play the game and watch the FSCommands we added in action. When you hit a bubble, the playback window shakes. At the end of the game, the application talks to you (on Windows 2000/XP) to let you know how many hits you made. If you've achieved a new high score, it's saved to the **highest_score.txt** file.

25) Close the executable file by pressing the Escape key, and then close Flash Studio Pro. Return to the Flash authoring environment and save your work as *Game2.fla*.

You have created an enhanced executable file using Flash Studio Pro. Flash Studio Pro and other third-party tools offer hundreds of custom FSCommands to enhance your content. You might find it interesting to read through the help files for Flash Studio Pro to learn about the other available commands. You might also want to play around with different Flash Studio Pro options when creating your executable files, such as assigning an icon to the file or having it fade in when the file is opened.

If you're bored with plain ol' ActionScript (yeah, right), learning to use third-party tools such as Flash Studio Pro can open up a new and powerful means of creating incredibly dynamic applications.

USING FLASHVARS

Have you ever had a situation where, aside from simple tweaks, a single Flash movie could be used in a number of different ways? For example, imagine having a Flash movie that loads and plays external MP3 files. To use this movie to play 10 different MP3 files would require you to open the original FLA, manually edit a small section of the code that specifies the MP3 to load, and export 10 different SWFs. Or you might have to script the movie to load the information from a database. The first option is too much work and has the potential of turning into a bandwidth nightmare. Even if each SWF contained only a single line that was different, you would still have 10 different SWFs. If each file was 30 KB in size, placing them all on a single page would result in a 300 KB download. The second option, setting up your movie to load data from a database, is generally fine, but might be too complex a solution in some situations. Fortunately, there's a third option that fits nicely in the middle: the FlashVars parameter.

FlashVars, introduced in Flash MX, is an HTML `<object>` and `<embed>` parameter/attribute that provides a quick and easy way to pass data into a movie embedded in an HTML page. Immediately upon loading the movie, the data passed in can tell the movie to do something. This essentially provides a means to configure an SWF via HTML without having to physically open the original FLA and edit its code. In other words, a single SWF can be used for multiple purposes. For example, suppose that a particular SWF plays MP3s. If you embed that SWF in an HTML page, with a few adjustments to the FlashVars parameter in the `<object>` and `<embed>` tags you can easily define which MP3 file that particular instance of the SWF should play. The greatest benefit about this functionality is that a single SWF can be repurposed multiple times throughout your entire site, and your visitor only needs to download it once. Your site's overall performance is enhanced.

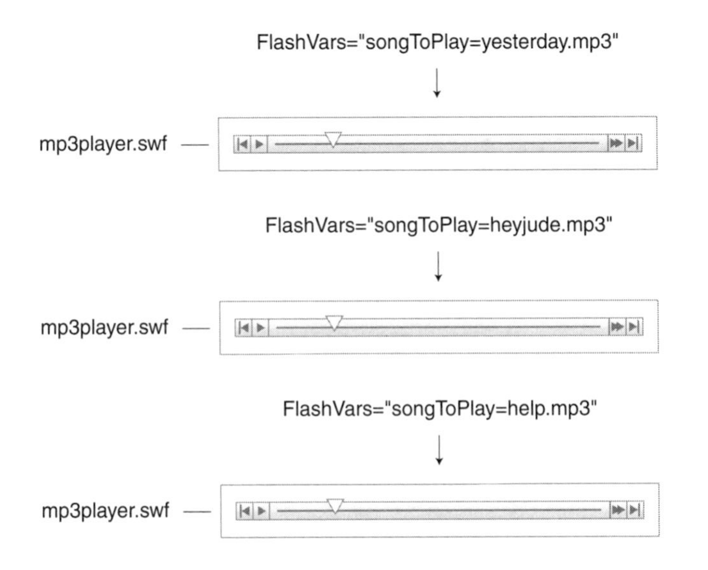

As mentioned earlier, FlashVars is an `<object>` and `<embed>` parameter. Implementation varies depending on which tag is used. For example, within the `<object>` tag, FlashVars is used within a nested `<param>` tag:

```
<PARAM NAME=FlashVars VALUE="hairColor=Yellow">
```

The attribute `NAME=FlashVars` tells the Flash player to push the contents of the `VALUE` attribute into the Flash movie when the movie is loaded. The content pushed is variable data loaded into the main timeline of the SWF. In this example, a single variable named `hairColor` with a value of `"Yellow"` is pushed in.

NOTE *All variable values pushed into an SWF using FlashVars are initially considered strings by Flash. Using some of the conversion tools provided by ActionScript, you can convert values to other data types within Flash.*

Within the <embed> tag, FlashVars is an attribute that can be added with the following syntax:

```
FlashVars="hairColor=Yellow"
```

In both sample scripts, we've only shown how the FlashVars parameter can be used to pass in a single variable and its value; however, more variables can be added by placing an ampersand (&) between name/value pairs, as shown in the following example:

```
<PARAM NAME=FlashVars
⇒VALUE="hairColor=Yellow&noseColor=Orange&occupation=Clown">
```

This example pushes three variables—hairColor, noseColor, and occupation—into the SWF when it's loaded. You can add up to 64 KB of variables by using FlashVars.

What if you need to use characters other than letters or numbers? When setting the value portion of the FlashVars parameter, special characters must be escaped by converting them to URL-encoded strings. This conversion is necessary because HTML uses special characters such as <, >, ?, @, and so on for interpreting how to render and process a page. Converting the special characters to URL-encoded strings makes them invisible to HTML.

Fortunately, you don't have to learn how to escape a string of characters. Flash provides the escape() function, which handles most of the dirty work. Let's look at an example.

Suppose you want to pass the email address *santa@clause.com* into a Flash movie by using FlashVars. This string contains both an at (@) symbol and a period (.) that must be escaped before the string can be used. You can create an escaped version of the string with the following script:

```
var str:String = "santa@clause.com"
trace(escape(str));
```

When this script is executed, the Output panel shows the following:

```
santa%40clause%2Ecom
```

Next, you copy this escaped version of the email address and paste it as the value for the FlashVars parameter, as shown here:

```
<PARAM NAME=FlashVars VALUE="email=santa%40clause%2Ecom">
```

Variable values are automatically unescaped by Flash after they're pushed in; therefore, Flash sees santa%40clause%2Ecom as its actual value of santa@clause.com.

All variables are passed into Flash before Frame 1 of a Flash movie is executed. This allows you to script your movie to react to this passed-in data immediately upon loading and playing.

In the following exercise, you'll create a simple Flash navigation bar for a Web site. You'll use the FlashVars parameter so that this same navigation bar (SWF file) can be used on multiple HTML pages but appear unique on each page.

1) Open *NavBar1.fla* in the Lesson20/Assets directory.

This movie has three layers—Background, Buttons, and Actions. The Actions layer will contain all the script for this project. The Buttons layer contains three movie clip instances: **home_mc**, **news_mc**, and **contact_mc**. These instances will act as both movie clips and buttons. In a moment, we'll look at the timeline of one of these instances.

The SWF created by this authoring file is used as a navigation bar on a three-page Web site. Each of the three movie clip instances on the Buttons layer represents a section of the site: Home, News, and Contact. When one of these instances is clicked, the user is taken to the appropriate HTML page. Using FlashVars, data is passed to our single SWF on each of these pages, enabling it to react in a certain way based on the current HTML page that has been loaded. For example, when the News page is visited, the News button on the navigation bar is highlighted and disabled, and a unique audio clip plays.

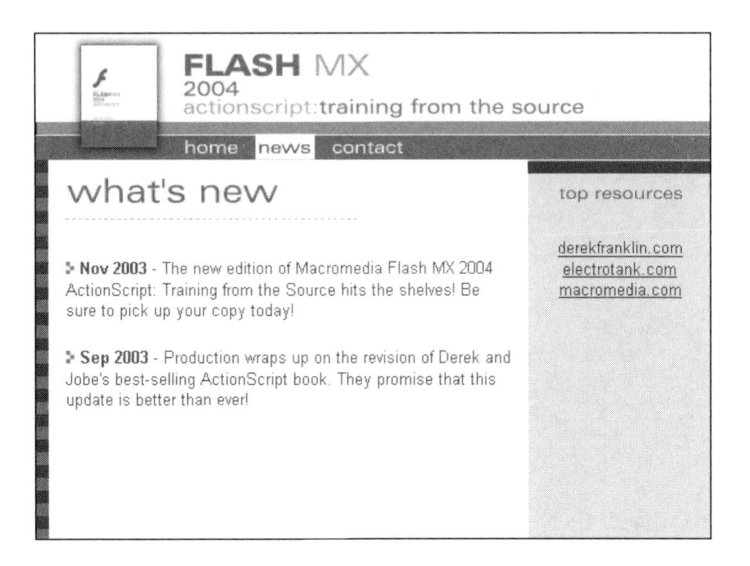

Our SWF will be scripted to use these passed-in variables:

- `currentPage` is a value representing the content of the current HTML page, such as `"Home"`, `"News"`, or `"Contact"`.
- `homeFileName` represents the name of the HTML file to load when the Home button is clicked. For example, we want **home2.htm** to open when the Home button is clicked, so `homeFileName` is assigned a value of `home2`.

- `newsFileName` represents the name of the HTML file to load when the News button is clicked.
- `contactFileName` represents the name of the HTML file to load when the Contact button is clicked.

Before we begin scripting, it would be a good idea to get acquainted with some of the elements in the movie that play a role in its end functionality.

2) Choose Window > Library to open the Library panel.

Notice that the library contains three sounds named Sound1, Sound2, and Sound3. Each sound has been given an identifier so that it can be dynamically attached using the `attachSound()` method. This will be explained in greater detail in a moment.

3) Double-click one of the movie clips instances on the Buttons layer to view its timeline.

The timeline consists of three layers and two frames. The main point to note is that when the playhead is moved to Frame 2, the clip appears highlighted. All three instances on the Buttons layer are constructed this way. This structure plays an integral role in how the navigation bar works.

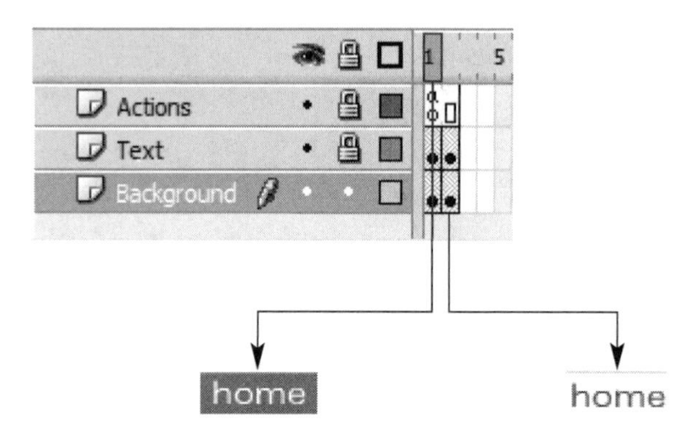

4) Return to the main timeline. With the Actions panel open, select Frame 1 of the Actions layer and add the following line of script:

```
var soundEffect:Sound = new Sound();
```

This line simply creates a Sound object that will be used in a moment to play a unique sound, depending on the page to which the user has navigated.

5) Add onRelease event handlers to each of the clip instances:

```
home_mc.onRelease = function() {
  getURL(homeFileName + ".htm");
};
news_mc.onRelease = function() {
  getURL(newsFileName + ".htm");
};
contact_mc.onRelease = function() {
  getURL(contactFileName + ".htm");
};
```

This script assigns onRelease event handlers to the **home_mc**, **news_mc**, and **contact_mc** movie clip instances. When any of these instances is clicked, it opens a URL based on the value passed into the movie using FlashVars (homeFileName, newsFileName, or contactFileName), plus the extension ".htm". For example, if we use FlashVars to set the value of newsFileName to news1, and then click the **news_mc** instance, **news1.htm** opens. Using FlashVars in this manner gives us the flexibility to change the URLs that are opened by the movie, without having to open the movie in the authoring environment and manually edit it there.

6) Next, add the following conditional statement:

```
if (currentPage == "Home") {
  home_mc.gotoAndStop(2);
  soundEffect.attachSound("Sound1");
  soundEffect.start(0, 1);
  delete home_mc.onRelease;
} else if (currentPage == "News") {
  news_mc.gotoAndStop(2);
  soundEffect.attachSound("Sound2");
  soundEffect.start(0, 1);
  delete news_mc.onRelease;
} else if (currentPage == "Contact") {
  contact_mc.gotoAndStop(2);
  soundEffect.attachSound("Sound3");
  soundEffect.start(0, 1);
  delete contact_mc.onRelease;
}
```

Each of the three Web pages (which you'll set up later in this exercise) uses FlashVars to pass in a variable named currentPage. The value of currentPage is "Home", "News", or "Contact", depending on the page that's loaded. For example, when the Home page is loaded, currentPage has a value of "Home". This conditional statement looks at that value when the movie is loaded and takes one of three sets of actions based on that value. Let's consider a scenario.

When the user visits the Contact page, `currentPage` has a value of `"Contact"`. As a result, the last portion of this conditional statement is executed. The **contact_mc** movie clip is moved to Frame 2, where the instance appears highlighted (indicating to the user that he or she is currently on the Contact page). Next, Sound3 in the library is attached to the `soundEffect` Sound object and played. The last action deletes the `onRelease` event handler from the **contact_mc** instance. This is done because if the Contact page is currently loaded, there's no need for that event handler, which is just used to navigate to the Contact page.

This step completes the scripting of our movie. Next, we'll export it to an SWF and place an instance of it on three HTML pages, using FlashVars to set it up to react differently on each page.

7) Choose File > Export > Export Movie to export this movie as *NavBar1.swf* in the Lesson20/Assets directory.

Next, we'll embed this SWF in several HTML pages.

8) Using your favorite HTML editor, open *home1.htm* in the Lesson20/Assets directory.

The main thing to be aware of in this file is the **placeholder.gif** image at the top of the page. Each of our starting HTML files has this image. In the steps that follow, we'll swap this image for the **NavBar1.swf** file generated in Step 7.

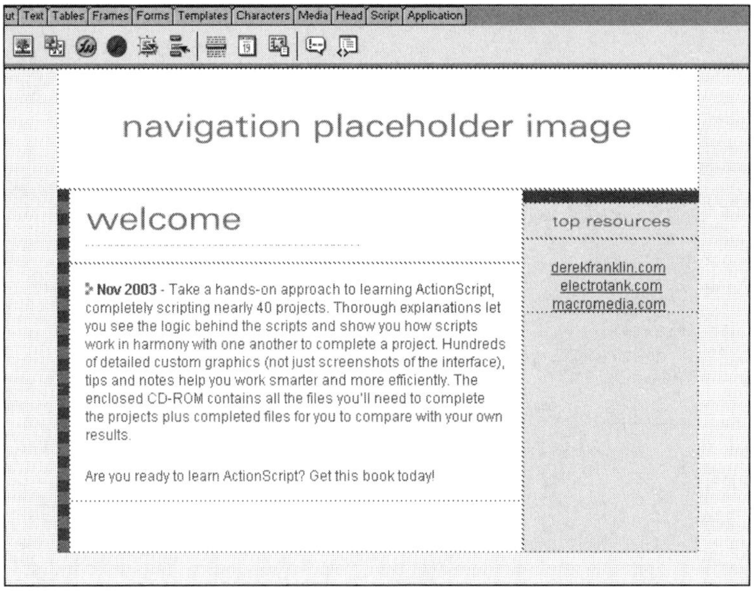

9) Swap the placeholder image for the *NavBar1.swf* movie (embed the *SWF* movie in place of the placeholder image). View the HTML source for the page, locate the `<param>` tags (nested in the `<object>` tags), and add the following tag:

```
<param name="FlashVars"
⇒value="currentPage=Home&homeFileName=home2&newsFileName=news2
⇒&contactFileName=contact2">
```

This step adds the FlashVars parameter to the `<object>` tag. The `value` portion of the tag contains four variables and their values, separated by ampersands (&):

```
currentPage=Home
homeFileName=home2
newsFileName=news2
contactFileName=contact2
```

When the SWF is loaded on this page, it receives these variable values and reacts to them as discussed in Steps 5 and 6. As a result, when this page is loaded, the Home button appears highlighted and disabled, a sound plays, and clicking the remaining navigation buttons in the movie opens **news2.htm** or **contact2.htm**, as appropriate.

10) With the HTML code still visible, add the following attribute to the `<embed>` tag:

```
FlashVars="currentPage=Home&homeFileName=home2&newsFileName=news2
⇒&contactFileName=contact2">
```

This step adds the FlashVars attribute to the `<embed>` tag, giving browsers that use that tag (such as Netscape) access to the FlashVars functionality.

NOTE *Dreamweaver MX 2004 supports the ability to add FlashVars tags to Flash content in an HTML page.*

11) Save this file as *home2.htm*.

The only thing left to do is edit our two remaining HTML pages.

12) Open *news1.htm* in the Lesson20/Assets directory. Edit this page in a fashion similar to that described in Steps 9 and 10, but change the value of `currentPage` to `news` (`currentPage=news`) in both the `<object>` and `<embed>` tags.

When the SWF is loaded on this page, it's passed the same four variables as discussed in Step 9, but the revised value of `currentPage` on this page causes the News button to appear highlighted and disabled, and a different sound plays, as defined by the conditional statement in Step 6.

13) Save this file as *news2.htm*.

Finally, let's edit one more page.

14) Open *contact1.htm* in the Lesson20/Assets directory. Edit this page as described in Steps 9 and 10, but change the value of `currentPage` to `contact` (`currentPage=contact`) in both the `<object>` and `<embed>` tags.

The revised value of `currentPage` on this page causes the Contact button to appear highlighted and disabled, and a different sound plays, as defined by the conditional statement in Step 6.

15) Save this file as *contact2.htm*.

The last step is to test your work.

16) Double-click *home2.htm* to open it in your default browser. When the page loads, click the navigation buttons in the Flash movie.

As you click the buttons, one of the three HTML pages is loaded. Each time a page loads, the FlashVars code on that page passes variable data into the SWF that tell it how to react on that page. This allows you to use a single 20 KB SWF on three different pages to take different actions, as opposed to creating three different SWFs to accomplish the same goal. As mentioned earlier, this can be a plus to someone visiting your Web site because they'll be required to load only a single SWF, not three.

Remember, FlashVars not only allows you to use a single SWF in unique ways on different HTML pages (as demonstrated in this exercise), but you can also use a single SWF multiple times on a *single* HTML page, with each instance configured to show a different frame, load a different MP3, show different text, or whatever your imagination suggests. This is an often overlooked yet powerful tool.

17) Close your browser. Return to Flash and save the file as *NavBar2.fla*.

This completes the exercise and this lesson.

WHAT YOU HAVE LEARNED

In this lesson, you have:

- Used FSCommands to extend the functionality of a Flash application (pages 701–707)
- Enhanced a Flash movie with Flash Studio Pro (pages 707–722)
- Configured movie functionality using HTML and FlashVars (pages 722–730)

printing and context menus

LESSON 21

Flash gives you a great amount of control over the process of printing content within the Flash movie window. You can print content that is not displayed onscreen as well as print the content within specific movie clips, frames, or levels. Unlike printing Web pages from your browser, where all graphical content is printed as bitmaps, Flash gives you the option to print certain graphical content as a bitmap or vector image (which produces results that are crisp and colorful). In addition, Flash allows you to gather information about a user's printer such as the dimensions of the paper and the default paper orientation so that printing can be customized even further. All this printing control is made possible by Flash's built-in PrintJob class.

Flash's new printing capabilities give you greater control over many aspects of printing Flash content, including the area to print.

In this lesson, you will learn how to use the PrintJob class to print content in various ways. You will also be introduced to the ContextMenu class so that you can add your own custom print options to the context menu (the menu that appears when the right mouse button is clicked and released).

WHAT YOU WILL LEARN

In this lesson, you will:

- Distinguish between printing from Flash and printing from the browser
- Learn how to use the PrintJob class
- Print content as a bitmap or vector
- Create a custom context menu
- Add custom items to a context menu

APPROXIMATE TIME

This lesson takes approximately 45 minutes to complete.

LESSON FILES

Starting Files:

Lesson21/Assets/PrintArea1.fla
Lesson21/Assets/ContextMenu1.fla

Completed Projects:

PrintArea2.fla
ContextMenu2.fla

FLASH PRINTING VERSUS BROWSER PRINTING

Despite all the interactive and exciting ways in which you can use Flash to create powerful multimedia presentations, sometimes it's appropriate to add print functionality to an application. Printing functionality would be both useful and appropriate for the following applications:

- Employee directory
- Word processor
- Drawing program
- Quiz with a results screen at the end

There are three ways to print Flash content:

- Using the standard Web page print option found in all Web browsers, if the movie is being viewed in a browser window
- Right-clicking (Control-clicking on a Macintosh) the SWF being played in the Web browser and then selecting the Print option from the context menu that appears. Support for this feature was first officially introduced with the Flash 5 player, although there was limited support in certain versions of the Flash 4 player.
- Having content printed as the result of ActionScript

Let's look at some of the advantages and disadvantages of each option.

Most people know how to print with the browser's Print command, but it doesn't give them much control of what's printed. Typically, when using this option, *everything* on the page is printed in addition to the desired Flash content. This includes text, graphics, buttons, banner ads, and any form elements that may be visible. The user ends up printing a bunch of extra, distracting stuff that probably has no importance to him or her.

Right-clicking (Control-clicking on a Macintosh) an SWF and choosing the Print option from the context menu that appears is a better option because it allows the user to focus printing efforts on the content within the SWF file; however, there are a few problems with this option. Users may not know that the context menu option even exists. Also, when printing with this command, only frames on the main timeline are printed; considering the fact that a Flash movie can contain many timelines, this restriction is somewhat limiting. And if you can deal with the first two obstacles, be aware that when you print using the context menu Print option, color and transparency effects used in the movie are lost. This could result in a printed page that looks nothing like you expected.

NOTE *For brevity, for the remainder of this lesson we'll assume right-click functionality for the opening of a Flash context menu. It should be understood that Control-clicking on a Macintosh is the equivalent to right-clicking on a Windows computer.*

Using ActionScript to print from Flash provides much more control over the printing process and the results, making printing Flash content easier and more efficient for the end user.

Using ActionScript, you have the following print capabilities:

- Print a level or specific movie clip, even if it's not visible
- Print a specific frame within a level or movie clip
- Specify the dimensions surrounding the movie clip or level that you want to print
- Print content as vectors
- Print content as a bitmap
- Perform various printing tasks, using various printing options, by opening a single Print dialog box

USING THE PRINTJOB CLASS

The PrintJob class is a built-in Flash class that gives the programmer control over what can be printed in an SWF as well as how it's printed. To use the PrintJob class, a new instance of the class must be created.

```
var myPrintJob:PrintJob = new PrintJob();
```

With this script, a new instance of the PrintJob class is created and referred to as `myPrintJob`.

To tell the PrintJob object what content to print, you must use the `addPage()` method of the PrintJob class. We'll get to this soon. Before you can use the `addPage()` method to add all printable content to the print job, however, you must first call the `start()` method of the PrintJob class:

```
var myPrintJob:PrintJob = new PrintJob();
var result:Boolean = myPrintJob.start();
```

The first line of this script creates the instance of the PrintJob class. The second line invokes the `start()` method. The moment that the `start()` method is called, a pop-up window (specific to the operating system) asks whether the user wants to proceed with printing. If the user selects Print, the Boolean value `true` is returned and stored as the value of the variable `result`. If the user doesn't have a printer installed or cancels the print pop-up window, the Boolean value `false` is returned. This feature allows you to program an application to react one way if the user successfully initializes the print option, and another if the user cancels the print request or doesn't have a printer. For example:

```
var myPrintJob:PrintJob = new PrintJob();
var result:Boolean = myPrintJob.start();
if (result) {
  //Successfully initialized print action
  //Add pages to print here
} else {
  //User does not have printer or user canceled print action
}
```

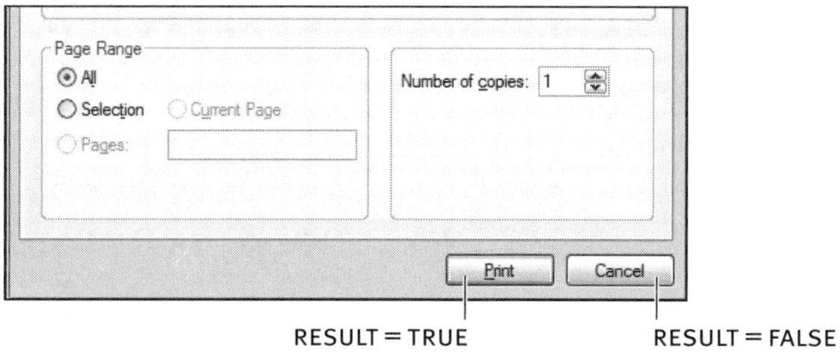

RESULT = TRUE RESULT = FALSE

NOTE *After the* `start()` *method is called but before the user responds to the pop-up window, Flash is paused and no frames are executed. All animations and code halt until the user responds.*

If the value of `result` is `true`, the user has a printer and has chosen the Print option. It's then time to use the `addPage()` method of the PrintJob class to add the printable content. The syntax for invoking the `addPage()` method looks like this:

```
myPrintJob.addPage(target, printArea, options, frameNumber);
```

The `addPage()` method has four parameters:

- `target`. This option defines the timeline where the page lives that you want to print. If this parameter is entered as a number, it's interpreted as pointing to a level of the movie. If the value entered is a string, it points to a movie clip.
- `printArea`. This parameter expects an object with four properties: `xMin`, `xMax`, `yMin`, and `yMax`. These properties together form a rectangle determining the printable area of the target. All of these measurements are relative to the registration point of the

target. For example, if `xMin` has a value of `-300`, the left border of the printable area is 300 pixels to the left of the registration point of the target. By default, leaving the `printArea` parameter blank prints the entire dimensions of the movie clip (or what can fit on the printed page).

- `options`. This setting specifies whether the page should be printed as a bitmap image or as vector graphics. The parameter value needs to be an object with a single property, `printAsBitmap`. This property has a Boolean value. If `true`, the page is printed as a bitmap. If `false`, it's printed as vector graphics. By default, leaving the `options` parameter blank prints the page as vector graphics. By printing as a bitmap you can print movies that maintain their transparencies and color effects, as shown onscreen.
- `frameNumber`. This parameter is a number specifying the frame within the target to be printed. It works only with frame numbers, not frame labels. By default, if this parameter is blank, the currently displayed frame of the target is printed.

All the parameters of the `addPage()` method are optional except `target`.

Let's look at some examples of this method in use. The following script creates a new PrintJob class instance, starts the print request, and adds a page to be printed. The currently displayed frame of the **myClip_mc** movie clip instance will be printed as vector graphics.

```
var myPrintJob:PrintJob = new PrintJob();
var result:Boolean = myPrintJob.start();
if (result) {
  myPrint.addPage("myClip_mc");
} else {
  //User does not have printer or user canceled print action
}
```

To use the default value of a parameter, enter `null`. The following line adds Frame 5 of the **myClip_mc** movie clip instance to the PrintJob class instance, and specifies that it should be printed as a bitmap:

```
myPrint.addPage("myClip_mc", null, {printAsBitmap:true}, 5);
```

To specify the dimensions of a movie clip to be printed, you must define the `printArea` (second parameter) using an object, as shown here:

```
myPrintJob.addPage(0, {xMin:30, xMax:250, yMin:27, yMax:300});
```

The target is level 0. This addPage() method instructs Flash to print all content in level 0 on the current frame that's shown between the x positions of 30 and 250, and the y positions of 27 and 300. Only content found within these dimensions will be printed.

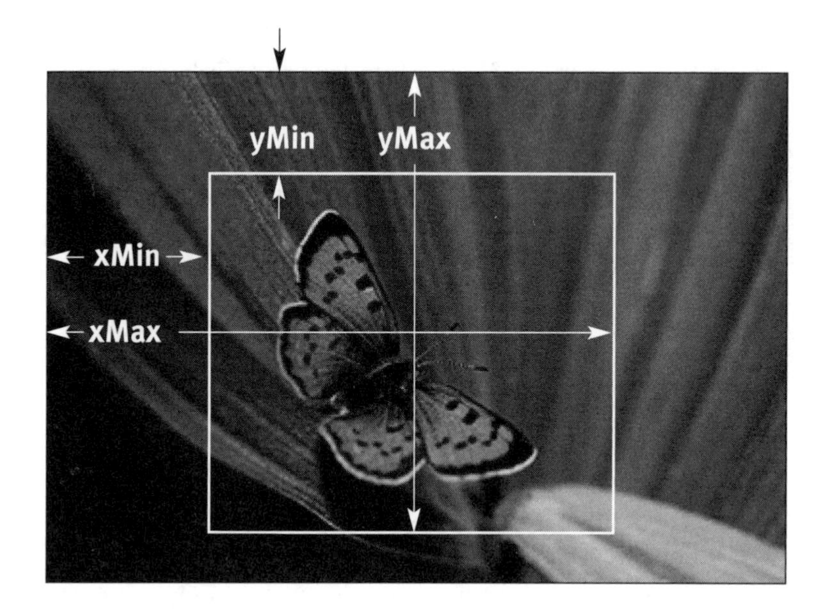

You can add pages from various timelines to a single PrintJob instance, allowing the user to print content from those various timelines from a single Print dialog box:

```
myPrintJob.addPage("invitation_mc", null, {printAsBitmap:true}, 2);
myPrintJob.addPage("map_mc", null, {printAsBitmap:false}, 1);
myPrintJob.addPage(1, null, {printAsBitmap:true}, null);
myPrintJob.addPage("guestList_mc", null, {printAsBitmap:true}, 4);
```

To add all frames of a timeline to a print job, use a looping statement:

```
for(i = 1; i <= myMovieClip_mc._totalframes; ++1){
  myPrintJob.addPage("myMovieClip_mc", null, null, i);
}
```

With each loop, a page is added to the print job. The current value of i specifies by which frame in the **myMovieClip_mc** instance to print for that page. This loop continues until i is greater than the number of frames in the instance.

TIP *Remember that a timeline needn't be visible to add frames from that timeline to a print job. This feature allows you to create hidden content in your movie that might only be appropriate for printing purposes, such as coupons, instructions, or maps that don't fit into your project's overall design.*

Main Movie

Hidden Movie

After all pages have been added to a PrintJob instance, you invoke the `send()` method of the PrintJob class to start the printing.

```
myPrintJob.send();
```

After you're done with the instance of the PrintJob class, you should delete it.

```
delete myPrintJob;
```

TIP *Don't leave instances around that no longer have any use; that's a waste of memory:*

A complete script for creating a print job will look something like this:

```
var myPrintJob:PrintJob = new PrintJob();
var result:Boolean = myPrintJob.start();
if (result) {
  myPrintJob.addPage("invitation_mc", null, {printAsBitmap:true}, 2);
myPrintJob.addPage("map_mc", null, {printAsBitmap:false}, 1);
myPrintJob.addPage(1, null, {printAsBitmap:true}, null);
myPrintJob.addPage("guestList_mc", null, {printAsBitmap:true}, 4);
for(i = 1; i <= myMovieClip_mc._totalframes; ++1){
    myPrintJob.addPage("myMovieClip_mc", null, null, i);
}
myPrintJob.send();
delete myPrintJob;
} else {
  //User does not have printer or user canceled print action
}
```

In the following exercise, you'll dynamically select part of an image and print it.

1) Open *PrintArea1.fla* in the Lesson21/Assets folder.

There are four layers on the main timeline: Animals, Interface, PrintArea Box, and Actions. The Animals layer contains six frames of animal pictures, the Interface layer contains the project's main interface graphics, the PrintArea Box layer contains a movie clip instance named **box_mc**. Frame 1 in the Actions layer is where you'll add all the ActionScript for this exercise.

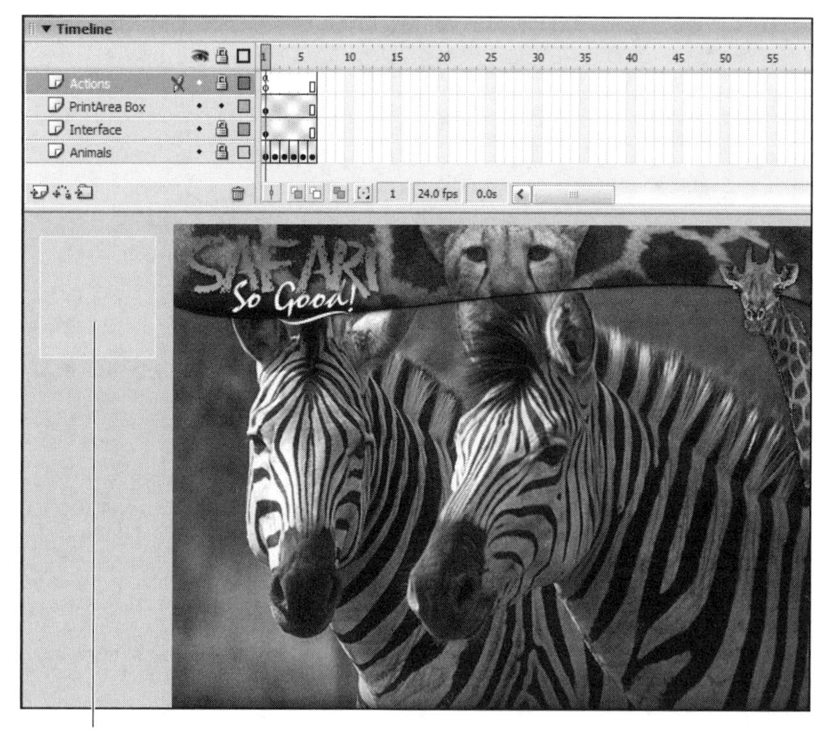

When this exercise is complete, you'll be able to navigate images using the Left Arrow and Right Arrow keys on the keyboard. Clicking an image and dragging down and to the right draws a box on top of the image. As soon as the user releases the mouse button, a print command is sent to print the area of the image that was just selected. The **box_mc** movie clip is resized as the mouse moves, to give the impression that the user is selecting part of the image.

2) With the Actions panel open, select Frame 1 of the Actions layer and add the following script:

```
stop();
box_mc._visible = false;
```

The first action prevents the timeline from moving forward until we tell it to do so. The second line makes the **box_mc** movie clip instance invisible initially. We only want it to be shown if the user has pressed the left mouse button and dragged to create a selection.

3) Add the following variable to track the state of the mouse:

```
var down:Boolean = false;
```

The movie initializes with the mouse button up. When the left mouse button is pressed, the `down` variable changes to `true`.

4) Add the following four variables to track the print area dimensions:

```
var xMin:Number;
var xMax:Number;
var yMin:Number;
var yMax:Number;
```

To specify the area of a target to print, you specify four values: `xMin`, `xMax`, `yMin`, and `yMax`. These values are declared here with no value. When the mouse button is pressed, the `xMin` and `yMin` values are set. As the mouse moves, the `xMax` and `yMax` values are set.

5) Add the following `onMouseDown` event to handle initializing the selection:

```
this.onMouseDown = function() {
  down = true;
  xMin = _xmouse;
  yMin = _ymouse;
  box_mc._x = xMin;
  box_mc._y = yMin;
};
```

When the left mouse button is pressed, the `down` variable's value is set to `true`. The minimum selection values, `xMin` and `yMin`, are set based on the mouse position when the event occurs. These two values are immediately used to position the **box_mc** movie clip.

6) To handle scaling the selection as the mouse moves, add the following script:

```
this.onMouseMove = function() {
  updateAfterEvent();
  if (down) {
    box_mc._visible = true;
    xMax = _xmouse;
    yMax = _ymouse;
    box_mc._width = xMax - xMin;
    box_mc._height = yMax - yMin;
  }
};
```

The updateAfterEvent function is a built-in function in Flash. It tells Flash to redraw graphics onscreen after the mouse moves, rather than waiting until the end of the current frame. This technique gives smoother results to objects that change as the mouse moves.

Every time the mouse moves, a conditional statement is evaluated. It states that if down is true (as it is when the mouse button is pressed), the **box_mc** instance is made visible. Next, the values of xMax and yMax are set based on the current position of the mouse. Finally, the **box_mc** movie clip instance's dimensions are set based on the distances between the minimum values (captured when the mouse button was pressed) and the maximum values (which change as the user moves the mouse around). The end result is that the **box_mc** movie clip instance scales as the mouse moves, to emulate selecting.

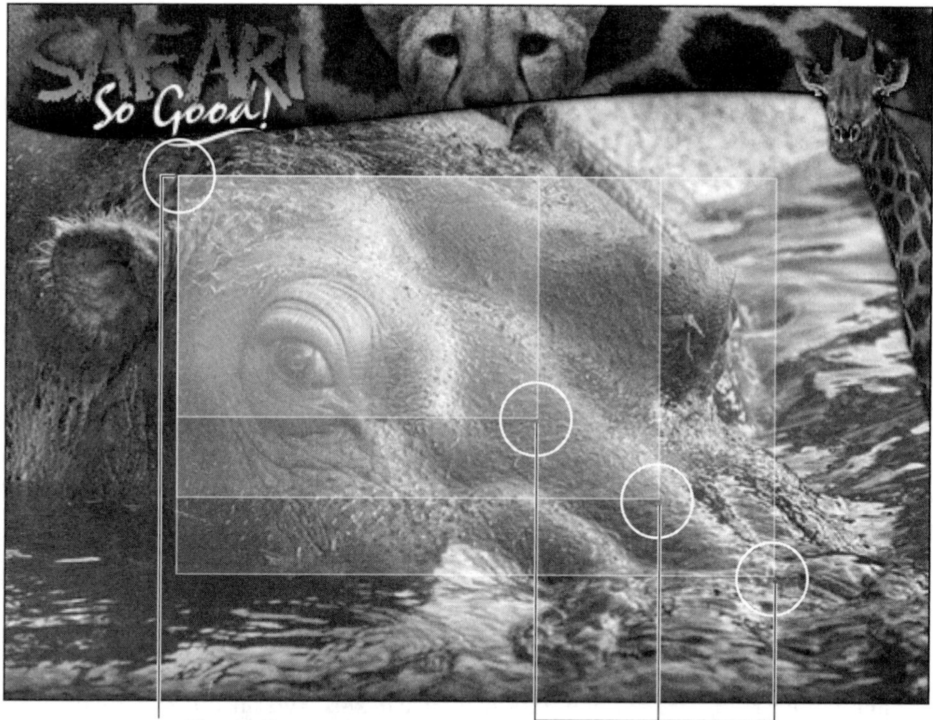

7) Add the following script to capture the onMouseUp **event:**

```
this.onMouseUp = function() {
  down = false;
  box_mc._visible = false;
  printImage();
};
```

When the mouse button is released, the down variable is set back to false and the **box_mc** movie clip becomes invisible again. Then the printImage() function is called; this function uses the dimension variables from the selection process to print an area of the image. Let's create that function next.

8) At the end of the current script, add the following function definition:

```
function printImage() {
  var myPrintJob:PrintJob = new PrintJob();
  var result:Boolean = myPrintJob.start();
  if (result) {
    myPrintJob.addPage(0, {xMin:xMin, xMax:xMax, yMin:yMin,
    ⇒yMax:yMax}, {printAsBitmap:true}, _currentframe);
    myPrintJob.send();
  }
  delete myPrintJob;
}
```

This function is called after the user has clicked, dragged, and released the mouse button. A new instance of the PrintJob class is created and stored as myPrintJob; then the start() method is called, the result of which is stored as the value of the result variable.

If the value of result is true, the user has a printer and has opted to continue the printing process. The addPage() method is then called and the target timeline to print is set as level 0. The second parameter passes in an object whose properties are the dimensions that were gathered during the selection process. The third parameter specifies that the image should be printed as a bitmap. The fourth parameter specifies that the frame to print is the current frame where the main timeline resides. Thus, if the user has navigated to Frame 6, a portion of the elephant graphic, as defined by the selection dimensions, will print.

After the addPage() action, the function sends the added page to the printer by using the send() method. When the send() method is called, the Flash player sends all the added pages (a single page in this case) to the printer to be printed.

The last line in this function deletes the instance of the PrintJob class because we're done with it.

The last thing we need to do is add the script to enable the user to navigate the animal images.

9) **At the end of the current script, add the following function definition:**

```
this.onKeyDown = function(){
  if(Key.isDown(Key.RIGHT)){
    nextFrame();
  }else if(Key.isDown(Key.LEFT)){
    prevFrame();
  }
}
Key.addListener(this);
```

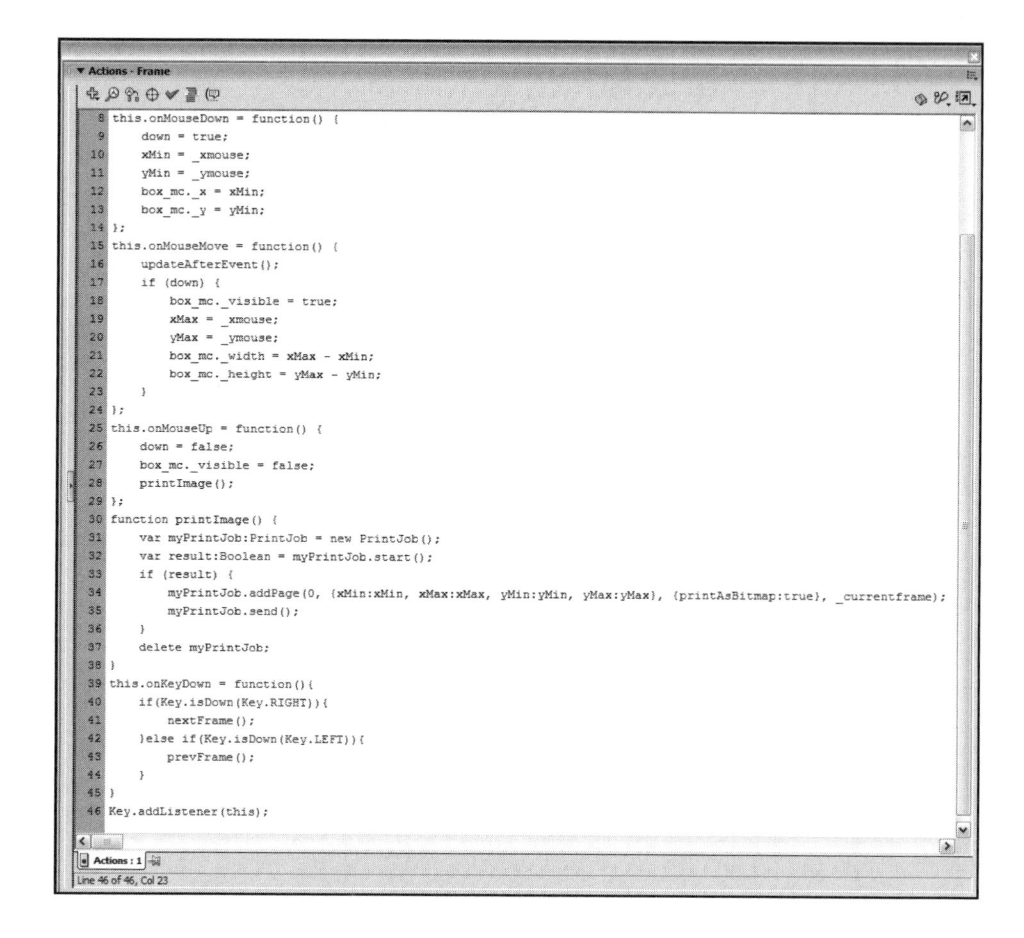

You should be familiar with how this script works. When the `onKeyDown` event occurs, a conditional statement checks whether the key pressed down is the Left Arrow or Right Arrow key. If the Left Arrow key is pressed, the main timeline moves to the next frame. If the Right Arrow key is pressed, the main timeline moves to the previous frame. If any other key is pressed, nothing happens.

Let's test our work.

10) Select Control > Test Movie. Select a portion of the image and then release the mouse button to print it.

After you select a portion of the image, a print window should pop up, opened by your operating system. If you proceed with the print job, the selected area of the image will be printed.

NOTE *The ActionScript that we added in this exercise supports selecting a portion of the image by clicking and dragging down and to the right. Using more advanced ActionScript, we could have supported selecting in any direction.*

11) Close the test movie and save your work as *PrintArea2.fla*.

You have successfully created a simple application that uses the PrintJob class. You can print a specific area of an image with this application.

CREATING CUSTOM CONTEXT MENUS

The context menu appears when you right-click a Flash movie (Control-click on a Macintosh). There are three different types of Flash context menus:

- **Standard menu.** Appears when you right-click anything in a Flash movie except a text field.
- **Edit menu.** Appears when you right-click a text field that's editable or selectable.
- **Error menu.** Appears when a Flash movie fails to load within a Web page and you right-click in the empty area.

The error menu cannot be changed, but the standard and edit context menus can be customized to display new items or remove the built-in default items. All the built-in context menu items can be removed except for the Settings item and the Debugger item.

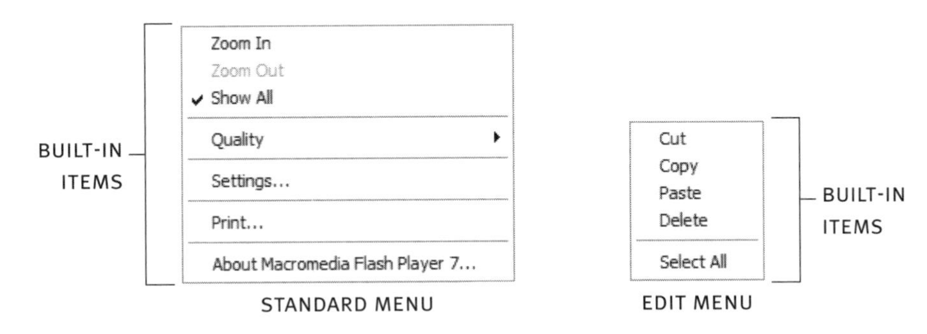

The Flash player includes two built-in classes to assist you in creating a customized context menu:

- **ContextMenu.** This class allows you to create a new context menu, hide built-in menu items (Zoom In, Zoom Out, 100%, Play, Stop, and so on), and keep track of customized items.
- **ContextMenuItem.** Each item in a context menu is an instance of this class. The ContextMenu class has a property (array) called `customItems`. Each element in that array is an instance of the ContextMenuItem class.

The ContextMenu class and the ContextMenuItem class are used together to build custom context menus.

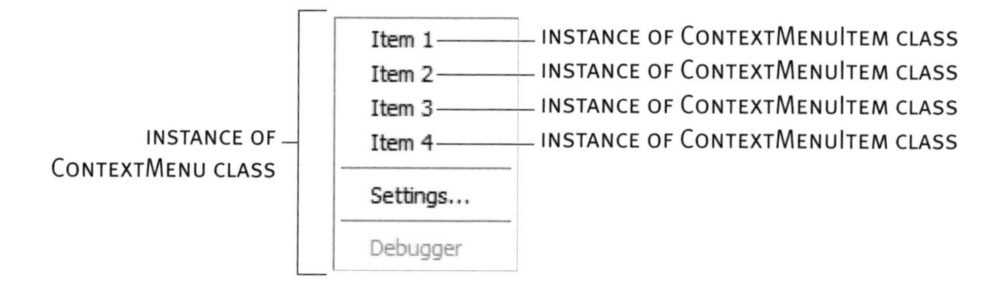

When creating a new instance of the ContextMenu class, you can specify a function to be called when that ContextMenu is displayed:

```
var myContextMenu:ContextMenu = new ContextMenu(menuHandler);
```

The `menuHandler()` function is executed just before the context menu appears. Script within the function can be used to evaluate certain conditions within the application and items on a context menu can be dynamically added, removed, enabled, or disabled. For example, a Save item may be disabled if nothing has changed since the last time the user saved.

You can dynamically change the function a context menu calls before it appears, by redefining its `onSelect` event handler. For example:

```
myContextMenu.onSelect = anotherFunction;
```

As a result of this script, the `onSelect` event handler is reassigned from its initial value to that of `anotherFunction`. The `myContextMenu` instance will call `anotherFunction()` instead of `menuHandler()`—or whatever function you passed into the ContextMenu constructor when creating it—when the context menu is selected (but before it appears).

When creating custom context menus, you may want to remove the default items that appear. To hide the built-in items in a context menu, you call the `hideBuiltInItems()` method:

```
myContextMenu.hideBuiltInItems();
```

With this method, all built-in items are hidden from the context menu except the Settings and Debugger items.

NOTE *In editable text fields, standard items such as Cut, Copy, Paste, Delete, and Select All are not removable.*

Instances of the ContextMenu class have only one property—`customItems`. This is an array that stores the custom ContextMenuItem objects that form the custom items that appear on the menu. To add a custom item to a ContextMenu object, you add it to the `customItems` array for that object:

```
myContextMenu.customItems.push(new ContextMenuItem("Next Page",
⇒nextPageHandler));
```

This statement adds a new ContextMenuItem object to the `customItems` array of the `myContextMenu` object. The first parameter is the text to be displayed in the menu. The second parameter is the callback function for that item. When the item is selected from the context menu, the callback function is called.

MYCONTEXTMENU.CUSTOMITEMS.PUSH(NEW CONTEXTMENUITEM("NEXT PAGE", NEXTPAGEHANDLER))

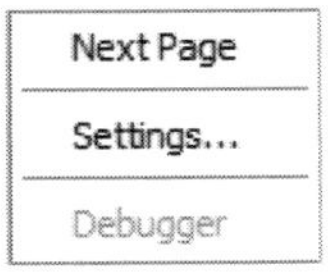

Next Page
Settings...
Debugger

MYCONTEXTMENU.CUSTOMITEMS.PUSH(NEW CONTEXTMENUITEM("PREVIOUS PAGE", PREVIOUSPAGEHANDLER))

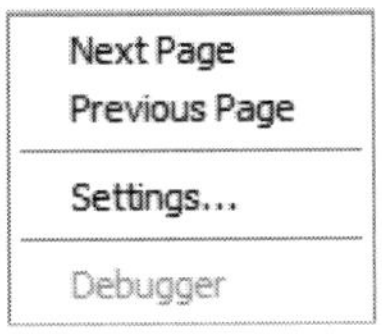

Next Page
Previous Page
Settings...
Debugger

MYCONTEXTMENU.CUSTOMITEMS.PUSH(NEW CONTEXTMENUITEM("FIRST PAGE", FIRSTPAGEHANDLER))

Next Page
Previous Page
First Page
Settings...
Debugger

Custom menu items in a context menu can be referenced in the following manner:

```
myContextMenu.customItems[0] // first custom menu item
myContextMenu.customItems[1] // second custom menu item
myContextMenu.customItems[2] // third custom menu item
```

Knowing this, you can enable and disable menu items dynamically:

```
myContextMenu.customItems[1].enabled = false;
myContextMenu.customItems[3].enabled = false;
```

Disabled menu items still appear on the custom context menu, but they're dimmed and won't function when clicked. Menu items are enabled by default.

You can dynamically change the function that a context menu item calls when selected, by redefining its `onSelect` event handler. For example:

```
myContextMenu.customItems[0].onSelect = differentCallbackFunction;
```

NOTE *Just to clarify, the context menu itself has a callback function that is executed just before the menu appears, and each context menu item has a callback function that's executed when that item is selected from the menu.*

To use a custom context menu, it has to be assigned to a particular movie clip, button, or text field instance. The assignment causes that custom menu to appear when the instance is right-clicked. Here's the syntax:

```
myClip_mc.menu = myContextMenu;
```

When the mouse is right-clicked over the **myClip_mc** movie clip instance, the `myContextMenu` context menu is displayed.

NOTE *A single custom context menu can be associated with as many movie clip, button, and text field instances as you want.*

When using custom context menus, the timeline with the highest depth always captures the right-click mouse event, which causes its custom menu to be displayed. For example, if two movie clips are overlapping and each has an associated custom context menu, the clip that's at a higher depth is the one whose menu is shown when the mouse is right-clicked over that clip. This principle also applies to the main timeline. If the mouse is not over a movie clip that has a custom menu, but the main timeline (`_root`) has a custom menu, the custom menu for `_root` will be displayed.

In the following exercise, you'll create a custom context menu with one custom item, used to print the contents of an editable text field.

1) Open *ContextMenu1.fla* in the Lesson21/Assets folder.

This file has three layers: Background, Text Field, and Actions. The Background layer contains the graphics for the project. The Text Field layer contains an input text field instance with the name **entry_txt**. Frame 1 of the Actions layer is where you'll add the ActionScript for this project.

When the project is complete, you'll be able to add text to the editable text field; when you right-click, you'll be able to select Print Fridge Note from the custom context menu.

2) Select Frame 1 in the Actions layer, open the Actions panel, and add the following line to create a new instance of the ContextMenu class:

```
var myContextMenu:ContextMenu = new ContextMenu(menuHandler);
```

This code creates a new instance of the ContextMenu class, named `myContextMenu`. This custom context menu will eventually be associated with the **entry_txt** text field. When the mouse is right-clicked over that field, this menu (and the menu items we'll eventually add to it) will appear. We'll add three custom items to this menu that give the user the following options:

- Print any text in the **entry_txt** text field.
- Delete any text in the **entry_txt** text field.
- Reformat any text in the **entry_txt** text field so that it's red and consists of uppercase characters.

In the constructor, a reference to a function called `menuHandler()` is passed in. This function is called whenever this menu is opened (the user right-clicks the **entry_txt** text field). Let's create that function next.

3) Add the following `menuHandler()` function definition below the current script:

```
function menuHandler() {
  var numberOfItems = myContextMenu.customItems.length;
  if (entry_txt.text.length > 0) {
    for(var i = 0; i < numberOfItems; ++i){
      myContextMenu.customItems[i].enabled = true;
    }
  } else {
    for(var i = 0; i < numberOfItems; ++i){
      myContextMenu.customItems[i].enabled = false;
    }
  }
}
```

This function is called just before the myContextMenu menu appears. The purpose of this function is to enable and disable custom items on that menu on the fly, depending on whether the **entry_txt** text field contains any text. If there *is* text in that field, custom items on the context menu are enabled; otherwise, the custom items are disabled.

The function begins by creating a variable named numberOfItems. The value of this variable is based on the number of custom menu items that have been added to the myContextMenu instance. In this project, that instance will eventually have three items added to it; thus, the value of numberOfItems is 3. The value of this variable will be used in a moment.

Next, a conditional statement evaluates whether the user has entered any text into the **entry_txt** text field. If the field contains text, the first part of the statement uses a loop to quickly enable all the custom items on the myContextMenu instance. If no text is found, all the items are disabled.

ENTRY_TXT CONTAINS TEXT	ENTRY_TXT IS EMPTY
Print Fridge Note	Print Fridge Note
Clear Fridge Note	Clear Fridge Note
Urgent Fridge Note	Urgent Fridge Note
Cut	Cut
Copy	Copy
Paste	Paste
Delete	Delete
Select All	Select All

After this function has executed, the menu appears. Now let's add some custom items to the myContextMenu instance.

4) Add the following line of script just below the menuHandler() **function:**

```
myContextMenu.customItems.push(new ContextMenuItem("Print Fridge Note",
⇒printHandler));
```

This line of script adds a new ContextMenuItem instance to the customItems array of the myContextMenu instance. This step defines the first item that will appear when the menu is opened.

The first parameter of the ContextMenuItem constructor method contains the text that we want to appear in the menu representing this item. The second parameter is the callback function that should be executed when the item is selected. We'll create this function next.

5) Add the following script to define the `printHandler()` **callback function:**

```
function printHandler() {
  var myPrintJob:PrintJob = new PrintJob();
  var result:Boolean = myPrintJob.start();
  if (result) {
    myPrintJob.addPage("entry_txt");
    myPrintJob.send();
  }
  delete myPrintJob;
}
```

This function is called when Print Fridge Note is selected from the context menu. The first line creates a new instance of the PrintJob class. The second line attempts to initialize the printer, capturing the result of printer initialization. If no printer exists or the user cancels the print request, the `result` variable has a value of `false`. If the user proceeds with the print request, the `result` variable is set to `true`.

If `result` is `true`, we use the `addPage()` method of the PrintJob class to add contents of the **entry_txt** text field to be printed. The remaining default parameters for the `addPage()` method are acceptable, so we don't need to set them.

Next, the page is sent to the printer, and the `myPrintJob` instance is deleted.

Let's add the remaining two items to our custom context menu.

6) Add the following script at the end of the current script:

```
myContextMenu.customItems.push(new ContextMenuItem("Clear Fridge Note",
⇒clearHandler));
function clearHandler() {
  entry_txt.text = "";
}
```

This script adds another custom item to the `customItems` array of the `myContextMenu` instance. `"Clear Fridge Note"` is the text for this item, and the `clearHandler()` function is called when this item is selected. The `clearHandler()` function is created with the three remaining lines of script. Its only task is to remove any text from the **entry_txt** text field.

7) Add the following script below the current script:

```
myContextMenu.customItems.push(new ContextMenuItem("Urgent Fridge Note",
⇒urgentHandler));
function urgentHandler() {
  entry_txt.textColor = 0x990000;
  entry_txt.text = entry_txt.text.toUpperCase();
}
```

This step adds one more custom item to the `myContextMenu` instance. The text for this item is `"Urgent Fridge Note"` and the function called when this item is selected is `urgentHandler()`. This function takes the text entered into the **entry_txt** field, makes it red, and converts it to uppercase characters.

8) Add the final line of script:

```
entry_txt.menu = myContextMenu;
```

This step associates the `myContextMenu` instance with the **entry_txt** text field. If the user right-clicks this text field, the custom context menu appears; otherwise, the custom menu won't be shown.

9) Select Control > Test Movie to test your work. Type some text in the text field, open the custom context menu, and select a custom menu item.

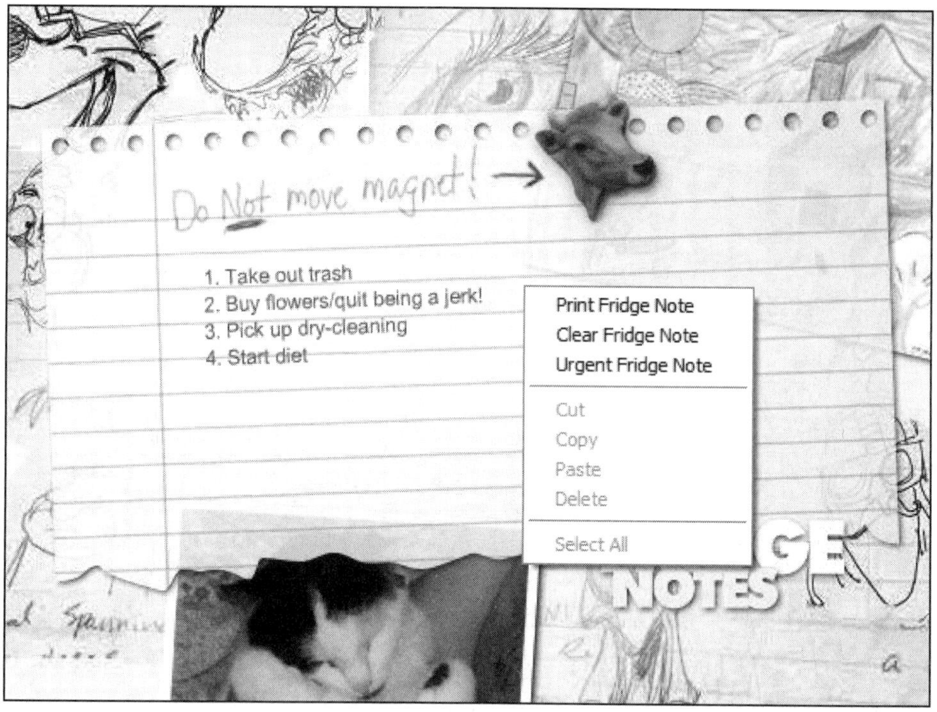

Notice that if the text field is blank, the custom menu items are disabled in the context menu. They're visible, but not selectable. If the text contains at least one text character, the menu items become available. This is the result of the `menuHandler()` function created in Step 3.

10) Close the test movie and save your work as *ContextMenu2.fla*.

This step completes the exercise and this lesson.

Custom context menus provide an entirely new way for users to interact with an application—without having to manually search for a particular button or control. If you use this new Flash feature, be sure to make users aware of it.

WHAT YOU HAVE LEARNED

In this lesson, you have:

- Learned the differences between Flash printing and browser printing (pages 732–735)
- Used the PrintJob class to print both vectors and bitmaps (pages 735–745)
- Created a custom context menu (pages 745–753)

index

C

D

W

X

Z

real world. real training. real results.

Get more done in less time with
Macromedia Training and Certification.

Two Types of Training

Roll up your sleeves and get right to work with authorized training from Macromedia.

1. Classroom Training
   Learn from instructors thoroughly trained and certified by Macromedia. Courses are fast-paced and task-oriented to get you up and running quickly.
2. Online Training
   Get Macromedia training when you want with affordable, interactive online training from Macromedia University.

Stand Out from the Pack

Show your colleagues, employer, or prospective clients that you have what it takes to effectively develop, deploy, and maintain dynamic applications–become a Macromedia Certified Professional.

Learn More

For more information about authorized training or to find a class near you, visit **www.macromedia.com/go/training1**

Macromedia Tech Support: http://www.macromedia.com/support

LICENSING AGREEMENT